D1028917

# Crown of Thorns

# Crown
## of
# Thorns

Stephane Groueff

★BOOKS★

Lanham • New York • London

British Cataloging in Publication Information Available

### Library of Congress Cataloging-in-Publication Data

Groueff, Stéphane.
  Crown of thorns.

  Bibliography: p.
  1. Boris III, Czar of Bulgaria, 1894-1943.
2. Bulgaria—Kings and rulers—Biography.  3. Bulgaria—
History—Boris III, 1918-1943.  I. Title.
DR89.G76  1987     949.7'702'0924     87-10727
ISBN 0-8191-5778-3 (alk. paper)

All Madison Books are produced on acid-free
paper which exceeds the minimum standards set by the National
Historical Publications and Records Commission.

# Contents

# Preface

ONCE UPON a time, between the two world wars, there was quite an engaging kingdom in the center of the Balkans called the Kingdom of Bulgaria. Foreigners may have heard about its Valley of the Roses, about the beauty of its mountains and Black Sea beaches, but very little else.

It was a small country with a vibrant, highly nationalistic population, sober and industrious people, mostly peasants, who fought valiantly in wars and strove to catch up with the rest of Europe in peacetime.

Dramatic events took place there during the twenty-five years between 1918 and 1943, upheavals and conflicts of much passion and blood. Those were times of agonizing soul-searching and momentous decisions, of illusions, hopes, and disappointments, of admirable actions and costly mistakes.

This kingdom is no more. But unlike other nations, whose recent past can still be discussed freely and read in detail, a veil of oblivion has fallen over the events of that period in Bulgaria. Today's student of pre-Communist Bulgaria would find it difficult to discover what exactly did happen in that country before 1944, nor would he understand how and why. A prism of distortion would most likely be put before his eyes.

Apart from the documents from the period, most of them unavailable abroad and inaccessible inside the country, the major depositories for this bygone Bulgaria, the 1918–1943 kingdom, remain in the memories of the hearts of Bulgarians who witnessed that period. Especially the hearts, I should say, because unrecorded remembrances fade with time; they tend to take on the color of things read and heard later, and are edited by the wisdom of hindsight.

It is imprudent, inside Bulgaria now, to reminisce aloud about certain aspects of that period; it is impossible to publish anything uncensored. As for exiled Bulgarians, we still dream at night, weekly perhaps, about "the good old country" as we remember it from our youth. Nostalgia, from a historian's point of view, is not a bad thing. Selectively picking events and images from the irrecoverable past, nostalgia is a good preservative for memories: it protects them with loving care, conserving not only the facts, but also the mood and color of the time.

I, for one, while I sometimes have difficulty recalling last year's occurrences and faces, can still recite the names of my schoolmates in the First Sofia Gymnasium and remember the precise composition of the then-national football team, heroes of our adolescent years. King Boris's nasal voice, which characteristically accentuated each syllable, still rings in my ears. I met him several times when I was growing up in the family of a court official.

I close my eyes and I can still smell the heavy odor of incense and candles in the centuries-old Sveta-Sophia church, where, every year on Good Friday, my grandmother used to cry her eyes out as she listened to the familiar tale of Christ's sufferings.

I can still hear the clop-clop hoofbeat on the paving stones in the days when horse-driven "phaetons" competed with the city's taxicabs. The bloodcurdling sounds of air alert sirens and bombs falling on Sofia still haunt me. Straining far back into the past, I can hear with disturbing clarity brass bands playing "Shoomi Maritza," the national anthem, and thousands of unmistakably Bulgarian voices screaming "Hurrah!" at parades and demonstrations. Then, the same voices reemerge a few years later, weeping inconsolably as the casket with the body of King Boris proceeds solemnly along the mountain road to the Rila monastery.

This is all so vivid in our minds, and yet, objectively, it exists nowhere else anymore.

Nostalgic recollections are too fragile and ephemeral to serve, alone, as a valid source for history. To reconstruct the events of that period, written testimonies are needed.

A few original fragments from the epoch can be found in old books and newspapers still available abroad. Others are mildewing in forgotten trunks of exiles scattered around the world. Another option is the official writings of current Bulgarian historians. In all fairness, historiography in Bulgaria has made noticeable progress in the last decade. Gone are the days of the vulgar pseudohistorical pamphlets by illiterate party propagandists of the Stalinist era, which, incidentally, enjoyed amazing longevity in Bulgaria. Some recent Sofia publications offer a more scholarly approach and well-documented research. But as objective as some among their more talented authors are trying to be, they cannot escape the constraints and taboos of a regime which openly professes that historiography, like all sciences and arts, must above all serve the party ideology.

The need for an accurate narrative of the events between the two wars, although universally recognized abroad among Bulgarians and their friends, would probably still be floating in the air were it not for the initiative of a patriotic Bulgarian who put the idea into concrete terms. James D. Velkov is one of those exiles who, along with his remarkably successful business achievements abroad, kept alive his feelings for Bulgaria. His is a case of an incurable longing for the homeland, involving him wholeheartedly in Bulgarian causes for four decades.

In chemistry, the addition of a new substance is often needed to cause and accelerate a reaction between different elements. The chemists call such a substance a catalyst. Velkov was the originator and the catalyst in the process that led to this book's materialization.

He, as the sponsor, and I, as the author, agreed that the best way to tell the story of the years between the two world wars was through the life of the one man who had been either the principal actor or the best-placed witness in these events—King Boris III. Our goal was a book that would describe this unusual man both as a ruler and as a human being, without partisan distortions, but also without flattery. At the same time, the episodes that marked his reign should elucidate the recent history of the nation and bring into focus the events that preceded the fall of the Bulgarian kingdom.

King Boris was genuinely loved by his people, as no other ruler had been in prewar Europe. But he was also accused of bringing Bulgaria into the German camp during World War II and criticized for exercising a "personal rule" during the last eight years of his reign.

This book is not an apology for the king, neither is it an attempt to justify or glorify his policies and his actions. It is not a book of polemics, but rather a chronological and, I hope dispassionate and objective narrative of the dramatic events that befell this unfortunate nation during the twenty-five years of King Boris's reign.

It is the result of several years of research, during which I was privileged to have access to unpublished private archives and intimate personal correspondence, and to speak to many of the last witnesses of the period. I must note with gratitude that none of the persons to whom I turned for help and advice—admirers as well as critics of King Boris, "monarchists" and "republicans," people of the political "right" or "left" refused to give me wholehearted assistance.

The research revealed an unknown and, in many respects, an unexpected human drama behind the official image of King Boris. An unusually complex, intelligent, engaging, and vulnerable man, he had the misfortune of being cast, like an unwilling but totally committed and conscientious actor, in the principal role in a Greek tragedy with no possible solution.

Once the project of the book was launched, all the research, selection of episodes, form of presentation, and actual writing, became my sole responsibility. The assessment of the described events, as well as the portrayal of the characters and the expressed opinions are exclusively my own, and are not necessarily shared or approved by the generous contributors of source material.

# Prologue

**H**E HAD just taken off his dusty boots and the wrinkled colonel's uniform and was about to change into civilian clothes, when the aide-de-camp knocked at the door and announced:

"Your Royal Highness, His Majesty wants to see you in about half an hour, at the end of the audience. He will call you before the visitor leaves."

"Is the visitor already here?"

"He has just arrived."

Prince Boris had been informed about the unusual meeting his father was to have in the Red Salon in the other wing of the palace, and knew how distasteful it was for King Ferdinand to receive "that man." The crown prince, too, had no reason to like the sworn enemy of the dynasty, but he was far more tolerant than his father and had always been intrigued by the crude flamboyance of this outspoken adversary, whom he had met three years before.

Boris was very tired that afternoon of September 25, 1918, physically and morally exhausted from his trip to the front. The heavy-heartedness he had felt for several months was turning into a mild depression, and the events of the past few days were only making it worse. Alarming rumors were spreading all over Sofia and the country. A creeping feeling of insecurity was permeating the palace, one could detect it in the voices, see it in everybody's eyes. Certain words that people whispered didn't sound so abstract anymore—"abdication," "dethronement," "exile" . . . or worse?

The martyrology of uncles, granduncles and other relatives was long, and Boris, the descendant of the Saxe-Coburg-Gothas, the Bourbon-Parmas and the Orléans, did not have to look as far back as Louis XVI and Marie-Antoinette. The family chronicle abounded with tragic episodes: Emperor Maximilian of Mexico facing the firing squad in 1867 . . . the nihilists' bomb killing Tsar Alexander II in 1881 . . . Elizabeth of Austria killed in 1898 . . . King Umberto of Italy murdered in 1900 . . . Serbia's King Alexander I and his paramour Draga assassinated in 1903 . . . King Carlos of Portugal and the crown prince killed in 1908, and two years later the deposition of Manuel of Portugal . . . King George of Greece in 1913 . . . the 1914 assassination of Archduke Francis-Ferdinand in Sarajevo, triggering World War I . . . and since the beginning of the war, the expulsion of King Constantine of Greece in 1917 . . . finally, only two months had passed since the abominable crime in Ekaterinburg, the massacre on July 17, 1918, of Tsar Nicholas II, Boris' godfather, together with his entire family, by the Bolsheviks-the tsarina, the four daughters, the crown prince.

They kill crown princes too . . . but, strangely enough, during those gloomy September days Prince Boris was not overly worried about his personal security. A fatalist, he had learned to accept tragedies and dangers as "les risques du métier."

Violent death was one of these risks. Boris was seventeen years old when the Russian prime minister Peter Stolypin was assassinated before his eyes. He could still see the glittering theater house in Kiev; the royal box with the emperor, the grand dukes and the grand duchesses; the splendor of uniforms, decorations and jewels; then the sound of two gunshots . . . Young Boris was visiting his godfather, Tsar Nicholas II, on his first official trip outside Bulgaria. The occasion was the inauguration in Kiev of the monument of Tsar Alexander II, the liberator of Bulgaria.

It was at the second intermission, he remembered. He was wearing the grand collier of the decoration of Saint-André that the Russian emperor had just bestowed on him. In the small foyer of the royal box, he was engaged in polite conversation with the members of the imperial family with whom he had spent the previous day at the military maneuvers outside of Kiev and at the lavish garden party that had followed. Then suddenly a young man in a black dress coat rushed toward Stolypin, who was seated in the first row of the pit, pulled out a Browning and shot twice, almost point blank. Boris remembered the echo of the two shots in the crowded theater house, the screams, the uproar, the blood reddening the white plastron of the prime minister. It was the first time he had seen blood run profusely from a dying man. What should be the right behavior in such circumstances for a prince on an official occasion? Boris looked around. In the emperor's box, hands were trembling and tears rolled down ashen faces. But, as the victim was carried out and the assassin seized, they were all—the tsar, the grand dukes and the grand duchesses—standing at attention, erect and solemn, as audience and actors burst into "God Save the Tsar."

Stolypin died. Death had been so close, only a few yards away. "Nous l'avons tous échappé belle!" "We were lucky to escape," Boris wrote later that evening in the coded telegram in which he described the event to his father.

Now in 1918, seven Septembers later, as the war was turning into disaster, the twenty-four year-old crown prince had no fear of death. Since

Stolypin's murder, he had seen, touched, and smelled blood in battlefields and military hospitals hundreds of times. The war only reinforced his fatalistic convictions. What he worried about was the probability of his family being forced to leave Bulgaria. What happens to a crown prince in such a case? Normally, he becomes the next king, of course. But did he *want* to become king? Having such doubts is very painful. But not everybody is born to be king. Not everybody is like King Ferdinand—so happy and eager to rule, delighted with his destiny and sure of himself, a true born monarch.

Was Boris meant to be monarch? At times, his own father seemed to have doubts. Boris's insufficiently "regal" posture, his lack of interest in the crown's traditional attributes, such as pomp and protocol, his penchant for befriending peasants and commoners, irritated the king. No one in the world loved and admired Boris more than his sister Evdokia, but even she could lose patience with his modesty and his overly democratic ways. She thought that he was the brightest in the family, but sometimes she wished that he were more assertive and acted with more authority and majesty.

His father's fate was going to be decided very soon, this week maybe, or even this day, and none of the rumors that circulated in Sofia were reassuring. If Ferdinand were forced into exile? . . . Boris's first impulse would probably be to renounce all rights to the crown and leave with the rest of the family. What a relief that would be! But, in fact, he never considered this option seriously. The notions of duty, the responsibilities which had been nurtured in him had become irremediably his second nature from which there was no possible escape. Moral codes impressed in infancy on malleable souls become an inseparable part of the character, to the point where trying to imagine a person without it is as futile as visualizing an ugly Venus or a poor Croesus.

A crown prince from his kind of lineage who would abandon his obligations to country and throne? Unthinkable! To betray what he was taught was his predestination and sacred mission? All the ideas about duty that he had ever heard—from his father, from Granny Clémentine, and every teacher and military instructor he had had—coincided and were in total accord. He had never known any other values. Every book he had read and word he had heard reinforced these values, and each one of the solemn portraits of his ancestors hanging on the palace walls reminded him daily of them. If there were other values, they certainly did not apply to honorable men.

It was not necessarily a particular merit, nor a question of great moral fortitude; Boris simply did not know any alternative. Could a dishonored samurai, no matter how afraid of dying, *not* commit harakiri? Could a young man, who is a real man, *not* run with the bulls in the streets of Pamplona? Could Prince Boris abandon the sinking ship?

Apart from duty, leaving Bulgaria was unthinkable for him for another, very personal reason. The young prince was incurably enamored of the country in which he had been born and raised. When Bulgarians talk about their attachment to their land, the talk may sound exaggerated and overly emotional to a foreigner. Yes, of course they love it, but who doesn't love his homeland? For the Bulgarians, however, the attachment has a different meaning. The feeling has such intensity that it can only be compared to the state of being in love—an obsessive, romantic, exhilarating, possessive feeling, a source of pride and jealousy, of continuous inspiration and reassurance.

It comes partly from the physical beauty of the land. True, Bulgarians are rather chauvinistic and absolutely convinced that their country is the most beautiful in the world. But, quite objectively, there is no foreigner who wouldn't agree that its mountains remind him of the Swiss Alps, that the lush valleys and fairy tale forests are among the loveliest in Europe, and that the unspoiled golden Black Sea beaches have no rival on the Riviera.

But there is something else, something intangible and yet unmistakably and unforgettably Bulgarian, that inspires a unique fascination with the country. No man knew Bulgaria better than Prince Boris, a hunter, hiker, and motorist, but even he would have been hard put to define the mysterious attraction of this land.

Maybe it was the air, an incredibly fresh and invigorating air that one never forgets, and one never finds elsewhere. Maybe it is the colors, or the way the sun shines and the wind blows. Poets and romantics speak of the brooks and the wild flowers, of the fragrance of "zdravetz," the exclusively Bulgarian wild geranium that covers acres of meadows and woodland. They speak of the hundred-mile-long Valley of Roses, another unique phenomenon, or of the smell of freshly cut hay. They insist that they would recognize the sound of native cowbells out of thousands in foreign pastures. The skies in Bulgaria have a different color, they like to say, the water tastes different. They describe the crow of roosters at sunrise in the villages and become nostalgic over the sound of dogs barking somewhere far away in the darkness of the night, as if roosters and dogs are different in other countries.

It is, doubtless, a biased and romantic outlook. But who knows, Bulgarians may be, objectively speaking, right. Maybe it *is* a special country, or in any case, a different one. Less sentimental words—latitude and longitude, soil, climate, altitudes, oxygen of the air, chemistry of the water, geological history—could perhaps explain the same reality in another, nonsubjective way. Be this as it may, the undeniable attraction of nature in Bulgaria is there, and countless men, far tougher and less sensitive than Prince Boris, have succumbed to it. King Ferdinand, the calculating and scornful Westerner, lost his heart to it only a few years after his arrival. For the crown prince, nature was the passion of his young life, probably the only real one, the place where he looked for peace, warmth, and reassurance. He was also attached to the Bulgarian people and felt closer and more comfortable with them than with his foreign relatives and friends. In fact, in this period of his life, he tended, somewhat naively, to idealize the so-called "simple people," attributing to them some marvelous purity and nobility of the soul, which is not uncommon with young men who have grown up in seclusive privilege, especially those deprived of family intimacy and affection, as had been the case with Boris.

No, there was no chance of Boris abandoning Bulgaria. Anyhow, things were still not at that point, the question had not been raised. But fall is conducive to this kind of meditation, and the frail prince with the purebred face and the extraordinary gray-blue eyes was a natural worrier.

In Bulgaria, September is the time when the first signs of sadness appear in the air. At the beginning, it is still very subtle, just ephemeral warnings of things coming to an end, momentary twinges drowned immediately in the summer brightness before they have a chance to take shape. It could be a whiff of wind carrying melancholy memories; it could be a shadow, slightly longer today than it was yesterday; or a different cloud over Mount Vitosha, or a nostalgic sound in the cathedral's carillon when the solemn bells ring for the evening Mass.

For an instant, one realizes that summer is over, the hot, radiant Bulgarian summer. Soon the skies will change color, and their grayness will descend over the red-tiled roofs of villages and towns. The streets' pavements will shine sadly in the rain, and mud will reclaim the harvested fields. It will be a different land, sadder, shabbier, and darker, as if the lights had dimmed over the set of a cheerful stage, and gloomy music had interrupted a happy festival.

Bulgarians do not always dislike this sadness. Although less than other Slavs and notably less than the Russians (who never pass up an occasion to enjoy a good sob, preferably in company), Bulgarians often indulge in melancholy. In fact, sadness is at the root of their esthetic life. Most Bulgarian art—music, poetry, painting—reflects a fascination with the beauty of sadness. While gaiety, humor, and joie-de-vivre in Bulgaria are earthy, lively and sensual, romance, dreaming, and meditation have invariably a touch of melancholy about them.

September is, nevertheless, usually a delightful month, the month of the pastel colors, the season of ripened vineyards and lush autumn flowers, the time when red-cheeked children flock happily back to school. Before getting ready for the winter sleep, the country basks in the mild September sunshine and seems to indulge in a last voluptuous stretch.

Not this year. The year of the collapse, the end of all dreams and all hope. Bulgaria, the kind of Bulgaria Boris had known, was about to die.

The aide-de-camp reappeared at the door.

"Your Royal Highness, His Majesty is expecting you. Mr. Stambolisky is about to leave."

There was a special way army officers, and for that matter many Bulgarians who considered themselves true patriots, pronounced the name "Stambolisky." If intonation could kill, the notorious peasant tribune would have been a dead man a long time since.

# CHAPTER I

# Defeat and Despair

**H**E HAD been released from his cell only seven hours ago, at ten o'clock that morning, and it felt strange now, after three years of prison misery, to find himself surrounded by the solemn luxury of the royal palace. A relative luxury, to be sure, as the Sofia palace was by no means Versailles, although the sumptuous tastes and majestic manner of King Ferdinand reminded many people of the Roi-Soleil. It was a rather elegant two-story, French-style structure in dark-yellowish stucco in the very heart of the capital, surrounded by a park and fenced by high walls of the same color.

As Alexander Stambolisky was led through the long dark corridors, he recognized the smell—a mixture of stale air, dried flowers, and freshly waxed parquet—and remembered the echoing footsteps in the silence of the palace. The fiery thirty-nine-year-old peasant leader had been here once before, three years ago, on September 18, 1915, to be precise. It was a dramatic visit that neither he nor King Ferdinand was ever to forget. It had taken place two weeks before Bulgaria entered World War I, when representatives of five opposition parties were reluctantly granted an audience with the monarch in order to express their alarm over the increasing indications that Bulgaria was going to abandon her neutrality in the year-old European conflict. The redoubtable king had received them in his imposing Red Salon hung with silk and damask, flanked by the crown prince Boris, a respectful youth of twenty-one, who listened intensely and politely but said little. He had looked uncomfortable while the opposition leaders criticized the government's policies; but when Stambolisky had lashed out in an angry, intemperate attack on the king, the young prince had been visibly embarrassed.

As expected, the other visitors had presented strong arguments against Bulgaria's joining the side of Germany and Austria-Hungary. They had tried to warn King Ferdinand of the devastating consequences a new war could have on the country, still badly wounded after the catastrophic 1912–1913 Balkan Wars. But they had spoken in a courteous manner, as loyal

1

statesmen dissenting from their constitutional monarch. Stambolisky, on the contrary, speaking for the Agrarian party had shown no respect for the king, but had been as violent, rude and insulting as few people had ever dared be in Ferdinand's intimidating presence. The king had been outraged.

"I will not be intimidated by your threats," he had shouted angrily. "I have my policy, and I will follow the road I have chosen, because in so doing I will serve my people much better than you."

"My path," Stambolisky retorted, "didn't end catastrophically like yours. This time, if you persist, you'll pay with your head!"

"Don't you worry about my head. I am an old man. But you are young; think about your own head!"

Fuming, King Ferdinand had turned his back on the agrarian and gone on talking to the other visitors. The meeting had been a total disaster and on leaving Stambolisky had turned to the young prince: "Let's hope, at least, that you and I will understand each other one day. It's clear that a chasm separates your father's ideas and mine."

Two weeks later, Bulgaria had joined the war on the side of Germany and Austria, the so-called Central Powers, against France, England, and their allies of the Entente. Stambolisky had been sent to jail for demoralizing the troops and undermining the nation's war effort.

As he was heading now for his second meeting with King Ferdinand, he could not help feeling bitter about the treatment he had endured because of his disagreement with the monarch. Three years in prison . . . three years in which momentous events had shaken the country. Years of epic struggle, of incredible courage and endurance, of glorious initial victories along with the ephemeral euphoria of fulfilled national dreams. But also years of suffering and sacrifice for the whole nation, of misery and bitter disappointment. Now it was all over. Disaster was looming over the unfortunate Balkan country.

Ten days earlier the front had been breached in Macedonia.

*       *       *

The military situation had taken a very bad turn in the last few months. Three years before, in October 1915, an Anglo-French expeditionary corps had landed in Greece, with the mission to open a Balkan front and rescue the defeated Serbian army. The positions were established north of Salonika, in Macedonia, the disputed territory between Bulgaria, Serbia, and Greece, over which the three countries had fought in 1913. Bulgaria had lost, and now, with her enemies siding with the Entente, it hoped to recover Macedonia by joining the Central Powers. The Bulgarian army had for a long time held its own against the Anglo-French on the Macedonian front. But the Greeks, although still proclaiming their neutrality, had joined the enemy forces, and the ninety-thousand-man expeditionary corps, including several French colonial regiments, had been continuously reinforced.

The first significant reverses had occurred three-and-a-half months earlier when, in May 1918, Greek and French troops pierced the Bulgarian fortified positions of Houma and Yarebichna, decimating an entire regiment. King Ferdinand had been mortified and enraged. Although alleged to be a Germanophile, the monarch blamed the defeat on the callousness of his German allies. The day after the debacle, he wrote an unusually strong letter to his representative at the German H.Q.:

General Gantchev,
Your rhapsodizing about the German victories is out of tune with the sad events on the front. Thanks to the criminal, heartless and extremely selfish orders of von Ludendorff,[1] we remain at 5 divisions, with 50 cannons, against 200 from the Franco-Greeks and, moreover, without a single German soldier in our ranks. May yesterday's defeat and the massacre of an entire Bulgarian regiment at Houma-Yarebichna fall like a curse over those who, in spite of my furious protests, so mercilessly withdrew their troops and exposed the Bulgarian soldier, against all treaties and laws of interallied solidarity, to evident slaughter! Moreover, these same beasts are now set on starving the Bulgarian people, by refusing to send the flour promised in the treaty.
The picture is really marvelous—hunger and defeat at the front, famine inside the country, the collapse of the Radoslavov cabinet, the opposition and the "narrow-socialists" (Bulgarian Communist party) in full action . . . May your honorable friends in Spa and elsewhere be proud of this great success of theirs! THE KING.

The letter was handwritten in Bulgarian, a language whose syntax and spelling the foreign-born monarch had mastered to near perfection.
In spite of the assurances of his allies, and the optimistic assessments of the situation by his hawkish prime minister Radoslavov, Ferdinand knew that since the beginning of the summer, things had been going from bad to worse. And if he still had any doubts, they were dispelled by the secret report he had received on June 13 by no less a believer in a final victory than the commander-in-chief of the Bulgarian forces, General Nikola Jekov. Having completed an extensive tour of the endangered Macedonian front, the general was sounding the alarm. Distrusting Radoslavov's government, his classified report was for the king's eyes only:

". . . Here on the spot I can witness the increasingly alarming plight of our troops. The food, especially the poor quality bread, is insufficient . . . The troops live from day to day, eating their last rations or

---

[1]Marshall Erich von Ludendorff, deputy-chief of the German general staff.

borrowing from the German depots. Sometimes they get meat only once a week. Now they are living on vegetables from their own kitchen gardens they keep behind the front line . . . There are no chances for improvement until the next crop.

The scarcity of clothing is even worse. The soldiers are almost naked and barefooted. In some units, 25 percent of the men go without shoes, and their uniforms are in rags. It's not rare to see the bare flesh showing through the torn and worn blouses and trousers of soldiers who have no underwear . . .

The general saw barefoot soldiers ordered on to bold counter-attacks, expected to charge enemy positions over sharp stones. Their overcoats were in rags, so threadbare they were useless. Instead of caps, some soldiers wore torn sandbags on their heads. "After the autumn rains, the uniforms will be nothing but cobwebs over the soldiers' bodies, already run-down from long immersion in humid trenches and lack of nourishing food," Jekov warned. "The officers' uniforms are equally miserable. By their appearance, they have lost their distinction from those of the troops. Both soldiers and officers feel shame and self-pity . . . Only a fraction of the artillery have enough draft horses for the cannons, thus precluding any major offensive."

The commander-in-chief urged the king to insist more vigorously on the allies' obligations, complaining that:

Since April, we have not received any military supplies from the Germans. The total lack of necessities, added to the realization that the war's end is not near and things will get worse, affects the morale in a disastrous way. Empty stomachs, naked bodies, worries about families back home, and the suspicion that our allies will not earnestly back our national aspirations—all this makes the troops apathetic, in spite of the victories we had been winning so far.

Inflated rumors of corruption and crime back home circulate on the front and anger the troops, magnified by the pitiful state of their supplies. "The guys back home steal and get rich, and look at us!" the soldiers say, pointing to their exposed flesh. The front-line troops have lost all hope and trust in the authorities: "Here we defend the Fatherland with our blood, but back there they sell it for money!"

After describing the troops' disgust with the government, General Jekov pleaded on behalf of the armed forces for a new "strong, honest, patriotic, nonpartisan government . . . The faults of Radoslavov's administration are indeed so many and so grave that no counterpropaganda in its defense among the troops is possible."

Jekov was well aware that the Germans' attitude was causing a growing popular discontent. It was tolerated in the hopes of fulfilling the national ideal—the liberation of Macedonia, Thrace, Dobrudja. But when Rumania was crushed and the Germans declined to turn liberated Dobrudja over to Bulgaria, mistrust and resentment filled the hearts of the soldiers. "It is the first treaty concerning Bulgaria, and it has already clipped the wings of its national aspirations," Jekov complained to the king. "It made of Bulgaria, in the words of the soldiers, 'a sheep that nobody can fleece.' "

King Ferdinand had been receiving similar reports for a long time from his son, the crown prince. Many cyphered telegrams of Prince Boris from the front (usually in French, and signed "Rylski"), mentioned the growing antigovernment feelings he had detected among the troops. For example:

Today we visited the 4th Division. Food unsatisfactory. Morale in certain regiments badly shaken. It deteriorated especially during the troops' transfer from Dobrudja to Macedonia. A number of soldiers infected with various propaganda. Discontent above all directed against the government. There are no deserters but, having not enough to eat, strong complaints against the authorities, saying that everything has been exported, especially that the Germans receive good bread. Some soldiers protest against the war's duration. Kiss your hand, RYLSKI.

And the following day, June 7, 1918:

Situation in the 3rd Division satisfactory, the soldiers have almost sufficient food, but what is far more critical is the pitiful state of the clothing. In the 5th and 2nd Divisions there are companies in rags. An upsetting thing is that soldiers returning from home leave talk about the tyranny of the tax-collectors in the villages. Biased rumors circulate behind the front, spread no doubt by partisans, in order to disturb the troops. Very devoted, RYLSKI.

\* \* \*

The lackey opened the door and Stambolisky found himself face-to-face with the king.

"Good afternoon, Your Majesty. The war minister informed me that you wanted to see me, and I am at your disposal."

"Good afternoon, Mr. Stambolisky."

The grandson of King Louis-Philippe and the farmer's son from the obscure village of Slavovitza shook hands and sat on chairs facing each other. "So we meet again . . ," King Ferdinand started cautiously.

"After three full years, Your Majesty."

"Yes, after three stormy years."

"And, once more, at a tragic hour."

"At a very tragic hour!"

"And this tragedy is the result of a definitely bankrupt policy which I foresaw on September 18, 1915," Stambolisky accused defiantly.

Ferdinand could not ignore the attack. His eyes were full of contempt and his voice turned icy. "This sad result is exactly what you desired. Now you can enjoy the results of your obstinate subversive action, Mr. Stambolisky. All these are your fruits. Yes, yours. You have worked for the disintegration of the front, constantly and systematically, and, finally, you have succeeded in achieving this result. A great result!"

It was the agrarian's turn to drop every pretense of polite conversation. "Your Majesty, remember that after our first meeting on September 18, 1915, I was sentenced to a maximum-security prison for life and thrown into jail, from which I did not emerge until ten o'clock this morning. Remember, that in jail I was treated like the most dangerous bandit and kept under special supervision by your government; that I was forbidden to see anyone and my letters were censored or burned. You cannot imagine my horrible treatment in prison! How then is it possible that the most strictly guarded prisoner in Bulgaria could be responsible for the collapse of the front? Do I have supernatural powers? Your Majesty, I indignantly reject any accusation of disrupting the front. I had neither the desire nor the capacity to do so."

Tempestuous, bitter, filled with mutual recriminations, the discussion went on for well over an hour. The men were as different as if they belonged to two totally unrelated worlds. On one side, the overbred, haughty nobleman with his delicate skin, pointed beard and prominent Coburg nose, a consumate master of sarcastic witticisms artfully delivered in a nasal foreign voice. On the other side, the clumsy peasant politician in his ill-fitting suit of coarse cloth, with his unkempt black hair and upturned mustache of a village roué, shrewd and loud, exuding a certain vulgarity but not entirely unattractive in his self-assurance and animal vitality, a charismatic Bulgarian Pancho Villa. To observe the movements of their hands as they exchanged accusations in the gilded palace salon was to understand their dissimilar genealogies. The aristocratic fingers, impeccably manicured and covered with precious gems, rarely unprotected by gloves, almost effeminate, with mannered gestures betraying a highly civilized sensitivity; and, opposite, the chubby plebeian hands with unclean fingernails, massive, callous, and determined; exuberant hands used to farm soil, thriving in handshakes and blows, gesticulating with vigor and arrogance against the unfamiliar brocade backdrop of the French armchair.

And yet, the scene was not totally incongruous. Although it seemed at first sight that no anthropological category could possibly hold both men, no observer could fail to notice the one similarity—each one in his own way was an exceptional man, of superior intelligence, bold and imaginative, a born leader, ambitious, authoritarian, and ruthless. They both knew it, and there was a large dose of respect mixed with the hatred they harbored for each other. In Stambolisky's eyes, Ferdinand was the archetype of the despot, while the king considered the agrarian leader a master of demagoguery. But today they shared the same overriding interest, and a similar fear. That was what made their encounter not only possible, but necessary.

On September 15 the Bulgarian lines on the Macedonian front were broken at the crucial point of Dobro-Polé, and the fall was turning into a rout. The Franco-British forces were advancing on the Bulgarian border, and the defeated troops, exhausted, hungry, and demoralized, were retreating in an ugly, mutinous mood. There was no time to waste; a catastrophe was imminent. As increasing number of units were openly revolting against their commanding officers; the government had to concede that the last chance of propping up the collapsing front was to seek the aid of Stambolisky, the mutineers' hero and foremost pacifist and critic of the king's policies.

It was a bitter pill to swallow for the imperious ruler. But the situation was all but hopeless, and he did not have any choice. "Something has to be done," he said, in a resigned voice, so out of character. "I thought hard. I pondered and reconsidered all options, but I still don't find the solution."

"Your Majesty, there is nothing left to reconsider. What is needed now is to act quickly. You almost gave the answer. The war minister told me that you were ready to agree to a proposal for an armistice. I approve entirely; the idea is reasonable and still possible. I beg you, in the country's interest, to act rapidly on this proposal, to comply totally and sincerely and wait for the enemy's answer. There is absolutely no other option. The continuation of the war will mean the ruin of Bulgaria."

"But what will the enemy say?"

"I suppose they'll demand our retreat back to the frontiers we had before October 1915. They'll ask us to lay down our arms and abandon our present allies."

"But this means capitulation."

"Total capitulation."

"Shameful capitulation!"

"Inevitable capitulation."

"And this does not disturb you?"

"As a Bulgarian, of course, it hurts me deeply. But as a politician, I predicted this sad end. I expected it. It could have been avoided if there had been bright and brave men in the country willing to sign a separate peace while there was still time."

"Unthinkable, impossible! It would have been monstrous treason, which I could never have committed."

The tempers flared anew. The politician's insolence and the monarch's contempt interrupted the precarious truce for a moment before the two men were able to resume their discussion, for they had urgent business to finish. The question was, "How can we save Bulgaria?" as Stambolisky put it grandiloquently.

His self-assurance was inflated because two days before the king's emissaries had visited him in prison to sound him out about eventually participating in the government. Then came the invitation for the palace visit. Obviously, he was a badly needed man, and he was not going to let the king forget it.

"I am glad to see that you appreciate my abilities," he said, undeterred by modesty. "Let me confess that I highly respect your talent as a student of the human soul, and I am pleased and proud that, in spite of all that has happened between us, you find me capable of governing the nation that your pupils, by their incompetence have exposed to terrible ordeals. I also believe in my ability to take care of the most difficult government problems . . . But let's come back to the vital question: what should be done at this moment? I insist that you agree immediately and without reservation to an armistice! Anything else would be stupid and fatal."

The time had come to speak of concrete matters, and the king asked Stambolisky what he suggested be done.

"The front must be consolidated at all costs so we can hold firm until our armistice offer is accepted," answered the Agrarian leader. "Then the roving units who have abandoned the front and are marching on Sofia must be stopped before they turn into savage mobs and cause extensive damage. I discussed this with the war minister, and we agreed that I and the representatives of other political groups and the War Ministry should use all our influence to reassure the troops. We should rush to the most endangered section of the front. I am ready to take on the mission."

To Ferdinand, the proposal made sense. In fact, he had no choice. The situation was so desperate that, distasteful as it was for him to accept favors from "this horrible man," he eagerly welcomed the idea. He stood up and extended his hand.

"A wonderful idea, Mr. Stambolisky! Let me shake your hand and congratulate you! Leave right away! You'll render a great service to me and to the country."

For once, the two men seemed to agree. As Stambolisky was about to leave, Ferdinand asked him, "You know my son, the crown prince? Would you like to talk to him?"

"With great pleasure, Your Majesty."

He was sincere. Only moments before, when the king was bitterly accusing him of being motivated by antidynastic hatred, Stambolisky corrected him by saying that while disgruntlement against Ferdinand personally had indeed assumed menacing proportions, it was not necessarily directed against the royal institution itself. "I repeat," the avowed republican had said, "that there is no resentment in our country against the dynasty, against the crown prince. He enjoys greater popularity than any politician who might try to compete with him, under another form of government."

Stambolisky remarked that Prince Boris had frequently visited the front and was aware, not only of the plight of the troops, but also of their determination no longer to endure the present conditions. Some ringleaders among them had fixed a deadline for the 23rd of September. Therefore, when the well-mannered prince entered the room at the end of the audience, Stambolisky cordially shook his hand and engaged him in conversation on the current conditions.

Boris was well aware of the gravity of the situation and visibly affected by it. In a way, he saw it more clearly than his father, because he had just returned from the front where he had spent the better part of the past three years surrounded by soldiers, talking to them, eating and sleeping among them, traveling from one battlefield to another, and witnessing daily the human side of the drama. His understanding of what was going on in the minds of most Bulgarians was better than the king's, who had a very good grasp of the military situation but only as reported to him by his generals and ministers.

Despite his rank, the young man was not intimidating, and people talked freely to him. In contrast to his imperious father, the prince's manner was simple, almost unregal at times, allowing for frank conversation. Especially during the last few weeks, with the military reverses eroding the morale of the troops, he had heard firsthand many complaints and grievances, many depressing tales. It was obvious that the crown prince was a deeply worried young man and Stambolisky, bidding goodbye to him felt a certain sympathy for him.

That evening Boris heard news from his father that only confirmed his fears. Events were unraveling faster than expected. In a few hours a Bulgarian delegation was scheduled to leave secretly for Salonika to meet with the Entente's commander-in-chief in Macedonia, General Franchet-d'Esperey, and ask for an armistice. The end seemed near.

It had been a terrible week for Prince Boris. Six days earlier, he had rushed to the Macedonian front when the Anglo-French and Serbian forces had broken the Bulgarian positions at Dobro-Polé. There he had found a desperate situation. The troops, largely outnumbered, were retreating in disorder and the demoralization was rapidly spreading to the other units in the area. The enemy was advancing with virtually no organized resistance. In the village of Dabnishta the crown prince met large groups of retreating soldiers in rags—the exhausted, angry defenders of Dobro-Polé—and tried to halt their retreat. In spite of their bitterness, the throng of defeated fighters listened patiently as he urged them to reorganize the resistance and maintain discipline. With the help of his aide-de-camp and the available officers, the prince started forming new platoons and companies. No hostility was shown to him. Since the Balkan Wars, he had become a familiar figure among the combat troops, and nobody, not even the pacifists, blamed the king's son for the policies of his father.

They listened and obeyed when the young prince, a handsome if frail-looking figure in combat uniform, harangued the makeshift battalions from the saddle and gave them their new assignments. Although soft-spoken, there was a definite competence and authority in the words of the youthful officer who had led men under enemy fire since he was eighteen.

Prince Boris ordered the troops to prepare new positions behind the village of Dabnishta, where the enemy had to be stopped. He then galloped to the various camps pointing out the correct emplacements for the machine guns. Night had fallen by the time he left the new defense position and drove his car over the bumpy village roads to Prilep to ask the German command for reinforcements. His request was turned down. He spent the rest of the night driving about the area, looking for scattered units, pleading with commanders to check the enemy until reinforcements arrived, trying to stop the retreat at the flank of the newly organized positions.

The next day, September 20, Boris cabled his father: "Condition of the army here more grave than I would have thought. Disintegration of the 1st Division is serious. There are signs of Bolsheviks. The Entente is stronger numerically than we. This morning the 3rd Division retreated. If this continues, the railroad is liable to be cut soon. Hindenburg's[2] refusal to give us real reinforcement is disheartening. If our situation does not improve tomorrow, feel it will be necessary to demand the German emperor personally to send one division. Very devoted, RYLSKI."

After sending the cable, as dawn was breaking, Prince Boris, binoculars in hand and equipped with a gas-mask, climbed the ridge near Dabnishta and joined the defenders of the newly established position. The battle started early that morning and raged throughout the day. Supported by intense artillery fire, the Anglo-French forces launched three consecutive assaults, causing heavy casualties among the poorly equipped defenders. But three times the attacks were repulsed. Boris remained at the advance positions, remarkably calm under the thunderous fire. At one point, a shell exploded between him and his aide-de-camp, and as the smoke obscured both men, the soldiers in the nearby trenches thought the prince had been killed. But he walked away unhurt and unruffled. His calm was as much a matter of fatalism as of courage: a superstitious man, Boris believed that "his hour" had not come yet.

---

[2]Field Marshal Paul von Hindenburg, chief of the German General Staff.

The Bulgarian positions held at Dabnishta, and the prince left in search of the division headquarters. On his way, he helped a wounded sergeant to his automobile, then transported two other wounded men to the field hospital, covering his car with blood. After looking in vain for the headquarters, Boris realized that it was too late. The entire sector was lost. He rushed back to Dabnishta and gave the command for an orderly retreat, lest the remaining troops be captured by the encircling enemy. Indeed, the French were advancing and had already blocked the road to Veless, the prince's next destination, where he was to meet his father. That night he was forced to drive with his headlights off, taking innumerable sideroads and detours, to avoid French patrols. King Ferdinand arrived at the headquarters in Veless soon after, and Boris had the opportunity to brief him personally about the debacle he had just witnessed.

The king had come from the German headquarters in Skopje, where he had made a last, impassioned effort to obtain from his allies the reinforcement of a few divisions. But the Germans had said they were in no position to send help.

Ferdinand returned to Sofia on the afternoon of September 23 in a morose mood after his unsuccessful visit to the Germans. But the telegram he found on his arrival discouraged him completely. Sent by the chief of the General Staff, Major General Bourmov, it read:

"I sent today the following telegram to Field Marshal von Hindenburg: 'Our situation on the Macedonian front extremely grave. If events continue to develop in the same way, we face certain catastrophe. The situation can be saved only with immediate and adequate help from you. Our present forces, aided by only two Austro-Hungarian divisions and some promised German battalions, cannot change the situation. The heavy fighting has completely exhausted many of our units.

" 'The recent reverses have strongly shaken the troops' morale and weakened their resistance. Our army can be helped only by sending immediately no fewer than ten German and Austrian divisions with powerful artillery. The critical situation is worsening rapidly, and if these reinforcements are delayed, even ten divisions will not be able to help.' "

Ferdinand read and reread the cable carefully. Then he took a red pencil and scribbled in the margin, in large letters, "KRAY!" (The End!). Immediately after, he summoned his ministers to an emergency Crown Council meeting for the following day and sent a message to Boris to return.

✳    ✳    ✳

As Prince Boris traveled to Sofia that night, he was increasingly distressed by the scenes along his way: a defeated army in disarray, mobs of disillusioned, angry men disobeying their officers, long columns of untidy soldiers with bitterness and revenge in their eyes. Reaching the capital, he sensed a new tension among the authorities: to the fear of the advancing enemy was added the threat of the mutineers.

The same tension pervaded the Crown Council meeting on the following day. As soon as it began, Prime Minister Malinov proposed that the government immediately request Germany and Austro-Hungary to start negotiations for a general peace treaty. Malinov, a democrat who had always opposed Bulgaria's alliance with the Central Powers, had replaced the pro-German Premier Radoslavov only three months earlier, and the people expected him to extricate Bulgaria from the war. If Germany and Austria-Hungary refused, he said, then Bulgaria should sign a separate armistice.

The chief of staff, General Bourmov, insisted that all was not lost, that Bulgaria was still capable of continuing the war. But none of the ministers was convinced, they all supported Malinov. The king remained uncharacteristically silent during the discussions, and he adjourned the meeting without expressing his opinion, and before a decision had been reached.

Alarming news continued to reach Sofia throughout that night. The army on the front was disintegrating, and mass desertions and mutiny were reported. In the western town of Kyustendil throngs of deserters had attacked general headquarters, killing two officers.

The ministers felt they had to act with no further delay. They met on the following morning, September 25, and without consulting the king, the cabinet unanimously voted to send a delegation to negotiate with the enemy in Salonika. Finance Minister Andrey Liapchev was designated to head the mission.

After the emergency meeting, Prime Minister Malinov wrote a letter to King Ferdinand in longhand, which was delivered immediately to the palace.

"Your Majesty," he wrote, "when the Crown Council convened at the palace yesterday, the situation at the front was different; today it is worse. Even yesterday, the council was already of the opinion that we must strive for an honorable peace. The chief of staff still believed it possible to consolidate the front, thus enabling us to ask for better armistice conditions.

"This morning, however, it was established that the situation is much worse." Here Malinov quoted top commanders who predicted a disaster and suggested an armistice. He also mentioned the large bands of deserters marching toward Sofia and the lack of German and Austrian help. For these reasons, "the government feels compelled to conclude that the war is lost and there is nothing else to be done but ask for peace. Only in this way can the country be spared destruction and all the horrors Bulgaria can expect if the enemy crosses her frontiers."

That was the very day the king received Stambolisky.

Although his back was to the wall, Ferdinand did not like the fact that his ministers had met and taken decisions without him, nor the defeatist tone of Malinov's letter. He did not reply to the urgent message.

The king had been aware for a long time that the situation was critical, but had refused to concede that everything was lost. He was torn by an inner conflict: abandoning his allies, being disloyal to Germany and Austria-Hungary and asking for a separate peace was repugnant to him and he resisted it as long as he could. Not, however, for the reasons alleged by his detractors. To explain his attachment to the Central Powers as being based merely on his German origin, on some stubborn conspiratorial loyalty to his royal cousins and former compatriots, was too simplistic and ignored his intricate character, his ambitions, and his long record as Bulgaria's ruler.

Ferdinand's reluctance had more to do with the prevalent ideas of military honor, of battlefield comradeship, of ideological affinity with, and gratitude for, the nations who had supported Bulgaria's territorial claims. This moral code was deeply ingrained in his character and perhaps overly honored in the tradition of the princely houses of the time. But, above all, his resistance had to do with the awareness that he was playing his last trump—the ultimate chance to achieve the task he had set for himself and for his subjects, which had reached the proportions of an obsession. In the thirty years of his reign, the national ideal of a Greater Bulgaria—the unification of the mother country with her lost territories in Macedonia, Thrace, and Dobrudja—had become a passionate personal goal for the foreign-born prince. It was his crusade. Every bit of political instinct and intelligence, of vanity and arrogance, of statesmanship and shrewdness, of lust for power and sense of duty that he possessed—and he had all of these in royal doses—had come to play in the pursuit of this dream. He had fully committed himself to its realization, in spite of his enemies, in spite of the entire world, and if necessary, in spite of the Bulgarian people themselves. And, now, with the goal within reach after the victories of the first two years of the war, it was inconceivable that he must abandon it!

After his audience with Stambolisky, he remained silent for the rest of the day. That evening, as no word came from the palace, the prime minister urgently delivered a second handwritten letter:

"Your Majesty, the Council of Ministers, which is in uninterrupted session, believes that every hour is being wasted and that it can no longer wait. News from the front attests that the routing of our army is complete. We are threatened by catastrophe. If Your Majesty does not accept the Council of Ministers' decision to seek immediately an armistice and then peace, it will refuse to take further responsibility. The acting commander-in-chief informs me that the situation is hopeless, that disaster is inevitable. He wants an immediate decision."

That evening two separate missions left the fear-stricken city of Sofia. Liapchev took the humiliating road to the enemy headquarters in Salonika. Stambolisky headed for the tumultuous center of the soldiers' mutiny.

*　　*　　*

A vivid, poignant memory from the past haunted the young prince these somber days of September 1918, a scene he had hoped never to witness again. He saw himself and his brother, barely nineteen and eighteen years old, silently riding on horseback next to their father at the head of the long, dust-covered columns of the defeated Bulgarian armies returning to Sofia at the end of the second Balkan War in 1913. Teary-eyed crowds were massed on both sides of the streets to greet husbands, sons, and brothers who had survived the cruel ordeal. It was a moving scene of sadness in dignity, like a giant procession of mourners returning from a funeral, the kind of moment a young man never forgets.

The Russian envoy to Sofia, Neklyudov, described it in his memoirs: "The soldiers, in their brown uniforms spoiled by sun and rain, bore traces of extreme fatigue on their emaciated and sunburnt faces, but nevertheless they marched with spirit and pride. Most of the generals whose names had become so popular in 1912 were with their troops. And the population of the town greeted them calmly and sympathetically, recognizing they had done their whole duty, and had deserved well of their country. Most of the soldiers were adorned with flowers, and so were King Ferdinand and his two sons, who were greeted by the crowd without the slightest show of hostility."

Without hostility . . . five years later, Prince Boris wished that could be said again.

# CHAPTER II

# Childhood and Youth

STANDING RESPECTFULLY in front of the gilded desk clustered with silver frames, leather-bound books, clocks and valuable objects, the two sons listen attentively to the king's bitter briefing on the critical situation. Seated behind the large table, "Le Monarque," as the children always referred to Ferdinand among themselves, was angry and frustrated, and his complaints were spotted with sarcastic comments.

Boris and Kyril, now twenty-four and twenty-two, had frequently endured their father's bad moods. The most terrifying were when some mischief or unfinished homework had been reported. Normally, the disciplining was done by the tutor, Captain Nikola Kourtokliev. But sometimes he would say, "I'll go and tell His Majesty!" and the king would summon them to his office: the same room as today, imposing and silent like a sanctuary; the same table covered with family photographs, Fabergé objects and personal relics; and the same frightened children standing at attention, waiting for the unsmiling monarch behind the desk to break the silence.

Ferdinand usually spoke to them in French, but if he addressed them in Bulgarian, the boys' hearts sank, for they knew then that Le Monarque was very angry.

"You lazy jackasses! Aren't you ashamed?" He would wave some school notebook. "Is this the homework of an intelligent person?" He would point at a few mistakes in their schoolwork, some misspelled words or faulty arithmetic. "Shame on you! Illiterates! Why did I create you?" Then he would give the boys repeated examples of how bright and studious other people's children were, and how mediocre his sons were.

But more often he did not scream or shout. His tone remained calm, but it was icy, sarcastic, cutting. And he always reminded the petrified children that they were his "creation," existing by his favor. The lecture over, the boys would be dismissed, with some extra homework assigned as punishment.

Relieved that the ordeal was over, Boris and Kyril would rush to the children's quarters on the ground floor hidden behind the palace park facing the Boulevard Tsar Osvoboditel, Sofia's main street. It was a cozy apart-ment—two double bedrooms, a small salon and dining room—that the four royal children shared through adolescence. They especially enjoyed the connecting veranda, leading to the garden. They used it for a playroom and kept their toys there—mostly models of trains and automobiles, as well as the girls' dolls. In good weather, they played outside the veranda, sheltered from the boulevard's traffic by the trees and the high park wall.

Evdokia and Nadejda, the younger sisters, would be waiting anxiously. "How was it, Bo? What did Le Monarque do to you, Kiki?" Then the confidences, the giggles, and back to the interrupted game.

Now, in this gloomy evening of September 1918, the sisters, young ladies of twenty and eighteen, are once again waiting in the same "chil-dren's" apartment. "How bad is it, Bo? What shall we do now, Kiki?"

"It's very, very bad. We may have to leave . . ."

*     *     *

They are still as close as they were throughout their childhood. Four children who grew up without a mother, in the shadow of an overpowering father who never gave them an affectionate hug or a tender word: "Bo," the eldest, the most sensitive, a very intelligent youngster and conscientious worker; "Kiki," a bigger, stronger boy although a year younger, more extroverted and mischievous, and a lazy student; Evdokia, or "Koka," four years younger than the crown prince, probably the brightest child, a girl with an unusually strong will and explosive temper, like her father's; Nadejda, called "May" or "Micky," a pleasant and obedient girl at whose birth their mother, Princess Maria-Louisa, née Bourbon-Parma, died.

They grew up without many friends of their own age, nor did they see much of their princely relatives abroad as most European monarchies were politically on bad terms with King Ferdinand. And Bulgarian playmates created problems of jealousy and intrigue among their parents. In addition, the absence of a mother and the iron discipline imposed by the father united the four children in an unusual way. For the twenty-four-year-old crown prince, there were only three people in the world with whom he was intimate: his brother and his two sisters. Of them, he was intellectually closest to Evdokia, who had a considerable influence on him.

Even at this age, the sound of The Monarch's steps and his cane still made them nervous when they heard him approaching on the long palace corridors. Ferdinand has remained a stranger to them, permitting no intimacy, even though he cared for them. He was most interested in their education, health and behavior, but he demanded their obedience, not their love. For them, as for everyone else, he remained on all occasions His Majesty the King. Even at twenty-four, Boris could not relax in his presence, did not dare show emotion, nor weakness, nor discuss intimate problems with him. Ferdinand seemed to prefer it this way. Their relationship was kept within the boundaries of education, duty, and dynasty.

When separated from his children, which was very often, Ferdinand was in constant contact, usually by telegram. From his frequent stops abroad he sent letters and postcards, sharing with them his excitement about the discovery of a rare mountain flower (described by its Latin name), or a butterfly. These messages were always educational, containing advice and instructions, but never affectionate.

The children were careful to observe a perfect regularity (and spelling) in the letters to their father. Whether vacationing at the seashore in Euxinograd palace, or in the mountain lodges in Rila, or remaining in Sofia, they had to report on their activities and state of health, with obligatory mention of the weather and the local flora and fauna. The letters, diligently copied from preliminary drafts, were usually written in French, starting with "Cher Papa" and ending with the respectful "baisemains"—kissing father's hand. These were formal letters, stiff and anxious to please, as was the entire relationship with the father-sovereign.

Yet, it was not an unhappy childhood. On the contrary, the closeness between the children and the privileges that go with royal position made for joyful times in the family palaces, villas, and lodges. The most frequented among them was the country estate of Vrana, seven miles out of Sofia, with its big white house that Ferdinand had built in a style inspired by traditional Bulgarian architecture.

The beautiful vast parks of Vrana, which Ferdinand designed himself, were a botanist-king's dream come true. The long alleys covered with yellow gravel and bordered by platans, linden, pines, birch, and rare species of shrubs looked like a most romantic bridle path. The rock gardens with edelweiss and other Alpine flowers, the rose gardens filled with every existing kind of rose, the cherry trees in the exquisite orchards, the ponds with water lilies and gigantic floating "Victoria Regia," the hothouses packed with exotic flowers, and the thousands of neatly labeled plants and bushes could match any European botanical garden. Vrana was a favorite place for the royal children, especially because of the miniature train that Ferdinand had built in the park and that he, and later the boys, would drive.

Another favorite residence was Euxinograd, built on a cape of the Black Sea, accessible from the port of Varna by a picturesque road resembling the French Riviera "Corniche" and crossing a countryside of vineyards and villas. The red-brick Louis XIII chateau, with its high windows, clock tower, and magnificent view of the sea, was surrounded by a masterpiece of a park, another of the landscaping extravagances of the king, who had imported fifty thousand trees from Marseilles and hired a French landscape designer. By night, the illuminated spectacle of maritime pines, groves of rhododendron, huge pots of geraniums, rose bushes, rock gardens, hothouses, and Japanese gardens enchanted the most blasé of foreign guests. But what the royal children enjoyed most at Euxinograd was the sailing and the motorboat excursions. They explored every beach and cove of the magnificent Bulgarian coast, from the Rumanian border in the north to the Turkish frontier in the south. Boris grew up to be an excellent sailor, and Kyril, very interested in sports and mechanics, later developed a passion for speedboats. Never were the children so happy as during their summers at the Black Sea.

Their father and Captain Kourtokliev, however, were there to remind them that vacations and fun were the exception in a responsible person's life. The king was particularly demanding on the subject of his children's education. "Kourto," as the children called their instructor behind his back, had orders to treat them like any ordinary schoolchildren, i.e., to be a strict tutor and a firm disciplinarian. An army officer, he filled the bill to perfection. He installed two classrooms in the palace, fitted with the customary wooden schooldesks, blackboards and relief maps of Bulgaria, and ran the private school (the children called it "the circus") with military efficiency. The pupils had to wear the uniforms of the public schools: black tunics, buttoned up to the high collar and caps with hard visors for the boys; and navy-blue dresses with large sailors' collars, pleated skirts, and black stockings for the girls. The teachers were selected from the Sofia schools and the curriculum was identical. Kourtokliev supervised the homework, the children's behavior, and the daily schedule. Light spanking and ear-pulling were popular disciplinary methods in Bulgarian education, and "Kourto" did not make an exception of the king's children. They feared, but respected and even liked, their strict but devoted tutor.

Naturally, the children missed having a mother, especially Boris, who was the only one who remembered her well. He was five when Princess Maria-Louisa died. He idealized her and missed her tenderness all his life. The story was told that on her deathbed, the twenty-nine-year-old mother, feeling her end approaching, sent for her children and told Boris: "Be kind, my boy, always be kind!" Apocryphal or true, her testament affected the child enormously.

Ferdinand was a widower for nine years until he decided in 1908 that Bulgaria needed a queen, the royal palace a housekeeper, and the children a stepmother and chaperon. Romantic love or physical attraction did not figure at all among the factors in the king's selection of the forty-eight-year-old German princess Eleonore von Reuss-Kostritz. Her name was suggested by matchmakers in the Russian imperial family, and she proved to be an excellent choice. While neither a beauty nor a wit, Eleonore, an earnest and well-educated lady with an impressive record of voluntary Red Cross work in Manchuria during the Russo-Japanese War, became a devoted and useful queen. The king treated her as any other member of his household, but he realized that his self-effacing and considerate spouse had won the respect of the country and the affection of his children. During Boris's teenage years, Queen Eleonore played the role of glorified governess and chaperon to the royal children. As Boris was already fifteen when his stepmother was brought to the palace, her influence on him was limited, although he liked and respected her. At times, he felt sorry for her and was embarrassed by his father's treatment of her as, for instance, once in 1911. At that time, Ferdinand had accused his wife of plotting against him simply because Eleonore had invited the Rumanian Queen Elizabeth to stay for a few days in Euxinograd while Ferdinand was abroad. In a furious telegram to the seventeen-year-old prince, the king referred to his wife and her guest as "the two half-mad royal women, who concocted this affair together, taking advantage of my absence."

Ferdinand was a man of sensual appetites, who indulged his hedonistic inclinations. Among them, his fondness for handsome young men nourished rumors about his homosexual tendencies. Recent writings tend to depict him as a homosexual satyr in pursuit of blue-eyed lieutenants and valets. But this portrayal should be accepted with the greatest reservations, because the allegations come from one single source: hearsay reports of a disgruntled former palace tutor who was fired by the king. Nor does it take into account the well-established fact that His Majesty had a long record of succumbing to the attractions of numerous ladies of humble position, and, in addition to his four official children, had sired a few illegitimate ones, some of whom he discreetly supported financially. Ferdinand continued his procreative activities even into his late seventies.

It is more likely that his homosexual ventures, if any, were due to an oversexuality in a period when bisexuality was still taboo.

The royal children received a solid education, although later other duties and trips took a considerable part of their time and interfered with their formal studies. But Boris completed the required high school classes taught by teachers who came to the palace, and followed courses at the military school. There was little time left for sports, except for horseback riding, an obligatory part of a future officer's education. Boris never became enthusiastic about horses but learned to ride properly, better anyhow than his father, who disliked riding.

When Boris was fifteen, a tutor for the two princes was brought in from Switzerland. French in manner and eloquence, Constant Shaufelberger stayed with them for five years, until World War I, and became very attached to the crown prince for his intelligence, sensitivity, and kindness. But he also noticed how deeply inhibited Boris was by his father's domineering personality. It seemed that the children could be themselves only when Le Monarque was away. Luckily, Ferdinand traveled incessantly, most frequently in his luxurious private train, shooting in Hungary and Slovakia, visiting relatives in Vienna and Karlsbad, vacationing on the Riviera or in Capri. "The moment the royal standard was lowered on the palace roof," the tutor remembered, "a deep sigh of relief escaped from all chests, a smile bloomed on all lips. It was like a liberation. The four children could breathe. They ran and laughed, played boisterously and enjoyed themselves tremendously."

Other memories from the years before 1912, when Boris "came of age" in more ways than one, were also happy: the first time he saw Paris, brought by his father for a few days in the summer of 1910 . . . and the following year, the first "independent" long trip abroad, alone with Kyril—one month in Turkey, walking incognito in the streets of Istanbul and Smyrna, paying visits to the Sultan, cruising on the Bosporus, trying a conversation in Greek with the Orthodox Patriarch of Constantinople, and, of course, several excursions in the countryside looking for butterflies and unfamiliar plants. "Found 'Serapias' in the vicinity of Smyrna today," he would cable his father. "Kiki caught a 'Camilla' and an interesting 'Thaise.' Kiss your hand. Rylski."

Then, the splendor of George V's coronation in London, where he had been sent to represent his father for the summer. The crossing of the Channel on the British royal yacht in the company of other royalty; the elegant house on Berkeley Square put at his disposal; the Grand Cordon of Victoria Cross he received from the king; and the kindness with which George V put him at ease in the intimidating atmosphere of the fabulous festivities.

What an exciting year that was! A second, longer visit to Paris followed, with Shaufelberger as his guide, and Boris thrilled to be an unrecognized tourist in the metro and among the strollers on the "grands boulevards." And the audience with President Fallières, who decorated him with the Grand Cross of the Légion d' Honneur. It seemed that he never stopped traveling that year. Representing his father at a family funeral in Turin and at the imperial maneuvers in Russia (when Stolypin was assassinated before his eyes). And the long Mediterranean cruise with Kyril and Shaufelberger, to Corsica, Corfu, the coasts of North Africa and Spain, the Canary and the Balearic Islands.

*　　*　　*

In spite of Ferdinand's coldness, Boris had great esteem for his father and was impressed by his competence. This was not the biased admiration of a son: if not the best-liked person, King Ferdinand was generally recognized as probably the most outstanding personality among all European royalty. Boris was also proud of the tremendous progress achieved in Bulgaria under his father's innovative leadership. The prince had never dared argue with him. The very idea of opposing the sovereign, absolute master of the palace, was inconceivable. It was a matter of characters, true, but besides, what would be the use of disagreeing with an autocrat who *told* people how things should be, but never asked for their opinion?

Ferdinand's competence in matters concerning court life bordered on the infallible. He knew each one of his numerous residences intimately—each room, every piece of furniture, the trees and flowers in the gardens, the name of every servant. His memory for details was phenomenal. He had personally devised the daily palace routine and the duties of each member of his household and he did not tolerate the slightest infraction of his rules. As a result his chancery and household functioned with clockwork precision. None of the European aristocrats employed in his court knew the intricacies of protocol better than he, no foreign chef had better knowledge of *la grande cuisine*, let alone the unsophisticated Bulgarians. How then could anyone question his instructions concerning rank and precedence, menus and wines, or the proper music for each occasion?

Or talk about natural history? The reports of his early scientific expeditions, "Itinera principum S. Coburgi," describing the flora and fauna of Brazil and Northwest Africa, were included in the textbooks before he came to Bulgaria. Many species discovered by him were classified under the name of "ferdinandi," such as the butterfly "Biston graecarius ferdinandi." He knew a great deal about minerals, especially gems, which fascinated him as much as the jewelry and medals he studied, collected, and designed. And he passed some of his knowledge on to his children.

He was intolerant of people who made grammatical or spelling mistakes, and his mastery of French and German was remarkable. He also spoke English, Russian, Italian, Turkish, Hungarian, and even Albanian. His Bulgarian—a language of which he was totally ignorant before he came to Sofia—became so good that, though he spoke with a foreign accent, his letters were written in impeccable style and rarely contained a spelling error.

How could young Boris, the obedient pupil, ever argue with his omniscient father? Ferdinand knew about guns and regiments (and a lot about uniforms!), about hunting (which became Boris's favorite pastime), about Wagnerian music—he saw the composer's widow Cosima regularly at Bayreuth and discussed music with her friends. He had driven cars since the early days of the automobile and knew a great deal about mechanics. And he passed on to his son his hobby of driving locomotives: Boris was as good a train engineer as any professional.

Ferdinand's competence in so many fields quite dominated the newly liberated peasant country whose development, although remarkably rapid and successful, had only barely begun. Unfortunately, he flaunted his superiority with a certain condescension and arrogance. He was not above making witty remarks in French in the presence of Bulgarians who did not understand foreign languages; nor above serving unfamiliar courses, such as artichokes or asparagus, to peasant-born politicians and be amused at their difficulty during official dinners.

Boris dutifully learned the princely skills and liked some of them: he became an accomplished linguist, hunter, natural scientist. He was equally good in other pursuits, but his heart was not in them. Thus, he mastered etiquette, but it bored him. He knew about uniforms and medals, but found them sometimes frivolous and embarrassing. An expert in ordering a gastronomic dinner, he was, unlike his father, not a gourmet; he was equally happy with a bread-and-cheese snack during an excursion. Ferdinand enjoyed galas, parades, pomp and pageantry, and it showed: he was excellent at it. The crown prince went through the motions, because it was his duty. And it showed, too.

He had still not overcome his timidity during the big state dinners he had had to attend since an early age. The palace looked especially festive on these occasions, with ADCs in gala uniforms, liveried footmen frozen like statues at each door, royal guards in silver-braided red tunics and astrakhan hats with tall feathers flanking the illuminated marble staircase, ladies-in-waiting in Parisian evening gowns. The guests begin to arrive: foreign diplomats in full-dress gold uniforms, ministers in white tie and decorations, ladies covered with jewelry. Then, the announcement of His Majesty's appearance. The imposing figure of the sovereign, graciously acknowledging the homages, an image of self-confidence and power. He would wear tails and white tie, or breeches and silk stockings *à la Française,* or resplendent military uniform bedecked with dozens of medals, like an overdecorated Christmas tree.

The king's place was at the center of the long banquet table, opposite the queen, who wore splendid jewels from his collection, selected by him. While dispensing charm and wit right and left, the king keenly observed everybody and everything. The bell, hidden under the tablecloth in front of him, helped him to control the pantry and direct the service of the army of busy lackeys and wine stewards.

In time, Boris became accustomed to these interminable dinners for eighty or more guests, served in Sèvres porcelain with the king's coat of arms, heavy monogrammed silver and the finest crystal glassware. He learned how to converse with his neighbors at table while the orchestra played Viennese waltzes. Since his adolescence, he had been familiar with calligraphed menus, in French of course, as for example:

Consommé froid
Zucco

———

Tartelettes à la Diplomate
Johannisberg 1868

———

Filet de bœuf à la Bordelaise
Château Léoville 1875

———

Mousseline de foies gras en aspic

Suprêmes de dindonneaux
à la crème
Clos Vougeot 1875

———

Sorbets de griottes au
vin de Romanée

———

Bécassines rôties sur canapés
Dry Imperial

———

Salade

———

Haricots verts à l'Anglaise

———

Profiterolles au chocolat
Château-Yquem 1878

———

Bombe gaufrée à la pistache

———

Dessert
Muscat Rivesaltes

But these lavish banquets were nothing more than a boring duty for the prince. So were the parades, the decorations, and the uniforms. His mind was elsewhere—in the mountains and the Black Sea, with the butterflies, the Alpine flowers, the locomotives. And ever since the wars, his prematurely aged adolescent heart had remained with the poor devils in the muddy trenches. For a young man of twenty-four, it was a heavy cross to bear.

*       *       *

The trouble with King Ferdinand, which turned out to be a disaster for Bulgaria, was that he was too grand a monarch for such a small country. There were elements of an operetta, but also of a tragedy, in the marriage between the dazzling, immensely ambitious European prince and the modest Balkan nation. The irony is that among the Western kings and princes (most coming from the same half-dozen Germanic families), Ferdinand was one of the most intelligent, dynamic, and well-prepared for the role. With all due respect to the royal institution, it must be admitted that some of his colleagues were no beacons of intelligence, and mediocrity was among their most obvious characteristics. But they nevertheless ruled over important nations in an epoch when monarchs still had considerable power. These countries should have had kings like Ferdinand, a sovereign with the imperiousness and the great vision of a Louis XIV or Peter the Great. Instead, the brightest descendant of the Coburgs and the Orléans found himself on the throne of a poor, powerless nation of less than 4 million inhabitants, 80 percent of them peasants, struggling to preserve their newly acquired independence against the continuous threats of hostile neighbors and intriguing Great Powers.

Bulgaria, an old kingdom, was founded in 681 A.D. when the Bulgars, a Hunnish tribe from Central Asia, invaded and conquered the eastern part of the Balkan peninsula and organized the indigenous Slavic population into a state. The kingdom had had a glorious past, reaching a high cultural level by the ninth century and extending its rule over the major part of the Balkans, but it had fallen under Turkish domination in the fourteenth century. The Ottoman rule lasted five hundred years, during which period the Bulgarians had no political rights. After bloody uprisings and massacres in the 1870s which horrified the world, Russia declared war on Turkey in 1877, defeated it, and liberated Bulgaria. Emperor Alexander II became Bulgaria's "Tsar-Osvoboditel," the king-liberator.

The initial euphoria was soon replaced by disenchantment in the face of international rivalries as Bulgaria became a helpless pawn in the Great Powers' game of spheres of influence. While Austria, Germany, and England refused to permit the creation of a strong Russian satellite in the proximity of the Straits and the Mediterranean, Russia was ruthlessly trying to use the new princedom for its expansionist designs, which were not very different under the emperors than they were later under the Soviets. Thus, while on the one hand, in the 1878 Berlin Treaty the Western powers amputated some regions, like Macedonia and Thrace, from the newly liberated Bulgarian state, on the other hand, the young princedom was increasingly suffocating in the bearlike hug of its Russian protectors.

The first Bulgarian monarch, Alexander Battenberg, a valiant German prince who was a nephew of the Russian emperor, fell out of favor with St. Petersburg when he became too popular with his Bulgarian subjects and too independent of the tsar. After a few plots by pro-Russian officers and politicians, the promising ruler was deposed and sent into exile after only seven years on the throne. Thus, in 1886, Bulgaria became a princedom without a prince.

To fill the vacancy was not an easy task. By its constitution, the country needed a ruler of princely descent, and as there was no titled nobility in Bulgaria, the selection had to be made abroad. But it needed the approval of the major powers, an almost acrobatic feat in view of their fierce competition for influence in Eastern Europe. There were few suitable candidates. Nor did the reports of Battenberg's ordeals during his short reign do much to inspire enthusiasm for the thankless job. Many Europeans considered Battenberg a lucky man to have escaped a more tragic fate after his years of constant maneuvering between Russian and Austrian schemes, of a war with Serbia, and a number of coup-d'etats and conspiracies.

How does an inexperienced nation go about finding itself a sovereign? The Bulgarians did it with innocence, which for a moment amused sophisticated Europe. The Sobranié (Parliament) designated a delegation of three prominent citizens and sent them on tour of the European capitals in search of a prince. After visiting Belgrade, Vienna, Berlin, and London, the candidate who impressed them the most was the dashing Prince Ferdinand of Saxe-Coburg-Gotha, a combination of a wealthy dandy and a serious natural scientist, who lived in splendor in Vienna and was a lieutenant in the Austro-Hungarian army. The blood in his veins could not have been bluer: a grandson of the last king of France, a nephew of Queen Victoria, a cousin of the Belgian and Spanish royal families, Ferdinand was related to every reigning dynasty in Europe. For the Bulgarian emissaries, he had another important quality: he was willing. In fact, he was more than willing, he was eager, and, a decisive factor, his mother had made up her mind that her youngest son, her favorite, whom she knew to be so much brighter than most of her royal relatives, would one day be a king.

Princess Clémentine of Orléans, a daughter of King Louis-Philippe of France, was a formidable, domineering seventy-year-old lady with a sharp mind and an iron will. Learning of the arrival of the three Bulgarians in Vienna, she knew that the moment to fulfill her ambitions had come. A meeting "by chance" was arranged between Ferdinand and the Bulgarians at the Vienna opera during the intermission, and the prince declared right away his interest in the Bulgarian crown. The next day when the three delegates called on him at the magnificent Coburg palace in Vienna, he confirmed his readiness, adding, however, that he hoped that Russia would not oppose his candidacy.

Ferdinand and his mother were in for a cruel disappointment. Not only Russia—who at the time was engaged in a bitter conflict with the anti-Russian Bulgarian government—but all the European powers declared their opposition to Ferdinand's candidacy. When the prince informed Tsar Alexander III of the Bulgarian Parliament's offer, the tsar answered that insofar as he was concerned, neither the Parliament nor the government in Bulgaria was legitimate. As he told his foreign minister Giers: "The candida-

ture is as ridiculous as the individual." Queen Victoria sent from Windsor
Castle a furious telegram to her prime minister, Lord Salisbury: "Hope no
truth in respect to Prince Ferdinand of Coburg as candidate. He is totally
unfit—delicate, eccentric, and effeminate. Should be stopped at once." Then
she wrote to her cousin Princess Clémentine, that she disapproved of her
son's candidacy.

Austria preferred to avoid confronting Russia and, in any case, neither
the Austrian emperor Franz-Joseph nor his foreign minister took Ferdinand
seriously. In the words of Ferdinand's biographer*:

> Neither could believe that this weird, rich and decadent young Prince,
> who abominated horses and hunting and adored chasing butterflies,
> armed with a net and killing jar, could succeed in a position which had
> broken Alexander of Battenberg, that contemporary model of martial
> valour.'

As for Prussia, Chancellor Bismarck's reply to Ferdinand's uncle, the
Duke of Coburg, read:

> Last December, the Vienna cabinet adopted a discouraging attitude
> and the Russian government one of harsh disapproval and hostility.
> There is no indication or likelihood that the views of these two major
> Powers have changed since. In these circumstances I advise you not to
> consent to an acceptance of Prince Ferdinand of the offered candida-
> ture. This undertaking, begun against the advice of Austria and against
> the will of Russia would, in my opinion, have no prospects.

A seven-month period of painful waiting and behind-the-scene maneuvering followed. Discouraged, Ferdinand often thought of withdrawing.
But his ambition and desire for the disputed crown grew. His mother was
constantly behind him, goading and mobilizing all relatives and friends who
might help.

The Bulgarians were growing impatient. The regents who ruled in Sofia
were determined to have a new prince as soon as possible, Ferdinand or
somebody else, with or without Russian approval. It took great courage for
a small country to defy the Russians openly, and for a European prince to go
against the will of the tsar and the Great Powers. But the Bulgarians
accepted the risk and again sent an emissary to ask the hesitating Ferdinand
whether, yes or no, he accepted the proffered throne. Although torn by
doubts, Ferdinand agreed. On July 7, 1887, Bulgaria's Grand National
Sobranié unanimously proclaimed him the ruling prince. When informed,

---

*Stephen Constant, in "Foxy Ferdinand"

the Russian emperor wrote on the report's margin: "What a disgusting business!," and his foreign minister called it "a slap in Russia's face." Queen Victoria, for her part, instructed Lord Salisbury to "make clear that we have no hand in Prince Ferdinand C's election."

The twenty-seven-year-old Ferdinand was received with enthusiasm and great hopes. The contrast between his private life and what he found in his new country was far more striking than anything he and his elegant entourage of French-speaking aristocrats had ever expected. The difference between the splendor of Franz-Joseph's Vienna and the muddy streets of Sofia, between the pomp and frivolity of court life and the frugality of rural and small-town society, between the carefree, hedonistic existence of Europe's privileged and the earnest commitment of patriots fighting to preserve their independence, would presumably preclude any affinity between the spoiled German-French, Catholic prince and his hard-working slavic, Eastern-Orthodox subjects. But things turned out very differently.

Ferdinand became deeply involved in his adoptive country, learning its language and history, and exploring the flora and fauna of the land. Quite simply, he fell in love with the country. The first years of his reign were extremely difficult. Denied recognition by the Great Powers and ignored by a hostile Russia, he found his ally in another young man, Bulgaria's strongman Stefan Stambolov, who was barely resisting Russia's attempts to dominate the country. Later the alliance broke, and after Stambolov's assassination, Ferdinand mended relations with the Russian emperor. Europe also came to recognize him gradually and grudgingly, but it never liked him. His reputation as a scheming, arrogant, and above all, too independent monarch, never changed.

In Ferdinand's thirty years on the throne (at first as reigning prince, then as proclaimed king in 1908), young, underdeveloped Bulgaria achieved spectacular progress, greatly due to his leadership. He built modern roads and railroads, organized education, the public health services, justice and administration, and modernized the army. Sofia, the sleepy Oriental town, began to look like a pleasant little capital, with a university, good theater and opera, museums, zoological and botanical gardens.

A man who loved his profession, Ferdinand's ambition was to be a great king. As far as Bulgaria's material and cultural progress was concerned, he succeeded brilliantly, but he was less successful in his foreign policy and military ventures. In response to his subjects' unanimous yearning to recover the territories of Macedonia and Thrace, he became almost more Bulgarian than the Bulgarians. As a consequence, he impetuously led the nation into three wars: gloriously in 1912, disastrously in 1913, and now, in World War I, in another abortive attempt to regain the lost lands.

*      *      *

One wonders whether there can be a clear distinction between public and personal in the life of a royal family. Where exactly does the one end and the other begin? How much privacy had Prince Boris known in his childhood?

His very existence began as a state function. He arrived in this world on January 30, 1894, greeted by a 101-gun salute, and his first gasp for air triggered thousands of church bells, many parades, and a general euphoria. Barely a few hours old, he was proclaimed honorary chief of a number of regiments, bestowed the decoration of Saint-Alexander and the military medal For Valor, and promoted to the rank of second lieutenant.

For his mother, the gentle twenty-four-year-old Princess Maria-Luisa, the childbirth was a semiofficial performance, as was her pregnancy. Prime Minister Stambolov, a hard man whom she could not stand, had to be present in the bedroom during her labor in order to attest to the authenticity of the crown prince. Unpleasant as this was for the sensitive mother, she hardly saw it as anything unusual. A descendant of the kings of France and Sicily and the dukes of Parma, she had been brought up to accept her duties. Obedience to tradition and protocol was an essential part of a princess's education. It was reflected in the way she would live, marry, produce children (preferably male), run the palace household, accept the treatment of her princely husband, and even in the way she would die. Duty and dignity. A princess did not know otherwise and therefore was not necessarily unhappy, especially if she had the luck to be singled out for the supreme mission—marriage to a reigning monarch.

Maria-Luisa was the eldest of the nine children of Duke Robert of Parma and Maria-Pia of Bourbon-Naples, a quiet girl who grew up with an English governess in Switzerland and Biarritz, spoke five languages, played the piano and guitar, painted well and read Italian poetry. Beautiful she was not, but her narrow long face with a long nose and, in the words of her future lady-in-waiting,[1] "beautiful eyes, the color of aquamarine, large and transparently clear behind their thick dark lashes," was pleasant and expressed intelligence and sensitivity.

Not that it mattered very much. Ferdinand, prodded by his mother and the prime minister, had consented to a consort, but like all royal marriages, it had to be a marriage of convenience. After unsuccessfully approaching various wealthier and more important princesses, his choice fell on the Duke of Parma's daughter.

But the duke posed an absolute condition for his consent: the future children had to be Catholic! An article in the Bulgarian Constitution, requiring that the crown prince be of the Eastern-Orthodox religion, had therefore to be amended. It was not easy, but Prime Minister Stambolov

---

[1] Anna Stancioff

badly wanted an illustrious princess on the Bulgarian throne and he obtained
the Sobranié's agreement. The current animosity toward Russia, an Orthodox nation, facilitated Stambolov's task. The Duke of Parma gave his
consent.

In January 1893, after visiting Emperor Franz-Joseph and obtaining his
approval of the marriage, Ferdinand met his future bride and the engagement was celebrated in Schwartzau, the Bourbon-Parma family's Austrian
castle. Princess Clémentine was delighted to see a union between the
grandson of King Louis-Philippe of France and a great-granddaughter of
King Charles X of France, thus reconciling the Orléans and the Bourbons.
Nevertheless, as a typical future mother-in-law, she wrote to Queen
Victoria: "Ferdinand is very happy and so am I. My future daughter is
unhappily not very pretty. It is the only thing which is lacking, since she is
charming, good, very witty, intelligent, and very likeable." The wedding
took place at Pianore, the Duke of Parma's Italian villa. Nine months later
Prince Boris was born.

The choice of the baby's name—Boris Clement Robert Maria Pie Louis
Stanislas Xavier, Prince of Tirnovo—was another political act, an exercise in
symbolism and family etiquette. Boris, for the great king who converted
Bulgaria to Christianity; Clement, for grandmother Clémentine, now living
in the palace; Robert, for the Duke of Parma; Maria, for the baby's mother;
Pie, for Pope Pius, Maria-Luisa's godfather. And "Prince of Tirnovo"?
What title could better please the nation than that of the ancient capital, the
picturesque North-Bulgarian town?

The christening also turned into a political affair, causing a tremendous
international uproar. Honoring the commitment made to his wife's father,
and the religion of both the Coburg and Bourbon-Parma houses, the
newborn prince was christened a Roman Catholic by the pope's delegate in
the Sofia palace. But bitter disappointment filled every Bulgarian heart.
Ferdinand sensed the popular frustration. And he had enough political sense
to realize that Boris's christening in the foreign religion was a setback in his
endeavor to identify the dynasty with the Bulgarian nation. He was also
thinking of ending Bulgaria's international isolation by seeking a détente
with Russia. Nothing would please the nation, consolidate the dynasty, and
gain the Russian tsar's favor more than a conversion of the crown prince to
the Orthodox faith.

Ferdinand's personal conflict was extremely difficult. A Catholic himself, he knew that neither the Vatican nor his family would accept the
conversion. This could lead to his excommunication. Having also solemnly
given his word to his father-in-law, his honor was at stake. On the other
hand, after eight years on the throne, the Bulgarian crown had become the
most important thing in his life.

He tried desperately to obtain a dispensation from the pope. For this,

his Catholic family's support was badly needed, but he failed to convince any relative, except his mother, after a year-long and vehement opposition. Ferdinand sent his trusted aide Dimitri Stancioff on a secret mission to the Vatican, but Leo XIII would not hear of such an apostasy. Meanwhile, the Bulgarian public was growing more restless, and more voices in the Sobranié were demanding the conversion of Prince Boris. Promising to consider the matter, Ferdinand went personally to the Vatican. The pope castigated him severely: "You want me to sanction your son's death, the death of his soul? It would be spiritual murder!" In vain Ferdinand spoke of Bulgaria's unanimous wish, the political imperatives, the dynasty's survival. Unmoved, Leo XIII reminded him that the Duke of Parma "gave me his word of honor and on your behalf, yours, that the children of this union would be brought up in the Catholic church. It was only then that I agreed to the marriage." Showing no sympathy for Ferdinand's problem, the pope's only advice was, "Abdicate, Prince, abdicate!," adding, "If you deliver your son Boris into schism, you are excommunicated, ipso facto!"

Back in Sofia, Ferdinand was so upset that for the first time he considered abdicating. But presented with a strongly worded government request, he decided to defy the pope, his family, and his wife by proclaiming that the crown prince would join the Orthodox church. An explosion of popular joy followed the announcement. Signaling a major shift of alliances, the king asked Tsar Nicholas II to be the crown prince's godfather.

Pope Leo excommunicated Ferdinand. The family was outraged and many relatives never spoke to him again. But the most deeply upset was Boris's mother. Maria-Luisa was crushed by the conversion which, as a devout Catholic, she considered an apostasy, and as the Duke of Parma's daughter, a betrayal. All during her husband's agonizing hesitations (she was pregnant again at the time), she had begged him not to break his promise. But she had little influence on her despot of a husband. When Kyril was born, however, he was discreetly baptized in the Catholic faith, as were the two princesses, who followed. Boris was the only one in the family who had to be an Orthodox.

At the announcement of Boris's conversion, Maria-Luisa, profoundly disturbed, left with baby Kyril for the French Riviera. A family friend, Princess Radziwill, wrote in a letter that Maria-Louisa's health was ". . . greatly shaken by all her recent emotions. Her parting from little Boris was horrible. They had to tear the child from her arms and the poor woman was in a faint for two hours." The lady-in-waiting Anna Stancioff noted that the Riviera brought a little relief, "but letters, telegrams and news of the forsaken child, all combined to crucify the unhappy mother, who seemed more fragile and ethereal than ever."

The Orthodox christening of Boris was celebrated in Sofia's cathedral, with the Russian special envoy, General Kutuzov, acting as godfather by proxy for Tsar Nicholas. Maria-Luisa was not present. (Convalescing in Europe, she returned only in May 1896, still sad but resigned.) In the presence of the country's leaders and elite, and the representatives of a few non-Catholic nations, the two-year-old prince, dressed in white with the red sash of Saint-Alexander's Order, was seated in an armchair next to his father's throne in the church. He remained remarkably quiet as the Exarch in his glittering robe and miter officiated, surrounded by nine metropolitans and fifteen priests in full regalia. General Kutuzov took the baby in his arms and repeated the consecrated words through which Prince Boris embraced the Orthodox faith. Afterwards, the Exarch anointed the child's forehead, ears, chest, hands, and feet. The prince received holy communion and Kutuzov returned him to his father, while gun salutes shook the city and tens of thousands of people massed around the church wildly shouting "Hurrah!"

It was difficult for Boris to extricate the official life from his childhood memories. In one of his earliest recollections, he was disembarking with his parents and his chaplain, Monseigneur Vassili, from some large boat in an unfamiliar place, amidst a multitude of foreign people cheering, bands marching, flags, soldiers, and speeches. For days the same excitement, in trains, in big palaces, at parades. He knew later that this was his first official trip—a visit to his godfather, the emperor of Russia. The royal party had been received with pomp in Odessa, in July 1898, then in Kiev, Moscow, and St. Petersburg. The little girls he vaguely remembered playing with were the Grand Duchesses Olga and Tatiana, the tsar's daughters. He did not, of course, see what Anna Stancioff, now the wife of the Bulgarian envoy, noticed:

Prince Ferdinand, generally so sure of himself, and inclined to be arrogant rather than amiable, appeared to me timid at the Russian court. The Emperor alone showed a little sympathy towards him, but there was a note of hostility in the crowd of Grand Dukes, as they stood grouped together, tall and proud, against the gilded panelling of the reception rooms, scanning the newcomers with sarcastic glances.

Nevertheless, continued Mrs. Stancioff, "much notice was taken of the charming little Prince, whose large, melancholy eyes, with their black lashes, won the hearts of all."

To Boris, even the memories of most normal events in every boy's life had their official dimension. His first exam, for instance: A cold December morning in 1904. Boris is almost eleven and is about to have his exam at the end of the primary school. He is quite nervous when, accompanied by his brother Kyril, he enters the palace room prepared for the occasion. All these solemn gentlemen waiting for him. A few familiar faces: "Kourto," the king's counselor Dobrovitch, the palace commandant, the prince's orderly, all looking ceremonious. He recognizes the education minister, who had questioned him a few days before to make sure the little prince was well prepared. But at the table facing Boris's desk, three unknown faces make him more bashful: the public school teachers of the examination committee. One of them breaks the silence: "Your Highness, we'll start with catechism. Please recite the Lord's prayer in Slavonic."

The boy is relieved. That's easy, he thinks, he knows it by heart both in contemporary Bulgarian and in the old church language, which is used in the Orthodox liturgy to this day. And Boris says the prayer, as he has done every single day since he could speak.

"When did Bulgaria embrace the Christian religion?" is the next question.

"In 865, under King Boris I."

He should know. That's his patron saint. The prince feels more at ease as he answers the other questions. "Christianity was spread among the Slavs by the disciples of Saints Kyril and Methody, the Bulgarian brothers from Salonika who invented the Slavic alphabet around the year 862. Their disciples translated the Holy Scriptures into Slavonic and carried Christ's message to all Slavic lands, all the way to Russia."

Bulgarians learn in school that their ancestors gave the other Slavs the alphabet that we now call "Cyrillic," and adopted Christianity before the Russians. These facts have always been a source of national pride, explaining in part the lack of any inferiority complex vis-à-vis the largest Slavic nation. It also accounts for the Bulgarian claims on Salonika, the city of Kyril and Methody, the most revered national saints.

The examination continues, Bulgarian language and history, Slavonic, arithmetic and natural history. Boris is a little worried about the dictation test, as spelling is not his forte. (Even later in life Boris, who showed exceptional talent for languages and spoke several with a perfect accent, grammar and vocabulary, was not always at ease with spelling.) But today's dictation is easy, and he makes only one mistake.

"Will you recite the poem 'Paissy'?" asks one teacher. This happens to be one of Boris's favorite poems, and he knows the verses of the national poet Ivan Vazov by heart:

In the darkness of the Mount Athos monastery, an obscure, pale monk was writing in his cell, bent under the flickering gas light . . .

There is no Bulgarian who doesn't know these verses. They tell, in Vazov's epic Hugoesque style, the story of the monk Paissy of Hilendari who wrote the first history of the Bulgarian kingdom in 1762, during the darkest years of Turkish rule. Totally subjugated, the Bulgarians had forgotten their past, and the nation was slowly losing its identity. This ardent patriot Paissy triggered the Bulgarian Renaissance by unearthing, in the monasteries of Mt. Athos, the historical facts of the glorious past and by telling the story of great Bulgarian kings from 681 to the Ottoman conquest. The heroic struggle for religious and political independence, kindled by Paissy's *History*, lasted for over a century.

The rest of the exam presents no problems, especially the questions about animals and plants. Due to his father's lessons, the boy knows as much about natural history as the teachers.

The entire nation watched the crown prince's scholastic progress. And when he was handed his primary school certificate, the event was chronicled in the press.

His eighteenth birthday, also a state occasion, turned into an international political event. King Ferdinand was secretly organizing the Balkan coalition against the weakening Ottoman empire, and he wanted to invest his son's "coming of age" with all the pomp possible. All Balkan crown princes—Serbian, Greek, Montenegro, and Rumanian—attended the spectacular festivities in January 1912 in Sofia, along with a Russian grand duke, an Austrian archduke, a Prussian prince, and envoys of many other states.

What young man would not be nervous, standing at attention on the podium erected in the middle of the Military School's court, with thousands of eyes fixed on him, while military bands played marches and troops presented arms? Behind him on the podium decorated with pinetree branches and tricolor ribbons, the royal family is surrounded by foreign princes and diplomats in full dress uniform, and the high clergy in their golden robes and crowns. Boris, in his lieutenant's uniform, steps toward the tattered Samara Flag, the Bulgarian army's oldest and holiest symbol that has seen action in the Liberation and the Serbo-Bulgarian Wars. The archbishop slowly reads the soldiers' oath, and Boris repeats it solemnly after him, his right arm raised. Then he crosses himself, kisses the archbishop's cross, the Bible and the flag, and shouts in a loud soldier's voice: "I swear!"

A thunderous "Hurrah!" from the troops massed in the large court breaks the silence, while the bands burst out with the national anthem and a twenty-one-gun salute announces that the crown prince has come of age. King Ferdinand, visibly moved, walks to his son and embraces him warmly. The troops form for parade, and march by the king. The Samara flag leads the review, followed by units of the IV Tirnovo Infantry regiment. Marching briskly at the right flank of its first row, younger and smaller than the men next to him, Lieutenant Boris, Prince of Tirnovo, salutes his sovereign and father.

This will be the last time he marches happily with his regiment. The Balkan War will start soon and many will never return.

# CHAPTER III

# The Ephemeral "Radomir Republic"

WHEN STAMBOLISKY, the war minister General Sava Savvov, and the rest of Sofia's emissaries on their way to the army headquarters in Kyustendil reached the small town of Radomir late in the afternoon of September 26, they discovered that the situation had deteriorated almost beyond repair. Several of the retreating units were in a state of open mutiny, and the last vestiges of discipline had disappeared at all levels.

At the railroad station and the nearby bivouac, the delegation of ministers and opposition politicians found itself in the midst of a crowd of three thousand agitated men, determined to march on the capital and punish the royal government. Stambolisky and his principal lieutenant Raiko Daskalov talked to the soldiers and later met with some of the rebels' ringleaders, the most influential of whom seemed to be a sergeant-major, Georgi Damianov. After some pleading, they succeeded in temporarily appeasing the mutineers.

Abandoning the front, the swelling streams of retreating soldiers had been transformed into disorderly mobs with no clear destination or goal, except to stop fighting and go home. Clashes had broken out with units of the regular army, deserters had been shot by army officers. The unruly mob was getting dangerously out of hand, when a few unexpected leaders, mostly noncommissioned officers with strong antiwar and leftist convictions, emerged from the ranks and tried to give direction to the rebellion. Men like Damianov, a viticulturist in civilian life who sympathized with the Agrarian Union, proved especially effective.

As the throngs moved from village to village, requisitioning food and supplies and recruiting more mutineers, something resembling an irregular army numbering about eight infantry companies began to take shape, still surrounded by noisy, anarchic deserters of no particular political persuasion. Two days before Stambolisky's arrival, a large part of the band had chosen Sergeant Damianov as their commander. He had requisitioned a few trains which transported his three relatively disciplined battalions to Radomir. When news of Stambolisky's release circulated among the troops, the reactions were mixed, from enthusiastic cries of "Long live Stambolisky!" to indifference and suspicion.

The arrival at Radomir was orderly. The soldiers were received by the town authorities, who offered them food and assistance. The commanding colonel urged Damianov to avoid confrontation and ask the soldiers not to proceed to Sofia. After some hesitation, Damianov accepted a truce for the time being and agreed to stay in Radomir. The troops in each arriving train were given a choice: those who wanted to march on to Sofia should disembark and join the rebels in Radomir. Those unwilling to take part in the "revolution" could go home.

The night after the arrival of the government delegates was relatively calm, but the loosely knit mobs already outnumbered Damianov's more or less organized "revolutionaries." The Sofia Emissaries spent the night in private homes in Radomir. Thus Stambolisky had ample opportunity to discuss the events of the day with his colleagues, and especially with his closest collaborator, Daskalov.

Dr. Raiko Daskalov, a fiery thirty-two-year-old Agrarian party activist, had been imprisoned and released with Stambolisky. He was a temperamental man with radical ideas who had worked briefly for an opposition newspaper and studied in Berlin, where he obtained a doctor's degree from a German commercial institute. Back in Bulgaria in 1914, he became fascinated with the ideas of the Agrarian Union, which he joined immediately. Daskalov's scholarly background seemed to impress Stambolisky, a man with no academic degree. The two party militants, who shared the same hatred for King Ferdinand and his policies, had become quite close in prison. There, Daskalov had done some writing about the Agrarian ideology and therefore fancied himself as a sort of theoretician of the "peasant rule" advocated by Stambolisky and his friends.

On the next morning, September 27, the delegates returned to the railroad station. A crowd of restless, disgruntled soldiers, larger than the evening before, packed the public square. Stambolisky climbed on a truck to address them. "I am Stambolisky," he shouted in the emotional voice of a popular tribune. "I came out of prison to tell you: Keep calm! No violence! Think of the Fatherland threatened by foreign invasion! Return to the front! Restrengthen it, while a delegation is asking the French general in Salonika for an armistice!"

But his charisma didn't work this time. The deserters were in no mood to return to the front. "The war is over!" shouted many voices. Stambolisky continued, but the unruly audience was losing patience. An angry sergeant took the floor: "We are not going back to fight! The war is over! Let's go to Sofia and punish those responsible!"

The soldiers cheered. It looked as if the efforts to contain the revolt had failed. Then the unexpected happened. Stepping forward and standing erect in his general's uniform, Savvov puffed up his chest and barked his orders, "Soldiers, attention!" There was a sudden silence and, miraculously, the men sprang to attention. The general waited a moment, then yelled: "In my capacity as war minister I am ordering you to disperse and go home! Go and take a rest with your families! And leave your guns here!"

There was a moment of hesitation. Some soldiers protested, "No, we won't disarm!" But Savvov insisted: "You have nothing to fear. You owe this to your country, which is about to sign a peace." In the confusion that followed, a soldier proposed a vote by raised hands. Savvov's offer won and the crowd began to disperse. The violence was avoided; the march on Sofia was canceled. The war minister's bravado had won the day. But not for long.

Savvov returned to the capital while the delegation proceeded to the headquarters in Kyustendil, thirty miles southwest of Radomir. But in the process, the Agrarian leaders switched allegiance. Immersed in the sea of defeated, disgruntled soldiers, spending hours in discussions with activists, hearing first-hand about the war's horrors and misery, Stambolisky and Daskalov felt closer to the mutineers than to the ministers and generals who had sent them to end the mutiny. Staunch enemies of the establishment by their background and ideology and naturally attracted to the rebellion, their conversion was not surprising. Daskalov's about face was total and immediate. As for Stambolisky, a less impulsive and shrewder politician, the shift was more gradual.

Total confusion had reigned in Kyustendil since the assault by mobs of deserters two days before. Growing crowds of runaway soldiers congregated at the railroad station, demanding transport to Sofia. The cadets of the Military School, sent to the Serbian border to stop and disarm fleeing soldiers, were ordered back to Kyustendil to protect the army general headquarters from the mutineers.

This was the situation Stambolisky, Daskalov, and their colleagues found when they arrived from Radomir. At headquarters, they were received by the army's chief of staff, Bourmov, who reassured them that the town was calm. Since dawn, the streets had been swarming with columns of soldiers in retreat, arriving from nearby villages and hills. But as the units looked orderly and still obeyed their officers, the commander directed them to the railroad station where the soldiers arranged their rifles in neat pyramids and sat, waiting for the trains.

General Bourmov accompanied the Sofia emissaries when they went to talk to the troops. Everything was quiet, until the group reached the station. There Bourmov, passing by a sloppily attired soldier who showed no respect, stopped and reprimanded him severely. Without saying a word, the soldier sprang to his feet and thrust his bayonet at the general. Another soldier grabbed the rifle in time to save the general's life. But now there was no doubt: the revolt had begun.

As the visiting politicians began to talk to the troops, Stambolisky was suddenly called to the telegraph office of the railroad station. "It's for you, Mr. Stambolisky," said the operator. "Dr. Daskalov is calling from Radomir." Surprised, the delegates looked around. Indeed, Raiko Daskalov was not among them. While they were at the army headquarters, he had slipped out quietly and gone alone to meet the soldiers at the railroad station. Then, without notifying his colleagues, he had left by car for Radomir.

Daskalov was no longer a member of the official delegation; he had become a rebel himself. He was more than that: back in Radomir, he became the rebel's leader. He had found thousands of disillusioned, angry men in a state of revolutionary fever, men ripe for violence and revenge, but lacking leadership and a concrete program. It occurred to him that what they needed now was a leader like himself, like Stambolisky, and their ideology. Daskalov had the energy and the fervor, and his rhetoric worked well that day.

"Ever since Ferdinand has ruled Bulgaria, the people have not seen a single happy day," he told group after group of cheering rebels. "He ruled the country like an absolute monarch, and anything he wanted, he got. All high officials were obedient puppets in his hands. He decided the nation's destiny as he pleased. He concluded secret treaties, declared wars, signed peace, forged new alliances and new disasters, without consulting the people, whom he treated as slaves. Today, Bulgaria is on its deathbed. If we want to save the country, we must dethrone Ferdinand and declare the people full masters of their destiny."

The foreign victors who wanted to punish Ferdinand would also punish the Bulgarian people, Daskalov preached. The only way for Bulgaria to escape the vengeance of the enemy was to overthrow the king before the enemy occupied the country. "The victors will demand an account, and we must give it to them," he said with passion. "We must put all the blame on him and his regime, which is the truth, and present the Bulgarian people in their real image—an innocent people and a great adversary forced to participate in the war. The same thing could have happened to the Rumanian people if the Germanophile Carol were still alive, and to the Greeks, if Constantine had not been dethroned. But it's getting late, and the victors may tell us, 'You were all for Germany and for Ferdinand, and only now that you have lost the war do you want to pass for innocent doves.' In order to stop such suspicions, we must act quickly and decisively. March on to Sofia! Overthrow Ferdinand, punish the criminals!"

The response was tremendous. Wave after wave of disaffected soldiers poured into Radomir, and the crowd in the town's square grew like a snowball. Daskalov felt that the moment had come to act.

Meanwhile, at the Kyustendil railroad station's telegraph office, Stambolisky received the urgent message from Radomir. "This is Raiko Daskalov. Do you agree with the following circular letter, 'Today, 27th September, the former King Ferdinand, his dynasty, and the former government have been overthrown. Bulgaria is proclaimed a people's republic.' "

Stambolisky dictated his answer, "Isn't all this premature?"

"No, it is exactly the right time," Daskalov wired back.

"All right then." But Stambolisky didn't seem very sure. "Ask him whether they have forces at their disposal, and how many," he told the operator.

"We have about fifteen thousand armed soldiers. You must come here at once." Then Daskalov suggested what roads his comrade should take to avoid danger, and Stambolisky promised to go to Radomir. When the conversation by wire was over, he demanded that the operator burn the tape in front of him. "Don't you dare say anything about this conversation! You'll answer with your head," he warned.

When Stambolisky joined the crowd massed in front of the station, he asked his colleagues to return to headquarters and leave him alone with the soldiers for a moment. Shortly after they departed, they heard a tremendous clamor from the station followed by thunderous hurrahs and jubilant cheers. Minutes later, throngs of men poured into the streets, chanting, screaming, and shooting in the air. The mob marched toward army headquarters and occupied it without meeting any resistance. General Bourmov, who tried to reason with some of the leaders when they reached the main entrance, was nearly killed before he managed to escape. The revolutionary orgy lasted late into the evening. All during the night, overloaded trains, trucks and horse carriages were leaving Kyustendil, transporting thousands of rebels to Radomir.

There Raiko Daskalov had just proclaimed the republic. After telegraphing Stambolisky Daskalov appeared before the mutineers and read the following proclamation:

Today, September 27, 1918, the Bulgarian people break the chains of slavery, throw down the despotic regime of Ferdinand and his henchmen, proclaim them enemies of the people, proclaim themselves a free people with a republican form of government, and hold out a hand of peace and understanding to the peoples of Europe. From this day, King Ferdinand and his dynasty and the former government are fallen. All provincial administrators, district officials, police commandants, mayors and military officers will carry out the orders of the provisional government of the republic.

President: Al. Stambolisky
Commander-in-Chief: Raiko Daskalov

While the crowds roared, Daskalov sent all railroad telegraph stations the circular message he had discussed with Stambolisky, announcing the overthrow of the monarchy and of the Malinov government. But he knew that for the moment his newly proclaimed republic was nothing more than a wishful boast and meant little outside of Radomir. If he wanted to overthrow the regime, the rebels had to march on Sofia. For that he needed Stambolisky; but Stambolisky had not shown too much enthusiasm during their telegraph conversation. That worried Daskalov, and while organizing the march on the capital, he scribbled a note to his friend and sent it on the first train to Kyustendil. In it he insisted that Bulgaria's situation made it imperative that the monarchy be replaced immediately by a people's republic. "I made use of your name, for I made you the president of the provisional government. This was the unanimous desire of the people and of the troops. If you do not wish to lead the provisional government, then my only prayer is that you do not condemn it now." Then the new commander-in-chief assured Stambolisky that the rebels were ready and strong enough to take over Sofia.

When Stambolisky received the message will probably remain a mystery forever. The fact is that the shrewd peasant leader did not show any eagerness to rush to Radomir and carry the banner of the revolution. His was a difficult position: he had been urged simultaneously to pacify the mutineers and to lead them. The mission the king and the government of the collapsing country had entrusted him with was critical, and Stambolisky could not fail to realize both its historic importance and his personal responsibility as a statesman and patriot. But on the other hand, emotionally and ideologically, he was on the side of the rebels and their cause. Quick decisions of this nature would be agonizing even under peaceful circumstances. In the total confusion that reigned, the wisest move was to gain time and collect as much information as possible about the state of mind of the troops and the chances of success. Therefore, Stambolisky, instead of joining Daskalov in Radomir, drove to the town of Dupnitza, fifty miles south, to probe the mood of the soldiers assembled there.

The rest of the delegation received a telegram saying that he had run out of gas and was unable to return to Kyustendil. The next morning, September 28, Stambolisky arrived in Radomir, where Daskalov was waiting impatiently. Since his proclamation, the self-appointed commander-in-chief had organized eight batallions with two machine-gun companies, and named the principal ringleader, Georgi Damianov, chief-of-staff. The night before, he had sent an ultimatum to the government: recognize the republic, or we'll march on Sofia in the morning!

Meeting his mentor and his appointed "president of the republic" turned out to be a cruel disappointment for the eager Daskalov. Instead of putting himself at the helm of the rebellion, Stambolisky criticized Daskalov's impatience and said that the proclamation of the republic had been premature and insufficiently prepared. "Instead of support, I only heard reproaches and complaints," Daskalov wrote later.

The meeting of the two friends, unexpectedly short, was tense and less than cordial. After talking for only half an hour, Stambolisky, still hesitating and unconvinced, left for Sofia, while Daskalov and his troops filled all available railroad cars ready to march on the capital.

*       *       *

The news of the Radomir rebellion had reached Sofia the previous evening and the capital was fearfully bracing itself for the assault. The insurgents' commander-in-chief had sent the following telegram: "To the former government: I understand that you still have not resigned. I am ordering you to do so immediately. I am coming tomorrow with the troops of the republic, and if you haven't resigned, I won't be responsible for the consequences. Signed, R. Daskalov."

The scanty garrison units were taking combat positions in the environs of Sofia, and the chief-of-staff, Colonel Ivan Shkoynov, was feverishly drawing up plans for the battle. Prince Boris, acting as liaison between the king and the military command, was kept informed by Shkoynov of the deployment of the troops. The government forces did not look very impressive and consisted largely of inexperienced units: eleven companies with twelve machine-guns, a leftover artillery of six disparate cannons, a cavalry of one squadron of the Royal Guards, and a half-squadron from the Military School.

Since the forces were alarmingly inadequate, requests were made to German and Austrian units to send help for the defense of Sofia. All soldiers on furlough were called in as well as many hospitalized officers. By evening, the new units occupied their assigned positions.

In the meantime, Stambolisky had vanished, and an order was issued for his arrest. Upon his arrival in Sofia, after his meeting with Daskalov, Stambolisky went straight to the Council of Ministers and denied any participation in the rebellion. But he failed to convince the government that he had been proclaimed president of the republic without his authorization and that he and Daskalov had been prisoners of the rebels. When he left the building, the ministers decided to have him arrested, but Stambolisky disappeared in the streets of Sofia. He spent the next several days in hiding, trying to rally support for the rebellion.

He found the official leadership of his own party peculiarly cool to the Radomir republic. A top Agrarian leader even came out with a proclamation condemning the rebellion as a fraud, and signed it with the names of the entire leadership, including Stambolisky's. The statement, published in the

Sofia newspapers and dropped on the troops from airplanes, gave the impression that the revolt was a personal venture of Daskalov, and caused considerable confusion and dismay.

Stambolisky also asked the support of the Narrow Socialist or Communist party, proposing a revolutionary coalition between Agrarians and Communists. The "Narrows," who did not have more than 3,400 members at the beginning of the World War, claimed 21,000 members by the end, due to the terrible wartime conditions. The success of the Russian revolution had also played a hand, encouraging the Bulgarian Communists and raising the circulation of their newspaper to thirty thousand.

But the Communists' head, Blagoev, a rigid doctrinaire, disliked the Agrarians and turned down Stambolisky's offer. In his eyes, the Agrarians were just ignorant peasants with petty bourgeois values, with no interest in nurturing socialism. Blagoev and his friends saw the entire insurrection as "ultimately reactionary, a rising of the peasantry against the urban population and against King Ferdinand." To them, the uprising was "not a fight of the proletariat and its party against the bourgeoisie, but rather a fight within the bourgeoisie."

But the Communists' refusal had other reasons. First, they were ill-prepared and not ready for action. In addition, they were convinced that the tidal wave of the Bolshevik revolution was about to engulf Bulgaria, and they saw no reason to risk their heads in a non-Communist uprising. And finally, Blagoev knew too well that Stambolisky was a much more charismatic and popular figure than he and that the Agrarians greatly outnumbered the Communists. He had no desire to settle for second place, as the minor partner in a venture which, in any case, he didn't believe could succeed.

All day and all night, Daskalov waited anxiously for some encouraging news from Sofia. He hoped that Stambolisky would succeed in rallying some support for the republic and that Sofia would surrender without fighting. But no word came from the capital, except that German troops were coming to reinforce the garrison. Left alone, Daskalov had to make his own decision.

At the palace, the king, briefed constantly by Prince Boris, followed the developments closely. At the same time, unwilling to accept defeat and abandon his allies, he was secretly considering an audacious, if not foolhardy, action, hoping for a mircale. He privately contacted the German and Austrian headquarters as well as some trusted Bulgarian diehards who still believed that Bulgaria should continue the war. As a precaution, the king's personal train was at his private station, ready to leave at any moment.

The government, in the meantime, was waiting nervously for news from the armistice delegation, which had left Sofia three days earlier, but no word had arrived from Salonika. The delegates were accompanied by the

American consul-general in Sofia, Murphy, and another American diplo-mat, Archibald Walker, representing the only Great Power not at war with Bulgaria. After a rough drive south across the battlefields, they were led to the headquarters of the Supreme Allied commander of the Macedonian front, General Franchet d'Esperey.

Everybody in the Balkans knew about the bellicose French officer and his authoritarian manner, although he had only that spring arrived from the Western front. After two-and-a-half years of unsuccessful attempts to pierce the Bulgarian defenses—the Macedonian front had become a quagmire for the Franco-British expeditionary forces—the previous commander, General Gillaumat, was recalled, and Clemenceau personally chose Franchet d'Espe-rey to replace him. He seemed to be the perfect choice. Louis Félix Marie François Franchet d'Esperey was a model of the professional soldier: a Saint-Cyr graduate who had served in Algeria, Tunisia and Indochina, fought in the Boxer Rebellion in China and during the pacification of Morocco, and distinguished himself on the Marne. In addition, having traveled on the Dalmatian Coast and in Greece, he had some knowledge of the Balkans; and in 1914, he authored a military plan to open a front in Salonika and from there mount an offensive against Belgrade and Budapest.

He was the archtype of the combat general, a sixty-two-year-old man of action who despised intrigue and felt at home on the battlefield. As a commander, he was tough and exacting, both feared and respected by his troops. (The British soldiers, unable to pronounce his name, nicknamed him "desperate Frankie.") A British general described him thus, "He kept all in their place by his manner. Never did he solicit or permit advice or sugges-tions, which indeed no one would have dared to offer."

The Bulgarian delegates didn't arrive with any illusions about Franchet d'Esperey's generosity. After all, he had no reason to like Bulgaria or to be understanding and magnanimous. On the contrary, he had developed friendly relations with its Balkan enemies, Serbia and Greece, and his troops had suffered heavy casualties at the hands of the Bulgarians. As a profes-sional, he admired his adversary's incredible bravery and endurance. But also as a professional, he was a strong believer in the relentless pursuit of an enemy until his final defeat and destruction. But the Bulgarians hoped that by asking for a separate peace they would at least obtain honorable condi-tions, in the spirit of President Wilson's idealistic declaration, which had given rise to great hopes.

Their delusion evaporated as soon as the delegates faced the French general. Cold and distant, Franchet d'Esperey appeared to them even tougher than his reputation had painted him. Instead of the aristocrat they expected to see, to judge by his nobleman's name, they found a short, stocky man, every bit the French peasant, thick and unswayable. The well-trimmed raven-black mustache over the unsmiling mouth and the strong chin fit perfectly with the role of the harsh judge that he assumed that afternoon in Salonika. His words chilled the hearts of the Bulgarian delegates. He was not negotiating; he was not bargaining. He was commanding them.

"Messieurs," he said, "we have every right to deal in a cruel way with Bulgaria. She has no army anymore, and she is at our mercy. However, we don't want to destroy her. We will not dictate humiliating conditions. We will not enter Sofia. We will not violate your sovereignty. But we shall demand from you certain guarantees indispensable for our security and for the pursuit of our military operations."

What guarantees, what conditions, worried the Bulgarian delegates. They had come with the idea of negotiating some acceptable terms. The Bulgarian troops, after all, were still fighting and could probably resist longer and inflict more casualties on the Allies. But Franchet d'Esperey showed no desire to continue the conversation.

"You'll receive the conditions tomorrow," he only said. "And I advise you to cooperate wholeheartedly if you want Bulgaria to be treated well. As soon as you accept the conditions, I'll order the immediate cessation of the operations."

And hardly saluting his visitors, the French general left the room.

*    *    *

On Sunday morning, September 29, Prince Boris, accompanied by two ministers, arrived at the Alexandrov Bridge, some ten kilometers west of Sofia. The large bridge just outside the village of Kniajevo, opens onto the highway which follows the Vladaya gorge, cut between two mountains: Vitosha, and Lyullin.

It was through this long gorge that the rebels had been approaching the capital on trains, on trucks, and on foot. It was at its exit that the capital's defenders had taken up position and were waiting, finger on the trigger.

A tragic event had occurred the previous day just outside the capital. A train, loaded with rebels, had been stopped by patrols of Military School cadets, and as the officers were trying to persuade the rebels to depose their arms, gunfire burst from the train. The cadets, galvanized into action, aimed their artillery at the train, pulverizing some cars. Many mutineers were killed and wounded; others were captured. The casualties among the insurgents had been very heavy.*

In spite of the destruction of the first train, the hard core of the rebel forces, inflamed by the spirit of Daskalov, were ready to fight. A battle

---

*Historians of the post-communist era quote five-hundred killed, but their reliability is questionable.

appeared inevitable, especially after the new ultimatum issued by Daskalov that morning: "If in the next 6 hours I do not receive confirmation from Sofia that the former authorities of the former kingdom of Bulgaria have recognized the new situation, I will be obliged forcibly to enter Sofia with the troops of the people's guards."

At the Alexandrov Bridge, Prince Boris and the war minister were briefed. The rebels had four to five thousand men in the village of Vladaya, and both Daskalov and Damianov were among them. They also had two trains full of insurgents in Radomir and one at the Pernik station. As for the government forces, they were deployed in four "ambushes"—the most important being at the Alexandrov Bridge. Their orders were to wait for the arrival of the "renegades" and to destroy them before they had a chance to continue on to Sofia. The cavalry squadrons were waiting in Kniajevo, the three companies of cadets had taken positions on the road north to them, and the infantry were deployed at three other suburbs. The few remaining artillery cannons and howitzers in Sofia were pulled out of town by oxen and the horses of the Military School and headed for action. In case of disorders in the streets of Sofia, a machine gun was installed in the belfry of the Sveta Nedelia Cathedral, in the heart of the city.

For Prince Boris, the battle would not be the first he would witness. He had received his baptism under Turkish fire in 1912; he had escaped Serbian and Greek bullets in 1913; and then for three years he had braved Allied shells on several fronts. But now, Bulgarians were shooting at Bulgarians. Soldiers from regiments he was familiar with were turning their guns against comrades wearing the same uniform. He had never felt a worse agony than on the Sunday when the Vladaya gorge resounded with the crack of rifles and the rattle of machine guns.

That morning groups of soldiers emerged from the gorge, on the road to Kniajevo, but most of them surrendered. Around noon, however, rebel patrols descended from the slopes of Lyullin, and soon after, large bands of insurgents appeared on the heights on both sides of the highway. The fratricidal battle, fierce and bloody, began.

In spite of the heavy artillery shelling, columns of rebels poured down from the hills and attacked the Alexandrov Bridge from the rear and the flank. Surprised and overwhelmed, the defenders retreated in disorder and had to fight their way through the lines in hand-to-hand combat.

The bloody fighting at the rear of the bridge was still raging when the main rebel force, led by Raiko Daskalov, exaltedly brandishing his sabre and shouting "Forward to Sofia!", attacked the Alexandrov Bridge. The cadets, unable to contain the insurgents, abandoned the bridge and fled. The other defenders were overrun by the raging rebel wave and swiftly massacred.

The defense seemed to be crushed as the government units retreated in disorderly fashion toward Sofia. But around four o'clock several officers managed to organize a new defense line around the artillery batteries on the heights of Boyana, the village at the foot of Vitosha, south of Sofia.

The rebels swept over the Alexandrov Bridge and crossed the village of Kniajevo and the nearby pine woods, but they met with heavy artillery fire and were forced to stop. Other bands of insurgents, meanwhile, began to descend the slopes of Vitosha in the direction of Boyana. The fighting spread over the entire area, but the attacks were repelled. Later in the evening, a German battery arrived and joined the battle.

At dusk, Daskalov decided to leave his position east of Kniajevo and to lead his forces on to Sofia. But once out of the pine woods, the searchlights of a special unit caught them out. Exposed to the renewed artillery shelling, they were met by the reserve units, and the heavy fire of two machine guns of the newly arrived Germans. Daskalov's forces had to retreat to the Kniajevo woods. Four times they renewed the attacks and four times they were repelled. During the battle Daskalov was wounded in the arm and was carried to the barracks in Kniajevo, now occupied by the rebels.

As the fighting continued, Colonel Shkoynov was summoned to the palace late in the evening. He was received by Prince Boris, to whom he described his plan for counterattack. When he had finished, Boris went to report to the king. When he returned, he said that his father had approved the plan and wished him luck.

The same night, Sofia was declared a "fortress." For the capital, the night was anxious, tense. The strict curfew kept the streets deserted. The noise of gunfire, only three or four miles from the city's center, did not stop the entire night. Nobody in Sofia slept; windows remained lit until morning.

At dawn, around Kniajevo and Boyana and in the outskirts of the capital, rebels and loyal troops faced each other, waiting for the decisive battle to begin.

\* \* \*

It was a dramatic night for the armistice delegation in Salonika as well. The delegates were heartbroken, indignant, and tempted to break off negotiations when an officer from General Franchet d'Esperey's headquarters handed them the draft of the armistice conditions, which were far worse than they had expected.

The former Serbian and Greek territories, now occupied by Bulgarian troops, will be evacuated immediately, said the document. The Bulgarian army will demobilize immediately, except for three divisions and four cavalry regiments. All weapons, munitions, military vehicles and horses will be surrendered to the Allies. All Bulgarian troops presently west of Skopie will lay down their arms and will be considered prisoners of war. Germany and Austria-Hungary will be given four weeks to evacuate their troops, diplomats and nationals from Bulgaria.

According to an additional secret agreement, Entente troops were temporarily to occupy strategic points in the country, and Bulgaria was to put her railroads, ports, roads, telegraphs, and telephones at the disposal of the Entente, to be used against her former allies.

For hours, Liapcheff and his colleagues tried desperately to ameliorate the conditions. It was a futile effort, especially as the news arrived of the collapse of the Skopié front in Macedonia. Franchet d'Esperey was intransigent, and the Bulgarians feared an even worse fate: Allied permission to Serbian and Greek troops to occupy parts of Bulgaria.

It was 10:50 P.M. when the delegates, almost in tears and completely devastated, signed the armistice agreement. Silent and businesslike, Franchet d'Esperey signed after them and went to give his order for the cessation of hostilities.

*     *     *

It was unfortunate for Raiko Daskalov that his troops did not achieve their goal in the first two days of the rebellion. By failing to penetrate the flimsy defenses of Sofia on the 29th of September, they allowed the garrison forces to regroup and receive sizeable reinforcements, including a German battalion.

Nor did the expected uprisings in Sofia and the nearby villages materialize. On the contrary, the alarmed population, with the horror tales of the recent Russian revolution still fresh in their minds, feared the arrival of undisciplined bands of mutineers and hoped they would be repelled. When even the local Communists did not join, the "Radomir Republic" was reduced to the proportions of a regional mutiny by embittered soldiers of three defeated divisions.

A deciding factor was the attitude of the officers' corps. Not one single career officer joined the rebellion, and the reserve officers who turned against the government were the rare exceptions. And this despite the fact that the officers, who suffered excessive war casualties, had liberally criticized the government "politicians." Most of them, moreover, came from peasant or small town families, real "sons of the people." But the rebel leaders had badly misjudged the officers' loyalty. This left the direction of the rebel military operations in the hands of incompetent amateurs. For all their revolutionary fervor, Daskalov and the ex-sergeant Damianov had not the least idea about strategy and logistics, and so committed many tactical mistakes.

But Daskalov's gravest miscalculation was his conviction that the capital would put up no defense. He wrote later, "We didn't need a big army to overthrow the bankrupt monarchy, we knew that not a single soldier from the front would remain on Ferdinand's side, and Sofia did not have more than 500 well-trained soldiers. These were the main reasons not to wait for larger forces to return from the front and join us before we started moving toward Sofia on September 28. We didn't expect any resistance in Sofia." Daskalov expected the government, already threatened by the advancing Allied forces, to resign voluntarily. He was so sure that he started his march without any artillery and with only twenty-five machine guns. And he was surprised when he met fierce resistance by a better-equipped and determined force.

On the morning of September 30, the defenders of "fortress Sofia" were considerably stronger than they had been the previous day. New units and artillery had arrived from other sectors, including four German companies, which held the access to the Kniajevo-Sofia highway. The government plan called for a decisive attack that day against the "renegades" in the Vladaya gorge and the Lyullin heights. The rebels were also preparing their final assault, and large numbers of insurgents were being loaded on trains at the Vladaya station. But as the devastating artillery barrage began at dawn, seriously hindering the rebel operations, the news arrived of Daskalov's injury and shocked the insurgents. Damianov sent an automobile to bring Daskalov from Kniajevo, but the "commander-in-chief" insisted on staying with his troops. In the morning, however, feeling weaker, he was brought on horseback to Vladaya where, despite his wounds, he addressed the newly arriving soldiers, trying to recruit them before they continued in the direction of Sofia.

Another major event that same morning considerably disturbed the insurgents. Thousands of printed leaflets carrying the long-awaited news—that the armistice had been signed in Salonika the previous night—were distributed to all army units and dropped by airplanes over rebel positions. One of the principal reasons for the rebellion had vanished.

In spite of fierce resistance on Lyullin and around Kniajevo, the insurgents were crushed that day, and the government troops entered the Vladaya gorge in hot pursuit. Damianov tried desperately to improvise some artillery support and defend the gorge, but that afternoon he suffered a leg wound and was captured. The defense of the pass never even got under way. At the end of the day, fifteen hundred insurgents were taken prisoner.

The pursuit of the defeated rebels continued during the following two days. In every town and village on their way back to Radomir, they fought furiously, and their single cannon played havoc with the pursuers in the narrow mountain pass. Many more casualties were suffered on both sides. But in the evening of October 2, Radomir, the capital of the ephemeral republic, was occupied by the loyalist forces. The rebellion was over.

Daskalov, his wounded arm badly infected, managed to escape and after hiding out for a few weeks, he crossed the border to Macedonia, where he surrendered to the French. Damianov was less lucky. After his capture, the wounded "chief-of-staff" was brought to meet his loyalist counterpart, who drove him to the capital in his car. There he went through rough interrogations and long weeks in prison, but, although a number of rebel leaders were executed or disappeared, Damianov's life was spared, for reasons he himself never understood. He was finally incarcerated in Sofia.

Stambolisky remained in hiding in Sofia, while the authorities searched for him. As the rebellion ended, he spent most of his time in a clandestine residence where he wrote articles for the party organ and received visits from a few trusted collaborators. Eluding the police, he even had the audacity to appear one evening at a meeting of the party's executive committee.

# CHAPTER IV

# The Abdication

THE BATTLE was still not over in the Vladaya gorge when, on October 1, the armistice delegation returned from Salonika. The chief delegate, Liapchev, made his report to the Council of Ministers before rushing to the palace where King Ferdinand was waiting anxiously.

It was a thankless, painful mission. Liapchev had to report that Bulgaria had capitulated formally and that foreign troops were going to occupy the country. He had put his signature to the document that accepted the evacuation, and probably the loss forever, of his own native land, Macedonia. But something else was bothering Liapchev as he entered the royal palace.

During the unpleasant talks he had had in Salonika, General Franchet d'Esperey had insinuated that the Allies had no confidence in King Ferdinand and that his presence on the Bulgarian throne would only complicate matters. Liapchev coldly reminded the Frenchman that he was a minister of the king and that he had not come to discuss Bulgarian internal affairs. Franchet d'Esperey did not insist, but he felt freer to discuss the subject with the secretary of the American legation in Sofia, Archibald Walker, who had accompanied the Bulgarian delegation. He told Walker frankly that the Allies considered Ferdinand an obstacle and that, under the existing conditions, only a change of monarchs would satisfy them. He indicated that Crown Prince Boris would be acceptable to them.

Ferdinand listened attentively while Liapchev described the harsh terms of the armistice. The only relative consolation, he said, was that no Serbian or Greek troops would enter Bulgaria. "That's a relief," agreed the king. "I expected worse conditions." Then, after a pause, he asked:

"So, they didn't say anything about me?"

"I didn't want to discuss Your Majesty with them," answered Liapchev. "But the Allies spoke in very flattering terms about the crown prince. Incidentally, some statements on the subject have been made to Mr. Walker."

49

The king remained silent for a moment. Then he whispered: "I understand . . ."

Shortly after, a member of the royal cabinet interrogated Walker who confirmed the worst suspicions of the king. But Ferdinand kept his silence. Nobody in the palace or in the government knew what he would do.

The next morning at nine o'clock Prime Minister Malinov summoned the representatives of all the political parties to a meeting. He was accompanied by Liapchev, the war minister, and the deputy chief-of-staff. After briefing the political leaders about the armistice, the prime minister left for the palace, asking them to remain in session until he returned. While waiting for Malinov, they began to review the military situation, until Liapchev exploded:

"Gentlemen, let's cut this out! These are details that belong to the past. I want to bring up for discussion another question." He was becoming emotional. "Macedonia, that the Bulgarian people desired to liberate and for which they made such sacrifices . . . I signed my name on its tombstone, me, one of her sons . . . But Bulgaria still remains ours. We must think of it now. King Ferdinand owes the nation retribution; he owes some reparation."

Liapchev's words were followed by total silence.

"I repeat," he said in a grave tone," King Ferdinand must make reparation to the Bulgarian people."

No one spoke, but it was obvious that they all agreed.

Meanwhile, in the White Salon of the palace, a determined Malinov was facing the king. Ferdinand asked first how the representatives of the parties had received the news of the armistice agreement. The prime minister answered, adding, "I take the liberty of suggesting that His Majesty concern himself only with his own person."

The king was not prepared for such a blunt answer. The pain on his face showed that Malinov's words had hurt him, but he collected himself quickly and managed to reply sarcastically, "Are you trying to tell me what I used to tell my prime ministers when I wanted them to resign?"

"That's right, sire, and as you see, the roles are reversed."

"Isn't there another way?"

"No, there is none."

It was a painful scene. The usually arrogant monarch became pensive, Malinov had never before seen him look so defeated and humiliated. "If you want to, sire, call the party leaders and hear their opinions."

Ferdinand waved his hand in a gesture of resignation and utter contempt. "Ah, the party leaders!" he said.

The same afternoon, however, he asked the leaders to the palace and received them one by one. What seemed to interest Ferdinand was whether Bulgaria could still reject the armistice conditions and continue the war with the help of Germany and Austria. The conservative Theodore Theodorov replied emphatically that this would be impossible, that not one single Bulgarian soldier would consent to fight any longer and that there was danger of the demobilized troops rebelling against the regime. As the king continued to avoid the question of abdicating, Theodorov said bravely, "That's why Your Majesty must get used to the thought that eventually you may be required to make the greatest sacrifice a sovereign can be asked to make for his people."

Jumping from his seat, Ferdinand burst out angrily, "What! You have the audacity to demand my abdication? Who are you and who gave you the right to be insolent with me? What wrong did I do to Bulgaria that you dare to talk to me in this way?"

Theodorov said that it was his duty to speak frankly and that the king should face the truth in the interest of the nation, and in the interest of his own dynasty. But Ferdinand, at the mention of the dynasty, exclaimed tartly, "Don't you want to make an agreement with Prince Boris to put me in chains and send me somewhere in Russia?"

Theodorov was horrified to realize the king was jealous of his own son. Ferdinand went on in a bitter soliloquy. "But tell me, how did I wrong Bulgaria, which I served for thirty-two years? How did I fail to rule it? How many worries, sleepless nights and fears I lived through during those years! Then why this black ingratitude?" He sincerely believed that he had been a very good king. And he readily accepted the responsibility for his policies. Unfortunately for him, entering the war on the side of the Central Powers had turned out to be a mistake. "I recognize it," he continued. "This policy was mine and is still mine, I affirm it."

"Sire, in that case why hesitate?" Theodorov asked. "Do you prefer to wait for your people to come under the window of this palace shouting, 'Down with Ferdinand!'? Believe me, sire, by abdicating promptly and leaving the country, you'll be able to present yourself in a much better light abroad, declaring that you didn't want to betray your allies nor to approve a separate peace, and that's why you left."

The king seemed quite moved but did not answer. He bade good-bye to the old statesman and went on receiving other political leaders. One after the other, they advised the monarch to leave the country. Only two statesmen shared Ferdinand's views and insisted that he stand firm and remain on the throne. The monarch listened but did not reveal to anyone what he was going to do—not even to Prince Boris. Late that night, when the crown prince visited the war minister for a briefing, he appeared unusually disturbed. "My father is making preparations for departure," he told him. "No doubt he has decided to leave. But he did not tell me anything."

Ferdinand had indeed prepared himself for departure, but had not yet accepted the inevitability of his abdication. He was still desperately clinging to the hope that the war was not lost, not yet anyway, and that his German and Austrian allies were still capable of resistance, at least until better peace conditions could be obtained. He was encouraged by the news that the "Radomir Republic" rebellion had been crushed. More German troops were arriving in Sofia, positioning machine guns in the royal manège and establishing headquarters in the Hotel Bulgaria.

The government was very nervous, as rumors of a *coup d'état* by the king with the help of German troops circulated in Sofia. And after news of the separate armistice spread, it was reported from Rumania that the German field marshal Makenzen was organizing an expedition of German and Rumanian troops to punish Bulgaria. It was also rumored that the German military attache, General Von Massow, had presented Ferdinand with a plan for the defense of Sofia and that the king had put himself under the protection of the German army.

During the night, following his consultations with the political leaders and the prime minister's request for his abdication, the king made a last attempt to reestablish his power and to avoid the break with his German and Austrian allies. He had already sounded out a few trusted people, suggesting that they try to form a new cabinet and prevent Bulgaria's defeat. But all of them declined. He then summoned the commandant of "fortress" Sofia, General Protoguerov, who had successfully defeated the Radomir rebellion, and, praising him and appealing to his patriotism, offered him the posts of prime minister and commander-in-chief. The plan was for Protoguerov to overthrow the government, arrest the ministers, and continue the war by moving the troops north to the Balkan mountains, where the resistance would continue until the arrival of the German divisions.

But after some hesitation, Protoguerov turned down the offer. The capital, all unsuspecting, woke up with the same Malinov government on the morning of October 3, a date which was to become memorable.

Twice that day, the prime minister urgently requested to see the king; twice he remained without an answer. As the luxurious private train waited in full readiness at the royal station in the suburbs of the capital, Ferdinand, locked in his Sofia palace, agonized in seclusion over one of the most difficult decisions in his life.

Late in the afternoon, the prime minister was finally received by the king. As soon as Malinov entered the salon, Ferdinand, unusually excited, greeted him with a long tirade, "This is the reward for a man like me, who never had another goal but the well-being of Bulgaria! I lifted the standard of agriculture in this country. I gave it the roads, the bridges, the railroads, the ports. I worked for it and thought of it day and night. I gave it all my forces. What was Bulgaria before me?"

Malinov grew impatient. "Sire, history will make the judgment one day."

Ferdinand continued, "Was there anything accomplished in this country without me?" He suddenly interrupted himself, as if he realized that there was no point trying to convince the prime minister, and angrily handed him a sheet of paper.

"Here is my abdication. Take it!"

As Malinov, trying to act calmly, folded the document and put it in his pocket, the crown prince entered the room, visibly perturbed. Only moments before, Ferdinand had called him and Prince Kyril, and announcing his decision, had them read his abdication. Although the decision was not unexpected, his sons were very moved as they read the document:

"Because the events require sacrifices and abnegation from every devoted citizen, for the good of our beloved Fatherland, I want to give the first example of such selflessness. In spite of the strong and sacred links that have for thirty-two years held me to this country, for whose prosperity and glory I have given everything according to my abilities, I have decided to renounce the royal throne of Bulgaria."

It was hard for Boris to control his tears in front of his father and the prime minister, as he stood at attention. Ferdinand, equally moved, turned to Malinov, "Let us two be the first to swear allegiance to the new king."

Malinov took a step forward, bowed to the young man and said in a voice trembling with emotion, "Allow me to be the first to salute you as king of the Bulgarians . . . King Boris the Third!"

Boris, still unbelieving, hesitated for a moment and looked at his father, as if he needed his permission. Then he shook the prime minister's hand and thanked him. It was a historic moment, and King Ferdinand, who had never lacked a sense of decorum, acted accordingly. Overwhelmed by emotion, he embraced his son and said, "From now on, I am your subject, but I am also Your Majesty's father." As he kissed the prince, both men let their tears run unabashedly.

Father and son had perhaps never been as close as they were that autumn afternoon. Soon after Malinov had left, Ferdinand asked Boris and Kyril to accompany him on a farewell visit to the Vrana palace, one of his favorite places in the world. During the hour of this almost unbearably nostalgic pilgrimage, the two sons, who still called their father "Le Monarque," saw the usually distant, haughty and exacting parent in a totally different light. Here was a heartbroken man saying good-bye to a paradise he had created and to which he had been attached for over three decades. But the time was short. The royal train was waiting at the station. After a slow walk through the lanes, the hothouses, and the farm, the three men drove back to Sofia for the final adieu.

The ex-king, hoping to be allowed to reside in his Austrian domain, had to leave that night by train for Vienna with Prince Kyril. The two princesses had already left. Ferdinand had asked that no officials, except for the prime minister and the war minister, come to see him off at the station. Only a small detachment of soldiers was present when he and King Boris arrived at eleven o'clock to board the private train. "Why these soldiers?" Ferdinand asked somewhat nervously, still worried about a last-minute arrest. Malinov and Savvov reassured him that it was just a protection measure. In the sumptuous salon-car the ex-king bade good-bye to the two ministers asking them to serve his son loyally. Always meticulous about hierarchy and formalities, Ferdinand informed the war minister that just before his abdication he had promoted his son to the grade of major-general. With that, the two ministers left the car, the station chief blew his whistle, and the royal train slowly pulled out of the station. King Boris stayed on the train to accompany his father and brother as far as the next railroad station.

After saying good-bye to his father, Boris returned to Sofia in the car that was waiting for him at the station. He took the wheel, as was his habit, letting the chauffeur sit on the seat next to him, and drove expertly and fast on the pitch-black road to the capital.

It was well past midnight; the city was asleep as the car drove along Moskovska Street and stopped at the palace's back north door. A uniformed policeman opened the black iron gate, clicking his heels and snapping his hand to his visor in a military salute.

Slow tires on the gravel in the silent park . . . the slamming of the car's door . . . the fading noise of the motor disappearing in the night . . . the echo of steps on the squeaky parquet of the long corridors . . . in the east wing, a door opens, then closes. The palace is silent again. Behind the door of what was called, only hours ago, "the princes' apartment," the new king is alone.

No one knows exactly what went through the mind of the young man in the solitude of that night. He did not keep an intimate diary, nor confide his private thoughts. His only confidants at that time were his siblings, especially Princess Evdokia, and they were gone. King Ferdinand's ghost was as present that night in the Sofia palace as was Hamlet's father on the ramparts of Elsinore, and the apprehensions of the new Bulgarian ruler were probably no less poignant than those of the prince of Denmark. The deserted palace rooms in the predawn hours of October 4 became his Gethsemane, but there was no evangelist to record the young man's agony.

At the moment when the state ship looked to be sinking, the helm was entrusted, by constitution, to a sensitive twenty-four-year-old prince, highly intelligent but not very decisive by character, a man of duty and self-discipline, to be sure, but also a man who wasn't quite sure whether he wanted to be king in the first place. And just at the moment he was called to assume responsibility for the failing state, under almost hopeless circumstances, he found himself abruptly cut off from his family, from the father who had instructed and guided him all his life, and from the only friends and advisors whom he could confide in and trust.

Events were unfolding with relentless speed, requiring immediate action, leaving no time for reflection and hesitation. Desperately, urgently, Bulgaria needed a king. The world did not care that he was only twenty-four, and Bulgaria could not afford to ponder his personal problems.

*     *     *

Long live the king! Congratulations, Your Majesty! Felicitations! Bells were ringing in every town and village. Telegrams poured into the palace, and smiles of hope reappeared on worried faces. Since early morning on October 4, military bands started rehearsing and Sofia's streets resounded with the familiar sound of proud patriotic marches, as thousands of citizens, suddenly transformed into festive crowds, converged to the Sveta Nedelia Cathedral.

A solemn Te Deum was sung at eleven o'clock by the entire high clergy of the Saint-Synod in full regalia, in the presence of the members of the government and the Parliament, the diplomatic corps, and most former ministers. An enthusiastic crowd greeted the young king with cheers and hurrahs when he appeared on his way to the ceremony, dressed simply in an army duty uniform with general's epaulets. He looked pale and deeply moved during the solemn Eastern-Orthodox liturgy as he stood listening to the magnificent church choir. He was still struggling to control his emotions at the end of the service when he received the congratulations of the congregation and later the public ovation in the streets. Upon returning to the palace, King Boris appeared on the balcony to address the assembled crowd.

"Thank you for the expression of your patriotic feelings," he said. "I have full confidence in the bright star of Bulgaria. I believe with all my might that the Bulgarian people, thanks to their qualities and strength, are headed toward a brilliant future!" The enthusiastic crowd burst into the national anthem, "Shoomy Maritza," and for a moment the tragic Bulgarian reality seemed to be forgotten.

By lunchtime, King Boris had signed his first decree, ordering the demobilization of the army. Early in the afternoon he went to the Military Club, where the officers of the garrison were assembled to take the oath of fidelity to the new king. Two hundred dapper men in uniform stood at attention in the grand ballroom as King Boris appeared, followed by the war minister. He looked frailer than usual and tired, as if he had suddenly aged by several years. He was wearing his general's uniform and, for the first time, the collar of the order of Saints Cyril and Methodius, the highest decoration of the kingdom.

It was a short and sober ceremony. The war minister asked the officers to swear fidelity to the new supreme commander of the armed forces. A priest said a few prayers, then read solemnly the oath which all officers repeated aloud. King Boris spoke briefly, thanked the men for their readiness to serve and obey him, and left the club. Shortly after, he was driven to the large parade and drill field outside Sofia, where the troops of the garrison took the oath.

Meanwhile, the proclamation announcing his accession to the throne was posted all over the country. It read: "Born on the beautiful Bulgarian soil, spiritual child of the Eastern-Orthodox church, having been raised among my dear people and having shared with them the joys of their glorious feats and constant progress, always inspired by their ideals and pervaded by the democratic spirit demonstrated in their historic struggle for freedom and independence as well as in our public institutions, I proclaim solemnly that I shall respect the constitution and will serve my country faithfully and devoutedly, keeping always as a goal the well-being and the prosperity of the people."

＊　　＊　　＊

# CHAPTER V

# The Debut
# of the Lonely King

THE SUMPTUOUS royal train with its polished mahogany and brass cars, comfortable bedrooms and salons had hardly left the Balkans when trouble began for King Ferdinand. His intention was to go first to the Ebenthal Castle near Vienna, where his two daughters were waiting for him, before deciding how to organize his life in exile between his properties in Hungary, Austria, and Slovakia. But when the train arrived in Budapest, he was sternly informed by the authorities that he could not go to his Murany estate in Hungary.

The *London Times* reported on October 8: "The ex-King of Bulgaria passed through Budapest on Saturday evening . . . but did not leave the train . . . A telegram from Vienna says that ex-King Ferdinand is suffering from a complete nervous collapse. Prince Kyril accompanied the ex-King. When during the short stay at the station of Mariatheresiopol, the ex-King read the Budapest papers which sharply criticized his attitude, he, according to the Prince, shed tears and protested that he had not deserved such a judgment after enduring so many tragic buffets of fate."

The trip continued without King Ferdinand leaving the train. On arrival at the border between Hungary and Austria, the ex-monarch was subjected to another unpleasant experience. In the middle of the night, at the station of Marchegg, he received a visit from a special emissary of his ally and brother-in-law, Emperor Charles. But the emissary, Count Berthold, had not come to convey the greetings of his sovereign. He boarded the train to ask politely but firmly, on behalf of the emperor, that King Ferdinand leave Austrian territory immediately, without stopping in Vienna or going to Ebenthal.

This was a terrible shock for the ex-king. He could not believe that his ally and relative would refuse him asylum, deny him the right to reside in his own estates. After much protesting and arguing, Count Berthold agreed to allow him to stop briefly at Ebenthal to see his daughters for a few hours before continuing to Germany.

Kaiser William was more generous and understanding than his Austro-

Hungarian colleague. Not only did he send Ferdinand a friendly cable expressing his sincere commiseration, but he insisted that the former king retain his honorary ranks of German field marshal and honorary commander of a German regiment. After exchanging several telegrams with the kaiser, King Ferdinand proceeded to Coburg where he was welcomed to establish his residence-in-exile.

Emperor Charles's refusal to admit Ferdinand to Austria shocked King Boris. He summoned the Austrian representative, Count Chernin, and protested vehemently, asking him to cable immediately to his government and demand that asylum be granted. "I am deeply indignant concerning this blatant injustice," he told his father in a coded telegram sent on October 6, informing him also that "for the moment the situation in Bulgaria is unchanged. A French colonel arrived yesterday and an Englishman comes today. I learned that beginning the day after tomorrow, the Entente will control the telegraph and will interrupt out coded contact with the Central Powers." The message was signed, "Your obedient, Rylski."

The young king's intervention was to no avail. Two days later, Count Chernin came to the palace with the negative answer of his government. The excuse was that there existed a strong feeling against Bulgaria in Austria-Hungary and fearful of demonstrations against Ferdinand, Emperor Charles was compelled to forbid, for the time being, the ex-king's sojourn in the territory of the monarchy. And Boris reported to his father, "The relations between us and Austria are not yet severed, and short of some flagrant provocation master-minded by the opposite camp, there is hope of avoiding a definitive break with our two allies. In general, the atmosphere becomes tenser, and resembles the Greek case [the king of Greece had been dethroned], but let us hope that with God's help we'll overcome. It appears that the government will resign in order to form a larger coalition cabinet."

The strong ties between the obedient son and the father who in his eyes was still "Le Monarque," were difficult to break. Partly because of habit, and partly because he had no other confidant for the affairs of state, Boris, in the first ten days of his reign, continued to share his thoughts with ex-King Ferdinand, until the cyphered telegrams were abruptly discontinued by the foreign occupier's censorship. "I have to be particularly cautious because the suspicions about me are great," Boris warned his father. One of his last messages, on October 11, said that "the situation is unclear. The Entente appears to be wanting to speed up the occupation. Yesterday I received the French and English colonels, both courteous, who declared that they did not look for reprisals but only wanted railroad cars to transport troops. For the moment, they'll bring an English division that will go to Serbia, and a French battalion here to Sofia. The German legation will leave before the French come, but the Germans will not break relations formally. The cabinet crisis is still not solved. The weather is good. I am in good health. I kiss your hand, Rylski."

In the meantime, Boris also worried about his sisters who were in the Austrian castle of Ebenthal, waiting for instructions to join their father and Prince Kyril in Germany. The situation in Austria was rapidly deteriorating and the dethronement of Emperor Charles appeared imminent. Fearing riots and the interruption of communications, King Boris strongly advised his father to call the princesses to join him in Coburg.

In October, the princesses could still speak on the telephone with their brother in Sofia and write to their father in Germany. Evdokia and Nadejda felt very lonely in Ebenthal, surrounded by new faces, and with the feeling that many of their friends and acquaintances avoided them as being politically embarrassing.

After a telephone conversation with Boris, Evdokia wrote to her father: "More than anything, Bo asked for your news and repeated again how infamous the behavior of IV [Emperor Charles] was . . . Bo has also had the Spanish influenza and was still coughing rather badly. About the situation, he said that his only hope was the reply of America and the possibility of gaining time before sharing 'the fate of my Southern colleague' [the king of Greece] . . . Then the line was cut and I couldn't hear anything more, except that he kissed your hand."

Evdokia and Nadejda soon after arrived in Coburg to share the exile of their father and Prince Kyril. It was a sad time of uncertainty and loneliness, waiting for news from Bulgaria, infrequent and usually disturbing. Poor Bo! the sisters thought constantly, how does he manage all by himself in Sofia? If only he could write! . . . A few loyal subjects still took risks and wrote to Ferdinand, but there was nothing cheerful in their reports from occupied Bulgaria.

The old Dobrovitch, who had served the king for twenty-four years, sent a letter through a foreign diplomat in October: "The way the Entente acts, we'll be completely cut off from Europe in a few days. The situation is grave, Your Majesty . . . Knowing how the Entente behaved in Greece, H. M. King Boris is certain that he too will suffer King Alexander's fate. In the beginning one thought that the Entente would be more magnanimous toward Bulgaria and would not make her feel too much defeat and impotence. But we were mistaken. The vise is tightened more each day, and the Entente's heavy yoke is being felt more and more. We hear that the Allied supreme commander of the Eastern front wants to move his headquarters to Sofia. In such an event, what will be the situation of the king? He'll be the prisoner of General d'Esperey, who will become omnipotent here. Let's hope that the peace treaty will be signed soon, so this occupation doesn't last too long! . . ."

The internal situation worried Dobrovitch too. The demobilization was orderly and most troops had returned, "but Socialists and Agrarians agitate the population against the state. They openly demand a republic. They were not at all embarrassed to declare it in the Sobranié when Malinov read your act of abdication and King Boris's manifesto. They shouted with all their force: 'We don't want any king anymore, long live the republic!' The idea of proclaiming a republic wins more partisans, and who knows whether we won't be forced one day to leave Bulgaria!" lamented the loyal monarchist. "If the extreme Left wins the majority in the cabinet, I think we could pack the suitcases, as such a government would bring to the Sobranié a Socialist and Agrarian majority, who will proclaim a republic." As a precaution, Dobrovitch thought it wise to pack the royal secret archives and send them to Ferdinand by a trusted foreign friend.

Another report of the royal chancery chief to his former master depicts the difficult position of the new king: "The situation here is not at all rosy, and young King Boris has to struggle against people hostile to the regime. The socialist newspapers, even the Ministry of Labor's organ, preach openly in favor of the republic. At the palace reception for the new cabinet, the new ministers were extremely polite and respectful, and in newspaper interviews they praise King Boris's talents and qualities very much, but one cannot trust them. . . . These ministers are capable of any crime and treason. Only the fear of Bolshevism forces them to keep quiet and not undermine the regime. Otherwise, they would have proclaimed the republic long ago. They fear Bolshevism because the Bolsheviks will not spare them either. . . .

"There is active Socialist and Agrarian agitation among the demobilized soldiers. As a result, the population in a few districts refuses to obey the authorities, to pay taxes or recognize any requisition commission. In one word: anarchy!

"The French and the English continue to arrive. The French are commiting the worst outrages, looting in the towns and villages through which they pass, the worst being Kyustendil and Radomir. Many cases of rapes are reported. In that respect, the worst are the colonial troops. The English behave quite correctly. . . .

"There are no French and English troops so far in Sofia, only officers who behave in a haughty manner, treating the Bulgarians like prisoners of war. They use our railroads as they please and they control the telegraph totally. In a word, they are the masters here, and we must swallow all humiliations. . . .

"The health situation in the capital is very bad, too. The Spanish disease is spreading horrendously, in its most malignant form. One hundred people die every day. Measures are being taken to stop it, but so far with no success. May God have mercy on us!"

But as the nation was licking its wounds, signs of order and peace began to appear. Passions were abating. Countless disrupted lives began to mend as the months went by. The demobilized soldiers, many of them in uniform for seven years, returned to the plows. The farms came to life again. In towns and villages, the peacetime routine was gradually cooling down the postwar fever.

Bulgaria, although poorer, traumatized, and occupied by foreign troops, was painfully returning to some degree of normalcy. And in the process, her unassuming young king seemed to gain an unexpected and genuine popularity, a fragile and vulnerable symbol of a fragile and vulnerable state.

In the first months after his accession, the politicians did not pay much attention to him, or at least did not feel threatened by him in any way. Boris was a modest, likeable young man who did not particularly bother anyone and who did not seem to have any ambitions beyond the ceremonial functions of a modern constitutional monarch. The dynasty's friends still looked on him as the son of *the* king, the real one, who was now in exile. For its enemies, he was a harmless and probably very temporary representative of an institution that would shortly be abolished. Stambolisky, for instance, referred to him condescendingly but not without a certain sympathy, as "Valchéto"—the little wolf, the likeable cub one should not let grow up with bad habits.

The Malinov cabinet was succeeded by a larger coalition that included Socialists and Agrarians. Amnesty was proclaimed for those responsible for both the Dobro-Polé defeat and for the Radomir uprising, thus opening the way for rebels like Stambolisky to return to political life.

All during 1919, the communications between King Boris and his family were extremely cautious, almost nonexistent, for fear of interception. Many circles, both in Bulgaria and among the Entente powers, were still fiercely hostile to Ferdinand and suspicious of the influence he might have on his son. Only occasionally would Boris send a message through a trusted traveler, like the one received in Coburg on July 26. "Prince Kyril, as well as the princesses, should under no circumstances return to Bulgaria now, nor raise this question at this moment. The king will inform them later, when he finds that the time has come."

Another letter, written by a devoted army officer, M. Nikiforov, was smuggled out of Sofia in October 1919. Nikiforov, who had returned from Germany, wrote: "I was happy to be received by His Majesty King Boris . . . He interrogated me in detail, mostly about your health, spirit and state. He asked many questions about his sisters and especially about H. R. H. Prince Kyril. It is obvious that he misses you very much. We spoke about the return of the whole family. He sighed and said, 'People here think that I am like a solitary stone.' He suffers a great deal, both as a man and as a ruler. Everybody loves him and sympathizes with him, including the republicans.

"... In August, he came alone in his automobile to pick me up at my home. He was driving himself. It was 2 P.M. Sizzling. The streets deserted. The few passers-by didn't recognize us. 'I don't have my father's figure,' he said, 'everybody recognized *him*.' ... We stop in Bistritza. Then at Sitniakovo and Sara-Ghyol.[1] The road is bad in many places. At one place, we have to push the car. The young king takes the shovel and digs. We reach the summit. A herd of wild goats crosses the road in front of us; a bearded eagle soars in the sky; the snow is melting; ... the panorama is indescribable! ... We drive at a terrifying speed. He is an excellent driver, I admire his skill and courage. He says, 'I've driven many times here by night with my father.' We stop to visit Sara-Ghyol, the most beautiful spot! In Sitniakovo one sees everywhere your taste and your hand. Bistritza has such a good collection of Bulgarian objects. I tell him, 'You should show these places to more people, so more people will appreciate King Ferdinand!' We dine in front of the roaring fire in the fireplace. We leave at eleven o'clock. One of the car's headlights doesn't work. The conversation continues in the dark. Silence. He sighs, 'I think that my father is standing next to me. He observes everything and notices everything.' I felt sorry for this young man from the bottom of my heart. At 1 A.M. we were in Sofia. We said good-bye and I felt even more attached to this man. He charms and attracts everybody who meets him. The republicans are also his admirers—Stambolisky, Kosturkov, Dimitrov, etc. etc."

Later, Nikiforov visited the Euxinograd palace on the Black Sea.

"The sun shines softly. The leaves are already falling," he wrote in the letter. "The palace is deserted. For years no master's foot has stepped here. The personnel are cautious and don't trust the visitors. Only when they understand that the visitor is a friend do they begin to talk. 'The old Master used to arrive suddenly and woe to us if the sand was not raked or if there was a single fallen leaf on the lawn!' "We came to the Cape of St. George. 'The old Master used to stand here and admire the coast. Only he could have found the best spot of the entire coast!' The servant continues, 'He loves this place very much.' He sighs and whispers mysteriously, 'As soon as things are straightened, some morning he'll arrive again, suddenly and secretly, from the sea.' This is the legend that lives now in Euxinograd."

*       *       *

Never had Boris felt so lonely as during the first year of his reign. Most of the familiar faces had gone, and the Sofia palace had become a somber place whose solitude was hard to bear. Evening after evening, the young monarch sat at the dinner table with the same collaborators with whom he

---

[1] Royal mountain lodges in Rila, above the fashionable resort Tcham-Koria.

had spent the working day, the few men whom he knew and who had remained. Often he looked disturbed, absorbed by his thoughts.

One night, after a long silence, he turned to his dinner companion, Pavel Grouev, a trusted palace secretary. "You have never seen war, have you?" he asked.

"No, sire, I have just done my regular military service in Sofia."

Usually, King Boris would tease the soft secretary, not very fit physically, for his eminently "civilian" appearance and manner. But this time he was serious.

"You don't know how lucky you are!" he exclaimed. "You don't know what a horror war is. I've witnessed death and suffering and atrocities so abominable as not to be imagined, if you have not seen them. Our men, Batcho Pavlé [his nickname for Grouev], Bulgarian soldiers, good men. Bleeding there, hungry and freezing, dying in pain, in the mud, hundreds of miles from home. . . . One never forgets these horrors."

He calmed down and his voice became solemn. "I'll tell you something," he intoned. "As long as I am king, no Bulgarian soldier will ever fight in a war again. I swear it! I won't allow any Bulgarian ever again to be forced to fight outside our borders! As long as I remain king!"

It was a weighty pledge, Grouev thought the first time he heard it. The king no doubt was a little too emotional that evening. But he had the occasion to hear it many more times, again and again during the long years he served the king. So did every person who was close to Boris III. Always the same words, the same determination. "As long as I am king. . . . Never! Ever!"

The year 1919 was a year of anguish, of waiting for the peace conference and its verdict. No one in Bulgaria entertained great illusions: the Entente statesmen and the Western press had indicated clearly that the conditions of the peace treaties would be hard. Some hope remained, however, that the spirit of fairness proclaimed by the American president Woodrow Wilson would prevail at the conference.

When in June the first two treaties were signed in Paris—with Germany in Versailles and with Hungary in Trianon—a great dejection was felt in Bulgaria. Vindictive and arbitrary decisions concerning ethnic minorities obviously were being imposed on the defeated enemies. The dismay increased in September with the St. Germain verdict on Austria. If King Boris was thinking of his personal future, the writing was on the wall: both the German kaiser and the Austrian emperor had abdicated and their countries had become republics.

Finally, Bulgaria's turn came. The Bulgarian delegation was summoned to be in Paris on the 26th of July. Six days before, the delegation left Sofia on a special train. Headed by the prime minister T. Theodorov, it comprised four other politicians, including the new member of the government,

Stambolisky. The delegation arrived in Paris on the morning of July 26 and was whisked immediately to its hotel in the residential suburb of Neuilly-sur-Seine—"Chateau de Madrid," an old castle built by Francis I near the Bois de Boulogne.

The comfortable residence turned out to be a golden cage. The delegation was informed that all visits to Paris were forbidden, all mail would be censored, and no visitors allowed. This humiliating treatment lasted for more than two-and-a-half months, during which period the frustrated delegates received no communication whatsoever from either the Entente's representatives or the French government.

Finally, on October 19, the five delegates were summoned to the Quai d'Orsay where they were handed the text of the peace treaty, in finished form, prepared without any prior deliberation with the Bulgarians. They were received in the Salon de l'Horloge by French Prime Minister Clémenceau surrounded by representatives of all the Allies. As they were entering the room, Clémenceau turned to his colleagues and asked loud enough to be heard by everyone: "Bulgarie? Est-ce un royaume ou une république?" ("Bulgaria? Is it a kingdom or a republic?"). Nadejda Stancioff (later Lady Muir), who was a secretary-interpreter for the Bulgarian delegation, described the painful scene.

"Clémenceau then handed a document to Theodorov declaring that the delegates would have twenty-five days to present their observations in writing. M. Theodorov made an eloquent speech, ending with indirect references to President Wilson's Fourteen Points. Clemenceau listened attentively, his small hands in the grey cotton gloves he always wore folded on the table, his small face grown wizened and his expression sullen; he bowed quite courteously to the delegates when they left. . . . Although the delegation expected the worst, the terms of the proffered treaty plunged every one of them into despair. . . ."

The delegates left the next day for Sofia for consultation. The king and the government were heartbroken when they read the clauses of the draft. Not only had Bulgaria to abandon Macedonia which it had occupied during the war, but it had to give Southern Dobrudja to Rumania, the frontier town of Tzaribrod to Yugoslavia and the Aegean coastline to Greece. A promise was made to provide Bulgaria with an outlet to the Aegean sea "at a later date." (This promise was never kept.)

The bad news caused a government crisis, and the cabinet was reshuffled, with Stambolisky becoming prime minister of the new coalition cabinet. Theodorov, however, remained the Chief delegate and returned to Paris with a counterproposal. But the Allies, in no mood to negotiate, declared bluntly that none of the territorial or military clauses of the treaty would be modified. Only a few changes were made in the economic clauses, which nevertheless remained very severe. The territorial conditions were so harsh—in many cases the frontier line divided villages in two, or separated cemeteries and water wells from the villages—that Theodorov, overcome by grief and indignation, refused to sign the treaty and returned to Sofia.

But cruel as it was, reality required that someone sign the harsh treaty. Bulgaria had no leverage whatsoever, no recourse, and no friends. Stambolisky took the responsibility and courageously put his signature to the document which was amputating Bulgaria and sentencing it to a future of misery. On November 27, he signed the Treaty of Neuilly, a name that became for every Bulgarian the synonym for injustice and humiliation. It is often said that emotions, much more than reason and goods determine the behavior of nations. In the case of Bulgaria, there is no doubt that the next twenty-five years of national life were irremediably and tragically marked by the indignation and despair sown on November 27 in Neuilly-sur-Seine.

Nadejda Stancioff witnessed the sad occasion:

"The ceremony took place without any pomp in the council chamber of the Mairie of Neuilly at 10:30 A.M.," she wrote. "I witnessed the entrance of most of the signatories: Polk, representing the USA, a fine-looking man with marmorean profile; Sir Eyre Crowe, sandy-haired, looking curiously absent; Clemenceau small, animated, with glittering restless eyes, grey gloved as usual; our friend Tardieu, who has gained weight; Venizelos, endeavoring not to look too pleased. No Serbs and no Rumanians were present; the handsome room gradually filled with onlookers who overflowed onto the stairs. The delegates sat around a table covered with green baize, and I saw another little table by itself a little further away. At 10:35 the formidable Stambolisky, quite impassive, entered with Stancioff[2]. . . . The whole assembly rose, including Clémenceau who rapped out, "La séance est ouverte." He then invited the delegate from Bulgaria to sign the Peace Treaty. Stambolisky rose with dignity, walked to the table and wrote his name resolutely on the open page. Stancioff then named all the delegates to him as they passed. . . . The ceremony had been very short. . . . Signatories, secretaries, and assistants went down the grand staircase, where this time the French guard of honor presented arms to Stambolisky and his colleagues."

There were many farsighted citizens of the victorious powers who, realizing that the peace treaties imposed at the Paris conference contained the seeds of future disasters, deplored the vindictiveness that had inspired them. The eminent British political writer, Sir Harold Nicolson, wrote in his book *Peacemaking 1919:*" We came to Paris convinced that the new

---

[2]Dimitri Stancioff, the distinguished diplomat and father of Nadejda Stancioff, acted as secretary-general of the Bulgarian delegation.

order was about to be established; we left it convinced that the new order had merely fouled the old. We arrived as fervent apprentices in the school of President Wilson; we left as renegades. . . . We arrived determined that a peace of justice and wisdom should be negotiated: we left it, conscious that the treaties imposed upon our enemies were neither just nor wise."

## Chapter VI

# The Stambolisky Regime

TO REIGN in Bulgaria in the early 1920s was an affliction that would forever cure even the most ambitious and power-hungry aspirant of the desire to be king. For Boris, who had never been enthusiastic about wearing a crown, it became a daily torment.

"The king reigns but does not govern" is the golden rule in every constitutional monarchy. Boris would not have had it any other way. Both this temperament and the experience of his father's mistakes reinforced his democratic inclinations. Under different circumstances, he would have been content with his role of "reigning." Unfortunately for him, the "governing" part was exercised by an extraordinary, overpowering hurricane of a man— Alexander Stambolisky. The inexperienced monarch had to live and work under the shadow of one of the most unorthodox and unpredictable dictators in postwar Europe.

The burly peasant leader was not merely the prime minister. With fervor and self-assurance, he undertook the ambitious task of changing the entire political, social, and economic structure of the state. He had started a revolution aimed at establishing the rule of the agriculturists—not the dictatorship of the industrial proletariat, as in the recent Soviet revolution, but of the class that fed the nation, the peasants, three-quarters of the Bulgarian population.

Stambolisky and his friends had been fighting for their rights since the creation of the Agrarian Union in 1899. They felt strongly that the rural population had always been exploited by the politicans, merchants, and middlemen from the cities without ever receiving their fair share. The Agrarian Union had opposed the policies of King Ferdinand and the "bourgeois" parties, and now that the Agrarians were in power, Stambolisky decreed several sweeping reforms, transforming, sometimes brutally, essential aspects of the society and the state. Some ideas of the maverick dictator—such as the mandatory labor service to replace military service, or the creation of a Green International for the agriculturists of Europe, attracted the world's attention and enabled the proud Stambolisky to boast,

"At home, the Agrarian Union has reached its apogee. Now it is more powerful than ever. All eyes are turned toward us. Not only in Europe, but all over the world people talk about the Bulgarian Agrarians. They have astonished the entire world. We can be certain: all the other peoples will imitate us!"

But the city people and the intelligentsia felt that the new regime treated them as enemies. The crude, indiscriminate methods of the ruling Agrarian Union frightened them. Intimidation, the brutal breaking up of opposition meetings, beatings, the dismissal of non-Agrarian officials, and favoritism had become common features of political life. The civil service was affected by the abolition of educational qualifications for public office. This opened the gates to all state jobs, including the highest, to a legion of illiterate and incompetent party members. Even the orthography was changed by simplifying spelling and grammar. But, curiously enough, this government of sworn republicans hesitated to abolish the monarchy.

Not that Stambolisky was not a 100 percent convinced republican. No Bulgarian politician had so flagrantly defied King Ferdinand as he. As far back as 1910 he had caused a tremendous scandal at the opening of the Parliament. Ferdinand had the habit of reading his annual Speech of the Throne sitting down, with his hat on, while all representatives listened standing up and hatless. As the king began his speech, Stambolisky ostentatiously sat down and placed his peasant cap on his head. The king was outraged, but ignored the affront and continued the reading. The following year, he delivered his throne speech on foot and with no hat. Throughout Ferdinand's reign, Stambolisky's editorials and speeches bristled with hostility to the crown.

Why then did he not attempt to abolish the monarchy when he assumed power? One reason was undoubtedly the surprising popularity of young King Boris and the loyal support of the army. Stambolisky was shrewd enough not to provoke a serious disturbance, possibly a civil war, by acting hastily against such a well-liked figure. He assured the Agrarian Congress that "the kinglet" had learned from his father's mistakes and that he would never be able to build a personal regime. But he added that all monarchs were "poisonous snakes" and that if King Boris tried to bite, the Agrarian Union had the means to pull out his fangs.

In fairness to Stambolisky, another reason for deferring the proclamation of the republic was purely patriotic. Boris was respected by the Western powers. To remove him now, during negotiations for the promised Aegean Sea outlet, the reduction of the exorbitant reparations, and other vital problems, would severely damage the Bulgarian cause. And no matter what one thought of Stambolisky, he was a man who loved his country.

But there was still another reason. Unlikely as it may seem, the radical antimonarchist came to admire the young king and even to have sympathy for him. A complex relationship developed between the nominal head of state and the real ruler of the country, woven from mistrust, mutual curiosity, and irritation, but also from complicity. A forced partnership, to be true, but nevertheless a complicity in which both men were conscious that they were working for the same national cause—and that each one was powerless to get rid of the other.

Early on, both had to accept, although reluctantly, the rules of the game. The first time the king summoned the prime minister to the palace, Stambolisky replied that if His Majesty wanted to talk to him, he had to come to his office. It took some courage for the twenty-six-year-old Boris to remind the dictator of the constitutional rules and to repeat the summons. This time Stambolisky obeyed. But from the beginning, he made it clear to the king that the governing was to be the responsibility of the prime minister and his cabinet. From then on, most important decisions were made without informing the monarch. Boris had to become accustomed to the *fait accompli.* However—and here was where the partner-rivals needed each other in their constitutional see-saw—the constitution prescribed that any decree required the signature of the head of state to become law. That was the king's leverage, probably the only lever still available to him.

A confidential letter from Dobrovitch to King Ferdinand describes the relationship between Boris and Stambolisky:

> . . . The situation of King Boris is most difficult. He is obliged to work with antimonarchist people who don't trust him and who proclaim openly that they'll keep the king as long as he works for their benefit. In spite of that, King Boris must keep them, because there is no other solution. The opposition is too weak to take over the power. The bourgeois parties still cannot form a bloc . . . Therefore, it is out of the question for the king to attempt a *coup d' état* and overthrow the government. If this were to happen, the Agrarians would go to the Communists, quickly make a new government and proclaim a republic. The result would be the partition of Bulgaria by Serbia, Rumania, and Greece, because Europe would not tolerate a Bolshevik nest in the Balkans. Therefore, there is no solution but to keep Stambolisky at the rudder. It is not pleasant for King Boris, but he has no other choice.

In his frustration, Boris often remembered that, curiously enough, his father also had to share power with a dictator, Stefan Stambolov, when he first mounted the Bulgarian throne. But the style and strategy of the father and the son were totally different. While Ferdinand expressed his disagreement in stormy confrontations, with mean sarcasm, outbursts of temper and occasional insults, Boris developed a technique of avoiding showdowns by postponement, maneuvering, or a convenient absence. When he did not want to sign a decree, he happened to be "out of town"; when expecting a minister seeking unpleasant decisions, he tried to defer the audience or to gain time before he had to act. His strategy was often successful, as time usually had a moderating effect. But it gained him a reputation for indecisiveness. In a country where political problems were seen in black and white, a man like King Boris, gifted (or afflicted?) with an extraordinary ability of seeing the grays in life, an objective observer with the tendency of looking at all sides of a problem, was condemned to continuous agony.

If he did not quarrel openly with his ministers, it did not mean that Boris was not subject to anger and discouragement. In fact, his temper was becoming worse and worse. He always managed to keep his composure and excellent manners during the tense meetings with Stambolisky or his ministers, but often, when the visitor had left, he would explode. The recipients of his outbursts were usually his intimates, the members of his immediate entourage. In such moments, they saw a side of the king very different from his mild and polite image. He screamed angrily, threatened to fire everybody and exploded in the most colorful idiomatic Bulgarian, mixed with rude words in Turkish or French. When his rage reached its zenith, his confidants would hear his perennial threat, "I've had enough! I am fed up! I'll take my hat and leave!" His intimates knew that it was useless to try to calm him down or to contradict him as long as his fury lasted. A few minutes later, the tempest spent, the young sovereign regained his composure and, feeling slightly embarrassed, made the first gesture of reconciliation toward his stunned courtiers.

Only a handful of men ever had the dubious privilege of seeing the young king in his off-guard moments. They were his closest collaborators, members of his civilian and military households, the nearest thing to confidants and companions a man without a family and without intimate childhood friends could have. Most of them—Ivan Bagrianov, Sirko Stanchev, Parvan Draganov, Dimitar Naumov—were army officers of his own age, bright and distinguished young captains, whom he had noticed during the war or during their service at the elite royal company assigned to guard the king's hunting lodges in the Rila mountains. They were all worldly, loyal and discreet, men of a certain culture, conversant in foreign languages. One after the other, Boris took them to his service as aides-de-camp. They were in attendance permanently, not only during their duty hours in the Sofia palace, but also frequently for dinner in the country palace in Vrana, at excursions and vacations, or at hunts in the mountains. A real comradeship developed between the lonely bachelor king and his aides-de-camp. They were the only company in which he could relax, be amused, laugh. Belonging to the same generation, they could share the same war memories and enjoy the same anecdotes and spicy jokes. They had nicknames for almost every Bulgarian politician and general, some of them quite cruel, all of them witty and original, invented mostly by the king. He had an extraordinary sense of humor centering on idiomatic expressions, old proverbs, and bawdy words, and he was delighted to have intimate and discreet companions with whom he could freely use his remarkable vocabulary.

Pavel Grouev, chief of his private cabinet, was another member of the inner circle, and probably the person with whom the king spent most of his working hours. Grouev was a mild, softspoken man from Plovdiv, who had a law degree from the University of Grenoble and a passion for French and Russian literature and classical music. King Ferdinand had brought him from the Ministry of Foreign Affairs to the palace chancellery two years earlier. The quiet pipe-smoking diplomat had above all two qualities that impressed both kings: he was proverbially discreet and he wrote remarkably well, both in Bulgarian and in French.

Boris's relationship with him was different from the one he enjoyed with his young aides-de-camp. First of all, "Bacho[1] Pavel," as he called him, was considerably older than he, fifteen years his senior. And, in fact, he looked and behaved even older, with his old-fashioned beard, his sloping shoulders and slow walk. King Boris trusted him completely, always respecting his advice. As Dobrovitch was growing older, all the coded telegrams and classified documents arrived in Grouev's offices, the first two rooms on the ground floor next to the main entrance of the palace, where the king came several times a day to read them. It was also in this office that Boris usually signed the royal decrees and worked on the speeches that "Bacho Pavel" wrote for him. Every morning he called him on the direct line to the Grouev home, and their telephone conversations, usually in French so the operators could not understand, often lasted for half-an-hour or more.

But Grouev was less involved in the king's private life than the younger officers. An avid reader, theater-goer and frustrated pianist, he had never done any sport in his life, never held a hunting gun in his hands, or been near a horse or an automobile steering-wheel. Consequently, he did not participate in the king's favorite extracurricular activities—hunting, hiking, motoring, sailing. Furthermore, although gifted with an exquisite sense of humor of the sophisticated kind King Boris appreciated enormously, there was a certain delicacy or even prudishness in Pavel Grouev's personality which made it difficult to tell earthy jokes or use obscene words in his presence.

Bagrianov and Draganov, who became the king's closest friends, were men of action, energetic and actively interested in politics. Grouev, on the

---

[1]"Bacho" is a popular appellation used to address an older brother, or someone older than oneself.

other hand, was a wise but rather slow and reflective adviser, certainly not a man of action and initiative. For all of them, being close collaborators of the king was not always easy, especially in his moments of discouragement or anger. But they were totally, almost unconditionally, loyal to him as their leader (they referred to him as "the nachalstvo," which means "the commander" or "the chief"), and also attached to him as a human being, even when they felt he treated them unfairly. On these infrequent occasions they sensed the extent of his frustrations and the poignancy of his doubts and insecurity. Obviously, the outbursts and the undeserved reprimands were merely symptoms of deep personal pain, of an inner conflict in which he recurrently saw the only solution in resigning. "I'll take my hat and leave!" In such moments, his close collaborators could not help but feel sympathy for him. They knew very well that he would never "take his hat," that he was incapable of not meeting the demands of his office.

His intimates' reactions reflected their different personalities. Grouev's patient, almost fatherly understanding was usually soothing, but at times, his passive philosophical acceptance of things could exasperate the king, especially when he needed to let out some steam. King Boris was so sure of the unswerving fidelity of "Bacho Pavel" that he often took him for granted and, as with other unquestionably loyal friends, did not make half the effort he sometimes put out to win over critics or unsteady allies.

Among Boris's intimates, the one who permitted himself to contradict the king most was Parvan Draganov. But he always did it very respectfully, like a disciplined junior officer standing at attention to report unpleasant facts to his commander. Draganov listened carefully when King Boris spoke of a problem, then, frankly and analytically, made his assessment of the situation. If he thought that the king should have acted differently, he said it firmly and explained why. When King Boris was irritated by advice he construed as criticism, he would cut the conversation short. For a few hours or days, he would show his displeasure with his aide-de-camp, avoiding him or treating him coldly. But he appreciated Draganov's intelligence and frankness and would soon call him again for advice. In time the outspoken officer became, together with Bagrianov, the closest man to the king, a confidant not only in political affairs but also in personal and family matters.

Because of his physical resemblance to King Boris, as well as his close relationship with the royal family, there had been rumors that Draganov was a son of King Ferdinand. And certainly not his only illegitimate child. Indeed, the old "Monarque" was known to be the father of a few children out of wedlock.

The veracity of these rumors is, however, questionable. In any case, the king and Draganov never acted as if they had such suspicions. In reading unpublished letters from the amazingly intimate correspondence the two men exchanged for over twenty years in a personal code, one does not find the slightest allusion to any blood relationship between them, nor any sign of brotherly familiarity. Even in his most intimate letters, Draganov invariably addressed the king as "Your Majesty," and never used the familiar "thou" instead of the formal "you."

Furthermore, in his bachelor years as an aide-de-camp to king Boris, the young Draganov had a brief romance with Princess Evdokia, who remained a lifelong close friend of his and his family.

*     *     *

Because of the antipathy and suspicion directed toward him from the government, King Boris was extremely cautious in corresponding with his father, who was still considered the main enemy of the new regime. The king's letters to Coburg became more and more infrequent, always sent through trusted travelers and written in a private code, which, except for some nicknames that only father and son knew, would not need a cryptographer to decipher. Who would not guess the identity of the receiver, addressed as "Cher Maitre," the usual address for a professor, and of the writer, "Your respectful and affectionate pupil, Stanislas"? (Stanislas was one of the names given to Prince Boris at his Catholic baptism.) Or the references to the volcanic prime minister, Stambolisky, in a letter announcing the mailing of some mysterious "two packages"? On February 21, 1921, Boris wrote his father ". . . one portion of the collection would be safe in a shelter, in case the Stromboli makes a final eruption in our garden. Such an eventuality should by no means be excluded. It can still happen. The seismograph is never quiet. The subterranean rumblings were especially strong around the date of poor Duc de Berry*, but this time we escaped it again."

The young king worried that his difficult and touchy father might not quite understand the reasons for his silence. In the letter quoted above, in which he sends his wishes for Ferdinand's birthday, Boris wrote, "I do it at a risk and in spite of all dangers. My thoughts and my prayers are with you. May God protect you and give you health, strength, and courage to endure all the horrors and sadness of the present times, and may the hard ordeals that you suffer be relieved in a not too distant future by less sad days! Let's hope that the Almighty will grant us the great joy of spending your next birthday together! This is the most ardent wish of your devoted and grateful disciple. Unable to say anything more for the moment or to manifest openly his attachment, he begs you to trust the sincerity of his feelings and his

---

*Charles, Duc de Berry, second son of King Charles X of France, was assassinated on February 13, 1820, in an attempt to "exterminate all Bourbons." Ever since, a family superstition attached special importance to the date of February 13th.

fidelity. He knows that many events and many actions of his car be badly misinterpreted or wrongly understood. It would be very painful to him if, unwillingly, he hurt his master. . . . With God's help, we may one day have the opportunity of seeing each other again, and *then* I'll be able to explain to you everything about the behavior of Tosho."

"Tosho" was the code name for Boris himself: "Tosho received your news," "the position of Tosho." In a cryptic letter sent to his "Cher Maitre" on May 25, 1921, "Stanislas" mentions some dangers for "Tosho." "There are always some dark clouds on the horizon. One of the closest and most dangerous cloud is the old idea of uniting the Momtschesie to the Mohatschanin. (Code names, probably for "Agrarians" and "Communists"). The current is very strong at this moment among the substitute for "Koie"[2] and his colleagues. Let's hope that Mohatschanin won't be clever enough for blowing in. Otherwise, things will turn out very badly. The end can come very fast, with a liquidation of the Tosho establishment, *à la portugaise*."[3]

"Tosho is doing not too badly," concludes his letter. "He is getting progressively bald and begins to have the ecclesiastic pate . . ." Indeed, at the age of 25 the young king had lost most of his hair.

Boris was fascinated by Stambolisky's personality. How could such a rustic man be so politically astute and have such original and advanced ideas? On the other hand, why was such a brilliant statesman encouraging the excesses of the regime and unnecessarily antagonizing so many segments of the population? What made this self-styled leader tick? What was the secret of his popular success?

One attribute was his phenomenal vitality. This exuberance, combined with the certitude of his beliefs that bordered on arrogance, could be very contagious. Also, he knew how to speak to the simple people, how to flatter and excite the peasants, by far the largest constituency in Bulgaria. If he was a demagogue, as his enemies maintained, he was a most talented and effective demagogue. His speeches were packed with the vernacular, most of his examples were taken from farm life, and his metaphors reeked of the stable. "Never elect for mayor a man who lets his chickens climb on his head!" he would advise his audience. Or, explaining the need for censorship, "You know that when a horse has to be operated on, they put shackles and blinders on him. That hurts, but he doesn't know what is happening to his behind. So with censorship: it permits doing surgery to the bourgeois political parties." His parables were not always noted for their delicacy, "It

---

[2]In his letters Boris refers sometimes to Stambolisky as "Koie." The origin of this nickname is unclear, but knowing the habit of the king of making fun of accents, it is possible that the name is derived from the provincial pronunciation of the Bulgarian interrogative pronoun "Koe?"—"which," "what?" At that time Stambolisky was traveling in Europe, with Raiko Daskalov acting as his substitute.

[3]The Portuguese king Manuel II was dethroned by a revolution in 1910.

wasn't we who took the power. It was the power that jumped on us. Like the cows, who when they are overexcited throw themselves over the bulls." In the parliament he once called an adversary "an old hen that can neither lay an egg nor cluck properly." In public speeches, he would refer to unfriendly politicians as "cat's shit" or "an acorn unfit to feed a pig."

Hostility toward the cities and the intelligentsia became the trademark of the Stambolisky regime. Everybody who had a diploma, lived in a town, or wore a necktie, was suspect in the eyes of the peasants in power, and they encouraged the growing polarization. "The agriculturist long despised by the cities, is now king in Bulgaria," Stambolisky proclaimed proudly. "By our legislative action, we began to break one after the other the chains of slavery. None of the people-eaters feels secure anymore. The tyrants are worried. The cities are upside-down. The bourgeois and all the intellectuals, with foam on their mouths, hurl threats against the victorious peasant party. But I am asking you, dear agriculturists, who sent you to the trenches? They did. Who made you lose Macedonia, Thrace, and Dobrudja? They did, always them. Look at them, however. They all swim in luxury, while you, peasants with sweat on your foreheads, continue to bear the burden of the hardest work in order to feed them. Let's continue the struggle! I predict that tomorrow the banners of the agriculturists will fly over all the nations ... Little by little, the peasant who used to be ridiculed and pressured, who was the eternal slave, raises the banner of emancipation. Soon he'll cease to carry the heavy load that the city-dwellers, the bourgeois, and the intellectuals have placed on his shoulders. Wars will disappear, the derision will end, and the city lawyers' contempt will be rejected. Yes, dear peasants, the world must know that he who provides the bread must be the master and the seigneur!"

His way of expressing his contempt could hardly endear him to the intelligentsia. "The imbecility is about to end: the generals, the professors, the journalists and the lawyers are excluded from the government," he said.

The shortcomings and excesses of the Stambolisky regime were outrageous, shocking. Few other governments could have survived them. And yet, Stambolisky's movement had an undeniable appeal for large parts of the population. It fit the mood and feelings of many Bulgarians of that period. His popularity was due to his ability to sum up and express clearly and courageously, albeit with large doses of over-simplification and demagoguery, a complete ideological program as an alternative to the previous disastrous policies. He had assumed the role of champion of the Bulgarian "Left."

His ideas were radical but consistent. They required courage because they contested traditional patriotic attitudes and challenged national ideas and priorities. The ground he chose to fight on was highly emotional, where accusations of betrayal could easily be formulated. But in the wake of the national disaster, the popularity of an ideology opposed to all previous values was only natural.

In contrast to the former government, it was pacifist rather than irredentist, international rather than national, republican rather than monarchist. It was willing to renounce part of Bulgaria's territorial claims and seek the friendship of yesterday's enemies, especially Yugoslavia, and was sympathetic to the idea of a Balkan federation. Such ideas, of course, made Stambolisky the mortal foe of many patriots, whom he considered chauvinists, and also of the dreaded IMRO, Internal Macedonian Revolutionary Organization. In a period when most Bulgarians were still mourning the loss of Macedonia, Stambolisky's words to Yugoslav journalists in Belgrade in 1922 sounded sacrilegious: "Since you've taken Macedonia, why don't you also take all Macedonians who still remain in Bulgaria? You can have them, good riddance! They have only been a nuisance to us. Because of them, Bulgarian sons perished. The Macedonians were harming us as much as they could. Take them all, and make them into human beings and citizens! I have been an adversary of the Macedonians. I fought against them. All political atrocities in Bulgaria are the doing of the Macedonians. I would never wage war with you for the Macedonians!"

But while alienating many circles, Stambolisky's bold innovations gained him prestige among the nation's peasantry, and also abroad. His new Compulsory Labor Services that recruited youths to work at public construction projects instead of doing military service became his most famous and admired reform, a precursor of many a future Peace Corps.

To most Bulgarian peasants, deprived of any modern comfort in their poor, underdeveloped villages, the agrarian utopia sounded very attractive. "In twenty years," Stambolisky wrote in March 1922, "Bulgaria will be a model agricultural state, whose towns and villages will no longer have muddy streets, provided with clean drinking water, electricity, the telegraph, telephone, wooded parks, modern fertilizers, model cooperatives, and a railroad network and storage facilities at every station. Lectures, plays, films, and recordings from the best speeches will be offered in every village. Local courts will settle disputes without any interference from lawyers. The old political parties will disappear. Women will gain the right to vote and earn a place in political life. And we'll get rid of all 'suckers of human blood'! . . ."

For Bulgaria 1922, this was quite a dream. King Boris himself thought that some of Stambolisky's ideas were good. In spite of their frustrating relationship, the better the king knew his prime minister, the more he was impressed by his talents. "If only this man had some education!" he often told his intimates with a deep sigh.

The king heard complaints about Stambolisky and his men every day. Their speeches and editorials were inflammatory and outrageous, and many of their actions provoked indignation or derision. But when seen in private, Stambolisky left a better impression than his public image suggested. Boris often thought that a considerable part of his bombastic rhetoric, his vituperation against the "city parasites" and the "Sodom and Gomorrah" of Sofia, was just a show for political purposes.

When alone with the king, Stambolisky was much less violent and radical. He could even assume the friendly, warm personality of a country uncle given to wise proverbs, small confidences and earthy laughter. He liked to talk about his native Slavovitsa, the small village near the market town of Pazardjik, where he was born in 1879. His father was a poor but enterprising peasant who had once gone to Istanbul to look for work, whence the name Stambolisky. Young Alexander's mother died very early, and he had a rather sad childhood, marked by the lack of maternal love, the abuses of a stepmother, and extremely poor health, with months spent in bed in his decrepit home. He suffered continuously from fever, an early symptom of the tuberculosis that became manifest later in his youth.

Luckily for Alexander, his illiterate father shared the common ambition of most Bulgarian peasants to have their sons educated. After finishing primary school in Slavovitsa, he was sent to a viticultural school, where an inspiring teacher, Yanko Zabounov, an early organizer of the Agrarian movement, took him under his wing. When Stambolisky later became a village teacher, he kept in touch with his mentor, sending articles for Zabounov's newspaper. In 1899, the Agrarian Union was founded. Stambolisky attended the first congress of the new organization, which was then intended more as a professional union than a political party.

Higher education in an agricultural college in Leipzig became possible for the penniless village teacher when he married an well-to-do colleague. Milena, a few years older and not a noticeably attractive lady, pushed her wifely devotion to the point of agreeing to support her bridegroom's studies in Germany while she remained teaching in the village, awaiting their baby. But during his studies in Germany, he came down with tuberculosis and, after undergoing long treatments, was forced to return to Bulgaria, a very ill man. After months of rest in his wife's care, he was cured. But, rather than returning to his family, he moved to Stara-Zagora, the Agrarian Union's headquarters, to become assistant editor of the union's organ.

Stambolisky had many qualities, but being a good husband and father was not prominent among them. Milena begged him to return to the village to help her support the family, but his answer was firm: he had a duty to fulfill, he couldn't abandon "the cause," she should join him in the struggle. She didn't. It had never, in any case, been a good marriage. All his life, Stambolisky bore the reputation of a man with an eye for the ladies and had numerous affairs. Such a reputation was not too harmful for a politician of this period in Bulgaria. Sexual exploits were commonly looked upon with a certain admiration and envy, the popular feeling being "there's a real man!" or "good for him!"

A journalist of extraordinary passion, combativeness, and capacity for work, Stambolisky wrote almost the entire newspaper, and as the Agrarian Union in 1901 and 1902 did not yet have a clearly defined ideology, his writings provided the official line. The union's first leaders saw it as a professional association for defending the peasants' interests. Stambolisky, on the contrary, believed in the direct exercise of power. Despising the "bourgeois" parties, he wanted the Agrarians to eliminate them and take over the government. The electoral campaigns gave him full opportunity to express his radical ideas and make himself widely known all over the country. There was hardly a village that did not hear his harangues against the ruling classes while he organized the local Agrarian "drouzhba" (fellow-ship). Soon he emerged as the leader of the Union's left wing and its bluntest spokesman.

Elected to the Parliament in 1908, he continued his fierce crusade against King Ferdinand and his governments. His positions frequently offended beliefs held sacred by nationalistic and conservative Bulgaria. Thus, in 1908, he protested when the principality of Bulgaria was pro-claimed a kingdom. In spite of immense popular enthusiasm, he opposed the Balkan War in 1912. And he violently criticized the Second Balkan War of 1913 and the entry into World War I. In consequence, he had been called unpatriotic, seditious, and even treasonous. But no one ever accused Stam-bolisky of being inconsistent or of lacking the courage to voice his opinions.

※       ※       ※

The reuniting of King Boris with part of his exiled family was achieved with the help of a most unexpected accomplice: Stambolisky himself. The king had suffered much from the separation. For three years he had hoped that his brother and sisters would be permitted to return, but the parties in power and the Entente were cool to the idea. But Stambolisky was becoming less suspicious and more sympathetic toward the young monarch. He had learned to appreciate his devotion, simplicity, and intelligence, and he frankly liked him as a person. He even surprised his partisans with state-ments such as, "I'm telling you: if one day we have a republic, we would find no better president than our "kinglet."

When, at the end of 1921, Boris again expressed his wish to see his family, Stambolisky told his associates: "The lad ['momcheto'] is lonely. I worry about him. Let's bring his sisters to him!"

On November 11, Boris sent a confidential letter to his father. "With anguish and remorse," he wrote, "I'm asking you a great favor: to permit my sisters to come here for a time . . . As far as 'Présalé' [Prince Kyril⁴] is concerned, it is still too early. But for the two others, things have lately turned out propitiously enough. 'Tosho' [Boris] handled things in such a way that the 'Koieides' [Stambolisky's associates] don't see any harm in it. There is, of course, suspicion and mistrust. The formula that 'Tosho' chose is that the sisters come for a visit. Tosho vouched personally that their reappearance here wouldn't cause any harm to the country. This reassured them and the 'Koie' [Stambolisky] accepted without quibbling."

The princesses returned in time to celebrate the birthday of Boris and Nadejda, both born on the 30th of January. It was the first time in ten years that they had been together on this day. So many dramatic events had happened since 1912! Two Balkan Wars, World War I, the defeat, abdication and exile, King Boris's accession . . . Now at last they were happy in their reunion, joyous, laughing, telling each other about their lives during the three years of separation, revisiting familiar places, remembering old jokes. For the double birthday, they went on an excursion, like in the old days, driving to Tsarska-Bistritza, in the Rila mountains. Princess Evdokia recalls the picnic they had at a nearby plateau, with the first crocuses showing through the melted snow. While enjoying the beautiful panorama and eating white beans with lard, they reminisced happily about their childhood: how on "Bo's" and "Mickey's" birthday the four children would go to church in the morning, and then visit Granny Clémentine in her drawing room on the corner, overlooking the Boulevard Tsar Osvoboditel and the guards' barracks in the palace park. On the white-clothed table in front of the fireplace, next to the azalea and cyclamen pots, waited the birthday presents. Granny and The Monarch would greet Bo and Mickey with bunches of flowers before offering the presents. They reminisced about Diado Vladika, Boris' religious instructor, Metropolitan Vassili, a huge, soft-spoken, bearded man wearing a black gown and toque, with on his chest a large cross and the Virgin Mary's icon glittering with pearls, who would arrive at the party bringing chocolate pastries.

Boris and the princesses talked about their childhood's Christmas tree, decorated by them, to which they used to bring the presents they would give to their father, "drawings and wooden boxes with pyrography made by us, or similar horrors," Evdokia giggled. "I must admit that Le Monarque was incredibly indulgent to pretend he loved them!" Boris recalled the boring official birthday luncheons they had to attend when they grew up, "with a lot of generals and ministers. Someone would make a speech, and who had to answer but poor me!"

---

⁴"Pré-salé" is a term on French menus for a kind of lamb. It sounds vaguely like Kyril's title, prince of Preslav.

"You practiced it so much that we also knew it by heart!" the sisters teased him. "We participated silently in your performance, ready, like prompters, to whisper the forgotten word if you were in trouble."

"I still keep the most horrible memories of those speeches," Evdokia added. "And I am sure that my aversion to champagne comes from those luncheons."

Late that afternoon, they drove through the winding mountain roads all the way to the Kritchim royal villa, a long, difficult drive, the kind Boris loved. They arrived very late at night, but in time to attend the Catholic memorial service for their mother the next morning in Plovdiv.

With his two sisters around him, the solitary life of the bachelor king changed considerably and some laughter and music could be heard again after dinner around the fireplace in Vrana and Tsarska. "The lad," as Stambolisky called him, seemed less lonely now and he appreciated the assistance that the prime minister had given him.

\* \* \*

Even though Stambolisky had his moments of correct relations with the palace and of statesmanlike behavior abroad, it became more and more difficult for the king to close his eyes to the incompetence and excesses of the arrogant government. Many circles already criticized the monarch for being too weak and accommodating and said with nostalgia that "the old king would never have permitted this." Indeed, even the most tolerant citizens were horrified by the brutal methods of the government and of its bullies, the regime's militia, the Orange Guard, named after the official color of the party banners.

The bourgeois opposition parties organized themselves into a Constitutional Bloc and declared war on the government. By the beginning of 1922, after some moderate Agrarian leaders failed in their efforts at reconciliation, the polarization in the country became total: the "bloc" against the "Drouzhbashi" (from "drouzhbi," the local Agrarian organizations). The hatred assumed dangerous proportions, and the situation became explosive because of the growing discontent of the army, the hostility of the Macedonians, and the presence of White Russian troops in the country. Several thousand officers and soldiers from the defeated anti-Bolshevik army of General Wrangel had retreated into Bulgaria with their weapons, uniforms, and headquarters, still dreaming of returning to Russia to fight the revolution. Tolerated and even welcomed by the previous Bulgarian government, the Wrangel soldiers met with hostility from Stambolisky, whose sympathies were on the side of the revolution (although he disliked the Bulgarian Communists). He succeeded in disarming the White Russians and forbade them to wear uniforms in the streets.

But disturbing rumors maintained that the Wrangelites were preparing a *coup d'état* in Bulgaria to help the anti-Stambolisky elements turn the country into a staging point for an anti-Bolshevik counterattack. The publication of a top secret letter (authentic or fabricated) from General Wrangel to his chief-of-staff revealing such a plan caused an enormous disturbance and fueled the Agrarians' accusations that the opposition had conspired with Wrangel's officers.

It was in this climate of tension that the opposition Bloc called a mass demonstration against the government. All opponents to the regime were summoned to a congress to be held on September 17, 1922, in the ancient capital of Tirnovo in northern Bulgaria. The Agrarian leadership saw in this initiative a serious threat to its survival, but also an opportunity to get rid of the bourgeois parties once and for all. It mobilized all of its militants, urging them to attend a "convention of sugar beet growers," to be held during the same weekend in Tirnovo.

As the day approached, thousands of partisans from the two camps started toward the old capital. The government, proclaiming openly that the sugar beet growers convention was intended to be a decisive and bloody showdown with its enemies, loaded several free trains with policemen, miners, peasants, and Orange Guard from all over the country. Stambolisky was abroad at a session of the League of Nations, and the acting premier, Raiko Daskalov, announced that he would address the convention. On the eve of the seventeenth, the leaders of the Bloc boarded the train in Sofia in a special car, including a few former prime ministers. Shortly before departure, a few new cars were added to the train. One was the "ministerial car," of Daskalov and several other Agrarian ministers; the others were loaded with their partisans. The clash seemed inevitable.

At two o'clock in the morning, as the train stopped at the small station of Dolni-Dabnik, the opposition leaders were awakened by a loud clamor and gunshots: their train was surrounded by a large crowd of people brandishing thick wooden sticks and shouting, "Death to the bourgeois!" "Death to the bloodsuckers!" The elder statesmen were pulled out of their compartments, hit, kicked, and thrown out onto the platform where the ugly crowd mishandled them brutally. Their supporters traveling in the other cars were submitted to the same treatment by the mob of thugs armed with slats and two-by-fours. Deafened by curses and screaming profanities, with bleeding heads, the distinguished party leaders, most of them old and frail men, were submitted to the last public humiliation: while some of the hoodlums held their hands and legs, others shaved their beards and mustaches, using rudimentary scissors or daggers. The ex-ministers might even have been lynched by the delirious crowd if it had not been for Daskalov, who restrained his overzealous troops. He suggested taking the opposition leaders to Tirnovo to let "the people" decide their fate. When the train finally arrived in the convention city, the "people's enemies" were forced into an open truck and paraded, standing up, disheveled and beardless, through the streets, preceded by a loud band and followed by a jubilant crowd of Agrarian militants. Later, they were imprisoned in the city's barracks.

Few of the opposition's followers ever reached Tirnovo. Most of their trains and trucks were stopped by angry bands of government supporters. The ancient capital was entirely in the hands of the Agrarians, who were marching triumphantly under banners and posters with slogans such as "Death to Wrangel's allies!" and "We demand a peasant dictatorship and people's tribunals!" At the sugar-beet growers meeting, Daskalov and the other speakers proposed to the cheering audience the establishment of courts to punish the members of the former cabinets who were responsible for the wars. For, as the Agrarian regime's analyst and scholar, John D. Bell, relates in his study, *Peasants in Power:*

"The captive Bloc leaders came perilously close to summary execution. [Some speakers] advocated finishing them off at once, and this appealed to the vast majority of the thousands of peasants who had come to Tirnovo with just this in mind. The principal difference of opinion was between those who wanted to drop them into the Iantra [River] from the high Stambolov Bridge, and those who favored casting them from the walls of the Tsarevets Fortress, a fate that had been meted out to the captives of the Second Bulgarian Empire."

By the end of September, most of the former ministers had been arrested. Others remained in exile or went into hiding. After a referendum, a tribunal was set up to try them. In effect, Stambolisky had a free hand to eliminate his enemies of the bourgeois political parties.

The events of Dolni-Dabnik and Tirnovo and the arrest of the former ministers caused an emotional turmoil in the country and gave rise to criticism abroad. Some sources say that Stambolisky had sent a telegram from Geneva disapproving of the excesses and the arrests, but that could have been for foreign consumption only, since in a later speech he described September 17 as a glorious, historic day. The fact was that his legal opposition was in jail or in exile, the country was deeply divided between his followers and enemies, and the conviction was growing among his critics that the only way to remove him was by force. For a long time, many opposition circles believed, or hoped, that the king would find a way to dismiss the prime minister. But as Boris seemed unable or unwilling to do so, the more impatient adversaries of the regime decided to take the law into their own hands.

The first to resort to force was the Macedonian Revolutionary Organization. On December 4, while Stambolisky was traveling abroad, two thousand Macedonian militants occupied the town of Kyustendil. Acting Prime Minister Daskalov, determined to deal with them as he had the bourgeois opposition in Tirnovo, mobilized the Orange Guard. Tens of thousands of the Agrarian militia vigilantes were armed with guns from the military depots, loaded on trains, and sent in the direction of Kyustendil. Daskalov, however, had badly overestimated the discipline and motivation of his troops. For the four days during which they converged in the vicinities of Sofia and Kyustendil, the Orange Guards became a terrifying, unruly horde of lawless ruffians, sacking stores, robbing and terrorizing the population in the towns through which they passed, and plundering the railroad stations. The local authorities were powerless to preserve order against the government's own irregulars.

The Orange Guards never reached Kyustendil. When the war minister went ahead to negotiate with the Macedonians, they read him the "death sentences" of Stambolisky, Daskalov, and the other "enemies of Macedonia" and "Serbian collaborators." Then, their point proved, they left the town voluntarily.

In the meantime, the Orange Guards had poured noisily into Sofia. The citizens were alarmed, and this time the government itself was no less worried. Fearing serious disorders, it decided to disarm its own militia. Regular Army units surrounded by night the barracks where the Orange Guards were billeted, took away their weapons, and sent them in small groups back to their villages.

Order was restored, at least temporarily. But talk of a coup against the government became more persistent. As 1923 began, it became an obsession to Stambolisky and his associates, a hope of the opposition, and a moral dilemma for the army. Of course talk reached the palace, too.

In March, the parliament voted, to prosecute the imprisoned former ministers. That day, Stambolisky paid a visit to King Boris in Vrana and left looking particularly sullen.

"Of course he was sulky," the king explained later to Draganov, "because I told him many things he didn't like to hear. I told him that he should not take the road of tyranny, because the greater the oppression, the more united in opposition the people become. That's the psychology of the Bulgarian. Allow him to relax, and everyone will take himself for Bismarck and nobody will unite to fight. But if you press him, then he will unite with everybody who is hurt or threatened and fight. And no tyranny has ever ended well for the tyrants. I told him not to count too much on the majority in a Parliament elected by force. The terror will cause reaction; one cannot bond the popular will by violence. This will bring us to civil war, which will provoke an occupation and intervention by our neighbors. That will be the end of Bulgaria."

Stambolisky had just appointed two new ministers who did not get along with some other cabinet members. "That's very good, very good!" the king commented to his intimates, with a mischievous smile. "Now they'll start quarreling among themselves, and that's all for the good; they'll devour each other all the sooner!"

But during dinner with his sisters and a few close courtiers, the king was very edgy. When an accident that had occurred the previous day was mentioned (one of the palace chauffeurs had been run over by another palace car), King Boris suddenly exploded and launched a furious diatribe against the palace inspector. He wasn't doing his job properly, the king contended angrily. Draganov suggested that, after all, it wasn't the inspector's fault if a chauffeur inadvertently caused an accident. King Boris went into a rage. "Then it is my fault!" he shouted. "The basic fault is that I am *not* a king as I should be. I always want to be the nice guy. I want to treat my collaborators as friends, instead of treating them as officials only. It wasn't like that with the old king, I can tell you that! What kind of a court is this, when they all left me alone on the 17th of September [the day of the Dolni-Dabnik events], with only a lackey, a chauffeur and a playboy?"[5]

As it was no use contradicting him, everybody stood silent while the king continued bitterly, "The strict kings, Louis XIV, Napoleon, and even my father, all ended up better than the benign kings—Henri IV, Louis XVI. It's better to die from syphilis, like Louis XV, than from 'the love' of your people!"

He had been very upset lately, his sisters and his intimates had noticed. He had been receiving representatives of the Bloc, who protested bitterly against the treatment of their leaders in prison and asked the king to interfere. He was extremely cautious in his replies. "I can't say or promise anything. No one can prophesy about how events will develop. But I am taking note. Thank you for your visit."

He became less communicative and very nervous. "The king has some plan," Draganov wrote in his diary on March 12, "but what it is exactly, I still cannot guess. He intends to go with Stambolisky, but for how long?" The same night, after being reprimanded for defending the inspector, Draganov went to bed disturbed, after writing the following entry:

"The King gets angry when the opinions of foreign circles are reported to him. It seems that he has stopped listening to other people, maybe not to be distracted from his own plan.

"He has excellent qualities. But he also has traits that . . . God forbid if things change and he starts revealing them! Perhaps he has

---

[5]It is unclear who the "playboy" was.

become a neurasthenic, but he has the tendency to terrorize people. The more one submits to his terror, the more brutal he becomes. The worst, almost cruel, is the tyranny he exercises over his sisters. And they, in order not to lose their position, get more and more submissive, and try to please him and not to contradict him, which in turn increases his tyranny. And they console themselves by talking about him and complaining to us."

As the tension grew in the country, the pressure on King Boris became too difficult to bear. Legislative elections were announced for April, fanning passions and sending all activists out on the campaign road. In the town of Yambol, the army clashed with demonstrating anarchists and some said that twenty were killed. Ten days before the elections, an agitated Stambolisky came to see the king to inform him that he intended to declare martial law in the Petrich district, to the Bulgarian portion of Macedonia. There, the IMRO had established a state within a state, controlling the administration and even collecting the taxes, Stambolisky reported indignantly. The government had decided to send in troops to dislodge the terrorists. He did not want to have elections in Petrich and allow Parliament members to be elected by the IMRO.

The king made a big effort to dissuade him. He advised him not to act hurriedly, not to provoke the Macedonians at this moment. A few IMRO representatives elected in Petrich would not present any danger, he said. And sending Bulgarian soldiers to fight against their brothers from Macedonia could be disastrous. "As a Bulgarian, and as a friend of yours, I cannot sign your declaration," the king said.

Stambolisky agreed to think it over, and left. Two days later, when he came again to ask the king to sign the decree for martial law in Petrich, Boris conveniently made himself unavailable: he went shooting wild cock, out of reach in the mountains. It turned out to be a wise move, because the following day the entire country, shocked by a massacre of Bulgarians in Yugoslav Macedonia, was demonstrating in the streets. For in the village of Garvan, the Serbian military had machine-gunned twenty Bulgarians. In such an emotional climate, any military action by Bulgarian troops against Macedonians in Petrich would have been unthinkable.

Boris was equally elusive with people he suspected of trying to involve him in plots against Stambolisky. When the king returned from the mountain, Pavel Grouev reported that the primate of Sofia, Metropolitan Stefan, had called asking to see him about a very important matter. The king's first reaction was to get angry with his chief of cabinet: why hadn't he asked the exact nature of the matter the Metropolitan wanted to discuss, and thus avoid an audience? Didn't he understand that the king did not want, at this moment, to be cornered by anyone like Metropolitan Stefan to discuss confidential matters?

The primate of Sofia was the most colorful and, perhaps, the least saintlike of all those of the Saint Synod. An extremely intelligent and well-educated layman who had been ordained relatively late in life, Stefan was a sophisticated and political man with good connections. He was the delight of Sofia's anticlerical cartoonists, who claimed that when traveling abroad, the good metropolitan donned his civilian clothes to frequent unholy places in Paris and Vienna. If recognized, the story went, he would argue that it was the duty of the good pastor to have firsthand knowledge of vice in order better to combat it. But if God hadn't bestowed on him the gifts of austerity and humility, He had generously blessed him with eloquence and astuteness. A highly cultured man and an amusing conversationalist, Stefan was on excellent terms with Grouev, a French graduate like himself. But this time he refused to tell Grouev why he wanted to see the king. What he had to say was for King Boris's ears only and no one else's.

The king, avoiding the audience, explained to Draganov:

"Metropolitan Stefan is a provoker. He plays both sides: he is on good terms with the Bloc, and on good terms with the Agrarians. He probably wants to report some kind of plot to me so that later he can wash his hands and say, 'The king knew.' I don't want to get involved in such things. I cannot now restrain either the Agrarians or the opposition. If I listen and a plot is prepared, successful or unsuccessful, then Metropolitan Stefan will say, 'I warned the king.' If I know of a coup against the government, how can I not warn them? Otherwise, I'll be part of the conspirators. For I feel that there may be something brewing. That's why I escape from Sofia all the time. I succeeded in preventing martial law in Petrich. I cannot intervene more than that."

"But why do you feel that something may be going on? Do you just feel it, or do you have some information?" asked Draganov.

"I have information, and I also sense it. I was told that a general had said, 'We won't allow the Agrarians to have elections! And as for that 'bed-wetter' ["piklio", very vulgar Bulgarian], there is no reason to ask him.' So you see, if I am a 'piklio' to them, I cannot restrain them if there is a plot."

The king became a master of little ruses and dodges. There were some decrees to be signed by him that evening. "What shall I do?" he thought aloud, while his aide-de-camp was waiting to bring the decrees from Vrana to Sofia. "If I sign, it means that I am in Sofia. But if I am in Sofia I won't be able to avoid Metropolitan Stefan . . ." So he decided to have a telegram sent on his behalf from the town of Samokov, telling the government that he approved of the decrees but his personal signature would have to await his return to the capital. Again he complained that his aides could not keep a secret and would not protect his privacy. His father had a different kind of servant, he mused wistfully. "He would ask for a special private train to be assembled to go to Paris. The train would be readied, would depart, and nobody would know. But look at me—everybody knows where I go and what I do! When my father hid in the stables, no one could find him. With me, everybody knows everything!"

# CHAPTER VII

# The Coup d'Etat

O N THE evening of June 8, 1923, ten men furtively entered the darkened courtyard of a house on Stefan-Karadja Street at short intervals. The house was the home of General Ivan Roussev, a leader of a clandestine group called the Military League and one of the principal organizers of the conspiracy to overthrow the Stambolisky regime. One by one, the conspirators climbed the stairs to the second floor where the general's mother led them into a soberly furnished drawing room, which was to become the headquarters of the projected *coup d'état*.

"Gentlemen, we can proceed now. I must ask you to be cautious when you speak, because we have an Agrarian official as a tenant next door," Roussev said in a low voice pointing at the wall. "Tonight the army will do its duty. It is up to us now to do ours. Let's start with the composition of the new government!"

The Military League had decided to act as a result of the April elections, a mockery of free voting, in which overzealous police and Orange Guards had used cudgels and similar methods of persuasion. This time the well of popular patience had overflowed. During the month of May, most garrison and military unit commanders had been initiated into the secret, as operational plans for the coup were drafted in detail.

The government was becoming increasingly nervous. Its allegation that the illegal IMRO had sentenced Stambolisky and a few of his ministers to death gave the authorities a new excuse to search private homes and conduct mass arrests. Even the Opera House was invaded by the police who searched the audience during a performance of *La Traviata*.

The Military League had been founded in great secrecy in 1919 by a small group of patriotic officers distressed by the Treaty of Neuilly, which had mutilated Bulgaria and caused her armed forces to disband. The members' initial objective was to preserve part of the army's weapons and ammunition by concealing them from the interallied occupational authorities. Without informing their superiors and the government, the officers had hidden considerable amounts of armament in old barns, in hay stacks, or underground.

The Neuilly Treaty required the dismissal of large numbers of officers, while the advancement of the rest came virtually to a halt. The overwhelming majority of the officers came from modest family backgrounds with no other income outside their meager salaries. Their forced retirement condemned a large number of them to a degrading existence of misery and hunger in the literal sense of the word. A few preferred to end their lives with a bullet through the head. With neither sympathy nor support from the government, the disgruntled officers turned more and more to the secret league for the defense of their interests. The alienation was further accentuated because the war minister was a civilian politician and the few pro-Stambolisky officers were hostile to the league. In addition, the Agrarians' leftist ideas and the excesses committed by their organs alienated the traditional and patriotic officers, pushing them into the hands of the league. In the process, the league itself acquired a taste for politics, along with considerable experience in conspiratorial organization. Some of its more active leaders, such as the colonels Kimon Gheorghiev and Damian Veltchev, emerged as particularly talented and ambitious political conspirators. The league's principal aim became the overthrow of the Agrarian government.

The Military League was aware that a takeover by the army alone would be unpopular in the country as well as unacceptable abroad. To secure political support, the league approached Alexander Tzankov, a strong-willed professor of economics, well known for his nationalistic, right-wing ideas and his dislike of Stambolisky. With Tzankov as leader, the league won the participation of several opposition parties, most of which had been systematically harassed by the Agrarian regime.

The hour for the coup was fixed for 3 A.M. on June 9. The final political decisions, and the distribution of the ministerial portfolios, had to be discussed on the eve of the operation in General Roussev's home. Beside the host and Professor Tzankov, the other participants were the league leaders, the colonels Ivan Vulkov, Christo Kalfov, and Kimon Gheorghiev, and representatives of the liberal, radical, democratic and populist parties. Some of the conspirators had never met before.

It took a few hours to agree on the composition of the future Tzankov cabinet and to approve the drafts for a proclamation to the nation and for royal decrees accepting the "resignation" of the Stambolisky cabinet and appointing the new government. The discussion revealed serious ideological differences.

Among them was the question of the king. The military members were in a particularly delicate position, as they had all taken an oath of fidelity to

King Boris. The overwhelming majority of the officers were enthusiastically devoted to him. Most of the conspirators even though convinced that by deposing Stambolisky they were saving not only the nation but also the monarchy, disliked the idea of presenting the king with a *fait accompli*. A few individuals, such as Kimon Gheorghiev, who had always disliked the dynasty, had no such scruples, but the other military men felt uneasy.

Boris's position seemed equivocal. Following the brutality of the progovernment thugs in Tirnovo and the trials of the former ministers, almost everybody had pleaded with the king to put an end to the tyranny by replacing the Agrarian government. But he refused to act. When his aide-de-camp Kalfov joined the chorus of indignant voices King Boris replied coldly: "Those who want a change, must first put an end to the quarrels that divide them. Then they should go among the people and gain their confidence. Only then will I have the right and the duty to intervene. I am not here to serve the interests of such-and-such a political party, but to respect the will of the people!" As a result, Kalfov, already deeply involved with the league, resigned from the palace service.

"We must decide what to do in case the king opposes our action and refuses to sign the decree," said Roussev. A long, painful discussion followed. Most of the military officers were deeply disturbed and hoped that the king wouldn't reproach them for ridding the country of Stambolisky who, after all, was making the monarch's life so difficult. The politicians were less concerned.

The three o'clock deadline was approaching. A long heavy silence followed, with everybody staring at the clock. "Only fifteen minutes left, gentlemen, and the army will move into action," a conspirator announced. Dimo Kazassov, an expansive socialist journalist, broke the silence: "It's too late to raise the royal question now," he said impatiently. "We are in the heat of action. Our heads, if not dearer, are in any case not cheaper than the king's head. With the king, or without him, we must complete the mission we have undertaken."

No decision had been taken when Kimon Gheorghiev announced calmly, "It's three o'clock. Good luck, gentlemen!"

The men rose to their feet and shook hands gravely. As the lights in the room were turned off, everybody moved to the windows. Sofia was asleep; not a sound could be heard from the deserted streets. Suddenly, the sound of gunshots broke the dead silence, very near, as if the bullets were flying in front of the windows. The shots were from the skirmish at the Central Post Office, a few blocks down the street. Again silence fell over the neighborhood. Had the troops succeeded in occupying the post office?

A few minutes later, machine-gun fire was heard from the southwest. Some fighting was going on at the infantry barracks. Then again everything became calm. At headquarters, the faces behind the windows were becoming more tense, the whispering voices more worried. Although it was almost 4 A.M., there was no sign to indicate whether the coup had succeeded or failed.

A loud knock on the door. A lieutenant-colonel in combat dress burst into the room, clicked his heels in front of Vulkov and gave the military salute. "Colonel, the operations have been successfully completed according to the given orders. Long live Bulgaria!"

A thunderous "Long live!" answered his report, and the conspirators fell into each other's arms, exchanging congratulations. "Any casualties?"

"Only one policeman killed."

A noisy group of jubilant officers invaded the apartment shouting, "Long live the new government!" hugging and kissing the new ministers. Tzankov thanked them warmly, assuring them that the new cabinet would justify the army's confidence.

And when the euphoria had subsided, he turned to the politicians, Kazassov and Boyan Smilov and said, "Let's go to Vrana to see the king!"

It was still chilly when they left Roussev's house at dawn. The courtyard was filled with excited officers, happily commenting on the night's events. A squadron of the Royal Horseguards in full battle gear was waiting in the street. The three civilians boarded two automobiles and the horsemen took off, one platoon galloping in front of the cars, the other behind. The noise of hoofs resounded on the pavement of the empty streets as the cavalcade reached the wooded Boris Park and continued trotting toward Vrana on the Tzarigrad Highway.

\*          \*          \*

On Friday evening, June 8, the king's aide-de-camp Captain Draganov went to the movies before returning to the palace to spend the night in the duty officer's room. He was soundly asleep when his colleague, Major Skoutounov, burst into the room at 4:30 A.M. "Something is happening in town," he reported. "The Military School cadets are around the palace. We heard that city policemen are being arrested, but our own palace police have been left alone." The aide-de-camp Dimitri Naomov also appeared, in his pajamas. "Nobody knows exactly what's going on," he said. "We suspect there's been a *coup d'état*. They say that the government has been overthrown." Both officers seemed rather pleased.

Draganov, hastily donning his uniform, rushed outside to make a quick reconnaissance of the streets around the palace before getting in touch with Vrana. King Boris was spending the night there after returning from Slavovitza, where he, his sisters, and two aides-de-camp had visited Stambolisky in his home.

It was already daylight when Draganov headed for the War Ministry.

The empty streets were patrolled by cadets and soldiers in combat dress. In front of the ministry, he stopped the commander of the Military School and asked him what was going on. "I don't know anything," the colonel confessed. "I don't even know who ordered the cadets out. But it looks like a coup."

Draganov continued to the Central Post Office. In the telegraph room, a couple of young women operators were busy sending messages, while sentries with bayonets on their rifles were guarding the building. As he looked and recognized the commanding officer, everything became clear: this officer, who had been fired from the army and had been a civilian for a long time, was wearing his full colonel's uniform. He was, however, reluctant to give any information. "I'm just following orders," he laconically answered Draganov's inquiries.

"But what about the provinces?"

"They preceded us."

Another officer arrived, visibly excited, rushed to the colonel, and the two men embraced effusively, congratulating each other. Draganov did not need more explanations. He hurried back to the palace where the other ADCs were waiting. It was 5:15 A.M. "Let's call His Majesty!" he said.

The telephone woke King Boris in Vrana. "The *coup d'état* is accomplished," Draganov reported in French. "The town is in the hands of the military. We still don't have detailed information. Should we go to the leaders for information?"

"No," the king answered, "you must come here first, right away, to tell me what happened."

Draganov jumped into one of the palace automobiles and asked Skoutounov to follow him in ten minutes with a second car. It was just before 6 A.M. when Draganov arrived in Vrana. Since there was no one to meet him, he climbed the staircase, looking for someone in the empty corridors upstairs. Suddenly, he heard the voices of the princesses at the front entrance, and rushed down to meet them. They told him that the king had gone out to the park with Bagrianov. Not knowing what exactly was happening in Sofia, King Boris did not want to be caught by surprise in his bed, or forced into precipitous action, the princesses said. So he had gone to the park, leaving his sisters to bring Draganov to him.

Princess Nadejda stayed to await the arrival of Skoutounov with the second car while Princess Evdokia led Draganov through alleys, lawns, and meadows, until they left the royal estate, and continued walking through the fields. They did not find the king, but bumped into his valet, Svilen, who was carrying a list with Bagrianov's instructions concerning the preparation of automobiles, horses, food, and other measures in case of emergency. The search for the king continued across trails and bushes, until they finally came across Bagrianov and Princess Nadejda. Luckier than her sister, she had managed to bring Skoutounov to the king. A few moments later, King Boris appeared from behind the trees with Skoutounov, who was briefing him on the situation.

"Your Majesty," Skoutounov said, "the coup took place also in the provinces. The power is in the hands of the army. A new government is formed, with Tzankov, Colonel Vulkov, and others."

The king wanted to learn how things had proceeded in Sofia and in the provinces before deciding what to do. Draganov gave his advice: "His Majesty must do everything to avoid bloodshed and civil war. Therefore, he must act only when he is fully informed about the situation. The ADCs should return to Sofia for more information. Meanwhile, His Majesty should wait before making any decisions." All the participants in the improvised council of war in the park agreed.

"I am sure that the coup-makers will come to ask me to sign decrees," King Boris said. "They'll try to blackmail me. But I am not going to be blackmailed into signing anything!"

The group discussed whether the king should wait in Vrana or go to Tsarska-Bistritza. But the Tsarska option was rejected: communications with Vrana were easier, and travel during these uncertain days carried the risk of kidnapping by some band of rebels, who would use the royal hostage for political ransom. The king's mood changed, he became very upset. "I can't stand it anymore!" he declared, discouraged. "I shall abdicate. I'll get out. Let them suffer the consequences! [In Bulgarian: "Let them eat it!"] They didn't ask me before they did it!"

"Your Majesty, your abdication now will throw the country into anarchy and civil war!" pleaded the others. The king calmed down. It was decided that he and Bagrianov would remain in the fields around Vrana, pretending that they were hunting. The other two officers would go reconnoitering in Sofia and keep in touch with the princesses in Vrana, who would transmit the messages to the king. In case anything went wrong and the princesses could not communicate, three secret dropping places were designated for messages: a desk, a mantlepiece, and a bench in the alpine garden. With that, the group disbanded. As the ADCs approached the entrance, they noticed a platoon of guardsmen on horses and two automobiles parked in front of the gates. The aides-de-camp rushed inside the house. Professor Tzankov, Kazassov, and Smilov, accompanied by three officers, were already there, arguing animatedly with the alarmed manager of Vrana.

"Good morning, gentlemen," the two ADCs greeted the early visitors. "What is the matter?"

Tzankov did not hide his irritation. "We are looking for the king. We are the new government and we want to see him. The manager first told us that the king was here. He went to the king's room, disappeared there for a quarter of an hour, then sent another man to tell us that the king is not there. The king is hiding!"

The ADCs tried to explain that His Majesty had really gone hunting, but the visitors did not seem to believe them. "Look, gentlemen, this is a very serious matter," Tzankov said. "You are hiding the king. We didn't expect such a thing. We don't want to do things that will put him in an unpleasant position. We don't want to search the palace. We wanted to treat him with all due respect. But he is hiding."

Kazassov grew more impatient. "If the king is hiding, let's leave! We can do without him," he proposed.

"If you don't believe us, come and see for yourselves!" the aides-de-camp suggested. The visitors followed them upstairs into the private apartments, looking in every bedroom. The king was not there. Perplexed and annoyed, they went out in the garden to wait. The ADCs sent more servants to look for the king in the park. But the morning was advancing without a trace of the vanished monarch. "If you don't find him by eleven o'clock, we'll go back to Sofia to announce that the king has abdicated," said Tzankov.

In the meantime, Princess Nadejda had returned to the palace, seen the guardsmen and learned that the visitors were upstairs waiting for the king. She rushed back to the fields, and alerted Boris.

While several palace servants and horse guards were searching the vast park for the king, the two aides-de-camp heard some details about the coup. The operation had been a success both in Sofia and in the provinces with virtually no resistance. All ministers were under arrest. And Stambolisky himself? He had also been arrested in Sofia, the visitors said. But hadn't Stambolisky still been in his home in Slavovitza last night? No, he was arrested together with his colleagues, the visitors insisted.

Draganov joined the search, while Nadejda galloped back to the palace where she met with the three visitors. She looked pale and frightened when Tzankov told her bluntly that the Agrarian government had been overthrown, Stambolisky and his ministers arrested, and the new cabinet formed. He complained about the humiliating four-hour wait for the king who seemed to be hiding from them. He then warned that if her brother didn't appear right away, the ministers would leave, and the consequences for the king and for the dynasty would be extremely grave. Nadejda noticed that when he mentioned Stambolisky's arrest, Tzankov had lowered his eyes.

The professor was not bluffing. At eleven o'clock, Tzankov called his colleagues in Sofia and, after telling them that the king was hiding, proposed to return to the capital to proclaim a republic. But his friends asked him to wait for another half-hour. If the king doesn't show up, Colonel Vulkov said, the delegation should return to discuss the new situation with them before taking this important decision.

Meanwhile, Draganov managed to alert Evdokia to the seriousness of the situation. She was able, after much difficulty, to find her brother. King Boris looked tired and his clothes were all wet when Evdokia finally drove him back to the palace. While he was changing into a dark business suit, his sisters and his ADCs informed him of the visitors' threats. The king explained that since he believed that only officers and soldiers had arrived, he had not wanted to risk talking to them before seeing their superiors. Meanwhile he had had sufficient time to assess the situation and on learning that the visitors were ministers of the new government, he had decided to return.

Boris received the visitors in his study in the old hunting lodge. Full of his usual charm, he greeted Tzankov as an old acquaintance, reminded Smilov that they had met at the Congress of Reserve Officers and told Kazassov that he read his articles in the Socialist newspaper. He apologized for keeping them waiting so long, explaining that as soon as he had heard of the coup, he had gone out to the woods to ponder in solitude.

Tzankov then explained the rationale for the coup, which was, he assured the king, the only way to end the disastrous peasant dictatorship. The king should now give his sanction to the change brought about by the army and supported by the people.

King Boris, evoking the coup's violation of the constitution, refused to sign the decrees. "Gentlemen, I only have one head; here it is, take it if you want! But this, I cannot do! I shall abdicate," he said. The visitors accused him of faintheartedness. He protested that it wasn't a lack of courage that motivated him, but that as a monarch and as a man he couldn't give his seal of approval to a violation of the constitution or to bloodshed. The three politicians answered that the best way to avoid bloodshed and civil war was for him to sign the decrees. But Boris resisted. "I am not a king anymore," he complained bitterly. "After what you did last night, what is left of the perogatives of the head of state? What is left of the monarch's obligation to ponder carefully each of his actions, to act only according to his wisdom and for the national interests? The constitution was not respected. Its precepts for solving conflicts were ignored. No, gentlemen, I am not the Bulgarian king anymore!"

The visitors insisted on the fatal consequences for the dynasty and the nation if the king refused to legitimize the new government. The arguing continued for an hour-and-a-quarter, interrupted only by a telephone message from Sofia. The news from the provinces was good, General Roussev reported, with the first foreign reactions favorable.

Boris finally had to concede that his abdication or his refusal to accept the new government would risk a civil war. Tzankov, taking the decrees out of his pocket, placed them on the table. A long silence followed. The king stood up, walked to his desk and took a pen. "May God help us!" he sighed. "With all my heart I wish success for our sorely tried country!" Then he signed the documents and handed them to Tzankov.

"Here are your decrees!" he said. "But as of today, I don't feel like a king. For me, this question remains open."

Relieved, the visitors begged him not to think of abdicating. Curiously enough, the most convincing arguments against abdication were those of the Socialist, Kazassov.

As the new ministers were leaving, King Boris pleaded with them to take every necessary measure to spare human lives. "Not a single drop of Bulgarian blood should be shed!" he admonished them. He also advised them strongly to include Agrarian representatives in the new cabinet in the name of national reconciliation. The idea seemed to appeal to Tzankov. The king then retired to his apartments for a short nap, suddenly looking terribly tired and unhappy. Bagrianov and Draganov assured him that, under the circumstances, signing the decrees was the best solution, the only possible one. But he remained unconvinced, shaking his head sadly.

*      *      *

By the time Tzankov came to see him in Vrana at 5:30 P.M. with General Roussev, the new minister of the interior, King Boris was feeling better. The night was relatively calm, in spite of sporadic skirmishes in a few areas where Stambolisky partisans were showing some resistance. In Vrana, a vigil of forty soldiers was organized in case of an attempt to kidnap the king.

The next day Boris went to Sofia. He was still most desirous to see some Agrarian participation in the new cabinet. The consensus among his intimates was that the government shouldn't give the impression of being against the Agrarian Union, but should assure the nation that it acted only against its corrupt elements. If honest and moderate Agrarians should collaborate with the new regime, the risks of violence will be lessened, the king and his advisors agreed. Not everything that Stambolisky did was bad, they added; on the contrary, some of his reforms should be kept. Most important now was to consolidate the new situation. As Draganov said, "What happened is bad. However, if it fails, the situation will become ten times worse."

Hoping for cooperation with the Agrarians, the king and his entourage disapproved of publicizing the discovery of vast sums of money, foreign currency, and indecent photographs in Stambolisky's house. That afternoon the king waited for an hour for the new ministers who were due at the palace for their first audience at 5 P.M. "They are paying me back for yesterday," he said. "Yesterday they waited for me, now it is my turn . . ." When they arrived at 6 P.M. Boris greeted them with the words, "Gentlemen, the prime minister told me that *you expressed the desire* [the king emphasized the words] of introducing yourselves to me. In my capacity as head of the state, and also as a Bulgarian, I granted with pleasure your request and summoned you here with the purpose of exchanging thoughts about the situation that *had already been created.*" [Again he emphasized the last words.] During the audience, the decree of the appointment of two new ministers was submitted to the monarch: Colonel Kalfov to Foreign Affairs, and Colonel Vulkov to the War Ministry. The king had not been consulted about these nominations. In addition, no Agrarian figured in the new cabinet. But he signed the decree. When the ministers were leaving, King Boris mumbled audibly, "Who would ever have thought that my former aide-de-camp would one day be my minister of foreign affairs!" On the way back to Vrana, he showed his displeasure with the nominations. "What can I do?" he said bitterly to his companions in the car. "They all take themselves for infallible gods. Yesterday I told them to keep some portfolios for Agrarians. Today they fill them with their friends . . . 'Bay Ganio'[1] always remains 'Bay Ganio,' whether he is dressed in peasant duds or in tails and top hat."

In Vrana, having drinks before dinner with his intimates, Boris seemed quite discouraged. "It wasn't for this that I have worked for this poor country for five years, spoiling my life," he complained. "God is my witness that I did not want the things that have just happened! But I regret that after so many efforts I will leave a bad situation. My idea was different, my plans were different . . . but what can you do? I already foresee trouble and disaster coming . . ."

The king and his confidants were pessimistic that evening. They had little hope that the Tzankov government would be capable of uniting and healing the nation. At the same time, they all deplored "the follies" and excesses of the Agrarian regime and understood the widespread desire to rebel. Why did Stambolisky's people have to behave in such a crude and intemperate way? The king reminded his company that he had told them that some Agrarian ministers' obnoxious statements had been fatal—they had shocked and alarmed the public, and triggered this reaction. What a pity! Because in many respects the Agrarians were not bad, Boris said. When will little Bulgaria have a great man like Stambolisky again? Meanwhile, rumors of fighting and shooting around Slavovitza, Stambolisky's village, had reached Vrana. "Let's pray that he survives and doesn't get killed!" everybody at the table agreed.

---

[1]Bay Ganio, the hero of a satirical book by Aleko Constantinov, became the prototype of the arrogant parvenu, the half-educated and obnoxious "Ugly Bulgarian."

✳        ✳        ✳

Stambolisky was, of course, not arrested in Sofia the night of the coup, as the government had claimed, because he had still been at his farm in Slavovitza. In fact, King Boris and his sisters had paid him a visit there the day before, on their way back from Euxinogard. It had been a pleasant occasion, with both the host and his visitors in excellent spirits. The guests had brought a present of freshly picked fruit and vegetables from the seashore palace's gardens, and the prime minister had offered the king a good-looking sheepskin overcoat.

The unexpected visit had surprised and alarmed the conspirators. Alexander Tzankov and his colleagues had suddenly become suspicious of the reasons for the visit. They also feared the highly embarrassing situation of staging a *coup d'état* against Stambolisky while the king was a guest in his house.[2] In such a case, a refusal by Boris to recognize the new government could have had disastrous consequences. The conspirators were greatly relieved when the royal party left Slavovitza.

When Stambolisky woke up on the morning of June 9, he did not know about the coup. The interruption of all telephone and telegraph communications that night by the military had been immediate and very effective. The first suspicions were aroused when a small detachment of about fifty soldiers appeared near the farm under the pretext of being sent to "reinforce" the prime minister's personal guard. But when Stambolisky's security unit composed of forty trusted men with two machine guns observed the unannounced soldiers mounting on the nearby hill, with two machine guns pointed at the house, the ruse was discovered. The bodyguards opened fire forcing the soldiers to retreat.

The unit had been sent to the farm by retired Colonel Slaveiko Vassilev, a leading Military League member, who was assigned to arrest Stambolisky. The first thought that occurred to the Agrarian leader was that the attack on his home was another IMRO terrorist operation, similar to the capture by the Macedonians of Kyustendil a few months earlier. But soon a gendarmerie platoon operating in the vicinity under the command of a friendly captain arrived at the farm, bringing the news that the government had been overthrown and all ministers arrested.

Stambolisky was stunned by the news. Somehow he had not believed that the army and the opposition would have the force and daring to organize and carry through a successful coup. There was no time to waste. As Stambolisky was organizing the defense with his bodyguards, the gendarmes, and the peasants who were congregating from the neighboring

---

[2]This was related several years later in Austria by Tzankov to the IMRO leader, Ivan Mihailov, who revealed it in his *Memoirs*, Volume II.

farms, a cavalry squadron arrived in a nearby village, ready to attack. The squadron commander sent an ultimatum demanding Stambolisky's immediate surrender. The Agrarian leader sent the emissary back with the following handwritten letter:

"Major, I am the prime minister of Bulgaria and of the Bulgarian people. In their name and in the name of the high interests of the fatherland, I order you to return to where you came from and wait for pardon. Renounce the stupidity that has taken hold of you, because the time when a handful of fanatical hotheads can trample and torment the Bulgarian people is past! Wars and heavy sufferings have taught this people how to defend their rights and freedoms. Once again I order you: go back where you came from as fast as you can, or you will never find a refuge!"

During the night Stambolisky, his brother Vassil, and a handful of aides decided to attack and capture the town of Pazardjik, where they could count on the assistance of thousands of faithful partisans. At dawn they advanced in the direction of Pazardjik forcing the cavalry squadron to retreat. But the lack of weapons was already apparent: most peasants were armed only with pitchforks, clubs and knives. The situation was so critical that in spite of the unfriendly, if not hostile, relations with the Communist party, Stambolisky turned for help to the local Communists, who appeared ready to join the anti-Tzankov resistance. However, when the district leader asked the Central Committee's permission, he was told bluntly that the party had proclaimed "strict neutrality" as far as the coup was concerned.

Left to themselves and miserably armed, Stambolisky and his column of loyal peasants postponed the attack on Pazardjik until the following morning. Unfortunately for them, army reinforcements with cavalry and artillery arrived in the interim. When the assault was attempted, the improvised battalion was badly defeated. And as another army unit occupied Slavovitza, any possibility of an organized retreat vanished. The battle lost, Stambolisky ordered his troops to return to their villages as discreetly as possible in order to avoid retaliation. His friends insisted that he should either try to escape abroad or put himself under the protection of some friendly commander. But he refused and, accompanied by his brother and two close collaborators, took the road northward along the river Topolnitza.

The Stambolisky brothers traveled on horseback to a nearby village, but lost contact with the car of their two companions. Continuing on foot, they spent the night of June 12 sleeping in the open fields. The next morning Vassil left for Slavovitza, but was captured on the way. Alexander, exhausted, hungry, and drenched by the rain, tried to enter a village to look for assistance. But he was recognized by the local authorities and arrested. He was held in the mayor's office in the same village where he had started his career as a teacher.

The new government, embarrassed by its failure to capture the fallen dictator five days after the coup and fearing his reappearance at the head of the resistance, dispatched a special unit with the mission to bring him to Sofia, alive or dead. But instead of driving directly to Sofia, the truck with the prisoner took the road to Slavovitza.

What happened that day is both unclear and horrible. The official version claimed that partisans stopped the truck and attempted to free Stambolisky. In the skirmish the fleeing prisoner was shot, the convoy chief reported to his superiors in Sofia. This story, which met with extreme incredulity, was quickly proved to be a complete fabrication. In reality, on June 13, Stambolisky was brought to Slavovitza, where he was submitted to "interrogations" of the worst kind. There are several versions of what happened that June day at the former prime minister's farm, with details concerning the participants and the methods of the inquisition and execution varying according to the sources. Was he cruelly beaten and tortured for hours by the henchmen of the "special unit"? Did a Macedonian terrorist, a certain "voyvoda" (guerrilla leader) Velichko, take part in the torture? Was Stambolisky stabbed sixty times, was his right hand chopped off, were his fingers cut one by one? Was the sinister mark "A.S., 14 June 1923" written in blood on the wall of the stable, his last signature before he expired? And was his body finally beheaded by his torturers? So many political groups wanted to use Stambolisky's assassination to accuse other factions or to justify future revenge that the complete truth has been obscured. But no matter the differences in the cruel details, the fact remains that Stambolisky was killed in the most abominable way.

That was the word King Boris used—"Abominable!"—when the war minister Colonel Vulkov came to announce the news of Stambolisky's death. At that time, the king had heard only the official version, the story of the attempted kidnapping and shooting. That alone was more than enough to fill him with indignation. As soon as Vulkov left, he rushed to the chancery and, fulminating, broke the news to his entourage. "What they did is abominable! It's also very bad for the government because it will prove either that it is so weak that it had to kill Stambolisky out of fear, or that it was too weak to protect him. This will also confirm the myth of our barbarism in the eyes of the foreign world. Imagine: only yesterday I was developing the thesis with (the French minister in Sofia) that, after all, this was an unbloody revolution because Stambolisky had just been put under arrest! And today—his assassination!"

The king went for lunch to Vrana, deeply disturbed. All during the meal he repeated, "Le pauvre grand homme!" The poor great man! "As a martyr, his death dishonors the new regime. This was a dirty thing to do! Europe will not praise us for it; the British won't forgive us. And now the government asks me to go abroad! What will people say? 'The king waited until his minister was killed to go abroad!' "

Needing to get away from his depressing thoughts, King Boris asked Princess Nadejda, Bagrianov, and Draganov to go with him for a walk in the fields. A heavy rain forced them to find shelter under a large plum tree. As they waited the king was silent, except for occasional remarks about Stambolisky's death. Completely soaked, they returned to the house, only to change their clothes and go out again. The king felt a need to walk. Silently they took the road to the nearby Guerman monastery, and did not return until eight o'clock in the evening. "I don't care what stories they are telling me," King Boris said, periodically breaking the silence. "I know that they wanted it to happen. I already saw it in the eyes of Vulkov the other day when I was warning him to avoid killing Stambolisky. Who knows whether they didn't eliminate him so that I wouldn't use him to overthrow them! Everything is possible. In any case, they were very afraid of him."

As the long June day was ending, the magnificent Vrana park was particularly peaceful. "Le pauvre grand homme!" the king kept repeating as they approached the house. "Now he has really become a great man. By making a martyr out of him, they have washed off all the mud that has been thrown on him in the last few days . . ." In an access of anger against Tzankov, the king remarked, "This deadly professor with the owl's eyes . . . Who knows whether he won't bring some evil to Bulgaria!" Then he concluded, "The dangerous man for Bulgaria now is 'Kalogeropolus,[3]! He is the real evil for Bulgaria, not Stambolisky. If he is liquidated, he would well deserve it!" ("Il ne l'aurait pas volé," in French.)

---

[3]It is unclear whose nickname he used: Tzankov? Vulkov? Roussev?

# CHAPTER VIII

# The September Uprising

THE JUNE 9, 1923, coup was generally welcomed in the cities; and while it caused some concern among the peasant population, it met with little initial resistance. The reaction of Stambolisky's followers had been weak, badly organized, and shortlived. The swiftness of the well-planned military coup had caught them by surprise: the whole operation had taken half an hour in Sofia, and less than one hour in the provinces. Most of the ministers and Agrarian leaders had been arrested immediately, together with a couple of thousand militants. The coup had also surprised Raiko Daskalov in Prague, where he had been sent shortly before as permanent envoy. The Orange Guards, in spite of their bullies' reputation, had neither the time nor the will to challenge the army. Some guards fought briefly in Radomir, led by the Agrarian president of the Sobranié. Another force was organized by the minister of commerce, Alexander Obbov, around Pleven. Obbov's troops, armed with clubs and scythes, fought bravely, suffering serious losses in a few skirmishes, but they were easily defeated by the army. Obbov then fled to Rumania. The attempts of the justice minister to lead the peasants in the Plovdiv area, and of Georgi Damyanov, the former chief-of-staff of the Radomir uprising, to mobilize the Orange Guards in the northwest, also failed in face of the well-organized forces of the new government.

Nor were the Communists of any help. The party's attitude during and after the coup amazed the entire Communist world. On June 9, the day of the coup, the Bulgarian Central Committee issued a proclamation of neutrality, denouncing the fallen Stambolisky regime more viciously than the military and the right-wing groups that had overthrown it. "Last night . . . the Stambolisky government which maintained its power . . . by terror and coercion, was overthrown. This government of the peasant bourgeoisie . . . used its power to defend its class and cliquish interests. Suppressing the rights of toiling people, it waged a merciless crusade against their only protector, the Communist party . . . Therefore, the workers and peasants must not come to [its] aid today . . . The working masses in town and village must not participate in the armed struggle between the urban and rural bourgeoisies, nor come to the aid of their own exploiters and oppressors."

Local Communist organizations in a few districts who were already mobilizing to fight the new regime were ordered by the Central Committee's secretary to disband and remain neutral.

The Bulgarian Communist party's (BCP) decision not to aid the Agrarians flabbergasted the Communist International, whose executive committee was meeting that week in Moscow. From the rostrum, its president Zinoviev expressed his disbelief and his hope that the news was not true. But, alas, it was true, the Bulgarian Vassil Kolarov, a high official in the International, admitted in Moscow. The shocked International strongly reprimanded the Bulgarian comrades. But the BCP's Central Committee defiantly defended the order, with its best-known member Georgi Dimitrov publicly agreeing.

In Moscow, Kolarov, although condemning his compatriots, meekly offered some attenuating circumstances, asking the assembly to "remember that the Bulgarian party had been engaged in a life-and-death struggle with Stambolisky whose persecutions had aroused fierce and justified resentment . . ." But in the eyes of the International, the Bulgarian party's passivity was the worst possible error, a sin against Lenin's dogma. An eminent international Communist, Karl Radek, was assigned to investigate the case and his report, read on June 23, was a devastating denunciation of the BCP.

The events of June 9, said Radek, were "the greatest defeat ever suffered by a Communist party." He accused the BCP of adopting a policy of servile passivity and spineless surrender instead of giving support to Stambolisky who, though not a Communist, nevertheless represented a genuinely radical, antibourgeois social force. "We in Moscow," concluded Radek, "have now been rudely disillusioned in our faith in the Bulgarian comrades."

Kolarov instructed the unanimous International to obtain the reversal of BCP's decision. On July 6 the Bulgarian Central Committee held a meeting to discuss Moscow's instructions to form a fighting alliance with the Agrarians. But again defying the International, the BCP insisted that the critisicm was due to insufficient knowledge of the Bulgarian situation. The idea of collaborating with the Agrarians was rejected unless the peasant union accepted the Communists' leadership. Also, the difficult relations between the Communists and Stambolisky were recalled, thus justifying the BCP's hostility toward him. Rejecting the International's accusations, the Central Committee challenged the correctness of Zinoviev's and Radek's views.

For a few months, a schism loomed between the BCP and the Communist International. But it was, of course, unrealistic, if not foolish, for any national Communist party openly to defy Moscow. Although the entire Central Committee approved the decision not to help the Agrarians, history was later rewritten to show that the error was committed not by the BCP, but by a few of its misled leaders. They, alone, were to be blamed. The party itself, infallible and eternally correct, remained blameless. Three months after the June coup, the BCP reversed itself and, following Moscow International's instructions, joined the remnants of Stambolisky's militants in a rebellion against the Tzankov regime.

*    *    *

From the military point of view, the September 1923 uprising was a total failure, an ill-prepared, amateurishly executed adventure with no serious popular support except for a few isolated counties. The short-lived revolt against the Tzankov regime began on September 23rd, much too long after the June coup to hope to ride on any wave of spontaneous protest or instinct of self-preservation. By September 28, it was all over.

The much delayed Communist decision to take up arms against the new regime found some support in the northwestern regions of Bulgaria, where the insurgence was organized by the comrades Vassil Kolarov and Georgi Dimitrov. The rebel peasants and workers briefly occupied the town of Ferdinand but were easily dislodged by the government troops, who were far more numerous and better armed. Bands of insurgents bearing red and orange banners advanced toward two other northwestern towns, engaging in fierce battles. They also fought at a couple of railway stations and small towns, suffering heavy casualties, but they were too poorly armed and organized to have the slightest chance. Contrary to the Communists' expectations, the local population did not rise. After three or four days of bloody battles, the insurgents were defeated in all the rebel counties.

The rest of the country remained calm. Sporadic fighting in Stara-Zagora and Nova-Zagora was quickly crushed. Vulko Chervenkov, top Communist leader (and later prime minister of Communist Bulgaria) summed up the reasons for the defeat: "The chief weakness of the uprising lay in the failure of the most important economic, military and industrial centers to rise in revolt . . . which led to the defeat of the insurrection . . . The main reason for the failure should be sought in the fact that the Communist party, while raising the masses in rebellion, had not purged itself—from top to bottom—of the erroneous tactical line of June 9th . . . The most appropriate moment to crush fascism—June 9th—had been missed through the faults of the Agrarian Union, as well as through the erroneous tactics of the Central Committee of the BCP . . . The uprising lacked an efficient and resolute unified leadership for the country as a whole . . ."

Chervenkov also deplored the hesitancy and inertness during the uprising. And in a surprisingly candid speech, Georgi Dimitrov, whom subsequent Communist hagiology proclaimed incapable of any error, confessed, "My only regret is that I myself and my party were not yet truly Bolshevik at that time. Hence, we were not able to organize and carry out successfully this historic popular uprising, headed by the proletariat. Our insufficiently Bolshevist organization, policy, and tactics, the absence of revolutionary experience and, more especially, our opportunistic, so-called neutral position on June 9th—at the time of the military fascist *coup d'état*— greatly aided the murderers and jailers of the Bulgarian people in quelling the uprising of the masses."

Although a complete fiasco, the September uprising was destined to play a tragic role in the country's history—not by its achievements, which were next to nothing, and not as an expression of deep national feelings, which it was not if one judges by the apathy of the enormous majority of the population; but the tragedy of September 1923 lay in the brutal repression that followed, unleashing enough hatred and cruelty to scar the Bulgarian national soul for decades to come.

How should the anger of the military, systematically humiliated by the Stambolisky regime, be judged? Was the passion justifiable in those who lost their homes in Macedonia and in Trace and who, rightly or wrongly, accused the "leftists" of collaborating with the enemy? Could the fear of Bolshevism be ignored, in a country so near the Soviets, hardly five years after the horrifying tales of the Red terror began to arrive from Russia? Could the Tzankov regime, or any regime, permit the victory of armed insurgents who openly preached its violent overthrow and its replacement by a dictatorship of the proletariat? Similar questions haunted every thinking Bulgarian when the sordid tales of jailings, beatings, and executions became known in the country. Some people were openly indignant. Others rationalized, found excuses in the concepts of self-defense, or of justifiable retribution for the Agrarian excesses or the Communist atrocities.

By the end of September, the insurrection was quelled. But the gap between the government and the king had become deeper and, perhaps, unbridgeable. A major reason for the disagreement was Boris's deep aversion to the death penalty, which the government sometimes considered necessary. Religiously, philosophically, and humanely, he was an enemy of capital punishment. This proved to be a tremendous problem in turbulent periods, at the constitution required the monarch's signature for all death sentences. Because his conscience and the *raison d'état*, as interpreted by the government, clashed frequently, he simply refused, or rather avoided, signing. His relations with the government turned from cool to cold, with Boris becoming even more isolated from his right-wing government than he had been from the left-wing Stambolisky regime. He disliked the men of the new regime and their methods. Speaking to his intimates about Interior Minister General Roussev he said, for instance, "I don't trust him. He is a stupid, fatal and false man." Outwardly, he was unusually calm during the uprising and its suppression. This worried his friends, for the king had often told them that when he was too calm it meant that things were bad. He was increasingly pessimistic about the near future. "Next spring the blood will ask for revenge," he kept saying.

A personal letter from the king to Draganov indicates that secretly, Boris kept some contacts with at least one Communist sympathizer, a certain Engineer Stoyanov, whom he visited in his home on the evening of October 13, walking in the darkened Sofia streets after a call to his ear doctor. "Tell your friends not to commit any more follies!" he told Stoyanov. "Now is the wrong time. I'll try to influence the government to give amnesty and to treat them better." He expressed his fear that some Communist leaders could be summarily liquidated after the fashion of two Agrarian ex-ministers who had been killed recently.

He was becoming more irritable and unhappy with himself. The approaching annual ceremony of the opening of the Parliament filled him with apprehension and even with disgust. He began to despise himself for the role he continuously played—an official accomplice of the government, giving public credit to men whose actions and mentality he disapproved of profoundly. He nearly bit off Pavel Grouev's head when the soft-spoken counselor reported late one November morning that the foreign diplomats in Sofia, certain that the Sobranié would be opened personally by the king, were all going to wear full gala uniforms and decorations. When "Bacho Pavel" mentioned the ceremonial open carriage and the horse guards, King Boris exploded, "Just to suit the whim of these haughty diplomats, I am supposed to organize spectacles so they can show off their decorations! We are going to bring back the times of Louis XIV. But don't forget that after him there was also Louis XVI! Why should I inaugurate this Parliament when I didn't open the previous ones, for reasons that you know very well? What have we gained in the meantime? What are our successes?" The king became more excited. "But that is the partisan mentality: we are in power, so it means that everything is well; we are not in power, so it means all is bad. You know how good things are now: Macedonia is under the Serbs. Thrace under the Greeks, Dobrudja is Rumanian—half of the Bulgarian people chased out of villages and towns or in jails—and they want ceremonies!"

Slamming the door, the king left the room. Grouev was very upset. "I should be like 'the Padre' Dobrovitch, [his predecessor who had just retired]," he complained. "He didn't report anything, he just kept silent. I am reporting what the foreigners say, and, you see, he gives me hell!"

The departure of "The Padre," the highly experienced chief of cabinet, was another blow to the king. Ever since Ferdinand's abdication, the governments had distrusted Dobrovitch whom they considered a potential agent of the former monarch, but Boris had managed to keep him. "After the fall of the Agrarians, I felt reassured," Dobrovitch wrote to King Ferdinand in December 1923. "I hoped that with the arrival to power of wise and understanding men, I would be able to play again the role of intermediary between the crown and the government and be of use to the king. But alas! I saw the same mistrust toward me shown by the present ministers, who asked for my dismissal." After thirty years of distinguished service, the most trusted of the old courtiers resigned. King Boris had received three anonymous letters saying that if Dobrovitch did not leave, he would be killed. Reluctantly, the resignation was accepted.

"The Padre's" letter to Ferdinand was entrusted to Princess Nadejda, who was leaving for Germany because she had recently been secretly engaged to the Duke of Wurttemberg. She also carried with her a confidential letter from Boris, dated December 3, 1923. Written in French, as usual, and using many code names, it describes well Boris's feelings toward the Tzankov regime:

"What I saw as a dangerous development last May happened in a much worse way, and with much wider consequences for the future, than I had feared. The poor Bolont [Stambolisky] has perished, horribly tortured by the descendants of the Pretorians, and with him, the boiler burst. That boiler, although primitive and made of copper, was nevertheless the only solid and durable one. It was replaced by a boiler made by the engineers Masson[1], Drangov[2] and Clotilde[3]. It is very elastic, but it only heats by using coal mixed with bones,[4] and has only secret regulators, which, as time passes, makes it dangerous."

A paragraph follows which leaves no doubt that King Boris took no part in, nor approved of, the June 9 coup and the bloody repression, as his adversaries continued to insinuate.

"The builders, in order to gain and maintain the confidence in the crew of Bremms [?], continue to say that Tosho [King Boris] took part in the construction of the 'elastic boiler' and that he approves entirely of it. This word is being spread around with the idea of exploiting all the prestige and sympathies that Tosho still has.

"Under these circumstances, the outcome is clear to me: it will, one day, either be Moscow, which will never forgive what happened in Septem-

---

[1]Masson: allusion to the Free-Masons. Tzankov and a few of his colleagues belonged to the secret Masonic lodge.
[2]Drangov: famous Macedonian hero. Allusion to the Macedonian support of the new regime.
[3]Clotilde: code name for unidentified person.
[4]Bones: allusion to the numerous victims of the reprisals.

ber; or it will be some admirer of the poor deceased [Stambolisky] or one of his acolytes who are now being helped by the Zahlkelner [Yugoslavia?/ Czechoslovakia?)."

Since he foresaw a dark future, Boris told his father that it would be a good idea to have his sisters married. "In principle I am not enthusiastic about marriages, as you know, and I will not change my convictions about it," he wrote, but in the case of Princess Nadejda he recommended a quick marriage, "while the firm has still some appearance of luster left." No one in Bulgaria knew about the wedding plans and, for political reasons, the king favored the "Bomben system"—to put before people a *fait accompli.*

Another important family event was in the making. Tzankov informed the king that he would have no objection to the return of Prince Kyril. The government even suggested that the prince's return would be useful to the king as well as to the country. Boris was both happy and worried to hear this unexpected offer. Suspicious as he was about any action of the ruling group, he was not sure of the real reason behind the invitation. Was the regime worried about his being killed without leaving an heir? "They want to have a member of 'the firm' in Sofia should that happen . . . " But was the danger that imminent, he wondered. Or did they know something he didn't know? In any case, as this was a good opportunity, he wrote to his father asking for his agreement for Kyril to return on a "temporary visit."

"The longer I continue in this *triste métier,* the more I admire you for your patience in enduring it for thirty-five years!" Boris's letter ended.

Six days later, on December 11, the king opened the Parliament. He did it exactly the way he had told his intimates he would. "I'll read the Throne Speech with no feeling. They want me to read it because of the effect abroad. Tzankov and Kalfov made me accept. Very well! I'll do it, but I'll recite it like a lesson." He kept his promise, reading the passages on foreign policy with eloquence and poise but mumbling when he came to the change of government. And as he spoke of the September insurgency, he mentioned that the government had taken the necessary measures, adding with exaggerated emphasis the word "un-for-tu-nate-ly." This word did not appear in the text of the preprinted Throne Speech.

*     *     *

The damp cold is particularly penetrating at three o'clock in the morning and, after one hour climbing in the dark, the steep mountain path becomes exhausting. Yet Boris, his eyelids still heavy with sleep, feels unusually happy. Indeed, he hasn't felt so at peace for weeks, maybe months. He follows the gamekeeper in silence, extremely careful not to make any noise, even though the mating place where the capercaillie has been spotted the previous day is still far away. Every metallic part of the equipment—the belt buckles, the canteen, even the safety latch on the rifles—has been wrapped to muffle a click that may frighten the shy bird.

The capercaillie, or *Auerhahn* in German, is reputed to have the sharpest hearing and sight of any forest inhabitant. It is extremely difficult to approach it within gunshot range. To add to the challenge, this turkey-sized grouse is becoming more and more scarce in Europe, living in mountains in barely accessible evergreen woodlands. Its attraction for the keen hunter is therefore irresistible, which explains the passion King Ferdinand had, and his sons inherited, for Auerhahn shooting.

The starry night is clear and the moonlight helps the party follow the narrow path through bushes, rocks, and trees along the wet grass. In early May the surrounding Rila peaks are still covered with snow. This is the best time for shooting, because, as cautious and perceptive as it may be, the capercaillie, much like humans, is apt to do foolish things during the mating season. And that is what the hunter counts on. Like most polygamous creatures, the male capercaillie is an incredibly vain lover, with a penchant for elaborate, conspicuous display, to the great joy of the rather dull-looking admiring hens in his territory. About one hour before dawn, the cock extends his large tail in a fan, takes up a posture much like that of the gobbling turkey and proudly performs his intricate love song. The display call is repeated again and again until sunrise, up to two or three hundred times, lasting well over an hour.

"Song" is perhaps too flattering a word for the clucking, popping, snapping sounds the bird utters, but the relevant point for the stalker is that during a specific part of this call, the capercaillie becomes totally deaf. These periods of oblivion at the height of the lover's ecstasy last for only seconds. But seconds are enough for the skillful hunter to advance a few steps nearer to the bird.

In Bulgarian they call the capercaillie *Gloohar*, which means "the deaf one." King Boris, an excellent ornithologist as well as a first-rate shot, knows well the gloohar's behavior and the technique for approaching it. He was amused by and saw a marvelous analogy in the weakness of the cock. "It reminds me of so many people we know," he would say. "People with such monumental vanity that they become totally oblivious to the rest of the world, deaf and blind, once they start talking. Have you ever watched an orator or a prima donna during performance? They are in such admiration of their own voices that if the universe collapsed around them they wouldn't notice it."

An old gloohar has been heard on a large Excelsea tree in the last few days. It is still dark, as Boris and the keeper stalk the bird over a carpet of wild geranium. This particular species, the *Zdravetz*, has a unique fragrance and only grows in the Bulgarian woods and mountains. Its scent, especially after a rain, perfumes entire meadows and forest pathways with a fresh, slightly spiced smell that evokes sensations of youth and health. *(Zdrave* means health.)

Suddenly, the hunters stop short and strain their ears. The familiar sound can be heard not too far away. "The liturgy," as King Ferdinand used to call it, has begun.

Cocked rifle in hand, moving slowly with extreme caution, Boris prepares himself for the final approach. In the predawn dimness, he discerns the contour of the bird perched on a branch of the Excelsea. But it is out of accurate range. Boris remains motionless, barely daring to breathe, for he knows that the moment of deafness has not arrived yet. It comes only with a particular "phrase" of the love call.

The gloohar is still at the first part of his four-verse song, a snapping double sound, repeated sometimes up to ten times. Then the separate sounds fuse together into a continuous trill, a warble that suddenly ends in a loud "klack," like a cork popping from a bottle. Boris comprehends the strict regularity in these successive sounds, like a music lover following the movements of a sonata. To move before the final phrase, the "hissing," would be as gauche and unforgivable for a hunter as it would be for a concertgoer to start clapping at the pause following the first allegro.

The hissing! This is the moment when the capercaillie loses his hearing and, some claim, even his sight. As soon as Boris hears this whetting sound—something resembling the honing of a scythe with a whetstone—he jumps to his feet, takes three or four steps forward, and freezes. The hissing stops. The pause seems endless, as he has to retain, in perfect immobility, the position he finds himself in. A few minutes go by, the rifle in the outstretched arm begins to weigh tons, the sharp rock on which he is kneeling hurts. The song resumes.

The champagne cork sounds again, immediately followed by the hissing. Boris rushes four more steps forward. Patiently he waits for a few more "whettings," repeating the leaps forward, until he places himself at shooting distance from the momentarily deafened bird. The superb gloohar is in the paroxysm of his ardor. Boris aims and pulls the trigger. The heavy bird crashes down through the branches, pierced by the 6 mm. bullet.

*      *      *

After each shoot, following the tradition inaugurated by his father, Boris and his guests used to sign the hunting log with a few commentaries. The leather-bound logs at the royal mountain lodge at Ovnarsko were filled with detailed accounts of capercaillie shoots, and Boris enjoyed reading the old entries. The first entry, dated May 13, 1908, is in the unmistakable bold writing of King Ferdinand: "Radiant night, incomparable moon. Departure at 3 A.M. We find three cocks there. One takes off noisily, silencing the others. After ten minutes waiting, the second cock flies over our heads. Finally, the third cock begins his call . . ."

Ferdinand switches from French to Bulgarian and back to French, with most hunting terms in German. The spelling in the three languages is impeccable, a virtuosity Boris could envy. "Furious climbing, perfidious twigs, I have to keep lying flat on my stomach in order to avoid the crack of the dead branches," continues the account. "At last I approach the place, but impossible to find the bird. Terrible anguish! Finally my old lorgnette discovers it, but the cock sees me and takes off. I shoot at the same moment, 4:37 A.M., and it falls like an enormous fruit. I was crazy with fatigue and also very nervous because of the 13th . . ."

Another superstitious mention appears in the entry of May 13, 1910: "A cock flies over my head. I shoot; it falls. But the bullet passes too close N.'s face. Anguish: Friday the 13th! I shiver at the idea of avoided danger."

At each turn of the pages, Boris discovered some unexpected aspect of his father's personality. In the intimacy of the hunting lodge, the formidable old monarch appeared to him like a different man:

"Monday, May 13, 1912." (The year of the Balkan war, Ferdinand's apotheosis). "I really don't feel well; three months of gout and rheumatism have ruined my strength, and the sorrow and disappointments of the recent times have ruined my nerves . . . As I leave at 4:15 A.M., my head feels heavy, my legs wobbly. Ah, the horror of feeling, at the age of 51, like a ruin, the beard already white, the head bald as a billiard ball!" But although exhausted and sick, Ferdinand spent the rest of the morning stalking the elusive cocks. The diary shows that he continued with the same passion on the following day: "Departure at 3:30 A.M.," and also the next morning, 3:45 A.M. The meticulous descriptions of every bird and each shot end with a few gloomy sentences: "Somber return. Mich freut nichts mehr auf dieser Welt. [I don't enjoy anything in this world anymore.] May God have pity on us!"

\* \* \*

# CHAPTER IX

# The Macedonian Drama and the IMRO

THE MOMENT his boss announced his travel plans, Ivan Mihailov didn't like the sound of it, as if he had some evil premonition. But then, "Vanché," as the twenty-seven-year-old IMRO (Internal Macedonian Revolutionary Organization) activist was called, had always been the epitome of a man obsessed with security and trained never fully to trust anything or anybody—anything but unconditional obedience to the secret organization, anybody but Todor, its undisputed leader.

Todor Alexandrov had arrived secretly in Sofia two days earlier, coming from one of his regular clandestine tours of Yugoslav Macedonia, and had summoned Mihailov on August 29, 1924, by confidential message.

"Stresov," he told his secretary (Stresov was Mihailov's pseudonym), "I'm going to attend a regional congress in the Pirin mountains tomorrow and I'm leaving tonight."

"I wish you wouldn't. To be frank, I don't trust Aleko's gang, and that's their territory. Do you really have to go?" Vanché-Stresov asked.

"Absolutely. There are many things to be settled and we'll resolve them at the congress."

Mihailov protested, respectfully but with insistence. Some recent developments in IMRO disturbed him. Dissensions had appeared in the monolithic, grimly disciplined organization. Some coolness in the relationship between Alexandrov and Protoguerov, another member of the Central Committee, had replaced the brotherly consensus. And in Bulgarian Macedonia, the regional boss was behaving in an overly independent manner bordering on defiance. But when Mihailov realized that Alexandrov had made up his mind and was going to attend the congress, he insisted that at least he take along several bodyguards. Alexandrov didn't like the idea of appearing as if he distrusted his hosts, but finally agreed to a compromise.

"O.K., but only two. And tell them that we'll leave tonight."

In other circles, Vanché Mihailov would appear exaggeratedly distrustful, almost paranoiac. But in IMRO, the revolutionary organization committed to armed struggle for the independence of Macedonia, this was an elementary instinct of self-preservation. It was not a club for timid souls nor a forum for intellectual discussions. Its members had agreed to live by the sword and, if necessary, to die by the sword. In romantic, if not sinister, rituals, they had taken an oath of total obedience and silence, swearing before a dagger and a revolver crossed over the Bible. To the occupier's oppression—the Turks yesterday, the Serbs and Greeks today—they retaliated with terror, bombs, and assassinations. Treason and disobedience were summarily punished by death. The slightest indiscretion was dealt with as a major crime.

Any evaluation of King Boris's actions which did not take into consideration the reality of IMRO would be as meaningless as an analysis of modern Lebanon without mentioning the existence of the PLO. And any description of Bulgarian political life during the first half of this century would be unintelligible without some understanding of the Macedonian problem.

There had been no more cruel and tragic history in Europe than the ordeals of contemporary Macedonia. Inhabited by Bulgarians, Turks, Greeks, Rumanians, Albanians, Serbs, and other minorities, this unfortunate land has known harsh Ottoman oppression, an unsuccessful popular uprising in 1903 followed by savage reprisals, the devastations of one Balkan War for its liberation and another for its partition between the liberators— all this before it became a ravaged World War I battlefield. Because of traditional hatred and rivalry between the Balkan nations, often encouraged by the Great Powers, and because of Bulgarian, Serbian, and Greek ambitions which led to reckless decisions, these events caused enormous suffering to the Macedonian population, who were mainly Bulgarian. In one short decade many Macedonians experienced four or five successive occupations and were subjected to intensive campaigns of denationalization and retaliation. Hundreds of thousands of refugees sought asylum in Bulgaria, thus creating an intolerable immigrant problem in that small country already impoverished and embittered from the war. In Sofia alone, there were hundreds of thousands of Macedonian refugees, permeating every layer of Bulgarian society.

Terror breeds revenge and retaliation; blood calls for more blood. The sons of the redoubtable Macedonian "komitadjis," whose bombings of banks and ports shook the Ottoman Empire at the turn of the century, became the new "tchetniks" or guerrillas, hiding in the mountains, killing Serbian policemen, and avenging persecuted Bulgarians in Yugoslav and Greek Macedonia. Their IMRO, composed of fearless fanatics and ruthless, well-trained revolutionaries obeying an iron discipline, became the terror of Yugoslav and Greek authorities, and a major concern for the Bulgarian government, who had little authority over them. Their large numbers, their hopelessness and determination contributed to the creation of a veritable state within a state.

While unequivocally proclaiming their Bulgarian nationality, IMRO members were not at the service of the Bulgarian state. In fact, IMRO was opposed to the annexation of Macedonia by Bulgaria, and the relationship between a future free Macedonia and the Bulgarian kingdom was the principal cause for division between different Macedonian groups. Most Bulgarians and many Macedonians did indeed dream of this tragic land becoming another Bulgarian province, reunited with the old country of their ethnic brothers. But the defeats after the 1913 war and World War I shattered this dream and showed how difficult, if not impossible, its realization would be. A growing number of Macedonians viewed the idea of a unified Great Bulgaria as unrealistic. Thus, the mainstream of the revolutionaries saw the solution in an autonomous Macedonia, a new and independent state composed of the three territories presently ruled by Yugoslavia, Greece, and Bulgaria.

The most militant "autonomist" group, IMRO, believed in an independent state in which not only the Bulgarian majority, but all the minorities—Turks, Rumanians, Greeks, Serbs, Albanians, Gypsies as well as Orthodox Christians, Muslims, and Jews—would enjoy equal rights and opportunities.

Other factions envisioned an autonomous Macedonia joining a truly "Yugo-Slav" federation-state of all Slavs of the south, including Bulgaria and Serbia as equal members. This idea was anathema to IMRO, who viewed it as a Serbian ruse to lure Bulgarians to the rule of Belgrade. The "federalists" were politically closer to the Left and entertained contacts with the Communists while the "autonomists" leaned generally to the Right.

The ideological and political differences between the actors in this Macedonian drama, all belonging to nationalities not particularly noted for their gentleness, moderation, and calm, had never had a chance to be discussed, let alone solved, with the civility of parliamentary or diplomatic procedures. Since the beginning, the debate had been soaked in emotion and blood, punctuated by gunshots and bombs, a debate from which few participants walked out alive or unharmed. The victims were not only Serbian or Greek oppressors. Fratricidal disputes tore apart the Macedonian emigrés in Bulgaria. Members of feuding factions killed each other in shocking numbers and with terrifying ferocity, often in broad daylight in the streets of Sofia.

IMRO took credit for several assassinations, referring to them as "punishments" and "death sentences" for traitors and informers carried out by "selfless patriots" in the name of the sacred cause.

Political violence creates its own moral and honor code, in which human life is less valued than qualities such as courage, loyalty, total obedience, silence, and commitment to revenge. Ivan Mihailov was a product of the IMRO world and its traditions and values in which violence was an unavoidable fact of life. To him the fratricidal struggle was a sign of patriotic involvement, certainly better than political apathy. He used to quote an eminent Macedonian professor who had told him: "I regret when Macedonians quarrel among themselves, or even have recourse to murder. But I prefer even these killings to not having Macedonian freedom-fighters, nor being concerned and suffering for Macedonia. Let there be differences, but let us not stop the struggle! The Macedonian internal strife is only a sign of the great dynamism of that struggle."

Ever since he could remember, Vanché Mihailov had been infused by the mystique of the Macedonian revolutionary movement. His father, his relatives, and every man he had admired as a child in his hometown of Shtip, were deeply involved in "the cause." As the Shtip region and most Bulgarian-populated areas of Macedonia remained under Turkish rule after the rest of Bulgaria was liberated in 1878, nationalistic activities were illegal and dangerous, and the struggle for liberation was pursued clandestinely. By the time Vanché was born in 1897, Shtip was an important revolutionary center of secret activities and proud that some of the apostles of the national liberation movement had been schoolteachers in that town.

Vanché's earliest memories were of strangers sneaking into darkened houses after the children had gone to bed, of his father whispering to late visitors or unpacking guns behind locked doors, of mysterious silhouettes carrying dim lanterns and crossing backyards when the Turkish *zaptiés* (policemen) were asleep. He remembered alerts in the neighborhood when the noise of the zaptiés' steps were heard on the cobblestones of the narrow streets, and the anxiety on the faces of grown-ups behind drawn curtains. He was only six when the great Illinden Uprising plunged Macedonia into a blood bath; and, like all Bulgarian children, he grew up spellbound by heroic tales of the brutally crushed popular revolt.

The sight of revolvers and bombs was familiar to every Bulgarian boy in Shtip. For Vanché, no thrill in the world could equal the excitement of the periodic visits of a "tcheta"—a guerrilla band—to their home. How marvelously strong, how handsome and proud the tchetniks looked in their uniforms! Oiling their guns and filling their cartridge belts with bullets as they cursed the Turkish authorities, the tchetniks represented the ultimate image of manliness and valor.

They would spend a few days in the house, resting and hiding from the police between guerrilla activities in the area, and then would disappear into the woods and mountains. The entire street was aware of their presence, but no one asked questions and no one, of course, talked about them. Even the children knew that one should never, ever, mention the tchetniks to strangers, no matter what the circumstances.

The tcheta chief, called voyvoda, was an almost mythological figure in the child's imagination, combining the authority of absolute commander with the supernatural power of demigod. The great hero of Vanché's youth was the legendary local voyvoda, Mishe Razvigorov. How unforgettable was the evening when the heavily armed Razvigorov tcheta slipped into town and Vanché's idol chose to spend a few nights in the Mihailov home, a bliss and an honor greater than anything the boy could ever dream of!

Another hero was the young schoolteacher, Todor Alexandrov, who lived only a hundred yards away from the Mihailov house. Todor used to vanish periodically from town, then reappear with other tchetniks, dressed in komitadji uniform—braids across the chest, the cartridge belt, the long leather laces crossed over the leggings from shoe to knee. Even then, little Vanché was impressed by "the domineering look in his eyes" and the "combination of severity and kindness" that Alexandrov projected.

It was also in his early years that Mihailov heard for the first time of people being "punished." Vanché was on the market street when he heard several gunshots and saw everybody around him running for cover. Women were screaming, merchants quickly shuttered the windows. Minutes later, the frightened child heard the news: somebody had been "punished." His bullet-ridden body lay in a puddle of blood in the public bar. Nobody used the words "murdered," or "assassinated." The victim had committed some indiscretion, he had talked too much. Therefore, "The Organization" had to punish him and a good, disciplined IMRO member had executed the sentence.

By the time Mihailov grew up, he had seen or heard of many similar "disciplinary actions." Later, he himself approved or ordered several executions. For decades to come, members and foes of IMRO were shot, knifed, bombed, or cut to pieces. Dispassionately, in the tone of someone reading a judiciary brief, the sinister euphemism "punishment" was delivered. In fact, the term corresponded perfectly to the beliefs of the militants: they saw the punitive measures as just and necessary retributions for crimes that endangered The Organization.'

Mihailov's case hardly requires psychoanalysis to trace the origin of such beliefs. The dramatic death of his hero Razvigorov was one of the events that marked his childhood. The voyvoda, surrounded by Turkish soldiers, had fought like a lion, and when he ran out of ammunition, he had killed himself rather than be captured, thus confirming how a voyvoda should live and die.

Then in 1907, when the police were searching for komitadjis, his father fled to Sofia. Soon, young Ivan joined him and continued his schooling in free Bulgaria's capital. The exile ended when a new era of good relations between Turkish authorities and Macedonia's population was proclaimed. Many fugitives, including the Mihailovs, returned to their homeland and for a period enjoyed the new friendship with the Turks. During various celebrations, many Macedonians showed off their hidden weapons, shooting joyfully into the air. To his infinite pride, Vanché discovered that his family also owned a gun, an old rifle kept concealed in the wall of the stables.

Unfortunately, after a period of relative respect for the human rights of the population, the persecutions resumed. In a sweeping campaign to confiscate weapons, hordes of soldiers swarmed into villages and towns, searching every house, arresting suspects by the hundreds, torturing and deporting. Soldiers invaded the Mihailov house, searching for the father and his gun. They beat Vanché's older brother in front of his mother and the other children and took him away, handcuffed and bleeding. A few days later the soldiers returned and took Vanché to the school building. The yard was packed with men under arrest. The child was promised that if he told where the rifle was, his brother would be released. Vanché repeated stubbornly that it had been "stolen" from the house. The inquisitor then pushed him to the end of a corridor and opened the door. The Dantesque scene remained indelibly engraved in his mind.

He saw a dozen armed soldiers with whips and truncheons in their hands. They were standing in a circle around a human heap composed of seven or eight Bulgarian men in a deplorable state. The grunting, bleeding, sweating prisoners, among whom Vanché recognized his brother Christo, were almost unconscious, their arms tied behind their backs. A short piece of wood was attached behind the shoulders of each body, and soldiers held the ends of the ropes with which the victims were tied. Each time the rope was pulled, the shoulders were forced back, the left shoulder nearly touching the right one, causing excruciating pain as the rib cage threatened to explode. The slightest movement of one body provoked unbearable pain to the rest of the prisoners. The petrified child discerned the face of Igno the baker, a man of sixty. Hadji Mishe, a septuagenarian, was attached to him, and also the pharmacist, Nakashev. Could Vanché help Christo out of this inferno? His brother looked half-dead, probably unable to recognize him.

"Look how your brother suffers! Why don't you tell us?" the zaptié asked again. And again the boy refused to talk. They took him out of the torture room and started beating him with a cane on the feet, until he couldn't feel them anymore. All he could feel when he was finally sent home was hate, a deep, overwhelming hatred and a thirst for revenge.

Several Shtip citizens died from the tortures. Others remained invalids for life. Christo returned home stunned and bruised all over his body. After a few more days of terror, the punitive expedition left town and headed for other regions.

There were happier memories too. The ecstasy of the Balkan War was one of them. No one who had not lived the feverish days of 1912 when the alliance of the young Balkan kingdoms attacked the crumbling Ottoman

Empire could have any idea of the euphoria that swept over Bulgaria and Macedonia. People cried with joy; volunteers rushed to enroll; singing soldiers sent off with gifts and blessings, marched on carpets of flowers as they left for the front.

Ivan Mihailov was a high school student in Salonika when the news of the glorious Bulgarian victories began to arrive from the battlefields. It was hard to concentrate on the lessons. No one in the boarding school could sleep from excitement, and martial marches resounded in the classrooms. The Turkish troops were retreating and leaving the large Macedonian city. Finally, the great day arrived, a rainy day when the entire Bulgarian population of Salonika poured out onto the highway to meet the first Bulgarian troops. What an unforgettable moment this was! Soaked to the skin by the rain, screaming "Hurrah!" from the depths of his lungs until he lost his voice, Vanché watched the long columns of soldiers enter the city, as overwhelmed by emotion as the delirious crowds. At the head of the first column on horseback, riding next to the division's commander, he saw an eighteen-year-old officer, whose distinguished frail adolescent face he recognized from many photographs: the crown prince himself, Prince Boris Turnovsky. And a little further behind, riding with the officers of the general staff, rode his former neighbor, the voyvoda, Todor Alexandrov.

∗    ∗    ∗

Six years later, Mihailov found Alexandrov again, this time in Sofia. Many tragic events had taken place since that glorious day in Salonika. The Balkan alliance had burst as a result of a bitter quarrel over the repartition of the liberated provinces, and after the 1913 war, Salonika was attached to Greece, and Shtip was taken by Serbia. The Inter-Allied war had exacerbated the hostility between Bulgarians and Serbs, and the condition of the Bulgarian majority in towns like Shtip had become almost intolerable. With Turkey no longer the main enemy, IMRO's action was redirected against the Serbian and Greek authorities in Macedonia.

When Austria attacked Serbia in 1914 and World War I began, a new hope was born in the hearts of the Bulgarian population. One year later, inspired by the same hope, Bulgaria joined the enemies of Serbia and Greece. At the end of the war, Vanché Mihailov arrived in Sofia where he became the secretary of Todor Alexandrov, who was by then unanimously recognized as the most important IMRO leader.

Vanché worked for Alexandrov for more than five years, before Todor's arrest and escape during the Stambolisky regime, as well as afterwards, when the voyvoda took the clandestine road and directed IMRO illegal activities from inside Yugoslavia. Thus Mihailov became the guerrilla commander's principal and most loyal representative in Bulgaria.

\*     \*     \*

Three days after Alexandrov's departure for the congress in the Pirin mountains, Vanché Mihailov and four of the voyvoda's most trusted collaborators in Sofia were summoned by coded message to join him and Protoguerov, the IMRO co-leader, immediately. Puzzled, the five men left for the Bulgarian sector of Macedonia. They were met near the small town of Melnik by a guide and continued on horseback along a narrow valley. The Pirin, an enchanted mountain rich in fir trees, brooks and alpine flowers, is known for some of the most picturesque landscapes in all of the Balkan peninsula.

It was evening when the men reached a poor hamlet with small dilapidated houses. They slept on the floor of a miserable room and at dawn three tchetniks came to lead them to Alexandrov and Protoguerov. After climbing a pleasant path fringed with bushes, they stopped for a rest. Then the oldest guide turned to the group and, choking with emotion, announced solemnly: "Brothers, it is my sad duty to inform you that our great Todor is not with us anymore . . ." The men were stunned. One of them started crying hysterically. Mihailov shouted to him: "Stop it! Crying won't help! Todor had been killed. Let's find out where he is now!"

The guides led them to a little chapel in the middle of the nearby fields. Most of the delegates were assembled there, all looking gloomy and shaken. The regional chief, Aleko Vassilev, and his deputy, Lieutenant Colonel Atanassov, both in tchetnik uniforms and armed with rifles, came forward and shook hands with Mihailov. These were the men Vanché suspected of being secret opponents of Todor. And yet, Aleko had tears in his eyes.

A close observation of Vanché Mihailov's face and behavior that morning would have been frightening. The young activist was in full control of himself, as cool and calculating as a master chessplayer forced into a dangerous position. Not a tear on the steely eyes. Not a word of regret or condolence. "What's happened has happened! There is nothing we can do about it!" he said icily to Aleko. "The important thing now is to pull ourselves together and work firmly to compensate for at least part of the loss."

In this manner he lulled the dissidents, even flattered them, telling Aleko that the organization would look to him for leadership. But there was something ominous in the determination in his eyes. Years later, he described his thoughts at that moment: "I decided that it was better to start playing my game right away. It would be either them or us! Protoguerov, Aleko, and Atanassov must be punished! Our only weapon now was the ruse, and our immediate goal to get out of there alive!"

Inside the chapel, Alexandrov's body lay in a makeshift wooden coffin. Protoguerov, visibly marked by the tragedy, told Mihailov: "We didn't want to bury him before you came." Then he told him what had happened. After meeting in Melnik, and escorted by three of Aleko's men, Alexandrov and Protoguerov took the steep path leading to the village, high in the mountain where the congress was to take place. They stopped for a snack in a meadow surrounded by woods and high peaks. As they were resting and eating, the three tchetniks, the escorts, suddenly opened fire on Alexandrov and his bodyguard. Then the murderers fled, disappearing into the woods.

The burial took place in front of the tiny chapel. The local priest said a prayer, Mihailov read the eulogy, and tchetniks fired three volleys into the air.

Mihailov stared at the magnificent mountain range to the south. A few kilometers beyond the ravine, one could see a white building—the Rojensky monastery. Next to it there was a tomb: the grave of Yane Sandanski, the late leader of the federalists, the archenemies of Alexandrov and Mihailov.

After the burial, all the delegates departed—some for Sofia, some for their operational districts, others for the Yugoslav or Greek borders which they would cross illegally. In the solitude of Pirin, across undisturbed forests, stony ravines, and meadows covered with wild flowers, the graves of the brothers-enemies, Todor and Yane, the autonomist and the federalist, remained to face each other.

\*    \*    \*

There was no doubt in Mihailov's mind that Protoguerov, Aleko Vassilev, and Colonel Atanassov were the real instigators of Alexandrov's murder. As the "Troyka" was taking over the organization's affairs, Mihailov secretly mobilized his friends and organized a plot to "punish" the guilty. Several conspirators, however, insisted that Protoguerov's life should be spared in order to ensure some continuity.

On September 12, 1924, eleven days after Todor's burial, the Troyka assembled, at Mihailov's request, in Gorna-Djoumaya, the principal town in Bulgarian Macedonia. But Mihailov did not appear, pretending that he was sick. Instead, his messenger opened fire, killing both Vassilev and Atanassov. Protoguerov was only roughed up and denounced publicly.

Alexandrov's death, kept secret, was only then publicly announced. The public also learned that the "culprits" had been punished. From that day on, Vanché Mihailov, a totally committed and ruthless twenty-seven-year-old genius of organization and conspiracy, became the uncontested and much feared leader of IMRO.

\*    \*    \*

The day the unsuspecting Troyka was heading for Mihailov's trap on September 11, 1924, events of a totally different nature were preoccupying

King Boris and his advisers, who were still unaware of Alexandrov's murder.

The previous day the king had told his aide-de-camp, Draganov, by coded telegram from his Black Sea palace of Euxinograd that he was coming to Vrana, but wanted his presence in the vicinity of the capital to be kept secret. He arrived in the evening by car, tired from the long drive and suffering from a bad earache. Draganov briefed him about the last minute preparations for the forthcoming event, the inauguration of the Alexander Nevsky Cathedral. The protocol for the ceremony had been completed; the diplomatic corps had been asked to come in full dress and decorations; Avram, the royal tailor, was ready to fit the king's new general's uniform.

"I wonder whether I'll be able to make it," the king announced worriedly. His illness was the reason he did not want anyone to know that he had come from Euxinograd. "I feel quite sick with my otitis. In any case, I'm against this kind of ceremony at the present moment. It's not a time for celebrations. But what can I do? I have to go through with it. If I don't get sicker . . . I'll see the doctor tomorrow, but tonight I'll try the old-wives' medicine." With that, he poured a few drops of warm olive oil in his ear before going to sleep.

The next morning, before 8:00, another aide-de-camp, Colonel Panov, arrived in Vrana, visibly disturbed and asking to see the king right away. "Another *cacade*, I suppose," said the king resignedly. "Very well. But let me at least put on a shirt!"

Panov had been told the previous night by the interior minister that the Communists intended to explode a bomb inside the cathedral during the inaugural ceremony. Believing that the king was still in Euxinograd, the government wanted the aide-de-camp to warn him and ask him not to come to Sofia. It also proposed to warn the foreign diplomats not to go and to announce officially that the church was going to be dedicated with only a religious celebration instead of a state ceremony.

King Boris received him sick in bed. The ear inflammation had worsened, and Panov's report upset him. He felt that his absence from the much publicized cathedral inauguration would make a bad impression. Alexander Nevsky's solemn dedication was indeed a great national event. The construction of the huge white marble church with its gold-covered cupolas had taken forty-two years, and it had become the pride of the nation. The magnificent neo-Byzantine cathedral, lavishly decorated with multicolored marble floors and walls, frescoes and icons by the best Eastern-Orthodox artists, was built by the Bulgarian people as a monument of gratitude to the Russian soldiers who had died in the Liberation War of 1877–1878. It was by far the largest church and monument in the country, and its inauguration was awaited impatiently by the entire nation. Could the king be absent from this important event?

After long deliberation with his advisers, Boris decided that he should not run the risk. Unless, of course, the ministers changed their minds and decided to go. In that case, the king, sick or not, would have to attend. It was agreed that he would wait for the decision of the government.

Grouev and Panov did not return to Vrana with the cabinet's decision until 8:30 in the evening. King Boris was impatiently waiting for them, all dressed and feeling a little better. They reported that the Council of Ministers took the bomb threat very seriously and appealed to the king not to attend. It has also been decided that the war and interior ministers would remain in their offices ready for action in case of trouble, but the other ministers would go to the cathedral.

The king carefully pondered the pros and cons of the government's decision and accepted it, adding: "But the foreign diplomats and the bishops should be warned that I will not attend."

Indeed, when the Alexander Nevsky Cathedral was solemnly consecrated the following day, the royal throne was empty. The bomb threat did not materialize, perhaps for that very reason.

*      *      *

Three mornings later, Pavel Grouev, uncharacteristically excited, rushed to Vrana and went to see the king.

"I think we delude ourselves when we imagine that our police know what's going on," he said. "The foreigners learn everything before us. Rinella [a diplomat] told me this morning, 'You know, of course, that Todor Alexandrov has been killed, don't you?' I was flabbergasted. And only now we are told that IMRO just announced it officially. Fifteen days after the murder!"

King Boris, who respected Alexandrov, was shocked. After the first surprise and indignation, he began to speculate about the reasons and the possible instigators of the crime. Maybe some people around the government won't be so unhappy, he mused. Now they'll have a good excuse to act against the Serbs, won't they?

Was the assassination a purely internal Macedonian affair, or was it linked to Bulgarian politics? "I warned Stambolisky not to involve the Macedonians in our political life," the king said. "But his lieutenants implicated him. I said the same thing to Tzankov. On June 9 in Vrana I told the coup's leaders: 'I hope that what you did today is for the good of Bulgaria, but the fact that the army and the Macedonians are involved is not a good thing!' And I said the same thing to Todor Alexandrov himself when I saw him shortly after June 9: 'Don't involve the Macedonians in our internal politics! It will end badly: you'll be contaminated by the vices of our partisanship, and our partisans will adopt your surgical methods.' But he did not listen. He thought that I was talking out of fear. Poor man, he paid for this mistake with his head!"

The king worried particularly about possible disorders in Bulgarian Macedonia, where Alexandrov's enemies, the federalists of Sandansky and the Communists, were strong.

But it was too early to tell, the available information was much too scant. King Boris became progressively discouraged and upset. God, couldn't there be one week, or even one single day, without some bad news! The Communists want to blow up the cathedral, the Macedonians kill each other, the Military League sulks because I refuse to sign the death sentences. What a job! Then his depression turned to anger. "I am fed up! I have had enough of all this!" he shouted to his confidants declaring that he was leaving town, he was going back to Euxinograd, and nobody was going to stop him this time! If the government wanted to start reprisals against some Macedonian factions, they could do it without him. He did not want any part of it. He refused to take sides in their fights.

"I don't care if the bandits that roam the roads get me and kill me. They may even do me a favor," he said in exasperation. He was of course exaggerating and Draganov, who was the bluntest of his advisers, told him so, adding that if things really went that badly, the king could always leave the country and lead a private life.

Boris exploded, "A private life, me? I wouldn't know what to do with a private life now. Don't you see that I have become *un vieillard rance, méchant et impotent?*"[1] He slammed the door and left the room in disgust.

---

[1]"A rancid, mean and impotent old man." Boris was thirty years old.

# CHAPTER X

# The Bombing of
# Sveta-Nedelia Cathedral

**W**ALKING NEXT to the officer in the snappy uniform and chatting cheerfully, the nondescript young woman felt assured that nobody was following her tonight, that she was not in immediate danger of being arrested. Tzola Dragoytcheva had almost forgotten this feeling, which she hadn't experienced since she had gone into hiding last year after the failed uprising of September 1923. Now an important Communist activist in Plovdiv, she had come to the capital to report on the recent arrests of Plovdiv's top party leaders, which had crushed the militant organization and frightened party members.

Captain Georgi Krotnev led her along the Boulevard Tsar Osvoboditel, past the imposing equestrian monument of Alexander II. With snow covering the streets and roofs, Sofia looked especially beautiful that late evening. The few passers-by paid no attention to the couple as they turned left at the university and continued on the squeaking snow, past the Boulevard Dondoukov, to the poorly lit streets behind the artillery barracks. It was a poor neighborhood, with small houses and snow piled on the sidewalks.

They stopped in front of an unimpressive cottage whose windows were totally dark. Krotnev knocked on the door in a certain way. After a short pause, he repeated the signal. Then, taking a key out of his pocket, he unlocked the door. Inside the entrance hall, there was another locked door on which the captain knocked again. A tall, bearded man opened it.

"Kosta Yankov," he introduced himself, as he turned to a second man sitting behind a desk. "And this is Ivan Minkov."

Tzola Dragoytcheva, or "Comrade Sonia," as the captain introduced her, now realized that the room was well lit, but heavy dark curtains covered the windows. She had seen the notorious Major Yankov, the head of the party's military center before, but she did not recognize him. Since the police were looking for him, he had grown a thick reddish-blond beard and flattened his abundant hair. Covering his blue eyes were pince-nez glasses.

This thirty-seven-year-old retired officer had impressive credentials as a Communist. Nephew of a famous heroine nicknamed "Princess Rayna," of the preliberation struggle against the Turks, Yankov was the son of a respected colonel of the royal army. He had been a Communist since his high school days when the founder of the party, Dimitar Blagoev, was his teacher in the Plovdiv School. In spite of his participation in all Communist demonstrations and of his expulsion three times from school for Marxist activities, he was accepted into the military school, and in 1908, promoted to second lieutenant. He fought in the Balkan Wars and in World War I and was decorated for bravery, and after the Russian revolution, he began to preach Bolshevik ideas to the troops. Leaving the army after the defeat in 1918, Yankov married Blagoev's daughter and entered the inner circles of the Bulgarian Communist party. Because of his military background, he became the editor of the newspaper, *People's Army*, glorifying the Bolshevik revolution. Yankov was among the organizers of the September uprising and the Central Committee's military expert.

His deputy at the party's military center, Ivan Minkov, was also a former captain of the royal army, the son of an officer, and had fought in the three wars. Younger than Yankov, he had retired in 1919 to become Yankov's closest associate at the *People's Army*. In 1921, he went to Moscow to a congress of the Comintern and remained for three months in Soviet military institutes specializing in explosives and sabotage.

A talented musician, Minkov had briefly studied piano abroad and had become known as the composer of the best-known Bulgarian funeral hymn when he was a cadet in the Royal Military School.

Krotnev disappeared discreetly, leaving Comrade Sonia alone with the leaders of the party's military branch. Yankov had heard of Tzola's Communist fervor since her student days in Sofia. Later, as an activist in Plovdiv, she had confirmed his first impressions. Now that the regional leaders had been killed or arrested, he and Minkov decided to entrust her with bigger responsibilities.

"Tell us about the losses at the Plovdiv committee," they said. Her tale was long and alarming. The police, discovering the committee's headquarters, had captured important secret documents. The leader was killed and three important members were captured. It was not known if they had talked during the interrogations. Tzola and another comrade had miraculously escaped only minutes before the police burst into their secret residences. The Plovdiv regional organization had been destroyed, or almost, she said.

Yankov and Minkov listened attentively before briefing her about the general situation. Yes, things were going very badly. The "fascist" government was intensifying its persecution against Communists and Left-Agrarians. Plovdiv was not the only disaster area, other regional organizations had also been hit cruelly.

"The center itself suffered heavy losses," Yankov said. "A comrade, sent to help with the uprising, was murdered in September. He was among the best party military leaders. The military center lost another valuable member, wounded during a gun battle." The list of the recent victims was getting frighteningly long. A Supreme Council member shot in the street; another disappeared; at least three Central Committee members, plus a Macedonian leftist activist . . .

"We are at the crest of a revolutionary situation, Comrade Sonia," Yankov said. "This makes it our duty to use all forms of civil war, to mobilize all potential forces for the approaching uprising. We shouldn't lose the combat initiative for a single minute! To each blow of the enemy, we must answer with a blow twice as strong. We mustn't leave him any time to recover. And when the earth bursts into flames under his feet, then we'll give the signal for the uprising."

The imminent uprising! The coming Bulgarian Red Revolution! That was what the Central Committee and the emigrés in Moscow led by Kolarov and Dimitrov were preparing feverishly under the instructions of the Comintern. For that purpose, the party had formed its military branch after the failure of last year's attempt in September.

Since October 1923, Comintern emissaries Kolarov and Dimitrov had set up an "External Representation" in Vienna of the Bulgarian party. Kolarov had returned to Moscow, while Dimitrov remained in Vienna to run it by relaying the Kremlin's directives to Bulgaria. The ideological line and strategy of the External Representation, which completely controlled the badly shaken internal party, were perfectly clear and simple: unconditional obedience to the Comintern. All instructions, financing, and weapons for the BCP came from the Soviet Union and were received with gratitude by the activists inside Bulgaria who proudly proclaimed that their first loyalty was to "The Great Soviet State."

With the party outlawed and its leadership in disarray, the Central Committee had organized a secret conference in May 1924 on Vitosha mountain. Twenty-four delegates, led by the Central Committee's secretary Stanke Dimitrov-Marek, had attended the meeting during which the future strategy was formulated and a new Central Committee elected, including Gheorghi Dimitrov. In an outburst of "self criticism," the Vitosha conference recognized and strongly condemned the "fatal mistake" of June 1923, when the Communists stood passive as the Agrarians resisted Tzankov's *coup d' état*. The delegates approved, on the other hand, the party's participation in the September uprising, as instructed by the Comintern, and unanimously adopted a new line, recommended by the Comintern: an "armed struggle for the overthrow of the fascist dictatorship and the establishment of a worker-peasant government; preparation of a new armed uprising."

A particular effort was made to attract other leftist groups into a "united front." Radical elements of the Agrarians agreed to participate in the military preparation of the revolution.

The party's military organization took shape: a group, under Vulko Chervenkov, was to undermine the regular army by forming secret Communist cells in the regiments. Another center, directed by Kosta Yankov, was to arm and train the militant Communists. Weapons had to be procured through bribery or by stealing from army depots, a method referred to as "expropriation." New guerrilla commandos, similar to the few tchetas already active in some mountain areas, were to be created.

But the Central Committee had to recognize that the revolutionary fervor in Bulgaria, if it existed at all, was weak: the masses showed little desire to revolt. The Communists admitted this frankly: "The recrudescence of fascist terror coincided with changes in the international and the internal situations, which were favorable to the government. By 1924, the revolutionary pressure in Europe began to weaken . . . By then, we had witnessed the beginning of the temporary and partial stabilization of capitalism in Europe . . ." Recognizing the growing postwar economic recovery in the Western world, the party concluded that "Bulgaria, as well as Europe, evidenced a certain fatigue from the incessant struggle, a certain withdrawal of the popular masses from the active revolutionary struggle."

As a result, some party leaders began to question the wisdom of any increased terrorist activity at that particular moment. By the beginning of 1925, the disagreement widened. While some Central Committee members, realizing that the campaign of assassinations only provoked harsher reprisals and alienated the population, favored its temporary postponement, others, and especially the party's military center, insisted on an even bloodier action. After the Comintern's condemnation of the Bulgarian comrades' "defeatist attitude" in 1923, a syndrome of being "more-revolutionary-than-thou" became prevalent and, in 1924, few Communists were willing openly to oppose "the ultras." The Comintern instructions received continuously through Gheorghi Dimitrov consecrated the party line—the preparation for a violent, bloody revolution sometime in 1925.

*       *       *

That November night, Yankov and Minkov did not seem to be discouraged by the masses' apathy, nor deterred by the police persecution. On the contrary, they made quite clear their conviction that terror should be met with terror. Terrorism had always figured in "the arsenal of our counteractions," as Tzola put it, "but now, given the increased wave of murders in our ranks, such actions are gaining legitimacy as a means of revolutionary retribution."

"Our military center's punitive actions against brutal hangmen and overzealous servants of the monarcho-fascist regime are harsh but neces-sary," Yankov agreed.

It was long after midnight when "Sonia" left the headquarters. "Now we must live with only one thought: the uprising!" Yankov told her at the door. "Everyone and everything must be subordinated to this goal! A clenched iron fist—that's what the party must represent from now on!"

She left for Plovdiv encouraged. The Sofia comrades were determined revolutionaries who did not panic when their friends were being liquidated right and left. She had had the same impression the previous day when she met, again secretly, with Marco Friedman, a thirty-two-year-old Jew who had studied law and had been a municipal councilor. Friedman had become an outlaw after the September uprising, and now worked as liaison between the military center of Yankov and Minkov and the Central Committee. A highly emotional man, he was deeply saddened by the bad news from Plovdiv, but assured her that the government "had not yet begun to see our fury and our might!"

When she saw Friedman on her next visit to Sofia in February 1925, he looked terrible: pale, with black circles under his eyes, nervous, chain-smoking. He told her about the latest police raids and gun battles in which several comrades had perished. "We are in a war now," he said. "The time for rhetoric and peacetime demonstrations is over. We are marching toward revolution in spite of all the risks, to fight to the last man, to the final blow!"

"These butchers have pulled out the sword against us, Sonia!" he said exaltedly. "There is no room for weakness or hesitation anymore! We'll make them understand that they'll pay with their blood!"

Friedman's menacing tone became icily official when he announced to Tzola: "This is the position of the Central Committee. The worse the conflict becomes, the better for us! When everything explodes under their feet, we'll rise up and assault them. And then . . . woe to them! This is our tactic!"

It was not long before Tzola understood what Friedman meant . . .

\*        \*        \*

The West Balkan mountain, where the meandering Iskar and its tribu-taries carve narrow passages through the old mountain range, is particularly picturesque in the spring. King Boris liked to go there for hunting and hiking. On April 13, 1925, he drove to the region of Orhanié, a small town situated 80 kilometers northeast of Sofia. He was accompanied by an aide-de-camp, Captain Stamatov, by the entomologist Delcho Ilchev, by his chief hunter, and by a chauffeur. The five men, who had a pleasant day hunting and looking for rare plants and insects, spent the night camping near the fire.

It was one of those enchanting spring nights fragrant with mountain air, with countless stars bright against the total darkness, unspoiled by the proximity of any town—a night conducive to meditation and metaphysics. That was exactly the topic of the conversation around the bonfire—the hereafter.

Early the next morning they took the road from Orhanié to Sofia, an old highway that cut through the Balkan range. The road climbs along the winding valley of a small river until it reaches Araba Konak, a mountain pass situated at 2,900 feet.

Just before Araba Konak, the royal car passed an old bus, painfully huffing and puffing on the steep road. King Boris, seated next to the chauffeur, was discussing with Ilchev their favorite subject—rare butter-flies—when the first shot was heard. The bullet struck the hunter, killing him instantly. Several other shots followed, coming from both sides of the ambushed road. As the windshield shattered, the driver lost control. The car was headed toward the precipice when the king, leaning over the stunned chauffeur, grabbed the steering wheel, trying to avoid the cliff, while Captain Stamatov opened fire at the invisible assailants. Boris, an expert driver, managed somehow to control the careening car, but as it came to a halt, it hit a telegraph pole throwing its passengers onto the ground.

The fusillade continued, and both Ilchev, who was badly wounded, and Stamatov, who was returning the fire, urged the king to run away. But Boris refused to leave them, even as Ilchev fainted from loss of blood. Meanwhile, the driver of the bus, realizing that it was headed straight into an ambush, was trying desperately to make a U-turn on the narrow road. King Boris ran through the gunfire in the direction of the bus, jumped on the driver's seat and, seizing the steering wheel, turned the vehicle and drove full speed to Orhanié.

In Orhanié, the king rushed to the barracks, collected a platoon of thirty soldiers and drove the bus back to the scene of the ambush. In a ditch near the car, Stamatov was still fighting off the assailants beside the bodies of his two dead companions. Under the command of the king, the soldiers chased the attackers, who disappeared in the mountain.

*     *     *

"Indescribable scenes of enthusiasm were witnessed in Sofia this morn-ing when a *Te Deum* was sung outside the Alexander Nevsky Church as a thanksgiving for the escape of King Boris," the *London Times* reported the next day. "Afterwards there was a spontaneous popular demonstration of loyalty and upward of 30,000 persons passed through the palace grounds cheering the King, who smilingly acknowledged this expression of good will. Later there was a military parade and the troops, led by the Minister of War, marched past the King."

The prime minister, Professor Tzankov, stated in the Sobranié that documents found near the scene of the attack indicated that the ambush was the work of political insurgents rather than ordinary brigands.

King Boris had never been more popular with his people than he was that day. The *Times'* correspondent wrote, "The whole country is rejoicing at His Majesty's escape, which certainly was greatly due to his own coolness and the great gallantry shown by his entourage."

*   *   *

The attempt on the king's life and his narrow escape provoked such a shock throughout the country, followed by such jubilation, that the news of another crime committed the same evening caused less of a sensation than it normally might have. A few hours after the Araba Konak ambush, an eminent army general and member of the Parliament was mysteriously assassinated in the street. Retired General Kosta Gheorghiev, one of the founders of the Military League, had entered political life after an illustrious army career and played a leading role in the Democratic Entente party. The assassins escaped, and the motive for the crime remained unknown.

Due to Gheorghiev's prominence, a state funeral was announced for the second day after the murder, the Thursday of the Orthodox Holy Week.

The capital, still recovering emotionally from the attempt on the king's life, was truly saddened by the death of the popular general. Large crowds lined the streets leading to the Sveta-Nedelia Cathedral, where the funeral services were to be held. At 2:30 on the afternoon of April 16, a solemn procession started from the home of the victim. The casket was followed on foot by the general's family, cabinet ministers, army officers, and a large number of friends. Preceded by military bands playing funeral marches, the cortege arrived at 3 P.M. at the cathedral packed with people. Metropolitan Stefan, archbishop of Sofia, was waiting, surrounded by the clergy in gold-embroidered robes.

As the bells tolled and the bands on the square played, Gheorghiev's comrades-in-arms carried the coffin on their shoulders into the incense-filled nave, followed by the widow with her two small children. Inside the church the choir was singing as the notables took their places.

The service began. Standing next to the archbishop's throne, Metropolitan Stefan looked over the illustrious assemblage: The entire government and almost all the elite of the capital were there. Over the open coffin, the younger child fixed his eyes on his dead father, as if hypnotized. Now it was the archbishop's turn in the liturgy. The deacon solemnly placed the open Gospel on top of his head and knelt in front of him. As the choir stopped singing, Stefan's "Pax omnibus!" rang out in the total silence, as he began to read the Gospel according to St. John:

. . . Verily, verily, I say unto you, he that heareth my word, and believeth in Him that sent me, hath everlasting life, and shall not come into condemnation; but is passed from death unto life.

He had hardly pronounced the words—"from death unto life"—when an indescribable explosion shook the cathedral, louder than any thunder, deafening the ears. As the roof of the nave collapsed, burying part of the congregation and filling the air with thick dust and smoke, the stunned multitude felt that the end of the world had come. Then the screams and wails of the wounded brought back reality, a horrifying reality of corpses, dismembered bodies, blood, and pieces of human flesh in the ruins of the church. While scores of men, women, and children were killed instantly, hundreds of wounded, many of them unconscious, were trapped under heaps of brick, mortar, and beams. It was a scene from the Inferno. More precisely, it was an "infernal machine" that the terrorists had exploded in the cupola of the church.

The first image to come to Metropolitan Stefan's mind was one of a tremendous earthquake "accompanied by a sudden hurricane of uninterrupted detonations, followed by a tornado and a profound darkness." Covered with dust, he cleared his voice and shouted with all his force, "God is great. He won't abandon us! The Lord will soon send us light and air." Strangely enough, a ray of sun came through a window at this moment and pierced the obscurity and dust, in a sense worsening the horror by making visible the crushed bodies, the agony of the dying, the hands extended in pathetic pleas for help.

Resembling ghosts returning from another world, wavering and dazed, the survivors looked through the thick dust for the exits, many of them bleeding in torn clothes. Prime Minister Tzankov was alive and, although wounded, managed to walk out. Interior Minister Roussev suffered several cuts, but his life was also spared. General Todorov, the war hero and ex-commander-in-chief, desperately searched for his wife in the debris, and found her dead body. After a time, Former Minister Liapchev told the horrified crowd in the square, "Suddenly a tremendous explosion occurred and all became dark. Fortunately, I was standing almost below a pair of arches so I escaped without injury . . . A minute later, the fumes began to disperse and I found almost everyone lying on the ground. Fragments of masonry were falling from the walls and the roof . . . Gradually, amid groans and cries, the congregation began to show signs of life. There was a general rush toward the doors and windows, many of which were now wide gaps . . ."

Although none of the ministers was killed, 160 people lost their lives, and more than 320 were seriously wounded in the bombing of Sveta-Nedelia, one of the worst political mass assassinations of the century. By some odd luck, King Boris, delayed, had not attended the service. But the casualties among the ruling elite were heavy: three members of the Parliament, eleven active or retired generals, and many senior officials and officers died in the explosion, as well as Sofia's mayor and chief of police.

When it became clear that the abominable crime was committed by Communists and pro-Marxist Agrarian militants, it was little wonder that a wave of fierce and uncontrolled popular wrath swept through the country.

*   *   *

King Boris, accompanied by Princess Evdokia, had spent the morning in the village of Bali-Iskar where he attended the funeral of his chief hunter, killed at Araba-Konak. On his return to Sofia, he rushed to the funeral services for Ilchev, the other Araba-Konak victim. King Boris was just about to leave the palace, when Sveta-Nedelia's formidable explosion shook the city. The first news was very alarming: all the ministers were killed, nobody was in control, the revolution had started! The king dispatched Draganov to the Ministry of War, where, in the absence of news from the government, the duty officer had decided to declare martial law immediately. The king, very worried but calm as he always was in moments of crisis, was annoyed by the War Ministry's haste. "What do they mean 'no government'? And I? What am I here for? Tell them that they must ask *me* first!"

Meanwhile, the ministers, appearing one by one from under the cathedral's ruins, were taking charge of the situation. General Vulkov arrived in the War Ministry, and the garrison's commander put his troops on alert. Tzankov called the palace where the telephone was ringing incessantly. Boris had assembled his aides along with Princess Evdokia in the military chancery and was talking personally to the garrison commander, Vulkov, Metropolitan Stefan, Foreign Minister Kalfov, and other officials, and listened as each one described the bombing and reported new casualties. Draganov shuttled between the palace, the War Ministry, and the Council of Ministers, where the members of the cabinet, many of them with bandaged heads and hands, deliberated about the security measures to be taken. They were considering the proclamation of martial law later in the evening, and the arrest of several suspects during the night. A massive house-to-house search of the city was scheduled for early in the morning.

In the deluge of telephone calls that evening, the king received a bizarre call which disturbed him considerably. It came from retired General Alexi Stoyanov, a friend of the palace, who said in a sibylline voice, "Tonight, nobody must know where you spend the night! . . . You understand what I mean, don't you?"

Boris knew what he meant. Stoyanov was the link between him and an unusual man, Lyubomir Loultchev, who had made some disturbing predictions in the past. Loultchev was a disciple of the mysterious guru, Petar Dunnov, whose theosophic-oriented religious sect enjoyed a great success. For this reason, the king hadn't taken Loultchev seriously at first. But some of his prophecies had materialized with astonishing accuracy and, half-jokingly, King Boris began to listen. Ten days before Araba Konak and the Sveta-Nedelia bombing, Loultchev had told him that "on April 14, 15, and 16, three buildings will be destroyed in Sofia." He had promised the king that when something grave was about to happen, he would give him a warning twelve hours in advance. Now Stoyanov was transmitting Loultchev's warning: the king should not stay in the palace that night!

Boris was far from sharing his father's obsession with superstitions. Ferdinand had a passion for the occult, a deep belief in all sorts of premonitions and omens. Although a devout Catholic, he took his superstitions with a seriousness that was almost scholarly. Boris, a truly pious Christian and an admirer of science, was not interested in things like spiritism or black magic. But, like the rest of the family, he had his own superstitions, along with an attitude that "one never knows!" and that, in some cases, it wouldn't hurt to pay attention to seemingly irrational prophecies.

Of course, on the day that the cathedral was blown up, it did not take the Delphic Oracle to predict that the king's life was in danger. With or without Loulchev's warning, the entire entourage of the king urged him not to spend the night in the palace. Boris hesitated about whether to stay with his old chief of cabinet, Dobrovitch, where nobody would think of looking for him. But finally he decided in favor of his own country palace of Vrana, where he could at least count on his platoon of guards.

But he had to wait for the cabinet to submit the martial law decree for his signature. At ten o'clock in the evening, Draganov was sent once more to the War Ministry, where he learned that while the ministers were still deliberating in Tzankov's home, many opposition leaders were being arrested. He reported to the king that the newly appointed Sofia police chief "was not going to forgive anyone tonight . . ."

King Boris was upset by this report. Both he and Draganov feared that some excessive repression was in the making, which would not only irreparably damage Bulgarian prestige abroad, but would also destroy any chances for national reconciliation. While they were talking, Tzankov telephoned, and Boris voiced his fears that "some underlings may show overzealousness" in the repression, which would be disastrous. "You must issue strict warnings to the authorities!" he insisted. The king then telephoned the foreign minister and repeated his apprehensions in even stronger terms, warning of the unfavorable effect any excessive repression would have in Europe. Meanwhile, rumors about new terrorist actions—even an invasion being organized in Yugoslavia—were circulating, making the royal entourage extremely nervous. Late in the evening, Draganov and the palace inspector Guenchev went on a reconnaissance mission to Vrana and returned reporting that the area seemed quiet. At midnight, the king, Evdokia, Draganov, Guenchev, and the king's valet, accompanied by three policemen, left for Vrana in two cars. Everyone carried a loaded gun.

*     *     *

Peter Zadgorski, the sexton of the Sveta-Nedelia cathedral, had been a Communist for a long time, since the days when he worked as a motorman in Sofia. Around New Year, he met a man who called himself Ivan. After seeing each other a few times Ivan told him that he was a member of the illegal Communist party and had some explosive material to hide. "Can you help us?" he asked. "We could hide it in the church. There is no danger of an explosion." As Zadgorski agreed, every week Ivan brought a package and gave him one thousand levas. When the sexton had received twelve thousand levas, Ivan told him that a bombing of the church was planned and asked him to carry it out. Zadgorski, frightened at first, refused, but Ivan's threat to murder him combined with the promise of an important job in the Soviet Union persuaded the sexton to help. Ivan even showed him the getaway car with the driver, a member of the party.

Ivan (later identified as Petar Abadjiev, head of the terrorist section at the central committee of BCP (Bulgarian Communist Party)) assembled the "infernal machine" in March. It was a package containing fifty kilograms of explosives with five wicks. It was laid above the attic, next to the central cupola. A bottle of sulphuric acid, meant to suffocate the victims who would not be killed by the explosion, was placed next to it.

In a café in Sofia, Ivan introduced Zadgorski to another Communist, "Vasco," who had lived in the Soviet Union. They told the sexton that the king was going to be killed, and at his funeral all ministers and high officials would be wiped out by the infernal machine. With that, the revolution would begin, they assured him.

On the evening of April 14, Vasco came to the church to tell the sexton that the attempt on the king's life had failed, but that the party was looking for another important person to be murdered in order to ensure a state funeral at the cathedral, attended by the entire government and the king. Vasco came again very early on the morning of April 16, announcing that the right victim had been assassinated and that the funeral was going to take place that afternoon. Then he asked the sexton to hide him in the attic and to alert him when the members of the cabinet arrived. Shortly after 3 P.M., Zadgorski went up and gave the signal—three knocks on the door. Vasco came out of his hideout, climbed to the explosives and ignited them. Then the two men fled from the church. In the square in front of the cathedral, Zadgorski, losing sight of Vasco, looked for the getaway car, but it was not there. Instead, an unknown person came to him, handed him a beret, and led him to an apartment, where he found Ivan in the company of two young men.

"Why did you lie to me?" Zadgorski asked Ivan. "Where was the car?"

"Don't worry," Ivan reassured the frightened sexton. "I am going to bring your passport right away." And he left the house.

The two young tenants of the apartment moved a table, lifted the carpet underneath, and dismantled two loose boards of the floor. Zadgorski saw a small cave in which he was told to hide until Ivan returned. But night came and went, and Ivan did not appear. More and more frightened, the sexton remained for two days under the floor. At the end, his nerves gave out. He left the house to walk in the streets like a hunted animal before going to his son-in-law, where he confessed everything and surrendered to the police.

\* \* \*

Soon after the crime, the government placed some recently captured Communist correspondence at the disposal of foreign diplomats. The documents clearly established the role of the Comintern and suggested the connivance of the Soviet government. For instance, the police had arrested, among others, a Soviet agent with a letter from the Comintern giving orders to prepare a general uprising in Bulgaria on April 15. Most interesting was a plan, professionally drawn up, for military operations following the projected uprising in two northwestern districts. The document contained plans for the launching of armed columns from the provinces to Sofia, to join the uprising which the Communists hoped would erupt in the capital.

The *London Times* concluded that "this again is reminiscent of the plans for the Communist putsch in Estonia last December, when it was intended to seize the wireless station, send out to the world the announcement of the formation of an Estonian Soviet Republic, and appeal to the Soviet in Moscow for help."

All Bulgarians, including the opposition, were outraged by the Communist plan. The Socialist leader Pastoukhov declared that both the cathedral bombing and Araba-Konak "were part of a plan inspired abroad, not solely directed against the present government, but against all Bulgarian authorities, who were to be disorganized and destroyed in order to proclaim a Soviet republic . . . The Bolshevist threat to Bulgaria is not provoked by the government's policies. Bulgaria has been chosen as a ground of action because they think that she is vulnerable to the plans of those who wish first to destroy peace in the Balkans and then to provoke a world wide outbreak." Another Tzankov foe, Malinov, was also convinced that the cathedral outrage and all the other terrorist actions were connected. "There is an organization directing these acts, with the object of provoking anarchy, and finally revolution."

What was this organization? The *London Times* revealed that Comintern activities were being energetically directed against the Balkan states in general, and the Bulgarian kingdom in particular. Since the failure of the 1923 uprising, "Communism felt it must alter its tactics in the Balkans . . . The Comintern formed a Balkan committee which prepared a new tactical program and submitted it to a conference." This conference, held in Baden, near Vienna, agreed that "the strategic objective of the Communist International must be the formation of a federal Danubian Soviet Republic." As for Bulgaria, wrote the *Times,* the conference decided "to re-form the fighting organizations and to begin pitiless extermination of agents and accomplices of the Tzankov government by application of individual and mass terror."

\*     \*     \*

On the morning four days after the bombing of the cathedral, somebody knocked on the door of Georgi Koev, a reserve army officer presently working as an accountant. An unknown man wearing glasses and carrying a package wrapped in newspaper under his arm was at the door, asking if he could come in. Only then did Koev recognize Captain Ivan Minkov of the Army Corps of Engineers, whom he had known for several years but had not seen since the September 1923 uprising. A Communist sympathizer, Koev was aware that Minkov was an important party member involved in terrorism. Admitting that the police were looking for him, the unexpected visitor asked for a place to hide. Koev had rented the cellar in his brother's house, a peaceful medical doctor who lived a few blocks away, under the pretext that he needed it for his work. In fact, he had installed a bed and used the room to receive occasional guests.

Koev led Minkov to the hideout, walking cautiously two-hundred yards behind so as not to be associated with him. Minkov had chosen him because, as an active member of the Reserve Officers Association, Koev was unlikely to be suspected by the police.

Koev did not know that the house was already under surveillance. Later in the day, two agents presented themselves at the house, demanding to inspect the cellar. The police surrounded the house and summoned Minkov to surrender, but he opened fire. The police returned the fire and killed him. Koev, his host, was arrested.

The next day the police discovered that the head of the conspiracy, Major Yankov, was hiding in the home of a friend, a retired lieutenant colonel. They surrounded the house, summoning him to surrender, but Yankov barricaded himself in the cellar, opened fire on the police, and threw a few hand grenades. The police sent Yankov's host, who had already been arrested, to induce his comrade to surrender. But once inside the house, the host joined his friend and the firing continued for several hours.

At midnight the police redoubled their fire until the house was nearly demolished. A bomb fell on the reserves of ammunition in the courtyard and caused a big explosion. The resistance grew weaker, then ceased. Policemen and soldiers rushed into the smoking ruins, where they pulled out the two bullet-ridden bodies. Several rifles and rounds of ammunition were found in the house, one of the secret headquarters of the Communist military center.

A court martial held in the artillery barracks in Sofia established that the Sveta-Nedelia bombing was part of a vast and minutely planned assassination campaign, masterminded by two terrorist centers working in close collaboration. One was the military branch of BCP, headed by Yankov and Minkov, with activists like Friedman and Abadjiev who carried out the bombing, and young terrorists like Chervenkov. The second center was operated by radical left-wing Agrarians.

The two illegal command centers, which had at their disposal large sums of money regularly brought from abroad, had organized an elaborate network of terrorist cells. They kept several clandestine apartments in Sofia, where considerable amounts of bombs, weapons, and ammunition were stored. Both committees were in close contact with the Soviet Union, where Bulgarian Communists like Kolarov held important positions in the Comintern, as well as with Agrarian and Communist émigrés in Yugoslavia. The latter were arming gangs of terrorists in preparation for the invasion of Bulgaria when the expected revolution erupted. Underground couriers shuttled continuously between Moscow, Belgrade, Vienna, Berlin, and the numerous Sofia hideouts, carrying secret messages, false documents, money, and weapons.

*     *     *

Large crowds filled the empty field in the outskirts of Sofia where the public execution was to take place on the morning of May 27. In the center of the field, against the backdrop of the Vitosha mountain, the three white gibbets looked even more sinister under the unseasonably dark skies. The van carrying the prisoners arrived at eight o'clock. Handcuffed and guarded by soldiers, Friedman, Zadgorsky, and Koev walked to the hanging platform where the executioners, three swarthy gypsies hired for the occasion, were waiting for them. Two priests spoke to the prisoners before the state prosecutor read the painfully lengthy accusation for forty interminable minutes.

Friedman remained calm until the end, repeating that he was innocent of the cathedral bombing and that he was being executed only because he was a Communist party member. The sexton Zadgorsky, who had confessed his guilt and had admitted taking money for his part in the crime, looked stunned and pitiful. Koev was on the verge of collapse, ceaselessly protesting that he was guilty of nothing but of offering shelter to one of the conspiracy leaders.

The hanging was expeditious, Koev being the first to die, then Zadgorsky, and lastly Friedman. The public remained immobile and silent, reacting with grave solemnity to the first public hanging in Sofia for many years.

Some of the other conspirators were executed a few days later. Still others like Yankov and Minkov, had been killed while resisting the police. Several participants in the outrageous crime, including the technical organizer of the bombing Abadjiev, had fled. Abadjiev, who was readily welcomed in the Soviet Union, returned to Bulgaria some twenty years later with the grade of general.

*      *      *

One year after the Araba-Konak ambush, during a skirmish in June 1926 with a band of anarchist terrorists in Northern Bulgaria, the police captured a hidden archive including a slightly damaged letter written in ink, addressed to the king. Dated "4 June 1926, the Balkan Mountains" and signed "Vassil Popov," it contained the confession of one of the Araba Konak assailants. The original had never reached the palace, but a friend of the king obtained a copy from the county chief to bring to the king.

"In 1919, thanks to a royal clemency, my father, St. Iv. Popov, was freed from the Sofia Central Prison, where he was serving a sentence imposed during the war," the letter began. "After a few petitions failed, I appealed with adolescent idealism to Your Majesty. When I went one day to the Supreme Military Court to inquire about the results, the archivist met me with a smile. 'Your father is already free. The King has signed a favorable resolution.' What a sublime joy I felt!" As a result of the son's plea, the King had signed an order freeing the elder Popov. Although the embittered youth chose the life of an outlaw by joining militant anarchist groups, he retained a feeling of deep gratitude to the king personally. Then destiny played a trick, he wrote, making him face an impossible moral conflict.

"On the morning of April 14, 1925, an attack was perpetrated against your automobile coming from Orhaniè. The press at the time presented it as an attempt against you, and because of the chronology of events which followed, it was assumed that the attack was based on a common plan for action, prepared by the outlawed Communist party. But the true situation was as follows:

"In the beginning of April, five men, including myself, reached the mountain Gulabetz. There, while inspecting the highway area in order to select an ambush location, two of our comrades were seen by passing travelers. Thus our plan for stopping cars driving between Pirdop and Sofia, to seize from the bourgeois passengers the means we needed to support our clandestine action, failed. We moved; and early in the morning of April 14, we found ourselves in the wooded heights of Araba Konak. We had not yet positioned ourselves when we heard the faint drone of an automobile. We quickly plunged from the steep cliff toward the highway. I knelt behind the ditch along the road so I could not be seen. Three men took up positions on my right, on the steep bank of the highway, while Comrade Vassil Ikonomov remained in the woods above. (Later, he was killed in a forest in the Ihtiman district, with your binoculars found on him.)" Both Ikonomov and Popov, like the majority of Bulgarian anarchists, firmly opposed any "united front" with the Communists and acted independently of them, often in hostility.

"I turned my field glass toward the curve," Popov continued," where the automobile appeared and I recognized you. Only minutes before, my comrades and I had talked about the king's frequent excursions on the Araba Konak highway and had wondered whether he would surprise us some day with his car,—a highly unlikely supposition! The comrades talked about capturing you so that they could present political demands to the Tzankov cabinet. Sheer fantasy! Because the bourgeois Cerberus would prefer to let a crowned head become a victim than lose thousands of their own.

"Your face was very well known to us. At this instant at Araba Konak my old gratitude to you reawakened. A king saved a family from shameful ruin. Now a member of this family has to save the king from certain death, regardless of my political credo.

"In one leap I am already on the road, with pistol in hand. Loudly I shout 'Halt!' and start firing to warn you of the imminent danger. At that moment, your car moves in reverse. The naturalist, Ilchev, and your guards officer lift their rifles to open fire on me. I lie down and continue shooting. When your car hits the telegraph pole, you all jump out of it, under the fire of the comrades positioned on my right. Only your hunter, badly wounded, remains motionless inside the car. The gunfire of the comrades finishes him. Ilchev would not have been killed if he and the guards officer had not taken up positions behind the car. When Comrade Vassil Ikonomov started throwing bombs from the heights damaging the car, they withdrew. It was just on the curve, behind the car, that Ikonomov aimed at Ilchev, killing him. I wish that the captain had been killed instead! We certainly do regret the loss of a man of science.

"When they understood that it was the king that they had let escape, my comrades accused me of spoiling the attack by signaling the car to stop from a distance, instead of waiting for it to come nearer the ambush. Of course, I turned aside these accusations to conceal the truth."

After Araba-Konak, the band undertook a few highway robberies in the Sredna-Gora mountains, and then split apart. Soon after Ikonomov was killed by the police. Popov moved into northern Bulgaria where he learned that several "innocent people" were held in prison in connection with the assassination of a police chief. One of them had been shot without sentence, and two teenagers were condemned to long prison terms. That was the motivation for Popov's confession to the king. Still hiding in the mountains, he wrote:

"The executed man not only had no contacts with us terrorists, but I don't even know him. The assassination of the police chief was committed by us—myself and my comrade, who was killed. I stated this in a letter I sent to the tribunal. A policeman testified that he recognized my comrade. Why then are innocent people convicted?"

Then Popov spoke of another trial in the area in which, apart from the "justified six death sentences of terrorists," several accomplices had been sentenced to life terms, and listed their names. "For them, and for their poor children and parents, I, as a 'bandit,' have decided to lift a dark curtain from my past, to reveal a secret, to commit a crime which violates the revolutionary ethic and, stressing the gratitude of an anarchist to a king, to plead for your clemency. It's strange indeed! A 'bandit' who asks royal mercy for people in prison! So let it be! But a king must show magnanimity and nobility toward a noble brigand. Among his other prerogatives, a king must be arbiter in the social struggle. I am a brigand of the type of [Schiller's] Karl Moore, and if the king can be noble, my nobility can rival his!"

The letter ended with an urgent plea to King Boris to pardon the listed prisoners and set them free.

(The king's reaction has not been recorded. Neither is there other proof that Ikonomov's anarchist band acted independently from the Communists. The authorities have always assumed that Araba-Konak and Sveta-Nedelia were closely linked as part of the same Comintern plan.)

\*    \*    \*

The Royal Family: Princess Maria-Luisa; King Boris; Crownprince Simeon; Queen Giovanna

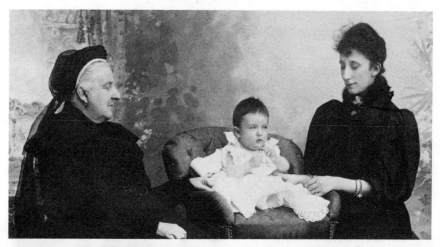

Right, King Boris' father, King Ferdinand (In Boris' handwriting: "Trop de fer-blanc" Too much tin ware)

Top, Baby Prince Boris, with his mother Princess Maria-Luisa, and grandmother, Princess Clémentine (daughter of the French King Louis-Philippe)

Above left, King Boris' mother, Princess Maria-Luisa of Bourbon-Parma

*Trop de fer blanc*

Above, King Ferdinand with his children;
Boris—Nadejda—Evdokia—Kyril

King Ferdinand's wedding to his second wife,
Queen Eleonore

World War I—Crownprince Boris at the front, with his father
King Ferdinand (face) and Austrian emperor Charles

Crownprince Boris

1918—World War I—Prince Boris with Generalissimo Jekov, and brother,
Prince Kyril, at the Macedonian front

Sofia, 1912—Coming of Age of Crownprince Boris (4th from left)—with his father, King Ferdinand, his two sisters, stepmother Queen Eleonore, brother Kyril, and all Balkan Crownprinces.

Vrana country palace, July 1927—relaxing with a few intimates. Closest confidant Draganov (moustache, violin), Princess Evdokia (piano) King Boris (drums)

King Boris' hobby: driving locomotives. (with brother, Prince Kyril)

Sofia, 1925. The cathedral "Sveta Nedelia," bombed by the communists, in an attempt to kill the King. (160 dead)

September, 1939—The popular King. Among Muslim minority population

Princess Giovanna di Savoia (future wife of King Boris), in Italian costume

Below, The Royal Wedding: the Orthodox ceremony in Sofia, which followed the Catholic wedding in Assisi.

# CHAPTER XI

# A Period of Reprisals

"**L**OOK, MY dear Parvan," King Boris said one day to Draganov soon after the Sveta-Nedelia bombing, "you advise me to strengthen the monarchy. Why should I do it? I hate the royal institution and have no desire to reinforce it. For a man to be a monarch means to have delusions that he is in direct telephone contact with God, that he is something more than the ordinary mortal. I despise this institution! I was not born to be a monarch. When I attend ceremonies, I cannot stand looking at myself sporting these dangling rattles. People treat me like a deity; little do they know that before I show myself in public I have to go five times to the toilet so I won't do it in front of them."

"But you are a different kind of monarch, Your Majesty!"

"Yes, but do you think that the type of king I represent is any good? Look, when I heard that Yankov and Minkov had killed themselves, I felt happy for them that they hadn't surrendered! What kind of monarch is that? No, that's political hermaphroditism. That's why I am always the one who gets raped. Do you think that I don't feel partially guilty for the 9th of June? Because of my weakness, I even feel guilty for the bombing of the cathedral. And you want me to stay, to prepare a new 9th of June. You want me to stay until I am completely poisoned!"

There were few periods in his life during which King Boris felt as discouraged and unhappy as in 1925. His disappointment with the politicians in power had turned into a contempt which he had difficulty hiding. At the same time, he was torn by doubts about his own ability to rule. "I'd better get out of here!" he'd often say in front of his sisters and the few intimates in his entourage. "The masses are healthy, but the intelligentsia and the semi-intelligentsia are contaminated. They interpose themselves between me and the masses, insulating me from the people. They did the same thing with The Monarch. But at least he was an imposing figure, whom they feared and respected. But I? I had contacts with the people; I am more Bulgarian than The Monarch was. I was born here; and I got used to the

'Bay-Ganios.' There is even a little of 'Bay-Ganio' in me: Look, I can swear like a trooper and use four-letter words; I tolerate being teased and I listen to vulgar jokes at table, which The Monarch would never permit. And the result? They use me as a towel, both the Agrarians and today's rulers; they use me to dry their hands . . ."

Then Boris would launch into long tirades against most of the politicians of the day. "How can you want me to work with them, when I know their past? I know their hypocrisy and their corruption. How can I respect them? I can't stand them! The Monarch also knew their weaknesses, but he used them. He never missed an occasion to remind them of some personal or family stain. He openly accused T. and L. of corruption. He told S. to his face about the commissions taken from the arms purchasing. It was The Monarch's fault. My father didn't create great statesmen around himself—in the army, yes, but not in government—because he wanted to be the only one to shine."

"The Agrarians," Boris used to say, "were crude, unpolished. They insulted me. They spoke openly against me. But they didn't have any of the perfidy of the bourgeoisie. At the beginning, they were primitive and simple. But the 'narodniaks'[1] made them cunning and taught them to lie."

The king was deeply disturbed by the repressive measures that followed the bombing of the cathedral and by the general attitude of the regime. He was receiving reports that the real power resided not so much in the hands of the Tzankov cabinet but in the leaders of the Military League—Vulkov, Roussev, Damian Veltchev, Zlatev, and other officers. Friends of the king warned him that some "cut-throat officers," some tough right-wing captains, were boasting that "if the king doesn't obey, one bullet—and that's it!"[2]

In his dark moments, King Boris talked constantly of abdicating, leaving the country, or even worse. "It won't work. These ministers are crazy. I can't do anything with them; they don't accept any advice from me. I feel like shooting myself!" When he learned that an attempt was made on the life of a prominent doctor with leftist ideas, he exclaimed, "Tout est fini! Let me end it once and for all, so nobody will have to worry about me anymore!"

This kind of talk was very upsetting for his intimates, who all had a great affection for him. Young Boris had an inborn charm difficult to resist.

---

[1]Members of the old Conservative party.

[2]Some thirty-three years later, in a letter dated July 12, 1956, Tzankov wrote to IMRO leader, Ivan Mihailov (both men living in exile), "It is clear that Stambolisky was killed by the people in whose custody he was placed. This was the same clique surrounding [General] Ivan Vulkov, which, during the entire period of my regime, purged Bulgaria from 'traitors' and 'villains.' This group was in the War Ministry, seven or eight active and reserve officers led by Vulkov."

In spite of his weaknesses (or partly because of them), people who came into contact with him invariably became attached to him. They were all sympathetic, especially his sisters who worshiped him. "I understand his indecision," Prince Evdokia used to complain. "But he should try, before he talks of quitting. He shouldn't be passive. He must act!"

Boris's deep depression did not begin with the cathedral bombing. Ever since June 9, 1923, he had been unable to adjust to the military coup or to establish a friendly collaboration with the new regime.

The polite, businesslike coolness between the king and the Tzankov government had continued into 1924 and 1925. In private, Boris had often made remarks such as, "More and more I come to the conclusion that the people of this unhappy country are good, but its leaders and its pseudointelligentsia are bad. Today's rulers are nothing but parvenus and intellectual zeros who think they are gods. In reality, they are little men, inferior, stupid, and arrogant. The present ministers have neither tact nor flexibility."

Periodically, the friction came into the open, especially on the question of the death penalty. "You should not link your name, and the prestige of your party, to the restoration of the death penalty," he told Minister Rashko Madjazov in June 1924, once more refusing to sign the decree. "If one day I ratify a death sentence, it will be only for recidivists, under the law against banditry. I won't sign death sentences under the 'Law for the Defense of the State.' " They separated without reaching an agreement.

After the meeting, Boris complained to Draganov, "Haven't they had enough blood, these people, without asking for more? They want to settle their accounts with their political adversaries by these methods. It's hideous; it's disgusting! I should quit. By staying, I don't contribute anything; on the contrary, I'm doing harm."

The ceremonial opening of the Sobranié, with Tzankov insisting on the king's reading the speech from the throne, haunted Boris as much in 1924 as it had the previous year. "The government, which is a government of Freemasons and the military, wants to use my prestige to consolidate its own position. By doing that, they are undermining the monarchical institution; by showing that I am their support, they are making me the target of Communists and Agrarians."

On the evening after the Sobranié's opening, King Boris was even more depressed. Draganov complimented him for his calm delivery of the Throne Speech.

"Calm?" Boris answered bitterly. "Yes, I read it calmly, because I have become like those girls who remain indifferent no matter who f. . . . them. I'm finished. They smeared me with their colors. I managed to preserve myself under the Agrarians, but this 'bourgeois' government has forced me twice to read their Throne Speech. The other side will never forgive me for that! Monarchs are held responsible for much lesser acts than that. Even the

Fascists in Italy spared their king: Mussolini didn't force the king to open the Fascist Parliaments."

Draganov tried to argue that if "the other side" were to return to power one day, the king would open their Sobranié too, and everything would be forgotten.

"You are too naive if you think that they'll forgive me. I survived once under them, but a second time will be impossible."

Draganov argued that if the king brought "the others" to power through a reconstruction of the cabinet, all the credit would be his.

"Reconstruction in our country? Impossible!" Boris scoffed at the idea. "I did form a coalition in 1918, but only because there were occupation troops in Sofia. Now I feel incapable of working anymore. Something inside me has been broken. Do you think that I can find peace again, after I had to hide in the fields on June 9 while people were searching through my shirt drawers? I have no feelings anymore. I performed my own Requiem on June 9. Now I am unable to love or to feel anything nice for anyone. Even with my forgiving nature, I cannot forget the morning of June 9. Now I cannot talk to nor have any feelings for anyone but the simplest peasant or worker. I am indifferent to the others. I even hate them."

"So you see, your contact with life is not lost, after all!" Draganov said.

"Yes, but on a human level only. Not as a king."

On October 24, Boris received the politician, D. Strashimirov, who had just come back from Belgrade with a message from the Agrarian exile leaders which upset him greatly. One faction of the émigrés, very much involved with the Serbs, wanted to overthrow the Sofia government with Serbian help, proclaim the republic with the imprisoned Agrarian poet, Tsanko Bakalov, as president, and work with Yugoslavia on an almost federative basis. The other faction preferred to achieve the same objective without foreign help. All of them, however, were determined to act unless King Boris agreed to replace the present government, call new elections, abolish the Law for the Defense of the State, and release Bakalov from prison.

The king became progressively irritated as he listened to the proposal. "The same Strashimirov, who only a year-and-a-half ago was pushing me to overthrow Stambolisky, insists now that I should overthrow this cabinet!" he told Draganov after the audience. "I told him that I do not make *coups d'état*. I am, and I remain, the same as I was when the Agrarians were in power. I reminded him of how many times I had warned them not to do certain things; for instance, not to fire capable army officers who would become a danger to them. But they didn't listen to me. They told me, 'We are the people's government, and you better sign whatever we propose!' Now my answer to the exiles is that I shall not pour oil on the fire."

The fall of 1924 was an unsafe period for traveling in the country.

Frequent reports of highway robbery and terrorist acts by anarchist or Communist commandos forced the king to take unusual measures for his protection. Returning from Euxinograd to Sofia, for instance, he would not board the train at Varna station but would go by motorboat to a small nearby station where he would sneak onto his train car. He would not even drive the locomotive, his great hobby. Before reaching Sofia, he would get off at another small station, where his chauffeur waited. Nobody would know that the king had spent most of the night on the train.

In early November, King Boris felt particularly discouraged and bitter after having spent a number of days with four ministers and realizing how bleak were the prospects of attracting other political parties into the government.

Boris had pleaded with them to abandon the plan for a trial against the former Agrarian ministers, which was being debated in the Sobranié. That would be "a stupid thing" to do now, he said. It would only swell the ranks of their adversaries, force other Agrarians to become political émigrés, and alienate the moderates among them, who might otherwise one day cooperate.

Boris foresaw a very dark future that day. "I see that this huge wave, the revolution, will ruin all our plans for survival and gradual stages," he said to Draganov. "You want me to do what I hoped to achieve through Stambolisky. But I can't. With my character, I am better as an appeaser than as a creator. For fifteen years, I've done nothing but that. Under my father, each time I raised my voice, he crushed me, but I was useful to him when there was a need to pacify. But now something more is needed that I can't give alone. Anyway, the events will overtake us. It will all end up in a *carambole* [carom—a billiard shot]. Ah, if my father could see me today, he wouldn't be angry with me anymore!"

Draganov insisted that things might improve for him, but Boris answered sadly, "No. We have regressed by thirty years." And he sighed, "Ah, why did my father try to do a transplant! Palms cannot grow on the Pole . . ."

Later that month, on November 25, one of the ministers arrived with a death sentence. Boris reacted strongly. "You know that I am against the death penalty," he said. "I've been fighting for this principle for five-and-a-half years, and, so far, I have managed to defend it. What you want me to do could be fatal in our circumstances. I had the same quarrel with your predecessor, Stambolisky, who forced me to sign by insisting that it was for the good of the country, that by not signing, I was encouraging brigandage. All right, I signed. But I didn't see any improvement. The brigandage continued. In any case, we agreed that I would approve death sentences only for recidivists. Now you want death for first offenders. That's a very dangerous thing. Don't think that repression is the only way to combat banditry; there are other ways. Repression and drastic measures are effective only up to a point, after which they bring the opposite results."

As the minister remained unconvinced, the king grew more adamant. "This right belongs to me and was given to me by the constitution. The legislators were very wise to put it into the constitution, otherwise you would have massacred each other. If you don't like it, then call an Extraordinary Sobranié and have it change the constitution! Then I will accede to your wishes. But if you cannot do that, then find yourself another king who will sign all your whims!"

Not only did the king refuse, he also pleaded the cause of the jailed poet, Tsanko Bakalov. "Why are you making a saint out of him?" he asked. "He has already paid for his sins; let him go! Are you so afraid of him? You act like Stambolisky who, by detaining your political friends, provoked a strong reaction and the June coup. By releasing Bakalov, you have everything to gain.

The same week, the king further irritated the government by making an unannounced visit to the railroad station's warehouse in Sofia, where he talked to the workers. The relevant minister was furious on hearing about it and wanted to punish the warehouse chief for not alerting him immediately. The government, after all, was responsible for the king's security, especially when he mixed with workers, the minister contended. Learning of the uproar, Boris asked that the warehouse chief be let alone, commenting "It's not my security that they worry about. It's not the first time I have gone incognito to the warehouse. I think they are afraid that 'the Red' in me will show in my meetings with workers."

Since the June 9 coup, Boris suspected almost all the politicians of ulterior motives. When Tzankov wanted him to go on a tour of Europe with him, especially to England, the king suspected that his real aim was to associate him in the eyes of the world with the new regime's controversial policies and actions. As Tzankov and some of his associates were Freemasons, Boris believed they were part of the war that "Freemasonry has been waging for two hundred years against all the thrones in Europe." "No, I won't go to Europe with Tzankov!"

Draganov tried to stress the positive sides of the June 9 coup which, after all, had taken care of the excesses and intransigences of the Stambolisky regime. But Boris disagreed. "That may be the way you see it," he answered, "but not I. I look at it with different eyes. And now, since they have rejected my proposal to include Agrarians in the cabinet, I see that things have taken a turn for the worse. We are headed for a revolution."

Princess Evdokia had just returned from a visit to her father and sister in Germany. "This time I found the monarch not as badly disposed toward Bo as he usually is," she told Draganov. "But he too no longer believes that Bo will be able to last much longer in Bulgaria . . ."

In summer, the Ossam River becomes very shallow and narrow and, if crossed at the right places, presents no problem for a sturdy automobile. King Boris, who was driving alone, was about to negotiate a seemingly easy passage when he heard somebody shouting,

"You'll drown, son! Don't enter, it's deep there!"

Stopping the car, he turned his head. An old, skinny peasant woman stood behind him, gesticulating animatedly.

"Where are you going, Grandma?"

"I was visiting relatives and I am returning to my village, to Doyrentzi."

"What's your name?"

"Grandma Yonka, sonny."

"Come, get in the car. Show me the road and I'll drive you to your home."

It was Sunday and the village looked deserted, as everybody had gone to the main square to dance the *horo*. Grandma Yonka's house was a very poor dwelling, but, in spite of the penury, she invited the driver to come in and share her dinner. While she warmed the dry bean soup and placed the homemade cheese and black rye bread on the table, her grandson, a soldier on leave, entered the room. He immediately recognized the king, froze at attention and shouted, according to the military rules,

"Your Majesty, I beg your permission to stay!"

Yonka was stunned. Then, overwhelmed by surprise and emotion, she started crying and apologizing,

"Please forgive me! I spoke to you like I talk to ordinary people!"

The king smiled and reassured her. "You did no wrong, Grandma! I enjoyed talking to you. I like old people."

After finishing the modest meal, he accompanied his hosts to the village dance. Long before reaching the square, one could hear the wailing of the bagpipe, the intricate variations of the clarinet, and the steady beat of the tympanum. Holding each other by the hands in a long undulating chain, two dozen cocky young men and pink-cheeked girls, all dressed in colorful peasant costumes and bursting with vitality, were vigorously stamping the ground to the rhythm of the band.

The *horo* is danced in all regions of Bulgaria and has many versions. Most Bulgarian folk dancing is choreographed for the men to display their virility and agility, and for the women to show their grace and femininity. The king admired the athletic performance of the village bachelors and the coquettish movements of the girls. They looked vibrant in their white hemp or cotton shirts, beautifully embroidered with silk of different colors, predominantly red—the women in ornate woolen skirts and aprons, the men with wide red sashes and fur caps.

Stories about the king's personal contacts with simple people, mostly peasants, had become part of the popular folklore. His reputation of being the best-liked and most accessible monarch in Europe was fed by reports of his appearing incognito in remote hamlets, helping stranded motorists, having friendly chats with illiterate old peasants, or surprising needy families with presents and financial help. People smiled affectionately at the countless anecdotes about their democratic king and his engaging simplicity.

Among the peasants—stopping his car in remote fields to talk to shepherds and harvesters—Boris felt at peace, as he only felt when hiking in the mountains or sailing on the waters. How good he felt away from the capital!

*       *       *

King Boris's moods and intimate feelings during the weeks following the Sveta-Nedelia bombing were expressed in a surprisingly candid way to one of his few childhood playmates, Ivan Stancioff, and his new American bride. The four children of King Ferdinand and the four children of the Bulgarian diplomat and courtier, Dimitri Stancioff, had been friends throughout their early youth, but the friendship between the Francophile Stancioff family and the Germanophile Ferdinand had ended during World War I. Seven years after the war, however, when King Boris heard that Ivan had brought his American bride, Marion, to Bulgaria, he invited them to Vrana.

On June 1, 1925, the Stancioffs were driven from Sofia to Vrana, where the king and Princess Evdokia met them at the entrance of the country palace. They were taken around the gardens where the flower borders were in full bloom and King Boris, acting like the internationally recognized botanist he was, proudly showed them his hothouses, pointing out the rare plants. Then he took them to dinner in the small old-fashioned dining room whose walls were covered with stuffed birds, horns and other trophies collected by King Ferdinand.

After dinner, they moved to another room for coffee. "I was riveted by the conversation that ensued," Marion Stancioff reported later. "It was more a monologue than a conversation. The princess was silent; she and the king had no doubt been through all of it together often enough." The surprised young American, a woman of great intellectual curiosity and almost militantly liberal ideas, continued, "We were all silent as the young king poured out what was weighing on his heart. He was speaking French as they had in their childhood.

" 'You can't imagine what's going on here. The horrors that have happened and are still happening. Yes, of course you know what's been in all the papers: the series of killings and attempted killings—they just missed me—the carnage at the cathedral, all those people crushed under the dome.

All that is dreadful enough. But it's a vicious circle. The horrors have been going on a long time. Repression in the villages, vengeance—personal vengeance, party vengeance—ever since they murdered the poor man, the poor great man [Stambolisky], who stood by me. Yes, Ivan, he did go too far. He lacked finesse, he was rough, I agree. He irritated people. But they didn't just *kill* him, they cut him up, they made butcher's meat of his body. It was barbaric. Of course, there was a reaction from his followers, uprisings. But then came the repressions, worse each time, and the peasants were the weaker . . . Our people are not a bad people. But with such lessons, they will learn to be savages. It was bad enough before, but now, since the events of April, it's worse. People disappearing, whole groups abducted and drowned in the Isker. People arrested for no reason. "Questioned" by the police; those they dare not let out again are thrown in the central heating. That poor Herbst—the journalist who married your mother's friend—and so many, so many, others, made out to be Communists and destroyed. Simply for convenience. Anybody who was in the peasants' party relentlessly pursued. They'll make Communists of them yet. And what can *I* do? They won't listen to me. They shed my people's blood and do it in my name. And I'm powerless. They're a mafia, with their sinister leader, and they'd like to get rid of *me*, too; you know their mentality. But for the moment I'm useful to them as a figurehead. But I'll try to last them out. Maybe I will; they are so hated. And *everyone* isn't in the gang. There are a few decent men left who are lying low. With tact and endurance and patience I might—in two or three years—be able to get a government together . . . But in the meanwhile, people suffer, disappear . . . my poor, poor country.'

"He stopped. We were stunned. The princess suggested a lemonade. She must have been worried lest he had said too much. After all, he had made accusations, named places and people which, however, being unknown to me then I soon forgot, and which my husband's loyalty kept him from ever repeating. What I could not forget was the refrain: 'Mon peuple, mon pauvre peuple,' and 'Le pauvre homme, le pauvre grand homme.'

"It was all soberly spoken, but clearly came from the depths of a tormented being. A man who knew he had to hold on to what little power the Tzankoff government allowed him, for any sign of giving up would precipitate the country into even bloodier confusion.

"Talking of it afterwards, my husband wondered what had prompted this extraordinary outburst, unique in a man who always kept his own counsel. He spoke with such deep feeling, spoke so openly (more openly than he ever did again, though I got to know him well in the next eighteen years) that we were puzzled. Why were *we* the recipients of all these unguarded, dangerous remarks? It was clear that he *had* to talk. . . . In the end we could only come to one conclusion: we were passers-by without any political ties, we were young and happy and would be able to share his human feelings without betraying him to the intriguers who were ruling in his name. We returned to Bulgaria three years later, and my husband entered the diplomatic service. Neither of us ever found King Boris in this mood or heard such words from him again."

*       *       *

# CHAPTER XII

# True Democracy

THE REPRESSION against the Communists and their allies after the abominable crime at the Sveta-Nedelia Cathedral was bloody, merciless, and effective. The Tzankov regime and the army saw it as a necessary and legitimate act of national self-defense. The public, revolted and frightened by the conspiracy, expected the government to take drastic measures for the sake of law and order and, initially, approved of the reprisals as just.

For the bombing had in fact been planned and executed by the Communist party as a prelude to a Bolshevik revolution in Bulgaria. Should it have succeeded it is possible that even so monstrous a crime might have been presented later as an "historical" and "heroic" act, or even glorified, as were the taking of the Bastille or the massacres of the Russian revolution. But since the plot failed and left a horrible stigma on the Communist movement, nobody was ready to take credit for it.

The party being infallible by definition, the blame had to be put on somebody else. But who? The Comintern and the BCP made a clumsy and totally unconvincing attempt to present the crime as a "police provocation," a pretext for massive reprisals against Communists, but soon abandoned this ploy and became silent on the subject.[1]

But the continual arrests and purges, and especially the excesses, dampened the original popular approval, disturbing many political leaders

---

[1] Even today, the Communist authorities carefully avoid the subject of Sveta-Nedelia. All documents concerning the planning and execution of the bombing are strictly classified. Although there is no doubt that no important action during this period was possible without the approval of the Comintern and BCP's Central Committee, the present official version denies the party's responsibility. It insists that the crime was an unauthorized act, a grave error committed by "ultra-leftist deviationists" and "adventurers," i.e., the party's "military center" directed by Yankov, Minkov, and Abadjiev, who acted on their own against the party's wise decision. Trying to absolve the top leadership, this version ignores the close and uninterrupted contacts of these "ultra-leftists" with their superiors, and especially with Gheorghi Dimitrov. In fact, Abadjiev found refuge in the Soviet Union.

151

and simple citizens, including members of the government coalition. As the
year 1925 advanced, the repression sapped the strength of the government.
The ruling Democratic Entente, corroded by disagreement and qualms,
began to crack.

King Boris was a major factor in the weakening of the Tzankov
government. His attitude was difficult for many people to understand,
because when Tzankov and the Military League overthrew Stambolisky in
1923, the king was a major beneficiary of the coup against the leftist regime.
Yet, in spite of the present government's professed allegiance to the king, the
nation felt that the heart of the most popular man in the country was not
entirely with his defenders.

This impression was right. As a person, King Boris simply could not
share the values and methods of the people who ruled in his name. Signing
death sentences, for instance, was something he could not force himself to
do, no matter what the *raison d'état*. In this respect too, he was different
from his father. Ferdinand approved of the death penalty, although being
superstitious, he disliked signing the execution decree with his own hand.
When a death sentence was submitted to him, he either donned his white
suede gloves before signing or, even better, summoned his aide-de-camp
General Stoyanov, whom he had taught to imitate his elaborate signature, to
sign for him. Boris opposed the very principle of the death penalty.
Learning about torture and police brutality made him sick, no matter how
monstrous the crime or how dangerous the conspiracy. He argued vehemently about it with his ministers. But he felt that they would never
understand certain sides of his character: his ability, for instance, to see the
point of view of his adversaries and even to respect some of their qualities,
and his belief that he was the king of *all* Bulgarians, the "bad" as well as the
"good," the royalists and the leftists.

In the beginning, he was highly disturbed by these "weaknesses" of his,
often doubting whether he was a good king. He felt that he had not lived up
to the standards of his father. ("Le Monarque wouldn't hesitate like this, he
was a real king, not like me!") At times he thought that perhaps he was
wrong, and the others, these nationalistic statesmen and patriotic officers
who expected him authoritatively to lead the merciless struggle against the
nation's enemies, were right. His doubts were all the more painful because
he shared most of the ideals of his officers, having fought in three wars for
the same national cause.

But time and experience helped him with his personal dilemma. Not
only did he realize that he could not change his values and feelings, but he
began to feel more confident that they were right. Excesses and brutality
cannot be justified. Good causes should not be defended by ugly methods.
There had been enough blood spilt in Bulgaria, staining Bulgaria's name.
Our Balkan neighbors are no better, he thought. Their treatment of the

Bulgarian minorities is inhuman and scandalous, but we solve nothing by hatred and terrorism. Having already achieved a remarkably democratic and civilized society in so many other fields, Bulgaria needed to behave maturely in politics as well, the king felt.

Boris never became close to Tzankov and his colleagues. By the end of 1925, as many disenchanted members of the ruling Democratic Entente became progressively restless, the king increased his contacts with them, tacitly encouraging them. As Tzankov's cabinet had outlived its effectiveness, Boris felt that the country was ready for a new government.

In the Parliament, growing numbers of the majority joined the government's critics. When the disagreement between Tzankov and his more moderate colleagues in the coalition became too deep to mend, he resigned in January 1926, and suggested as his successor the veteran Democratic leader, Andrey Liapchev.

The resignation pleased King Boris, but he remained extremely nervous and suspicious. The new development seemed too good to be true. For the first time in more than five years, a cabinet was going to change peacefully, according to the rules of the parliamentary system. Everybody in the capital was skeptical. Rumors of an impending coup circulated widely; warnings that the king was in danger came from all sides. Boris was sure that Tzankov and the Military League would cling to power. He was wrong.

In a most proper manner, Tzankov came to the palace to submit his cabinet's resignation, bringing with him his colleagues for a farewell audience. The king thanked him for doing a service to parliamentary democracy and decorated him. Then he gave Liapchev his mandate to form the new government. The crisis Boris had feared did not materialize. He sent for Princess Evdokia and Draganov, who were waiting anxiously in Draganov's office. They found him in bed, with a wet towel around his head. The migraine he had been suffering from during the last tension-filled days had become worse, but he was relieved and happy. At last, the parliamentary system had been restored in the country, he said.

The years that followed became a period of true democracy in Bulgaria. For five years, the Liapchev government, representing the center and the Right, and enjoying a majority in the Sobranié as well as the king's confidence, ruled in strict observance of the constitution. Led by respected statesmen, experienced and moderate Democrats, the government offered the country the much-needed time for recovery and normalization. As the political passions seemed to cool off, the parties of the Left resorted to parliamentary channels to express their opposition.

Other state branches also acted in the spirit of the constitution. With judges and teachers in Bulgaria enjoying a legal tenure in office, justice and education were as politically independent as in any Western democracy. The press was totally free, except when military and state security matters were

concerned, and attacks on the government, even on the king, were published regularly with impunity.

It was a period of renewed optimism in Bulgaria, of hope that the
country's ordeals were over and an era of stability and progress beginning.
In foreign policy Bulgaria adopted a more conciliatory tone, proclaiming
her unequivocal allegiance to the principles of the League of Nations and her
readiness to settle all grievances through the honorable international body.
In response, the league helped arrange two foreign loans for Bulgaria. It also
gave the league its first and, alas, only successful intervention in an international armed conflict. This unique occasion occurred during a Greco-
Bulgarian border incident in October 1925 when Greek army units crossed
the frontier to start a small-scale invasion. Instead of ordering out its troops,
the Sofia government sent an urgent appeal to Geneva. For once the league
reacted energetically, forcing the Greek forces to withdraw immediately.

The relative peace and stability encouraged a strong cultural trend,
interrupted too frequently by wars and internal unrest. In a country only
recently liberated, with no hereditary aristocracy, no big landowners, and
no really great fortunes (if one discounted a few "wealthy"—by Bulgarian
standards—families in the tobacco, rose essence, and banking businesses),
social hierarchies were based not on money but on culture. Formal education was the first prerequisite in this system, the diploma being the key to
social and professional preference. It was as hard for the grammar-school
graduate to compete in the world of the "gymnasium" (high school) alumni,
as it was for the holder of a gymnasium diploma to aspire to the privileges of
a university graduate.

The drive for a formal education, an earnest and often touching
endeavor, had top priority in every Bulgarian family. Poor, hard-working
peasants and factory workers made extraordinary sacrifices in order to send
their children to school. The studies were thorough and the methods strict
and demanding: long texts had to be learned by heart, lessons copied and
recopied, and mountains of homework absorbed. Latin was taught in high
school and, in addition, many students took classical Greek. A foreign
language—French or German—was mandatory.

A diploma though indispensable, was of course only a starting point.
What made the class difference was the degree of culture—how well read a
person was, how well versed in the theater and music, how well informed
about world affairs and scientific progress. In less than fifty years, the young
kingdom had succeeded in producing a noteworthy culture, and quite an
impressive intelligentsia, though it was not a sophisticated culture, in the
Western sense of the word. Bulgarians are not by nature sophisticated
people, nor had they had time to develop the refinement or the skepticism of
the European civilizations, let alone to become cynical or blasé. They tended
to be studious and sober, a little naive, wholesome and ready to put the

established world masters and thinkers on a pedestal. Hence, their cultural life had the vigor and simplicity of a young nation, more eager to learn and admire than to criticize and defy.

Far more than money, culture—genuine or sham—was the main status symbol, the coveted value, the "in" thing. Among the intelligentsia, it was customary to use quotations from the classics in ordinary conversation and, sometimes, a few words in Latin. Lovers borrowed verses from Lermontov and Verlaine to impress their sweethearts. It was quite fashionable to suffer from *Weltschmerz,* the cosmic anxiety of the romantic heroes, discuss Nietzsche and Kant, be interested in reincarnation and Karma. Young lieutenants' romantic dreams, rich with hussar exploits, gypsy violins and duels, followed scenarios by Dostoyevsky and Tolstoy. And everybody in town could, of course, whistle, with different degrees of accuracy, Beethoven's Fifth and Carmen's "Toreador."

Proficiency in foreign languages—at least one, usually French or German—was a must at the higher social levels. Even after the inauguration of Sofia's university in 1889, many Bulgarians continued to study abroad, primarily in Germany, France, Austria, and before the revolution, Russia. A few studied in Switzerland and Italy. The national university developed into an excellent center for higher education, but studying in the West, like traveling abroad, remained one of the ultimate status symbols. Even those who stayed home, however, had to learn foreign languages if they wanted to advance. Speaking three or four languages was not exceptional among the educated classes.

In spite of the relatively limited number of cultural events, or maybe because of it, cultural life in the small capital had an intensity unknown in most of the world's great cities, where the abundance of choice tends to have a diluting effect. In Sofia, the publication of a new book or the opening of an exhibition automatically became the talk of the town. The première of a play or an opera at the National Theater was an event awaited avidly and commented on with passion. Long before opening night, the new production would be discussed in the newspapers, with the public reading extensively about the author and the actors. When the curtain rose, all Sofia would already have a good idea of (and even strong opinions about) Ibsen's and Pirandello's Second Act or the soprano in *La Traviata.*

The new foreign films became another favorite subject of conversation, as large audiences, following the dialogue from the Bulgarian subtitles, cried with Garbo and Barrymore or laughed with Chaplin.

Native writers and poets, enjoyed tremendous popularity and were treated as celebrities, opera singers and actors and their works were studied in the schools. Reading was one of the principal forms of entertainment. No educated person would possibly admit to not having read a book that everybody was talking about. As new translations hit the bookstores, everyone would rush to read them—André Maurois one month, Knut Hamsun the next, followed by Jack London, Gerhart Hauptmann, or a new edition of *Portrait of Dorian Gray* or *Anna Karenina*. And, again, the relatively limited number of books, along with the concentration of readers, made reading masterpieces not only possible but socially essential.

Parallel to the cultural blossoming, the late 1920s were years of increased technology, rural electrification, and improved living conditions, including new road construction and public works. King Boris wholeheartedly welcomed this effort to catch up with the Western nations and his role in it became vital.

He had matured enormously during the turbulent first eight years of his reign. Physically he had aged; his face had become thinner and his head balder; and his eyes had the expression of a man much older than thirty-two. Stambolisky, if he could have seen him, would hardly recognize the "cub-wolf" of the postwar years: King Boris had gained some self-assurance and authority; his indecisiveness and doubts were less noticeable, and his moments of agonizing less frequent. He had been forced to learn the rules of the game and, having mastered them, he was now a skillful player, even if the game did not always appeal to him.

His was the kind of assurance that comes from disillusioning experiences, and some loss of inocence. He was still a lonely king, although now as an emancipated man, he felt almost free of his crippling filial dependence and the insecurity he had felt facing elder poiticians and generals. He had been too conscious of his limitations; now he was discovering his powers. Boris still did not like his *métier*, the "trade" he had inherited. But his enormous sense of duty did not leave him any alternative but to persevere in his job with the best of his talents. This duty was often a heavy burden, but, paradoxically, it made things easier, for it was among the few things in life about which he had no doubt.

The democratic atmosphere of the Liapchev years suited Boris better than the previous left-wing and right-wing governments. But he also realized that Bulgaria's condition was alarmingly precarious.

Indeed, wherever he looked, he found reason for concern. The economy was still bleeding from the exhorbitant reparation payments imposed in Neuilly, amounts as unrealistic as they were cruel. Even the Allies had to recognize the complete inability of Bulgaria to pay the astronomical sum of 2,250 million gold francs, and reduced it to one-quarter. But even this sum represented a crushing burden to the impoverished nation: the yearly payments amounted to 20 percent of the budget! In addition, since 1918 Bulgaria had supported the total cost of the Allied occupation forces, while Bulgaria's coal was going to Yugoslavia as "indemnities."

The prospects for improvement of the economy were bleak, especially without an outlet to the Aegean Sea. Although the Neuilly Treaty explicitly guaranteed Bulgaria a free Aegean port with "conditions to be fixed at a later date," Bulgaria never received one.

Another colossal burden was the growing refugee population. Since the loss of Macedonia, Thrace, and Dobrudja, more than 250,000 refugees had entered the impoverished country of barely 5 million inhabitants. By 1926, 150,000 of them still lived in great misery, waiting to be resettled. The government was trying its best, but the task was beyond its means. Conditions became so appalling, that the League of Nations and other international organizations finally began to listen to the pleas for assistance. The League of Nations appointed a special commissioner for the refugees in Bulgaria, René Charron, and approved a loan of 2.2 million pounds. New villages were built for refugees, small loans for tools and cattle were granted. The king frequently saw Charron, and the Frenchman developed a great respect for the monarch, who played a major role in arousing international interest in the Bulgarian refugees' plight. But the difficulties were enormous.

By forbidding the military draft, the Neuilly Treaty put another stress on the precarious Bulgarian budget: the 33,000 men, to which she was entitled, had to be recruited as volunteers, a costly and inefficient system. As a result, Bulgaria in 1926 was a nation with practically no military defense.

The country badly needed help from abroad. But with the memories of the last war still painfully vivid, who would sympathize with an insignificant, defeated nation vilified by its neighbors? Bulgaria had no talent for public relations. Its connections abroad could not compare with the influence other Balkan countries, the Greeks in particular, had always enjoyed; and, in the art of lobbying foreign chanceries and courting European public opinion, the Bulgarians were naive amateurs.

There was only one Bulgarian known and respected abroad. Because of his background, his achievements and his personality, Boris, "the lonely king," intrigued Westerners. There was hardly a foreign visitor who had not succumbed to his charm after being exposed to his intelligence, sense of humor, and proverbial simplicity. Even Bulgaria's critics always had a kind word to say about its moderate and benevolent ruler. If anyone could successfully plead the Bulgarian cause abroad, it was King Boris. And he decided to do so. In 1926, for the first time since becoming king, he left the country to tour Europe.

Boris's approach of moderation and appeasement was appreciated in the foreign capitals. The conciliatory tone of his Throne Speech in 1926 is typical: "Start with the positive," he said to his compatriots. "Before you accuse, before you present demands, start by expressing your gratitude: Bulgaria is on good terms with all the Balkan states; our nation enjoys the sympathy of the world. "(Which, unfortunately, sounded more like wishful thinking . . .) Counting on "the collaboration of the civilized world," he acknowledged that, "thanks to the kindly intervention of the League of

Nations, we were able to record a successful start, though it be but modest in comparison with the country's needs. The refugee loan is proof of the benevolence and sympathy felt for Bulgaria by the Great Powers, who have speedily responded to our appeal."

Apart from the opportunity it gave him to renew his contacts in Europe, King Boris was in bad need of rest. In addition to the pressure of his job, he was worried about new personal problems. His brother, Prince Kyril, had recently returned from exile deep in debt and involved in lawsuits over a family inheritance in Europe. Boris was, of course, very happy to welcome him after their long separation, but at the same time, Kyril, a charming man with no particular talents and interests in life, was totally dependent on him and could become a burden.

The two brothers, inseparable friends in their youth, had led completely different lives since 1918, which had accentuated the differences in their personalities to the point where their relationship was radically altered. The prince, an attractive, handsome man, taller and stronger than his older brother, easygoing and intellectually uncomplicated, possessed all the attributes of an aristocratic bon vivant and big spender who enjoyed the pleasures that the more sophisticated European capitals and spas could offer. Unlike Boris, he never had to face any responsibilities, to work hard, or to agonize over fateful decisions. As he was the presumed heir of the best part of Prince Philippe of Coburg's colossal fortune, Kyril enjoyed considerable credit all over Europe. Unfortunately, the inheritance was challenged and after interminable lawsuits and enormous legal expenses, the case was lost. Penniless, pursued by creditors, the prince returned to Sofia.

Those years marked the brothers for life: Boris, the serious man of duty, brilliant but tense and constantly worried, a busy worker with not enough time for his many interests; Kyril, the pleasant sportsman and playboy, relaxed, uncomplicated, a man with no particular ambition nor duties to perform. In a way, the ant and the grasshopper of La Fontaine's fable.

Kyril was given a room in the palace, had his meals with the king and Princess Evdokia, and spent his weekends with them in Vrana on Tzarska-Bistritza. But Boris, worried about him and his future, was annoyed by the gossip in the foreign press about his brother's debts, his nightclubbing and his girlfriends. The king was more than willing to pay off Kyril's debts but, having no money himself, he was unable to do more than give him bed and board.

The king, with no personal fortune, lived almost entirely on the "civil list" provided by the state. The immense family fortunes of the Orléans and the Coburgs had not benefited Boris. His grandmother, Clémentine d'Orléans, had spent enormous sums during her life, with considerable amounts financing not only the grand life style of her son, Ferdinand, but also a number of public projects and charities profiting the Bulgarian nation. King Ferdinand had also been a rich man, but his fortune had diminished considerably by the end of the war. What was left was taken by the old monarch into exile in Coburg, together with all the precious family jewelry and objets d'art. Boris, who lived very modestly for a king, had suggested a reduction in his own allowance in line with the pitiful condition of the state's finances. The upkeep of the palaces and the entertainment expenses were kept at a minimum, as were the salaries of the royal entourage and servants. There were no big receptions, galas, and state dinners at the palace, no pomp and luxury, no court life whatsoever.

Another disturbing factor in Boris's personal life was his father's increasingly capricious attitude. The old monarch, never an easy man or a loving father, became more and more difficult as the years passed in exile. Ferdinand's desire to see again "his" Bulgaria—a sincere, deeply felt nostalgia—had become an obsession; and this was combined with the suspicion that the only obstacle to his return was his son. In the first years of his reign, Boris suffered greatly from his father's criticism, his coolness and suspicion, but now he felt less hurt than annoyed by his continuous complaints and accusations.

It was a very unpleasant situation for a son who still respected his father. Ferdinand's hints about returning to Bulgaria became open requests that worried Boris. He knew that the old monarch's return was impossible at the moment—not only were all political parties categorically opposed to it, but Bulgaria's neighbors and the Great Powers had also warned against such a move. Yet Ferdinand refused to accept these arguments, accusing his son of not wanting to let him in, and even insinuating that Boris might be jealous of the former king.

In spite of all this, Boris tried hard to remain a good son. Not an anniversary nor a holiday passed without his sending affectionate telegrams and presents, no trusted traveler left for Germany without carrying a missive—all grudgingly accepted by the moody ex-king. But, it was also true that Boris was not enthusiastic about Ferdinand's return. He knew his father too well to expect him to behave in Bulgaria as a quiet, retired, old man on a nostalgic pilgrimage, looking for butterflies and edelweiss in his beloved mountains or sweetly reminiscing from a solitary rock near Euxinograd. He knew that the presence of "Le Monarque" in Bulgaria meant trouble. Ferdinand's letters still referred to "my Vrana," "my Euxinograd," "my Zoological garden," "my Bulgaria." He criticized the way Boris was running the country in front of visitors to Coburg: his lack of authority, decisiveness, and regality. He was authoritative with his sons and daughters, offering unsolicited advice, or rather, instructions. All this was not only irritating, but also politically dangerous in a country where ultranationalist groups were often disappointed with King Boris's moderation and his "softness" toward Serbs, Greeks, Communists, leftists and other "mortal enemies." In the emotionally laden atmosphere, the mere presence of the old monarch could serve as a rallying point for different forces, even if Ferdinand were sincerely determined to remain aloof.

*     *     *

King Boris first traveled in Europe in the summer of 1926 and then again in the fall of 1927. He started his trips in Switzerland, his favorite foreign country. There he relaxed, shopping incognito in Zurich and Geneva, climbing the mountains in Zermatt and Arosa, and admiring the incomparable lake views at Montreaux and Lucerne. For a few weeks, the Baur-au-Lac Hotel in Zurich became the headquarters for his Swiss excursions and trips to other countries. In the Alps, which reminded him very much of his native Rila, he spent many days hiking, discovering similar mountain flowers and comparing Bulgarian and Swiss ferns and pine trees.

He was thrilled to see, after thirteen years of separation, his former Swiss teacher, Constant Schaufelberger, who had tutored the princes in Sofia between 1909 and 1914. Prince Kyril accompanied his brother and the encounter between Schaufelberger and his former pupils was quite emotional. The Swiss noted in his diary:

"Boris has not changed much, just aged a little, naturally. The facial features have become more pronounced and the nose more prominent with a beginning baldness making the forehead look higher, but the blue eyes are still vivacious and bright, while the firm mouth under the small black mustache opens in a charming smile over his magnificent teeth. He's rather thin, looks tired, has lost the soft, sweet grace of adolescence, but not his natural elegance nor his delightful simplicity. All his personality emanates an aura of intelligence and wit, of goodness and cordiality."

In contrast, Shaufelberger found Kyril very changed, "transformed to the point where I did not recognize him: the hair turned black and wavy, the almond-shaped eyes, the Bourbon nose, the Habsburg lip, the high complexion, big and strong, the large chest thrown out, the long legs, a splendid allure, the air of a seigneurial bon vivant and sportsman untormented by an exaggerated intellectuality or moral scruples."

The days spent together in Switzerland confirmed the ex-tutor's admiration for Boris: "The older brother, who has always been superior to the younger prince in intelligence and in heart, has become a man weathered by trials, matured by misfortunes." As for Kyril, "He has remained the same nice guy as before, light, pleasant, gay, never taking things tragically, knowing conveniently how 'to open the Orleans' umbrella of indifference.' Life's vicissitudes have not marked him nor made him a deeper man. He wants to enjoy life, and his practical mind and his realism help him in satisfying his thirst for pleasures."

In Switzerland, King Boris visited the League of Nations, talked to members of the government in Bern, and met celebrities like Albert Einstein and the philosopher Henri Bergson. In between visits, he saw personal friends and relatives, had his medical checkup with Swiss doctors, indulged in shopping (mostly for official and private presents), and pursued his usual hobby of searching out shoes for his especially narrow feet. He had a hilarious time trying to speak in Schwitzerdutch, a dialect that amused him enormously and that he had mastered less well than Prince Kyril, who had studied at the Polytechnic School in Zurich.

With Schaufelberger, he crossed the high mountain pass of Furka, and went on to Zermatt, where they climbed the Gornergrat, picking flowers, and collecting butterflies. Many of the Alpine plants in Vrana and the other royal gardens had been collected personally by the king during his Swiss excursions. On these climbs, Boris sometimes opened his heart, talking about himself and his problems. He struck Schaufelberger as an unusually mature, sensitive man without personal ambitions, who had dedicated his life, with great courage, to the crushing and ungrateful task of serving his people. Boris told him about all the "obstacles, humiliations, treasons, intrigues and calumnies he had had to endure." ("What a terrible job!" noted the Swiss.) The king described how he had been "mortified and crushed by the peasant-dictator, Stambolisky, and then, after the fall of the tyrant, taken in a net of plots and intrigues by ministers who tried to compromise him . . . how he had fought back, defended himself and threatened to abdicate, an efficient weapon because of his great popularity and because only the king can rehabilitate Bulgaria, plead her cause and win precious sympathies abroad." And the king concluded his tale, smiling bitterly, "I am the mender of broken dishes!"

During his trip, King Boris went to Coburg to see his father for the first time since Ferdinand's departure from Sofia in October 1918. Many things had radically changed in these eight years, but the old monarch had not become a warmer father. After paying the respect of a devoted son in an atmosphere of polite formality and trying to ignore a few nasty remarks and complaints, Boris left Coburg feeling more upset than when he had arrived. He joined Kyril and Evdokia on a visit to their sister, Nadejda, in Wurttemberg. Comparing notes, the four children of "Le Monarque" had to admit sadly that their relationship with their father had not changed much since their nursery days.

In Paris, Boris was received by President Poincaré and President Doumergue and left a very favorable impression. In England, King George V invited him to shoot grouse in Balmoral. In Belgium, he was warmly greeted by King Albert, and in Italy, he visited King Victor Emmanuel III and his family at their summer residence in San Rossore. It was there, in 1927, that he met the king's daughter, Princess Giovanna, whom some newspaper gossip columnists had already listed among the possible choices for a future Bulgarian queen.

He kept a very busy schedule, seeing dozens of officials, political personalities, diplomats, and journalists in each country. Between the official visits, Schaufelberger suggested that he should rest in Montreux, on Lake Geneva. But Boris, who had received information that terrorists had been hired to assassinate him abroad, told his Swiss friend, "I don't want to stay in Montreux. They already have the monument of Empress Elizabeth there. I'll have mine in Lucerne, where they don't have any royal cenotaph yet."

The trips ended, however, with no incident. Everywhere Boris went, the young king of the ex-enemy nation was well received, occasioning articles in the Western press about Bulgaria that for once were not hostile and disparaging. On the contrary, many European journalists and politicians discovered a new friend—an attractive, bright and democratic king.

*         *         *

# CHAPTER XIII

# The Royal Romance

PRINCESS GIOVANNA di Savoia saw him for the first time on September 25, 1927, when he came to San Rossore to have lunch with her parents, the king and queen of Italy. She immediately noticed his aristocratic profile, the very unusual gray-blue color of his eyes, and the well-tailored dark suit he wore with distinction. Of course, she found him a bit too old for her—King Boris was thirty-three and she was just short of twenty—but she liked his maturity and sophistication as he discussed the world situation with her father. Maybe a little too serious, she thought.

They exchanged a few words in French, which she realized he spoke perfectly. Then King Victor Emmanuel made some remarks in Italian and the guest switched smoothly to Italian. During the rest of the lunch, he spoke exclusively to her parents, who seemed to be charmed by the remarkably well-informed and entertaining visitor. Giovanna did not have a chance to say anything else to him.

After all, she was extremely nervous that day, feeling very shy in his presence, but, at the same time, very curious about him. The reason this particular guest especially intrigued her was that newspapers and gossip columns had recently linked her romantically with the bachelor Bulgarian king. Their photographs had appeared side by side in illustrated magazines, predicting a forthcoming engagement. This was, of course, preposterous— the two had never even seen each other—and for a moment Giovanna considered going to Turin to visit her brother in order to avoid meeting Boris, but she was persuaded to stay.

King Boris and Prince Kyril, on their way from Rome, were spending the night at the Royal Victoria Hotel in Pisa, not far from the huge royal estate of San Rossore. Boris had seen parts of Tuscany before—his mother Princess Maria-Luisa had lived near Pisa in the dukes of Parma's Pianore palace—but had never visited San Rossore.

The vast estate near the sea, containing farms, stables and pine woods, and comfortable houses, built in the 1830s, had served as a summer and autumn retreat to King Victor Emmanuel's father and grandfather, and was the favorite vacation place of the king's children.

The royal family received Boris very warmly and, after lunch King Victor Emmanuel and Queen Elena invited Boris to bring Kyril that same night for a quiet family dinner. That evening, Giovanna had a good opportunity to talk with the guests; she discovered that the serious-looking Bulgarian king could in fact be quite amusing and warm, especially when he laughed, and that he had an excellent sense of humor. He, in return, found the young Italian princess very attractive. This was quite a pleasant discovery, because Boris's visit was not entirely without motive. Yielding to all sorts of pressures to give Bulgaria an heir to the throne, he had vaguely considered a few possible choices among the available European princesses, with Giovanna among the first on the list. Marrying a Bulgarian was out of the question: Bulgaria, according to the constitution, does not have any titled nobility, and the Bulgarians would disapprove of their king marrying a commoner. A few suitable candidates had been mentioned, such as the Grand Duchess Kyra Kirilovna, daughter of Grand Duke Kyril, the pretender to the Russian throne, or Sybille, princess of Coburg, but Boris was not overly thrilled.

Not that the king necessarily had to be thrilled and enamored to enter matrimony. A king's duty was to marry a future queen, a future mother of kings and princes, not a romantic Dulcinea. Indeed, one look at old portraits of the homely infantas at the Prado or royal princesses at the Louvre would be enough to give any nonroyal bachelor nightmares, and yet there were always dutiful (or courageous) kings and princes to marry them. But kings, after all, are human, and royal unions are obviously far more appealing when the prospective bride is blessed with looks that gratify a male eye and make the heart race. Boris was therefore eager to see what the Italian princess, about whom he had lately heard so much, really looked like.

He was delighted, but also a bit puzzled, because Giovanna was different from the young ladies he knew. Her delicate narrow face, with lovely light skin and receding small chin, was animated by a pair of lively, mischievous hazel eyes. One could not call her face beautiful in the classic sense because of her aquiline nose, a feature which, however, gave her an aristocratic distinction. Young, fresh, and graceful, the princess gave the impression of a cheerful, chirping bird.

To Boris, such a young woman was new and refreshing. The fashionable clothes she wore, her talk about the current theater and concerts, her interest in tennis, skiing, and dancing, indicated an enviable capacity for enjoyment or even frivolity. There was a quality he could not quite put his finger on—something happy, light, and feminine. Her life appeared more relaxed and joyous than his had ever been. Nor did Giovanna have much in common with most princesses he knew—his hale and hearty Germanic cousins, thoroughbred, serious maidens with schoolteachers' hairdos and large flat shoes who were excellent shots and horsewomen.

Giovanna was different from his sisters too. To begin with, she obviously did not know anything about politics—the main topic of conversation in Boris's family—nor did she seem to care about it. But in other respects, the twenty-year-old Italian was more worldly than the Bulgarian princesses. Boris, for instance, had never heard Evdokia and Nadejda discuss haute couture or hairdressers, nor seen them wear makeup or fancy jewelry. When they were girls, their stepmother, Queen Eleonore, dressed them, invariably, in austere old-fashioned garb, prim and proper enough to satisfy the monarch, who personally decided on the family jewelry they wore, on special occasions only. Later, in the sober atmosphere of the postwar years, the princesses never developed the slightest interest in clothes, girl talk or frivolities of any sort. Instead they became, especially the brilliant and politically minded Evdokia, the closest confidantes of their harassed brother, who often discussed important public affairs with them.

Yes, Giovanna is a very different girl, Boris was still thinking when he returned to his Pisa hotel. A child. But he was stimulated enough that night to continue talking about her to his brother and to Draganov until they all went to bed.

*       *       *

Compared to King Ferdinand's children, Giovanna had had a happy childhood. Born in 1907 in the Quirinale palace in Rome (where, by coincidence, Boris's mother, Princess Maria-Luisa, had also been born thirty-seven years earlier), her youth had been spent at the Villa Savoia, the Roman palace where her family had moved when she was seven. Her father, Victor Emmanuel III, a taciturn, short man not blessed with good looks, had a solid education and possessed all the virtues of a valiant soldier, but without any of the proverbial Italian light-heartedness and charm. He could speak Latin and was probably the world's leading collector of rare coins. But the unexciting, frugal monarch was a kind, if undemonstrative, father. He had succeeded his father, Umberto I, who was murdered in 1900; and since 1922 the country had been governed by the flamboyant Benito Mussolini and his Fascist party, while the king was progressively reduced to the role of a respected but powerless constitutional monarch.

The more colorful parent was Giovanna's mother, Queen Elena, a tall, stately looking but simple and warmhearted Slav, the daughter of King Nikola, the former ruler of Montenegro, the tiny Balkan principality incorporated into Yugoslavia after World War I. Educated in St. Petersburg and Vienna, the queen was a talented painter and was particularly interested in archeology. Diggings sponsored by her led to the discovery of the "Discobolo," the famous statue of a Greek discus-thrower, among other treasures. But her main activity was philanthropy, and her charitable contributions were impressive enough for her to be named "La Signora della Carita," the Lady of Charity, by Pope Pius XII.

As Victor Emmanuel and Elena were not strict parents, Giovanna never experienced the fear that Boris had of his father. But the traditional upbringing of European princesses was based on rigid rules that required a severe discipline, and that was the job of Miss Biglino, Giovanna's governess. She was very strict about the princess's studies and manners, but on the other hand capable of round-the-clock vigil when Giovanna nearly died of typhus at the age of sixteen. As a result, the princess received a solid education, primarily in history, literature, Latin, and the arts. She also spoke French and English, painted, sang, and played the piano, the violoncello, and the harmonium.

Unlike the Bulgarian royal children, the Italian princesses grew up surrounded by friends of their own age. They had parties and dances at home, went to picnics and excursions, and played tennis with young Italians of proper families. But there was no question, of course, of ever going anywhere without a chaperone: some youngish *dame-de-compagnie* had to escort them on all occasions. This strict upbringing instilled in Giovanna a strong sense of discipline and duty, but underneath her perfect behavior there was an independent, headstrong young girl with a mischievous sense of humor.

Politics was never discussed in the presence of the Italian princesses, nor did they meet any statesmen. Giovanna was eighteen when she attended her first official palace dinner for the king and queen of Afghanistan. But she and her sisters were accustomed to public appearances: since their childhood they had represented the royal family at openings of schools and hospitals, at ship launchings and galas—sometimes as often as twice a week.

But also there were vacations, the carefree weeks of playing and laughter. Giovanna was inseparable from Mafalda until her favorite sister was married, after which Giovanna became closest to Maria, the youngest. Yolanda, much older, had been married since 1923 to Count Calvi di Bergolo, while Umberto was always away at military school or with different garrisons. Giovanna never cared much for the mountain vacations, but she adored San Rossore, with the beaches, swimming, walks along the Arno and the Serchio, and the night-time fishing expeditions. She loved their tours of Tuscany, and shopping incognito in Florence, Pisa, and Lucca.

After Giovanna turned eighteen, suitors began to appear, usually cousins or scions of European princely families, with hovering old aunts who yearned to get involved in the matchmaking game. There was, of course, no way that a daughter of the Italian king could marry a commoner.

The princesses of that period thought this quite natural and would not think of marrying somebody outside their class. But the time when marriages were arranged by parents was over in the Italian royal family. Victor Emmanuel and Elena did not impose their choices on any of their children, all of whom personally decided on their spouses. Until Giovanna met Boris, she had not found any prince that interested her, and her parents, knowing her rebellious nature, never tried to force a husband on her.

One evening at the opera, soon after Boris' visit, Queen Elena took Giovanna aside during the intermission. "I have something to tell you," she said with a mysterious smile. "Mafalda told me that Prince Kyril went to see her, to ask her whether you would marry his brother, King Boris. What do you think of him?"

Giovanna was taken by surprise, although the news was not totally unexpected. "I don't know him well enough. I need some time to think about it," was all she could answer. Later, she told her father the same thing. He had never hidden his sympathy for the Bulgarian king and had always held Boris's impressive war record in high esteem, although they had fought on opposite sides.

But if she needed some time to make up her mind, Giovanna never expected not to hear from her suitor for two entire years. The idea of marriage with the Bulgarian king seemed to have died when they met again in January 1930 at the festivities in Rome for the wedding of her brother, Umberto. It was difficult to talk together during the ceremonies, especially on the day of the wedding when Boris in full uniform rode on horseback side by side with King Victor Emmanuel and the crown prince through the streets of the Eternal City. But the following day, Boris found Giovanna in her sister Mafalda's Roman house where they could finally be alone to speak freely.

There, finally, Boris told her of his desire to marry her, which she had previously only heard from some relatives. But he was pessimistic as he related the religious obstacles he had to face. It would be extremely difficult to receive the pope's approval of a marriage between a Catholic princess and an Eastern-Orthodox king, especially after the scandal, some thirty years earlier, when Boris was converted to the Bulgarian church in spite of King Ferdinand's solemn commitment. The Vatican was not about to repeat the same error. And it was impossible for the next Bulgarian crown prince not to share his subjects' religion. But Boris assured the princess that he would do everything in his power to surmount this obstacle, adding, "I have a friend in Sofia on whom I can count. He is an Italian, who I know cares for me."

The friend to whom he was referring was Monsignor Angelo Roncalli, the apostolic delegate in Sofia (the future Pope John XXIII). Roncalli, a good-natured, true man of God, bursting with peasant vitality, who had been posted in Sofia since 1925, had literally fallen in love with Bulgaria. A big-hearted, humble man with simple tastes, the Vatican delegate had learned the language and traveled so extensively in the country, by car and by mule, on foot and on horseback, that he knew its mountains, villages and inhabitants better than many Bulgarians. Many years later, he wrote to the Bulgarian Catholic bishop Stefan Kurtev: "I still keep a fine collection of photographs of these beautiful country places, and when I am tired I look through them again. Believe me, when I remember those dear people, my heart is moved and my eyes are full of tears." All Bulgarians, though most of them were Orthodox, liked Monsignor Roncalli enormously and considered him their true friend.[1]

King Boris was always delighted to chat with the bright and witty Italian, and members of the royal circle, such as the Catholic Stancioff family and the Orthodox Pavel Grouev, kept in close contact with him.

Once back in Bulgaria, Boris went from periods of great hopes to days of discouragement concerning the possibilities of his marriage ever taking place. The American chargé d'affaires in Sofia reported to Washington after the Italian trip: "Apparently, the king has not given up hope of marrying Princess Giovanna, and I understand that the ecclesiastical obstacles have not as yet been overcome. That evening, Mlle. Petroff-Tchomakoff, the lady-in-waiting, remarked that in spite of the optimism prevailing in the press, the king himself knows nothing more about the situation than what was apparent some months ago. At that time, Monsignor Roncalli told me that the question was an exceedingly difficult one and that the church could not cede on the point involved. It is obvious that the Bulgarians will not change their constitution in order to permit the heir to the throne to be other than Orthodox . . ."

A few weeks later, the same diplomat wrote pessimistically: "The impression prevails in Sofia that a marriage with Princess Giovanna is almost out of the question." People resumed speculations about other candidates. When asked why the king had not picked out the best-looking of the princesses who attended Prince Umberto's wedding, Mlle. Petroff-Tchomakoff replied, "They were all more or less *moches* [homely] with the exception of one Russian princess, Grand Duke Kyril's daughter."

Another American diplomat wrote from Belgrade: "Prince Paul of

---

[1]When leaving Bulgaria, Monsignor Roncalli made the following pledge in his farewell address: "Wherever I may go in the world, anyone from Bulgaria who might be in distress and who passes by my house at night will find a candle lit at my window. He has only to knock for the door to open to him, whether he be Catholic or Orthodox. 'A brother from Bulgaria' will be title enough for him. Two fraternal arms will welcome you, and the warm heart of a friend will make it a feast day." He remained faithful to his promise when he became Pope John XXIII, during the time of the Communist terror in Bulgaria.

Yugoslavia told me today that the young Grand Duchess Kyra, daughter of Grand Duke Kyril, at present pretender to the Russian throne, would not be averse to marrying the Bulgarian monarch, as the young lady had expressed herself favorable to this idea only recently. As Kyra is of the Orthodox faith, this match would in all probability be agreeable in Bulgaria."

Succumbing to the Serbo-Bulgarian hostility of the period, Prince Paul surprised the diplomat, John Dyneley Prince, with his wicked remarks about his Bulgarian cousin: "I asked Prince Paul whether he thought that either of these girls had a real admiration for King Boris, and he replied with vehemence, 'Certainly not. How could any girl fall in love with Boris with his wizened little face!' I could not help laughing at this sally which is quite in accord with the already recorded dislike of the Karageorgevich House for its Coburg neighbor." Then Prince Paul switched to Balkan politics: "If Boris were only friendly to us, all might be well, as we certainly do not want to and cannot absorb Bulgaria *now*, for such an addition would only give us more political indigestion, from which we are suffering badly in Croatia."

Back in Rome, Giovanna waited for another six months without any definite word. Then in July, Princess Evdokia came to see her at a royal mountain retreat near Turin, bringing the latest news from Sofia. Things were progressing slowly, she reported, but Boris was more optimistic after his conversations with leaders of the Bulgarian government and church, and with Monsignor Roncalli. It was still difficult to find a formula acceptable to all, but it was encouraging to see that everyone sincerely wanted to help the popular king.

Finally, in the beginning of September, Boris arrived in San Rossore where the royal family put him up in the seaside villa, Gombo. He was happy to tell Giovanna and her parents that he had succeeded in obtaining the blessings of the head of the church's Synod and of the archbishop of Sofia. The problems with the Catholic church had been discreetly eased, thanks to the friendly understanding of Roncalli. He was not overly insistent on a solemn commitment in advance concerning the future children's faith, even though he had to issue some pro forma warnings.

The next evening, September 3, 1930, in San Rossore, Boris and Giovanna decided to get married but not to announce their engagement officially until all formalities were settled. They both felt very relieved and very happy. For once King Boris stopped worrying. The radiant thirty-six-year-old fiancé was delighted at the thought that he, too, would at last be allowed to experience some of the joys of simple mortals.

\*　　\*　　\*

King Boris had seldom been as tense and nervous as he was on the day of October 2, 1930. He was restlessly pacing his office, crossing for the tenth time the long corridors of the Sofia palace, and impatiently calling Draganov on the telephone every half hour. "Any news from Zoupe? For Heaven's sake, what takes them so long?" Then he would go to Princess Evdokia's apartment to complain, "I'm going crazy. I can't wait anymore. Something went wrong, you'll see!"

Three days earlier, Boris had sent his counselor Handjiev ("Zoupe") to San Rossore with a personal letter to the Italian king informing him that on the previous day Prime Minister Liapchev and Metropolitan Stefan had come to Vrana with happy news: both the government and the church gave their blessing to the king's marriage to Princess Giovanna. Boris asked for Victor Emmanuel's permission to announce the engagement officially on the 3rd of October, simultaneously in Sofia and in Rome. If the Italian king agreed, he should simply cable, "The book well received," addressing the telegram to "Sokolsky, Sofia, the Palace."

Ever since Handjiev had left, the vigil had begun at the palace, involving Princess Evdokia, Prince Kyril, and Draganov. The suspense after two days grew oppressive as the hours passed, becoming unbearable by the 2nd of October. Why doesn't Victor Emmanuel answer, the king wondered. At the lunch table, he did not touch his meal while Evdokia, Kyril and Draganov speculated: maybe the Italian king had been absent, maybe he had decided to consult the duce. At dinner, King Boris was really worried. And what if the telegram were lost? The engagement would then be announced in Rome and not in Bulgaria. What a terrible blunder that would be!

Finally, late at night, a coded telegram arrived from Pisa: "Letter transmitted. Have letter for His Majesty. Am leaving for Sofia, arriving 4th October evening." Nothing more. This telegram caused even greater concern. King Boris did not sleep well that night, although he had to get ready for the celebrations on October 3, the anniversary of his accession. "King Victor Emmanuel received the letter and he still doesn't answer . . . Why? Does he disagree with the proposed date, or did he change his mind about the engagement?" Nobody could answer. The solemn *Te Deum* at the cathedral felt more like a funeral mass that day, Boris said later.

Discouraged, he went in the afternoon to the Botanical Gardens. At six o'clock a telegram arrived from San Rossore: "Happy to be able to send the book today. Please answer whether you will publish it on the 3rd or on another day, so I do it the same day. Signed: Uncle."

Alerted on the telephone, the king rushed to the palace, raced his car down the Tsar Osvoboditel Boulevard, and arrived just as Kyril, Evdokia, and Draganov, all overjoyed, were congregating in the military offices. Boris burst into the room, smiling and unusually excited. Making no effort to conceal his joy, he took off his hat and happily threw it up in the air. A few minutes later, a telegram left for Italy: "Publication of the book 4th of October 11 o'clock."

Boris's love life had been rather limited. He did not inherit any of his father's lust and taste for sensual adventures. Sex and sensuality do not seem to have played a very important part in his life. Apart from a few adolescent platonic crushes on girls, like his childhood playmate Feo Stancioff, research on his bachelor years fails to uncover any serious romantic involvement or passionate affairs.

Until the age of thirty when he resumed traveling abroad, the opportunities in Bulgaria were in any case virtually nonexistent, for he was overworked and under constant pressure in a country where every move of the king was highly visible. The period between 1925 and 1930, however, when he visited Western Europe frequently, may have been a different matter. There is no reliable information about it, but chances are that a young man with his vitality, charm, and sensitivity did not always resist a lady's appeal. Very discreetly.

"What an unforgettable day!" Draganov marked in his diary on October 4, 1930. Liapchev was expected for an audience at 9:30 A.M. to be told about the official engagement. But at nine o'clock the director of the Bulgarian telegraph agency called to ask what to do because the Italian news agency, Stefani, had already reported that King Victor Emmanuel had announced the engagement. Draganov asked him to hold the news until the prime minister was officially informed. But in the meantime, the happy news spread like brushfire and jubilant crowds began to assemble at different points of the capital. As Liapchev left the palace to inform the cabinet, Draganov took the news to Metropolitan Stefan. In the streets of Sofia, the excitement was growing by the minute. Smiling people were congratulating each other as festive throngs marched in the direction of the palace. Soon, they entered the royal gardens, shouting congratulations and hurrahs, as the members of the diplomatic corps and other officials filled the palace hall to sign the register.

At noon, the king, returning from the Council of Ministers, appeared in his car on Tsar Osvoboditel Boulevard. The cheering crowd engulfed the car, everybody trying to shake his hand, congratulating him and wishing him happiness.

"But what happened in the evening surpassed anything that I had ever seen in Sofia," writes Draganov. "Leaflets calling the population to a mass celebration were distributed during the day. The entire city was quickly decorated with flowers and flags. By six o'clock, a cortege formed in front of the Military Club and, led by the members of the government, started moving in the direction of the palace, rapidly swelling like a torrent in a flood. King Boris, looking very happy, met the procession just inside the gates. The prime minister tried to make a speech, but he had hardly uttered a few sentences when a thunderous hurrah drowned out his words. The deafening cheer, coming from thousands of throats, until some lost their voices, never stopped for two hours, as group after group and delegation after delegation crossed the palace park." After officials, students, and patriotic organizations had marched past the king, the palace gardens were literally invaded by enthusiastic crowds of simple citizens, as if the entire population of the poor neighborhoods and suburbs had congregated in the center of Sofia to celebrate the event. The popular outburst was more delirious than any previous demonstration, even more emotional than the day of the Araba-Konak assassination attempt when all Sofia had rushed to the palace to congratulate Boris on his miraculous escape. And now, five years later, there was at last a happy event to cheer about, and because it was happening to the nation's most popular citizen, everybody genuinely shared in the joy.

After shaking hands for one hour in the garden, King Boris went up on the balcony, waving and smiling to his frenetic well-wishers. When the demonstration was over, he served champagne to the ministers and the church leaders before withdrawing to his office with a few intimates.

Handjiev arrived during dinner carrying the letter from the Italian king. As Boris read it carefully, the happy expression disappeared from his face. "You see, you always blame me for not letting myself rejoice completely," he said, "but I always know that something may go wrong. I know my bad luck. Now the Italian king writes that because of their family traditions, the wedding can't be on the eighteenth as we had agreed, but has to be postponed. I know the Italians! They're not like the English. Before you even start to deal with them, they play games. But what can I do? We have to comply. I told you that one shouldn't do these things in a hurry, but you pressed me and pushed me. Now see the results!"

He was unhappy again, worrying that the wedding might be delayed for two months, even longer. After much deliberation, a coded telegram was sent to King Victor Emmanuel, suggesting a date later in October. The next day the answer arrived from Italy: the princess's family proposed October 25 as the new wedding date. Giovanna had chosen the date: her parents' anniversary was on the twenty-fourth, but in 1930 the twenty-fourth was on Friday, not a good day. The smile reappeared on Boris' face.

The three weeks that followed were the most feverish the palace had known since Boris had become king. All wedding and travel arrangements had to be made at once, celebrations had to be planned in detail, and a general amnesty was to be prepared, while thousands of telegrams and letters poured in from around the country and abroad.

Boris was under enormous pressure, happy but worried, personally taking care of minute details, noticing the few but conspicuous omissions on the long list of congratulatory telegrams (the heads of state of France, Greece, and Czechoslovakia), getting annoyed by insinuations in the newspapers that religious problems were being raised by the marriage. Happily,

Metropolitan Stefan was on his side. The shrewd churchman devised a procedure that would satisfy both the Orthodox and Catholics. He planned to meet the royal bridegroom and bride at the entrance of Alexander Nevsky holding a gold chalice, a gift from the Bulgarian church. He would then lead them halfway, to the center of the nave, where he would say a prayer, bless them, and offer them Holy Communion. Only then would the couple proceed to the royal throne in front of the altar, where the clergy would celebrate the solemn Mass. Thus, technically, no second wedding ceremony would be performed, the Orthodox prayer and blessing merely sanctioning the Catholic wedding that was to be celebrated in Italy. "A stroke of genius!" exclaimed King Boris when he heard of the plan. "The metropolitan really deserves the Grand Cordon!"

Stefan also advised the king to hurry with the wedding, lest some ultraconservative church leaders and politicians, who objected to any Catholic ceremony, attempt to create obstacles.

Boris worried about his mother's tiara, given to her on her wedding by the Bulgarian people. Would Giovanna wear it at her wedding? King Ferdinand had taken it, along with all of the valuable family jewelry, to Coburg when he abdicated. The bridegroom thought that his father might use the tiara to "blackmail" him into letting the old monarch visit Bulgaria. Or what if it had been sold in the meantime? What jewels could Boris offer his future wife? He had, himself, no jewelry worthy of an Italian king's daughter. Again he felt the old dependence upon his father, a feeling he hated by now.

As a modest man ruling over a poor country, Boris was also concerned about the wedding expenses and eager to avoid any lavish ceremonies. But Prime Minister Liapchev expressed the unanimous feeling of the ministers, and, in fact, of the entire nation when he said, "We may not be as rich as the Italians, but we'll show the world that Bulgarians know how to give their king a wedding!" A budget of 5 million leva was granted by the government.

The preparations in Sofia, and especially the amnesty decree that King Boris was determined to sign before the wedding, delayed his departure for Italy by a few days. On October 10, his fiancée cabled jokingly: "If you don't come soon I'll run away." "Please don't run away. I am coming at once!" he replied before leaving the next day by train via Yugoslavia. Prince Kyril had strong misgivings about his brother crossing Yugoslavia, advising him to travel by boat via Istanbul, but the king had no time to waste. Fortunately, the trip went without incident. A special Italian train waited in Venice, where the official trip began. In Pisa, the bridegroom was met at the station by King Victor Emmanuel, Princess Giovanna, and her sister, Maria. There the fiancés embraced and kissed each other for the first time in public.

In San Rossore, King Boris and his small party were again put up in the villa at Gombo, a charming wooden cottage on the beach, three miles from the main villa of the royal family. The same evening Boris was received by Victor Emmanuel for a private discussion. His future father-in-law told him about the agreement he had reached with the pope. At first, the Holy Father had insisted that the bridegroom address to him a personal handwritten letter asking permission to marry Princess Giovanna and promising that the children of the marriage would be Catholic. But Victor Emmanuel objected, saying that King Boris should not have to do more than the prince of Hesse, who had married Giovanna's sister Mafalda, had done. He should, that is, simply countersign the letter that the princess would write to the pope without putting specifically his own commitment in writing before or during the Catholic wedding ceemony. After some insistence by the Italian king, the pontiff accepted the compromise.

Boris was greatly relieved and put his signature next to his fiancee's on the letter she had written to the pope. When he returned that night to the villa, he told Draganov, "I am happy about this arrangement. But I know that one day I'll have to pay for it. I don't know how exactly, but I'll pay for it. You'll see! . . . The pope is a hard and intransigent man. No wonder that Cardinal Maffi, who knows him well, says that prayer about him: 'Please, God, either open his eyes, or close them forever.' " That same evening Victor Emannuel proposed that his daughter's money be deposited in Boris's name. A very wealthy man himself, he knew that his future son-in-law had no fortune of his own: King Ferdinand and Princess Clémentine had spent the larger part of their Orleans inheritance, while Boris's mother, Maria-Luisa, one of twenty-four children of the duke of Bourbon-Parma, had inherited very little and left nothing. But Boris refused. "No, it's better to leave it in her name," he said. "That way, if I am killed, at least the money will remain hers."

The following morning, Giovanna arrived at Gombo in her car to take Boris for a ride. They spent the whole day alone together for the first time, and then met the family for dinner.

Two days later, Boris left on a short trip to Munich to meet his father to talk about the diadem and the jewelry. He returned very pleased with full hands: King Ferdinand had given him the tiara of Princess Maria-Luisa and a jewel of Boris's grandmother, Princess Clémentine. "Le Monarque," who was gratified to see his son marry a princess of an important dynasty, had also promised to attend the wedding.

The wedding, a splendid affair that delighted the Italians and thrilled all Bulgaria, took place on October 25 at the St. Francis Cathedral in Assisi, the favorite church of the bride. Assisi and its celebrated patron saint had, indeed, a special place in the heart of the pious princess. Giovanna, like millions of Catholics, considered the compassionate thirteenth-century protector of the poor and of animals among the most inspiring and lovable figures in Christianity. Since her childhood, Princess Giovanna had visited

Assisi at least once a year, staying sometimes for an entire week to attend services at all the churches and to visit monasteries and places connected with St. Francis. She had spent months embroidering a magnificent vestment that she offered to the poor Assisi church of St. Damian. There was never a doubt in her mind that when the time came for her to marry, she would have her wedding in the old town she knew and loved more than almost any place in Italy.

The day came and the church of the poor man's saint filled with glitter, uniforms, and princely titles. An unending succession of trains and ten thousand automobiles poured festive crowds into the narrow steep streets of the ancient town. One hundred thirty-five correspondents invaded Assisi. Behind a cordon of schoolchildren, carabinieri, bersaglieri, royal guards, and milizia men, all in full uniform, the sidewalks were packed with people by the early hours of the morning. Three hundred little girls in white dresses, each carrying a white rose, waited impatiently in front of the gates of the "upper" church while the guests began to arrive.

Prince Kyril and Princess Evdokia were there. Nadejda, expecting a baby, could not attend. Old King Ferdinand, resplendent in his Bulgarian general's uniform, adorned with an incredible amount of decorations, cordons, and ribbons, managed to walk majestically with the help of his cane in spite of his gout. Mussolini was there, in diplomat's uniform, leading his ministers and Fascist leaders. Next to him was Liapchev, a paunchy white-bearded figure in white tie and top hat, accompanied by his Bulgarian colleagues.

King Boris, in general's uniform with britches and black boots to the knee, wearing the collier of the highest Bulgarian decoration—"Sts. Kyril and Methodi"—arrived in the Italian king's car. At that moment, a heavy cloud burst, and a violent rain mixed with hail drenched the cathedral square. But the crowd did not budge an inch, chanting delightedly: "Sposa bagnata, cento anni fortunata!" ("The raindrenched bride has a hundred years of happiness!")

Princess Giovanna was brought to the church by her brother, Crown Prince Umberto. The Bulgarian general, Stoyanov, A.D.C. to King Ferdinand and the A.D.C. of Prince Umberto escorted them in the car. In spite of her stage fright, the young princess could not keep from giggling when the brave general, trying to make conversation, declared solemnly, "Yes, I know your country. I was here when they killed your grandfather."

Giovanna looked magnificent when she appeared, radiant in her white velvet wedding dress with an extralong train, a veil of old lace, and a small bunch of orange blossoms from Sicily in her hand. The crowd greeted her enthusiastically as all the church bells in the holy town rang festively.

The ceremony, celebrated by a Franciscan Father Antonio Risso, was short. After Boris and Giovanna were proclaimed husband and wife and the rings exchanged, the bridegroom took the arm of his bride to lead the official cortege to the "lower" church where St. Francis is buried. King Ferdinand with Queen Elena walked behind the newlyweds, followed by King Victor-Emmanuel escorting the queen of Greece, Prince Kyril with the duchess of Parma, Prince Umberto with the bride's younger sister, Maria, still crying, and finally the remaining princesses, princes, dukes, counts, and high dignitaries. After a brief service at which a 160-voice choir sang, Giovanna prayed at the altar of St. Francis. Finally, the bridal couple signed the wedding certificate at the altar containing the relics of the Assisi saint. The witnesses for King Boris were Prince Kyril and his brother-in-law, the duke of Wurttemberg. Crown Prince Umberto and Giovanna's brother-in-law, Count Calvi di Bergolo, signed for the bride.

After the religious ceremony, the crowds rushed to the center of the city where the newlyweds and their witnesses signed the civil marriage act at the Town Hall. Benito Mussolini acted as Crown's Notary. (On the day of her wedding, Giovanna saw the Duce for only the second time in her life; she had seen the Fascist leader only once before at the Opera.) The Senate's president Federzoni officiated on behalf of the state. After receiving a thunderous ovation from the crowd outside the Town Hall's window, the couple drove to the Villa Costanzi outside Assisi where three hundred guests attended the wedding luncheon. Giovanna was wearing a tiara and the red ribbon of the Bulgarian order of St. Alexander across her chest. Daring aviators of the air force, the pride of Italy, flew low over the villa, dropping bunches of flowers decorated with Bulgarian and Italian tricolor ribbons.

The departure scene at the Assisi railroad station was filled with emotion—hugs, kisses, tears—as Giovanna called "Arrivederci" to relatives, friends, and old servants. The band was playing "Shoomi Maritza," the Bulgarian national anthem, a melodious anthem, she thought, but unfamiliar to her ears. She took a last look at the familiar faces as she headed to the train's car where her new compatriots were waiting. They all looked friendly, the uniforms were good–looking, their voices pleasant, and yet everybody and everything was so new and so foreign. For a brief moment, she was seized by the kind of panic that most brides experience at the realization that their maiden life has just ended. But before she could think, "What have I done!" Boris smilingly took her hand to lead her to the car, reassuring her. He had had his bridegroom's moment of panic, but that was *before* the wedding. Now he looked happy, anticipating their honeymoon voyage across the Adriatic, the Aegean, and the Black Sea.

The voyage to Giovanna's new country was not an unmitigated success, as cruises go. It started at Brindisi, where the newlywed's train from Assisi arrived in the morning. The *Tzar Ferdinand*, the best of the three ships that formed the entire Bulgarian civilian fleet at that time, was waiting at the dock, shining in her new white paint. The snappy sailors looked immaculate in their navy blue uniforms. The couple was welcomed by an admiral in a splendid black uniform, the only Bulgarian admiral, a man with no great looks but with great charm and a name unlikely even for a Bulgarian—Varyklechkov. Bidding a tearful good-bye to her brother Umberto and her sister Mafalda, who had come with their spouses on the train from Assisi, Giovanna boarded the spotless ship.

As the sea was heavy, the courteous Varyklechkov offered the royal couple his own cabin, situated in the middle of the boat where the rolling of the waves is least felt. As the ship's orchestra continued to play romantic music, the new queen, deeply moved, closed the door and lovingly examined the bridal cabin. Suddenly, her hand felt something hard under the pillow: the nice admiral had forgotten his pistol. Customs seemed to be different in her new country, she thought.

The romantic music did not last long. The *Tzar Ferdinand* encountered heavy weather, huge waves furiously smashed the deck, forcing half of the seasick orchestra to retire to their cabins for the rest of the trip. After an hour, the royal bride also disappeared to her stateroom, violently seasick. Four small Italian destroyers escorting the honeymoon ship were so badly buffeted by the wild sea that King Boris asked them by radio to return to Brindisi, which they reluctantly did. The sea calmed down a little when the ship passed the Isthmus of Corinth and spent the night between the Greek islands. The next morning she crossed the Aegean and entered the sea of Marmara. King Boris was pleasantly surprised by the warm reception from the Turks, for Istanbul greeted the newlyweds with cannon salutes and cheers.

Passing through the Bosporus, the *Tzar Ferdinand* entered the Black Sea. Soon, four shark-like, metal-gray vessels appeared from the north and as multicolored signal flags were hoisted on their masts, their cannon fired salutes. That was the entire Bulgarian navy—four old, minuscule torpedo boats that had come to salute their supreme commander and his bride as they reached Bulgarian waters. From the deck of the ship, King Boris delighted in showing his wife the coast he knew so well and loved more than any in the world. "Here is Ahtopol . . . Now, there is Ropotamo, an enchanted tropical river, with the flora and fauna almost untouched," he pointed out proudly. "Sozopol, with its windmills and ancient wooden houses, a painters' paradise . . . you'll never see beaches like that in the rest of Europe . . . This is the Little Island, where our Naval Academy is, . . . Sveti-Ivan which they call the Big Island . . . and Bourgas."

The end of the sea voyage! Bourgas, largest Bulgarian port on the Black Sea after Varna, was where the new queen set foot on Bulgarian soil for the first time. An enormous crowd was assembled at the port, cheering wildly. As a small party boarded the ship, the queen recognized two familiar faces: Prince Kyril and Princess Evdokia. With them was Metropolitan Illarion who offered her an exquisite icon of Jesus Christ. As the royal couple disembarked, the military bands played "Shoomi Maritza," the crowds broke through the cordon of soldiers and police, and scores of enthusiastic citizens poured water over the magnificent carpets in front of the rather surprised queen. "An old custom," explained Boris. "May everything run smoothly like floating on water."

The crowds at the Bourgas railroad station were equally frenetic, cheering the royal couple and nearly crushing them, offering blessings and small gifts, trying to shake their hands. Giovanna, delighted, was moved by such an outpouring of popular affection. The train left for the overnight trip to Sofia, where the newlyweds arrived in the morning amidst an indescribable noise: the engineers of all the nearby locomotives were saluting their royal fellow-engineer with their whistles.

Sofia's mayor greeted the couple with the traditional offering of bread and salt as the king and queen stepped out of the train onto the red-carpeted platform, where all the members of the government had come to meet them. A gilded open carriage drove them through the garlanded streets, where the entire population of the capital was converging toward the Alexander Nevsky Church.

Metropolitan Neophyt, the ranking member of the Holy Synod, gave the benediction and a solemn *Te Deum* was sung by all the bishops in the church, which was packed with the highest state officials, members of Parliament, diplomats, generals, and prominent citizens. Outside, gun salutes shook the windows of the festive city as all the town bells rang wildly, announcing that the popular "tzar" had given the nation their "tzaritza." Officially, and with the blessing of the Orthodox church, Princess Giovanna had become *Tzaritza Ioanna*.[2]

*　　*　　*

---

[2]The Orthodox celebration in Sofia infuriated Pope Pius XI, who severely denounced "the second marriage" and reproached his delegate Monsignor Roncalli for not having prevented it. Roncalli, a less rigid and more understanding prelate, preferred to interpret the Alexander-Nevsky service as a mere blessing ceremony rather than a second wedding. But he accepted part of the blame. "More painful to me," he wrote two months later, "is the sense of the uselessness of my attempts to persuade the king to make a simple declaration that would have explained the significance of the October 31 marriage, a declaration that would have averted the solemn words of the pope that cannot have been very pleasant for his Majesty. . . . In any case, the Holy Father's language could not have been more balanced and kind."

# CHAPTER XIV

# The Bloc Years

A MOST SURPRISING event—so unusual in Balkan politics that the cynics were talking of a miracle—occurred in Bulgaria in June 1931. General elections had taken place and, although organized by the ruling Democratic Entente, the government lost! King Boris regretted seeing Liapchev go, but, like all believers in democracy, he saw the orderly defeat of the respected statesman almost as a tribute to his regime of lawfulness and moderation. It was, indeed, an encouraging sign of democracy in action.

Five-and-a-half years in power had worn out the Liapchev government, and a new middle-of-the-road coalition—democrats, agrarians, radicals, and liberals—came to power under the name of the Popular Bloc. The old Democrats' leader, Malinov, became prime minister, to be replaced only a few months later by his close associate, Nikola Moushanov, a distinguished-looking gentleman with a well-groomed mustache, Western manners, and a skill for political mediation and maneuvering. The urbane Moushanov worked in harmony with the king.

For another three-and-a-half years, parliamentary democracy flourished in Bulgaria, with all its advantages and shortcomings. The Bloc regime continued to assure a high level of freedom for citizens, opposition parties and the press, and found respect and understanding abroad. If the regime was criticized, it was not for civil rights abuses, but for its factionalism and for the partisanship of the professional politicians. The proliferation of small splinter parties and factions took on ridiculous proportions. The ruling coalition was kept alive at the price of continuous bargaining between the partners for ministerial and high administrative jobs, resulting often in the appointment of eminently incompetent officials. Stories of nepotism, illiterate ministers, and favoritism became the daily staple of satirists and cartoonists, badly eroding the popular respect for politicians.

In other periods, such flaws of the parliamentarian system have mattered less, because, in spite of them, the record of democracy in Bulgaria was impressive. The proliferation of political parties was a common disease shared by most Western democracies. But the wind of totalitarianism was blowing with increasing strength in the world of the 1930s. In comparison with the weakening central authority in France, Germany, and other democracies, the Fascist experiment in Italy, with all its vitality and glamor, had impressed various circles abroad, including Bulgaria.

The Democratic Entente, now in opposition, was also going through an internal crisis, with its younger members grouped around the former premier, Alexander Tzankov, against its more parliamentary minded leaders. In July 1932, the Entente split. Tzankov's wing, favoring basic state reforms, grew rapidly, proclaiming itself a national "movement" rather than a "party," thus showing its disenchantment with the traditional parties. Ideologically, Tzankov's movement, without shedding its democratic credo, was interested in some aspects of the authoritarian philosophy.

The Fascist experiment—as later the Salazar regime in Portugal— appeared very successful at the time and appealed to another political circle, the group called Zveno. (The word means "link" or "bond.") Zveno brought together some of the politicians and reserve officers who had masterminded the overthrow of Stambolisky in 1923, as well as a few independent intellectuals critical of the party system. It was a very small circle, but because of the drive and ambition of its leaders and its army connections, it gained considerable political influence. Zveno was critical of King Boris and, in general, skeptical about monarchy as an institution.

This was the political climate in 1931 and 1932, the first "Bloc Years." Welcoming the relative peace, and immensely popular with the people, King Boris played the role of a somewhat aloof arbiter between squabbling, but otherwise respectful, politicians. At the same time, he kept a watchful eye over would-be innovators from the Right and the Left who were bent on reforming Bulgaria and this imperfect world.

*       *       *

Holding its breath, Sofia waited and counted. Everybody had heard the first cannon at ten o'clock that morning, but one or two isolated gunshots do not necessarily mean much. Then a third salvo resounded in the bleak January day, with a fourth coming at exactly the same interval. As the regular succession continued, it became clear that the event had taken place.

Friday the thirteenth, January 1933. Wasn't it a little early, earlier than had been predicted? Nine, ten, eleven shots . . .

Smiling faces appeared behind frosty windows. In the snow-covered streets, pedestrians in heavy overcoats and galoshes stopped in their tracks to listen. The king had a child! The great, long-awaited news! But a boy or a girl? Fifteen, seventeen . . . At the twenty-first gun salute, the city stood still in silence. A few moments passed . . . nothing happened . . . the cannons were mute. It was a princess.

Soon after, exuberant crowds filled the streets, joyously marching toward the palace. Children left their classes, employees emptied the offices, and an enormous, noisy procession formed spontaneously as on the day of the royal wedding. People shouted "Hurrah!" until their faces turned blue. Many wept for joy.

The new thirty-nine-year-old father appeared on the balcony, looking happier than ever, eyes shining, voice trembling, controlling his emotions with difficulty. The crowd burst into "Shoomi Maritza" as King Boris tried to thank his people for sharing his joy. Once again, for a few unforgettable hours loaded with emotion, the transfiguration of the modest monarch into a symbol occurred, as people eagerly merged their identities into his. It was one of those sublime, almost mystical, moments when thousands of people suddenly see their aspirations, fears, ordeals, and joys personified in one human being, see themselves and their own lives represented by the personal life of another.

Without seeking it, without even trying, King Boris possessed the quality capable of triggering such national feelings. At certain moments, he *was* the nation: on his day of accession in 1919; on the day he escaped the Araba-Konak ambush; on the day of his wedding. And he was the nation today, when his first child was born.

It was as though every Bulgarian shared the joy of being the parent of the child. Was it possible then for the newborn princess of Orthodox Bulgaria to be anything else but Orthodox? But because King Boris had committed himself to baptize his children, except for the future crown prince, in the Catholic faith, he had a serious problem. The painful negotiations with the Vatican before his marriage came to mind, reviving memories of the excommunication of his father. But on the other hand, he could not afford any political mistake at this moment: the campaign in favor of an "Integral Yugoslavia," meaning the incorporation of Bulgaria into a larger Yugoslav federation, had intensified, and taking away a king's child from his subjects' religion could have serious consequences for the dynasty.

Boris decided to act swiftly. Only two days after her birth, the baby was christened into the Eastern-Orthodox rite. The day before, the king explained his action to his confidant Draganov in a coded telegram to Berlin: "In today's extremely difficult conditions and in view of the 'Integral,' I have no recourse but a *fait accompli*. Therefore, I have decided with the prime minister to have an Orthodox baptism tomorrow morning, the fifteenth, although the child is a girl . . . I know already the anger that this will provoke in the Vatican. As Roncalli here threatens to pour all this out on my wife, I am acting hurriedly in order to use the arguments that my wife, who is still recovering from the birth, has nothing to do with it, nor is her mother an accomplice. The latter will arrive the afternoon of the fifteenth. Tell all this to Firmen [Mussolini]. Make him personally aware of the secret, that although my wife has given me *carte blanche*, I don't want to pay her back for her noble and patriotic moral support by letting her drink the bitter chalice of the Vatican's wrath. I beg Firmen to give me his powerful support when the bomb explodes so that the Vatican's thunderbolt falls on me. In my wife's present situation, I am the only one who bears all responsibility . . . I am fully aware of the gravity of my decision, but under today's conditions, there is no other solution. Anything else will profit the 'Integral' neighbor. Therefore, remembering Firmen's advice in Assisi that often in life there are moments when the best thing a man can do is to offer a *fait accompli*, and accepting personally full responsibility, I have decided to do it."

The baptism, performed by Sofia's Metropolitan Stefan, took place in the small palace church of Saints Peter and Paul. Except for the Sobranié's president, the venerable statesman Alexander Malinov, who was chosen as godfather, and the baby's nurse, no one attended the christening, not even Prince Kyril or Princess Evdokia, both Catholics. The baby was given the name of Boris's mother, Maria-Luisa. The king had considered the names of Elena, in honor of his mother-in-law, or Clémentine, after his grandmother. But Queen Giovanna, always fascinated by the image of the gentle Maria-Luisa, dead before her time, preferred the name of her romantic heroine.

For the Catholic relatives and the Vatican, the whole affair had a familiar look, a déjà-vu quality. Bulgarian monarch wants to marry Catholic princess; the pope is opposed unless all children are Catholic; monarch accepts the conditions and the wedding takes place; child is born; monarch forgoes his promise and child is baptized Orthodox.

But, in fact, the situation was quite different. Ferdinand was Catholic, but Boris was not and, therefore, could not be excommunicated. Besides, the Vatican's power in 1933 was not the same as it had been in 1895 when Ferdinand broke his promise. The world had changed, and the Orthodox baptism of a Bulgarian royal child hardly sent shock waves around Europe. The world was realistic enough to understand the compelling political reasons. Even the Italians were not overly distressed, especially after Draganov transmitted King Boris's confidential message.

Draganov, the military attaché in Berlin at that time, left in secrecy the same evening he received the king's telegram. He arrived in Rome the next day and went to the Palazzo Venezia, where he was received by Mussolini. The duce, seated behind the desk of his huge office, listened carefully as Draganov told him about the Orthodox christening which had taken place the morning before. At the mention of King Boris's worry about reprisals from the Vatican, Mussolini twisted his mouth in a grimace of contempt.

"Of course His Majesty had to act the way he did!" he said. "One shouldn't give the campaign in favor of Integral Yugoslavia any ammunition. That would mean the obliteration of Bulgaria."

Draganov reminded him of the advice the duce had given King Boris at the wedding in Assisi. Mussolini smiled, gladly confirming it. "Yes, the *fait accompli* is sometimes a necessity." Repeating that King Boris had done the right thing, he went on, "Now, what complications can be expected and from where? From the royal family, none. From the Vatican? What can it do? To him, nothing. To the queen? There is a gradation in Vatican sanctions. I think the pope cannot remain silent and will protest. I'll send our ambassador to the Vatican to see the pope's secretary, Pacelli, to try to find out what the mood is there. We'll explain what you just told me, without mentioning that it comes from His Majesty, of course. The Vatican has no interest in seeing an Integral Yugoslavia either. I believe that the whole affair could be settled with a letter from the pope, through his secretary, to the Italian royal family, congratulating them over the happy event and expressing his sorrow that the commitments pledged at the wedding have not been honored. And with that, the case will be closed. The worst he can do is excommunicate the queen. We'll try to avoid that. But even if this should happen, for Heaven's sake, we are not in the Middle ages; we are in the twentieth century! Anyhow, I don't think the pope will force things now. It's a bad moment for the Church: Russia, Lithuania, Mexico, and now Spain . . . no, the Vatican has no interest in opening a new wound."

The duce promised to help and, as Draganov was leaving, he said, "Give His Majesty a private message for me. Even if the Vatican does something, tell him that he shouldn't give a damn about it. We are in the twentieth century. And if there is a God, He is neither Catholic, nor Orthodox; He is the same for everybody. And if He doesn't exist, then He doesn't exist for anybody!"

The Italian king, hearing of Draganov's presence in Rome, sent a message that he wanted to see him the next morning. He received him with a big friendly smile and asked many questions about Germany and the German army, of which he had a high opinion. Then he talked about the birth of his granddaughter Maria-Luisa, announcing happily that he had talked to Queen Giovanna in Sofia one hour after the birth. A few hours ago, he said, the Italian queen had telephoned from Sofia, saying that the baby was beautiful. Draganov started explaining the reasons for the Ortho-dox christening, but Victor-Emmanuel interrupted him, "Of course! The king couldn't do anything else! It's very natural: the country is Orthodox and the king's children must be Orthodox too."

He then asked what Mussolini had said about the matter, adding: "I am not as optimistic as he is about the Vatican. I know the priests too well. They are not people you can rely on completely. When I talk to an army officer and he says yes, I know that it is yes. It's not the same with the priests. Today they'll tell you yes, and tomorrow they'll do something else, explaining that the circumstances have changed and that, anyhow, they meant something else when they said yes. But in this case, the king has nothing to worry about. What can they do to him? They'll be angry, they'll protest, and that will be the end. And the queen? She must follow her husband. She's in an Orthodox country, so her children have to be Orthodox. God doesn't distinguish between Catholic and Orthodox. I am not very good about religion; I still haven't understood the difference between the Catholic and Orthodox explanations of God the Father, and the Son, and the Holy Ghost . . . Those things don't belong to our time anymore."

Both Mussolini and Victor Emmanuel turned out to be right: the Vatican issued a restrained protest, more of a formality, without taking any drastic sanction. In Sofia, a Catholic friend, the young diplomat Ivan Stancioff, was sent to break the news of the baptism to the papal delegate. Upon learning that the Orthodox ceremony had already been performed, the understanding Monsignor Roncalli only asked: "But Her Majesty the queen doesn't know it, does she?" He was too diplomatic to expect an answer. He had, however, to write an official letter of protest to King Boris, more in regret than in anger: "I think of the pain of the Holy Father and of all good Catholics around the world; and then I myself grieve that no real advantage can accrue either to your royal family or to the Bulgarian people from these continued outrages [soprusi] to the human conscience . . ."

But in fact, Roncalli understood well Boris' position and was not surprised when he received the king's reply: "You know perfectly well, Your Excellency, that by family and baptism I was a Catholic. If I have acted as I have twice over, it was solely out of concern for the interests of my country. The Holy Synod was beginning to doubt my loyalty toward the Orthodox Church. The Communists seize upon anything that can turn the people against me. I have to do all I can for this torn and divided country."

The pope was highly displeased but did not punish the innocent queen. But in order to avoid any risk of sanctions, the queen and Monsignor Roncalli discreetly agreed that she should in the future attend Mass privately at the delegate's private chapel rather than in Sofia's Catholic church.

As Giovanna's mother, Queen Elena, arrived only after the baptism, she was spared any embarrassment. A Slav by blood and educated in Orthodox Russia, she was in any case not likely to show any great Catholic zeal. King Boris and all Sofia made a great fuss over her. She was the honor guest at the traditional *Te Deum* for the troops and the splendid military parade celebrated yearly on January 19 in front of the palace, usually in freezing weather. A gala performance of Tchaikovsky's *Eugen Onegin*, one of Queen Elena's favorite operas, was offered in her honor. She left Bulgaria the happiest of grandmothers. There was no sign of any family resentment about the Orthodox christening of little Maria-Luisa.

*      *      *

The world's Great Depression affected Bulgaria during the Bloc years. Although there was no hunger—the country always produced abundant food—money was painfully scarce. Many public construction projects had to be postponed, and the unemployment increased alarmingly. Salary payments were several months behind, with periods when the state could only pay half-salaries. Officers and teachers were forced to borrow money in order to subsist; it was a time for drastic economies. King Boris set an example in 1931 by voluntarily reducing his "civil list" from 6 million levas per annum to 5 million. The queen and Princess Evdokia followed his example.

It was during this period that Bulgaria's economic dependence on Germany began, a gradual process with grave consequences which soon became irreversible because of market imperatives and the shortsightedness of the other Western powers. The world crisis forced the big food producers such as the United States, Canada, and Argentina to sell their products at prices so low that small agricultural countries like Bulgaria could not compete. Besides, England, France, the United States, and most Western nations were simply not interested in trading with Bulgaria.

If many Bulgarian exportable goods were not always of the quality offered by competitors, Bulgaria's vegetables and fruit, dairy products, eggs, tobacco, and rose essence were first class. Nevertheless, the Western markets judged them inferior, not quite fit for their people; in addition, the absence of Aegean Ports made them uneconomical to transport. Moreover, the lack of solid foreign currency discouraged most Western exporters. It was a vicious circle: with almost no exports, Bulgaria was deprived of hard currency, and without currency, it was unable to import from England, France, or the United States.

Germany was the exception. The Germans, also hard up for currency, started buying tomatoes and poultry, grapes and pork, wheat and tobacco, everything that Bulgaria could offer, and they asked for more. Less choosey than the rich countries' consumers, the Germans would buy mediocre, even low quality goods—Germany was insatiable. Unable to pay in hard currency, they bartered their industrial goods—machinery, automobiles, electric equipment, household appliances—that developing Bulgaria needed badly. It worked beautifully for both nations. For Germany, especially after the Nazis took over in 1933, the trade became a political tool. Imperceptibly, but inexorably, Bulgaria's dependence on the Reich started spreading from the economic sphere into the cultural, technological, and military fields.

Some foreign diplomats in Sofia, aware of the danger, strongly advised their governments to counter the creeping German infiltration, by resuscitating trade with Bulgaria. They implored London and Paris to consider commerce with the former enemy, even at a financial disadvantage, for political reasons before it was too late. But to no avail. The West, disinterested in Bulgarian chickens and beans, felt that if it needed Oriental tobacco, the Turkish and Greek leaves would do.

During his European travels, King Boris repeatedly urged the English, French, Swiss and Italians to buy his country's products, but without much success—business and commerce were not his forte. Nor were the Sofia governments very enterprising or successful. In fact, few Bulgarians at the time had reason to complain: the "Deutscho," as the population called the Germans, were buying everything in abundance, while supplying them with tractors, cranes, bicycles, and all sorts of manufactured articles at reasonable prices. The Germans were efficient and friendly and, as old comrades-in-arms, showed understanding for the injustices done to Bulgaria.

\* \* \*

Travelling abroad had become a pleasant annual habit for the royal couple, and in the summer of 1933 the king and Queen Giovanna visited Italy, Germany, Switzerland, England, and France. For Boris, it was the best time for relaxation, his only opportunity to mix with people without being recognized, to go shopping, or to the theater, or to dine out incognito. Registering in hotels as "Count Rylski," he took enormous enjoyment in these little pleasures of private life (including obsessively trying on new shoes for his narrow feet), and when he had a chance to hike in the Alps and collect botanical specimens, he was a very happy man. Sometimes, on the way home, he enjoyed the extra bonus of driving the Orient Express locomotive, a hobby that made foreign railroad officials rather nervous but delighted the train personnel in Bulgaria, where his machinist's skill had been admired for years.

There were additional reasons for the 1933 trip. The queen, not recovered completely from the birth of her first child, was having problems in conceiving a second child, which the king wanted fervently. They consulted specialists in Germany and Switzerland, where the queen underwent some treatment. But there were moments when the anxious king lost hope of ever having a son.

He tried to combine the medical visits with meetings with foreign statesmen. The royal couple accepted an invitation from King George V to spend a few days at Balmoral, where Boris had shot grouse as a bachelor in

1927. This time he went shooting with the king and his son, the duke of York (the future King George VI). While there, Boris had ample opportunity to talk politics with George V and with Prime Minister Ramsay MacDonald, also a guest at the Scotish castle.

After a brief stay in London to see the Prince of Wales, Boris and Giovanna spent a few days in Paris, where the king met with the president and with a few French politicans and journalists. With his remarkable French, and the Orleans and Bourbon blood in his veins, his cosmopolitan manner charmed the Parisians; many ears and hearts, closed so far to anything concerning Bulgaria and her Saxe-Coburg-Gotha dynasty, became receptive. Pleasantly surprised, the usually critical press turned very favorable, and when the royal couple left France, Bulgaria could count on several newly acquired friends.

*     *     *

His conversations in England helped King Boris make up his mind about a bold step he had long been contemplating: to take the initiative in meeting with the king of Yugoslavia. By coded telegram, he instructed his aide-de-camp in Sofia, Colonel Panov, to approach Belgrade discreetly and probe the terrain. The time was not propitious for an official visit, which would certainly provoke a strong emotional reaction in both countries. But what about an informal, "improvised" encounter when King Boris and Queen Giovanna's train passed through Yugoslavia? At the Belgrade railroad station, for instance.

It takes courage to extend a friendly hand to an enemy. In the eyes of most Bulgarians, King Alexander of Yugoslavia was the symbol of Serbian chauvinism, the nation's number one enemy. Hatred and feelings of revenge had poisoned relations between the two neighbors ever since the Second Balkan War of 1913. The loss of Macedonia—still a national trauma—the harsh treatment of Bulgarian minorities in Yugoslavia, and the presence in Bulgaria of a large number of embittered Macedonian refugees made it difficult for the two Slavic countries to overcome their mutual resentment. The IMRO's terrorist activities represented another major obstacle: Belgrade was outraged that Bulgaria tolerated the terrorist organization, but the Sofia government was powerless or unwilling or simply afraid to curb it.

In the early 1930s, the revival of German nationalism began to worry the victors of World War I. Revisionist feelings—never dead in the nations punished by the 1919 peace treaties—were reawakened in Bulgaria and Hungary, causing considerable concern in Central Europe and the Balkans. The Little Entente, dedicated to the preservation of the status quo, was formed in Central Europe, made up of Yugoslavia, Rumania, and Czechoslovakia. These nations, afraid both of Bulgarian revisionism and Italian aspirations in the area, envisioned in addition the creation of a Balkan Pact. Among the chief architects of this regional project, obviously aimed at the neutralization of Bulgaria, was King Alexander.

In fact, Alexander Karageorgevich, a true autocratic ruler, hoped that Bulgaria would join the pact, thus recognizing permanently the status quo. And although the idea—an anathema to IMRO—was not acceptable to the Bulgarians, King Boris, the born conciliator, had not rejected outright the few advances made by his neighbor. At the risk of offending the IMRO and many nationalistic Bulgarians, he looked for ways toward a reconciliation with Yugoslavia. He had to act discreetly, but as he began to gain in self-confidence, he felt ready for bolder initiatives. In May 1933, thanks to the more conciliatory attitudes of both governments, the two countries, which had had no economic relations for thirty-seven years, signed their first commercial treaty. Suddenly, conditions began to improve in other areas, the atmosphere became less hostile, and a new hope for friendship was born.

This did not mean, however, that King Alexander was prepared to make concessions. A true heir of the native Serbian dynasty of the Kara-georgevichs (in contrast, the Bulgarian, Rumanian, and Greek royal families were all of German origin), he wanted peace with the Bulgarians, but on his terms. As a Serbian nationalist who had fought valiantly against them in two wars, he had no particular sympathy for his traditional adversaries. But he cherished the idea of a Greater Yugoslavia, a true federation of all southern Slavs, including Bulgarians.

Alexander was Queen Giovanna's first cousin: their mothers were sisters, the daughters of the former king of Montenegro. Giovanna, al-though much younger than he, had known him since childhood—"Sandro" was a favorite nephew of her mother, Queen Elena, and had visited her family on many occasions. Boris had met him in 1912, when they were both crown princes: Alexander, six years his senior, had come to Sofia for the ceremonies attending Boris's coming of age.

Alexander had succeeded his father, King Peter, under peculiar circum-stances. Peter, who had reigned since 1903, had gone into exile in Greece during World War I; and not until one year after the victory in 1918 did he return to the newly created Yugoslavia and then as a private citizen wearing a long white beard. He no longer considered himself king and refused to live in the palace, but moved by himself into a villa outside Belgrade. Peter was not close to his son Alexander, but having disinherited his oldest and favorite son, Prince George, Alexander had by necessity become regent at the end of the war, taking over the state's affairs.

Alexander had hardly any family around him. He did not get along with his brother George, a violent and emotionally imbalanced young man. His sister chose to live in Switzerland, while his uncle Arsène, a colorful bon vivant, lived in Paris. His only friend in the family was his cousin, Prince

Paul, Arsène's son, a cosmopolitan Anglophile educated in France and at Oxford, whom King Peter had brought back to Belgrade and treated as an adoptive son.

Alexander had acted as regent until his father died in 1921. One year after being proclaimed king, he had married the Rumanian Princess Marie. He was then thirty-five years old.

Alexander had always been the consummate soldier, both in appearance and in soul. The military uniform he wore constantly, was not the splendid flashy model in which monarchs are usually painted but the old worn-looking service garb that he sent periodically to be cleaned and mended. As a rigid and sober bachelor, he had led a Spartan life in a modest house across the street from the palace, sleeping in a soldier's bed in rooms furnished more like an officer's garrison quarters than a royal residence. Comfort, family life and other civilian pleasures had not seemed to interest him much. He read and went hunting. True, the Karageorgevich dynasty had no fortune, but he had pushed frugality to the point of wearing mended socks and using darned handkerchiefs. His only self-indulgence was the cigarettes that he smoked constantly.

If Alexander's lack of fatherly affection, lonely bachelor's years, war record, or late marriage reminded Boris of his own past, there was nothing similar in the way the two Balkan kings ruled their countries. Alexander, for a start, was resented as a Serb by his Croat, Slovene, and Macedonian subjects, while at the same time he was considered too European by the Serbs, and thus he never had the popularity Boris enjoyed among the Bulgarian people. The old King Peter was entirely Serbian. "We are peasants. My grandfather was a peasant," he used to say. But the Western-educated Alexander, who tried to be not only king of the Serbs, but the unifying symbol of all Yugoslavs, had lost contact with his popular roots.

He was, moreover, a cold authoritarian man with enormous self-confidence, a ruler and commander who, unlike Boris, never hesitated or showed doubt. He had also changed from a constitutional monarch to an autocrat. For sensing the danger of disintegration within the fragile Yugoslav federation, tired of the quarrels among its heterogenous population, and disappointed by the ineptness of the political parties, Alexander felt that the only way to preserve the state was to dissolve Parliament and personally assume all power. The metamorphosis intrigued King Boris, the conscientious practitioner of limited monarchy, and he followed it with the fascination any professional feels for the experiments of a colleague in the same trade.

Colonel Panov's answer reached Boris just before he left England. King Alexander had agreed to the meeting on condition that it be presented as a Bulgarian initiative. Boris accepted.

The Orient Express carrying the Bulgarian royal couple stopped at the

Belgrade station on September 18, 1933. If Alexander was overjoyed to welcome the king of Bulgaria, he certainly did not show it. As Boris, smiling and friendly, greeted him with a warm handshake, the Serbian host stood there, still and formal, mumbling some polite formula of welcome. It had the effect of a cold shower. But then Queen Giovanna appeared from the door of the sleeping car, beaming and making no effort to conceal her joy at seeing her cousin. "Sandro!" she exclaimed cheerfully, "I'm so happy to see you again!" A smile appeared on the severe face as his cousin hugged him spontaneously. With the ice broken, the meeting in the station's VIP reception room proceeded cordially.

As they sipped Turkish coffee, Alexander brought up the subject of the Balkan Pact. The project had advanced to the point where Foreign Minister Yevtich was working out the last details with two of the most brilliant diplomats of the epoch, Rumania's Foreign Minister Titulescu and Turkey's Ruzhdy Arras. Boris, listening with interest but without committing himself, assured his host of Bulgaria's desire for friendly relations. When Alexander told him of his impending visit to Rumania, Turkey, and Greece, Boris extended an invitation to him to stop in Bulgaria.

At the end of September, King Alexander and Queen Marie's destroyer, *Dubrovnik*, sailing from the Rumanian port of Constanza to Turkey, stopped in Varna. At the pier, decorated with Bulgarian and Yugoslav flags, King Boris and Queen Giovanna received their guests with honor salutes and military bands and drove them to Euxinograd for tea. The two Balkan monarchs resumed the conversation begun at the Belgrade station, and it continued through dinner. By this time they were talking like old friends. After dinner, the Yugoslav couple returned aboard the *Dubrovnik* to proceed to Istanbul.

By the end of 1933, as the four Bulgarian neighbors were frantically laying the foundation of the Balkan Pact, an alliance obviously directed against Bulgaria, King Boris, undaunted, was sparing no effort to develop friendly relations with them.

Thus, after initiating the ice-breaking meeting with Alexander, Boris improvised an encounter with Turkey's Ruzhdy Arras, another architect of the Balkan Pact. Again the meeting had a railroad setting. For when the diplomat was crossing Bulgaria on his way to Europe, the king unexpectedly boarded the Orient Express and was able to talk to him all the way to the Yugoslav border. Then, on October 30, he met with his northern neighbor, Rumania's King Carol, at the Danube port of Rousse. The two monarchs sailed for several hours on the Rumanian royal yacht allowing Boris to review the situation with his colleague and with that virtuoso of Balkan diplomacy, Titulescu. A promise of a new friendship was born that day, with Carol extending an invitation for an official visit to Bucharest in January of the following year.

Meanwhile, after his visit to Turkey, King Alexander proceeded to Greece where in February 1934, the Balkan Pact was signed. Bulgaria, who saw the new alliance among its neighbors with apprehension and suspicion, did not join. But Boris, still determined to pursue his quest for reconciliation, did not decline his new friend Alexander's official invitation for a visit to Belgrade. Early in December, King Boris and Queen Giovanna arrived on a state visit to the Yugoslav capital, where they stayed at the royal palace. The Moushanov government and a large segment of the Bulgarian public, seeing new hope for peace in the Balkans, applauded the visit. But in many Macedonian and nationalistic Bulgarian circles, fears of a sell-out caused considerable dismay.

Alexander received the Bulgarian guests warmly, but did not fail to say in his welcoming speech that only "the consolidation of the existing order" could guarantee a better future for the two nations. Boris spoke of peace and friendship, but carefully avoided the thorny subject of consolidating the status quo in the Balkans, which every Bulgarian knew meant the renunciation of claims to Macedonia, Thrace, and Dobrudja.

When the German foreign minister von Neurath later visited Sofia, the king told him that he had originally found the idea of a Balkan Pact acceptable, and that he had even told Ruzhdy that Bulgaria might collaborate. "But when the Greeks insisted that Bulgaria should recognize the status quo, and therefore forever reject any revisions, the king felt forced to refuse his collaboration," von Neurath reported. "But in order to dispel the impression that Bulgaria is the perennial troublemaker in the Balkans, the king tried to communicate with the kings of Yugoslavia and Rumania on a personal basis."

Boris told von Neurath that he was trying to reach a rapprochement with Yugoslavia, "on which all Bulgaria's future depends," but that he had to do it very quietly, because the Macedonian faction would totally misunderstand any friendship with Yugoslavia. "The king believes that only through this kind of policy can the Macedonian interests be best served. He is also convinced that by following this policy, he is in great danger of being shot, at any time, by Macedonian bullets."

\*     \*     \*

In February 1933, the names of three Bulgarians appeared in front-page headlines all over the world: the Comintern activist, Georgi Dimitrov, and two of his compatriots were arrrested in Berlin and accused of participating in the sensational burning of the Reichstag.

In fact, Dimitrov, a fifty-one-year-old Communist militant who has fled to Moscow after the 1923 abortive uprising in Bulgaria, was more a Soviet citizen than a Bulgarian. A totally committed party member, an effective organizer, and audacious conspirator, he belonged, together with Kolarov and other Bulgarian Communist exiles, to the group of expatriates who lived in Moscow, were schooled there, and operated under Russian instructions. Dimitrov had been involved with the perpetrators of the Sofia cathedral bombing, and was, like Kolarov, active in the affairs of the Comintern, the international branch of Bolshevism.

After the arrest of Marinus van der Lubbe, an obscure twenty-three-year-old Dutch Communist caught at the scene of the Reichstag fire, the police searched for three foreigners who had been seen repeatedly in Lubbe's company in a Berlin coffeehouse. A few days later, the suspects were recognized by a waiter, arrested, and accused of complicity. Dimitrov, Blagoy Popov, and Vassil Tanev admitted being Communist militants traveling on false passports but vehemently denied any connection with the fire.

It was indeed doubtful that the three Bulgarians were involved with the Reichstag burning, and later evidence pointed to the Nazis themselves as the real perpetrators of the crime, for the new regime needed a pretext for a massive purge of its enemies.

The trial of the Communist "arsonists" that started in Leipzig in September caught the attention of the entire world. After the incoherent Van der Lubbe had pathetically admitted his guilt, Dimitrov emerged as the star of the trial, an eloquent, arrogant, and brave defendant, who, defying Goering himself, unabashedly proclaimed his Communist beliefs. Seeing a great opportunity for publicity, he transformed the Leipzig courtroom into a world tribune for Communist causes. Dimitrov became a sort of national hero when he shouted his pride in being Bulgarian, citizen of a nation that had, he said, a highly developed culture when his German accusers' ancestors were still half-civilized.

The Leipzig trial caused considerable emotion in Bulgaria, and King Boris, true to his abhorrence of capital punishment, used all his influence to prevent a death sentence for the three Bulgarians. When he visited Germany in the summer, the pretrial investigation was still going on under the supervision of Goering, then minister of the interior. When the king paid him a visit, he brought up the question of the accused Bulgarians. Queen Giovanna reports that he told Goering very firmly: "You are not going to condemn Dimitrov who is absolutely innocent in the Reichstag fire, as you know better than I do!"

It is difficult to determine the impact of Boris's intervention. But it is well established that the new German leaders had good reason to court the king of Bulgaria. The fact remains that while van der Lubbe was condemned and executed, Dimitrov, Popov, and Tanev were acquitted, though deported. They left for the Soviet Union where in due course Dimitrov was promoted to a key position in the Comintern. Within twelve years, Georgi

Dimitrov, a man totally obedient to Stalin, became the person responsible for all Communist activities in Bulgaria, often overruling the Bulgarian party leadership itself.

*   *   *

Ever since the National-Socialists started assuming power in Germany early in 1933, King Boris had been worried about his sister Nadejda and her family. As the relations between the Nazis and the ducal House of Württemberg deteriorated, Boris, through his confidant, Draganov, warned his sister and her husband Albrecht several times to restrain their criticisms of Hitler and his party.

In the summer of 1933, Albrecht's older brother, the duke of Württemberg, was continually harassed by the Nazis. On August 19, 1933, the day of the plebiscite that gave the final victory to Hitler, bands of SA thugs in brown uniforms arrived at the duke's residence in Stuttgart demanding that the duke vote. The Württembergs had never voted since the German monarchy was abolished in 1918, nor did they vote this time. By midnight, an angry mob had invaded the palace, broken down the door, seized the duke, and brought him to police headquarters, where he was submitted to humiliating treatment. It took Goebbels' personal intervention to release him. Soon after, the duke was expelled from the German reserve officers' association.

Nothing had happened so far to Nadejda and Albrecht; and as the tensions grew in Lindach, the palace where they lived, they kept a low profile. But not low enough for Draganov—a trusted friend of the former Bulgarian princess since her days in Sofia and Vrana—who was alarmed by her outspokenness. He warned King Boris that the mail and telephone conversations were in all likelihood being read and tapped, and they themselves followed. But because of the importance the Nazis attached to the Bulgarian king, his relatives in Germany were not harmed. Nadejda was nevertheless relieved when the Bulgarian minister in Berlin received instructions from King Boris to be at her disposal in case of trouble.

A few weeks later, King Boris was distressed by terrible news. Doctor Arthur Meyer, one of his few personal friends in Germany, had come one evening, very perturbed, to the home of Colonel Draganov to tell him that the Nazi authorities had submitted him to a rough interrogation and searched his house after telling him that they had received several anonymous letters accusing him of illegal foreign currency transactions. Meyer, a good friend of the Bulgarians in Berlin, was a Jew. Draganov called the Bulgarian minister Pomenov, who arrived immediately and, knowing that Dr. Meyer had been close to the king since his childhood, offered to intervene.

Meyer, still very upset, returned to his apartment. The following morning Pomenov and Draganov learned that the doctor and his wife were dead. Unable to bear the harassment, Meyer had shot his wife and then himself.

Boris was profoundly shocked by his friend's death. On November 17, 1933, the few friends of the Meyer family who dared attend the Jewish funeral were surprised to see the entire staff of the Bulgarian legation, headed by Minister Pomenov. The wreath he laid had a large ribbon with an inscription in bold letters: "From your good friend, Boris of Bulgaria."

The wreath did not pass unnoticed in Nazi circles. It was the first of many future acts which made the Bulgarian king suspect in their eyes. A future ally? Maybe. But never a truly sincere friend, they must have thought.

*   *   *

On December 1, 1933, Draganov received a message that King Ferdinand wanted to see him at the Hotel Bristol in Berlin. On arrival, Ferdinand received him as imperiously as ever in his hotel suite. After a brief exchange of amenities, he started asking questions about Boris's last trip. Why had King Boris not come to see him before he returned to Bulgaria, as he had promised? Was it premeditated? Draganov explained that unforeseen complications had prevented the king's visit—a meeting with the prince of Wales in London, a delayed appointment with Hérriot in Paris. Then the wait for Belgrade to confirm his meeting with King Alexander. That's why, instead of coming to see him personally, King Boris had written a detailed letter about the trip.

At this point King Ferdinand exploded. "I received this letter. But I was flabbergasted by my son's insult! I never expected such an affront from him, and I don't deserve it!" The old monarch was getting angrier and angrier. "I'll never forgive him for this, never, and I want you to cable him that right away, today. I wanted to tell him of my indignation in an open telegram, but I restrained myself. Instead, I came to Berlin especially, to do it through you."

But what was the insult, Draganov asked. Still shivering with anger, Ferdinand pulled out his son's letter.

"I am not in the habit of reading my mail to others, but I'll read you this," he said. In the paragraph in question, Boris had complained that during an earlier meeting his father had denied that he had made an application to visit England. But when Boris went to Balmoral, the king of England confirmed that Ferdinand had indeed taken such steps. Boris was hurt by Ferdinand's not telling him the truth, which he interpreted as a lack of trust.

"That's not true! That's an insult!" raged the old monarch. "The Ornithological Society, in preparing their international congress in Oxford, sounded the British Foreign Office about my presiding at the congress. The society took this initiative without my knowledge and the Foreign Office rudely turned them down . . . "

"But, Your Majesty, you cannot blame King Boris for not knowing this, especially when King George himself told him that the application had originated with you."

Ferdinand turned the verbal barrage against George V. "And what does my going to England have to do with the king of England's sermon to my son about my desire to return to Bulgaria? That is none of his business. It's not up to the English king to give me permission to return to Bulgaria. This question is entirely in the hands of King Boris, who thinks that present conditions don't allow it. But how could he permit the king of England to talk like that about me? To say that my returning to Bulgaria would be 'unfair'? I can't understand how King Boris could allow this crowned imbecile to discuss my affairs instead of minding his own business! To talk like this about me, King Ferdinand, in front of my own son!"

"Do you think, Your Majesty," Draganov intervened, "that King Boris liked him speaking like that? But what could he do? After all, this is the king of England, and an older man. I think that you should be pleased that King George is preoccupied by your return to Bulgaria. You are not a private person, and probably all diplomatic chanceries are discussing the problem of your return. It doesn't depend only on King Boris; it depends on the foreign governments."

Ferdinand handed Draganov a pencil and paper. "I can forgive him only if he apologizes," the ex-king said. "You must send him a cable. Now that you know my position, I want to see what you tell him."

While Draganov started drafting a telegram suggesting an apology, Ferdinand asked many questions about his son's meetings with the Rumanian and Yugoslav kings.

"I saw the photos of him and the Rumanian king . . . he looks vulgar and cynical. I am curious to hear how he behaved with King Boris. You know, we are related more closely to him than to the Serbian king. It's a blood relationship while the Serbian is a relative only through Queen Giovanna."

Draganov could not provide much detail, except that King Boris was pleased and that the talks had been cordial.

"I have always said that King Alexander is a very intelligent and positive man," Ferdinand commented. "He is doing a great job for the Balkans and for Serbia, but he has been the most dangerous enemy of the Bulgarian people. And though I am pleased that King Boris has started this policy, he should have taken the step long ago. Three years ago, when he went through Belgrade I told him to arrange a meeting. Remember, I was the first one to receive poor King Peter in Nish, a good fellow, an honest gypsy. I worked well with him, although the English King Edward was angry with me for three years! Finally, he came to me one day in Marienbad and said, in German: I couldn't forgive you until today for shaking hands with the man who came to the throne after such a terrible massacre."[1] But now it is very difficult to work with the Serbs; they are too intransigent. Maybe it would be easier with the Rumanians."

The anger had subsided enough for Ferdinand to make some flattering remarks about his son. He had heard that the Hungarian foreign minister Goembosch, after a visit to Bulgaria, was telling all Budapest that King Boris was the most intelligent man he had ever met. Then Ferdinand spoke of what an excellent impression King Boris had made on him at their last meeting, what a brilliant mind, what logic, what wisdom—a real pleasure to hear him talk! He was also very complimentary about Queen Giovanna: he had found her matured and was impressed by her talent to observe, her understanding of the Bulgarian character, and her quick mastery of the Bulgarian language. "That must come from her Montenegro blood," he remarked.

Ferdinand then ventured an analysis of his son's character: "He goes too far in pondering over things. He cogitates too much over each step he has to make. He thinks too much about the consequences. But politics is not mathematics; one has to practice it with great élan, as I did. He should steer the wheel in the direction he wants, as I did, even though I had to fight against the distrust the entire nation felt for 'the foreigner' that I was . . ."

"But in a way it was easier for you, Your Majesty, because you were alone at the steering wheel, while today there are many who are trying to hold it. Now, if the king wants to turn the wheel to the right, they pull to the left, and vice versa. So he has to steer it very slowly and with great effort."

Not very convinced, Ferdinand again brought up the insult he had suffered from his son and from the British once more. Draganov advised him to ignore it.

"This is just a misunderstanding between father and son, Your Majesty. Try to forgive and forget." He took a matchbox from the desk and handed it to the old king. "If this letter upsets you so much, why don't you burn it?"

Ferdinand quickly put the letter in his pocket.

"Letters are not to be burned. Letters should be preserved."

Draganov, who had finished drafting his telegram to King Boris

---

[1]King Alexander Obrenovich, of the rival Serbian dynasty, and his wife Draga, were savagely murdered and hacked to pieces in June 1903 by members of the secret officers society, The Black Hand.

suggesting an apology by cable, showed it to the old monarch. Ferdinand seemed pleased, if one could judge by the uncustomary gesture with which he graciously bade farewell to his visitor: taking off one glove (he had kept on his gloves during the entire audience), he tended his bejeweled hand to his former subject. He then said, "I do hope that your mediation will end the war between father and son."

*  *  *

King Boris spent the evening of March 2, 1934, with his brother-in-law Duke Albrecht Württemberg at Berlin's Stadtische Opera, where they heard *Die Fledermaus.* Draganov joined them for supper afterwards at the Traube Restaurant to eat oysters, a delicacy for which the king had a real passion.

But in spite of the operetta and the oysters, Boris looked preoccupied and depressed. When the duke left at midnight, the king asked his old confidant to accompany him to the Bristol Hotel where he was staying. Once in his private suite, the conversation turned immediately to the present situation with the Bulgarian army. A crisis was brewing there because the war minister was about to be replaced and rival factions were pushing their candidates.

Few things were more upsetting to the king than politicizing in the army. Disloyalty and intrigues, when coming from politicians, did not disturb him much anymore. He had lost his illusions about them. But each time army officers engaged in politics behind his back, he felt betrayed and deeply hurt. Having fought in three wars, he felt at home with soldiers and officers and loved the army. The affection was mutual: the army adored him.

But ever since the Military League had been formed, some officers periodically tried to meddle in political life, which always disturbed Boris, especially since he could not trust the loyalty of some of them. He was extremely sensitive on the subject; each new case revived his old disenchantments.

Colonel Draganov, no friend of the league, gave his advice.

"Your Majesty, it doesn't matter who the next war minister is," Draganov advised. "The important thing is to restore discipline and spirit. The army is decaying because the high command has abdicated its duties. The league infected the military with politics. Now is the moment to act, Your Majesty! Before you appoint a new war minister, ask him to commit himself to your program, to swear that he'll obey only you. To declare that he will depoliticize the army and reestablish discipline and hierarchy!"

King Boris was particularly discouraged that night.

"You're asking me to do the impossible," he said sadly. "What war minister would make such a promise and keep it?"

"If he doesn't, then you'll pick somebody else."

"You want me to command. You always make the same mistake—you assume that I'm capable of ordering people to do what I want them to do. But I can't, don't you understand? You can't make a Hitler out of me."

Draganov had not seen him so dispirited for a long time.

"You want me to be a fighter," the king continued, "but to be a fighter, one has to be motivated. I have no stimulus left anymore."

"Your motivation will be the fate of 5 million people who depend on your actions," the colonel insisted. "And the army . . . the army needs you badly to heal it. Otherwise, you're contributing to the decay, and it will all end badly."

The king exploded. "Haven't I worked for them all this time? I can't do it anymore. I don't want to do it! I hate this army that I served with such devotion and that hurt me so deeply. I can't stand the Pretorian spirit of our officers!"

Draganov knew that the king was speaking out of anger, not meaning what he said.

"This way you only encourage this spirit, Your Majesty," Draganov continued. "Let the army feel your firm hand; show them that you're the leader! They will all applaud."

But Boris was too upset and excited to listen. He jumped to his feet, screaming in his friend's face. "You want me to tell you why I can't do what you want me to do? All right, I'll tell you why! I am not born to command. I inherited many talents from my father, but that talent he killed in me. He only trained me to negotiate and persuade, but not to command. I fulfilled the most delicate missions, even in cases when we were wrong, and I always managed to convince the others. Yes, I am good at that. But I remain the same, even now. My father crushed me. He molded my character to be more like a lackey than like a master."

Then, furious at his confession, he disappeared into his bedroom without saying good-bye.

It was past 2:30 in the morning when the colonel returned home, deeply shaken. As Mrs. Draganov asked worriedly what had happened, he could only say, "The king is finished. Poor, poor man!"

He did not sleep the rest of the night.

\*　　\*　　\*

# CHAPTER XV

# The 1934 Coup

"I S IT true," the war minister asked bluntly, "is it true that a *coup d'état* is in the making?"

He looked straight into the face of General Pentcho Zlatev, the inspector general of the cavalry, whom he had summoned to his office. They had been classmates at the Military School and for many years, close friends and leading members of the Military League. Ever since General Vatev had assumed his new function of minister, only nine days before, he had been hearing rumors about an impending coup by the league. Strange, he had first thought, am I not the president of the league? True, we had planned to get rid of the ailing Moushanov cabinet, but now that the king has brought the head of the league into the government, things have changed. Or have they?

As the rumors persisted, General Vatev had second thoughts. He had felt a coolness lately on the part of his colleagues in the league, and, as a matter of fact, he had not been invited to any of their meetings since King Boris had chosen him as his war minister. Was it possible that the league would act without informing him, its president? My friend Zlatev will tell me, he thought.

Zlatev had never less willingly faced his classmate than on that afternoon of May 18, 1934. But recovering his poise, he answered firmly:

"I haven't heard anything. But, look, you have your means and sources. You can find out easily what's going on in all the sixteen sectors." He had hardly finished his sentence when he regretted it. The military sectors numbered fifteen, not sixteen. They were sixteen only in the secret plan for the coup, because it included the takeover of the War Ministry building. But Zlatev was relieved to see that the minister had not noticed the gaffe. Instead, Vatev later called in Sofia's commandant, another league member, and asked him the same question.

"Not at all, General!" the commandant answered without hesitation. "Nobody is preparing a coup at this moment."

"Do you give me your officer's word of honor?"

"Yes, general! My officer's word of honor!"

They later confessed, Zlatev and the commandant, how difficult it had been for them to conceal the truth from their comrade and superior; for they had both lied. Only a couple of hours before, Pentcho Zlatev, one of the plot's military leaders, had left the home of a friend where the conspirators were to meet on the eve of the coup. At this meeting, the future ministers were to assemble for the first time, together with the officers who were to carry out the coup.

The Military League had made up its mind six months earlier to overthrow the Moushanov cabinet. Totally disillusioned with the various parties' ability to govern, and angered by many cases of incompetence and injustice, many politically minded officers had became impatient. Their mood was ripe at the league's annual congress in November 1933 to hear the gloomy reports of the regional delegates. One of the most critical reports was presented by General Vatev, then commanding the Plovdiv military region, who recommended the overthrow of the government. The original impetus stemmed from their opposition to the flaws of the party system, a popular view shared by the majority of army officers, most of whom were staunchly monarchist. But as plans developed, the leadership of the conspiracy fell into the hands of ambitious league members, many of them veterans of the June 1923 coup and supporters of former Colonel Damian Veltchev. They were also ideologically close to the political club "Zveno," which had no great sympathy for the monarchy, and was attracted by the ideas of an "authoritarian state."

Looking for "nonparty" civilian partners, the officers had approached Zveno. Colonel Veltchev was at first proposed by his followers as the future prime minister. But Veltchev was, by temperament, a man who shunned the limelight and preferred to be the *éminence grise* behind the power. He declined the offer and his friend, Kimon Gheorghiev, a Zveno member, was designated to be the future premier. The officers, anxious to secure support from the principal political forces, gave a mandate to Gheoghiev to obtain the participation of the Agrarians and of Professor Tzankov's Movement, thus he sounded out the Agrarian leader Dimiter Guitchev, some of Tzankov's closest collaborators, and other prominent personalities.

The first reactions seemed encouraging. As the party regime was showing signs of decomposition, most officers did not see any conflict between their desire to improve the system of government and their loyalty to the crown. On the contrary, the monarchist league members saw a confirmation of their view when the king chose General Vatev, their president, for his cabinet. General Zlatev, emerging as the new head of the league, made a special effort when recruiting junior officers for the conspiracy to emphasize that it was directed against the Bloc government, not against "His Majesty, our beloved Supreme Commander."

It must also be said that in many respectable circles the prestige of Zveno at that time was high, a reassuring note. Many of its intellectuals were respected and articulate critics of the system's obvious shortcomings. They were few in number—"just enough to fill a phaeton,"[1] their detractors used to say—but they were all highly educated city intellectuals, most of them free of party attachment, some of them disappointed politicians, others former army officers. Zveno had no structured organization nor was it a political party. It was a loose, elitist circle in which political ideologies, philosophies and modern sociological problems were discussed on a relatively high level, maybe somewhat preciously and irrelevantly for peasant Bulgarian realities.

Be that as it may, the Zvenars' criticism hit a sensitive chord. While no exceptional perspicacity was required to notice that "something was rotten" in the kingdom of Bulgaria, they formulated the grievances more eloquently and more cogently than others. As a result, many Bulgarians who had had enough of partisan squabbles and incompetence, of Macedonian terrorist acts, or of unfriendly relations with the neighboring countries, found the Zveno positions attractive. As long as Zveno was perceived as a courageous and uncompromising faultfinder, the "phaetonful of people" enjoyed a certain respect. It was later, when they went beyond the role of diagnostician and began to prescribe their questionable medicine, that public opinion turned skeptical. Indeed, Zveno's fascination with authoritarian ideologies, its republicanism, its readiness to abandon the Macedonian cause, and, also, the transparent personal ambitions of many of its leaders, made the group highly suspect in the eyes of the traditionalist segments of Bulgarian society.

In the beginning, the officers involved with Zveno did not dominate the league. For several years, most members were nationalistic, right-wing and monarchist, occasionally critical of King Boris for not being firm enough with politicians and left-wingers. But as time passed, they lost control of the league, which fell into the hands of the more radical minority grouped around Veltchev.

After overthrowing Stambolisky, the Military League had imposed itself as a powerful, albeit behind-the-scenes factor in Bulgarian political life. Whether salutary or not, the military coup of 1923 created a dangerous precedent: once involved in politics, many officers were hesitant to return to their barracks; they had known the sweet taste of power.

King Boris, as well as all statesmen, believed strongly that once the Stambolisky dictatorship had been overthrown, the league should no longer have meddled in politics. The military, however, had been divided. Some of the league's leaders had shared the king's opinion. But the majority of the leaguers led by Damian Veltchev, had opposed the depoliticization and had

---

[1]Phaeton was a horse carriage for hire, gradually replaced by taxi-cabs.

organized themselves into an antimonarchist faction. Little known to the
larger public, the enigmatic colonel had by 1934 become the real power
behind the Military League.

*     *     *

With his tight, lipless mouth, energetic chin and serious dark eyes,
Veltchev, the fifty-one-year-old colonel, looked rather severe and cold.
Taciturn and immaculate, almost sanitized, he was obviously a man of great
self-discipline. But the voice did not fit the face: Veltchev spoke softly and
with a certain warmth. The awkward, self-conscious gestures did not
correspond to his commanding personality either, but belonged to an
introverted, shy man. But his smile, revealing a range of white teeth, gave
the stern face an unexpected expression of kindness, charming friends and
followers. The followers, mostly younger officers, were few but devoted,
looking up to him like disciples.

Veltchev had kept the sober tastes of the modest family in which he was
raised. He neither drank nor smoked and showed no interest in common
pleasures. He was sent to the Military School at the age of fifteen, and later
fought in the Balkan Wars. An excellent officer, decorated for bravery and
respected by his subordinates, he liked the military life. But the horrors of
battle and defeat became real to him during World War I, when one brother
had his leg amputated and another was killed. The two tragedies, along with
the deaths of thousands of soldiers in a war that he disapproved of, marked
Damian for life.

He believed that Bulgaria's defeats were the fault of King Ferdinand,
and he transferred his animosity to the entire dynasty, including King Boris.
Ideologically, Veltchev was a convinced republican whose hobby was studying Bulgarian history and the French Revolution, whose great figures were
his heroes. He believed that Bulgaria's tragedy had begun in 1878, when the
short-lived San Stefano Peace Treaty recognized Bulgaria's rights over all the
territories inhabited by Bulgarians. The fatal mistake, according to Veltchev
and his friends, was to try to win afterwards a "San Stefano Bulgaria" by
chauvinism and force. The only possible way to recover at least part of the
lost territories, he thought, was by peaceful collaboration with the Great
Powers and the neighboring countries, primarily Yugoslavia. And seeing the
monarchy as a major obstacle to a Balkan understanding, he became an
active adversary of the crown. His interest in politics brought him early to
the Military League, and he took part in the 1923 coup against Stambolisky.
But he was quickly disappointed by the Tzankov regime, and when frictions
developed with the leaders of the coup, he was dismissed from the army.

As a civilian, politics became his main activity. His friend Kimon
Gheorghiev had also left the army after disagreements with the other leaders
of the 1923 coup, and the two men became close political collaborators. But

whereas Gheorghiev threw himself into the arena of political parties and civilian groups and became a founder and leader of Zveno, Veltchev's activity was concentrated exclusively on the military. Although he was the only civilian among the league's leaders, he became its secretary general. When the league became dormant after the 1923 coup, Veltchev organized its more militant members into a faction with an antimonarchist orientation. Among his most fervent followers was a small group of ambitious cavalry captains, all of them trophy-winning horsemen of international reputation, who held the king responsible for their slow advancement in the army.

For ten years, between 1924 and 1934, Veltchev worked effectively, but always in the shadows, among active and reserve officers, keeping contacts with Zveno and especially with Kimon Gheorghiev. Although he never joined Zveno formally, he shared its ideology entirely.

The hold Veltchev had on some younger officers was not due to any rhetorical talents; in fact, he was a poor public speaker and generally a taciturn and not very sociable man. But in their eyes, he was an example of uncompromising morality and courageous straightforwardness. Curiously enough, in the most political of all officers, they saw the antithesis of the typical politician—an honest man, devoid of demagoguery and public-relations skills.

His alter ego, Kimon Gheorghiev, one year his senior, was also a brilliant Military School graduate. He had distinguished himself in the service and at the front, where he had lost an eye and been decorated for bravery. The son of a modest state employee who had died early, Kimon was nicknamed "the Greek" because his mother was of Greek descent. Like Damian, he was a sober, disciplined man devoted to work, an exemplary father and husband. But the personalities of the two friends—or rather close collaborators, as they were not of the type to have intimate, affectionate friendships—were essentially different.

Kimon was perhaps the brighter of the two, in the sense of having a quicker mind and a shrewd awareness of the realities. Although usually a silent man like Damian, he was a better speaker and had more presence in public. But he was colder, more skeptical and calculating than Veltchev, with no personal charm whatsoever. Always in control and emotionless, exacting with subordinates, and difficult with collaborators, contact with him was not made any easier by the cross-eyed look from behind his glasses, caused by the white of his blind eye.

When appearing together at reunions, Kimon showed more self-assurance than the timid, awkward Damian. An ambitious man, and a better politician, he commanded respect, and his cool, dispassionate analyses carried great weight with his antidynastic followers. But while some officers were humanly devoted to Veltchev, nobody was ever known who personally liked Gheorghiev.

The Moushanov cabinet resigned on May 14. The news did not surprise anyone. The schism inside the ruling Popular Bloc was beyond repair, and a quarrel between the coalition's four parties over the distribution of ministerial posts ended in an impasse. King Boris accepted the resignation immediately, and on the same day gave a mandate to Moushanov to form a new cabinet.

It was a difficult task. Most parties, afflicted by factionalism, were on the decline. An exception was the vigorous "Movement" of Professor Tzankov. The movement was busy that spring organizing its National Congress, a huge affair scheduled for May 20. According to persistent rumors, Tzankov was to make a pitch for power if the congress ended with the anticipated success. The king would then give him the mandate to form the new government and reform the institutions, the rumors said.

The resignation of the Moushanov cabinet occurred at a particularly bad time, because it coincided with a serious crisis in the army. Discontent had been spreading for a long time among the officers. Because of budget deficits and the Neuilly Treaty restrictions, a painful overcrowding in the army, blocked promotions. The frustrated young officers had expected the former war minister to make some bold reforms. When he did not, they pressed for his removal.

The king, for his part, favored the retirement of a number of generals, especially those known for their IMRO sympathies. Such a move would have the double benefit of appeasing Yugoslavia and creating openings for capable junior officers. The war minister, however, was reluctant to act. He happened also to be disliked by the league. King Boris, although deploring the league's increasing power, was well aware of its dangers and could not afford to ignore it. Thus on May 9, to everybody's surprise, he appointed the league's president, General Vatev, as the new war minister.

The non-league officers were stunned. Vatev did not have the seniority of other generals who had been groomed for the job. The chief of staff and the Sofia garrison's commander resigned in protest. They were replaced by two royalist officers. The new war minister himself, although a leader of the league, was considered a monarchist. With such officers in key positions, Boris stood a good chance to succeed in depoliticizing the army, his most ardent desire at that time. But the question was whether he had the time to act, or if it was already too late.

                                    *        *        *

In addition to the Bloc's disintegration and the malaise in the army, the king worried about another source of popular indignation. The recrudescence of assassinations of Macedonians all over Bulgaria, and especially in the streets of Sofia, had reached intolerable proportions. The feuding factions—Mihailovists and Protoguerovists—were killing each other in broad daylight with audacity and impunity, and the Bulgarian authorities seemed unable to stop them. The IMRO followers of Vanche Mihailov had the upper hand, but the minority of Protoguerov's partisans (he himself was assassinated in 1928) fought desperately to prevent their physical extermination by equally bloody retaliation. The results were horrifying.

Between August and December 1932, the press reported thirty-three assassinations or attempted assassinations of Macedonians. Most victims belonged to the Protoguerov wing of IMRO. The Mihailovists justified their "punitive action against traitors" on the grounds that the Protoguerovists were in the pay of Belgrade or were agents of Moscow. The Protoguerovists denied these charges, called their murderous activities "acts of self-defense" and said they were hunted down simply because they refused to submit to the leadership of Mihailov, whom they considered an usurper. They denounced Mihailov's policy of terrorist actions against Yugoslavia as counterproductive. They preferred a campaign of propaganda abroad and the organizing of the popular masses in Macedonia for an ultimate uprising.

A December 1932 editorial in the Protoguerovists' clandestine newspaper urged the emigrants to organize counterterrorist groups and use eye-for-an-eye tactics against the "Mihailov band." A few days later, the editor of the pro-Mihailov newspaper was attacked in front of the royal palace by two gunmen, wounding him and his three bodyguards. It was noon; the streets were crowded. Several policemen and passers-by pursued the attackers and apprehended them, but not before one policeman had been shot dead. Three passers-by were wounded, and the editor and one bodyguard died in the hospital.

The same night, Mihailov henchmen tried to kidnap one of the wounded assassins from the hospital, but they failed. The following evening, however, the night nurse shot the patient dead, readily admitting that she had followed the orders of IMRO. This was a chilling reminder, if anyone still had doubts, that IMRO's long arms left no offender unpunished.

The Mihailovists accused the government of indifference in the face of "murderous attacks of patriotic leaders by traitorous bands," and the Macedonian organizations organized a gigantic funeral, with five thousand people parading behind the coffin through the streets of Sofia.

After this murder, the relations between IMRO and the Moushanov government deteriorated. Paradoxically, each of the Macedonian factions accused the authorities of favoring the other. As for the general public, it demanded that the government put an end to the terrorism of both wings. But the authorities seemed incapable of acting decisively, and the wave of assassinations continued. Two leftist Macedonian members of Parliament were murdered in January 1933. A few days later, three prisoners accused of killing a school teacher in Petrich were kidnapped as they were taken by train to trial and executed. With this new humiliation for the Sofia government, a wave of indignation swept the country.

To show their distrust of Sofia, when the official Macedonian emigrant organizations convened their 1933 annual congress in Gorna-Djoumaya, the chairman declared that the Macedonians had come to work for the unification of Macedonia into an "independent" political entity. A message from Ivan Mihailov and IMRO's Central Committee was read. "We are not fighting simply for churches and schools," the message said. "We seek the creation of independent Macedonia." Mihailov asserted that "time has proved that Belgrade understands only the language of bombs and guns." After identifying the Serbian police and Bolshevism as IMRO's principal enemies, the message continued, "We must also mention, with profound indignation, the necessity of forming a defensive front against opposition from Sofia. Although the Bulgarian people cherish a fraternal love for Macedonia, political circles in Sofia raise obstacles to the success of our efforts." And the message concluded, "Sofia becomes as dangerous to the Macedonian cause as Athens and Belgrade. The attitude of the Sofia political leaders concerning Macedonia is determined by considerations of party politics."

The government was incensed. Commenting on the convention's desire for an independent Macedonia, its organ wrote: "The right of a people to determine freely its destiny is sacred and inalienable. But distinct from the right is the problem of possibilities. This is no time for maximum demands. Such demands brought the Bulgarian people to their present state. The formula of an independent Macedonia is a chimera which means war, whereas the formula of an autonomous Macedonia means peace and assures freedom of action in the realm of the possible." The government's reply continued angrily, "We must recall the 200,000 sons of Bulgaria who lost their lives fighting for the liberty of Macedonia. Bleeding Bulgaria has the right to greater respect and gratitude from the Macedonian emigration which resides within its borders."

There was more tough talk all through 1933, but nothing could stop the bloody war in the streets of Sofia. The casualty list was horrendous: May 29, a member of the Macedonian National Committee shot in front of his home; June 1, on returning from the funeral of the above, aborted attempts on a deputy and on the new editor of "Makedonia"; June 12, an assassination near the National Bank; June 14, a leftist leader shot to death in the street; a few hours later, a former bodyguard murdered; June 21, a man shot while sitting in a Sofia coffee-house (when arrested, the killer realized that he had mistaken the man for someone else—the victim had no connections with Macedonians). The macabre list continued to fill the pages of the newspapers.

Not only was the government powerless to put an end to the massacre, but it had lost almost all jurisdiction in the Petrich region, the heart of Bulgarian Macedonia. This district had become a state within a state: IMRO controlled the appointments of the local officials, had its own tax collectors for "voluntary contributions," and punished its enemies, with little interference from the Sofia central authorities. Although there was hardly a Bulgarian who did not sympathize with the cause of Macedonia, the emergence of IMRO as a formidable force in Bulgarian politics shocked the public. Without voicing it, most Bulgarians were deeply disturbed that IMRO was strong enough to make and unmake ministers, police officials, military commanders, and civil servants. Everybody in Bulgaria—especially the politicians—knew that it was highly unhealthy to antagonize the IMRO.

\* \* \*

King Boris's intimates found him often in a peculiar mood that spring, a mood of serene fatalism. The accidental death of his favorite Coburg uncle, Albert I, the king of Belgium, during a solitary mountain hike, had left a very deep impression on him. Did Boris identify with another overburdened monarch, who also loved mountain solitude? Boris did not seem to believe that the fatal fall had been accidental. The communiqué of the February 1934 tragedy read: "His Majesty, having climbed a rocky point, reached the summit, where very obvious traces of his passage remain. He leaned against a big block of stone, which must have seemed to him firmly fixed. The block fell away, carrying His Majesty with it."

For a long time after the Belgian king's death, in moments of discouragement, Boris would repeat with a mysterious, dreamy look in his eyes which worried his entourage: "Good old Albert. He knew very well what he was doing!" Boris neither elaborated, nor explained what he meant, but the look in his eyes indicated his agreement with the uncle who went to his death on this solitary mountain, the king who "knew what he was doing," whatever that meant.

\* \* \*

King Boris was trying desperately to solve the three crises which had simultaneously reached their boiling points by the spring of 1934. With regard to the political crisis, he had come to the conclusion that it was high time for basic reforms of the existing party regime. But, contrary to other critics of the system, he was absolutely adamant that the desired changes should be made by constitutional means. For him, the then fashionable authoritarian regimes held no appeal.

As to the military crisis, the king had but one desire: that the army get out of the political arena. He disliked the Military League and would be delighted to see it dissolved. His intention was to defuse its conspiratorial spirit by bringing its moderate president into the government. For that, he had regretfully to sacrifice a few superior officers who were devoted to him and also bitter enemies of the league. For reasons of secrecy, he could not explain to them that he was dropping them in order to split the league and destroy it from within.

As for the Macedonian crisis, King Boris attempted to reconcile the feuding factions, but his emissaries had no success: the brothers-enemies were absolutely intransigent and had sworn to obliterate each other. The Mikhailovists had a respectful but cool attitude toward Boris. They did not attack him directly, for fear of helping their own worst enemies: Communists, left-wing Agrarians, Zveno, and the Republicans of the league. But IMRO did not like Boris's policy of rapprochement with Yugoslavia and followed his flirtation with King Alexander with growing hostility.

By May of 1934, King Boris was determined to act. His plans had ripened, but only his very closest advisers were informed of his intentions. It is interesting to read how the American envoy in Sofia, F. A. Sterling, described the king's plans in a report to Washington:

"The Legation has heard from a confidential and fairly reliable source that His Majesty did have strongly in mind a plan to rid the country of the political confusion caused by the inability of the parties to come to an agreement. Together with the general public, he had become disgusted with their moral corruption, self-interest, and decadence; and had neither Mr. Moushanov nor Mr. Guitchev been able to form a government, as seemed likely, he would have dissolved the Sobranié. Pending the general elections, which must take place within two months after the dissolution, he would have appointed a cabinet of his own choosing composed of the best elements of the country, regardless of political affiliations, and above party interests; an honest, strong and patriotic government which, when the elections took place, could have been returned to power. Generally, the policy and program of his government would have been along the lines of . . . that of Tzankov. All this was to be accomplished with the influence behind him of the army, which he did not doubt solidly supported him, and was to be achieved by constitutional means. There is no question that if this plan had been put into effect, the king's prestige would have been greatly enhanced." That is where things stood on May 18.

\* \* \*

That day, the conspirators were to meet in the afternoon in a private home where Kimon Gheorghiev was to introduce the future ministers. Three days before, he had informed his coconspirators that he had obtained the agreement of the Agrarian leader Guitchev, the president of the Reserve

Officers' Association, a representative of the Democratic party, and Peter Todorov of Zveno. Most important, he affirmed, the Tzankov Movement had also agreed to participate: their representative was not to be Tzankov himself, a controversial personality, but his close associate, General Roussev. The league's General Pentcho Zlatev had accepted the post of future war minister. It looked like a very impressive and representative cabinet. The conspirators decided that the coup should be carried out on May 19.

But just before the meeting, General Zlatev had received an unexpected visit at his home from General Roussev who informed him that he was unable to represent the Tzankov Movement in the future cabinet. "I suggest that you invite Tzankov himself," he said as he bowed out of the plot. Disappointed, Zlatev rushed to the meeting. A second disappointment was in store for him there. Guitchev was not in the room. Instead he saw Nicola Zahariev, a dissident Agrarian of doubtful reputation for integrity and of no influence in his own party. Zlatev, in charge of the military execution of the coup, was also told that a friend of Tzankov might join the new government but could not come this afternoon because his wife was sick . . . It became clear to Zlatev that the two principal political forces on which the officers had counted, Guitchev's Agrarians and Tzankov's Movement, were not going to participate in the coup.

His first impulse was immediately to cancel the action for that night. But it was too late. The orders had already been issued, the movements of the units had aroused suspicions, and the war minister was summoning him to his office. For better or for worse, the die was cast.

And the king? What if King Boris refused to sign the mandate for the new government and ordered some loyal troops to resist? The same question had been asked before the 1923 coup, with many of the same participants. Then, they had gone into action before they had time to decide on the course to be taken should the king resist. Now things were much clearer. The leaders of the plot, under the influence of convinced republicans like Kimon Gheorghiev, Damian Veltchev, and Petar Todorov, decided that in the unlikely case of the king's resistance he would be dethroned and a republic proclaimed. General Zlatev, still professing that the coup was not directed against the crown, did not oppose the decision.

Sofia was asleep when the conspirators' military units began to occupy their posts. As the leaders of the coup assembled in the Fourth Police Precinct, next to the War Ministry, Zlatev toured the darkened streets of the capital, inspecting the deployment of the troops. Everything was progressing smoothly with no incidents reported. Two army majors, placed in front of the war minister's home, saw him leave the house and rush in the direction of the ministry. They followed him in the dark to his office; the duty officer that night was a league member. The moment Vatev reached for the telephone, the majors jumped him, grabbed the receiver, and arrested him. A few moments later the alarmed garrison commander arrived, and he was also arrested. It was well past midnight, and reports from the provinces began to arrive: so far, the operation had been successful, with no resistance and no victims.

At the conspiracy's headquarters in the Fourth Precinct, the authors of the coup waited nervously for the climax of the drama: the moment of truth, when they would wake the king with the news of the coup and ask him to sign the decree appointing the new government. Only two blocks away, behind the silent palace park, King Boris was sound asleep. Or so they thought . . .

Suddenly the entrance hall of the precinct came alive—it was exactly 3:30 in the morning. As the door of the room opened, the conspirators, stunned, could not conceal their surprise: there stood General Panov, the king's aide-de-camp. "Gentlemen," he said, "His Majesty is expecting you. He is ready to receive Mr. Gheorghiev and General Zlatev."

*    *    *

King Boris in full officer's uniform, sabre, holster and all, stood in the middle of the salon when Gheorghiev and Zlatev were introduced. The conspirators looked tense and ill-at-ease, especially General Zlatev, the holster of whose parabellum was unbuttoned, as though he feared an ambush. He stood at attention, and saluted in the military manner: "Your Majesty, the inspector of the cavalry introduces himself to you!" They then reported to the king that the Moushanov cabinet had been deposed and that they had taken over the government. They carried two drafts—one for the decree appointing the new cabinet, the other with the text for the king's abdication in the event that he refused to accept the change. Before leaving for the palace, they had been cautioned by their worried coconspirators to be careful not to present inadvertently the abdication text first.

The *coup-d'état* had not taken King Boris by surprise. He had been kept well informed by devoted officers, some of them members of the league, and had been expecting the coup for the last two months and "sleeping only with one ear," he later told his intimates. Since the beginning of the month, he had been busy implementing his plan for reforming the regime through constitutional means, knowing that he was racing against the clock. He could only pray that, in the meantime, nobody would do something foolish. The day before, the director of the Royal Museum of Natural History, Dr. Bouresh, had informed him that the coup was scheduled for that night. Bouresh had a very important connection who had been in on the secret.

"You made a mistake, general," the king said sadly to Zlatev. "You made a mistake to act prematurely."

"I beg your pardon, Your Majesty!"

"You don't have to apologize to me. Let's hope that Bulgaria will pardon you."

He turned to Kimon Gheorghiev: "Do you remember what I told you when you were appointed commander of the Sixth Infantry Regiment?" Gheorghiev blushed. He remembered well King Boris's words: "I am entrusting you with a regiment which has *never* betrayed its oath."

For two hours, they discussed the newly created situation. King Boris was confronted with a *fait accompli,* but he tried to limit the damages. "As constitutional head of state, I cannot give you my approval," he said. "But let's find a formula which would respect the constitution." He had given Moushanov a mandate to form a new cabinet, with May 19 as a deadline.

"I asked them to free the unfortunate 'Optimist' [Moushanov], who had been arrested in his underpants," the king wrote later to his confidant Draganov. "He came to see me at 7 A.M., crying and asking me to forgive him. He returned the mandate, and I sent him to see them . . ."

At 9:30 A.M., Kimon Gheorghiev again came to the palace, bringing the new mandate to be signed by the king. After some bargaining in which the king succeeded in reducing the number of officers to be fired by the new regime, Boris signed the decree appointing the new cabinet. When Kimon Gheorghiev left the palace at 11:15 A.M., he was the new prime minister of Bulgaria.

A little incident occurred as he was taking leave of the king. He slipped on the parquet and, losing his balance, kicked the wall next to the doors, his black shoe leaving a mark on the exquisite wallpaper. As soon as the door closed behind him, a lackey rushed to clean the spot.

"Don't touch it!" King Boris, a believer in omens of all sorts, cried. "I want to keep a souvenir of this meeting." "Kimon's stain" was kept intact for several years.

At noon, the king received the visiting mayor of Paris as if nothing had happened.

But in fact, the previous night was a turning point in Boris's life, for from the moment he learned that the coup was in progress, he was conscious of the crucial stakes in the unfolding drama. This time, he did not let the conspirators surprise him, as they did in 1923. This time, he was the one who sent for them. "I cannot stress enough the fact that there is nothing in common between my attitude on June 9, 1923, and now, on May 19. This time I couldn't care less about my life," he wrote in an unpublished letter.

". . . Judging this an unusually solemn moment, I remembered the godfather of Eliezer [code name for King Ferdinand][2], the photograph of whose hat I had seen the previous evening. I said to myself that if my destiny

---

[2]Emperor Maximilian of Mexico, executed by a firing squad.

is to take the same road, I'll do it in appropriate attire. That's why I only pinned my 'For Valor,' third-class medal on my chest, fastened my Gabrovo-leather belt, and donned the sabre I carried in the old glorious times when I solemnly entered Salonika."

The coup was executed without any physical violence. But it could have ended in a bloodbath had the king followed the advice of some of his aides who were on palace duty that night. At 3:15 A.M. two of his devotees had insisted that he assume the command of the troops to redress the situation.

"That's all we needed!" King Boris wrote later. "An operetta with not only a tragic, but, also, which is much worse, an immortally ludicrous ending! I told them that I prefer to be either Boris III or Boris the Last, but that in no case did I want to be known as Don Quixote of the Balkans. If you don't agree with me, I told them, then you should shoot me!"

*          *          *

The new cabinet was announced the same day. There were eight members instead of ten, with Kimon Gheorghiev as prime minister and General Zlatev as war minister. It was not merely a change of cabinet; it was a change of regime. Its first decrees dissolved the Sobrané, banning all political parties. Censorship of the press was next. The no-party authoritarian regime launched the usual campaign of rhetoric about a social and moral "renovation" and a just and incorruptible "New Order."

Another spectacular act was banning the IMRO, a courageous measure that no previous government had dared to take. In what amounted to a declaration of war against the organization, several Mihailovist activists were arrested, and public officials connected with IMRO summarily fired. The new regime was more friendly to the Protoguerovists. Ivan Mihailov went into hiding for four months in northern Bulgaria, then fled to Turkey where he was kept under surveillance for four years. The Petritch administrative district was abolished, and Bulgarian Macedonia was placed under the jurisdiction of the Sofia and Plovdiv districts. Simultaneously, the government proclaimed its determination to cooperate with all neighboring countries, especially Yugoslavia.

For a few days, the public reaction was generally rather favorable. The participation in the coup of several officers and a few politicians gave the impression that the army, and probably the king himself, supported the new regime.

But when the dust settled, things became disappointingly clearer. The army realized that contrary to the assurances it had been given, no major political force supported the coup, and that the new leaders represented the radical wing of the Military League. Although still in the shadows, Damian Veltchev, together with Kimon Gheorghiev, directed the policies of the new regime. All major decisions rested with a triumvirate composed of the responsible minister, Gheorghiev, and Veltchev.

Many officers and supporters of the coup became suspicious, but it was too late for regrets. More disturbing, the dominant roles of well-known republicans—Gheorghiev, Veltchev, Todorov—and the noticeable omission of the king's name in the first proclamation clearly indicated a hostility to the crown.

The American legation reported that "the facts seem to preclude all complicity, direct or indirect, or even advance notice of the plot," as far as King Boris was concerned. "This belief is founded on the king's known respect for constitutional government and constitutional procedure, so that any forceful taking over of the government by the military forces would be against his principles."

The American minister Sterling noted further that the king was compelled to dismiss not only his newly appointed war minister Vatev, but also the commander of the Royal Guards and one of his personal aides-de-camp. As no mention was made of the king in the government's first manifesto, "which would appear to be a direct disregard of his authority, if not an intentional insult," Sterling concluded that the king had obviously no real choice in the formation of the cabinet. Otherwise, he would not have appointed Peter Todorov, who had openly and contemptuously criticized him at public meetings in the past. The report concluded:

"The king knew nothing of the plot and is not now behind the government except by reason of *force majeure*. Furthermore, it is said that upon receiving his 'orders' he was only dissuaded from abdicating by the knowledge that such action might lead to civil war and because of his love for his country and people."

Five days had not passed before the entire country knew that the new regime was not friendly to the king. People also realized that the constitution had been violated against the will of the king. Even those who had favored the dissolution of the parties and desired the ending of the Macedonian killings were disillusioned. The national mood was demonstrated on May 24 at the annual parade commemorating Saints Cyril and Methodius, inventors of the Slavic alphabet. King Boris, wearing his general's uniform and accompanied by Queen Giovanna and Prince Kyril, arrived at Alexander Nevski Cathedral where the entire new cabinet and most former ministers were assembled. After the religious service, the royal party returned to the palace and retired to the garden, surrounded by the ministers.

From eleven until two o'clock under a bright sun, the troops, the school children, the veterans and, finally, the general population marched through the palace gardens, passing close to the king and cheering him widely. The *New York Times* report from Sofia said:

"This correspondent witnessed this morning the most amazing demonstration for King Boris he had ever seen here. . . . The king was evidently moved by the enthusiastic demonstration, which was attributed by government circles to the satisfaction by the population over the king's decision to inaugurate a new era in Bulgarian politics. Independent quarters noted, however, that the enthusiasm was for the king alone and not for Premier Gheorghiev and his colleagues, who were received coldly by the crowds. The citizens are said to have cheered their 'constitutional king,' whose opposition to a dictatorship had become known by the Bulgarian people."

The *Times* headline summed up the situation: "SOFIA CHEERS KING BUT NOT CABINET. LEAVING PALACE FIRST TIME SINCE CHANGE IN REGIME, BORIS GETS OVATION. OPPOSED COUP, IT IS SAID."

※　　※　　※

# CHAPTER XVI

# The King
# Takes the Reins

POLITICS MAKES strange bedfellows, but the Military League was quick to come to its senses. Most officers woke up wishing they were elsewhere, with the same guilty feelings of embarrassment and regret that one feels when awakening next to a homely stranger, picked up unwisely the night before. The partners who had shared the army's bed on the night of May 19 turned out to be either ambitious politicians who were using the army for their own ends or well-meaning dilettantes with no experience.

Certain changes of the new regime were implemented efficiently: the parliamentarian system was abolished, the political parties dissolved, the Mihailovist IMRO banned and its members (but not the Protoguerovists) prosecuted, and friendly relations with Yugoslavia were strengthened. But the routine management of the state machinery was amateurish, raising criticism. The obvious anticrown bias and the experiments with authoritarian measures—the censorship, the banning of public reunions, the propaganda campaign for National Renovation—left the general public cold, sarcastic, and outright hostile.

Before long, there arose within the government a latent conflict between republican Zveno members, led by Prime Minister Gheorghiev, Minister Peter Todorov, and the real power behind the cabinet, Damian Veltchev, on one side, and, on the other, the military who felt that Zveno was not living up to the mandate it had received from the army. A spokesman for the second group was War Minister Zlatev.

Neither of these groups, nor the politicians in opposition, nor the army, nor the bulk of the population, suspected that the political scene was being prepared for the entrance of a new, unexpected factor—the king. His republican enemies called him contemptuously the "Gentleman with the Fedora Hat." For sixteen years, hardly anyone had considered the unassuming monarch capable of risky decisions and resolute actions.

Perhaps they had been right all those sixteen years, but not now in 1934. If a single night can transform a man, the night of May 19 had done it for King Boris. That night, he lost his illusions and rid himself of his scruples and doubts. One more time, "they" had disappointed him—the politicians and, alas, the army; one more time, he felt betrayed and humiliated—one time too many. If these were the rules of the game, very well, he would show them who was the better player! The stain on the wall left by Kimon Gheorghiev's shoe was still there as a reminder.

His principal weapon would be his patience. ("Tarpenié" is the Bulgarian word.) He would outlast them and then outsmart them. True to his fondness for nicknames and pseudonyms, he signed private letters of this period, "Yours truly, Tarpeniev." "I am firmly determined to swallow everything from the conspirators, without giving them any pretext for accusations that I am conspiring. I'll close my eyes and wait. But it is not easy. They fired Draganov, they fired Drandar[1], and Grouev is the next target," not to mention the commander of the Royal Guards regiment and many other monarchist officers. The important thing immediately after the coup was to survive, and to be extremely careful not to give his enemies any pretext to depose him.

At the same time, he was watching them very carefully. It was not difficult to know what was going on in the government, as many league members were devoted monarchists and kept him informed. When he saw the first cracks in the government's walls, he began to look for potential allies inside the fortress. The military were the natural choice, beginning with General Zlatev.

The Bulgarian officers might have had many faults, but, with few exceptions, they were all extremely sensitive where honor was questioned. King Boris had his discreet ways of reminding them of their allegiance and solemn oath. Nor did he leave unexploited any friction, jealousy, or personal ambition among the cabinet members. He was very good, almost Machiavellian, at this sort of thing. And, he had learned to wait.

He was ready for everything, even the worst, and he remained totally calm. With republicans in power, the monarchy's future looked bleak. His confidant Draganov, who had been in Berlin as the military attaché, was forced to resign from the army. And as Princess Evdokia was visiting Nadejda in Germany at this time, Boris sent her a message not to return for the moment.

*         *         *

Thank Heaven for mountain retreats! Each time the pressure became unbearable, Boris took the winding road to Tcham-Koria to drive the forty miles to his Tzarska-Bistritza mountain house. Once in the wooded wilder-

---

[1]Drandar was the chief of the Royal Chancery.

ness, walking among the pine trees, or in the lodge, reading in front of the fireplace, he could unwind and relax. From Tzarska, depending on the season and the companions he had brought with him, he would go shooting capercaillie in Ovnarsko, hunt around Sitniakovo, or climb some mountain peak. The worse the political crisis in Sofia, the more urgent was his need to withdraw to nature with his nonpolitical pals: Elin-Pelin, the writer; Alexander Bojinov, the cartoonist; Dr. D. Balabanov, his ear-and-nose physician; Velizar Bagarov, the industrialist. Prince Kyril, an excellent shot, always accompanied him, Princess Evdokia very often, plus a couple of aides-de-camp. There were no political discussions—just a comparing of notes on who saw or shot what wildcock where, and, of course, a little boasting and teasing too. Sometimes, Boris stayed there for the entire weekend, but often he only spent the night in the lodge, went hunting well before dawn, and drove back to Sofia later in the morning. But even such short retreats did miracles for the restless, high-strung king. His peace of mind restored, he was ready to face the stress again in the capital.

Only three weeks after the May 19 coup, an entry in the Ovnarsko log reads: "In good weather conditions we climbed Malyovitza" (a Rila mountain peak). Signed: "Boris." Under his name, another signature, also in Bulgarian: "Ioanna."

Since their marriage, the queen had become the new member of the old gang, accompanying her husband on many excursions, hunts, and skiing trips. She had gradually become accustomed to her new country and her role as queen and mistress of the palace. But the beginning was not easy. The twenty-two-year-old Italian princess had found herself in a totally foreign environment in unfamiliar houses, surrounded by strangers, polite and friendly people, but nevertheless, strangers. She found the Sofia palace less enchanting than the castles of a Prince Charming are supposed to be, dark and rather severe for her taste. The formal salons in Louis XVI style, with gilded chairs and sofas, damask-covered walls, and ornate doors, looked sumptuous and bore the mark of King Ferdinand. The palace, while furnished in good taste, could hardly be called luxurious, as royal palaces go. Most rooms had been left intact since the time of Ferdinand with his furniture, his portraits of ancestors and paintings of battles, and his innumerable clocks in each room. Even Ferdinand's clothes were still hanging in some closets. In the Sitniakovo lodge, for instance, Giovanna discovered all the Macedonian costumes in which he used to pose for photographs.

King Boris had given orders to leave his father's rooms as they were, even those he himself never wanted to enter again. Giovanna could not believe her eyes when she finally obtained the key to one locked room in Vrana that nobody had been allowed to enter since the departure of the old monarch. Heavy black curtains blocked all sunlight, and the air smelled of mildew. Death masks of deceased relatives, in plaster and wax, were displayed in what used to be Ferdinand's "funeral room," a sordid place where the mystic-minded king could indulge in meditations about the hereafter.

Boris had none of his father's morbid tastes but because of an exaggerated conservatism and filial respect, he kept postponing the redecoration of the paternal rooms. But Giovanna did not wait one day to get rid of the macabre relics.

In her Sofia bathroom she found a locked safe, unopened for some thirty years. As nobody was able to open it, a jailed bank robber was brought from prison to force it. Several jewelry cases and gift boxes were found inside. They were all empty.

Fortunately, the queen loved her apartment in the Sofia palace, in the corner of a wing whose walls were covered with luxuriant mauve wisteria. These were the rooms that belonged to Boris's mother, Princess Maria Luisa—a bedroom, study, small blue drawing room, and larger pink salon—to which Giovanna had added a new cheerfulness with masses of flowers and photographs, and beautiful aquarelles, a gift from her parents. A copy of the most famous Bulgarian historical bas-relief, the huge ninth-century *Madara Horseman*, hung over the mantlepiece in the study, where she spent a large part of the day. Giovanna's violoncello and her grandmother's old piano were in the pink salon.

Boris's quarters next door consisted of Ferdinand's old bedroom, also overlooking Tsar Osvoboditel, and an adjoining working office. But most of the time the king worked either in Grouev's office or in the palace military chancery, where she never disturbed him.

With her husband constantly busy, Giovanna's days during the first year or two were long and lonely. She did not know much about his work, and less about state affairs. Boris was not the kind of husband who burdened his wife with his problems. But having grown up in the Italian royal court, where politics were never discussed with the women, she did not miss that at all.

What she was missing was her own family, mostly her sisters Maria and Mafalda. Boris's family could not fill the void, although she maintained good relations with Evdokia and Kyril. As for her exiled father-in-law, she could never feel any warmth for him, knowing what a despotic and unloving father he had been to Boris. Even now, Ferdinand had not changed much. He never asked about his granddaughter, not even as a matter of politeness, when Boris and Giovanna paid him visits in Coburg. He always managed to say something unpleasant or to criticize his son, even though Boris tried hard to please him, never letting an anniversary or birthday go by without sending warm letters, telegrams, and presents. Boris and Giovanna, for instance, sent him a large case of mango fruit, a rare delicacy in Europe. Came the cable from Coburg: "Received your mango. Tout-à-fait inutile" (utterly useless). In spite of this treatment, Boris asked his wife to be tolerant to Le Monarque. But she angrily insisted that Ferdinand was nothing but a selfish, spoiled, and bitter old man, who was also jealous of his son.

Giovanna did not see her husband during working hours. However, they met daily for lunch in the ground floor private dining room, always in the company of Evdokia, Kyril, and the officer on duty. The same group also shared dinner every night. She found Prince Kyril a pleasant and likeable man, but somewhat phlegmatic, without his brother's and sister's quick minds and intellectual curiosity. Somehow she had the feeling that he was uncomfortable alone in her company. Her relations with Princess Evdokia were no different from the usual relations between two sisters-in-law with strong personalities. At times, she felt that Evdokia was watching her—maybe criticizing her.

The princess, ten years older, was a remarkably interesting and witty companion to those whom she liked. But she was an impatient and critical person too, often blunt, short-tempered, and sarcastic. Authoritarian as she could be with others, she was totally, even submissively, devoted to her brother, whom she constantly tried to please. For almost a decade, Evdokia had played the role of first lady, closest friend and confidante of her bachelor brother. Since she could remember, they had spent most of their happy moments together and had shared ordeals and reverses, standing side by side when the crown faced attacks. Even Evdokia's personal life revolved around Boris: the romantic attachments she had had were all among her brother's close circle of ADCs and friends. One romance reached the point where she contemplated marriage. But marrying a Bulgarian commoner was politically unwise, as well as unacceptable to the family. Heartbroken, she was forced to abandon all ideas of marrying for love. Nor had she ever found a suitable prince to marry: she was much too involved with Bulgaria to think of foreign candidates. Like Boris, and in spite of the foreign blood in their veins, Evdokia was incurably attached to the Bulgarian land—its colors, sounds, and odors, and its language. More than Kyril and Nadejda, she belonged, almost organically, to the country in which she had been born.

With the arrival of Giovanna, things of course, had to change. Evdokia realized quickly that the lovely young girl was not as helpless and docile as one might believe and had quite a strong character of her own. The Italian newcomer was not about to let herself be pushed around. Her first task was to learn Bulgarian. Her teacher, the daughter of Plovdiv Gymnasium's principal, came twice a day until Giovanna, a good linguist, learned to speak, read, and write excellent Bulgarian.

At first a politely silent outsider at table conversations, Giovanna gradually asserted her presence. The occasional sister-in-law sarcasms and critical remarks did not remain unanswered. The usual Bulgarian talk and inside jokes of her table companions had to be extended to topics which were of interest to the queen, too. Before long, it was established that she was now the mistress of the house.

The only time during the day Boris and Giovanna were alone was during their daily visits to Vrana after lunch, in his sturdy, uncomfortable Stayr (or, in later years, his convertible Packard). They would walk for a half-hour in the park, play with the dogs—his favorite dachshund and her bulldog Bonzo—and talk to the gardeners before returning to Sofia. They both loved these trips to Vrana, which gave him some time to relax.

Of the other houses, the king preferred Euxinograd, and also loved his hunting weekends in Tzarska and Ovnarsko. Giovanna also adored Euxinograd (although she thought the furniture was ghastly) on the Black Sea. She never cared for the mountains, but was happy to see her husband thoroughly enjoying himself in his hunting lodges. But her favorite house was Kritchim.

In Sofia, he was usually tense and preoccupied. Even when he retired to their apartments after a busy day, it often took him a long time to unwind. He would pace the room until Giovanna could not stand it anymore. "Will you please stop it? You're making me nervous too!" she would plead. Then she would add in a conciliatory gesture: "If both of us get that nervous, it will end in an explosion. But, all right, you are the older one, so I'll keep quiet and try to calm you."

Boris controlled himself well in front of outsiders. However, one day, after a very upsetting meeting with a politician, he showed Giovanna his mouth. He had made such an effort to contain his rage that he had clenched his teeth until he had broken the tip of one of them. After another angry argument, the queen's lady-in-waiting surprised him as he smashed a jar of jam against the wall, thinking that he was alone. Boris used to release his emotions after the crises, when he was alone with his intimates. Then all his frustrations would come out in a verbal thunderstorm, surprisingly rich in curses, epithets, and colorful metaphors from the most vivid Bulgarian and French folklore. Words were said sometimes that no "jeune fille de bonne famille," let alone a Savoia princess, was supposed ever to have heard.

Boris never ceased to amaze his wife. Since she had first met him, she had noticed his extraordinary, almost phenomenal memory, curiously synchronized with some kind of built-in calendar mechanism. Not only did he remember the most minute details of events that had occurred several years before, but he could also quote the precise date: "It was on April 24, 1922," or, "It happened on Friday the 15th of July, at 5 P.M." He never forgot a face, no matter how plain, or a name, no matter how complicated. Another unusual feature was his eyes. Giovanna had never seen eyes whose color so reflected mood changes. One day they were gray-green, the next day one could swear that they were the lightest of blue, but one must beware when they turned dark gray! It was a sure sign that His Majesty was very, very angry. His vision was extraordinary too: his eyes were like a combination of natural binoculars (he could see for miles) and an infrared device (he could see in the dark).

But mainly she was impressed by his knowledge. Everything seemed to interest him, while in certain fields—like botany, zoology, and engines—he was an expert. He knew as much about mountain plants, butterflies, and snakes—his specialities—as any professional scientist. He worked very closely with the director of the Royal Museum of Natural History, Dr. Bouresh; and he could repair any automobile. Everybody in Bulgaria knew stories about the king stopping on the road personally to repair the broken-down cars of motorists. When new locomotives were bought, he would join the selection committee to test the engines in person.

His use of humorous words in every language made Giovanna laugh. Apart from Bulgarian, French, and German, the languages he spoke perfectly, and Italian and English, which he spoke very well, King Boris had a good grasp of Turkish, Russian, Greek, and Albanian. He spoke French with the queen but adored inserting colloquial foreign expressions in the conversation.

Boris read a great deal, mostly memoirs, and historical and scientific books. He loved the theater, the opera, and certain kinds of music, including Wagner and Viennese operettas, but although he could paint quite well, he was not particularly interested in collecting art. Although not a gourmet (except for his passion for oysters, which were very difficult to find in Bulgaria, he was not particularly interested in food and his tastes were very simple), he knew a lot about cuisine. The daily meals were ordered by the queen, but recognizing Boris expertise, she let him decide on the menu and the wines for special occasions.

By the time Princess Maria-Luisa was born, Giovanna was no longer an outsider in the palace, nor a foreigner in Bulgaria. She had definitely asserted herself as the "Tzaritza," the queen. The king's everyday habits had changed considerably, and the entourage of his bachelor days realized that his free time now belonged to his wife and daughter.

By 1934, Evdokia brought up the idea of building a separate house for herself somewhere near Sofia. Boris did not object. An architect, Yordan Sevov, was recommended to the princess—a tall, distinguished man with a slight limp and much charm. Nobody, of course, could have predicted at that time that his selection would have far-reaching consequences in the political life of the country.

*       *       *

The rapprochement with Yugoslavia, inaugurated by King Boris the previous year, was one major policy of the new regime with which he was in full accord. The timing of King Alexander's state visit to Sofia on September 29 could not have been more propitious for the Bulgarian monarch. Deliberately or not, Alexander thwarted attempts by Bulgarian republicans, most of them friends of Yugoslavia, to overthrow the monarchy.

A few weeks after the May 19 coup, the Bulgarian minister in Belgrade, George Kiosseivanov, arrived in Sofia to report to the new government that "the palace circles in Yugoslavia are not indifferent to whether Bulgaria is a republic or a monarchy." This warning was a result of Alexander's fear that a republic in Bulgaria could be a "contagious example" in his own country, where the ruling Serbian minority was surrounded by antimonarchist Croatian, Macedonian, Albanian, Slovene, and other populations. At the gala reception for Alexander in the Sofia palace, King Boris told Kiosseivanov personally: "He came to stress our professional solidarity . . . "

The visit required considerable courage, both on the part of the royal visitor, whose name headed the hit list of every Balkan terrorist, and on that of the host, who knew that any attempt on Alexander's life on Bulgarian territory would be a catastrophe, maybe a *casus belli.* For the security services, the unprecedented visit of the hated "Serbian king" to the hated "Bugarashi" enemies was a nightmare. Several hundred Macedonians and extreme Bulgarian nationalists were put under preventive arrest or sent out of Sofia. The tension grew almost unbearable. King Boris was, of course, perfectly conscious of the tremendous risks, but he could only repeat, fatalistically, for the thousandth time in his life: "These are *les risques du métier,"* the professional hazards.

But the visit of King Alexander and Queen Maria turned into an enormous success. The Sofia crowds received the two royal couples, flanked by the new pro-Yugoslav government, warmly. There were receptions, speeches, parades, and ovations everywhere. It was the consecration of the Bulgaro-Yugoslav reconciliation, of the new friendship which had to bring—everybody so hoped—security for the Yugoslavs and important concessions to the Bulgarian minorities.

It was strange, and unprecedented, to hear inside the walls of the Sofia palace speeches and toasts in the Serbian tongue (Boris spoke in Bulgarian, Alexander in Serbian) extolling the friendship between the two long-quarreling nations. Meanwhile, a sincere personal friendship was also developing between the two royal couples. They enjoyed each other's company very much during the deer hunt and pheasant shoot Boris organized at the Kritchim villa. From there, incognito and on the spur of the moment, they drove to nearby Plovdiv, Bulgaria's second largest city. Romantic Plovdiv, the ancient Philippopolis, built around 340 B.C. on seven steep hills ("Tépés," in Turkish) on the banks of the wide Maritza River, was Queen Giovanna's favorite town. She had said to Boris: "If your father were still king, I would have loved for us to have lived in Plovdiv!" And he answered with the kind of black humor she did not appreciate: "When you become a widow, you can go live in Plovdiv."

She was delighted to show the guests the town's old quarters with their narrow cobblestone streets, the old wooden houses with carved ceilings and eaves—typical examples of Bulgarian architecture—and the home on Djambaz-Tépé where Lamartine lived in 1833. The two couples, still unrecognized by most passers-by, climbed the rocky Nebett-Tépé on foot to admire the magnificent panoramic view over the picturesque town, all the way to the first contours of the remote Sredna-Gora Mountains. In the meantime, as word spread of the royal visitors, crowds of friendly citizens rushed to greet them. This unscheduled contact with crowds, with no security escort was quite a new experience for the Yugoslav dictator-monarch. Taken by surprise, tense and rather nervous in the beginning, he soon relaxed and enjoyed enormously the handshakes and spontaneous greetings.

Nevertheless, when Alexander left Bulgaria unharmed, a gigantic sigh of relief was heard on both sides of the border.

The visit, of course, did not endear Boris to the IMRO. The Macedonians did not see much difference between the Yugoslav policy of the new regime and the king's. "As far as the rapprochement with the Serbian king is concerned, King Boris took this road even before the coup. Circles close to the palace insinuated that the purpose was to snatch the banner of Serbo-Bulgarian rapprochement from the hands of the Agrarians and Zvenars," wrote IMRO leader Ivan Mihailov in his *Memoirs*. "Long before the coup, highly placed military officers informed friends of ours in Sofia that King Boris had often, openly, and unequivocally expressed his lack of sympathy for the Macedonian cause and his desire for friendship with Belgrade. . . . The large masses in Bulgaria did not know it, but in certain political circles, it was no secret that King Boris's crown was saved by the Serbian king."

Mihailov writes that in conversations they had after World War II, Kiosseivanov told him that King Boris had instructed him to emphasize to King Alexander that his visit to Sofia "would do a great personal service" to the Bulgarian king. After the May 19 coup, Kiosseivanov (as quoted by Mihailov) was asked by King Alexander to leave immediately for Sofia to tell the new rulers that he, the Yugoslav king, desired that they not touch the crown of Bulgaria. "When the neighbor's house is burning, the fire may engulf my house, too," said Alexander.

\*    \*    \*

Then, on October 9, 1934, hardly one month after the Yugoslav royal visit to Sofia, tragedy struck again: King Alexander was assassinated on his arrival in Marseilles. It was lucky, in a way, that he was shot in France rather than in Bulgaria—another Balkan war may have been avoided.

The open car with the king and French Foreign Minister Louis Barthou was rolling slowly along the Marseilles boulevards lined with cheering crowds, when the assassin emerged from the crowd. Shouting, "Vive le Roi!"—he jumped on the automobile's step and shot Alexander almost point blank. After also shooting Barthou, the attacker was cut down by the sabre of the mounted French colonel escorting the official car.

The assassination was attributed to the Croatian Ustashi organization, mortal enemies of Serbian domination, but it was established that the actual assassin was Bulgarian, the IMRO member Tchernozemski, alias "Vlado the Chauffeur."

Tchernozemski, a loner and a fanatical Macedonian nationalist, had joined Mihailov's organization at an early age, participating in tchetnik raids inside Yugoslavia. This quiet man, who tried to write verses in his free moments, was one of the 1930 assassins of a Protoguerovist leader.

While international opinion was profoundly shocked by King Alexander's murder, the action of "Vlado the Chauffeur" was acclaimed in many Croatian and Macedonian circles as a great "exploit" and a patriotic self-sacrifice. Ivan Mihailov reports in his *Memoirs* that "millions of people praise him and bless him because he is a hero against tyranny . . . What he did in Marseilles cannot be called a murder. It is so clear to anyone who knows anything about the regime of King Alexander and the plans of Belgrade . . . Vlado emerged merely as the executor of the punishment that, through thousands of curses and rivers of tears and blood, was pronounced against him by entire nations, like the Macedonian Bulgarians, the Croatians, the Albanians, and millions of other discontent citizens of Yugoslavia, including many Serbs.

"The words of Mrs. Raditch [the wife of the Croatian leader Stiepan Raditch], 'God bless the hand of Tchernozemski!' are the words of millions of wives, mothers, and sisters."

            \*      \*      \*

On January 22, only eight months after the coup, the Kimon Gheorghiev government fell. The unrest in the army, spurred mostly by the Zveno elements in the government and their disloyalty to the king, had been growing for several months. The officers who had put Gheorghiev in the premier's seat with the intention of ruling the country through his cabinet realized that the real power was eluding them and decided to withdraw their mandate. The idea of a military cabinet was gaining ground. As a first move against the Gheorghiev government, the officers insisted on replacing the National Renovation director, a Zvenar, with a colonel. Then they started openly to criticize Damian Veltchev for allowing his Zveno friends to play such prominent roles in the cabinet. In December, Veltchev made another attempt to undermine the king's power by transferring some of the crown's prerogatives to a newly devised state council, controlled by Veltchev, but the proposal was opposed by the monarchist officers. The American legation reported to the State Department: "Rumors, true or possibly exaggerated, were rife that Veltchev, whose lasting hostility to the crown was well known, was only waiting for an opportunity to force the hand of the king and even remove him entirely, if necessary. The effect was very harmful to the government: it resulted in an increased loyalty on the part of the leading military men who realized that no greater harm could be done to the new regime than the current rumors of its 'republicanism.' Moreover, it was recognized that the only way to overcome the increasing hostility of the people was to manifest a complete unity between the king and the government and, thus, utilize his personal popularity."

The American minister F. A. Sterling also reported that in order to avoid the crisis, the Military League discussed with Veltchev the various ways a cabinet could be dominated by them. But Veltchev responded with personal demands that alarmed the officers. He wanted to be the minister of war or the president of the cabinet and also have full power to choose the ministers. The league decided that they had to choose between their loyalty to the king and their loyalty to Veltchev. "The former was the stronger and Veltchev was eliminated."

General Zlatev, who lately had been courted and discreetly encouraged by unofficial emissaries of King Boris, was asked to form the new cabinet. It included three officers and three political ministers from the former cabinet, but eliminated the Zvenars and the coup's *éminence grise*, Veltchev. With the king's approval, Zlatev proclaimed that some of the "positive achievements" of May 19 would be preserved: the ban of the political parties, the administrative reforms, and the outlawing of the Macedonian organizations—both the Mihailovs and the Protoguerovists. In the moderate (or repentant?) leader of the league, General Zlatev, the monarch had found a precious and discreet ally who helped him to purge the league of its radical and republican elements and quietly to deliver the organization to the crown.

The fall of the Kimon Gheorghiev-Damian Veltchev regime was a major victory for Boris. In the king's plans, the Zlatev cabinet had only a transitional role, a first step toward the return to the barracks of *all* the military.

Sterling commented: "To the extreme loyalists, the king has proved once more that he is a good tactician, a man of political wisdom, self-control, and great ability in handling difficult situations. On May 19, the Military League and Veltchev check-mated him; eight months later the league stands by the king and Veltchev is check-mated. Undoubtedly, the king, by approving the change (and it is likely that he was instrumental in its accomplishment), undertook a great responsibility, which he previously did not assume when the Gheorghiev cabinet was forced upon him. He is thus given another opportunity for real leadership if he cares to take advantage of it."

*    *    *

As expected, Zlatev did not last long, not even three full months. Unable to gain the strong support of the Military League, he soon became a target of its younger, politically ambitious members, who were impatient to put the government under full military control.

The Zlatev cabinet crisis was precipitated by the unexpected arrest of former Prime Ministers Tzankov and Kimon Gheorghiev, followed by their internment on a small Black Seas island. Both men were accused by the interior minister of antigovernment activities. On his way to internment, Tzankov was given tremendous ovations from large crowds of his followers at each railroad station. But since the cabinet had not been consulted, three civilian ministers resigned immediately, and that same evening Zlatev presented the king with the resignation of his cabinet.

King Boris spent the next day in consultation with the leaders of the league, who pressed for the appointment of Dimo Kazassov, then minister to Yugoslavia, as prime minister. The officers intended to exercise the real power behind Kazassov. That day, they had their first surprise: King Boris, the usually amenable "Gentleman with the Fedora Hat," simply refused. He suggested instead a totally unexpected man—Andrea Toshev, a respected sixty-eight-year-old retired career diplomat who had for a long time kept out of politics.

Taken by surprise, the league representatives did not refuse outright, but the next day when the negotiations resumed they voiced strong reservations. For they had begun to worry about the king's plans concerning the future cabinet's program and composition, and the role of the army in it. The league's council met that evening, splitting into two groups. The senior officers recommended moderation, cooperation with the king, and acceptance of his candidate, Toshev. But the more radical officers were intransigent. Feeling strong enough to force upon the king a government chosen by them, they refused to make any concession, causing an impasse. In face of the opposition of the officers, the discouraged Toshev returned the king's mandate. It seemed that the king had lost and that, once more, he had to submit to the league's will.

But that Sunday, April 21, 1935, things happened quite differently. People had not counted on the "new" King Boris. Calling Toshev, he told him in no uncertain terms that he insisted that he form the cabinet. Then, ignoring the league's official delegation, he summoned to the palace three of its moderate members who the night before had opposed the radical officers. The Sofia garrison commander, the War Ministry chancery chief, and the assistant chief of staff were told by the king that, whether the league liked it or not, he was appointing Andrea Toshev prime minister. He demanded the cooperation of the three officers. The generals saluted and left, promising to try to convince their colleagues.

The king's action was as uncharacteristic as it was risky. His friends and advisers were delighted to see him act so firmly, but they were also scared. How would the league react? Would the republican-minded officers stage another coup, impose their will by force? Without waiting, Boris publicly announced the Toshev appointment in a personal manifesto which was published and distributed the same evening. The league, divided and disconcerted, did not budge. The monarchist officers, an overwhelming majority, disavowed the disobedient members and proclaimed their readiness to follow the king.

It was a veritable *coup d' état*, but this time a coup executed by the king himself. That day, Boris took full control of the state affairs. The role was not of his choosing, but the May 19 coup had forced the democratic monarch to abandon one of the basic dogmas of his credo, "The king reigns but does not govern." From now on, the king was going to reign *and* govern. It was not, however, "La Restauration," the return of the old regime, for Boris publicly endorsed some of the principles which had inspired the league to intervene and abolish the party system. He got rid of Zveno and most of the authoritarians, but he did not resuscitate the parties. The king's manifesto of April 21 proclaimed solemnly that "There will be no turning back!" But at the same time, he made clear his determination to return to a constitutional government, elected in free elections, and to submit to the people's approval constitutional reforms "corresponding to the present complications and to the requirements of the new times."

The role of the Toshev cabinet, comprising three generals, three non-aligned specialists, but also three respected political figures, was to achieve the "normalization" of the regime as a transition to a future constitutional system: The word "normalization" became used more and more frequently by the king and by the politicians. It became to mean much desired panacea for solving all the political problems of the restless nation.

Toshev started immediately to draft a new constitution which would be submitted to a special commission of eminent jurists before being presented to the people for approval. The cabinet was still discussing the eventual form of the people's involvement—a referendum, or a Grand National Assembly?—when an emergency forced it to delay work on both the constitution and the "normalization."

The new war minister was quietly but effectively purging the army of the republican-minded officers involved in the May 19 coup. The league's old leadership was gradually stripped of its power. After his fall from power, Damian Veltchev had been expelled from the League and placed under surveillance. On the verge of being completely eliminated from political life, Veltchev undertook a desperate action. In the summer, he went in exile to Belgrade, where he reestablished contacts with his followers and with left-wing Agrarian émigrés.

In September 1935, with the assistance of Serbian unofficial circles who feared a worsening of the Bulgaro-Yugoslav relations (Andrea Toshev was of Macedonian origin and had written, in his youth, strong anti-Serbian articles), the veteran-conspirator Veltchev organized a plot for a new coup against King Boris.

On October 2, as he was illegally crossing the Yugoslav border into Bulgaria, Veltchev was arrested. Prime Minister Toshev, announcing that a large conspiracy had been uncovered, stated that Veltchev and his group had planned to assassinate the king during a military parade and seize power. Several league members, including General Kyril Stanchev, former minister Kroom Kolev, and the pro-Soviet General Vladimir Zaimov, were put in jail, together with left-wing Agrarians such as Dr. George M. Dimitrov, accused of participating in the conspiracy.

It was a new shock for King Boris, but he reacted calmly, almost philosophically. It was a period during which he was increasingly attracted to meditation and religion. At the first opportunity, just one week after the discovery of the plot, he went to his mountain lodge in Ovnarsko with his brother. The entry for October 9 in his hunter's log reads: "In times of grave importance, we came here, during a draught and summerlike heat. Yesterday we went to Edy Gyol. Today, at 7 in the morning, we are leaving for Sofia. God be with us!" On the bottom of the page, in another handwriting, one reads: "May God be always with Your Majesty!" signed Lyubomir Loultchev. The king had brought his mystic friend, the Dunnovist, to the mountain with him.

After a much publicized trial before a military court in February 1936, Veltchev and three coconspirators were sentenced to death. General Zaimov was released. But one month later, King Boris, as usual, commuted the sentences. Later, in a conversation with Draganov in Germany, Marshal Goering expressed his frank opinion about the commutation of Veltchev's death sentence. "You know my admiration for His Majesty King Boris," the Reichsmarshal said. "That's why I'll permit myself to say what we think here about this Veltchev affair. I think that His Majesty made a big mistake. I know how hard it is to sign a death sentence. But sometimes higher state interests require such a difficult decision. Look at our party: early in our regime we had to be ruthless and liquidate our colleague Roehm and all his supporters. It was a terribly painful decision. They were our comrades; some of them were personal friends. But there was no other way. And you see, since that purge, nobody has thought of plotting and dissenting, nor will they ever do so. We assured our back and can now devote our time and energy to accomplishing our task, without worrying." Having evoked the example of the horrible bloodbath of the S.A. troopers, Goering gave his grim advice: "One should never keep an adversary or a potential adversary in the house. Compared to our agonizing decision, King Boris's choice was easy: Veltchev is no friend of his; Veltchev is an adversary."

In the meantime, Premier Toshev, discouraged by the lack of full support from some of his colleagues in the cabinet and shaken by the discovery of the Veltchev conspiracy, resigned on November 23. His foreign minister George Kiosseivanov, a trusted advisor to the king, was named prime minister.

\* \* \*

# CHAPTER XVII

# The Non-Party Regime

WITH THE boat leaving in one hour, the two old friends still had so many things to say to one another. King Boris, on his way to England on this cold afternoon in January 1936, had not seen his confidant since before the 1934 coup, when Draganov, then military attaché in Berlin, was forced to resign from the army. Recently appointed minister to Germany, Draganov had come now to Ostende to see his king off and to hear from him personally the inside story of the latest events in Bulgaria.

"What are your plans now, Your Majesty?" Draganov asked, when the king finished telling how he had managed to neutralize the authors of the coup, gradually replacing them with a government headed by Georgi Kiosseivanov, a loyal monarchist. "How do you envision the makeup of the future system? You can't go back and restore the past with all its faults. But neither do we want any of those authoritarian rules, so much in vogue nowadays, nor can you put the normalization off too long. The banned parties are restless and may act. What is the solution?"

They left the cabin to go up to the open deck. As they walked to and fro while the past passengers were boarding, the king confessed that the question of normalization had been his main preoccupation for the last several months.

"The situation is indeed very difficult," he said. "To return to the old system would be dangerous: the army bristles so at the idea, that it may intervene again. Besides, I signed the manifesto last year: no going back! But a way must be found to discard the outworn politicians. Here is what I intend to do: first, devise a procedure to call municipal elections. That will be a good test, buying us some time. Then I'll reshuffle the cabinet, drop some of the old faces, and replace them with younger members of the parties. I have come to realize that I can't work with the old-time politicians! With such a reconstructed cabinet, we'll call general elections for the national assembly, which will then make a few small changes in the constitution."

Draganov liked the plan, but he cautioned the king: "No matter how much we disavow the old parties and politicians, we must keep in mind that they still have their influence in the country. To appease them, Kiosseivanov should at least make contact with them."

The boat blew its horn. It was departure time. Draganov took leave after King Boris instructed him to meet him in Paris, when the London visit was over.

*     *     *

The man King Boris had chosen to carry out the normalization process was particularly well qualified for the mission. Georgi Kiosseivanov, the foreign minister in the last cabinet, was not a politician and, although he had grown up in a politically active family (or perhaps because of that?), he had never had much respect for the parties. That, in the present circumstances, constituted a valuable advantage. He was a career diplomat, among the most brilliant at the Foreign Ministry, who had served in all the Balkan countries, leaving an excellent impression. In a period when Bulgaria wanted better relations with her neighbors, that was another fortunate quality. In addition, before joining the Toshev cabinet, Kiosseivanov had served briefly as chief of the palace chancery and was considered a trusted "Tsarsky tchovek"—king's man.

Refinement and graciousness were not among the principal qualities of Bulgarian statesmen. The gentlemenly, soft-spoken Kiosseivanov in his well-tailored morning coat, striped trousers, and top hat was, therefore, not a typical figure on the political scene. A portly, balding man in his early fifties, with the pleasant face of an oversized baby with extraordinarily pale blue eyes, the new prime minister exuded the qualities of serenity and wisdom rather than energy and will power. His slow, almost phlegmatic, gestures and movements concealed a vivid mind, inclined to sharp and sober analyses.

Kiosseivanov, a cosmopolitan man of great culture, had studied in France, receiving a doctor's degree in law in Paris. He had spent his entire career in the diplomatic service, except when he served as an officer during the wars, and when he resigned during the Stambolisky regime.

King Boris saw in "Kiosseto" (as he was called by his colleagues) personal qualities promising a smooth collaboration: a highly civilized person of impeccable integrity, who was calm, polite, and discreet, and who spoke foreign languages well. An excellent bridge player and a charming and convincing conversationalist, he had the ease of a man of the world. He was less at ease as a public speaker, however; and having never lived near the peasant masses, he had nothing of the man-of-the-people about him.

All the ministers in his first cabinet were political newcomers: two retired generals with no connections to the league; an energetic war minister, General Christo Loukov, a declared opponent of the league; and a few technocrats. The first task of the government was to balance the budget and to consolidate the administrative apparatus, demoralized by the recent frequent changes of government. At the same time, Kiosseivanov, who was also minister of foreign affairs, continued to improve Bulgaria's relations with her neighbors, especially Yugoslavia, where he was highly respected personally. Loukov, on his part, continued firmly to purge the army of politically minded officers and to redirect it to perform its professional duties exclusively.

To King Boris, this task was as urgent and primordial as it was delicate. The politicization of the military had become a personal, emotional problem for him, a painful subject about which he felt strongly. "I am disgusted with the army," he used to tell his entourage after the republican elements had gained influence in the Military League. To a foreign diplomat he confided,[1] "Three times the army has risen to take over control: once against Prince Alexander Battenberg; once against Stambolisky; and once against me [May 1934]. The next time it will be against Bulgaria herself!"

To depoliticize the army had become an obsession, and after his successful maneuvering in 1934 and 1935, the process was well underway. But Boris also realized that high morale and strict professionalism could not be expected if the army was deprived of the most elementary equipment, and the Bulgarian army in that period was, materially speaking, in a deplorable state—too small, equipped with obsolete arms, and without munitions. King Boris mobilized his personal contacts abroad to convince foreign governments to allow Bulgaria an adequate defense force and to assist with the necessary credits.

His chosen policy, in contradistinction to the traditional, nationalistic and right-wing forces in the country, emphasized Bulgaria's commitments to peace and international cooperation—renouncement of the use of force to correct past wrongs, attachment to the League of Nations, and friendship for all countries, including former foes. The new regime's goal was to change Bulgaria's image abroad and erase the unfavorable impressions left by the impulsive policies of King Ferdinand. Nobody was better equipped to implement this policy than Kiosseivanov, who was willing to make unpopular decisions. Thus, when sanctions were proposed against Italy after she invaded Ethiopia, Bulgaria, in order to prove her adherence to the League of Nations' principles, voted in favor of the sanctions, in spite of its close friendship with Rome.

The Bulgarian image still suffered among the victors of World War I— the antiparliamentarian coup of May 19 had revived some of the old

---

[1]U.S. minister, F. A. Sterling, in June 1936.

suspicions—although King Boris's repeated visits to England and France and his conciliatory attitude toward the Balkan Pact nations had achieved some success.

✻   ✻   ✻

After his January visit to London, he cabled to Pavel Grouev from Paris, on February 2, 1936, in the special private code to which only Grouev in Sofia and Draganov in Berlin had the key. "Yesterday [in London] I had a long talk with Sargent."[2] In general, they appreciate any effort to preserve our national independence. But unfortunately, the current events at home, especially their impressions of a politicized army, have greatly undermined our prestige."

Three days later, he sent a five-page typewritten letter from Paris, summing up his talks with English and French statesmen. "Grouev, read this letter to the prime minister before putting it in our private archive," he began. Reporting on his talks with Eden, Vansittart, Sargent, and Mac-Donald, King Boris wrote: "It is incredible how well informed they are about our sad internal situation, and it is very painful to hear with what condescending compassion they regard our military. They do not feel confident about it and believe that if we don't have elections and a parliament in the next few months . . . there will be new unhappy ordeals in store for us. When our officers' corps is mentioned, they speak in the tone we use to talk about the Rumanian army."[3]

The same unflattering impression of Bulgarian officers was rife in Paris, where President Lebrun compared their unfortunate involvement in politics to the politicking of the Greek military. "What a pity!" the French president said. "Your country used to be famous for its excellent officers' corps."

Lebrun was more friendly and trusting than on any of King Boris's previous visits. He asked questions about the Damian Veltchev trial, which had started in Sofia, and the king explained that the outcome depended not on him but on the tribunal which, incidentally, had to apply laws reinforced by the regime of Veltchev himself. "When Lebrun realized that I didn't want to be another Alexander[4], he tapped me amiably on the knee and said: 'You have had a very rough time. But try to continue on the road of normalization, and when you have laid the groundwork, bring back the parliament.' "

The problem with the military seemed to torment King Boris con-

---

[2]Orme Sargent, under-secretary of the British Foreign Office.
[3]Bulgarians had no great respect for Rumanian officers, whom they considered to be vain and frivolous men, not to be taken seriously.
[4]King Alexander of Yugoslavia, after suspending the Parliament, took all the power into his own hands.

stantly. On his arrival in Paris, while receiving Draganov in the Hotel Majestic, he could not get off the subject of the politicization of the military. Boris was in a bad mood that day. He had hit his head on the boat crossing the channel, and the wound was still bleeding. He was also annoyed by the unusual number of French police assigned to protect him. The Paris authorities had received information that two dangerous Bulgarian anarchists had left Varna for France, Draganov told him.

"That's the best thing that could happen to me!" King Boris said, as usual exaggerating when upset or frustrated. "Maybe it's the best way for me to end, like King Alexander. Otherwise, the way things are going at home, I'll end up disgraced." He tried to explain: "This time I return from London discouraged; I realize how people look at us. You should hear what the English think of us! They still have some esteem for me, but the Bulgarian people, and especially the Bulgarian army, are finished for them. Vansittart, for instance, told me that if it weren't for me enduring all this, Bulgaria would have perished. And the captain who was my escort told me that in the War Office they regretted that the Bulgarian army, which they used to esteem is now worth nothing because of its politicization. I can't stand it anymore! I hate this army. I am worse than Le Monarque, because I hold grudges and don't forget . . ."

They also talked about the Damian Veltchev trial. What to do if the tribunal sent the king a death sentence with a recommendation for clemency. Many Bulgarians wished that the king would ignore the recommendation and have Veltchev, the perennial conspirator, executed. "If a death sentence is brought to me with a plea for clemency, I cannot be untrue to myself," King Boris said. "I'll have it commuted." (Which, of course, he did.)

It seemed to be a period of constant problems. King Ferdinand announced to his daughters during a visit that he intended to celebrate his seventy-fifth birthday in Bulgaria. "It will be either in Bulgaria or not at all! Let them stop me at Dragoman!" (the frontier station) Le Monarque declared. Boris was very upset when Evdokia broke the news. That was all he needed with the delicate position he and the country were in. "He's quite capable of doing it!" Boris exploded. "He wants to sink me at any price. But let him come! Then I'll take my hat and quit!"

King Boris took advantage of the favorable atmosphere he felt in Paris to open the question of Bulgaria's need for modern armaments. Foreign Minister Flandin listened attentively to his arguments and encouraged him with a "Let's hope you succeed!" Alexis Léger, the real power at the Quai d'Orsay, was cool at the start. He obviously wanted to "understand where I was headed, toward normalization or toward King Alexander's model," Boris wrote to Grouev. But when the king explained his plans and demonstrated that an independent Bulgaria, capable of defending itself, would be in everyone's interest, Léger's attitude changed completely. He complimented

King Boris for his moderating influence and said with a smile, "So, you want weapons, do you?"

"Yes, I do, not to wage war, but, in accordance with the treaty, to replace obsolete matériel. We need new armaments in order to normalize the situation at home, and, especially, to encourage our military to attend to their real business, rather than meddling with politics."

\*     \*     \*

During the first half of 1936, the Kiosseivanov government achieved a series of successes in the economy and in public works, and a certain stabilization was felt throughout the country. Large portions of the public seemed to believe that the state could, after all, be run without the political parties. That was not, of course, the opinion of the increasingly restless old politicians, who considered the king's "personal regime" a purely transitional one.

Another who also believed that the "personal regime" should lead to some popular participation in the government was King Boris. The exact form of the future government was not yet clear, but Kiosseivanov's cabinet—as Toshev's before it—worked assiduously on different proposals for constitutional amendments and electoral laws that would somehow bypass the old system. After a conversation with the king in June 1936, the American minister Sterling reported to the State Department: "The present government is of the King's own choosing. He is now responsible for its success or failure. Of this he is well aware and anxious, true patriot that he is, to lead his country back to tranquility and a surcease of the political unrest which has disturbed Bulgaria for several years. Neither by nature nor inclination a dictator, he wishes to bring back normal political conditions and a return to constitutional government as soon as possible. It was evident from the King's manner that he is worried, as well as earnestly endeavoring to find a solution."

Anxious to give the no-party government a wider popular support, the king tried to associate it with the two largest political forces, the Agrarians and the Movement of Tzankov. He asked the prime minister to approach their leaders, Guitchev and Tzankov, and invite them to join the cabinet as individuals. Kiosseivanov, a sincere believer in the nonparty system, was not enthusiastic about the idea, but he loyally obeyed the king's wishes.

Parallel to consultations with Kiosseivanov, political figures were sounded out unofficially by the king's personal emissaries. It was a habit of Boris to rely on private sources of information outside the government, mostly members of his palace staff, but at times also personal friends. Grouev, for instance, was his contact with the foreign diplomats and with the Ministry of Foreign Affairs; Colonel Panov informed him about developments in the army and the mood of the military; and Petar Kostov lived among newspapermen and reported on their information. For delicate, discreet missions with ministers and opposition politicians, the king at that period used his inspector of the palaces, Dimitar Guentchev.

Guentchev, a former army officer, was an energetic, sometimes blunt man, totally devoted to the crown. He had an impressive record of bravery during the war, where he had lost part of his hearing as a result of an injury. Boris trusted him, and between 1935 and 1938 used him as the principal liaison between the palace and the ministers. As inspector of the palaces, Guentchev also ran with a firm hand the royal estates and their personnel. Boris once wrote of him: "I know well the good and the bad sides of Caligula's character. ["Caligula" was the king's nickname for Guentchev.] But he has two valuable qualities: a brave loyalty and, thanks to his deafness, when you beat an idea into his head, he will repeat it and plant it in the right place without changing it or adding to it. And if it doesn't work, he'll take on himself the responsibility for an idea advanced by me, without betraying me."

Neither Kiosseivanov nor the king's emissaries succeeded in convincing the Agrarians to join their former Tzankovists foes in support of the nonparty government. "It's unrealistic," their leader Guitchev answered. "Have you ever seen sweet water and bitter water run from the same faucet?"

Tzankov, on the contrary, was ready to cooperate, and two of his close collaborators became ministers. "With two of our members participating not only with my permission but by my instructions," Tzankov told the prime minister, "His Majesty links the destiny of the throne with the government and, also with our movement." But Tzankov reminded Kiosseivanov and the king of their commitment to hold elections no later than October, a condition for his movement's participation.

The government solemnly proclaimed its "determination to achieve in the immediate future the normalization of the situation and to prepare the conditions for bringing the people into the government; free general elections will be held in the second half of October," i.e., only three-and-a-half months later.

Suddenly, all former politicians woke up and became agitated, hoping that the elections would disavow the nonparty regime and resuscitate the parliamentary system based on parties.

The plans of the king and Kiosseivanov, however, were different. With no desire to restore the party system, they wanted a gradual return to some form of parliamentarian democracy in which the voters would not be obliged to pass through the party clubs to elect their representatives. King Boris, especially, was very desirous of seeing such a Sobranié. Concerned about the worsening of the international situation, he told Dr. N. P.

Nikolaev, a respected statesman and later a minister in Kiosseivanov's cabinet, "A storm is gathering in Europe, and we should not be caught in our present state, with the country being ruled by myself and ten ministers appointed by me. Events may put us in very difficult situations, and we, just a handful of people, cannot decide the fate of the nation without the participation of the people."

The deadline for the elections being unrealistically short, they had to be put off, and the king had to revise his plans. In a confidential letter he sent to Draganov via Guentchev ("Caligula"), he explained his new strategy:

"Caligula sees the solution in a radical restructuring of the state and made a few proposals to that effect. But I think that such a radical upheaval of our political life, without the cooperation of the people, and given the incredible cowardice of our present statesmen, would entail intolerable burdens and responsibilities for me. There is also another problem: many people forget a terrible mortgage whose terms are running out—my last year's manifesto on which I cannot default, as some politicians would like me to do. I must do, or try to do, something in this direction.

"I came to the idea of calling *municipal* elections, based on the law that was made by the 19th of May people. We will see where the people stand. If we are successful, it will mean that the people have approved of the nonparty, or half-partisan, system. If we don't, the failure will be much smaller than it would be with general elections, and we'll still have a clearer orientation. We'll know that the people don't want those things, and I'll contend that I have tried honestly and loyally to follow the road of my manifesto, but that the people don't care for it. In which case, I'll have to revise my position. Thus, the army cannot accuse me of being a liar."

The less ambitious municipal elections took place in 1937. Women were allowed to vote for the first time. To the surprise of the parties and to the delight of the government, the voters were favorable to the government candidates, thus indirectly approving the nonparty system. The king and Kiosseivanov were immensely encouraged by the results and proceeded to organize with greater assurance the legislative elections for the following year.

\* \* \*

In the summer of 1936, King Edward VIII, together with a group of friends, including Mrs. Simpson, his future wife, returning from a cruise around the Dalmatian coast, the Aegean Islands and the Dardanelles, was traveling incognito through Bulgaria. The acting chief of protocol, Stoyan Petrov-Tchomakov, was sent to welcome the royal party at the station of Svilengrad, at the Turkish border, and to accompany it to the Yugoslav frontier.

The special train arrived early in the morning, with the civil and military authorities, the schoolchildren and a brass band waiting impatiently at the station, lavishly decorated for the occasion. But the blinds on the train's windows remained drawn, and King Edward did not appear, although the children broke out into lusty cheers and the band struck up a lively march. Only a Negro steward popped his head out of a window and grinned broadly. Petrov-Tchomakov, well known for his witty reports, wrote: "Merely to say that the people of Svilengrad were disappointed would be an understatement. For a whole week they had been looking forward to the great day when they should see a mighty King and Emperor, and all they were given to behold was a Negro. A nice Negro, it is true, but a poor substitute for the glory and majesty they had been expecting. But to some of the children, who had never seen a Negro in their lives, it must have been, all the same, a thrilling experience and, no doubt, their anthropology teacher was quick to seize the unique opportunity which was offered her to show them a live specimen of the African race."

Petrov-Tchomakov boarded the train and was introduced to King Edward. He had seen the king more than ten years earlier in London, but found that "he had the same boyish appearance, and the same irresistible fascination emanated from his original personality. The people who assembled at the next stations felt it too, as he mixed freely with them, asked questions, received gifts and flowers from gaily attired country girls, and took snapshots of them with his Leica."

Petrov-Tchomakov, invited to have lunch with the king and Mrs. Simpson, was asked by King Edward: "How many Bulgarians are there?" "Eight-and-a-half million," he replied, "of whom only 6 million are in the kingdom." The king asked worriedly: "Where are the others?" Petrov-Tchomakov answered: "The Peace Treaty has placed one-and-a-half million of them under Yugoslavia, another half-million under Greece and a further half-million under Rumania." The king looked surprised but made no comment.

A telegram was handed to Edward announcing that King Boris would meet him at the next station. While everybody was surprised and excited, Petrov-Tchomakov remembered how "I could not help feeling proud when I saw how highly King Boris was thought of by King Edward." Boris boarded the train and the two rulers greeted each other with great cordiality. Apart from their common Saxe-Coburg ancestry, they knew each other from Boris's visits at Balmoral and Windsor. Then the two kings drove by automobile to Vrana, and after the host showed his parks and house, he drove his guest to Sofia. There he showed him the Alexander Nevsky Cathedral and other points of interest in the capital, and then took him to the palace to introduce him to his family.

Princess Maria-Luisa, almost four, talked politely to the English guests for a moment, then abruptly took leave, saying in German, "I must go now.

I have to go to work." King Edward, who adored speaking in German and never missed an opportunity to do so, found the little princess's words hilarious. Roaring with laughter, he answered "Leider muss Ich auch!" ("Me too, unfortunately!")

For the rest of his life, King Boris referred to Edward VIII as "Leider muss Ich auch!" and later, during the war, the phrase became the code word for the British royal family.

Boris did not know that his guest had also coined a nickname for him: in Edward's ear, the names of the lady-in-waiting Petroff and the king's secretary Handjiev became "Petrol" and "Handkerchief." That was how the Bulgarian royal family was designated during World War II in all coded messages from Buckingham Palace. Except when the British were really angry. Then they used a code word derived from the name of one of Boris's friends, which Edward VIII had found very funny: Mr. "Baggarov."

Boris accompanied Edward on the two-hour train journey to the Yugoslav border. Petrov-Tchomakov reports: "In the dining-car, where the other members of the royal party were introduced to him, he held the company under the spell of his conversation. Whoever had the opportunity to approach King Boris was struck by the astounding amount of detailed information he possessed on every possible subject. Endowed with irresistible charm, he was most democratic in manner and could mix with everybody with unaffected simplicity."

After saying good-bye to his guests at the frontier station of Dragoman, Boris joined the crowd of town people, shaking hands and talking to them. Petrov-Tchomakov writes: "He seemed to know them all by name, and probably did. He stood in the midst of a knot of happy and smiling people and fondled, as he talked, the head of a rather dirty little boy who stood unceremoniously with his back turned to him. He was happiest when he chatted with peasants about politics and crops."

\* \* \*

The gun salutes that resounded in Sofia on June 16, 1937, did not stop with the twenty-first salvo, as they did when Princess Maria-Luisa was born. They went on 101 times, but as soon as the 22nd shot was heard, people rushed into the streets, congratulating each other on the happy event: the country had a crown prince, an heir to the throne! (The Bulgarian Constitution stipulates that only male children can succeed the king.)

For personal, as well as for state reasons, Boris had yearned for this son for the last four years, and now he was overwhelmed with joy. So once again was the whole nation, for the same old reasons which defy any entirely logical explanation but lead to emotional outbursts of surprising magnitudes. In a matter of hours, the entire nation was in a state of euphoria which lasted for several days. Festive crowds from the provinces, bringing presents

of fruit, little lambs, and calves, invaded the capital, joining Sofia's population in giant processions through the palace grounds, parades and dances in
the streets. For an entire week, the king had to appear several times a day on
the palace balcony and, deeply moved and smiling, acknowledge the
crowd's frenetic ovations.

To celebrate the event, delinquent taxpayers were pardoned, four
thousand prisoners were released, and the marks of all schoolchildren
increased by one point. There was no hesitation over the name to be given
the newborn prince: following the popular will, the king chose the name of
the greatest king in Bulgarian history, Tsar Simeon, who had reigned
beween A.D. 893 and 927. During that most glorious period in the nation's
past, Bulgarian rule was extended over the quasi-totality of the Balkan
peninsula, with Simeon reaching the walls of Constantinople, the capital of
the Byzantine Empire. It was also "the Golden Age" of the old Bulgarian
culture, whose emissaries spread Christian Scripture and the Cyrillic alphabet to other Slavic countries, including Russia. Now, in the troubled 1930s,
the name of the illustrious Tsar Simeon had become, once more, the symbol
of national pride and hopes.

The war minister announced to the army that the baby, Prince Simeon
of Tirnovo, had become a first lieutenant and named patron of a few
regiments. In another symbolic act, King Boris selected for godfather of the
crown prince the oldest army general, Danail Nikolaev, a revered hero of
the 1885 Serbo-Bulgarian War. The Orthodox baptism (there was no
question concerning baptism in the Catholic rite) was performed on July 12
in the palace chapel by the entire Saint-Synod of the Bulgarian church. A
major of the young Bulgarian air force flew to the Holy Land to bring water
from the Jordan River for the occasion. The Royal family, the entire
cabinet, former prime ministers, the highest state officials and generals,
and—typical of Boris's democratic style—simple soldiers and sergeants
attended the ceremony and the palace reception that followed. It was a day
on which everybody—government and opposition, intelligentsia and peasant—felt happy and optimistic. Only Princess Evdokia was trying to
suppress a feeling of dark premonition that the Orthodox baptism had once
again triggered. For some mysterious, mystical reason, she had always
believed that all the misfortunes of the royal family had begun the day
Ferdinand, her father, had violated his solemn oath by christening Prince
Boris in the Orthodox faith some forty-two years earlier.

*       *       *

After receiving many requests, the League of Nations authorized
Bulgaria to replace some obsolete materiel with more modern armament.
For the purchase of new weapons, Bulgaria approached France, England,
and Germany. The first two showed little interest, while the Reich re-

sponded very favorably, opening serious negotiations in Berlin and Sofia. King Boris and his government insisted, however, that the military purchases should in no way lead to an alliance with Germany, and formal assurances to that effect were given by the Reich.

The chief negotiators were War Minister General Loukov and the finance minister Gounev and, on the German side, Goering and Finance Minister Schacht. By 1937, the purchase of important supplies was approved. But at about the same time, frictions appeared between Prime Minister Kiosseivanov and his dynamic, strong-willed war minister, who had proved himself a resolute and popular leader of the army. Certain authoritative traits of Loukov had begun to annoy King Boris, too. He wrote to Draganov in Berlin: "Concerning the frictions between me and 'our Goering'[5] lately, he has thrown himself recklessly into procurements, and without waiting for the arrival of the first installment, costing 2 billion, he now wants to commit us to another 5 billion. Without asking me, he presented his plan at the conference of the senior commanders 15 days ago, hoping to present me with a *fait accompli!* What would you have done in my place? I summoned him to tell him that since all the responsibility is mine, I cannot blindly commit the Bulgarian people to pay annually for 15 years, 500 million for servicing such a debt. The quarrel wasn't small! I hope that he'll remember what I told him; it will spare him law suits and accusations one day. A point on which we also disagreed was the mania of 'our Goering' for motorizing everything in five minutes. But where we shall get the gasoline and where we shall find the tires, only God knows! Another thing I didn't like was that he wanted little by little to take over the police. I opposed all this with my veto."

The problems of aviation and anti-aircraft defense "are the first things that we should pay attention to," wrote the king. "Afterwards, heavy and half-weight artillery will follow, and for naval defense—four submarines and two 600-ton torpedo boats."

"I had a long talk with Christophor (another name for Loukov) today, trying to open his eyes to the need of dealing only with the responsible factors in Germany and through the official channels of our Finance Ministry, so that we won't be accused one day of wheeling-and-dealing. He begins to understand, but like every Bulgarian, he still thinks that he knows better than the king!"

The conflict between Kiosseivanov and his strong-willed war minister worsened to the point where, in January 1938, Loukov had to leave the cabinet to be replaced by General Theodossy Daskalov. King Boris, already concerned by Loukov's growing authority and independence, did not try to retain him.

The same year, the first general elections after the 1934 coup took place,

---

[5]General Loukov

as promised by the king and Kiosseivanov. Instead of party lists, the voters
chose among individual candidates. The results confirmed the popular
approval of the nonparty system, with the government gaining a majority in
the newly elected twenty-fourth Sobranié. The prime minister and the
interior minister N. P. Nikolaev assured the Parliament that the government's goal was a "new democracy," rejecting both the totalitarian Fascist
and Communist regimes and correcting the weaknesses and divisiveness
afflicting the Western democracies, party systems. At the May opening of
the Sobranié, King Boris also solemnly insisted on a middle-of-the-road
domestic policy of national reconciliation and a foreign policy of neutrality
and friendly relations with all countries.

In November 1938, however, the Parliament refused a confidence vote
to some cabinet members and Kiosseivanov formed a new government in
which elected members of the Sobranié participated. It was a first step in the
direction of parliamentary democracy. To sit among the new ministers, the
king chose: his former aide and confidant, Bagrianov, a man close to the
Agrarian party; Professor Bogdan Filov, an eminent archeologist and president of the Academy of Sciences; and Dobri Bojilov, the director of the
National Bank. The prime minister had other preferences for his cabinet,
but he loyally accepted the king's choices.

*       *       *

By 1938, the Bulgarian economy was slipping deeper and deeper into
the German sphere of influence. King Boris and many of the statesmen,
although pleased with the new prosperity brought by the export of local
products, watched the country's trade gradually becoming a monopoly of
the Third Reich with great concern. While the British and the French
showed no interest, the Germans bought almost the entire Bulgarian
tobacco crop, and most agricultural products. At the same time, German
industrial products, offered at very advantageous conditions, inundated the
country, improving spectacularly its standard of living.

The dangers of this economic colonization—a benevolent one, to be
true, profiting both sides—were obvious, especially in a period when the
Great Powers were splitting into two competing hostile blocs. But there was
little that small Bulgaria could do to restore at least a relative balance
between the foreign influences on its economy.

King Boris was determined to keep Bulgaria out of the Great Powers'
rivalry. "When the horses start kicking each other in the stable, the donkeys
get hurt," he used to say quoting a popular proverb. At each visit to
England, he pleaded with the British to start trading with Bulgaria. In Paris,
in February 1936, after his conversation with Flandin, he wrote to Grouev,
for the attention of Kiosseivanov: "I seized the opportunity to emphasize

that it would be very good if we could find some economic backing from France, lest we be exclusively dependent on our only buyer, Germany. He [Flandin] said: 'I understand,' but he didn't seem to be willing to listen further."

The French minister in Sofia, Labouret, met with Kiosseivanov to express his concern about the increasing German economic expansion. The prime minister reiterated Bulgaria's desire for trade with France, pointing out that this depended exclusively on France, which was buying almost nothing from Bulgaria. Indeed, French goods accounted for only 3.3 percent of the Bulgarian import, with only 1.6 percent of Bulgaria's export going to France, while the German import and export represented 54.8 percent and 43.1 percent respectively. Kiosseivanov assigned N. P. Nikolaev to examine, together with the French minister, the possibilities for increasing trade between the two countries. The two men prepared a list of goods available for export, and Labouret did his best to convince Paris, but "this excellent man," reported Nikolaev, "was soon forced to recognize with regret that in France people did not attach any importance to trade with Bulgaria."

The British minister in Sofia, George Rendel, was also alarmed at the degree of the German economic presence when he arrived in Bulgaria in 1938. Commenting on the tobacco export, for instance, he wrote that "our weakness was also partly our own fault," As British smokers had switched from Oriental to American cigarettes, "the British tobacco companies lost interest in Balkans . . . and were not prepared to risk the interests of their shareholders for political reasons." Rendel noted too that when opportunities arose for the British to compete for some major Bulgarian enterprise, the "British firms were not prepared to take either the financial or the political risks involved," despite his urgings. He reports that in 1938, "the Bulgarians were still trying to escape from the steadily tightening German economic fetters, if only because they did not want to be at anyone's complete mercy."

But try as he did to counteract the German economic penetration, Rendel also realized that politically Germany possessed one special advantage. "The Bulgarians had been severely punished after the Second Balkan War and after the First World War," he wrote. "The case in equity and common sense for treaty revision in this area seemed to me very strong. Germany stood for treaty revision on principle. We, on the other hand, not only feared any form of treaty revision . . . but made no secret of our unqualified—and perhaps not always very discriminating—support of Rumania and Yugoslavia, countries we always thought of as potential allies, in contrast to Bulgaria which we were inclined to think of as a potential enemy."

Rendel, an astute diplomat, saw Boris often, becoming friendly with him, especially when the king discovered that Rendel had been a collector of rare butterflies. After spending two years in Bulgaria, the British minister could say that "there was no doubt in my mind that King Boris was systematically trying to improve Anglo-Bulgarian relations [and] that his anxiety to improve and consolidate his relations with us was sincere. For one thing, I believe that he was still at that time genuinely anxious to prevent Bulgaria from becoming irretrievably committed to the German side. For another, I know that he had a real and profound admiration for the British royal family, dating from the time when he had been sent as a boy to represent his father at the coronation of King George V, and the latter had, as King Boris often told me, shown him great kindness and gone out of his way to put the shy and awkward young Balkan prince at his ease."

These are not words of some uncritical foreigner who succumbed to the well-known charm of King Boris. Rendel, a first-rate professional, saw Bulgaria and her king with remarkably sharp and objective eyes, noting scrupulously the qualities and the faults he observed. Here is how King Boris appeared to him:

"Although essentially a Coburg, King Boris was in some way curiously un-Germanic, both in manners and in appearance. He always seemed happiest speaking French, which was, in fact, the language most used in the court. In appearance he was dark and slightly built and looked more of a Latin than a Teuton. His dark hair—already rapidly thinning into baldness—his dark moustache and his quick disarming smile had little that was German about them. At the same time, he had some strong Germanic characteristics, both in his domestic tastes and in his meticulous and encyclopedic approach to every form of factual knowledge. His houses were full of knick-knacks. The walls were a mosaic of small trophies of the chase and mementos of travel. In approaching a subject he liked to begin at the beginning and go through to the end, and much of his conversation consisted in imparting or acquiring, information . . . It was easy to imagine him taking his young queen for walks in the grounds at Vrana and telling her which trees were which and all about the bees."

One of Boris's most engaging characteristics, Rendel found, was a natural courtesy which led him to show friendly civility to everyone, from all classes, "for he was singularly free from snobbery." At a reception in England, for instance, he turned to talk to a British ex-sargeant, who had fought at the Macedonian front. The king immediately identified the sergeant's battery and found something amiable to say. Another time, Rendel noted, he stunned the British naval attaché with his knowledge of all the ships in which the officer had served, of their captains and their armament, and of recent developments in the British navy. Rendel also mentioned that the king was famous for being on the spot, giving practical help in earthquakes, floods, and other emergencies.

But, Rendel wrote, his Germanic thoroughness did not make him tedious in conversation: "He was too well informed and too acute an observer to fail to be interesting. But he instinctively preferred the complicated to the simple explanation, and, occasionally, his analysis of a political problem would lose itself in intricate accounts of the secret causes which had really led to quite simple events . . . He was always quick to follow up a hint, sometimes allusions which had not been made or intended. It suggested at times that, despite his apparent frankness, he was inclined to look too much, as it were, round the corner."

Rendel thought it was a pity that Boris's family should have lived so long in "a tradition of manoeuvre, if not of intrigue, rather than of real leadership." What he called "the Coburg political technique" had become dangerous and mischievous in Ferdinand of Bulgaria, when he tried to play off Russia and Austria against each other. Boris, he believed brought up in this tradition had a Coburg instinct "to rely on manoeuver rather than on a straight and open policy. As the European situation became more complex, these manoeuvers necessarily became more complicated, and he himself became, in consequence, less and less able to adopt a completely frank and straightforward attitude: thus he seldom told anyone the whole truth, and gradually lost first our confidence and, finally, even that of the Germans."

According to Rendel, "this reliance on manoeuvre also complicated his relations with his own government. He was always obsessed by the fear that a national leader might arise who would be able successfully to challenge his authority. He thus constantly sought to keep a balance between his various ministers . . . This failing was, I believe, partly due to weakness. There was, in fact, a streak of Jekyll and Hyde in him which made it difficult ever to trust him completely."

Behind all this, the British envoy suspected a kind of restless uneasiness, a consciousness that to many foreign governments he was always more or less suspect, if only because he was his father's son and because his country was unpopular. It was perhaps not unnatural that he should give the impression of being haunted by his past." Rendel saw two reasons for this: the treatment Boris had received from his father, and the dramatic circumstances in which he had been called to the throne. He had grown up amid disasters and catastrophes, Rendel noted. He had witnessed as a young officer the Bulgarian defeat in 1918 and the army's disorderly rout, followed by the humiliating occupation by French troops. He had inherited "a bankrupt kingdom on the verge of anarchy." But by the time he arrived in Sofia in June 1938, Rendel could affirm that "the country was beginning to make real headway toward recovery and prosperity."

Another English visitor, the author Harold Nicolson, also wrote of meeting King Boris in 1938: "He is certainly one of the most delightful people I have ever met. You know that I am not a royalty snob, and that I am generally bored by the artificiality of one's relations with kings. But this man would be delightful if one met him in a wagon-restaurant and got into conversation. His stories were thrilling."

\*    \*    \*

No film director could have staged a more eerie scene. The mountain, still asleep, is black and silent in the cool predawn hour. The summer stars have vanished over the sky of Rila, and as the pale light slowly appears along the eastern horizon, one begins to discern the jagged rocky peaks that surround the high mountain cirque in the area of the Seven Rila Lakes.

The darkness dissipates gradually to reveal a most surrealistic sight. There are hundreds of people in the large meadow at this unseemly hour: men, young and old, women, children, maybe six hundred or seven hundred, maybe more. Orderly, sliently, in rows of three or four, they form a huge circle around an improvised platform, where a dozen musicians, mostly violinists, are about to play.

The horizon is already afire; another gorgeous July day is about to break. The orchestra begins to play. Hundreds of silhouettes start moving rhythmically in a strange mixture of gymnastics and slow dance, as the solitary mountain peaks echo the words of their chorus:

Here it comes, the Sun that shines on us!
We dance happily on the dewy grass and flowers.
Bright joy illuminates us,
And constantly pours new forces into our souls.
At dawn we greet the mighty Sun . . ..

The first rays of the sun escape from the darkness behind the horizon to pierce the sky. Genuine joy brightens the faces; the lips whisper words of gratitude. Glory to God! Glory to the Sun! Glory to the Teacher!

He is there, among them, an alert old man with a white beard and shoulder-length white hair, very neat in his pale-gray suit, white shirt, and diamond necktie pin. Peter Dunnov, the founder of the "White Brotherhood," is well over eighty, but he performs the "paneurhythmic" with more ease than many of his younger disciples.

The orchestra switches to a waltz tempo and the "brothers" and "sisters" start singing another hymn composed by Dunnov, an accomplished violinist himself.

As they do every year, the Dunnovists have come to their Rila camp to spend the summer in the midst of Nature, sleeping in tents, eating vegetarian food, mediating, and listening to the Teacher's lectures. The subjects vary from Karma and reincarnation to "The Invisible World," from the importance of suffering and the lost continent Atlantis, to the techniques of correct breathing, and, above all, to the powers of Universal Love. After the paneurhythmic ritual that morning, Dunnov's sermon is on music.

"Music contains the supreme laws of Genesis," he intones. "It is the link between the world of angels and the world of men. As breathing is necessary for the cleansing of the blood, so music is indispensable for the purification of the sentiments. There is a connection between the musical sense and intelligence. On this earth, the sublime expression of intelligence is music, because music is condensed light, and light is the expression of thought . . ." Dunnovists should sing and dance, because through music they can communicate with "the conscience of Nature" and with "the superior Beings of the Spiritual World."

This kind of talk, expressing a doctrine where Christianity, theosophy, and pop-science were mixed with large doses of mysticism and the occult, had gained the Teacher considerable popularity. His White Brotherhood could boast several tens of thousands of disciples, not only in Bulgaria, but also in many foreign countries, from France to Japan.

Peter Dunnov, a charismatic guru with magnetic, kind eyes, was the son of a priest, born (or "incorporated physically," as he preferred to say) in 1864. At the age of twenty-four, he left for the United States to study theology and medicine for seven years. On his return to Bulgaria, he lived as a hermit for five years until 1901, when he began to travel across the country preaching. He gradually developed his own religion and by 1918 founded the White Brotherhood. The sect believed that once in every several centuries a "Master" was born to help men to become one with the "Cosmic conscience." Orpheus, Zarathustra, Lao-tse, Krishna, Buddha, Christ, and Mohammed were such great teachers. The latest Messenger to Earth, Dunnov taught with disarming candor and total assurance, was himself.

His followers were convinced that the Teacher possessed the gifts of clairvoyance, levitation, and healing. As their number increased steadily, their main camp, outside of Sofia, called "Izgrev" ("the sunrise"), became a sizable suburb of the capital. Every brother and sister contributed one-tenth of his revenue ot the community with free food and shelter available to the needy. Contrary to many sect leaders, Dunnov was disinterested in material gains and led a spartan life. Dunnovists, usually peaceful people who condemned violence, were not involved in political activity, although some of them occupied important public offices.

Lyubomir Loultchev, a handsome man of fifty-two, sporting a pair of luxuriant mustachios, left the group of dancers to follow the Teacher into his tent. A widower, fomerly an army major until his dismissal fifteen years before when the Stambolisky regime was overthrown, he now considered himself a writer.

Loultchev informed Dunnov that he was going to meet King Boris that day. The Teacher listened carefully, then uttered softly a few words of wisdom. The stars in that July 13, 1938, sky were propitious for the monarch, he told his disciple, who was also relieved to hear that there was not going to be any war. Provided, of course . . . Provided that "the right road was followed" and that the king listened to his right rather than to his wrong instincts. The Teacher also mentioned some dreams he had had and gave some cryptic advice. Like most gurus and oracles, Dunhov spoke primarily in parables, and his prophecies and advice were usually expressed in an enigmatic and equivocal way. Advice such as, "Observe the pear tree and you'll learn how to lead your life!" or "Don't wash in a river that has no source!" were acclaimed as pearls of wisdom by his more admiring followers but failed to provide much practical guidance to the less well initiated. Even Loultchev, a White Brother since 1919, had been disturbed lately by the lack of precision in the Teacher's pronouncements.

It was 7:00 in the morning when Loultchev left the camp to take the path down the hill leading to the place called "Váddata." He was accompanied by another brother, Yordan, who carried a kettle filled with water from the camp's fountain and a bag of food. At Vàddata, they had hardly had time to start a fire when a hiker appeared far way at the edge of the meadow. He was wearing a tweed sports suit with knickers, binoculars hanging around his neck, and was carrying a walking stick and a small rucksack. Noticing the two Dunnovists from a distance, he saluted them cheerfully by lifting and waving his cap. Loultchev returned the greeting, and when the king approached, he rushed to him, shaking his hand warmly.

"I brought you tea for breakfast," Loultchev said, and offered the king freshly baked pita bread, cheese, and a green pepper. When talking to the king, he mixed with folksy familiarity the polite form of "you" with the informal "thou," which nobody was supposed to use in addressing the monarch. Boris pretended not to notice, addressing him, as always, by the polite "you."

"And I am bringing you fruit from Kritchim," he said. His rucksack was filled with peaches and apricots.

"Welcome, Your Majesty," Yordan greeted him with his arms raised in the air. "Love of God alone brings us a meaningful life!"

"I quite agree," Boris answered, as he shook the brother's hand. Then the king and Loultchev talked about the present situation in Sofia and the latest Kiosseivanov speech at the Sobranie delivered on July 7.

"The seventh day of the seventh month," noted the Dunnovist. "You chose magic numbers for him!"

They talked about the new bill that would reinforce censorship of the press. A bad idea, said Loultchev, who also complained that the interior minister threatened to ban all White Brotherhood meetings. "The world is like a house. If you close the windows, the entire house is plunged into darkness. And even worse things may happen," he said ominously, in a Dunnov–like statement.

Loultchev habitually spoke to the king in an unusually blunt, direct way, but with the implied affection of an unpolished peasant talking to his kid brother. For some reason, Boris tolerated his familiar, coarse language and was even amused by it.

"You have very good intuition," Loultchev said, "but your reason is your main handicap. Your brain is what hampers you."

"Yes, I think you're right," Boris conceded.

The time came for the king to leave. He had left the car with his chauffeur far below the hill to avoid being seen in the vicinity of Dunnov's camp. Rumors had already circulated that he and Evdokia were disciples of the Teacher. The rumors were false. Boris, a deeply pious and practicing Orthodox, had never met Dunnov. But his contacts with Loultchev, as well as his curiosity about metaphysical subjects, fed the gossip.

He handed the remaining fruit to the brothers, who counted them carefully. "Nineteen!" Loultchev beamed. "This is the best terrestrial number! Nine for me and ten for the Teacher."

Bringing the ten Kritchim peaches back to Dunnov, Loultchev told him about his meeting. Dunnov, however, was critical of King Boris. "He is only preoccupied with his throne and has no ideological motivation," he told his disciple. "He is willing to listen to the Divine only as long as it helps him. He follows a 'feminine' line: when women look at a man, they want to know whether he is rich, powerful, and what there is to gain from them. That's a feminine approach to policy. But if the king wants the help of the Invisible World, he should act according to God's will."

The curious relationship between King Boris and Loultchev, a man interested in astrology, clairvoyance, and phrenology, had begun in an unusual way. Loultchev, a graduate from the Military School, spent some time at an aviation school in England and fought in World War I, where he was wounded. Suspected of sympathizing with Stambolisky, he was fired from the army after the coup of 1923, leaving him unemployed and in financial difficulty. He tried various jobs and started writing novels, but without much success. One day in 1925, he asked friends of his, the family of retired General Alexi Stoyanov, who were close to the palace and also to the White Brotherhood, whether they could arrange for him to see the king, to explain his difficulties. A few days later, the general brought him to the Zoological Garden and led him to the director's house. Suddenly, King Boris appeared at the door.

Loultchev, taken by surprise, was very embarrassed: he was wearing an old cheap suit, a shabby overcoat, and worn-out sneakers. Probably out of confusion, he said somewhat defiantly as he shook the king's hand: "You are no king to me!"

"I know, I know, dear Loultchev. For you, Christ is the king," Boris replied gently.

In spite of the tactless beginning, the conversation went well. Loultchev depicted the country's bad internal situation, as he saw it, and the people's discontent. The king listened with sincere interest, as he had the habit of doing in his frequent conversations with simple citizens and strangers. "Unfortunately, I am not the sun, to shine everywhere," he said sadly. Loultchev then made a prophecy. A big storm would hit soon, he predicted, and in the storm, lightning strikes the highest peaks."

Soon after this conversation, the king was ambushed at Araba-Konak and the cathedral was bombed. Superstitious or not, Boris remembered vividly Loultchev's words.

There are no indications that they kept in contact until 1934. In the meantime, personal tragedies involving Loultchev's family had pushed him definitively into mysticism. Boris heard about him occasionally through General Stoyanov, who also relayed some of Dunnov's opinions. In 1934, during another meeting arranged by Stoyanov, Loultchev predicted that someone in the king's family was about to die. The next day, the Belgian king Albert, Boris's uncle, was killed in the mountain accident. The prediction made a deep impression on the king, and he saw Loultchev more often—at the palace, in Vrana or Tzarska, or at Stoyanov's home—occasionally asking his opinion about various people and events. Except for Guentchev, the other court officials did not know Loultchev. And though Boris seemed to be interested in the information he brought, there is no evidence that he ever followed any of the advice that the Dunnovist so readily and outspokenly volunteered.[6]

As for predictions and dream-interpretations, Boris was certainly intrigued and, although scientifically minded, he did not reject entirely the possibility that there might be some truth in the phenomena of telepathy, bad omens, and extrasensory perception.

*       *       *

In August 1938, during their annual trip abroad, King Boris and Queen Giovanna spent a weekend with the British royal family at Balmoral and saw an international exhibition of butterflies in which the king was particularly interested. It was a period of great international tension. Since the Anschluss

---

[6]To judge by the alleged *Loultchev Diary*, uncovered during the period of the Communist People's Tribunals, Loultchev claimed to have played an important role as a political adviser to King Boris. Some reservations are in order: (1) No handwritten diary has ever been produced—Loultchev maintained that he recopied his original entries on a typewriter in 1940, so it is probably an edited version; (2) Loultchev was a fiction writer, had a taste for colorful stories, and liked to brag about his friendship with the king; (3) Almost none of Loultchev's assertions have been corroborated, by other participants in the political meetings he describes, not even in testimonies edited and produced by Communist investigators.

of Austria in March of that year, the fear of armed conflict had increased enormously, and now the German claims on Czechoslovakia's Sudeten region brought Europe to the brink of war.

Before coming to England, Boris had visited Italy, where he had seen Mussolini. Upon his arrival in London, he met the Foreign Office's top men, Lord Halifax and Alexander Cadogan, and relayed to them the duce's expressed desire for improving Anglo-Italian relations. This information, coming as it did from Hitler's ally during the Sudeten crisis, was received with special interest and hope by the British.

When Prime Minister Neville Chamberlain heard that King Boris was going to pass through Germany on his return to Bulgaria, he asked to see him. Normally, protocol would require a visit of the prime minister to the Bulgarian head of state's hotel. But with the Czechoslovakian crisis at its peak, Chamberlain could not leave his residence that day. Boris, therefore, readily agreed to pay him a visit at 10 Downing Street. The meeting went very well. The prime minister emphasized Britain's desire for peace, if Hitler did not push too far. The king, eager to help prevent a catastrophic clash between the Great Powers, accepted an unofficial mission of mediation.

Boris sincerely wanted an agreement between Germany and England. As the German minister in Sofia, Rümelin, had reported to Ribbentrop, the king was impressed by the might of Great Britain. Boris also believed that by offering to help Chamberlain, "I open wider the English doors, so far closed to Bulgaria's interest."

Later in September, after a short visit to Paris and Switzerland, King Boris arrived in Berlin, where he met first with Goering and then with Hitler. Goering was in a belligerent mood, asserting cockily that the war could be localized and would not last more than two weeks. Boris replied that the localization of the conflict was impossible. England, he said, would certainly enter the war and would be helped by its dominions; it is slow to declare war, but once the fighting starts, it would fight to the end. The king's advice was that it would be supreme folly for Germany to provoke a war, because that would turn the entire world against it, with the same disastrous results as in 1918.

He spoke in the same vein to Hitler, whom he saw on September 25, at the climax of the crisis. The fuehrer was in a state of high excitement, but as King Boris was one of the rare persons in the world for whom Hitler had respect and, curiously, even a kind of admiration, he listened attentively. Boris assured him that he was speaking as an old friend of Germany, who had fought next to the German soldiers in World War I, and who wanted to spare Germany the next "fatal disaster." It was a dangerous illusion, he said, to believe that Great Britain would not intervene in Czechoslovakia. He described candidly what he had just seen in England—the strength, the resolve of the population, and the readiness to face a long struggle. The British Empire has never been defeated in a major war, he argued, and you can be sure that it will not be beaten now.

Later in the day, the king offered similar arguments to Ribbentrop, but the foreign minister dismissed his logic, most particularly the danger of an American intervention, because the threat of Japan. Boris found him "arrogant and inflexible," and expressed his skepticism about Japan's ability to keep the United States out of the war.

King Boris later told Rendel that he had found Hitler more difficult than Goering, with both men inclined to believe in British weakness. "The king had assured them that they were totally mistaken," Rendel reported. "Not only would England react sharply and with increased effectiveness if she were pushed too far, but she had a well-known way—however unprepared she might be at the start—of winning the final battle." When Goering expressed doubts that the U.S. would join England, because "Japan should look after U.S. neutrality," King Boris replied that Japanese-German cooperation would be more likely to provoke America than to tranquilize it. Rendel wrote that King Boris told him "that he thought he had convinced Goering—and, he believed, Hitler, at any rate at that time—that England was ready to fight and that a war would be a serious risk for Germany.

The Nazi leaders, however, were determined to annex the Sudeten region, either by marching into Czechoslovakia, or by negotiating, under threat of war, the acquiescence of the Western democracies.

Four days after King Boris's talk with Hitler, the French and British prime ministers met with the fuehrer and the duce in Munich, and agreed to the return of the Sudenten to Germany. There are indications that Hitler had planned to invade Czechslovakia that week, which would have led to an Anglo-French intervention. In that case, World War II would have started in September 1938 instead of September 1939.

It is not possible to determine whether King Boris's intervention convinced the fuehrer to choose the Munich Conference rather than an immediate military action. The fact is that the war was delayed by one year. After the Munich Conference, which later became a symbol of appeasement and surrender, Chamberlain instructed Rendel to "thank King Boris for what he had done and to tell him that it was felt that he had acted as 'a great European.'" Rendel wrote: "King Boris was pleased and touched by the message . . . He turned to me and, in asking me to thank Mr. Chamberlain for his message, said rather sadly: 'Nous deux, nous sommes les seuls vrais pacifistes, lui et moi.'" ("We two, we are the only true pacifists, he and I.")

# CHAPTER XVIII

# Pressure from All Sides

THE CONSOLIDATION of King Boris's personal rule came at a time when his relations with his old confidants were undergoing changes. Earlier, he would discuss any problem—political as well as personal—with two people: Princess Evdokia and Parvan Draganov.

The role of Evdokia had changed since Boris's marriage. Indisputable First Lady until 1930 and her brother's confidante, she had been constantly around him and had had a great influence on him and his entourage. Now, relegated to second place, she saw him *tête-à-tête* less and less frequently. Although her relations with the queen were polite, there was a felt tension in the palace. Nor did they always resist the temptation of criticizing each other and dropping caustic remarks. When, for instance, the invading Italian army suffered humiliating defeats at the hands of the tiny Albanian forces, Evdokia remarked at table in front of the Italian-born queen: "Have you heard of yesterday's earthquake in Albania? It turned out to be the Italian army quaking under Albanian attack."

King Boris, who like any husband, wanted peace at home, could not stand these family frictions. When he realized that things were not improving, he suggested to Evdokia that she have her own house, near enough to be with them when she liked, but independent of them. The proud princess soon moved out, and subsequently insisted that she was happy in her lovely villa. But in moments of bitterness, she complained about being "thrown out of my father's house."

Draganov, to whom Boris so often opened his heart on political as well as intimate family and financial matters, became minister in Berlin. The king saw him for long periods each time he traveled abroad, and they corresponded regularly by coded telegram and letter, but the distance affected their relationship as did Draganov's blunt tongue. Boris trusted him, because the former ADC was one of the few people who spoke to him frankly, daring to disagree openly with him. Yet, at times, the king resented his telling him unpleasant truths. At such times, the king would temporarily cool toward him, not contacting him for weeks or months, until he once again needed his opinion.

Relations with other intimates were more compartmentalized. He did not talk politics with the family, for instance, nor discuss private matters with his political advisers.

Apart from his work, he spent most of his time with the queen, who was interested in her family, the arts, and charities. Giovanna kept out of state affairs, motivated both by inclination and by upbringing. Besides, Boris was not the kind of husband who brought home office problems. As a result, politics never became a topic of conversation with his wife.

Boris also kept his brother out of public affairs, although Kyril lived in the palace without much to do. They remained close hunting and traveling companions and enjoyed relaxing together, during those rare weekends they could share childhood memories and family jokes.

It was Pavel Grouev who saw the king most during the working week. Grouev, as chief of the king's private cabinet, would see him several times a day and talk to him even more often on the telephone. In fact, King Boris used to sign decrees, read classified reports and letters, and discuss drafts for speeches in "Batcho" Pavel's office. He felt comfortable in these two rooms on the ground floor, with walls crowded with large paintings of war scenes and tall windows looking onto the palace park. Grouev was probably the most trusted among his aides, and the king especially valued his extreme, almost exaggerated discretion. When visitors asked if the king was in town, Grouev would walk to the window, look up at the palace roof, and answer: "It looks as if His Majesty is here: I see the standard is up." At other times, journalists would ask where the king had gone the previous night. "Has he really left?" Grouev would ask, surprised. "He didn't tell me that he was going to travel." When the reporters complained that photos showing Grouev seeing King Boris off on the Orient Express, were in the morning papers, Batcho Pavel would smile mischievously: "Then it must be true, I suppose . . ."

When alone with Grouev, the king could eschew all caution and freely voice his candid assessments of people and events, as well as his intimate thoughts and political plans. Often, his talk took the form of a long soliloquy, starting matter-of-factly, rising to a crescendo, and covering the entire scale of emotions—from sympathy to indignation, from humor to resignation, swinging between optimism and self-recrimination. The monologue was punctuated only by Grouev's patient, "Oui . . . oui . . ." (they had the habit of speaking in French, in case they should be overheard by the palace staff) or a noncommittal, "hum . . . hum . . . ," meaning neither approval nor disagreement, but indicating interest and understanding. The king's language was often violent, always colorful. Grouev knew that when the king worked himself into a rage it was useless to contradict him.

Therefore, shaking his blond-white beard, he would wait until the storm passed. Then, in a most detached, tolerant manner, he would respectfully give his opinion. Boris would usually leave the room appeased and reassured.

The king both respected and relied on Grouev's objectiviy, and thus listened to his advice. But when he had to act, Boris needed the help of other trusted aides in order to maneuver among rival poilticians. Grouev, by nature a quiet, self-effacing man, lacked both the energy and the taste for the political arena. Furthermore, a recent sinus operation and phlebitis of the legs had aged him prematurely; at sixty, he was showing signs of fatigue.

It was in the king's character to seek advice and reassurance from outsiders, occasionally to bypass the official channels, no matter how much he trusted a prime minister or his own, appointed advisors. Without falling under the influence of an *éminence grise,* Boris' nevertheless, frequently entrusted confidential political missions to people with no official positions. Thus, in the past, military officers like his aides-de-camp, Bagrianov and Draganov, used to advise him and act as king's emissaries in purely political matters. More recently, the inspector of the royal palaces, Guentchev, had served as go-between with politicians and ministers. But by 1938, the king had stopped using Guentchev as his main confidential emissary, assigning the role more and more frequently to a man with no political background whatsoever, the architect Yordan Sevov. By 1939, when Sevov's gray Ford sports car was seen parked circumspectly behind some ministry, it was apparent that some issue of interest to the palace was being discussed inside. Sevov did not need to make appointments in advance with the ministers. When he walked in unannounced, they usually dropped their other business to receive him.

Sevov, a tall, well-built man of forty-seven, who walked with a slight limp, was a successful Sofia architect who had done a few jobs for the royal family. He grew up in the small town of Targovishte in northeast Bulgaria, raised by his mother, a widow of modest means. After graduating from the Military School and serving in the Balkan and World Wars, he went to study architecture in Dresden. A professor of his, an Austrian whose daughter he later married, was designing the city plans for Ankara, and Sevov eventually went to Turkey as his assistant. Like many natives of Targovishte, a town with a large Turkish minority, he spoke Turkish. In Ankara, he was introduced to Kemal Ataturk, with whom he developed a lasting friendship. The Turkish dictator who in his early career had lived in Sofia as military attaché, knew Bulgaria well and liked Bulgarians. He commissioned the young architect to design his farm outside Ankara and, later, to build one of his residences near the capital.

Sevov was very impressed by Ataturk's strong personality and by the bold ideas implemented by his authoritarian regime. The example of the

Turkish president's successful reforms marked his thinking for life. But he had no desire to go into politics, and when he returned to Bulgaria, he became totally absorbed in his profession. He remarried, had two children and, as he was not very social, led the quiet, uneventful life of the well-to-do Sofia bourgeoisie.

He was related to Bagrianov, the king's former ADC, which is probably how he came to be recommended as the architect for Princess Evdokia's house. As the villa was a success, Boris hired him to remodel Kritchim, and later, the Queen commissioned him to build a children's hospital which she personally financed.

Relations with the architect were pleasant, although he proved to be an independent-minded professional, who firmly defended his concepts, even in the face of royal disagreement. The king respected this and on occasions gave in. Evdokia was less flexible, and after some disagreements about roofs and windows, she stopped seeing Sevov. The true reason for her cooling toward him, however, was more complex: the architect was an admirer of Germany, while the princess had developed, ever since Hitler had come to power, a strong, almost visceral, resentment of everything German.

Apart from a few jobs for the royal family, Sevov was quite independent of the palace and the government. He did not belong to the politicians' world, he was making a good living as a private architect, and he had no ambitions in public life. This, added to a vivid mind and an absence of vanity, intrigued the king. When asked for an opinion, Sevov was sure to give objective and disinterested answers. Before long, Boris saw him as a man reflecting the common sense of a nonpartisan and honest citizen, the genuine expression of "public opinion."

Sevov impressed Boris as an intelligent, quiet man who did not want anything for himself. The king began to see him more often, using him as a sounding-board to test various ideas and find out how "the people" would react. Sevov, always available and willing to oblige, always calm and unemotional, seemed to make sense. With time, Boris began to send him to sound out people on his behalf.

Although his influence was growing, Sevov remained discreetly in the shadows, never attending official functions, never speaking in public, never appearing in a newspaper. When visiting the palace, he used the back door, going straight to the king's apartments. Most of the court aides did not meet him, though he always left the number where he could be reached with the palace telephone operators. When the king had a visitor, Sevov was never present, even if he had arranged the audience. During his political errands for the king, he would ask questions, listen attentively, but would seldom express his personal opinion.

Acting as Boris's eyes and ears, he attended sessions of the Sobranié, sitting anonymously in the crowded press box. He belonged to the conservative Reserve Officers Association as well as to the secret Masonic lodge, liberal and pro-France and Britain; and maintained contacts with right-wing, pro-German organizations. And everywhere he listened, always polite, never arrogant, saying little. By the time World War II broke out, Sevov had become the king's closest adviser.

Boris continued to see Loultchev, but less frequently as Sevov's influence grew. It remained a special relationship, not necessarily political. Through him the king sought to satisfy a personal curiosity about mysticism and the occult, although he himself never got involved with the White Brotherhood. Loultchev, at the same time, was a good source of information about an often neglected, silent minority, for whom Boris felt sympathy—the humble and the poor—who gravitated around the brotherhood.

The king sometimes picked Loultchev's brain about political figures and politics: it was Boris's habit to collect the opinions of different people on the same question.

The rumors about Loultchev's political weight irritated Boris. Once, in November 1938, he told the minister Dr. N. P. Nikolaev: "I'm shocked by the stupidity of people who imagine that such influences can affect my decisions when the national interests are at stake! One does not govern a state in the twentieth century with occult data from prophets, astrologists, and fortunetellers!"

By the summer of 1939, it was clear that Germany and Italy were on a collision course with the Western democracies. Hitler had occupied the Czechoslovakian regions of Bohemia and Moravia without any Anglo-French reaction, while Mussolini had invaded Albania. But now that the Third Reich's objective was Poland, it looked as though Britain and France would have no choice but to use force.

In case of war, Boris had made up his mind: Bulgaria was to remain neutral, to stay out of the conflict at any cost. This was also the firm conviction of Prime Minister Kiosseivanov, and unanimously shared by his cabinet. The opposition, too, emphatically supported neutrality.

Important as the ideological basis of the imminent conflict was for the Western world—a global struggle between democracy and totalitarianism—the Bulgarian viewpoint was understandably different. Preservation of peace in the Balkans was the top priority and the paramount concern, and as the storm approached, the main objective, the first duty of the tiny bark's captain, was to keep it out of the tempest. 1919 peace treaties were important factors as well. Every Bulgarian perceived the Neuilly Treaty as not only cruelly unjust but as the principal cause of the nation's misfortunes. Consequently, it would be unrealistic not to expect at least some sympathy for Germany's revisionism. The third main element in Bulgaria's decision was the fear of Communism.

Ever since the horror tales of the Bolshevik revolution had become public, Bulgaria—a weak, vulnerable, and geographically close country—had felt a fear that was genuine, intense, and almost universal among the bourgeoisie and the peasantry. Only a fraction of the working class and an insignificant minority in the cities regarded the Soviet regime with sympathy. The rest of the country viewed it as a brutal dictatorship, given to atrocities, and with a total contempt for human life. Russia, as a nation and a culture, had traditionally enjoyed popularity in Bulgaria, although the original enthusiasm for the Big Brother-Liberator had cooled considerably in the post-liberation days when the bear-like embrace had become somewhat suffocating. But even the ardent Russophiles in Bulgaria resented and feared the revolution which, in their eyes, had destroyed most of what they had loved about Russia: the civilized life, the culture and religion, and many of its respected leaders.

King Boris fully shared this view. It was not only because he had heard, firsthand, shocking stories from victims he had known personally, or because his own godfather, the tsar, and his family had been massacred by the Bolsheviks. It was also because the Soviet regime promoted as state doctrine everything he stood against and abhorred as a man, philosophically, ethically, and esthetically: the disdain for human dignity, the bloody terror, and the total lack of compassion and tolerance. He, who was physically sick each time he had to sign a death sentence for common murderers, could never understand the ruthlessness of the Lenins, the Stalins, and their like, even if perpetrated in the name of the highest interests of state and humanity.

The British minister to Sofia, Rendel, thought that Boris's profound fear of the USSR was the decisive influence in his policy. When Rendel suggested that Russia had "settled down" and that she might not be so dangerous after all, King Boris replied impatiently:

"It is all very well for you in England to make light of the possibility of revolution," he said. "Your own revolutionaries are respectable and law-abiding people, who would be the first to call the police or the fire brigade in case of need. A Red revolution here, Russian-inspired, would be a very different matter if it involved this fierce and fighting Balkan race. Centuries of struggle, oppression, and bloodshed have left the Bulgarians—under a crust of civilization which is still thin—a potentially cruel people. Once law and order have been shaken, unimaginable horrors will follow."

In spite of the deteriorating international situation, 1939 was a relatively good year for Bulgaria. The standard of life had improved tremendously, relations with the neighbors were friendlier, and the recent legislative elections indicated that the majority of the population approved the general lines of King Boris's policies and Kiosseivanov's no-party government.

There was, of course, a vigorous and articulate opposition, well represented in the twenty-fourth Sobranié by former party leaders and a few Communists. But on the paramount issue of the day—Bulgaria's position in case of war between the Great Powers—the national consensus was almost total: all political groups felt strongly that Bulgaria should remain neutral.

Although his prestige as prime minister was increasing steadily, Kiosseivanov was not without problems. Apart from the criticism of his no-party regime, the opposition attacked his foreign policy. The government, although firmly in favor of neutrality, saw it in terms of remaining "in step" with the general German policies in order to avoid antagonizing or provoking the mighty Third Reich. A different attitude would be unrealistic, the government believed, both because of Bulgaria's economic dependence on Germany and the affinity between Germany's revisionism and the Bulgarian ideal of national unification. King Boris shared this feeling, but both he and Kiosseivanov were determined to do everything to keep the country out of the war. Personally, Boris was convinced that Germany could not win a war against the Western powers.

The opposition, however, was anti-German. But, while the so-called "bourgeois" parties, as well as the Agrarians and Socialists, were sympathetic to the British and the French, the Communists obviously leaned toward the Soviet Union. The opposition believed that a neutral Bulgaria stood a better chance to see its national goals fulfilled through peaceful negotiations with Great Britain and France, than in siding with Germany.

Meanwhile, disagreements had put Kiosseivanov in conflict with some people from his own majority. The most serious were the frictions with the Speaker of the new Sobranié, Stoytcho Moshanov (a nephew of the Democrat leader Nikola Moushanov), who seemed to be gravitating toward the opposition, and the minister of agriculture, Bagrianov. This second conflict was essentially a clash of personalities, a rivalry between the prime minister and the former confidant and friend of the royal family.

In the summer of 1939, King Boris, finally convinced that the war could not be avoided, concentrated his efforts on maneuvering between the Great Powers, all of whom were increasingly courting him. He defended—before Germany, Britain, France, Italy, and the Soviet Union—the thesis that a strong and neutral Bulgaria would best serve their respective interests in the Balkans. He convincingly conveyed these arguments to the various diplomats in Sofia as well as to the procession of foreign emissaries who began to visit the country. Speaker Moshanov presented the same arguments before King George VI and Lord Halifax in London, and in Paris to Premier Daladier and the Speaker of the Parliament, Edouard Herriot. The same thesis was heard by Hitler and Ribbentrop during Kiosseivanov's visit in July, together with the prime minister's assurances that Bulgaria would never support any coalition or action directed against Germany. Kiosseivanov was sincere, reflecting the feelings of large parts of the Bulgarian population, when he evoked both the old World War I camaraderie between the two nations and their present common interests, including a just revision of the 1919 peace treaties. He also expressed concern about the recent Turkish maneuvers near the Bulgarian border and the sudden increase in Turkish military preparedness. Kiosseivanov argued that Germany should deliver promptly the requested armaments, in order to have a strong, although neutral, friend in the Balkans.

Hitler showed an understanding of Bulgaria's positions and did not press for a military alliance. But he explained, quite eloquently, Kiosseivanov thought, his own vision of the world. Nations, he said, fall into two categories: the ones who have but a limited access to the world's vital resources and those who have secured for themselves the larger share of living space and wealth. The first group of nations tries to change the status quo, while the second tries to preserve it. As Germany belonged to the first group, economic factors compelled it to demand a revision of the existing situation, preferably by peaceful means. But if this were impossible, Hitler added, the Reich would go to war. Because Bulgaria, too, belonged to the first group as a peace treaty victim, the Fuehrer pointed out, its destiny was to march side by side with Germany.

As a result of Kiosseivanov's visit, the arms deliveries to Bulgaria were speeded up. King Boris was relieved that Hitler had not insisted on signing a military pact. Moreover, the prime minister brought back some extremely important information: Ribbentrop had spoken of the likelihood of a dramatic improvement in Germano-Soviet relations. The Bolshevik danger no longer existed inside today's strong Germany, Ribbentrop had argued, and the Soviets were too busy rebuilding their country to interfere in the European conflict. Besides, the Reichsminister had said, "The Fuehrer is no Napoleon to look for a Moscow adventure . . ."

A reconciliation between the two bitter enemies would have enormous repercussions in Bulgaria. As the storm approached Europe, the immediate concern of King Boris and his government was not England or France, relatively distant powers with limited economic and political influence in the country. The immediate, alarming danger was a forced choice between the other two giants, both of them capable of crushing small Bulgaria in a matter of weeks, or even days: Hitler's Reich and Stalin's Soviet Union. As long as these superpowers were not warring against each other and did not force Bulgaria to participate in suicidal actions against either one of them, Boris, the master diplomat, still had a chance of dancing and dodging and saving his country. But a Soviet-German agreement seemed illogical—wishful thinking, a total impossibility. What about the sacred Nazi crusade against Bolshevism? What about the much-heralded Communist struggle "to the last drop of blood" against Fascism?

And yet, the unthinkable happened. On August 22, 1939, the fateful

Molotov-Ribbentrop pact was signed, with the Soviet Union thus giving Hitler a free hand to attack the Western democracies. To Britain, France, Poland, Czechoslovakia, and all their allies, the astonishing agreement appeared as a monstrous, cynical, and immoral act—a betrayal. But to Bulgaria, strategically, economically, and politically vulnerable to any Russo-German armed confrontation in the Balkans, the pact came as a relief, a postponement of a dreaded deadline. Two days later, Kiosseivanov expressed his satisfaction to Richthofen, the German minister in Sofia.

But King Boris had nurtured other hopes. "I wanted *you* to come to an agreement with Germany," he told the British envoy Rendel. "But instead, Russia signed a pact with her! The future lies in an agreement between the Reich and the Western powers. Why do you destroy one another?" When Rendel suggested once again that Bulgaria should align herself with the British and French side, the king replied: "We'll wait for you, the Big Powers, to reach an understanding among yourselves and, then, you can help us solve our problems . . ."

Rendel, who had an exaggerated idea of the pro-Russian feelings in Bulgaria, noted that "the effect of the unholy alliance between Germany and Russia was electric . . . Had Germany and Russia not become virtual allies, the country would have been profoundly divided . . But the Molotov-Ribbentrop agreement united practically everyone and strengthened the overriding hope that it would enable them to keep out of the conflict. It united practically everyone, except, perhaps, the king.

"Thus to the Bulgarian people as a whole, except for the king, the distinction between Germany and Russia came to mean less and less. It was the cooperation of the Russians with the Germans that impressed and seduced them."

Rendel believed that "the virtual Russo-German alliance of August 1939 enabled the pro-Russian majority to accept a pro-German policy without hesitation." And he noted that the agreement made his task far more difficult, "since the full weight of Russian influence, which in Bulgaria is very great, is now thrown exclusively on the German side." Once again the British diplomat repeats that "King Boris was practically alone at this time in not believing in the permanence of the Russo-German understanding."

For a short period, the Nazi-Soviet Pact totally disconcerted the Bulgarian Communists—many felt betrayed. But party obedience prevailed over idealistic scruples; the leadership managed somehow to justify the ideological correctness of the agreement, using rationalizations which sounded like an insult to the intelligence. The position of the party, however, improved markedly as harassment of the Communists by the authorities temporarily ceased.

War broke out on September 1, 1939, and two weeks later, on September 15, Bulgaria officially declared her neutrality. The same day, King

George VI wrote a personal letter to King Boris, assuring him that Britain would respect Bulgaria's neutrality if "it is not violated by others."

\*        \*        \*

At the opening of the Parliament's second session, set for the end of October, Kiosseivanov still felt uncomfortable with Speaker Moshanov, whose pro-Western sympathies had brought him closer to the opposition than to his own majority. The prime minister also thought that the new international situation called for a popular consultation to reaffirm both Bulgaria's determination to remain neutral and the country's support of the regime. Therefore, he proposed to the king that he dissolve the twenty-fourth Sobranié and call new general elections.

Accepting the idea, which involved the automatic resignation of the cabinet, the king proceeded to hold consultations with sixteen political figures, including the leaders of the opposition groups. The latter criticized the no-party regime and urged an end to the system of a cabinet of technocrats. But they all confirmed their support for neutrality.

A new Kiosseivanov cabinet was formed and elections were announced. The king had asked his friend Bagrianov to remain in the government in order to assure victory for the regime. The relationship between the king and Kiosseivanov was cooling, however. During the cabinet reshuffle and the consultations with the opposition, Boris had constantly conferred with Sevov and Loultchev, discussing some of his plans with them. Sevov had even suggested the replacement of the prime minister, but the king decided that Kiosseivanov should stay, at least until after the elections. The list of the new ministers was made by the king personally, and then submitted to the prime minister, who had no choice but to accept. There were four new ministers, three of them recommended by Sevov.

Kiosseivanov, feeling increasingly frustrated and hurt, suggested a later date for the elections but was overruled by the king. Kiosseivanov especially did not want Bagrianov in his cabinet, and the king sent Grouev, who was close to Kiosseivanov, to pacify him, but the prime minister had been deeply wounded by the monarch. "I don't want to be used as a springboard for Bagrianov," he said, suspecting that Sevov's friend was being groomed for premiership.

As the campaign started, reports began to arrive from the provinces to the effect that Bagrianov was picking his own candidates, without consulting his colleagues. Exasperated, Kiosseivanov sent his written resignation to the king just one day before the elections.

Boris was furious. By then, he had become thoroughly irritated by the prime minister, whom he considered touchy, obstinate, and determined to have his own way, and it is unlikely that advisers such as Sevov or Bagrianov did much to dispel the monarch's displeasure. The king, refusing to accept the resignation, ordered the interior minister to proceed with the elections as agreed upon.

In spite of these dissensions, the elections brought a resounding victory to the government. The Twenty-fifth Sobranié had only nineteen opposition deputies out of 160 members, much less than in the previous Parliament. King Boris and the government greeted the results as a new proof of popular support for their policies.

Kiosseivanov, for his part, interpreted them as a popular vote of confidence for the way he had presided over the nation's affairs for four years, and their success encouraged him. Commanding an overwhelming majority in the new Parliament, the prime minister was determined to assert his authority without the interference of unofficial royal advisers. His friends also counseled that now, in the wake of *his* electoral success, he should pick his own ministers rather than rubber-stamp the personal appointees of the king. Kiosseivanov conveyed as much to the king, very respectfully and politely as always, but very firmly.

But he had musjudged his real position. Several ministers and deputies of the majority had gone over to his rival Bagrianov. More importantly, he had not fully realized that as the year 1940 dawned, King Boris was in full charge of the country's policies. All the others, including the prime ministers, were nothing but his assistants. King Boris—the doubting, indecisive, soft monarch of yesteryear, a man with no inclination for ruling—had taken the reins in his hands. For him, it had not come as the crowning of a lifelong ambition. Quite the contrary, it had more the air of the resigned acceptance of a tragic destiny. After a twenty-year ordeal, peaked by the May 19, 1933, coup against him, he had decided to carry the nation's cross by himself. Was he strong enough for such a burden? Deep inside, he was not sure. Occasionally he felt that he would not have the strength to persevere. On taking over in 1935, he hoped with all his heart that he would succeed in "normalizing" the situation created by feuding politicians and ambitious officers, gradually to bring Bulgaria back to democracy and internal peace. But the war came too soon, there was little hope for democratization, now, in the eye of the storm. This was an emergency situation, with survival the first priority. King Boris saw no choice but to hold onto the rudder, alone.

In February 1940, during a bitter scene in Vrana, Kiosseivanov exploded, maybe for the first time exchanging harsh words with the king. Boris shouted, "You forget whom you are talking to!" and at the same time informed him that his old letter of resignation was now accepted. Professor Bogdan Filov, minister of education, was appointed prime minister.

Soon after, Kiosseivanov was sent as envoy to neutral Switzerland. "Bulgaria may need you one day in Bern," the king told him equivocally, as if he wanted to add something else. But the close, friendly relationship between the two men was never restored. On the day of Kiosseivanov's departure, the entire diplomatic corps and a crowd of former colleagues, collaborators, and admirers came to see him off. But there was nobody from the palace at the railroad station.

King Boris's foreign policy during the entire year of 1940 was an adept maneuvering between Scylla and Charybdis. To remain evasive while the Great Powers, engaged in a life-and-death struggle, applied formidable pressures on the small Balkan states, required a rare virtuosity. Boris, whom Hitler was not alone in comparing to a fox, was an accomplished master of dodging. He managed to practice his art successfully at a time when big and small countries in Europe were being crushed and their populations massacred. His goals were clear: to spare Bulgaria the horrors of war; to maintain neutrality, no matter how strong the pressures; and never to send one single Bulgarian soldier to fight outside the country.

Boris kept personal relations with the envoys of all the powers, seeing them in private, conversing fluently in their own languages, using his charm to the maximum. In the reports to their governments, they all described him in most favorable terms. Baron von Richthofen, a member of the old nobility, reported that King Boris was a sincere friend of Germany, who would never turn against the Reich. The shrewd, gentlemanly Rendel, realistic enough to know that Bulgaria could not become Britain's war ally against Germany, tried to promote a Balkan neutrality bloc in which Bulgaria would play a key role. He hoped that, if its neighbors made a few minor favorable frontier corrections, Bulgaria might consider such a neutrality pact. But London was not interested. The scheme failed partly because of the uncompromising opposition of Yugoslavia's prince-regent Paul, reported Rendel. There was "the bitter personal hatred which Prince Paul felt for King Boris, and our still unshaken confidence in Prince Paul . . . We were not prepared to do anything which he might dislike, and this, of course, made any concession, or even friendly gesture, to Bulgaria much more difficult."

The American minister George Earle, former governor of Pennsylvania and a personal friend of President Roosevelt, also fell quickly under Boris's charm and sent commendatory reports to Washington. Earle, an extrovert and an eccentric who had caused a sensation in Sofia by keeping a pet cheetah at the legation, became even more famous after a much-publicized uproar in a Sofia nightclub. The exuberant diplomat was enjoying himself with friends, when a group of German customers asked the band to play the Nazi song, "Horst Wessel Lied." Earle demanded that in fairness the musicians also play "Tipperary." The Germans objected, and after exchanging insults, one of them hurled a bottle at the American. Earle skillfully caught it in the air and smashed it on the German's head, which earned him no little admiration in Sofia's nightclub circles.

But in spite of his occasional rambunctious behavior and his reputation as a heavy drinker, Earle was an acute observer with excellent connections with the Bulgarian government, the opposition, and Sofia's elite. "The king and foreign minister have the highest regard for our country and government and are on the friendliest terms with me," he reported to the secretary of state.

*         *         *

Can territorial claims be solved by peaceful means? Can a nation be asked to return a territory to a neighbor without resorting to war? Modern history does not offer many examples. Yet this issue became a test of King Boris's policies. Braving the fierce irredentist sentiments in the country, he had the courage to proclaim that Bulgaria would not resort to force to fulfill her national aspirations but would seek solutions through negotiation. He let it be known to the Great Powers, who were all courting him, that now was the time to see who really cared for a just settlement in the Balkans.

Realistically, he did not stand a chance as far as the claims to Macedonia and Thrace were concerned. Yugoslavia and Greece were the traditional protégés of Britain and France; and even Germany, although committed to revision of the status quo, was wooing them. But Rumania, with the collapse of her protector, France, and threatened with the Soviet claims to her Bessarabia region, would probably be more amenable to discussing Dobrudja, the rich strip of land between the Black Sea and the Danube, north of Varna.

In fact, the Bulgarian character of Dobrudja was not contested by Rumania. A border territory between the two countries, its population had always been predominantly Bulgarian. But in 1878, when Russia annexed Bessarabia, the Great Powers decided to compensate Rumania by giving her northern Dobrudja. As Rumania had to accept the exchange, it brought its own populations in. After the Second Balkan War of 1913, Rumania invaded Bulgaria and seized southern Dobrudja. But Bulgaria never ceased to feel that this land belonged to it.

In April 1940, the government concluding that the situation in Europe was now propitious for raising the question of some territorial revisions, decided to launch a diplomatic campaign for the return of southern Dobrudja. If successful, the campaign might eventually lead to Bulgaria's claims to a free outlet to the Aegean.

The reaction among the powers was favorable. When Russia occupied Bessarabia and Bukovina in June, and the new right-wing Rumanian government sought an understanding with Germany, it became clear that Rumania would not resist if the powers pressed her to return southern Dobrudja to Bulgaria. Suddenly, Germany, England, Russia, Italy, and even the United States became interested in receiving the credit for an eventual peaceful solution of the Bulgaro-Rumanian conflict, thus appearing as true friends of Bulgaria and international justice.

Soon after the Soviet sent its ultimatum to Rumania concerning, Bessarabia, Earle reported to Washington:

"Now that the Rumanian territorial subject had been opened by Russia, Bulgarian claims to southern Dobrudja would be considered because they were so just that not even a devil's tribunal could reject them. But this would definitely be done by Bulgaria through peaceful negotiation and not by military force."

The American diplomat, who had become a friend of King Boris, informed Washington that ". . . my impression is that the king and government sincerely want their claims to the Dobrudja acceded to peacefully, since it would mean a much more permanent settlement. However, the Bulgarian people and the army feel so righteously justified in their Dobrudja claims that there is a possibility that the king and government might be forced by the army to take military steps if fighting breaks out in Rumania."

King Boris warned the German envoy Richthofen that after the Soviet takeover of Bessarabia, Bulgarians would clamor for the return of Dobrudja. Reminding him of the active local Communist party, the king said: "The situation will become intolerable unless Bulgaria at least receives a promissory note. If not, there will be danger of a violent revolution, followed by a very close association with Moscow." He hinted that although Bulgaria would rather receive southern Dobrudja from Germany, she would accept it from the Soviets if necessary.

At the same time, Draganov told the German Foreign Ministry that "what disturbed him especially was the danger that Bulgaria might now receive Dobrudja as a gift from the hands of the Soviet Union rather than from Germany."

As usual, Germany acted ahead of the other powers. On July 26, Hitler and Ribbentrop, assuming the role of arbiters, summoned the premiers and foreign ministers of both Bulgaria and Rumania to Salzburg to discuss a peaceful settlement of the Dobrudja question. Given the Reich's overwhelming military might in the summer of 1940 and the hopeless position of Rumania, already invaded by Germany's ally, the Soviet Union, Hitler's suggestion to Bucharest was tantamount to an order.

It was marvelous news for Bulgaria, a development full of promise. But happy as King Boris felt, he could not suppress certain suspicions about the German invitation. "My joy would be full if there were not a few dark points," he wrote to Draganov. "Why do the Germans suddenly raise this question now, after recommending calmness and sang-froid before?" For Boris, the danger for Bulgaria resided in the relationship between the Third

Reich and "Grandpa Ivan" (Russia). He thought that "Germany had dealt with the eastern problems in a naive manner and had made many mistakes regarding the Russians." Now, to correct this, the Germans "bring into the limelight the equitable settlement of our problem with Rumania. They consider Rumania sufficiently sick to pressure it to our benefit, but they also count on it to sustain later pressure from Grandpa Ivan. Therefore, hard as it is for us Bulgarians, it's imperative that we be extremely cautious, lest we become an illusory dam of 'Varbanism'[1] [Hitlerism] against Stalinism."

Boris was also suspicious of the sudden British interest in the restitution of Dobrudja to Bulgaria. "If I'm not wrong, the British hope that we become the apple of discord between the Eagle and the Bear," he wrote to Draganov.

Because of these "dark points," the king recommended caution and moderation. "We should not aim too high! We should not overload the boat and have it capsize at the first lash of the storm, which is going to last," he told Draganov in a letter of instructions for Filov and Foreign minister Ivan Popov who were due to arrive in Germany. "We should not be guided by the vain thought that our names will go down in history as the statesmen who returned *everything* to our unfortunate country. Because, in that case, we would repeat the mistake of our predecessors: to settle things under abnormal and unclear circumstances, for fear of missing the prize, and then, when the situation becomes normal, our edifice collapses because it has been built too fast and with provisional materials on the sandy and hazardous Balkan soil."

Bulgarian and Rumanian delegations, meeting in Craiova, Rumania, in August, reached an agreement, signed on September 7. Bulgaria received southern Dobrudja, including the towns of Silistra and Balchik, but northern Dobrudja remained Rumanian. The Bulgarian and Rumanian populations in the two zones were to be exchanged.

On September 21, 1940, units of the Third Bulgarian Army crossed the border to recover this old Bulgarian territory, welcomed with flowers by the ecstatic local population. All over Bulgaria, the jubilation reached delirious proportions. Seldom had the nation had a happier day, felt more enthusiasm and pride. In spite of the war approaching from the West, a wave of optimism, perhaps unreasonable and naive, swept over the country. The first step toward the long-awaited national unification had been crossed: southern Dobrudja was Bulgarian again! The mass demonstrations lasted several days. King Boris decreed an amnesty for all political prisoners. In a speech in Parliament, he warmly thanked Germany and Italy. The British support was also acknowledged by the government but to a much lesser extent. (Churchill said in a speech on September 5: "Personally I have

---

[1]Varban—King Boris's nickname for Hitler.

always thought that the southern part of Dobrudja ought to be restored to Bulgaria.") The Soviet Union was not given any official credit, though the Communists and a few opposition leaders gave it some public recognition.

It was a great psychological and diplomatic victory for the German-Italian Axis. The majority of Bulgarians, convinced that the return of southern Dobrudja was due to the Third Reich, felt deep gratitude. Streets in Sofia were renamed "Hitler" and "Mussolini." The British envoy Rendel assessed the situation very correctly: "Dobrudja was formally ceded under German and Italian auspices, and the jubilation took the form of enthusiastic gratitude to our two principal enemies and did our cause an infinity of harm . . . Many waverers who had not yet committed themselves to the German side were swept into the vortex of pro-German enthusiasm."

\* \* \*

The pressure on Bulgaria to take sides, rather subtle in the first year of the war, was felt more clearly after Germany, Italy, and Japan signed the Tripartite Pact on September 27, 1940. Twenty days later, Ribbentrop formally invited the Bulgarian government to join, asking it by telephone to do so within three days.

The dodging tactics of King Boris, determined to remain neutral, were put to a hard test. Among his ministers, the policy of evasiveness was best served by Ivan Popov, minister of foreign affairs, a quiet but convinced opponent to any involvement in the war. Popov instructed Draganov to decline the invitation by invoking Bulgaria's delicate international and internal situation, as well as its insufficient armaments. Draganov, who shared the same opinion, accomplished the mission readily.

Popov, a professional diplomat who believed that the Reich could not possibly win the war and who was skeptical about the Germans in general, had found himself in the curious position of heading the Foreign Ministry just at a period when inexorable factors seemed to be pushing Bulgaria into the German orbit. A tranquil bachelor with conciliatory manners, he had spent ten years as head of the ministry's press department and, since 1933, had been minister in Budapest, Bucharest, Prague, and Belgrade. In that last post, he had been very effective in implementing Kiosseivanov's policy of friendship with Yugoslavia, and this accomplishment plus his well-known neutralist feelings, were the main reasons King Boris had chosen him as foreign minister in the first Filov cabinet.

Popov had studied both in France and Germany, speaking both languages equally well, and had a far greater affinity for the French democracy than for the Third Reich. Although possessing integrity and intelligence, he was a phlegmatic man full of doubts. He was also a somewhat inactive Freemason, which did not endear him to the Nazis. In fact, the Germans did not know to what extent he could be trusted. A confidential report from a German agent read: "Our informer was told that Foreign Minister Popov tells the American envoy Earle everything he learns from the German embassy."

Pressure was coming from all sides. On October 17, Mussolini sent a letter to King Boris informing him that he intended to occupy Greece by the end of the month, which, he said, might possibly solve "the just Bulgarian aspirations for an outlet to the Aegean." The king's reply, although friendly and polite, declined the veiled offer to join the Italian troops against Greece. "Without renouncing its sacred rights and its historic mission, Bulgaria is compelled to restrain itself from any armed action against Greece," he wrote, invoking Bulgaria's military unpreparedness and her encirclement by "neighbors that you know well."

On October 18, Germany clarified Ribbentrop's invitation: the deadline was not three days, but ten. Still, as the pressure to join the fact had not diminished, King Boris attempted to explain his reluctance directly to the Fuehrer.

"Bulgaria's policy of neutrality not only met the deepest approval in the hearts of our people," he wrote to Hitler on October 22, "but it had accomplished another important task of our common policy, namely, the preservation of peace in the Balkans." Recalling warmly the World War I camaraderie between Germany and Bulgaria, the king assured the Fuehrer that in the future, too, the interests of both nations would coincide. He warned him that Bulgaria's neighbors would feel threatened by an alliance between Berlin and Sofia, and said: "I would be deeply grateful to Your Excellency if you would reconsider the question whether it is absolutely necessary to subject the present unequivocal and imperturbable policy of Bulgaria, which has heretofore kept our and your enemies in check, to a change which might result in immediately exhausting our modest forces, aside from the fact that full mobilization would bring to a standstill our entire economic life." In conclusion, Boris offered to send the prime minister and the foreign minister to clarify these questions further.

Hitler was not convinced. And instead of discussing the problem with the Bulgarian ministers, as Boris had suggested, he invited the king to come personally.

On November 17, the Fuehrer's plane flew the king from Sofia to Salzburg, where Hitler and Ribbentrop greeted him and drove him to Berchtesgaden, the Fuehrer's mountain resort. Expecting a great deal of arm-twisting, Boris used a little strategem: he took with him the foreign minister Popov but not Premier Filov. Thus, if need be, he could defer any definitive commitment during the visit under the pretext that the cabinet had first to be notified.

The first impression Hitler made on the small Bulgarian group (palace officials Handjiev, Colonel Burdarov, and Balan accompanied the king) was rather favorable. The Nazi leader seemed friendly and courteous, with an obviously brilliant mind. Tea was served in an informal atmosphere by the fireplace, in the large living room, while the host proved to be an entertaining raconteur. Later on, however, they realized that this was only one facet of the Feuhrer's personality: as soon as he was in a larger group of people or in the presence of subordinates, he turned into an overexcited orator and despot.

After the amenities, King Boris and Hitler withdrew for private talks which lasted, with short interruptions, for four full hours. Meanwhile, Popov had a tense, unpleasant conversation with Ribbentrop who, contrary to his master, had remained cold and aloof during the entire visit.

Hitler began by describing the spectacular success of the Wehrmacht on all fronts. But he did not hide his grave concern over the Italian military reverses in Greece. Mussolini had invaded Greece without consulting him, he said, and Italy's setbacks were jeopardizing the German war plans. Italy had created a "boil" in the Balkans, which had to be lanced, Hitler said, because he could not allow it to endanger his own forces. The Fuehrer saw no choice but to secure his ally by smashing the Greek resistance. To do this, the German troops had to cross Bulgaria. As friends, he emphasized. As allies in the Tripartite Pact, in which, by the way, all European nations were invited, including France and the Soviet Union. Hitler did not press Bulgaria to enter the war. But he insisted that it sign the pact.

Boris listened patiently, then repeated his arguments for declining the invitation. Bulgaria was not ready to join the pact, he said. It would create dangerous complications with its neighbors, with Russia, and with the internal opposition. The Bulgarian army, so far poorly equipped, was unable to participate in military operations in Greece or anywhere else. But, even more importantly, a Bulgarian signing of the pact was likely to provoke a Soviet-Turkish alliance, Boris argued, which would be a "mortal danger for Bulgaria." He tried to convince Hitler that "by remaining neutral, Bulgaria kept in check twenty-four Turkish and seven Greek divisions, better than if it were to fight, underequipped as it was, or even if it were well-armed . . . "

Hitler seemed impressed by the arguments concerning Turkey. Boris reminded him that Turkey had a mutual defense treaty with Greece, and a Bulgarian involvement, even a passive one, might force the Turks to honor their treaty obligations by entering the war against Germany. The Fuehrer, however, maintained that Turkey would not dare attack Bulgaria if it was part of the Tripartite Pact.

As for the Italians in Greece, Boris told his host about Mussolini's attempt to secure his help by insinuating that Bulgaria could in doing so recover Thrace, and was surprised to note that Hitler appeared not to know about it.

Furthermore, if the Reich was determined to attack Greece, the king continued, the direct road to Salonika was through the Vardar Valley in Yugoslavia, not through Bulgaria. The Yugoslav frontier was moreover not fortified, while the Greeks had the strong Metaxas Line along the Bulgarian border.

Hitler did not seem to agree. Because Yugoslavia had signed an alliance with Greece, he pointed out, its territory would not be available for an attack on her ally without some resistance. He wanted to spare the Wehrmacht an unnecessary war against the tough Yugoslavs before reaching Greece. He preferred, of course, that the German troops pass through friendly Bulgaria. Trying to postpone as long as he could a definitive answer, Boris advised the Fuehrer that winter was in any case a bad season for military operations in the Balkans. Bulgaria might reconsider joining the pact in the spring, especially if Yugoslavia were also to join.

Hitler more easily accepted King Boris's argument that a peaceful Balkans would better insure Germany's food supply, and even offered a ten-year contract for all exportable Bulgarian foodstuffs, payment to be made by barter.

The talks concluded without Hitler having persuaded Boris to join the Axis. Characteristically, the king did not say "no," but rather "not now." This was to become a pattern in his dealings with his omnipotent conqueror of Europe. But as Boris was leaving the next day, the Fuehrer let him know that the German troops were going, one way or another, to cross the Danube in the beginning of spring. That gave the king enough time, Hitler said, to decide how he wished to receive them in Bulgaria—as friends and allies, or otherwise.

Five days later, Draganov personally converged the formal Bulgarian reply to Hitler: The government declared itself willing "in principle" to join the Tripartite Pact but requested that the signing be postponed to a later date.

The king returned to Sofia quite disturbed. This time, he had succeeded in buying more time, but he knew that from now on, he could rely less and less on his delaying tactics. The circle around him was becoming alarmingly tight.

In spite of Boris's refusal to sign the pact, the Berchtesgaden talks made the Kremlin very nervous. On November 19 in Moscow, the Soviet commissar for foreign affairs, Molotov, told the Bulgarian envoy Stamenov that his government supported Bulgaria's territorial claims and was ready to give it economic assistance, but would not accept Bulgaria becoming a "Legionnaire State." He then proposed to guarantee Bulgaria's sovereignty by signing a bilateral pact. King Boris, after discussing the offer with his four policymaking ministers, decided to decline. By then, the important decisions were discussed not by the entire cabinet, but by a "quartet" of ministers: Premier Filov, Interior Minister Gabrovsky, Foreign Minister Popov, and Defense Minister General Daskalov.

The Russian overture in turn alarmed the Germans. Two days later, the Reich's envoy to Turkey, Franz von Papen, on his way through Sofia, was received by the king. He warned Boris of the pitfalls of a Soviet guarantee, insisting again on the advantages of Bulgaria joining the Tripartite Pact. The king repeated the same arguments he had given Hitler. "Bulgaria should not become the apple of discord between Germany and Russia," he told the diplomat, and this required loyal relations with both powers.

In spite of Bulgaria's refusal, Moscow intensified its diplomatic offensive. On November 25, it dispatched the secretary general of its foreign affairs commissariat, Arkadi A. Sobolev, to Sofia with a formal proposal for a bilateral pact of nonaggression and mutual assistance. The chips were down. Sobolev's offer required a "yes" or a "no" answer.

"This was one of the most unpleasant days of my life," Boris confided later in a conversation with the leader of the opposition, Nikola Moushanov. Sobolev met first with Filov, to whom he read the proposal, without however leaving the text with him. Then he was received by the king, to whom he formally presented the Soviet offer, which also contained a promise of noninterference in Bulgaria's internal affairs.

King Boris, expressing his reservations, told Sobolev that Bulgaria did not feel threatened by anyone at this point and, therefore, did not need guarantees from a Great Power. The country was determined, he said, to maintain its policy of strict neutrality. He promised, however, that the Bulgarian cabinet would examine the proposal thoroughly and reply formally within a few days.

On November 30, after the Sobolev offer was discussed by the cabinet's "quartet," the Soviet envoy Lavrishchev was informed that the government rejected the offer. The official reply pointed out, among other arguments, that it would be unfair to negotiate with Moscow while Bulgaria was still considering the invitation to join the Tripartite Pact, issued by Germany, "a country on friendly terms with both Bulgaria and Russia."

The conversations were supposed to be kept secret, but the Communist party deliberately began to leak some selected items. A cable from the U.S. envoy Earle, for instance, read: "The secretary of the illegal Bulgarian Communist organization informs me that Sobolev asked the King for naval and air bases in Bulgaria. Russia in return offered to force Turkey to give Adrianople and Turkish Thrace to Bulgaria and to exert all possible pressure on Greece to cede Grecian Thrace. [The Secretary] says that the King has courteously but firmly refused Russia's proposals."

After the Sobolev offer was rejected, a massive and well-orchestrated propaganda campaign was launched in Bulgaria by using the leaked terms of the proposal. At the instigation of the Communist party, thousands of letters and telegrams poured into the palace and the Council of Ministers, demanding the acceptance of the Sobolev proposals. The party gave wide publicity to the campaign, trying to present it as a sort of national referendum in favor of Russia, which gravely alarmed the government. The London *Times* wrote that "Bulgaria has been profoundly shaken by what may be considered as the greatest subversive activity originated from abroad in the country's recent history."

Afraid that Bulgaria might yield to Soviet and internal pressure, Berlin strongly argued against such a move. Hitler himself declared that "as soon as Russia sets one foot on Bulgarian soil, she won't keep promises and, as happened in the Baltic countries, will quickly flood the country with propaganda and terror, and, eventually, any respect for the King and the regime will vanish." These problems would not have arisen, he reminded Sofia, "had Bulgaria joined the Tripartite Pact right away." Not signing the pact had been "a psychological and tactical error," he insisted, which allowed the present widespread propaganda campaign to be launched in favor of a Soviet-Bulgarian pact. Hitler stated that "as long as the Russians know that Bulgaria is not a member of the Tripartite Pact, they will try to blackmail her in every conceivable manner."

Similar arguments were frequently heard in Bulgaria also. A large and dynamic segment of public opinion, spearheaded by nationalistic organizations and groups such as the National Legions, the Ratniks, the Reserve Officers Union, and the Macedonians, did not hide their sympathy for the German cause and their disenchantment at the government's hesitation in joining the pact. Led by prominent figures like General Christo Loukov, former Premier Tzankov, the old Generalissimo Jekov, and many young members of the Sobranié, the right-wing groups gradually became an opposition force, critical not only of the Filov government, but also of the king's cautious policies.

The pressure on King Boris, both from abroad and from within, became tremendous, making him wonder whether he would be able to withstand it for long. World events and the national history had trapped him into a position where he had to make a fateful decision. All he could hope for now was more time for maneuvering and delaying. Would he be able to deny passage to the victorious German armies next spring? "We adjourned the trial this time, but with a fixed date for the next session," he told Moushanov after his visit to Hitler. And as the opposition leader urged him not to grant the German troops a free passage through Bulgaria, Boris snapped impatiently: "And with whom do you want me to link our destiny? With your grand, glorious France who was not able to last even one month under German assault? Rendel advises me to fire at least one artillery round at the Germans on the Danube and thus prove our protest. It's easy for him to talk, with the channel separating the Belgian coast from England! Earle is more reasonable. He doesn't ask us to resist with arms but recommends Denmark's attitude. However, I prefer to quit, rather than be a prisoner in my own country! The choice is Germany or Russia. These are the two powers who will seal the fate of Europe. Your feelings tell you Russia. But if you listen to your reason, you'll answer Germany!"

*     *     *

King Boris in the Alps—
August 1933

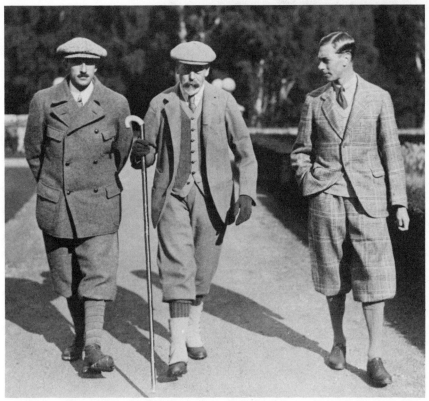

Balmoral Castle, Scotland, 1933. King Boris with King George V and future King George VI

September, 1934—at Kritchim country house, Bulgaria. Rapprochement: a former enemy, King Alexander of Yugoslavia, visits King Boris

Queen Giovanna, King Boris, Sofia's archbishop, Metropolitan Stefan

State visit to Rumania. King Boris with Rumanian King Carol

King Boris with Premier Filov behind them: Pavel Grouev and Queen Giovanna, Sofia, May 1941.

Sofia, 1940—The royal family at the balcony of the palace. Popular rejoicing: Rumania returns the territory of Dobrudja to Bulgaria

King Boris visits Scotland with King of
England, George VI and Queen
Elizabeth

August 1936—King Boris, hunting with Marshal
Goering, at Goering's hunting estate Schorfheide

Crownprince Boris, age 2-and-a-half, at a soldiers bivouac in Rila Mountains

King Edward VIII (later the Duke of Windsor) visits Sofia's "Alexander Nevsky" church, with King Boris and Prince Kyril (September 7, 1936)

King Boris' son, Crownprince Simeon, in Rila Mountains, 44 years later.

King Boris visits Hitler's
Headquarters

King Boris at Hitler's mountain retreat

King Boris' last trip to Germany, August 1943, in the co-pilot's seat

Sofia, 1943—King Boris' funeral—Crowds in the streets

Sofia, 1943—King Boris' funeral

Sofia, September 1943—King Boris' funeral. The widow, Queen Giovanna, with Prince Kyril. Boris' sisters, Evdokia and Nadejda; Giovanna's sister, Princess Mafalda; and Duke of Würtemberg (husband of Nadejda)

King Boris' funeral, Sofia 1943, crowds in villages along the railroad between Sofia and Rila monastery.

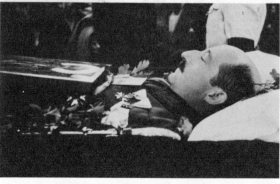

Sofia, 1943—King Boris' body lying in state in the church "Alexander Nevsky"

# CHAPTER XIX

# The Tripartite Pact

"THE PRIME minister is going to Vienna for medical reasons, to consult a specialist during the holidays," the government spokesmen were instructed to answer all inquiries. (Christmas was celebrated on January 7 in Bulgaria.) There was an acute sensitivity about the increasing Bulgaro-German closeness, both in the country and abroad, and any publicity given a visit to Hitler and Ribbentrop would have been unwise. To make the ruse more credible, no other minister accompanied Filov. He and his wife were alone with their good friends, the German envoy and Mrs. von Richthofen, when they boarded the Orient Express on New Year's Day.

The following evening, Draganov, the Bulgarian minister in Berlin, met them at the Vienna station in the midst of a snowstorm. The heavy snow during the night clogged the railroads, preventing Ribbentrop's train from arriving in time for his meeting with Filov, scheduled for January 3. That gave the Filovs the opportunity to do some sightseeing in Vienna. It also permitted Draganov to brief the prime minister thoroughly and to remind him of King Boris's instructions regarding the talks in Germany: Filov was to try and gain time, to postpone Bulgaria's signing the Tripartite Pact.

Filov listened but appeared to be absent-minded and rather impatient. The Bulgarian envoy to Germany was not his favorite. He had complained on a few occasions about Draganov's slowness in replying to Sofia's requests and his failure to follow strictly the ministry's instructions. His intimacy with the king also disturbed Filow, who was aware of the continuous flow of ciphered messages between the two men. The prime minister wondered, sometimes, whether Draganov could be trusted entirely. Lately, the Bulgarian envoy, although considered a true friend of Germany, had been skeptical about Bulgaria's joining the pact, which annoyed Filov.

As for the prime minister himself, he had made up his mind. He had become convinced that Bulgaria had no choice but to become an ally of Germany. The question for him was no longer *whether*, but *how* and *when* to join the pact, in order to obtain the best conditions and avoid the worst risks for the country. He felt that this was now the real mission of a patriot and a statesman.

Professor Filov's statesmanship was of recent date. As an archeologist of international caliber, his credentials were impeccable and his reputation as a scientist solidly established. He was president of the Academy of Sciences when Kiosseivanov chose him to be minister of education in his cabinet of technocrats. Filov had previously not been a member of any political party nor participated in political life. A roly-poly man whose plump Mongolian face was accented by a dark mustache, he was fifty-seven when King Boris chose him to replace Kiosseivanov.

Although an academic intellectual, his shrewdness and determination were not to be underestimated. After a few months in office, he managed to conquer the essentials of governing and to assert his authority among the members of the cabinet, most of whom were equally lacking in political experience. It did not take long before the professor began to enjoy the challenge of being prime minister. His relationship with the king was good, as it was with Sevov, which was essential.

As Filov's experience in diplomacy was next to nil, he left the technicalities to Ivan Popov and the Foreign Ministry, while the general direction of Bulgaria's foreign policy was directed by King Boris. In time, however, he discovered in himself an unsuspected interest and, he began to think, a talent, for international affairs. More and more, he devoted his personal attention to foreign policy. Therefore, the unsolicited and slightly patronizing advice of more experienced diplomats like Draganov irritated him.

Filov's talks with Ribbentrop began the next morning, January 4, at the Vienna railroad station, where he boarded the Reichsminister's car. By the time the train arrived in Salzburg at 12:50 p.m., the two men had covered most of the topics they intended to discuss.

Filov briefed Ribbentrop about the Russo-Bulgarian relations, the rejection of Sobolev's proposal, and the virulent pro-Soviet propaganda campaign that followed. There was no pressure from Moscow at the moment, Filov said, but he reaffirmed Bulgaria's determination not to bow down to the Soviets, even to face them with arms if need be.

Bulgaria would have avoided all these unpleasant problems if it had joined the Tripartite Pact, Ribbentrop replied. He did not hide his disappointment at Bulgaria's procrastination, given that in the meantime, Hungary, Rumania, and Slovakia had joined the pact. What was Bulgaria, supposedly a great friend, still waiting for?

Filov had to repeat the old arguments. Although we have not signed the pact, we agree entirely with its spirit, he assured Ribbentrop. Since 1915, our fate is linked to the fate of Germany. This friendship exists not only in the government but also among the people. Look, the peasants designate German victories as "ours"! The Reichsminister, however, did not appear overly touched by Filov's sentimental verbosity. All the more reason for you to join us, he replied coldly.

The Bulgarian had to resort to more concrete arguments. We are not prepared militarily, he said. We risk complications with Russia, with Turkey . . . Ribbentrop scorned the risk: Russia will cease to bother you as soon as you join the pact, he assured Filov. As for Turkey, there is no danger there. They will not attack you if they know that Germany is behind you! And, in case the prime minister did not realize fully what that German power represented, Ribbentrop provided details which did not fail to impress Filov. The war will, in fact, be over by the end of 1941, he predicted. The world will be amazed at what will be accomplished during this year!

He revealed that the Germans had recently used a new method of aerial bombardment, thanks to which the city district of London had been almost completely destroyed two days ago; real submarine warfare would begin in March, Ribbentrop said; and "if God gives us fair weather," it would be possible to launch an invasion of England in fourteen days. Germany possessed a formidable war machine: 238 divisions, twenty Panzer divisions, eighteen motorized divisions. The war on the continent was already won—Albania was just an incident without great significance. The English fleet in the Mediterranean would be destroyed, the Reichsminister assured Filov, and England could not continue to wage war with her colonies alone. Nor could American aid save her—Roosevelt was, in any case, a sick man and under the influence of his wife. The Americans would never send men into the war because the Japanese were just waiting for a pretext to pounce on their fleet . . .

Filov thanked him for the information and assured him that Sofia's and Berlin's positions were very similar indeed. They only differed as to the date of Bulgaria's signing the pact. There was no doubt about the joining itself, he said. Ribbentrop remained suspicious. "We have information that you don't believe in Germany's victory, which is why you don't enter the pact," he said bluntly. Filov protested vehemently, assuring him that this was not so.

As the train by this time was arriving in Salzburg, there was not much time left for him to bring up the subject he most wanted to discuss: would the Germans assist Bulgaria in reclaiming its territories in Thrace and Macedonia if it joined the pact? After helping with Dobrudja, Germany had made no promises concerning Bulgaria's old litigation with Greece and Yugoslavia. On the contrary, the recent rapprochement between the Reich and Yugoslavia worried Sofia.

Ribbentrop indicated that Bulgaria had a good chance of recovering Thrace, but as soon as the word Yugoslavia was pronounced, he insisted they interrupt the conversation in order to get ready for the meeting with Hitler.

Filov arrived at the Fuehrer's mountain residence Berghof at 4:30 P.M.. Hitler received him cordially and the conversation started in the presence of Ribbentrop and the Fuehrer's secretary-translator Schmidt. Filov repeated the reasons for the delay in signing the pact.

Unlike Ribbentrop, Hitler admitted that Russia might try to cause difficulties but was equally sure that Moscow would accept the *fait accompli* as it had the German entry into Rumania. He then revealed that Molotov had told him that the Russians wanted to enter Bulgaria as the Germans had Rumania. But Hitler had objected, pointing out that the Germans had acceded to a request of the Rumanians, while, as far as he knew, no such request had been made by the Bulgarian government. Filov confirmed this vehemently. If the Soviets intervened, Hitler declared, he would crush them with his army. But as the prime minister still fretted, the Fuehrer said that he was ready to put any force at Bulgaria's disposal—ten divisions, more.

After pointing out that he would not repeat the mistake of World War I by letting the English open a Balkan front, and after expressing his regrets over the Italian reverses in Greece (the Italians had not informed him in advance), Hitler declared categorically that no military participation would be expected from Bulgaria—he did not want Bulgaria to enter the war. Thus, he insisted since there was no danger in joining the pact, Bulgaria should do it promptly. Otherwise, Hitler warned, Bulgaria would be taken over by the Bolsheviks, just as they had the Baltic countries.

Since both Hitler and Ribbentrop declared themselves in favor of Bulgaria's claim to an outlet to the Aegean, Filov thought the time was propitious to raise the Macedonian question. But Hitler interrupted him by saying that as all problems could not be solved at once, the matter should be discussed at a later date. Let's first win the war, he said, and then many problems will find their solutions.

*     *     *

It was not the happiest Christmas that King Boris could remember. True, the family celebration around the Christmas tree the night before, with the delighted children opening their presents, could not have been more pleasant. Boris loved that January holiday, a day of peace in snow-covered Sofia: a touchingly simple church service in the morning, Christmas cards and telegrams arriving by the hundreds, and rest in the serenity of Vrana or Tzarska-Bistritza.

But this year he had lost his peace of mind. His intimates noticed his deepening piety. Sentences such as "God willing," "with God's help," or "if God so decides," began to appear more often in his personal letters. Even his hunting log abounded with references to the Almighty. Boris had always been a religious man, who liked visiting churches and convents, talking to priests, and spending an occasional night with monks in some isolated monastery when traveling around the country. But his religiousness had increased lately, as had his irritability and distrust of people.

At moments, he felt that he could not trust anyone entirely anymore. Filov and Sevov were complaining about Draganov, suspecting him of secretly wanting to become a Bulgarian "gauleiter." They also disapproved of Bagrianov's influence in the palace. Inside the cabinet, Gabrovsky and General Daskalov were engaged in a bitter personal quarrel. And while Princess Evdokia was criticizing him for becoming too "pro-German," right-wing leaders like Tzankov and General Loukov suspected him of not being a totally loyal friend to Germany. Boris himself was irritated at the continuous praise of these leaders by the Germans, and suspected certain Nazi circles of plotting to have these pro-Germans replace the present government. Well aware of the strong pro-German feelings in the army, the press, and the nationalistic organizations, Boris knew that if he were to give up the reins, there would be many people willing to lead the country to the German side.

That Christmas day, he waited impatiently to hear what news Filov would bring from Berghof. After the talks with Hitler, the prime minister had stopped for a day in Vienna for a check-up with Dr. Eppinger, an Austrian doctor. He arrived in Sofia on the evening of January 7 and was met by Gabrovsky and Popov who accompanied him to his home where he briefed them about the meetings. Popov, who was, as usual, not at all impressed by the German arguments, ridiculed Ribbentrop's explanations. At ten o'clock in the evening, before Filov had finished his report, Sevov arrived to take him to the palace, as the king wanted to see him right away.

The nocturnal meeting, the most dramatic that Filov had ever had with the king, lasted for over four hours. Boris, tense and nervous, exploded as soon as the prime minister told him that in his opinion there was no other course left for Bulgaria but to join the Tripartite Pact.

Filov, who had never seen him so angry, was stunned. The king's reaction was indeed unusually violent. "No, no!" he shouted, "I'd rather abdicate! I prefer to throw myself in the arms of Russia, even if the country becomes bolshevized!" It took him a long time to calm down. He described himself as "a republican king" who cared only for the fate of the people and complained that all this talk of joining the Germans once again was attributable to "the graybeards," the old folks around General Jekov, with King Ferdinand the leader of the group.

"Le Monarque and his former generalissimo just cannot accept the thought that we have so far achieved without war much more than they ever did!" King Boris said angrily. He sounded extremely pessimistic that night, telling Filov that if Bulgaria signed the pact, he feared the British would bomb the country. He also expressed doubts that the people would be willing to fight. Disorders would probably erupt, he predicted; nor did he trust the army.

The vehemence of the king's outburst was quite unexpected. But equally unexpected was the prime minister's reaction. If the mild-mannered Professor Filov, politically a total creation of King Boris, had ever felt insecure and inexperienced, something had happened in the last weeks to change him. Was it the taste of power, the discovery, after one year of governing, that he was stronger, more resolute and—why not?—probably more competent, than his colleagues? Was it the attention the most powerful man in Europe, Hitler, paid to his opinions? Was it that the German arguments had not only convinced him but also confirmed his own feelings, thus giving him self-assurance? Or did he see in Boris's furious outburst all the king's indecision and doubts, all his weaknesses?

The fact is that Filov did not back down. After the first shock passed, the king's anger failed to intimidate him. On the contrary, he retorted energetically and with assurance. He said that if a nation was unwilling to fight for its ideals and make sacrifices, such a nation was ripe for slavery. But this was not the case with our people, he affirmed. If they were presently inert and spiritless, the government was partly to blame, "because our attitude has been hesitant. If, however, we decide to act, they also will be encouraged, Your Majesty, since between the government and the people there is the same kind of bond that exists between the army and the people."

Filov's words became personal. "I appeal to you, sire, to be a soldier, as you have been in the past, and not to abandon the country which has full confidence in you! Permit me to tell you that I have not been a soldier myself, but I come from a military family and I have never surrendered in a struggle. I have always fought and always succeeded. And I believe that I'll succeed again!"

"If we must fail," Filov went on, "let's fail with honor. Even if we wanted to bring Bolshevism to the country, we could not avoid a fight, because there are still people in our country ready to fight against it, who won't surrender easily!"

By then, King Boris had calmed down enough to listen carefully as the prime minister repeated his conclusion:

"For us there is no other course, because war is unavoidable. If we realize this, it is best to arrange conditions that are the least painful for us. If we allow the Germans simply to pass through our country, they will treat us as an occupied land, like Rumania, much worse than if we ally ourselves with them. We cannot gain anything from an English victory, for the failure of German arms inevitably means we shall be bolshevized."

As Boris had become pensive, Filov believed he was accepting his arguments. It was half-past twelve. The king excused himself for a moment, saying he wanted to say goodnight to the queen. When he returned, the conversation continued until 2:30 in the morning. His attitude had changed completley. He even complimented Filov, telling him that his visit to Berghof had been very useful, his questions well put. Calmly, they discussed in detail all eventualities, deciding that it would be best to accept the German offer. But some conditions should be posed. The Germans should clarify their position on the Aegean outlet and the Bulgarian territorial claims. Preliminary talks should be held by military experts in order to make sure of the German reaction in case of an invasion from Turkey or Yugoslavia. The conditions of supplies and requisitions should also be negotiated. With all these bilateral talks, Boris told Filov, the signing of the pact might be delayed a little . . . He insisted that the signing should take place on the very eve of the German troops' arrival and not earlier.

The king appeared less pessimistic as the prime minister left the palace. Despite the late hour, Filov did not go to sleep right away. Instead, he drove with Sevov, who was waiting for him, to a village in the outskirts of Sofia to tell him about the audience. He urged the architect to try to boost the morale of the king. He needs much encouragement at this time, he said.

\* \* \*

The kind of encouragement Filov was talking about was certainly not what King Boris received from the confidential report Draganov sent him after Filov's visit. Draganov felt that Filov had come "to plead a cause in which he was not convinced himself; therefore, he could not be convincing," and that he had not attained the objectives of his visit. Filov had not expressed them well to Ribbentrop, not even mentioning the question of Macedonia and Salonika, Draganov wrote to the king. "Filov told me himself that he did not argue much with Ribbentrop, because he didn't want their talk to end as Popov's had." (In a previous meeting, Ribbentrop had been curt and impatient with Popov.) "It appears that he [Filov] mainly listened to Ribbentrop's arguments and accusations, without convincing him of the justness of our position—that our official joining of the Tripartite Pact should be postponed."

Draganov reported that Filov's conversation with Hitler had followed the same pattern. "So, what he heard from both of them was that Bulgaria must join the pact soon, this said by Ribbentrop in a categorical manner, and by Hitler a little more mildly, because he is Austrian. Filov told me that he himself is in favor of a quick signing of the Tripartite Pact, mainly for reasons of internal policy, which, of course, he cannot tell the Germans. He is very afraid of the Russian propaganda at home and thinks that the bolshevization of Bulgaria may even occur within the month, before the signing of the pact . . . He judges that once we sign the pact, we would have a more defined policy, a clear position, and the possibility of fighting the Bolshevik danger more efficiently."

Draganov thought that after the visit Ribbentrop was "angry at Bulgaria, to say the least," and that the Germans could not fail to notice that Filov was not firmly convinced of the cause he was defending. Therefore, Draganov warned the king, if the pact is not signed soon, "the impression here would be that Filov would have signed, but that the cabinet, and mainly you, do not agree. It would be easy to foresee the consequences: Germany interferring in our internal political life, discarding the inconvenient people, and bringing to power the convenient."

Draganov was already noticing signs of German displeasure: the party and government circles evinced a mistrust of Bulgaria, an interest in bringing Yugoslavia into the Tripartite Pact, which meant sacrificing Bulgaria's interests, and a desire to replace the Bulgarian government by a strong military cabinet.

Draganov wrote this confidential report convinced that King Boris was still absolutely determined to avoid, or at least delay, Bulgaria's entry into the pact. The old royal confidant was unaware that Boris, who had cooled toward him lately, was listening increasingly to Sevov and Filov, no admirers of Draganov.

*        *        *

". . . The cabinet met through the night from 6 P.M. to 2 A.M. . . . This was without doubt the most important meeting which we have had to date," Filov marked in his diary on January 20, 1941.

It was during this tense, eight-hour session that the Council of Ministers decided the future of Bulgaria.

The three questions the ministers had to answer that night were terrifying in their simplicity and clarity, three brutal "yes" or "no" questions that none of the men around the long conference table could dodge anymore:

Can we oppose the inevitable German passage through Bulgaria?

Should this passage follow a preliminary agreement with Bulgaria?

Is it necessary and in the interest of our country to sign the Tripartite Pact?

No one entertained any illusions about the gravity of the situation and the responsibility each minister was taking. The German might was at its apogee, with nobody able to stop the victorious march of the Wehrmacht through Europe, not even France or England, giants in comparison to miniscule Bulgaria. The Third Reich was in fact their mortal enemy, whereas it pretended to treat Bulgaria as a friend. Who could come to Bulgaria's rescue if it refused to sign the pact? Russia? But the Soviets were Hitler's allies, officially in any case. And every minister knew, in any case, that turning for help to the Russians meant certain bolshevization of the country, a fate they all dreaded above all.

In the Balkans, Greece and Albania were ravaged by war, German and Russian troops had entered Rumania, and Turkey was massing divisions on the Bulgarian border. Hitler was flirting with an increasingly receptive Yugoslavia, with indications that he had promised them Salonika if the Yugoslavs joined the Tripartite Pact and let the Germans through. If Belgrade signed the pact before Sofia, Bulgaria would have to forget its territorial claims forever and would moreover be surrounded by hostile pact forces.

And would the country, would the army, follow a government order to resist the Germans by force? There was not one minister who did not have serious doubts. In fact, persistent rumors and recent articles in foreign newspapers insisted that a government crisis was imminent, that some friend of the Germans like Tzankov, or General Loukov, or even Bagrianov, was going to replace the hesitant Filov and his cabinet. And there was no question that, as 1941 dawned, the victorious Germans, proclaiming their crusade for a New Order in Europe, were very popular in Bulgaria with the officers corps, the youth organizations, the majority of the press, and the so-called bourgeoisie.

Most of the ministers were not fully informed of the talks with the Germans and the other powers. Filov and Popov briefed them on the general lines of foreign policy, but the highlights were discussed only by the four favored ministers who were in permanent contact with the king, directly or through Sevov. Of the quartet, Filov and Gabrovsky believed in a German victory, and if they had any hesitations about signing the pact, they no longer voiced them. Both men believed sincerely that the worst that could happen would be a suicidal war against the Reich and the triumph of Communism. They had no doubt that the only solution for Bulgaria was to accept the unstoppable Germans as friends and allies.

The foreign and defense ministers, however, were far from being convinced. They had equal fear of the Bolshevik menace, but they did not believe that Germany could win against the Western powers. General Daskalov was even more unenthusiastic about joining the pact because, as a military man, he estimated that the Bulgarian army was not at all prepared or equipped to wage a modern war if the need occurred.

Foreign Minister Ivan Popov faced a true conflict of conscience. He understood equally well both sides of the dilemma, too well for his own peace of mind. And as they were contradictory, he saw the only solution in procrastinating, in helping King Boris defer the moment of truth. He was therefore distressed when Filov summoned him and Gabrovsky the day after the prime minister had reported to the king. Filov told the two ministers that King Boris had accepted his arguments in favor of signing the pact. "Popov tried to prolong everything some more," Filov wrote in his diary. "He remains decidedly an opponent to the signing and does not believe in a German victory. Nevertheless, he admits that the pact must be signed, but *after* the Germans enter Bulgaria. He insisted, however, on his resignation so that he need not personally sign the pact. I strove along with Gabrovsky to convince him that we would talk to the king some more on this matter . . ."

Popov did not resign. Filov and Gabrovsky convinced him that his resignation would confirm Germany's suspicion that the government was playing with it, putting the king in a delicate position. But Popov's doubts and sporadic outbreaks against the pact did not end. A few days later, after talking to British and American diplomats, he rushed to Filov in the evening, bursting with anti-German feelings. "He began once more to curse them," Filov wrote, "and declared that on no account would he sign the pact, although he is cooperating in its signing. He preferred that we drive him to suicide, rather than sign it. He insisted on leaving the cabinet beforehand."

The pressure during the two weeks that preceded the decisive Council of Ministers' meeting had been unbearable. Rendel, alarmed by Filov's visit to Vienna, repeated his warnings: if Bulgaria joined the Tripartite Pact and permitted the Germans to pass through, England would be forced to regard her as a hostile nation and to attack her. Turkey would attack as well, he said, and the English fleet would enter the Black Sea. At the same time Momchilov, the Bulgarian envoy in London, cabled that Britain would consider the presence of German troops in Bulgaria as Bulgarian complicity in the operations against England.

At this point, Richthofen returned from Berlin to convey in no uncertain terms the Reich government's irritation at Bulgaria's procrastination and its insistence on immediate action. In an unusually tough message Ribbentrop warned of "the grave consequences any further delay would have on Bulgaria's present and future political situation." Draganov arrived in Sofia on January 17, confirming that the Germans, extremely displeased, could not wait any longer.

Russia, too, became agitated. In a special communiqué, the Soviet government denied rumors of having given its consent to an eventual passage of German troops through Bulgaria, declaring that it had not been informed about such a passage.

Meanwhile, after King Boris had met several times with Filov and the "Group of Four," and in spite of the reservations of Popov, Daskalov, and the king himself, a consensus was reached on the inevitability of joining the pact. Their attention focused now on the conditions of the signing. A military delegation was dispatched to Rumania to negotiate the details of the Wehrmacht's passage with Field Marshal List, the German commander in the Balkans. A financial delegation was sent to Berlin for economic talks, while the Germans sent a special representative to Sofia to discuss the problems of currency, supplies, jurisdiction, and logistics connected with the eventual arrival of the Reich's troops. At the same time, the king and the government entrusted Draganov with another mission of crucial importance: to obtain concrete commitments from Berlin concerning Bulgaria's outlet to the Aegean Sea, a promise about which the Germans continued to be vague.

But most important, the king insisted on two conditions: that the German troops be sufficiently large to preclude any enemy intervention, and that the signing of the pact occur simultaneously with the arrival of the Wehrmacht. Boris felt that all these negotiations had a double advantage: appeasing the impatient Germans, and buying time for him. He realized, of course, that the chances of some miracle occurring in the last hour were infinitesimal, probably nil. But, alas, that was all he could hope for now.

On the morning of January 20, The Four met with the king in Vrana to review the instructions for the military delegates and confirm their agreement that Bulgaria had to sign the pact. When the long session of the Council of Ministers began that night, the four men told their colleagues that they could see no other choice and explained why. By 2 A.M. the cabinet had unanimously answered the three questions: No, we can not oppose the German passage. Yes, we must agree to this passage. Yes, it is necessary to sign the Tripartite Pact.

\*   \*   \*

King Boris was well briefed about Colonel William J. Donovan and his mission in the Balkans when he received him on January 22, and very curious to see the man who headed American intelligence. President Roosevelt's close friend had arrived in Sofia two days before, coming from Cairo and Athens en route to Belgrade and Ankara. He had already seen Filov, Popov, and Daskalov, and the king knew that the frank, blunt American was going to try his best to dissuade him from letting the Germans pass through Bulgaria.

The previous day, Filov had found Donovan to be militant and uncompromising. Afterwards the American had spoken with Popov extensively, advising him strongly that Bulgaria should defy the Germans. When the foreign minister suggested that the United States mediate between England and the Reich, Donovan replied that Washington firmly believed in

Britain's victory and did not want to hear of peace until the Nazis were definitely crushed. He reminded Popov of Bulgaria's "key position" in the Balkans.

"Keys are often unable to lock doors tightly enough to prevent anyone from entering," Popov said with a sigh. His only hope, he added, was that events would develop in a way which would preclude undesirable situations.

Donovan asked how the government would react if a great power wanted to cross the country's territory? Diplomatically, the foreign minister replied: "If I said that Bulgaria would oppose it, this would be a provocation to a mighty power; and if I said that we would allow it, this would be tantamount to an invitation."

Donovan did not like this elusive answer. "Such conduct could only confirm the belief that Bulgaria would not resist a foreign invasion," he said, pointing out that the Greek leaders were determined to resist a German attack through Bulgaria with all their forces, and that he himself had recommended that Washington send them aid immediately. Donovan nevertheless felt a certain sympathy for Bulgaria's predicament. He also felt that the foreign minister personally shared most of his ideas, but was not allowed to express them. "I'll tell you an anecdote," Popov said. "A criminal, sentenced to death, begged the sultan to postpone his execution for a year while he taught a camel to talk. To his friends, at a loss to understand how he was going to do this, he explained: I have a whole year at my disposal; God knows what may happen in one year—the camel, or the sultan, or I may die." (Rendel, who together with Earle acted as Donovan's guide in Sofia, remarked that it was the best illustration of Bulgaria's efforts to play for time, hoping against hope that something might happen to remove the danger.)

King Boris received the American cordially, and a mutual sympathy sprang up from the first moments of their hour-and-a-half conversation. Donovan stressed that the United States would help England by all possible means until victory, and that it was going to send aid to Greece to defend its independence. The king explained the tragic situation of a small country vanquished in the first war and cruelly punished. Bulgaria had been sentenced to death for doing what its geographic position had dictated, he claimed. Recently, he said, he had believed that peace could be secured, and had discussed the matter with Chamberlain. Earlier, he had tried to reach economic agreements with England and France, but London had wrecked them. He had hoped that the war would not expand into a world war, that a neutral U.S. would play the role of mediator. Now, to his regret, he learned that America too was rushing to war. All this filled him with anxiety about the fate of civilization.

"Civilization will be destroyed only if Hitler prevails," Donovan retorted, repeating that in this ideological conflict, the United States would not mediate until Hitler was defeated. Then, with unexpected frankness, he told the king the proposed content of his report to Washington. "Please correct me if my conclusions are not accurate," he asked Boris, as he started reciting:

"Complete economic dependence on Germany; introduction of antisemitic legislation; presence of German officers in the country; German uneasiness about my visit; Bulgarian officers expecting the arrival of German troops . . ."

The king, taken by surprise, did not correct him. Instead he stated that as the head of a small nation he had the duty to play for time in his relations with a Great Power and not allow it to crush his country, to avoid every risk that might expose the country to an invasion, and to try to cushion any blow the country might receive.

Donovan, realizing that he was not going to have a direct answer, offered to voice his own interpretation of the king's words. By maneuvering, Donovan said, the king was trying to avoid a German ultimatum; Sofia had not yet been compelled to make a decision, but if it could no longer be delayed, Bulgaria would neither put up any resistance to nor participate in military operations on the German side. Was this interpretation correct?

King Boris said nothing. He looked straight into the colonel's eyes and smiled. Donovan did not need more. The king had confirmed his conclusions.

When, later in the conversation, Boris described how, during the coup of 1934, he had outsmarted the conspirators who were reportedly ready to kill him, Donovan could not help thinking that in his dealings with Hitler, the king was probably applying the same tactics: taking the edge off the despot's demands by playing for time.

As he left for Belgrade after the audience, Roosevelt's special envoy declared: "I am leaving Bulgaria with pleasant impressions of a small but splendid country, of a sturdy and enlightened people, of a courteous, democratic and frank king." He reported to Washington that the Bulgarian monarch was an honest, but easily frightened idealist who sincerely wanted to avoid war. "But I fear that he has been so successful in maneuver, that he has placed too great a reliance upon it, even when the time has been reached when decision, and not maneuver, is essential," he wrote. Donovan believed that the king, not yet tied up with Germany, was trying to offset the Nazi pressure by certain concessions, playing for time in the desperate hope either that peace would be established, or that developments would deflect German pressure. In Donovan's view, the king was doing everything possible to avoid the entry of the German troops and to preserve peace, as well as Bulgaria's integrity and neutrality. But in the case of a German attack, he would yield, hoping that the United States and the other nations would not condemn him for the act.

Donovan's visit was disappointing for Boris. He had hoped that with American mediation a compromise between the two belligerent blocs could still be reached before the war came to the Balkans. In spite of Roosevelt's December speech, rejecting the idea of mediation, the king had hoped that something would happen to prevent the extension of the war, and he had impatiently awaited Donovan's visit. Now he heard from the envoy's own mouth that America intended to wage war until Hitler was totally destroyed.

He did not, of course, tell Donovan that on the very day of his arrival, the government had made its decision not to resist the German troops' entry into Bulgaria. But the colonel's words reinforced his determination to limit, as much as possible, Bulgaria's direct involvement in the war.

✳    ✳    ✳

As if King Boris did not have enough problems with the Germans, their enemies, and his internal opposition from the Right and the Left, a crisis exploded right in the middle of his own government. A speech of Agriculture Minister Bagrianov on January 31 had, indeed, the effect of a bomb. The prominent cabinet member and personal friend of the king unexpectedly attacked the agricultural policy of his government and proposed radical reforms which amounted to a planned economy.

Filov, taken aback, was outraged. He took it as a maneuver aimed at provoking a ministerial crisis, and suspected that some German sympathizers in Sofia, not satisfied with his government, believed Bagrianov the most suitable person to form a more Germanophile cabinet. That day he noted in his diary: "Sevov thinks that the King will do very well to get rid of his old friends like Bagrianov, Draganov, etc. . . . The King does not need such people. From the looks of things, Sevov now has the greatest influence on him. . . ."

Boris was very upset. In these crucial days for Bulgaria, the government's stability was jeopardized by none other than Bagrianov, his trusted friend, who had not even consulted him!

Filov interpreted the king's hurt feelings differently. He suspected that "Bagrianov's popularity especially frightened him. He is afraid that [Bagrianov] might become another Ivailo."[1]

Bagrianov resigned, triggering many speculations in Sofia. Had he become too prominent for the king's taste? Or, on the contrary, was he being groomed by the king for a "pro-German" role? In any crisis precipitated by German pressure, it would be advisable for the king to have ready at hand a potential prime minister of unquestionable loyalty.

---

[1]Ivailo—a shepherd who became Bulgarian king (1277–1280) after leading a popular revolt.

\* \* \*

In fact, the decision regarding Bulgaria's fate had already been made. But not by the king or Filov, nor by the ministers and generals, nor by the Parliament or public opinion. It is frightening to think how little, in the final analysis, Bulgaria counted in the unfolding of the drama, how little it was able to influence events.

Other factors, other powers, incomparably mightier than puny Bulgaria, had predetermined the fate of the Balkans. With hindsight, there is something pathetic in the small countries' efforts and illusions about controlling their own destinies. Their programs and policies, their passionate struggles and speeches, partisan coalitions or rivalries seem almost pitiful. The right decisions or mistakes of their leaders appear almost as irrelevant as the painstaking endeavors of ants building their hill on a path of approaching heavy boots . . .

Bulgaria closely escaped becoming an unwilling Soviet satellite when the Reich and the USSR were bargaining about Russia's joining the Tripartite Pact, which Stalin had accepted in principle. But one of Moscow's conditions stipulated: "that within the next few months the security of the Soviet Union in the Straits is assured by the conclusion of a mutual-assistance pact between the USSR and Bulgaria . . . and by the establishment of a base for the Soviet land and naval forces . . . within range of the Bosphorus and the Dardanelles." Stalin also demanded Finland, as well as control of the Straits and the Arabian and Persian oil fields. Unbeknownst to Bulgaria, Hitler judged the price much too high and rejected the deal. "Stalin is clever and cunning," he told his top commanders. "He demands more and more. He's a cold-blooded blackmailer. A German victory has become unbearable for Russia. Therefore, it must be brought to its knees as soon as possible."

Also unbeknownst to Bulgaria, the fate of the Balkans had been sealed by the Italian attack on Greece. This "regrettable blunder," as Hitler called it, endangered Germany's position in the Balkans because Britain threatened to send troops to the Greek mainland. In order to prevent it, the Fuehrer ordered the Wehrmacht to prepare plans immediately to invade Greece through Bulgaria, with a force of at least ten divisions. Directive Number 20, "Operation Marita," was decreed on December 13, 1940. Its first paragraph read:

1. . . . In the light of the threatening situation in Albania, it is doubly important to frustrate English efforts to establish, behind the protection of a Balkan front, an air base which would threaten Italy in the first place and, incidentally, the Rumanian oil fields.

The second paragraph of the directive is perhaps that which sealed irreversibly the fate of unwitting Bulgaria:

2. My intention is therefore:

(a) To establish in the coming months a constantly increasing force in southern Rumania.

(b) On the arrival of favorable weather—probably in March—to move this force across Bulgaria to occupy the north coast of the Aegean and, should this be necessary, the entire mainland of Greece ['Operation Marita']. We can rely upon Bulgarian support.

In another paragraph the Fuehrer stated:

4. (a) The first objective of the operation is the occupation of the Aegean coast and the Salonika basin . . .

(b) The flank of the attack will be protected against Turkey by the Bulgarian Army; but German units will also be held in readiness to strengthen and support it.

(c) It is not yet certain whether Bulgarian formations will play any role in the attack.

Signed: Adolf Hitler


The plan called for an army of twenty-four divisions under Field-Marshal Sigmund List to be assembled in Rumania, ready to descend on Greece through Bulgaria. Hitler ordered personally that the transfer of troops from Rumania to Bulgaria begin immediately so that "Marita" could start on March 26.

By the third week of February 1941, the Germans had massed a formidable army of 680,000 troops in Rumania. With the Italians still unable to conquer Greece, Hitler had serious fears of the British opening a front above Salonika, as they had done successfully in World War I. As the Fuehrer had already decided to attack Russia ("Operation Barbarossa"), he could under no circumstances allow such a development to endanger his southern flank. With or without Bulgaria's consent, the German troops were going to pass through its territory, headed for Greece. It was irreversibly spelled out in the plan "Marita," drawn up over a month before Sofia's cabinet meeting of January 20, 1941. And "Marita" was the absolute prerequisite for initiating "Barbarossa."

Would things have been different if Mussolini had not launched his ill-fated Greek adventure? To King Boris, who had refused to help him, it was now an academic question, for 680,000 of the best-equipped soldiers in the world were waiting for their marching orders on the northern border.

\*       \*       \*

The Bulgarian delegation for the signing of the Tripartite Pact, headed by Prime Minister Filov, arrived at the Vienna airport on March 1 at 12:30 after a considerable delay. Hitler's private plane, sent the previous day to Sofia, had sunk in the mud on landing at the Bojourishte airport. It took five emergency tractors working the night through to pull the *Condor* out and several hours for the Fuehrer's pilot Hans Bauer to inspect all the systems. It was not until ten o'clock that Filov and Richthofen, accompanied by two Foreign Ministry high officials and the king's secretary S. Balan, took off for Vienna.

Foreign Minister Ivan Popov was not in the party. Two days before departure, he fell sick and stayed in bed with a heating pad. In view of his repeated statements that he would rather resign, or even commit suicide, than sign his name to the Tripartite Pact, the king and Filov, irritated by his faint-heartedness, saw his sudden illness as psychosomatic. But as the prime minister was willing to go, the Germans were satisfied, to the relief of Popov.

Filov seemed to thrive during the preparations for his trip to Vienna. And yet it had been a tremendously tiring period for him, defending his policies, negotiating with the Germans, fighting the pessimism of close associates like Popov and Daskalov, and having continuously to encourage the unenthusiastic king. Although the decision to join the Tripartite Pact had been made, Filov felt that some of his collaborators were dragging their feet. Draganov, for instance, had returned to Berlin on February 1 with explicit instructions to see Ribbentrop immediately and explain the government's position on the timing and size of the German intervention. But pretending illness, Draganov did not see Ribbentrop until February 8, after repeated proddings from Sofia. The Reichsminister agreed that the pact could be signed at the same time the Germans passed through Bulgaria.

Meanwhile, the opposition leaders, alarmed by the rumors that Bulgaria would sign the pact, demanded explanations from Filov. Not satisfied by his evasive answers, they formally requested an audience with the king. But King Boris declined, replying that he could not see representatives of political parties since no parties legally existed under the present regime.

The reception at the Vienna airport impressed Professor Filov. "There was a ceremonial greeting," he remarked in his diary. "Ribbentrop, honor guard with music, two generals and fifteen high officials in uniform standing in line at the airport."

On the way to the hotel, Filov told Ribbentrop that he was concerned by the mobilization in Yugoslavia. Ribbentrop reassured him: the Yugoslavs had promised not to interfere, and he was confident that they would also join the pact. The Reichsminister admitted, however, that there was no explicit agreement with the Russians, who would not be pleased when Bulgaria joined the pact. But he was sure that the Soviets would put up with the new situation. The only threat to Bulgaria was from Turkey, he said, but the Turks would behave themselves.

The Bulgarians, and particularly King Boris, had their own reasons to believe that the Soviet Union would not strongly oppose Bulgaria's entering the pact. Only two days earlier, the king had sent Pavel Grouev on a delicate mission to the Soviet legation in Sofia. Grouev, who spoke Russian, had kept up contact between the palace and the Soviet envoy Lavrishchev, with whom he entertained polite relations, talking about Russian literature and sampling caviar. That day, the king's chief of cabinet told the Russian: "We intend to join the Tripartite Pact. What will your government say to that?"

To Grouev's surprise, Lavrishchev raised no objection. On the contrary, he said: "Why, we are allies of the Germans." He even hinted that the Soviet Uion itself might join the pact . . . King Boris, who had been very concerned, was enormously relieved when Grouev reported his conversation with the Russian diplomat.

Continuing his conversations with Ribbentrop, Filov recalled the Fuehrer's explicit agreement that no Bulgarian soldiers actively participate in front-line action. Ribbentrop answered that, in any case, Germany would not want anything with which Bulgaria would not be in agreement.

Filov left his hotel at 1 P.M., more than two hours behind schedule, to drive to the Belvedere Palace in the company of Richthofen. In the splendid setting of the old palace, the representatives of the pact signatories were solemnly waiting. Here are Filov's impressions:

> At our entrance into the palace, a detachment of soldiers saluted us again. Ribbentrop greeted us. We went into a vast hall, where Count Ciano, the Japanese, Hungarian, Rumanian and Slovak ambassadors, and some other people were presented to me. About 1:30, we went into a salon with two enormous Gobelin tapestries, where the signing was to take place. I was at the right of Ribbentrop; to the left of him was Ciano; to the right of me, the Japanese ambassador. The ceremony lasted some time since it was necessary to affix 64 signatures. Ribbentrop opened the ceremony with a few words. After the signing I read my declaration. (My calm tone and clear pronunciation made an impression, as it was heard on the radio very well.) Afterwards, Ribbentrop closed the meeting with a slightly longer speech. There were about two hundred people there. Many photographs and movies were taken.

Filov then followed Ribbentrop and Ciano to a small salon where they handed him letters, stating that an access to the Aegean Sea, between the mouths of the rivers Strouma and Maritza, was to be recognized as Bulgarian when the Balkan frontiers were arranged. This was to be kept in the greatest secrecy and announced only with the agreement of the two governments.

Filov and Ciano proceeded to a meeting with Hitler during which the Bulgarian prime minister expressed his concern about the threat of the Turkish army. Afterwards, "lunch was served in the Golden Circular Hall of the palace, on a great round table covered entirely with dark red roses," Filov continued in his description. "I was at the right of the Fuehrer; at his left was Ciano; at my right Field Marshal Keitel. Before the meal, the Fuehrer spoke little and, then, only sporadically. We exchanged some words, touching again on the question of Yugoslavia . . . I conversed more with Keitel, who is a very likeable fellow. I told him about our wish that the German soldiers not pass through Sofia, in order that we avoid English bombings . . ."

After lunch, Filov had an hour-long talk with Hitler, mostly about Russia and Yugoslavia. The Fuehrer repeated that it was very important for Germany to prevent the establishment of an English front in the Balkans, and for that reason, the Russians should keep out.

Hitler then said things about the Yugoslavs that Ribbentrop had not told Filov: if they tried anything, he would crush them! The Fuehrer's opinions had changed drastically since Filov's talk with him in January. At that time, he had considered the regent Prince Paul to be the chief Anglophile in Belgrade and had hoped that some sort of reversal would occur when King Peter came of age. Now, he thought that with the English-educated Peter, the Anglophiles would be even more powerful. Filov then pointed out the equivocal behavior of Yugoslavia which had suggested an eventual alliance between Yugoslavia, Bulgaria, and Turkey. Hitler did not like this at all. "He winced as if he suddenly had made a decision—just as when he made the decision on Dobrudja. He summoned the Hungarian envoy and Ribbentrop, who came quickly, and he declared that the Yugoslavs, whatever they did, would never be able to be our friends. At the settling of Balkan affairs, revision must affect them. They must make concessions both to Bulgaria and to Hungary. When I spoke more about Yugoslavia, he thought that we should once again raise claims for Macedonia."

Hitler then talked about the war. The Suez Canal, closed by sunken ships, was almost irreparable. The submarine war, difficult in winter, would resume in April, with ten times as many German submarines. The American aid was ineffectual. In industrial production, the "superiority of Germany over the U.S. is great." The Germans already had a significant head start, he said, and would remain ahead. Satisfactory large-scale war production was not possible in a democratic parliamentary regime, because centralization was indispensable. "American aid can come only after two or three years when it will be too late," Hitler predicted. And Ribbentrop continued to repeat that the war was already won for Germany, "restlos" (completely).

Filov was very pleased with the rest of his day. After dinner, Ribbentrop took him to "gemütlich" small beer hall, crowded with party people, who sang with the piano and collected money for the soldiers in winter. "People showed a very good disposition toward me," Filov wrote. "Ciano was very taciturn and sullen. He was probably dragged over the coals when he met with the Fuehrer before dinner."

He also noted Hitler's excellent mood at the Vienna reception. "At lunch, he took two portions of dessert and said that all his good intentions not to eat too many sweets had failed. This he does only when he is in good humor. The Bulgarians joined the pact at exactly the right moment, when we were gravely threatened and the Axis had suffered setbacks, and this is valued very much. It is as if a great power, and not little Bulgaria, had joined the pact."

The next day, a Sunday, Filov returned to Sofia by lunchtime, going straight to the palace from the airport to report to King Boris. He found him "very excited . . . evidently very satisfied."

The king had indeed been in a state of great agitation ever since Filov had left for the signing ceremony. But it is most doubtful that the prime minister found him "satisfied" upon his return, except to hear about the Germans' explicit agreement to Bulgaria's conditions—no active participation in the war and recognition of Bulgaria's rights in Aegean Thrace. But, apart from that, Boris would have preferred to see the signing of the pact postponed. In fact, just after saying good-bye to the prime minister on the eve of his departure to Vienna, the king had asked Grouev to come to his office. The chief of cabinet had seldom seen him so disturbed. Saying that Filov had left to sign the Tripartite Pact, King Boris added with a deep sigh in French: "Quelle fin!" (What an ending!) He repeated it several times. Grouev, who knew him intimately, understood what he meant. The king felt that a grave decision had been made, with consequences which would probably be fatal.

The reaction of the governing majority was quite different. The same afternoon, an enthusiastic Parliament greeted Filov, interrupting his speech with an acclamation and singing the national anthem. The prime minister, visibly delighted, presented the treaty for approval by the Sobranié, asserting that joining the pact did not mean war and that the government was 95 percent sure that Bulgaria would preserve her peace policy. "For twenty years we spoke about revision, and we waited for this moment. Now we cannot surrender, refusing to act. Our policy is a logical consequence of all that has occurred since the war," he declared.

The small group of opposition deputies tried to protest, but their words were drowned out with hurrahs. The Sobranié vote overwhelmingly approved the signing of the Tripartite Pact.

The same day, March 2, the gigantic army of Field-Marshal List entered Bulgaria, on the heels of the advance units which had crossed the Danube the previous day. The population watched with friendly curiosity as column after endless motorized column passed through the streets of Sofia.

England broke diplomatic relations with Sofia. Rendel went to the palace for a final audience with King Boris. "I found him petulant and evasive and very different from the friendly sovereign with whom I had got on so well up till the autumn of 1940," the British diplomat wrote. The king repeatedly reminded him that England had acquiesced when the Germans entered Hungary and Rumania. "You did not object or react when your friends the Rumanians let the Germans in," he said. "Why are you so much more upset when the same begins to happen here?"

King Boris brought up every Bulgarian grievance, professing complete helplessness before the vast might of Germany, but Rendel replied that this was no excuse for becoming an accomplice, rather than behaving like the Danes. "We parted sadly but coldly," Rendel wrote.

\*    \*    \*

# CHAPTER XX

# A Non-Belligerent Ally

**Y**UGOSLAVIA IS the first country that westbound planes from Sofia must cross. So it was only minutes after King Boris took off from the Vrajdebna airport on his way to Vienna that he was flying over the valleys and hills of Serbia.

Colonel Hans Bauer, Hitler's pilot, who had come to fetch the Bulgarian king, did not adhere to any particular altitudes or detours, as he was accustomed to do when passing over combat zones. The land below was ominously quiet. The guns had been silenced. The last fires were dying slowly in the ruins of the burned cities. The Luftwaffe was the total master of the Yugoslav sky.

The German attack, swift and devastating as a tornado, had been over in less than a fortnight. Thirteen days ago, on April 6, 1941, the formidable legions of the Reich had crossed the Rumanian and Hungarian borders. On their savage drive southward the Panzers and the Stukas turned towns and villages into piles of rubble. Operation "Marita" had begun.

Belgrade had been razed. Whatever resistance had been offered—and at several points the Yugoslav army had fought valiantly—had been crushed as if the defense lines had been made of match sticks. Thousands of people had perished. The day before, April 17, Yugoslavia had been forced to surrender and sign an armistice.

Could so much suffering and destruction have been avoided? What had happened?

On March 25, 1941, pressed by Germany, and with the seemingly invincible Wehrmacht on her borders, Yugoslavia had signed the Tripartite Pact, as Hungary, Rumania, and Slovakia had already done and as Bulgaria had done that same month. It had been a harder decision for the regent prince Paul and for Yugoslavia, a creation and major beneficiary of the Versailles treaties, than for Bulgaria or Hungary, who shared Germany's desire for treaty revisions. But the Belgrade regime had, in the end, joined the pact in an attempt to avoid war. But two days later, Yugoslav nationalists and the army, led by General Doushan Simovitch, overthrew the government and refused to ratify the unpopular alliance. In brutal retaliation, the Germans invaded the country, crossing its entire territory to the Greek war theater, where their Italian allies were in serious trouble.

In the wake of these momentous events, Filov insisted that King Boris talk to Hitler in person, especially now that the future of Macedonia was at stake. Fearing that the Fuehrer might ask him to participate in the new war, the king initially declined. But after some hesitation, seeing Yugoslavia so quickly conquered, he requested the meeting.

On April 19, beneath the Fuehrer's plane carrying the Bulgarian king to the Vienna meeting, Yugoslavia's martyr population had good reason to ponder who had acted in the better interests of the country: Prince Paul or General Simovitch? The question may remain open forever.

But for King Boris, there had never been any real doubt as to the course he would take in a similar dilemma. Unlike his father, whose priorities were of a historical and national order, humanitarian considerations weighed predominantly in Boris's decisions. He knew personally many "Uncle Ivans" and "Grandma Penas" in every Bulgarian village, had shaken hands with them, had shared their meals. He felt that they relied on him, trusting him as children trust a parent, which was a great reward as well as a terrible responsibility. "Don't worry, the king knows his business!" was the general public attitude.

For him, sparing those trusting people the kind of horror and devastation that the land he was flying over had just suffered had precedence over all other considerations. Last month, by signing the Tripartite Pact, Bulgaria had escaped the destruction of war. In a couple of hours, the king and Hitler were going to discuss the problem of Macedonia and, who knows, the Fuehrer might come up with some new ideas or some new demands.

The German attitude toward Bulgaria's territorial claims had changed completely since General Simovitch's coup. Reserved and noncommittal during their courtship of Yugoslavia, the Germans had begun openly to favor the return to Bulgaria of large parts of Macedonia. The Bulgarian government was delighted but, at the same time, worried about the price Germany was going to ask in return.

Relations with the passing German troops were very good at that time, with no serious complaints from either side. Field Marshal List and his staff had praised the reception in Bulgaria, expressing pleasure with the temporary headquarters at the Rila mountain resort of Cham-Koria. On March 16, in the presence of Filov and War Minister Daskalov, King Boris had received List in Vrana, and the field marshal had asked whether Bulgaria would be willing to occupy parts of Greek Thrace. At the same time, Draganov had confidentially informed the king that Hitler had summoned him, and in the presence of Ribbentrop, spoken angrily against the Yugoslavs, saying that now the Macedonian question could be solved to Bulgaria's advantage. On March 30, Draganov reported that Ribbentrop, showing great interest, had requested a briefing on the Macedonian problem, asking whether Bulgaria could, within forty-eight hours organize a propaganda campaign for Macedonia.

Though the king and Filov had been willing to examine the propaganda aspect, Foreign Minisiter Popov insisted that the suggestion be completely rejected. Filov wrote in his diary: "I said that if we rejected the proposal, it would appear as if we were not interested in Macedonia. At this point, Popov again expressed his hostile disposition toward Ribbentrop. He still does not believe in their victory. After a long argument, we agreed on a compromise formula, since Popov is terribly afraid lest we widen the war and still thinks that we could gain a little good will from the English and Americans and their friends. I objected to him once more that we could expect absolutely nothing from them and that they would show us no mercy if they are victorious. However, we must be very attentive not to impair our relations with the Germans. No people can secure their national ideals without struggle, merely by standing with folded arms and expecting everything to be offered them when ready. We must realize that, for us also, a battle is imminent and be prepared for it."

In the first days of April, as the war between Germany and Yugoslavia appeared inevitable, King Boris and his four chief ministers had maintained firmly that Bulgaria should stay out of the war, even though the Yugoslavs had provoked some rather serious border incidents. During the deliberations, general Daskalov was as pessimistic as ever, while Popov went on with his anti-German remarks. The policy of neutrality was also defended by the king during the lunch he had given on April 3 for Field Marshal von Brauchitsch, the chief of staff of the Germany army, who requested that Bulgarian troops join the Wehrmacht in the forthcoming campaign against Yugoslavia. King Boris refused.

On April 8, two days after Germany invaded Yugoslavia, Ribbentrop asked Draganov to leave for Sofia at once with a request from Hitler that three Bulgarian divisions occupy Yugoslav Macedonia, taking over its administration, so that the German troops could be freed. King Boris wanted to accept the proposition, but as a way of "maintaining order and peace in territory captured by the Germans" rather than as an "occupation." Filov suggested accepting in principle right away, without waiting for the arrival of Draganov, in order to demonstrate to the Germans the government's will and readiness. But he had to face other opposition: The foreign minister was decidedly against the proposition, and the war minister insisted on asking for one German armor division for protection against the Turks. Filov was exasperated. "I spent more than an hour arguing with them, but these two did not budge, asking that we not hurry into this but wait for the arrival of Draganov. Popov began to speak again about resigning, saying that he was sorry he had not persevered earlier. He admitted he did not believe in a German victory. He envies me because as I am such an optimist, I am serene, while he is troubled constantly, with the thought that all will end badly."

Architect Sevov joined Filov in his efforts to convince Popov. It took several hours and much persuasion, but, finally, the foreign minister agreed that Bulgaria had to hasten the occupation of Macedonia, especially since there might be conflicts there later with the Italians. General Daskalov also ended by approving. That same day the government informed Germany that Bulgaria was ready to accept Berlin's requst.

When asked about the date of the three Bulgarian divisions' entry into Macedonia, the German government did not answer for several days. The puzzling delay caused a certain nervousness in Sofia. Had the Germans changed their mind about letting the Bulgarians into Macedonia? The news that the Italians had occupied Ochrid, a Macedonian town of special sentimental value to Bulgaria, was received with disappointment and concern. Richthofen reported to Berlin that the Bulgarian public had once again begun to accuse the king and his government of not defending Bulgaria's aspirations with sufficient energy. "A Bulgarian occupation of Serbian Macedonia would crown the feeling of gratitude to Germany and the Fuehrer, which is now at its peak . . . It would also reinforce the position of the king and the government," wrote the Germany envoy. Finally, on April 18, Ribbentrop's cable defined the territory that the Bulgarian troops would occupy.

Meanwhile, British war planes had dropped a few bombs on Sofia's railroad station; Bulgaria had broken diplomatic relations with Yugoslavia; and King Boris and Hitler had agreed to meet to discuss the problems of the occupation of Macedonia.

On April 19, the day of the meeting, three Bulgarian divisions began to enter German-occupied Yugoslavia.

\* \* \*

The new master of Europe, the most powerful individual that the world had known since Napoleon, waited at the Wiener Neustadt airport to greet the king of defenseless, humble Bulgaria. Surrounded by uniforms and swastikas, the two men shook hands smilingly, passed the honor guard in review, and headed for the Fuehrer's car.

It would have been a most typical meeting between heads of state were it not for a curious, even amazing detail: Adolf Hitler was behaving like an insecure, awestruck man in the presence of a much-admired guest of superior rank. The intimates of the two leaders had already noticed Hitler's uncustomary deferential attitude during his previous meetings with King

Boris. There was no doubt about it: faced with the Bulgarian monarch, the Fuehrer looked unusually attentive, as if he were flattered by the honor, and a little ill at ease. It showed even in photographs. "Look, isn't it typical?" the queen's lady-in-waiting Nadia Stoyanova exclaimed when the king's secretary Balan showed her pictures of King Boris with Hitler and Ribbentrop. "Here is His Majesty, perfectly at ease, aristocratic, nonchalantly elegant. Then there is Hitler, friendly but tense, like a soldier standing at attention in his captain's presence. And then Ribbentrop, of course: haughty, sure of himself and distant."

Pavel Grouev, who had never seen Hitler but had heard all the detailed and confidential descriptions reported by King Boris, had his own explanation for the Fuehrer's strange deference: "It's the same old story, the prince and the corporal—the childhood inferiority complex of the humble commoner *vis-à-vis* born royalty—especially for a dynasty of Germanic origin: the Saxe-Coburg-Gotha. It's funny, but certain pecking orders of our youth remain with us forever and nothing in our later life can possibly alter them— neither success, nor fortune, nor power. No matter how powerful, the corporal feels deep in himself that he has remained basically the same old commoner while the prince continues to be a blueblood. . . ."

This theory did not account, however, for the contempt in which Hitler held almost all other royalty, including German princes and dukes. "Yes, he has a very special respect for the king," Grouev agreed. "Maybe he recognizes in him personal qualities and characteristics that he himself lacks but wishes he had. Who knows? . . ."

During the meeting at the Wiener Neustadt headquarters, the Fuehrer once again showed his respect for King Boris, receiving him cordially. Before leaving Bulgaria, the king had been worried; when preparing the strategy for the meeting, he had confessed to Filov and Popov that the visit rather troubled him. But he was relieved when Hitler did not try to pressure him into sending combat troops.

Von Papen, the German ambassador to Turkey, was also present at the meeting. After the king thanked Hitler for liberating territories that Bulgarians considered theirs, the Fuehrer expressed his grief over everything that had occurred in Yugoslavia and confessed that he was unhappy about the war with Greece. Then he revealed his plans concerning Yugoslavia: he intended to reduce her to a small state, parceling out parts of her present territory to the newly independent state of Croatia, to Bulgaria, Hungary, Rumania, and Italy.

Boris brought up the Bulgarian claims on Greek Thrace and Salonika. But Hitler did not wish to commit himself before the completion of the war with Greece. They also talked about the Italian occupation of Ochrid, and the Fuehrer instructed Ribbentrop to discuss the problem the next day with Ciano. When the talks resumed in the afternoon, King Boris produced a detailed map of the territories claimed by Bulgaria. His German hosts showed considerable interest in the map, keeping it for further study. After the meeting ended in a friendly atmosphere, Ribbentrop invited the king to dinner at his favorite Viennese restaurant, The Three Hussars.

The next morning, Easter Sunday, King Boris returned to Sofia, satisfied with the visit to Hitler's headquarters. At six o'clock in the evening, he received the four policymaking ministers in Vrana to brief them in detail.

*   *   *

The news of the occupation of Macedonia was received with enormous enthusiasm in Bulgaria. Twenty-three years after its loss to Yugoslavia, the land for which so much Bulgarian blood had been spilled had again been integrated into the Motherland. And although the official status was one of temporary occupation and administration until the end of the war, when Macedonia's future would be decided at a peace conference, the Bulgarian public saw it in terms of "liberation" and national "unification." The ecstatic nation named Boris "King Unifier" as huge spontaneous demonstrations broke out all around the country. The frontier between Bulgaria and Yugoslav Macedonia was not, however, abolished—anyone crossing the border in either directions submitted to strict formalities.

Taking over the occupation of the conquered regions just conquered by the German army was a delicate and costly task. At the king's insistence, the administrative personnel for the "newly-liberated lands" was recruited from among Macedonian Bulgarians, with most county and municipal jobs reserved for the local people. Large quantities of food had to be sent from Bulgaria; roads and public works in the badly neglected province began to be rebuilt; and special privileges and tax exemptions were granted to the Macedonian population. The military were under strict orders to treat the local people with extreme consideration.

Soon after the decision about Macedonia, the Germans authorized Bulgaria also to occupy Greek Thrace with the islands of Tassos and Samothrace. All the occupied territories were organized administratively into three regions, with headquarters in Skopie and Bitolia for Macedonia, and in Xanthi for Thrace. After the previous year's peaceful return of Dobrudja, most Bulgarians believed that the national dream of unification seemed finally to have been achieved. But King Boris, a pessimist by nature, was more skeptical, still feeling that Germany could not win the war.

As he toured Macedonia and Thrace, mostly unannounced but quickly recognized in every town, he was given wild ovations by the population and the troops. Meanwhile, the celebrations back in Bulgaria went on with uninterrupted enthusiasm. In a highly patriotic speech in the Sobranié, Filov proclaimed solemnly that the long-awaited hour of the Bulgarian Unification had finally arrived. The country was in a state of euphoria. A flame ignited in the ancient capital of Preslav, in northern Bulgaria, was carried in triumph across the country all the way to Macedonia and Thrace, met in every town and village with speeches, military bands, and popular festivities. Everybody, including the members of the anti-German opposition, was overjoyed. It reinforced, of course, the pro-German feelings in the country, as most people attributed the unification to the victorious Germans.

News coming from the liberated territories, however, somewhat dampened the euphoria. It was reported that the pro-Bulgarian feelings in Macedonia and Thrace varied from town to town, according to the age and education of the population. In Shtip and Ochrid, for instance, people were enthusiastic, but they were more reserved in Skopie and Veless. The young were cooler to Bulgaria than their elders; the peasants more demonstrative than the intelligentsia. Twenty-three years of intense "de-Bulgarization" in Yugoslavia and Greece had borne fruit. In many regions, especially in Thrace, there had been population exchanges with massive resettlements of ethnic Greeks. In Macedonia, the majority of the old Bulgarian elites had emigrated, and the young generations growing up under Serbian rule were losing their national identity. Most Bulgarian schools had been replaced by Serbian schools, many teachers and priests deported or intimidated. In addition, in territories which had in brutal circumstances changed hands five or six times in the last thirty years, ethnic loyalty was an extremely risky and rare quality. People had learned the hard way to wait and see before declaring themselves prematurely or openly.

These observations were disturbing to a few Bulgarians, including King Boris. It also became clear that most Macedonian immigrants in Bulgaria, especially those who had found some security there, were not keen to return and start all over again in Macedonia, particularly while the war was going on. And—a most disturbing factor to many who dreamed of the "Great Bulgaria"—IMRO, the militant anti-Serbian Macedonian organization, continued to fight for an *independent* Macedonia, rather than for a Macedonia integrated into the Bulgarian kingdom.

The most urgent problem on the agenda of King Boris and the Filov government, in addition to the organization of an efficient Bulgarian administration in Macedonia and Thrace, was to convince Germany to fix the boundaries of the occupied lands to conform to historic Bulgarian claims. This question, as well as Bulgaria's rights and obligations in Macedonia and Thrace, was negotiated by the senior German diplomat Dr. Karl Clodius, who arrived in Sofia at the end of April.

Clodius was amenable concerning the borders of Macedonia, but made several requests of an economic nature, especially about mining concessions in Macedonia. He informed the king that the Fuehrer had still not made a decision about Salonika and Greek Macedonia, but that Serbian Macedonia to the Shar mountains would be given to Bulgaria. In a second audience with the king, Clodius was able to announce that Ochrid would remain in Bulgarian hands, but six other disputed towns would go to Albania. Originally, he said, the Italians had had bigger claims in favor of their new protectorate Albania.

Boris and Filov, finding the Italian demands excessive, feared they would trigger anti-Italian feelings in Bulgaria. Filov noted in his diary: "It appears, however, that the Germans cannot force anything more upon them, since they are anxious that the Italians not renounce them. Like all other Germans, Clodius rather cautiously expressed ill feelings toward the Italians."

*    *    *

King Boris paid another visit to Hitler in June 1941 during a three-week private trip abroad, which took him to Germany, Italy, Switzerland, and Slovakia. This time the meeting took place at the Fuehrer's mountain retreat in Obersalzberg in the Austrian Alps.

Hitler had personally designed the plans for his house, the Berghof, incorporating into it the old small chalet with the overhanging roof, which he had used regularly since the early years of his career as a retreat. King Boris had known this magnificent mountain area since childhood, and he had visited Berchtesgaden with his brother and sisters in 1908 as a fourteen-year-old boy. But the unspoiled wilderness of the place had changed since then. As the car climbed the steep highway past Berchtesgaden and headed toward Berghof, it was disappointing to see fences and paved roads, barracks, garages, and several annexes for the Fuehrer's entourage and guards. The entire Obersalzberg area, with its newly confiscated state forests and old farms, had become a huge, 2.7 square mile private estate, extending from the top of the 6,400 foot high mountain all the way down to the valley. From a distance King Boris was shown the houses of three of Hitler's closest collaborators: Goering, Martin Bormann, and Albert Speer.

The king, accompanied by Draganov, Handjiev, Bardarov, and Balan, was offered tea in the large, split-level living room of Berghof, comfortably but sparsely furnished with a few oversize pieces of furniture. The guests admired the large oil paintings on the walls, the nude by Titian, the landscape with Roman ruins by Pannini, and the big bronze bust of Richard Wagner by Arno Breker. Hitler was particularly proud of the superb view from the immense picture window of the salon overlooking Berchtesgaden, Untersberg, and Salzburg. According to legend, Emperor Charlemagne still slept in Untersberg and one day would rise up to restore the past glory of the German Empire. "It is no accident that I have my residence opposite it," Hitler liked to tell his visitors.

It was obvious that he loved his Berghof, the private retreat where he used to come with Eva Braun (she discreetly stayed in her rooms when the Fuehrer received official guests) and where he watched movies every evening until the early morning hours. As for the beauty of nature, his architect friend and neighbor Speer wrote that "he frequently admired a beautiful view, but as a rule he was more affected by the awesomeness of the abysses than by the harmony of a landscape. It may be that he felt more than he allowed himself to express. I noticed that he took little pleasure in flowers and considered them entirely as decorations."

After the amenities, King Boris and Hitler withdrew alone into an adjoining room.

The convesation with Hitler was friendly. The Fuehrer remarked that he considered the Bulgarians Germany's best friends, declaring himself very pleased with the reception of his troops in Bulgaria. He spoke very harshly about the Soviet Union, making no attempt to maintain the appearance of an alliance. The Germano-Russian Pact was indeed still valid officially, but King Boris, who was aware of the enormous troop concentrations at the Soviet border, had reliable information that the Wehrmacht was preparing a strike against the USSR. Hitler was equally bellicose when speaking of England, repeating bitterly that before the war he had made attempts to come to terms with the English. As for Bulgaria, he suggested that its Cyrillic alphabet might be replaced by the Latin one, in order to lessen the Russian influence. The king politely ignored the suggestion.

In his talks with Hitler, and then at the Foreign Ministry in Berlin, Boris raised the delicate question of Italian designs on Macedonia, a matter of concern in Sofia. The Germans were themselves increasingly annoyed by their ally's ambitions in the Balkans but avoided any overt arguments with Mussolini and Ciano over the few Macedonian towns and mines which Italy had annexed on behalf of Albania. Without intervening directly in the nascent Italo-Bulgarian dispute, Germany's sympathies were on the Bulgarian side.

After the Obersalzberg meeting, King Boris went to Rome to speak of the problem with Mussolini, who promised to give it his full attention. But the demarcation of the Bulgaro-Albanian border and jurisdiction over a number of mines in Macedonia were postponed to the following month when Filov and Popov were due to visit Rome. The squabbles, however, continued for another year-and-a-half before a final agreement was reached.

Boris took advantage of his trip to pay a visit to his father who was complaining and sulking more than ever. King Ferdinand had celebrated his eightieth birthday on February 26, with hurt feelings that not only was he not invited to celebrate it in Bulgaria, but none of his children had come to spend the day with him. However, they had all written long, warm letters, expressing their deep regret at being unable to travel because of the military situation. King Boris could not, of course, write him that as Bulgaria was going to sign the Tripartite Pact in three days, the moment was hardly auspicious for visits and celebrations. The old monarch was not about to forgive.

From his estate in Slovakia, he wrote to his old friend Ekaterina Karavelova, the widow of an eminent Bulgarian statesman:

"In spite of my expectations of spending my eightieth anniversary in Bulgaria, I spent it here alone, lonely, and forgotten by the country for which I worked and still work even now. Suspecting the unfavorable mood of our responsible circles, I knew that no joyous celebration of popular festivities would be organized for the occasion, but I did not expect Destiny to be so cruel as to find myself abandoned by everybody and, even, by my children. The Bulgarian people, for whose progress, I dare rightly say I did so much, silently ignored this anniversary. My bitter disappointment is immense, because the anniversary coincides with events touching Bulgaria, events that not only do not let me be indifferent but in which I took part and tried, according to my abilities, to make profitable for Bulgaria. And what can I say about our press, which barely mentions this date with two or three lines, while in reality this is a historic date for Bulgaria, because my person cannot be separated from the history of the Bulgarian people, with whom I am bound forever. Is not the present political harvest the fruit of grain sowed by me? Was due homage given to the Ploughman and to the Sower?"

Again, King Boris had to arm himself with all his patience and tact to face The Monarch, listen to his litany of complaints, and explain why the moment was not propitious for his return to Bulgaria. As usual, he left exhausted and upset. No matter how much the caprices and unreasonable demands of "Bitternus" or "Saint Illia" (code names for Ferdinand that Boris used when corresponding in cypher with his sisters or with confidants like Draganov and Grouev) exasperated him, the king never found the strength to sever relations with him or even to put him in his place once and for all. The respect for Le Monarque was still there, hidden in the depths of his complicated nature, alongside a residue of childhood intimidation. And, annoying and politically dangerous as Ferdinand's insistence on his return to Bulgaria was, Boris could not fail to recognize the sincerity and intensity of his father's dream. The nostalgia of the old man for "his" country had, after twenty-three years of exile, taken on psychosomatic proportions, and although Boris was absolutely determined not to let him return, there were moments when he could not help feeling a certain guilt.

Only two days after Boris returned from his European trip, the world was stunned by news that was to change the entire situation on the global chessboard: On June 22, 1941, the armies of the Third Reich invaded the Soviet Union. For Bulgaria, it meant that many of the premises on which her foreign policy had been based were of a sudden radically altered.

In fact, Hitler had long since made up his mind to attack Russia. On December 18, 1940, he had issued the secret (nine copies only) Directive Number 21 for "Operation Barbarossa." His detailed orders to the military chiefs began with the words: "The German Armed Forces must be prepared, even before the conclusion of the war against England, to crush Soviet Russia in a rapid campaign ('Operation Barbarossa')."

Neither King Boris nor the Filov government was overly surprised by the news. Since the beginning of May, Bulgarian liaison officers at the German headquarters, as well as the Bulgarian legation in Berlin, had been reporting in confidential cables that the Wehrmacht was preparing something against the Russians. King Boris had himself brought back similar impressions from his trip abroad.

The announcement, nevertheless, caused a sensation in Bulgaria. Filov noted that "according to information heard in Sofia and the provinces, our people reacted with surprise and despondency." The cabinet met the same morning and decided there was no need to take any special measures except to reinforce surveillance on the Communists. At Filov's suggestion, the Communist deputies were expelled from the Parliament and placed under house arrest.

The American minister in Sofia reported that the "first reactions of Bulgarians to the Russo-German war are confusion and shock, mainly on account of distinct division of sympathy for the two countries. Some Bulgarians recall with apprehension Hitler's words in *Mein Kampf* that Slavs are only good to be slaves, while others who hitherto looked upon Hitler's frequent breach of word with equanimity have been struck pretty hard by Hitler's complete lack of good faith as exemplified by his latest aggression. Others fear involvement of Bulgaria in the war."

That was the predominant feeling: fear of involvement. During the first days of the new war, the government worried that Germany might pressure Bulgaria to participate, or at least assist, in the military operations. There was a consensus among the political and military leaders that any involvement in the war should definitely be avoided: in view of the traditional friendly feelings toward the Russian people, it was felt that such a war would be unpopular. And, as King Boris had stated on several occasions, the Bulgarian soldier was an excellent fighter only when fighting on his land for his own cause, not in foreign lands for obscure reasons. The king and his ministers had made this point very clear to Hitler, Ribbentrop, and all visiting German officials.

The fear of involvement subsided when it became clear that the Germans were not asking for Bulgarian troops. Operation Barbarossa did not call for Bulgarian participation. Sofia was greatly relieved when Ribbentrop, informing Draganov officially about the war, did not even mention assistance by Bulgarian troops, but instead asked Bulgaria to represent German interests in Moscow. King Boris's policy of benign evasiveness seemed to be paying off, at least for the time being: while Italy, Hungary, Rumania, Slovakia, and Finland declared war on the Soviet Union, Bulgaria retained diplomatic relations with the USSR.

But as the fire further engulfed the entire continent, the balancing act would become more and more difficult. Close to home, King Boris saw the harbinger of things to come—the replacement of the German minister in Sofia, the aristocratic von Richthofen, a diplomat of the old school, with a Nazi party man, the SA Obergruppenfuehrer Adolf-Heinz Beckerle, a former police chief of Frankfurt. Beckerle arrived in Sofia six days after the beginning of the Russo-German war.

The initial German victories in Russia were so overpowering that many Bulgarian circles hoped that the war might end soon, without directly endangering Bulgaria. But despite the daily communiqués announcing the fall of yet another Soviet town and the surrender of hundreds of thousands of Russian soldiers, Boris remained skeptical. On August 8, Filov noted in his diary: "The king sent me a confidential report from Draganov. It is very pessimistic. In Berlin, it is acknowledged that the war with Russia caught the Germans by surprise. But they do not yet wish to admit that there is much anxiety and fear among the people because of the great number of German casualties and the difficulties which have arisen. Everyone sees, however, that there is no other alternative. The bombardment of Berlin and other German cities has increased, becoming more effective. This winter there will be many hard days."

The mood in Bulgaria began to change markedly. The people, who had been lulled into a sense of relative security by the Russo-German pact, became deeply disturbed by the sudden rupture between the two powers on which Bulgaria's future depended. And now, with the first setbacks on the Eastern front, the smiling German soldiers and friendly diplomats of yesterday seemed to have put on new faces—tougher, arrogant, overbearing. Another consequence of the German attack was that the Bulgarian Communists, who until then had observed a tacit truce with the authorities, switched tactics, resuming their acts of terrorism, sabotage, and vicious antigovernment propaganda.

King Boris's regime seemed nevertheless, to be well in control of the situation. On October 14, 1941, the American minister in Sofia cabled to the secretary of state:

To be communicated to the President. Summed up as I see it, the situation in Bulgaria is as follows:

One. The king is more popular than ever before because he has kept his country out of war and acquired for Bulgaria more territory than was ever hoped for. His popularity will continue so long as his country remains at peace.

Two. Today the king's power is absolute. In an unobtrusive and subtle way, almost never showing his hand, he governs Bulgaria exactly as he wishes.

Three. While not going to war, he is helping Germany in every way possible against Russia, feeling as do nearly all well-to-do Bulgarians that Bolshevism is a far greater menace to Bulgaria than Nazism.

Four. I think the king does not like the Germans but believes, though not so strongly as heretofore, that they will win the war. However, should Germany begin to show signs of cracking, Bulgaria will be among the first to desert the sinking ship.

Five. That the king does not want to burn all his bridges is shown by his considerate and very friendly attitude toward me personally and the legation, in spite of the fact that several of my colleagues inform me that I am the most unpopular man with the Germans in the Balkans.

Earle

Two months later, some of the most important bridges were burned. Immediately after Pearl Harbor and the American entry into the war, Draganov cabled from Berlin on December 12: "It is proposed to the country signatories of the Tripartite Pact to declare war on America." Simultaneously, the German and Italian ambassadors in Sofia presented the same request to Foreign Minister Popov.

The request was immediately transmitted to the king, who was in his house in Kritchim that day. While waiting for his return, the cabinet met urgently in the afternoon. The Axis demand posed a serious problem of legal interpretation of the Tripartite Pact, Article 3 of which obliged each member to give full assistance to any other member who became victim of an aggression. The Axis thesis was that the United States was the first formally to declare war on Japan and was thus, technically speaking, the aggressor. Bulgaria, like all the other signatories, had therefore the contractual obligation to declare war on America and its ally Britain. Beckerle visited Filov three times that day, pressing for an affirmative answer. Ribbentrop, who was making a speech the following day, wanted to announce that Bulgaria too had declared war. Under Filov's prodding, the cabinet agreed with this interpretation, accepting the Axis request, with only two ministers expressing hesitation. The rationalization behind this momentous decision was that, since the U.S. and England were so far away, the declaration was a purely "symbolic" act with no practical consequences.

The same evening, Filov and Popov saw the king, who was very unhappy about the new development, although the prime minister emphasized that the "symbolic war" would in no way entail fighting by Bulgarian troops anywhere. "He approved the decision, but obviously reluctantly," wrote Filov. "He was nervous and worried."

According to Loultchev, King Boris told him that he had had nothing to do with the war declaration, that it was the ministers' doing, not his. He had even angrily berated Filov and Popov: "You should have resisted," Loultchev quoted the king's coarse outburst. "Let them rip your pants first and then f. . . you! But you not only pulled them down yourselves, you also supplied the vaseline."

The next day, December 13, Filov announced in a stormy session of the Parliament that Bulgaria, "true to her obligations under the Tripartite Pact," was declaring a symbolic war on the United States and Britain. The opposition protested strongly, but the majority voted in favor, accepting Filov's assurances that the declaration was only symbolic.

The country received the news with consternation, torn between apprehension of Anglo-American retaliation and the hope that they would understand that "we did it only because of German pressure and it actually doesn't mean anything." The Bulgarian minister in Washington, D. Naoumov, not informed in time, learned the news from the newspapers. Hoping the press had mistaken a breaking of diplomatic relations for a declaration of war, he cabled to Sofia that "the rumors about declaring war seem to be more than incredibly ridiculous. Please instruct me by open telegram and in just one word—'breaking'—so I will be able to dispel the unbelievable impression that could be left here that Bulgaria has declared war on America!" Draganov, also surprised, cabled that the adherence to the Tripartite Pact did not necessarily require Bulgaria to declare war.

Late in the afternoon, after the dramatic vote at the Sobranié, King Boris left the palace alone, and no one was able to locate him. Later in the evening, he was found in a remote corner of the darkened Alexander-Nevsky Cathedral, a solitary figure, praying.

※　　※　　※

During the winter, the Germans put pressure on Bulgaria to break diplomatic relations with the Soviet Union. They considered it increasingly unnatural and annoying for an ally to tolerate the presence on its territory of a Russian legation and consulates, convenient centers for espionage and sabotage against the German troops passing through the country. The other allies meanwhile could not understand why Bulgaria should be exempt from sending troops, even a token unit, to the eastern front where their soldiers were fighting against the Russians. When the pressure became too heavy, King Boris once more resorted to his talents of personal persuasion on Hitler.

The meeting on March 24, 1942, at the Fuehrer's headquarters started at 11 A.M., with the two men talking alone until 2 P.M. Hitler invited Boris for lunch and continued the conversation until five o'clock in the afternoon. Hitler, very talkative, seemed pleased as usual to see the king and again accepted his arguments. He spoke mostly about the incredibly hard conditions at the Eastern front which the German army had faced through the winter. There had been no preparation for a winter campaign, he said. His field marshals insisted that the armies be withdrawn a considerable distance, but he did not agree, lest he repeat Napoleon's history. This had led to a rupture with Field Marshal von Brauchitsch. Hitler then took full charge, but the Germans sustained about a million casualties, he admitted. He described in some detail the way they tried to cure the frostbitten victims.

Hitler told king Boris that, because of the unusual cold, the machine-gun mechanisms would not work. The Germans needed 120 trains daily to feed their soldiers, but as the locomotives could not operate normally during the great cold, only ten trains per day ran. There were many critical moments, but the soldiers held out, he said. The Sixteenth German Army was encircled, holding out because of the supplies brought in by plane. But, with his 4 million reserve troops, Hitler revealed, he planned his main strike for the Caucasus, in order to establish connections with the Japanese at the Persian Gulf.

After urging Boris to be more amicable to the Turks, the Fuehrer said that Germany would want additional help in Serbia. The king answered that more Bulgarian soldiers were also needed in Macedonia. Hitler confided that he found Italian claims in Macedonia excessive; however, he stressed his friendship for Mussolini. He was impressed and surprised to hear Boris urging the Germans not to relinquish Crete or Salonika; until now, the Bulgarians had been interested in occupying Salonika themselves. Finally, the king briefed him on the interior situation in Bulgaria, complaining that the Bulgarian army was not yet properly armed.

King Boris also saw Ribbentrop, who went straight to the point. He insisted strongly that Bulgaria should sever diplomatic relations with Russia. The Soviet legation in Sofia was a dangerous center for espionage and propaganda, he said. Boris declined, as eloquent and evasive as ever when he meant no. He repeated his arguments: a rupture now would lead to Soviet military action against the Bulgarian Black Sea coast. It should be postponed, until the German naval forces on the Black Sea were strengthened, as the undefended Bulgarian ports of Varna and Bourgas, of great potential use to the Germans, could easily be attacked. He also stressed that the Bulgarian army was useful in its present position—relieving the Wehrmacht from occupation duties in Macedonia and Thrace and guarding the Turkish frontier. A rupture with Russia would increase tensions with Turkey, whose precarious neutrality was of great importance both to Bulgaria and Germany.

As for the Russian legation in Sofia, Boris assured Ribbentrop that the danger was not serious, as its activities were kept under close surveillance by the Bulgarian authorities. True to his diplomatic style, the king did not answer with a clear refusal but rather side-stepped the issue with a promise. "Let's discuss this issue again very soon, Herr Reichsminister, shall we?"

Boris brought up two other topics which bothered him: some concessions that Germany in her courtship of Turkey, was making to the Turks in Thrace, and the Italian designs on the mines in Yugoslavia, along with the greedy attitude of Count Ciano, a man who was not among Boris's favorites.

The king ended with a personal complaint. He was very annoyed, he confessed, to learn that in Sofia German officials were secretly involved with Bulgarian right-wing opposition circles. He mentioned General Christo Loukov, the former war minister, who had become president of the National Legions Organization. King Boris did not hide his displeasure. He also gave the names of two Bulgarians who, he said, served as liaison between Loukov and the Germans: the correspondent of the German news agency Weltpresse, and an engineer prominently involved in arms procurement.

Boris was extremely sensitive on the subject of the right-wing opposition, which criticized him for not siding more openly and actively with the Third Reich. An important part of this opposition was the National Legions, a patriotic organization led by Ivan Dochev, a dynamic young man who recruited members chiefly from among university and high school students. But, since its nationalistic ideology—revision of the Neuilly Treaty, unification of Bulgaria, and militant anti-Communism—had enjoyed considerable success in the prewar years, the legions had attracted many older sympathizers. Having become a felt political force, the legionnaires elected as head of their organization two of the generals they admired the most; the old World War I Generalissimo Jekov and the energetic Loukov, both of whom were strongly pro-German. Ivan Dochev continued to be the main organizer and propagandist of the movement.

While practicing his policy of maneuver and delay, the king constantly had to worry about this strong, impatient, and openly pro-German opposition from the Right. Professor Tzankov and Loukov, both with large followings and important connections in Germany, were the most serious right-wing challengers to the king-appointed government. Boris felt that his freedom to maneuver was limited by the knowledge that the Germans could, at any moment, encourage a more friendly government in Sofia.

Ribbentrop answered that he was not aware of any connection between Reich officials and Bulgarian nongovernment personalities. He promised to investigate and, if such contacts existed, see that they ended.

He kept his promise, immediately demanding explanations from Beckerle, who replied that although Loukov's pro-German sympathies were notorious, the Reich's legation had no links whatsoever with him. Beckerle would only confirm that the engineer in question, because of his good connections in the German Air Ministry, had in the past carried letters between Loukov and Goering.

Ribbentrop was not satisfied with this answer. He resented especially the assertion that Loukov exchanged letters with Ribbentrop's rival, Goering—an example of the interservice rivalry between the Foreign Ministry and the Luftwaffe. After further private investigation, Ribbentrop sternly told Beckerle what he had discovered: Loukov did indeed have contacts with German officials, as King Boris had said—not with the German envoy, but with the air attaché, Colonel von Schoenebeck, whom he had befriended. It was Schoenebeck who transmitted Loukov's letters to Goering. Another liaison was a former German press attaché, who was now back in Germany serving at the Air Ministry. Ribbentrop directed Beckerle to tell Schoenebeck to cease all contacts with General Loukov and to stop meddling in political affairs, which were none of a military attaché's business.

During the same March 1942 visit, the king met with Goering, the economy minister, Walther Funk, and Joseph Goebbels. Funk was very concerned about supplies, especially gasoline, and bitterly criticized Rumania for not sending enough oil and food. Boris was made to understand that if Bulgaria did not share something with Germany that year, relations between the two countries might deteriorate.

Before meeting him, Goebbels had not been an admirer of King Boris. Only two months before, he had written in his diary that the king "is said to be playing a somewhat doublefaced game. He is a sly, crafty fellow, who, obviously impressed by the severity of the defensive battles on the Eastern front, is looking for some back door by which he might eventually escape." But Boris's charm worked with the propaganda minister too, as a March 1942 entry in Goebbels' diary reads: "The King is extraordinarily charming and has returned from the Fuehrer full of new ideas and suggestions . . ."

\*        \*        \*

Addressing his three aides in the German hotel, King Boris looked slightly embarrassed. "Please . . .," he started uneasily, and the way he said it, Handjiev, Bardarov, and Balan knew that he was going to ask for something unusual.

"I ask you to do me a favor," he continued. "I am going to Coburg to visit The Monarch. This time he expressed a desire to meet you, to see what kind of collaborators I have. I have enough difficulties with him, so I accepted. So, after I leave him, he is expecting you, at seven o'clock, alone."

"Of course, Your Majesty. We'll be honored."

"But . . .," and King Boris swallowed before going further, "When he greets you, please kiss his hand. He loves it. You know his weaknesses, but that's how he is."

The king was apologetic. It was difficult for him, a simple-mannered democratic man who hated this kind of thing for himself, to ask his aides to humor his father.

"I know it's silly, but do it for me! I don't want any more unpleasant comments from him," he pleaded.

The three men did it readily. It didn't cost them anything, especially since it was customary in Bulgaria to show respect to old people by kissing their hand. The audience, however, made them quite nervous, having heard so much about the formidable King Ferdinand, about his haughty personality and difficult character. But after Boris introduced them to his father and left the room, it took them only a couple of minutes to feel reassured. The exiled monarch was in an excellent mood, polite and full of charm. He thanked them for helping his son, told them how much he missed Bulgaria, and went on reminiscing about the beauty of nature in Bulgaria. He switched back and forth from Bulgarian to French to German, as if he wanted to hear how proficient his son's aides were in different languages. Then he brought up the subject of a new German book on Pirin Mountain.

"This writer did a remarkable job," he said. And with a mélange of nostalgia and erudition, the old king went on to recite names of villages in the Pirin, along with mountain peaks, flowers and pinetree species. None of the visitors, of course, knew even half the names. Then, suddenly, Ferdinand turned to Handjiev and asked, somewhat aggressively:

"Have you read this book?"

"No, Your Majesty," the counselor admitted.

"Then you don't know anything!" The tone was sharp, almost rude. With that, Ferdinand abruptly turned his back on Handjiev, never addressing another word to him until the end of the visit.

After Handjiev's inquisition, the other two anxiously waited their turn. Colonel Bardarov's examination, mostly on military subjects, went off without major slips. Then The Monarch turned to Balan and, after assuring himself that the secretary could handle the German syntax and the use of "der," "dem," and "des," tested him on Bulgarian geography.

"Rila Mountain. What a beautiful mountain! . . . Sara-Ghyol! One of my favorite spots!" Then, aggressively, "You know Sara-Ghyol, don't you?"

"Yes, Your Majesty, very well. I go there quite often. And that superb spruce, where Your Majesty shot his first cock, it became an enormous tree, which every tourist visits now."

"Don't tell me that people still remember the places of my hunts?" Ferdinand was absolutely delighted. "Yes, I remember my first Bulgarian capercaillie, a huge bird he was, and a tricky one to shoot! How amusing that you know the spot, after all those years."

"Every mountaineer knows it, Your Majesty. It is quite an attraction now and very well marked." And Balan went on describing in detail the tree and the local lore of the legendary hunter king.

The audience was over. The old monarch, enormously pleased, extended his ring-laden hand for them to kiss.

King Boris was amused to hear the account of his aides, particularly when Balan confessed that the Sara-Ghyol spruce story was a total fabrication. No such tree, of course, existed, but why not make the old monarch happy, the secretary explained. "Excellent, Balan, excellent!" And he roared with laughter.

*    *    *

Increasingly sensitive about his right-wing critics and feeling threatened by their fraternizing with the Germans, King Boris contemplated a reshuffling of the cabinet—unloading its most criticized members, Popov and Daskalov. Working with the two pessimistic men had become so difficult that the government was losing its efficiency. That was, at least, the complaint the king heard almost daily from Filov and Gabrovski, and Sevov seemed to agree with them. In his painful moments of hesitation, Boris found comfort in the optimistic assessments of Filov and Sevov, in the certitude of their convictions, in their purposefulness.

Paradoxically, the king himself better resembled the indecisive, troubled Popov. His feelings about the Third Reich and its chances of victory were much closer to Popov's and Daskalov's than to those of Filov and Sevov. But, as he recognized in the foreign and the war ministers what he perceived as his own weaknesses—his own doubts and fears—he became highly irritated by them.

Was he like Popov, about whom Filov had written, "He envies me because I am such an optimist and thus I am serene, while he constantly is troubled with the thought that all will end badly"? King Boris had no need, surely, of any more skepticism or fears than he had himself.

On April 11, after consultations between the king, Filov, Gabrovsky, and Sevov, the cabinet was reconstructed. Prime Minister Filov took over foreign affairs, while General Nikola Mihov replaced Daskalov as war minister. Most of the ministers were chosen by the king personally. Filov wrote in his diary that the king "signed the decree exactly at 8 P.M., as he noted that this hour was good for him, but seven o'clock was evil."

These were distressing times, leaving King Boris very discouraged, especially after the declaration of war against the United States and England. He talked about Germany losing the war, predicting the "bolshevization of Bulgaria" as being almost inevitable. Loultchev reported that on January 9, 1942, the king had talked to him about abdicating, and on March 6, he had mentioned the temptation to commit suicide.

# CHAPTER XXI

# The Jewish Dilemma

**T**HE TERRIFYING rumor spread rapidly among the Jewish communities—first in Sofia and Kyustendil, then in Plovdiv, Doupnitza, and other cities—and it made hearts stop.

The dreaded KEV (Bulgarian acronym for the Commissariat for Jewish Questions) was making secret preparations—the rumor went—to round up all Jews and deliver them to the Nazis. According to the information circulating in the first days of March 1943, deportation to German-occupied Poland was imminent, with the police action beginning on the tenth of the month.

Similar rumors had circulated before, ever since the new Law for the Defense of the Nation, voted in January 1941, had restricted the civil rights of the fifty thousand Bulgarian Jews. During the first year-and-a-half, these now second-class citizens had not been overly alarmed: although their new status was unjust and humiliating, they did not feel in physical danger in a country where antisemitism was virtually unknown. But when the infamous commissariat was formed in the early fall of 1942, no rumor, no matter how incredible, could be safely ignored.

The KEV's boss, Alexander Belev, one of the rare Bulgarian militant antisemites, had a secretary, a certain Liliana Panitsa, who was friendly with the family of Buko Levi, a Jew from Sofia. At the end of February, Miss Panitsa confided to her friends that the KEV was preparing to deport Jews from Macedonia and Thrace to Poland. A few days later, she informed the Levis that they, along with other Jews from the old borders of Bulgaria, were on the list for deportation. Levi, who happened to be vice president of the city's consistory, the governing body of the Jewish congregation, alerted some of the Jewish leaders. The same alert was sounded by another consistory member, Avraham Alfasa, to whom Liliana Panitsa had also revealed the secret.

During the same week, while visiting the capital, a Jew from Kyustendil, Haim Behar, met by chance the KEV's office physician, Dr. Iossif Vatev. For a certain sum, the doctor revealed that deportations were imminent.

The next day, back home, Behar received the same information from Kyustendil's governor Lyuben Mitenov. The governor told him confidentially that if the town's Jews collected 300,000 leva, he would try to bribe the officials and save some families. Behar informed the local consistory leaders, and by the next day, the entire Kyustendil Jewish community was seized by panic.

The money for the governor was quickly raised, with additional sums collected in an attempt to bribe KEV officials. A delegation of five Bulgarians from Kyustendil was sent to Sofia to try to stop the deportation, should the rumors prove to be true. Governor Mitenov disclosed the secret to another Sofia Jew, Samuel Baruch, who had been mobilized in Kyustendil as a pharmacist. Samuel's brother, Yako Baruch, a clandestine Zionist representative in Sofia in charge of issuing immigration visas to Palestine, had important contacts in the capital. Alerted by his brother, Yako Baruch joined the emergency efforts of the Sofia consistory and the Kyustendil delegation.

They called on every prominent Bulgarian friend that they could locate during the ensuing days. The king's confidant Loultchev and an influential member of IMRO, Vladimir Kourtev, were contacted, as well as Archbishop Stefan, Parliament members, writers, and opposition leaders, such as Nikola Moushanov, Petko Stainov, Dimo Kazassov, and Damian Veltchev. All of them were shocked and promised their support. But how reliable was the confidential tip leaked by Miss Panitsa, Dr. Vatev, and Governor Mitenov? There was no official confirmation to the rumor.

Yako Baruch knew many officials who had asked him in the past for visas to Palestine for friends. He went to see a number of them, including Nikola Zahariev, the minister of trade. Zahariev, afraid to commit himself, did not say anything officially. But he gave Yako an important tip in confidence. The cabinet had been notified of the deportation of Macedonian and Thracian Jews, who were under German jurisdiction and not Bulgarian citizens. But, Zahariev said, it had *not* authorized any deportation of Jews from the old Bulgarian borders. Yet, according to the leak from the KEV and Kyustendil, Bulgarian Jews were also included. Who was telling the truth?

Baruch then remembered an old classmate, Dimitar Peshev, an important progovernment and pro-German member of the Sobranié from Kyustendil, who was now vice president of the Parliament. He paid him a visit on the morning of March 7, telling him everything that he had heard about the KEV deportation plan.

Peshev had never heard of it. He could not believe that such a major, and also inhuman, decision could be made without the knowledge of the leaders of the Parliament's majority. He called Governor Mitenov. Is it true that the Jewish citizens of our town are going to be deported to Poland, he

asked? Yes, the governor had to admit regretfully: Commissar Belev personally had brought the secret orders this week. Peshev then called Kyustendil's
police chief. What are your orders, he asked? The police chief confirmed the
news: in three days, on March 10, Jewish residents will be arrested, taken to
the Fernandes tobacco warehouse, and prepared for transfer.

Similar orders had been received by the police authorities of every
major city in the country.

*    *    *

The Jewish population was plunged into a state of shock and depression. In addition to the fear and anger, there was also a considerable dose of
disbelief. How could this happen in Bulgaria, where Jews and Christians
lived as good neighbors and where, contrary to most Central and Eastern
European countries, no racist feelings existed? Bulgarians even used to take
pride, when comparing themselves to Germany, Poland, or Rumania, in
quoting the old aphorism that "every nation deserves the Jews it has." It
meant that most Bulgarian Jews were perfectly loyal citizens, genuinely
attached to their country, and happy to live among Bulgarians. Moreover,
there was no "Jewish problem" in Bulgaria because there were fewer than
fifty thousand Jews in a population of 6 million. With no great hold on rural
land, excessive wealth, or monopoly in any profession, the Jews did not
represent a threat to anyone.

If some prejudices existed, such as "Jews do everything for a profit" or
"Jews are cowardly," they did not go much deeper than stereotypes about
any other ethnic or regional group. People from Gabrovo, for instance,
were reputed to be excessively stingy: they bury their dead in upright
positions to save on grave space, the story went, and only to the waist,
because the tops are whitewashed to serve as monuments. In the case of
Armenians, they were said to embellish facts and rumors into fables. The
Jews, that is, who went to the same schools and spoke Bulgarian like
everybody else, were regarded as circumcised Bulgarians who went to
synagogues instead of churches and had their Sundays on Saturdays.

The Bulgarian Jews were mostly Sephardim, speaking a mixed Spanish
and Hebrew dialect, with a minority of German-speaking Ashkenazim.
They lived mostly in the cities, where they engaged in commerce, banking,
and the liberal professions. With few exceptions, they were not represented
in Bulgaria's political life or in the army, although they maintained friendships and business relations with many influential Bulgarians. The Zionist
Movement had a strong influence on them.

Although still largely undisturbed, the Jews had felt certain changes
when the war brought the increased German influence. Extensions of
residence permits for noncitizen Jews had been denied, and a few Bulgarian

right-wing groups began to copy Nazi ideas and methods, including antisemitic slogans; but at no time did important Fascist organizations exist in Bulgaria or play a political role, as was the case in Rumania, Hungary, and even France and Belgium.

The situation worsened when the Filov government, ready to sign the Tripartite Pact, had imposed the Law for the Defense of the Nation ("ZZD") in January 1941. One of the four sections of the law, aimed mainly at the Communists, and strongly influenced by the prevailing ideas in Germany, deprived the citizens of Jewish faith of their political rights. In the months that followed, new decrees further restricted their rights, imposed new taxes on their possessions, and established Jewish quotas for certain professions.

The ZZD had triggered a wave of protests. Several opposition deputies, including the pro-German Professor Alexander Tzankov, vehemently fought the bill in the Sobranié, invoking article 57 of the constitution which stated that "all Bulgarian subjects are equal before the law." But they lost the vote. The Writers' Union, the Union of Lawyers, and the Medical Doctors Association, among others, sent strongly worded letters of protest to Prime Minister Filov. The Holy Synod of the Orthodox Church denounced the law officially and unequivocally. Most Bulgarians disapproved and felt embarrassed *vis-à-vis* their Jewish friends. But the general belief was that the government had acted under heavy German pressure and had little choice.

The Jewish community distrusted Filov and Interior Minister Gabrovsky, a founder of the far-right Ratnik organization, although he was no longer a member. As the Ratniks' antisemitism grew militant—even though it was a fringe organization with no government support—its noisy activities were a source of concern.

But the Jews had confidence in King Boris. He was considered their friend, and with his reputation for fairness and compassion, they trusted him to prevent anything worse from happening to them.

It was no secret in Bulgaria that the palace disapproved strongly of the antisemitic measures. When talking to his family and close friends, Boris spoke with deep indignation and disgust about the inhuman treatment of Jews by the Nazis. Without even suspecting the forthcoming horrors of the holocaust, the king considered the Hitlerists' antisemitic obsession an aberration of a disturbed mind. He was very upset when his own government, pressed by the Reich, decreed anti-Jewish laws. But he accepted the new legislation as the lesser of two evils, as the only possible way to gain time with the Nazis and prevent the worst: delivering the Bulgarian Jews into their hands. That, Queen Giovanna revealed later, he was absolutely determined to avert. "The poor people!" he would say each time the conversation turned to the Jews.

Nor did Queen Giovanna hide her revulsion of the Nazi cruelty to Jews and other minorities. She intervened discreetly in many cases, mostly through the Vatican and Italian diplomats in Sofia, helping Jews of foreign nationalities who resided in Bulgaria. One day, for instance, she surprised the Italian envoy, Count Magistrati, Ciano's brother-in-law, at the opening of the Italian Fight against Malaria exhibition in Sofia. Leaning over to examine some exhibits, Giovanna whispered softly but firmly into the count's ear: "I need Italian passports urgently for some Jewish people!" Caught short, Magistrati mumbled that it was not possible to accept Jews in Italy at that moment. Still smiling to the photographers and showing a great interest for the antimalaria techniques, the queen murmured: "I give you my personal assurance that they will not stay in Italy. I only need transit visas for them; they will go to Argentina." No later than the following day, the Italian diplomat personally issued the requested visas. Neither he nor the queen ever mentioned the case again. But as discreet as these humanitarian interventions were, they became a matter of public knowledge, adding to suspicions in Nazi circles that "the royal family protects the Jews."

Boris's friendly relations with many Bulgarian Jews was well known. His personal dentists, for instance, were the brothers Djerassi; the Rosenbaums were the court-appointed clothiers; and the king selected his cars with the help of the Packard representative, Lazar Gheron. Most of his entourage—Pomenov, Handjiev, Balan—had good personal connections with Jewish families, and the king used to call his chief of cabinet Grouev, "the Jewish consul," teasing him about all the Rosenbaums, Eliases, Goldsteins, Bakishes, and Berahas that Grouev and his wife saw constantly. Boris often received foreign Jewish leaders visiting Bulgaria, like the prominent Zionist Nahum Sokoloff, who declared after the audience: "You can be proud of your king; he is a friend of ours."

King Boris remained their ultimate hope. While the harsh laws and decrees were discussed publicly, he kept curiously silent. But the Jewish community interpreted certain actions of his as quiet signals of sympathy. In June 1942, in the midst of the debates on the anti-Jewish bill, the king made a special point of sending a warm telegram to the Jewish consistory in thanks for its telegram of good wishes to crown Prince Simeon on the occasion of his fifth birthday. The consistory published both messages in its bulletin, prompting the German envoy Beckerle to report that this "incident" had caused much comment throughtout the nation.

The following month, the king took the trouble personally to explain the new law to the chief rabbi of Sofia, Dr. Asher Hananel. The Nazis were disturbed, and Beckerle complained to Filov. Boris replied that if Beckerle had a complaint, he should come directly to him.

Jews close to the court were aware of the king's feelings and were philosophically accepting some of the painful treatment as inevitable tactics that would save their lives. They knew that the king could not, and should not, talk about the problem publicly. In the extremely touchy Germano-Bulgarian relations of this period, they feared that any open challenge to Hitler's anti-Jewish plans would trigger a confrontation with disastrous consequences for them.

Many Jewish families quietly were sent personal messages of sympathy and commiseration from the palace. At the height of the antisemitic campaign, the Jewish orphanage Queen Eleanora, to which the palace contributed regularly, received an unusually large gift of textile from Queen Giovanna personally, destined "to help in these hard times." The departure of many Jews from the country was eased and administrative measures against them rescinded thanks to the palace. Often Jewish applicants for passports or other permits arrived at government offices preceded by telephone calls from the royal chancery to the responsible minister or agency head with the magic phrase: "His Majesty would like you to . . ." In a period when it was extremely difficult for Jewish citizens to emigrate, many received their passports with royal help, as, for instance, the Samuel Rosenbaums, who left for the United States. To prevent a mishap, the king's chief of cabinet Grouev accompanied them to the airport, got them through the police and customs control, and saw them right to the door of the plane.

Up to the summer of 1942, the hardest consequence of the ZZD law had been the special tax on Jewish wealth, which led in many cases to confiscation of property. But still the Bulgarian Jews did not fear for their lives, for they were unaware that a specially appointed group of German Nazis had secretly reached a monstrous decision. Hitler and Himmler had already decided to exterminate the Jews in the conquered Russian territories, but there remained some hesitation as to the best means of getting rid of *all* European Jews. Deportation to Palestine was one possibility. Sending them to Africa was another. Or herding them into permanent concentration camps.

The SS chief of staff Reinhardt Heydrich had been ordered to prepare a plan for a "final solution" of the "Jewish problem" throughout Europe. Heydrich had called a conference of fifteen representatives from various ministries, including Adolf Eichmann, to meet in Berlin in his Wannsee Street offices on January 20, 1942. As a prelude to the Jews' physical extermination, the conference had approved a plan for the deportation to Poland of Jews from all over Europe, including neutral countries like Spain and Portugal and countries yet to be conquered, such as England. Also on the list were 48,000 Bulgarian Jews. In the axis countries, like Hungary, Rumania, and Bulgaria, the SS planned to rely on the local governments' cooperation in delivering their Jews, which was to be arranged by the German foreign office. To keep the project absolutely secret, the deportation had to be presented as the "resettlement" of Jews to a Jewish homeland in Poland.

From the Bulgarian Ministry of Interior, the person in charge of Jewish problems, Alexander Belev—Ratnik, antisemite, and protégé of Minister Gabrovsky—went to Berlin to familiarize himself with the German antisemitic laws. He returned with the recommendation that the Bulgarian government prepare the Jews for deportation and confiscate all their property. But, believing this would not happen until after the war, or after the German capture of territory in East Africa, he reported that "for the time being, there is no possibility of deporting the Jews unless Germany agrees to accept them and settle them in Galicia or elsewhere in Russia. In the meantime it is imperative that the measures concerning the Jews be strengthened." Strongly influenced by the Nazis, Belev suggested a tightening of existing exemptions—such as those that applied to Jews of mixed blood or those baptized or married to Bulgarians—their expulsion from the capital, strict control over Jewish organizations, and the creation of a special government agency with full powers to deal with all Jewish problems.

Under enormous pressure from the Germans, the government accepted Belev's recommendations. An August 1942 decree established a more rigorous regime for the Jews and created a Commissariat for Jewish Questions (KEV), with Belev as its first commissar. KEV took direct charge of all Jewish matters—the cabinet's approval was required only for the most important decisions—and the effect was felt immediatley. As of the fall of 1942, Bulgarian Jews were forced to wear yellow Stars of David on their lapels; their homes and businesses were marked with special signs; several businesses were closed; many families were expelled from Sofia; radios, cars, and telephones were confiscated; and men between the ages of twenty and forty-five were mobilized in labor brigades to work on the roads. In most cases, these measures were applied with deliberate laxity. Metropolitan Stefan managed to obtain exemptions for the families of baptized Jews, and Filov excused Jews in mixed marriages from wearing the star. Jewish citizens with the "right" connections had no difficulties in obtaining all sorts of favors. But—most important—everyone believed that the Jews were still in no danger of deportation.

The anti-Jewish measures were implemented during the fall and winter of 1942, but each time the Germans suggested deportation, the Bulgarian government balked. The main excuse was that Jewish labor was badly needed for road construction. Even Beckerle was hoodwinked, assuring Berlin that the need was "genuine." Ribbentrop, as well, advised the security arm of the SS, the RSHA[1], to be patient with Bulgaria and wait for the proper moment.

But RSHA began to be suspicious. In a secret report on Bulgaria's recalcitrant attitude on the Jewish question, Walter Schellenberg, its espio-

---

[1]RSHA (Reichssicherheitshauptamt)—the central administrative arm of the SS.

nage chief, complained that "the Bulgarian people believe that the anti-Jewish laws have gone too far." He remembered that Princess Maria-Luisa's godfather, the old statesman Malinov, was married to a Jewess, and so was the granddaughter of General Nikolaev, Prince Simeon's godfather. Those were trivial facts indicating only the assimilation of Jews into Bulgarian society, but the antisemitic thinking of RSHA tended to smell out a trend. And what about the king's secretary, Balan, intervening at the KEV on behalf of a Jew, saying "the king orders"? Schellenberg reported that other people of the royal court had also intervened in favor of Jews.

Schellenberg distrusted some ministers, even Gabrovsky. He reported that when three hundred Jews marched on the ministry carrying a petition, Gabrovsky personally met them in the courtyard, accepted the petition, and reassured them that they "should not be disturbed: the worst had already passed." Gabrovsky had argued with Commissar Belev, contending that the palace and the cabinet wanted a milder Jewish policy, said Schellenberg, disturbed that the interior minister had not yet forbidden Sofia Jews from entering public places.

The espionage chief also complained about Minister of Justice Konstantin Partov's disapproval of the policy of forcing yellow stars on Jews, and, especially, about Metropolitan Stefan's sermons castigating the antisemitic policy of the government. It is interesting to note that Beckerle, although a Nazi himself, disagreed with Schellenberg's report; his own reports tended to find excuses for the Buglarians' lack of enthusiasm.

Borrowing King Boris's tactics, his government had not flatly refused the German demands for deportation. Avoiding confrontation, it preferred to say, "yes, but later, not now." On November 2, the foreign ministry once again explained that Bulgaria was willing to deport its Jews, but that at the present time they were needed for public works.

The impatient RSHA sent one of Eichman's deputies, Theodor Dannecker, to Sofia to speed up the deportation arrangements. After working for three months in close cooperation with the Bulgarian KEV, a secret agreement was reached between Belev and Dannecker, signed on February 22, 1943. According to its terms, twenty thousand Jews from the new territories (Thrace and Macedonia) were to be assembled at six points and deported to German-occupied Poland at Bulgarian expense. The deportation was to begin in March and be completed by the end of May. The Jews were not to be told that they were being deported but rather that they were merely being relocated elsewhere within Bulgaria.

On March 2, the cabinet consented to the deportation, issuing a confidential decree (Number 127) instructing the KEV "to deport from the borders of the country, in agreement with the German authorities, up to 20,000 Jews, residing in the recently liberated territories." In the meantime, however, Belev had changed the original text of the Belev-Dannecker agreement by crossing out the words "from the new Bulgarian territories [Thrace and Macedonia]." Thus modified, the document could mean deportation of Jews of Bulgarian nationality from the old borders, too. The change was made by Belev personally (the same green ink was used for the deletion as for his signature), probably because of his antisemitic zeal. As the total Jewish population in the new territories was less than fourteen thousand, it seemed a pity to waste the six thousand places on the twenty thousand quota that the Germans had agreed to accept for a starter. The discrepancy between the texts of the agreement and the government's decree there created an ambiguity, which allowed the KEV to add more than six thousand "undesirable" Jews with Bulgarian citizenship to its deportation orders.

When the secret plan was leaked, the shocked Sobranié vice president Peshev and a number of other Parliament members decided to act at once. On the morning of March 9, they met at Peshev's office with Yako Baruch, Colonel Avram Tadjer (the highest-ranking Jew in the army), and other Jewish leaders, agreeing to bring the issue to the Sobranié floor that same evening. At 5:00 P.M., when Gabrovsky arrived for the evening session, Peshev and his colleagues took him aside to warn him that unless the deportation orders were cancelled, they would introduce an interpellation leading to a vote of confidence, which could trigger a government crisis. Gabrovsky at first denied the existence of such a plan but, on realizing that the secret had been broken, he left the building to discuss the matter with Filov. He returned at seven o'clock to announce that the deportation of the Thracian and Macedonian Jews (not Bulgarian citizens) could not be revoked, but the orders concerning the Bulgarian Jews would be canceled.

As the rounding up of the Jews was to begin at midnight, Peshev and his colleagues insisted that Gabrovsky telephone the district governors to stop the action. In their presence, the interior minister called his secretary to dictate a telegram to all the cities concerned. As an extra precaution, Peshev picked up the phone to Kyustendil and personally instructed Governor Mitenov on behalf of Gabrovsky.

The arrest of the Jews was thus prevented with only minutes to spare. But in several cities, the telegrams did not arrive until the next morning, causing hundreds of Jews the terror of a midnight arrest, transferral to temporary camps, followed by relief a few hours later at being set free. When the arrests began in Plovdiv, Metropolitan Kyril cabled a strong protest to the king and demanded that Plovdiv's governor warn the Sofia authorities that if the measures were not revoked, he, the metropolitan, would cease to act as a loyal citizen and would personally lie across the rails, in front of the first train carrying deported Jews.

What actually happened between five o'clock and seven o'clock on the afternoon of March 9 that made Filov and Gabrovsky abruptly reverse the deportation order of Jews from old Bulgaria? Had they received an order from the king? Considering that this was the period of Boris's personal rule, when he had the final word in all major decisions, it is almost inconceivable that Filov and Gabrovsky did not consult him on that day. Besides, Filov's lack of sympathy for the Jews' plight was well known, and it is most unlikely that he would on his own suddenly instruct Gabrovsky to spare them.

The report of the German legation, countersigned by Beckerle, elucidates the matter. Written after Peshev's intervention, it states: "It is more than certain that the interior minister was instructed from the highest place to suspend the execution of the planned deportation of the Jews from old Bulgaria. In any case, on March 9, the interior minister—without the commissar for Jewish questions taking any part whatsoever—ordered the release of the Jews from old Bulgaria."

In Bulgaria in 1943, *"the highest place"* could only mean one person: King Boris.

The cancellation order did not dispel the Jews' fears, nor appease the indignation of their Bulgarian friends. Eight days later, on March 17, forty-two members of Parliament, mostly from the progovernment majority, led by Peshev, sent a long letter of protest to Filov, vigorously condemning the government's Jewish policy. The names of several opposition figures, including the right-wing leader Alexander Tzankov, also figured among the signatories.

Filov was incensed. He took this public protest as an act of disloyalty and rebellion, as well as another proof of the "great harmful influence of the Jews in Bulgaria." He called a cabinet meeting to ask for Peshev's dismissal as vice president of the Sobranié. Then, in a special session of the parliamentary majority, the prime minister insisted on a censure motion against Peshev and all members who refused to withdraw their signatures (a few did). A couple of days later, a tumultuous plenary session of the Sobranié voted to strip Peshev of his functions, amidst shouts of "shame!" and strong protest.

The Bulgarian Jews were badly shaken by the experience. Had they known the entire truth about the Thracian and Macedonian Jews, officially being "resettled to work camps," they would have been even more panic-stricken. But at that time, nobody yet knew of the secret Nazi plans for a "final solution."

In March 1943, 7,144 non-Bulgarian Jews from Macedonia, 4,058 from Thrace, and 185 from the Pirot region, were rounded up for transfer to four departure centers, organized by the KEV. Only citizens of neutral and allied countries—Turkey, Spain, Italy—escaped the deportation. (The governments of Spain and Italy, though authoritarian, took energetic measures to protect their Jewish citizens both in Bulgaria and in the occupied territories.) In the four centers—Dupnitza, Gorna-Djoumaya, Skopie, and Pirot—the deportees were loaded on trains bound for Treblinka in Poland, either directly through Yugoslavia or by ship from the Danube port of Lom.

Although not deported this time, the Bulgarian Jews by no means felt safe. The distressing news about their brethren from the occupied territories revived their fears that the danger was not over. Indeed, the KEV had not given up its original scheme. Commissar Belev was enraged and deeply frustrated on March 9, when his deportation orders were rescinded from "the highest place" without his even being consulted. But, interpreting the counterorder as a postponement rather than a definite cancellation, he started preparing a new plan. It called for the deportation to Poland by the end of September of all Bulgarian Jews, except those in mixed marriages or mobilized. The KEV divided the Jews into two categories: those in Sofia, about 25,000, and those in the rest of the country, about 23,000. Belev decided to start by evacuating all Jews from the capital, where they could best use their political influence; Peshev's intervention had taught the KEV a good lesson. Lists were prepared of sixteen thousand Sofia Jews, targeted to go to the provinces pending deportation to Poland.

Once the Jews were out of the capital, the deportation procedure should begin. All Jews would be rounded up and sent by rail to the two staging centers established by the KEV in Lom and Somovit (near Pleven) at the rate of ten thousand per week. From there, they would go to Vienna, where they would be delivered to the Germans. The plan was discussed with Gabrovsky, who asked for an audience with the king to present the Belev project for approval.

On May 21, the Sofia Jews began receiving expulsion orders, with three days to pack and leave the capital for the provinces. Only the sick, the mobilized, the converted, and the spouses of Bulgarians could stay. Desperate, the consistory leaders knocked on every door for help. Most Bulgarians responded, but neither Filov, nor Gabrovsky, nor the king could be reached. A group of the opposition, led by Mushanov, Kazassov, Damian Veltchev, Bourov, Nikola Petkov, and Kimon Gheorghiev, sent a strong letter of protest to the government. Jewish leaders contacted the king's secretary Handjiev and the widow of the old statesman Karavelov, who promised to speak to the king. Metropolitan Stefan and the bishops of the Holy Synod pledged their full support. Three of them—Stefan, Kyril, and Neophyt—had had an audience with the king the previous month and, in the presence of Filov, had presented the church's strong objections to the government's Jewish policy. Boris had explained the reasons for the policy, stressing that the question should be seen in the general European framework and not solely as a Bulgarian problem. But he did not make any promises.

Sixty-three intellectuals, writers, and opposition politicians sent three separate letters to the king, enjoining him to cancel "this cruel, inhuman measure which is foreign to our nation's spirit," and holding him personally responsible for the results.

But the government stood firm. Belev declared that the expulsion of Sofia's Jews would be completed as ordered. On May 23, King Boris, still silent, left the capital.

In total despair, a few thousand Jews from the poor Jewish neighborhood of Yutch-Bounar and other city districts met in the Central Synagogue's yard and decided to hold a mass demonstration the following day. Communist and other anti-government activists, finding an ideal cause for agitation, urged the frightened and helpless Jews to resort to violence if need be for their own defense.

May 24, Saints Cyril and Methodius Day, is one of the biggest Bulgarian holidays, celebrated with giant parades of students and youth organizations. It was almost certain that a Jewish street demonstration that day would provoke bloody clashes with parading right-wing groups, adding fuel to KEV's anti-semitic zeal. The consistory leaders, aware of the danger, used all their power and influence to dissuade their most agitated coreligionists, closed the Central Synagogue, and succeeded in canceling the planned march on the center of Sofia.

Many Jews, however, arrived that morning at the meeting place in front of the synagogue and were furious to find its gates closed. As tempers mounted and people discussed what to do, a familiar figure appeared at the door of the temple to address the excited crowd. Rabbi Daniel Tsion was one of the most controversial leaders of the community, but what he had to say that morning stunned the assembled multitude.

Tsion's actions on behalf of his endangered coreligionists had taken, since the previous autumn, a most bizarre form, coming as they did from a rabbi. So bizarre, in fact, that the congregation disavowed him, relieving him of his duties. A well-respected rabbi, Daniel Tsion was interested in mysticism and comparative theology, which had put him in contact with representatives of other religions, including the Eastern Orthodox church and Dunnov's sect. He had even been accused of joining the Dunnovists' teachings.

When the first anti-Jewish measures were announced in 1942, Tsion had made a strange announcement: he had, he said, received a message from God, warning against persecutions, that he had to deliver to the Bulgarian leaders. He printed several copies of "God's message," handing them in all earnestness to leaders he knew, such as Finance Minister Bojilov, the director of police, and Metropolitan Stefan. He prepared a copy for King Boris, attached a personal letter to it, and brought it to Pavel Grouev. Another copy of the message and the letter were given to the king's personal chaplain. Even if they thought this mode of communication with God rather curious, all addressees received the good rabbi with the courtesy due his position and prestige. Metropolitan Stefan assured him that he indeed considered these words as coming from God. And a few days later, the royal chaplain told Rabbi Tsion that King Boris gave his assurance that the Jews would not be moved outside the borders of Bulgaria. But the Jewish consistory, embarrassed by Tsion's unorthodox actions, fired him.

Now, in the dramatic morning of Saints Cyril-and-Methodius Day, Rabbi Tsion reappeared on center stage in a role no more conventional than before. Accompanied by a Zionist leader, he had gone at dawn to the Dunnovist camp to meet the king's "advisor" Lyubomir Lultchev at the sunrise ritual dances to ask for advice. Loultchev had sympathy for the Bulgarian Jews. (His brother, a deputy of the government majority, was among the signatories of the Peshev protest letter.) In his opinion, the planned Jewish demonstration should take place.

Rushing to the closed Central Synagogue, Tsion comforted the assembled Jews and led them to the synagogue on Clementina Street, where he and Sofia's chief rabbi Asher Hananel addressed the crowd. While preparations for a demonstration were under way, the two rabbis, accompanied by a small group of Jewish leaders, headed for the residence of Metropolitan Stefan. The prelate was already leaving the house for the celebrations at Alexander-Nevsky Square, but he invited the visitors in and listened to them. Then, full of indignation, he asked them to wait in his house while he went to the palace, a few blocks away. In the king's absence, he saw his chief of cabinet Grouev and asked him to advise King Boris to revoke the orders at once. The metropolitan wrote a letter, warning the king not to persecute the Jews, "lest he himself be persecuted," as written in the Bible. Grouev promised to deliver the letter.

Stefan returned to his home, told the Jewish delegation about his conversation with Grouev, and reassured the delegates, saying that in the meeting in April with the king, Boris had promised the prelates, in the presence of Filov, not to deport the Jews. The metropolitan also advised the chief rabbi to call on the palace to intervene personally on behalf of his congregation. Following his advice, Hananel immediately led a few of the delegates to Mrs. Karavelova's home, where they drew up a petition to the king. Mrs. Karavelova signed it too; and the group proceeded to ask Princess Evdokia, the papal nuncio, and Queen Giovanna's Catholic chaplain, all of whom were known to have sympathies for the Jews, to support the petition.

Metropolitan Stefan meanwhile addressed the festive crowds assembled in front of the cathedral. He publicly deplored the absence this year of Jewish students, who had always taken part in the parade, alongside their Bulgarian schoolmates. Persecutions were contrary to traditional Bulgarian tolerance, he said, daring the wrath of the KEV and the pro-German circles.

Later that day he spoke to Filov, but the prime minister, insisting that the operation was politically necessary, advised him to stop interfering in the matter. Stefan, spurning the advice, prepared another message to the king, that same evening.

As the parade started from the Alexander-Nevsky Square, unrest was growing on the other side of town. Groups of agitated Jews attempted to form a procession on Clementina Street to march on the palace, but police and KEV agents quickly broke up the demonstration and arrested numerous participants. While scores of demonstrators were loaded on police vans, KEV agents knocked on the doors of Jews scheduled for expulsion that day, arresting them, and sending them that same night to the center in Somovit. Several Jews, however, escaped by hiding in the homes of Bulgarian friends. Rabbi Tsion, who was arrested as soon as he returned from Metropolitan Stefan's house, was sent to Somovit. Rabbi Hananel was not found until the next day, when he was brought before Commissar Belev who berated him furiously for having sought the king's and the metropolitan's help. Belev did not hide that he hated Stefan and despised his opinions. But, restraining himself from criticizing the king, he shouted to the rabbi: "You should be grateful that you have powerful supporters behind you! If this were not so, I would lock you and your entire congregation up this very evening and send you to Germany, not Poland!"

The commissar was telling the truth. No one was sent to Germany. But no one was sent to Poland either. During the weeks that followed, thousands of Sofia Jews were summarily sent to the provinces. Leaving the capital, most of them were sure they were being deported outside the country, to be delivered to the Nazis. They were mistaken. Unbeknownst to the consistory, unbeknownst to the Bulgarian political and church leaders, the fate of the Jews in Bulgaria had been decided four days before the emotional events of Saints Cyril and Methodius Day. On May 20, after reviewing the new Belev plan with Dannecker and the Gestapo representative Hoffmann, Gabrovsky had brought it to the king for approval.

Though the project called for the deportation of all Jews to Poland and in spite of the Bulgarian assurances that the government was "in principle" favorable to deportation, the doubts and suspicions of the Germans had increased with the continuous excuses and postponements. Reports had reached Berlin that many Bulgarian leaders, even Gabrovsky himself, were deliberately deceiving the Germans—that they had no intention of deporting Jews outside Bulgaria. Then, as recently as April, when King Boris had met with Hitler, he had told Ribbentrop that he had not accepted the deportation of the Jews from Bulgaria, even though the Macedonian and Thracian Jews had already been ousted. Ribbentrop icily expressed his disagreement with the king, insisting once again that the only correct solution to the Jewish question was the radical one adopted by Germany, i.e. deportation to Poland. Boris answered that Bulgaria might deport "Communist elements" among the Jews, but the remainder (he quoted the figure of 25,000) would be interned on Bulgarian territory and employed in public works. But even on that point, the Germans distrusted the Bulgarians. One SS report said that in one Bulgarian labor camp two thousand Jews loafed most of the time, living comfortably, while Greek prisoners nearby worked a twelve-hour day . . .

The Nazis would have been even more suspicious had they known about the quiet activities in aid of European Jews of an old friend of King Boris, Monsignor Angelo Roncalli, then Apostolic delegate in Istanbul. Reporting on the humanitarian efforts of the future Pope John XXIII, his secretary in Venice and in the Vatican, Monsignor Loris F. Capovilla, writes: "Through his intervention, and with the help of King Boris of Bulgaria, thousands of Jews from Slovakia who had first been sent to Hungary and then to Bulgaria and who were in danger of being sent to concentration camps, obtained transit visas for Palestine, signed by him."

At this point, Roncalli intervened directly in favor of the Bulgarian Jews. On June 30, 1943, he wrote from Istanbul to King Boris, enclosing a list of several Jewish families and pleading their cause. "I know that it is only too true—according to what I read coming out of Bulgaria—that some of the sons of Judah are not without reproach. But alongside the guilty, there are also many that are innocent; and there are many cases where some sign of clemency, over and above the great honor it would bring to the dignity of a Christian sovereign, would be a pledge of blessings in time of trial."

On the copy of this letter, Roncalli wrote, by hand and in Italian, that King Boris had replied to his message, verbally, through the Vatican's representatives in Sofia, Monsignors Mazolli and Jean Romanoff. "The king has acted ('Il Re ha fatto qualche cosa')," reads the note, "but he also has his own difficulties, which he asks us to understand. To deal with individual cases arouses the jealousy of others. But I repeat, he has acted ('Pero, ripeto, ha fatto')."

Aware of Bulgaria's unreliability on Jewish matters, Dannecker had suggested that Belev's plan should provide for an alternative in case King Boris did not approve the deportation. Therefore, when Gabrovsky went to the palace, he took along two versions of Belev's plan: plan "A" for deportation of all Jews to Poland, and, if this were unacceptable, plan "B" for the expulsion of the Sofia Jews into the provinces.

Boris immediately rejected plan A but had to settle for plan B. Once again the KEV was overruled at the last moment. And once again the Germans were left to guess whether the king was sincere and really meant eventually to deliver the Jews to them. The price the Jews had to pay was high—hardships, deprivations, humiliations, lasting for three long years. But King Boris's quiet, unspectacular maneuvering paid off. Not one single

Bulgarian Jew was ever deported from the country or delivered to the Germans.

Belev was crushed—he complained to his Nazi friends that Filov and Gabrovsky had spoiled his plan—but he was determined to try again. The German police attaché Hoffmann agreed that there was no way Bulgaria could get out of its commitment to deport. But Minister Beckerle reported that Belev was not to be trusted, as the commissar belonged to a group in opposition to the king and cabinet. Beckerle furthermore advised Berlin to consider the Bulgarian mentality—its "lack of ideological strength." The Bulgarians had grown up with Armenians, Greeks, and gypsies, he said, and they had no innate prejudice against the Jews as did the people in northern Europe. Berlin should not press Sofia on the Jewish matter, the envoy concluded, for such pressure might alienate the Bulgarians.

The German RSHA was unpersuaded and wrote back that the Jews were spies for the Communists and the Allies and once more insisted on their immediate deportation. But Beckerle had to admit to the RSHA that every effort to impress the Bulgarian government with the need for deportation had failed. In his report of August 18, 1943, the Nazi diplomat concluded that only a German victory could compel the Bulgarians to change their minds. It was counterproductive and even dangerous for the Reich, he said, to continue to put pressure on Sofia.

\*     \*     \*

# CHAPTER XXII

# Communist Subversion

"**T**HANK HEAVEN that at least one of my secretaries likes mountain climbing," King Boris said, rewarding Stanislav Balan with a grateful smile, as the two men stopped to catch their breath on the steep wooded path. "The others are weaklings! None of them would join me on a hike."

At the beginning of the war, Balan, the forty-year-old son of an eminent philology professor, had been transferred from the foreign ministry to the royal palace, where he worked in the king's private cabinet as one of Grouev's two assistants.

The king had been in an excellent mood ever since they had left Tzarska-Bistritza that Sunday morning, knapsacks on their backs, for the Rila lakes. "Now is the moment to talk to him," Balan thought. "I will never have this opportunity at the office."

It would be inadmissible, indeed, for a junior secretary to discuss during working hours at the palace any subject that the king did not bring up himself. Although Boris was always very polite to the junior staff, his relations with them, usually through Grouev, remained strictly formal. Only when Balan accompanied him on his Sunday excursions did the king talk about topics other than business.

The path left the pine wood, the thick ferns and wild blackberry bushes, and continued above the tree line, among lichen-covered rocks and gravel. The July sun, hot even at this altitude, caused perspiration to run down Boris's forehead under the tweed visored cap, which protected his balding head. Just as Balan collected his courage to speak, the king turned to him: "You don't know how happy I am here! No cables, no audiences, no telephones! I can forget my worries for a moment. It's been a rough week, Balan. A very difficult year . . ."

How could he talk about his problems now? Balan lost his nerve. But minutes later, the fresh memory of a desperate woman came to mind, a young woman he knew well, who was crying and pleading. The words came out of Balan's mouth in a stutter: "Your Majesty, permit me . . . I wanted to report to you but . . . I know that it's not my business but . . . Seven men are about to be executed in the Communist trial. One of them was a schoolmate of mine. Kostov. Traytcho Kostov. His sister came to see me, and I promised to talk to you. It would be a tragedy, sire, and also a mistake!"

The happy expression disappeared from the king's face, shocked for a moment that his secretary had dared to spoil this beautiful excursion. He continued walking in silence, then said, almost angrily: "But he *is* a top Communist organizer, isn't he? He *did* conspire. He was found guilty by the tribunal. I have nothing to do with it. His guilt was proved beyond any doubt; even he himself didn't contest it."

This was said in a "you-should-know-your-place" tone of voice. A long unpleasant silence followed. Clearly, the Sunday hike was ruined. But a few moments later, Boris stopped again to ask grudgingly: "Tell me about your friend Traytcho."

"He's an exceptional man, Your Majesty, although a Communist. We were together throughout high school. He was the best student and always wanted to help the other boys. He taught me shorthand, for instance; he's a remarkable stenographer. Then he was always organizing all sorts of cooperatives in our class, to help us put together our pennies to buy things and share with the other children. He spent all his free time doing things for the others. I remember when our class was doing poorly compared to other classes, Kostov, always an A-plus student, organized us to arrive at school half-an-hour before the classes started so that he and the better students could tutor the poorer ones. As a result, in the final grades our class was the best in the whole school . . . We all knew he was a Communist, and we were quite the opposite. But somehow it didn't matter with Traytcho . . ."

Boris listened attentively, and although he seemed unconvinced, Balan voiced his last argument: "This is a superior man, Your Majesty. It is too bad that he turned against the state, but he sincerely wants to help people. Why kill him? Who will gain by killing a man like him? We are a very small nation. How many exceptional men like him do we have? We need every one of them. He may be useful one day, who knows? He'll be harmless in jail, so why destroy a gifted Bulgarian?"

The king, visibly annoyed by the lengthy plea, gave him a cross look, as if to say, "That's enough, Balan! The matter is closed." Then he returned to Tsarska in a bad mood.

\* \* \*

The desire to change the world had always been strongly inscribed in the Bulgarian soul, particularly among the literate. A sincere, almost messianic urge to improve man's condition and to right all wrongs animated thousands of schoolboys hearts as soon as they learned to read and write.

Emotional and impulsive, Bulgarians possessed a great capacity for indignation against injustice. With a touchingly immodest claim of having a
mandate to reform the world, the romanticism of many generations took the
form of dreams of a just society, of a perfect world without hunger, war, and
cruelty of man to man.

The daily struggle for life in defeated, mutilated Bulgaria, with the
rigors of its widespread poverty, made this dream particularly appealing
during the two decades following the disastrous first World War. It was also
a naive dream, cherished in innocent young hearts eager to believe in miracle
solutions to the human plight. A large portion of the youth, for instance,
believed that misery and hardship would disappear if only Bulgaria could
recover her unjustly lost territories of Macedonia and Thrace. Therefore,
thousands of students and schoolboys braved the mounted police each year
on November 27, the Neuilly Treaty's anniversary, fervently shouting,
"Down with Neuilly!" to be brutally dispersed with police truncheons
when trying to demonstrate in front of the Yugoslav and Greek legations.

Other youths, concerned with the entire human race, dreamed of
reforming the wicked world with the noble formulas of Socialism, redistrib-
uting wealth more equitably and giving every man and woman a fair chance.
In the existing internal and international realities, however, the chances of
the handful of Bulgarian Socialists to achieve a better society on earth were
rather slim. King Boris used to be amused by the remark of Grouev,
paraphrasing an old maxim: "A man who is not a Socialist before the age of
twenty is a man without a heart; a man who is still a Socialist after twenty is
a man without a head."

Then there were the young Communists. Compared to the nationalistic
and apolitical youths, they represented only a small minority. Most of them,
combining Bulgarian sensitivity to social injustice with Slavic romanticism,
belonged with those indignant witnesses to Bulgarian poverty who were
impatient to depart on a crusade against the dragons of inequity and
privilege. In a tragic paradox, their high school idealism naively led them
into the service of moral monsters of the type of Stalin and his colleagues,
high priests of oppression and inhumanity. In the name of building a perfect
society, many idealistic young Bulgarians, expertly manipulated by callous
professionals, became involved in the clandestine activities of the BCP,
whose leaders—many of them Soviet citizens—worked for the interests of a
foreign power. Akin to zealous Catholics of the Dark Ages who, in the
name of God, threw their twigs on the stakes of the Inquisition, these
Communist idealists were able to support abominable systems of oppression
with no particular moral qualms.

All of this came to play in the case of the condemned Communists in
1942, which was a very serious business. They had been sentenced, not for
their ideas and party membership, but because they were guilty of grave

subversive acts, involving weapons, explosives, and sabotage. Hence, Balan's assurances that Kostov was "a good person, an idealist and an exceptionally capable man" did not seem relevant. The BCP had declared war on the state. After Germany attacked the Soviet Union, Bulgaria's political exiles in Moscow, led by Georgi Dimitrov and Vassil Kolarov, had undertaken to incorporate the Bulgarian national Communist party into the military effort of their Russian protectors.

The first initiative was to open a militant radio station, "Christo Botev," operated from Moscow under the direction of leading exiles—Vulko Chervenkov, Karlo Loukanov, and Ferdinand Kozovski—whose "Radio Moscow's Bulgarian program was controlled by Kolarov. A second station, "Naroden Glass," began broadcasting from inside Bulgaria, directed by a local leader, Stanke Dimitrov.

Soon afterwards, starting in July 1941, Bulgarian Communists, trained in subversive activities in Soviet schools, were parachuted in or sent by submarines from the USSR. A Soviet submarine landed fourteen saboteurs in August, led by the Red army colonel Radoinov. Other groups landed or parachuted in during September and October. But of the fifty-eight commandos, twenty were discovered and shot on arrival, and most of the rest were caught later, with the almost general cooperation of the population. As the operation was a total failure, it was not repeated until the end of the war.

In another effort, about one hundred Bulgarian exiles were recruited in an international brigade and sent to fight under Soviet command. One Bulgarian, Ivan Vinarov, rose to the position of regiment commander in the brigade.

Inside Bulgaria, the local Communists were not very successful either. In February 1942, the police apprehended important party members, which led to mass arrests in March and April of top Communists all over the country, including Traytcho Kostov and the "submariner" Radoinov. The back of the internal party organization was broken.

In the first trial, eighteen "parachutists" were sentenced to death and later executed, while nine received prison terms as minors. A second trial against sixty-two party activists ended in July with seven death sentences, which included Central Committee members Kostov and Anton Ivanov, and several life-term sentences.

The day after his excursion with the king, Balan was working in the Sofia palace when Boris dropped in for a talk with Grouev in the adjoining office. When they finished, the king came to examine the map of the Russian front in Balan's room. He seemed cooler than usual while listening to the secretary's briefing and made no mention of their conversation of the previous day. Balan still felt embarrassed about having pushed his unsolicited advice. Leaving the office, King Boris hesitated for a moment at the door and, turning to the secretary, said casually: "Balan, this sister of your classmate. . . . She can relax and sleep well now." With that, he walked out and never again uttered one word on the subject.

On July 23, 1942, six of the Communists were excuted. The seventh man, Traytcho Kostov, was not among them. Surprisingly, the sentence of the principal secretary of the Central Commitee had been commuted to life imprisonment.

*        *        *

A Japanese top-level military delegation, including the emperor's brother and the army chief of staff, was visiting Europe and accepted an invitation to attend some big Bulgarian maneuvers. Having heard of King Boris's reputation as an entomologist, the Japanese decided to take advantage of their stay in Bulgaria and bring back a special and meaningful gift to their emperor, also a great amateur student of butterflies.

"We would like to be taken to the Rhodope mountains and catch a few butterfly species discovered by your king and named after him," they announced upon their arrival in Sofia, thrilled by this symbolic way of enhancing the amity between Bulgaria and Japan.

When the bewildered Bulgarian liaison officer reported the unusual request, King Boris couldn't help but burst out laughing. He imagined the faces of the perplexed Bulgarian officers and soldiers, in the midst of the maneuvers, watching cheerful Japanese generals with butterfly nets leaping and frolicking on the Rhodope meadows and snapping pictures of each other—and he found the scene irresistibly funny. He had to use all his diplomatic tact to dissuade the enthusiastic guests, offering instead to supply them with a few Lepidoptera borisii specimens for the emperor Hirohito.

He was a master at preventing the *faux pas*, without hurting any feelings, of well-meaning but sometimes embarrassing visitors.

A most delicate situation, for instance, arose when Goering came for a shoot at Boris's country estate in Kritchim. The reichsmarshal was particularly pleased to hear that they were going to stalk fallow deer, a favorite game, he said, that he was accustomed to shoot "in his own, special way." King Boris could not believe his eyes when his guest appeared early the next morning: Here was the huge marshal in a sort of Robin Hood leather outfit, wearing thigh-high boots with turned-down cuffs, a Tyrolean hat with a long feather, and carrying, in place of a gun, a large bow and a pack of arrows—the grotesque image of a fat, cherubic William Tell. "The best way to go after fallow deer! Your Majesty should try it one day," Goering, an accomplished archer, suggested.

Having a highly developed sense of the ridiculous, Boris almost panicked at the thought of the gamekeepers and his other hunting companions' reaction to this anachronistic spectacle. It took him a great deal of coaxing and some fancy inventing of fictitious local traditions to make the disappointed reichsmarshal change into less-theatrical hunting clothes and abandon his bow for a conventional gun, which, incidentally, Goering handled with equal expertise.

\* \* \*

General Christo Loukov had gone too far, King Boris thought. It annoyed him that all through 1942 the general and his Legionnaires had maintained very close relations with various German circles behind his back and had criticized his determination not to send Bulgarian soldiers to the Russian front. This was, after all, the basis of Boris's entire foreign policy: Bulgaria would not send even a symbolic contingent, to show solidarity with the Axis nations or demonstrate hostility to Communism. Who was, after all, in charge here? Who bore the responsibilities? The head of state and his government, or unauthorized retired generals and young nationalistic hotheads?

Even though Boris sometimes admitted to a certain suspicious nature, the menace of Loukov, the Legionnaires, and the Ratniks could not be dismissed lightly. In spite of the official German assurances to the contrary, he suspected that the contacts between "our Goering," as he called Loukov, and the real Goering had not ceased. Other Nazi circles also held the former Bulgarian war minister in high esteem. In May, for example, the king learned from Berlin that Gestapo agents were reporting to their superiors that Boris was following an anti-German policy, that the Sofia government was Masonic, protected the Jews, and so on. "The only man in Bulgaria who could possibly manage the situation is reportedly General Loukov," the report said.

Prime Minister Filov also began to press for greater involvement with the Germans. After an audience with the king on July 10, Filov wrote in his diary: "I spoke to him extensively and very urgently, saying that we also would now have to take part in the struggle against the Bolsheviks, although only symbolically, with a volunteer detachment. We are practically the only ones in Europe who are not taking part in this struggle. Our behavior would embarrass us very much at a [future peace] conference, and Italy would exploit this circumstance to the utmost . . . I emphasized that now, after the victories on the Eastern front and in north Africa, would be a convenient moment for us to step in, since there is no immediate danger to us."

Soon after, informers told Filov that Loukov, speaking at a private meeting of twenty persons, had criticized the government. Bulgaria should have taken its place in the war a long time ago, he had declared. After accusing the government of following an erroneous interior and social policy, of turning the country into a police state, of not enjoying the popular confidence, and of an incapacity to cope with Communism, Loukov had circulated some legionnaires' membership applications for signatures.

At the end of the summer, the king's suspicions deepened when a prominent legionnaire sympathizer, Colonel Atanas Pantev, requested a passport to go to Germany. Pantev, a former head of the police, was well known for his pro-German feelings. King Boris was disturbed by Pantev's plans and feared that he might be going there to prepare a change of government with German help. On September 1, the king told Filov that he believed that Nazi party circles would be able to effectuate such a change even against the wishes of Hitler. In such a case, Boris would not, he declared, remain in Bulgaria to play the role of the Danish king. Filov noted that day: "The danger of such a violent change of government in Bulgaria seems more than likely, according to the information which [Boris] has from his father. Although the latter has always 'spoken up' on behalf of Germany, now even he is afraid of a decisive intervention by the Germans and has warned the king through Evdokia. The king insisted that we find some pretext not to permit Pantev to go to Germany."

Filov answered that it would be easy to stop Pantev and Loukov, but that the king should discuss this problem openly with Hitler and Ribbentrop. And the diary entry continues: "[The king] was very nervous and convinced that the Germans are preparing a *coup d'état* for the end of September."

Pantev did not leave, and no preparations for a coup were detected that fall. In his October Throne Speech, King Boris proclaimed pointedly that Bulgaria was doing its share in the war. There was no noticeably bad German reaction; on the contrary, the new Bulgarian minister in Berlin, Slavcho Zagorov, who had replaced Draganov, reported that "our situation in Berlin is very good. They consider us true friends. They do not wish more from us than we are giving, and they are ready to help us."

But Boris still worried about the right-wing opposition and its contacts abroad. He was displeased to hear that the German, Italian, and Hungarian envoys had attended a party for three hundred people given by the legionnaire students on December 8, at which the generals Jekov and Loukov were present. Loukov gave a speech full of attacks on the government. It was not clear whether the diplomats realized that their invitation came from the legionnaires or whether they thought it was just a student reunion.

On February 13, 1943, a sensational news bulletin jolted the capital, sending tremors of fear and emotion throughout the country. General Loukov had been assassinated by unknown gunmen at the door of his house in Sofia.

Some legionnaires quickly spread a rumor insinuating that the king had a finger in the elimination of their chief, his "rival." But the general assumption was that Loukov had been killed by his declared enemies, the Communists, in the tense atmosphere created by the recent capture of the Soviet parachutists. As the assassins were not found, the question of who had ordered the murder of the popular former war minister remained an enigma for a long time.

\*      \*      \*

Outside of the abortive venture of the few dozen agents sent from Russia, one could not speak of any attempt of armed resistance in Bulgaria before the Soviet military successes in Stalingrad in early 1943. Indeed, when German troops crossed the country in 1941, the Soviet Union was their official ally; therefore, the Bulgarian Communists had no reason to oppose them. Later, when the Reich invaded Russia, the BCP—with many of its leaders arrested or under police surveillance and its ten thousand-odd members greatly disheartened—did not represent an important enough movement to be able to defy the authorities by force.

The incentive was, moreover, missing. The example of the Yugoslav, French, or any other Communist resistance, was not applicable: these were *occupied* countries, under foreign authority, while Bulgaria kept its own national institutions and administration. The government, no matter how pro-German, remained the government of a sovereign state, conducting a policy which it considered to be in the best national interest. This last point could, of course, be subject to disagreement, but nobody could say in good faith that the Bulgarian state apparatus was run by Germans. To say that the Germans exercised a great, sometimes excessive, influence, was true; that they interfered, sometimes heavy-handedly, was probable; but to maintain that the Bulgaria of 1941 and 1942 was an occupied country ruled by the Germans and, therefore, that the population ought to take arms, was manifestly false and totally unconvincing.

On the contrary, the royal government frequently turned down German requests or declined to follow German suggestions. Furthermore, during these two years, the population in general did not seem to be too unhappy about the German presence: indeed, not only had Bulgaria remained miraculously out of the war, but it had also recovered Dobrudja, Macedonia, and Thrace. The economy was booming, the country, considered an "ally," was not occupied by the Germans, technically speaking at least; and, most important, no Bulgarian soldier so far had been sent to combat.

The BCP propaganda had still another weak point. While the Filov government, or right-wing opposition leaders such as Loukov, or even the king himself, were unmercifully labeled "German agents" or men "sold" to the Germans, these accusations were, of course, allegorical. These men were, after all, *Bulgarian* citizens, serving the *Bulgarian* state, even though the opposition felt they were serving it badly and leading it to disaster.

On the other hand, the BCP was openly and unconditionally directed from abroad, by comrades (such as Kolarov and Georgi Dimitrov) who lived in Moscow, obeyed the Kremlin, and were paid Soviet functionaries. Most of them were Soviet citizens, proudly dedicated to serving the Soviet state above all else. The party organizers inside Bulgaria were all instructed, paid, and armed by the Soviets. They were Soviet agents, not in any allegoric sense, but in the most literal meaning of the term. And they never denied it.

Anyone who knows the independent Bulgarian psychology would understand, therefore, why so many people who were opposed to the pro-German policy nevertheless distrusted the BCP and received any Communist call for action with the utmost suspicion.

With the conditions for a mass armed resistance totally lacking in Bulgaria, the BCP militancy was reduced to individual and sporadic acts of terrorism and sabotage. Acting on his own, for instance, a Communist blew up the German gasoline depots in Rousse, small commando units derailed a few trains, saboteurs burned warehouses of the Wehrmacht or disabled factories that presumably supplied the Germans, and a train loaded with gasoline barrels exploded at the Varna station. But, audacious as they were, such isolated actions were hardly noticed by the gigantic Nazi war machine.

The only campaign that caused serious damage and took important victims—Bulgarian victims, not German—was the city guerrilla activity during the first half of 1943 carried out by terrorist commandos designated as "combat groups."

The BCP instructed its Sofia district secretary to organize small squads of between three to six gunmen (or rather "gunpersons," as many of them were women) for the liquidation of "people's enemies" and "provocateurs." The latter category consisted of Communists suspected of having turned informants. An early assignment of one of these "combat groups" was to "punish" an active Communist suspected of collaborating with the police. Believing that well-dressed teams of one young man and one woman looked less suspect on Sofia's streets, a girl, Violetta Yakova, was selected as the partner of the male gunman. At her eager request, she was granted the privilege of shooting the "traitor" first. But when she pulled the trigger, the pistol did not go off, and her partner had to do the job. Yakova was so frustrated, that when her group received the next assignment, a most important job, she begged for the opportunity to make up for her first failure. Her request was honored. With her appointed coassassin, she spent one month in meticulous study of the victim's daily routine.

On the afternoon of February 13, General Loukov met with friends in the Tsar Osvoboditel Café, a favorite meeting place of politicians and intellectuals on Sofia's main boulevard. The conversational topics were, as they were at every other table and in all Sofia cafés, the same: war and politics. When the group left the café around 6 P.M., the general and one of his friends decided to go to the movies. Violetta and her partner followed them in, and when the two men left the cinema and said good-night, the couple started walking behind the general, hugging and kissing, pretending to be lovers. Loukov, keeping a rather fast pace given his considerable corpulence, reached his home in twenty minutes and was met by his daughter. Turning to close the front door, he suddenly found himself face to face with the assassin, wearing dark glasses, who fired almost point blank. Although fatally wounded, Loukov tried to retreat into the vestibule, as his daughter and his wife, rushing from the living-room, screamed in horror. But the killers followed him, emptying their pistols into the dying man before fleeing into the dark street.

The assassins were never caught, nor were the gunmen who, two months later in April, shot the prominent Sobrané member Sotir Yanev, an articulate advocate of the government's policies and an ardent anti-Communist. The executioners waited for him early in the morning in front of his lawyer's office and murdered him as he entered the building. Then, less than three weeks later, a "combat group," a young man and a young woman— protected by Yakova and another terrorist—assassinated the former police director, Colonel Pantev, well known for dealing roughly with Communists terrorists, in broad daylight in front of his apartment building.

The assassinations of Loukov, Yanev, and Pantev caused deep public distress and provoked energetic police measures. Hundreds of Communist activists in hiding were apprehended by police forces helped by military units in a house-to-house search during a twenty-four-hour blockade of Sofia. The party was badly shaken. A few days later, luck abandoned the combat groups. A male terrorist of twenty and a girl of seventeen were wounded and captured during the shooting of a radio technician responsible for the jamming of the secret Communist radio station. Though the victim survived, the young man was sentenced to death and hanged and the girl, a minor, received a life sentence. In an attempt to avenge their comrades, the combats groups struck again at the same radio technician by placing explosives in front of his door. The four killers were seen, however, and chased in the streets by several citizens, joined by the police. After a long pursuit and many exchanged shots, three of the gunmen were killed, while the fourth escaped into the underground sewer system. But after a thirty-six-hour siege of the sewer, he shot himself.

The party's Central Committee, realizing that the assassinations, while having no effect whatsoever on the German troops, led to devastating reprisals against the Communist militants, ordered an end to individual city terrorism. Thus, after four months of bloody activity, the combat groups were disbanded and the surviving gunmen ordered to join partisans bands which were beginning to form in the mountains that summer of 1943. Instructors and weapons for the nascent guerrilla groups were arriving from the Soviet Union, and, in the western frontier regions, a common effort was developing in conjunction with Tito's Yugoslav guerrillas.[1]

But, in spite of the prodding, recriminations and, in many cases, outright threats by the Moscow-directed Central Committee of BCP, the formation of these guerrilla groups, or "tchetas," proved to be an extremely slow and disappointing undertaking. Faced with the total apathy of the population and such drastic police measures, the rank-and-file received the exile Communists instructions with reluctance. Many members had lost their nerve, with almost all of them questioning the wisdom and timeliness of the risky call to armed struggle. But the wide-spread conviction that the party was being bled, without the slightest chances of success, was labeled "capitulation attitude" and "shameful defeatism" and proclaimed a cowardly heresy. Even Traytcho Kostov had warned his colleagues that by its campaign of violence the BCP risked "isolation from the masses and the possibility of having to bear the burdens of the fight all alone." But the party continued to state that no defeatism would be tolerated, which convinced some Communists to stay in prison rather than be forced to join the guerrillas and risk their lives.

A few small tchetas, initially near the Yugoslav border, with not more than a dozen poorly armed partisans each, began limited activities in the summer of 1943, attacking village mayors and tax collectors. Some of the victims were publicly "punished" as "people's enemies" in most savage ways. As the police, assisted by army detachments, pursued them energetically, the partisans spent almost their entire time simply trying to survive in the mountains. For food they robbed peasants working in the fields and for weapons they attacked isolated police stations.

The best-organized and most politically dedicated guerrilla group was the tcheta of Slavcho Trunski, a well-trained Communist activist with some talent for leadership. He operated as an outlaw in the vicinity of Trun, near the Yugoslav border, a particularly poor area and a traditional Communist stronghold. (Trunski's tcheta, like the entire partisan movement in Bulgaria, began to grow only after the German military reverses in Russia—the partisans were not significant in Bulgaria before the end of 1943.)

That year, King Boris was much more concerned about the infiltration of Bolshevism in some army units, where conspiracies had been uncovered, and the individual assassinations by urban terrorists, than about an armed resistance. But even though he had little fear that Communism could ever

---

[1]Violetta Yakova and the girl assassin of Yanev, along with the leader of the combat groups, joined a partisan gang. Violetta, captured one year later, was killed.

win in Bulgaria through the popular will, he felt that the danger of bolshevization was increasing because of the Red army's advances.

The king had been skeptical about Germany's chances of victory in Russia since the first winter of the campaign. By the summer of 1942, his predictions seemed to be confirmed. "He is disturbed by the results on the Russian front—namely, the success of the Russians at Rzhev," Filov wrote in his diary on August 30, "and he believes that Hitler is a bad strategist who surrounds himself with flatterers who always view his deeds approvingly, which for a man like himself is more dangerous than for monarchs with traditions. He [Boris] continues to categorize Ribbentrop as a dangerous man, who is prepared to sacrifice everything to his ambitions . . ."

One month later, the king told Filov that he was very much disturbed by the news of changes in the German high command. Field Marshal List had been removed from the Caucasus command and Colonel General Franz Halder from his post as chief of the army general staff. Boris thought these changes were "inauspicious."

Then, on November 23, Filov wrote after an audience with the king: "We touched further upon the military position and the setbacks of the Germans at Stalingrad. The king again expressed his concern that the frequent changes in the military leadership have perhaps upset the German army and in this the mentality of the *feldfebel*[2] is apparent. He has been impressed by how easily the spirit in our country drops at the smallest setback."

When Stalingrad fell in the spring of 1943, it became obvious that, far from being "the smallest setback," the German advance was stopped. King Boris's grim jokes about "when the Bolsheviks come here" were heard more frequently, and those who knew him well believed that he was not joking at all.

---

[2]Feldfebel (first sergeant in German and in Bulgarian)—the reference to "Corporal" Adolf Hitler is obvious.

# CHAPTER XXIII

# Meetings with Hitler, Feelers to the Allies

KING BORIS did not like at all the message Beckerle transmitted to him on March 28, 1943, on behalf of Hitler. It was not so much the invitation to Berchtesgaden that disturbed him; he was getting used to these meetings, and had been, so far, successful in warding off suggestions that he involve Bulgaria more actively in the war. But this time, Hitler was asking Boris to bring with him the army chief of staff to meet with the German chief of staff for important military discussions.

Against the backdrop of the Wehrmacht's defeat at Stalingrad, the Fuehrer's unusual demand worried Boris. It revived his fears that, sooner or later, his determination to keep Bulgaria out of the war would be put to a test. Had this moment arrived? How much longer could he postpone the day of reckoning? Boris knew that the hour was late and the Germans were growing impatient. Their military, so far willing to accept his arguments against helping with troops and holding him in high esteem, could now definitely use a few divisions of the untouched Bulgarian army. As for the Nazi party organs, always suspicious of the king's loyalty, they were reporting quite openly that he was an unreliable and insincere ally.

By this time, even Hitler had begun to be irritated by the Bulgarians' reluctance to help more actively, while also increasing their territorial demands. Recently he had remarked to his entourage: "The Bulgarians are now behaving as if the developments in the Balkans were all the results of their own decisive action. In reality, Boris, caught between cupidity on the one side and his cowardice on the other, was so hesitant that the strongest intervention on our part was necessary to make him do anything at all."

And now Hitler's invitation. Reviewing Bulgaria's position with Prime Minister Filov, Boris agreed that the meeting's agenda should include the Bulgarian claim to part of Greek Macedonia. The two also reviewed the arguments against participating in the war against Russia: the numerous Bulgarian obligations in the Balkans; the danger from Turkey; the guarding of the Black Sea and the Aegean Sea coasts; the occupation of Serbia; the possible broadening of the occupation in the Salonika region, and all the rest.

But Boris was, in Filov's words, "very exceptionally disturbed" by the summons of the chief of staff to the meeting. The prime minister noted in his diary: "This trip does not please the king; he is going without heart; he considers that in the last analysis the German cause is already lost. I tried to encourage him by emphasizing Germany's still great chances, saying that even if its position is not good, the position of its enemies, among whom there is great discord, is no better."

The king left on March 31 accompanied by the chief of the general staff, General Konstantin Loukash, and his usual entourage of Handjiev, Bardarov, and Balan. The two-day conversations in Berghof, where Boris and Hitler were joined by Ribbentrop, opened on the question of the new danger in the Balkans following the recent Anglo-Turkish secret talks in Adana. The Germans believed that the Turks would remain neutral and, if forced to join the Allies, would choose an alliance with England though certainly not with the Soviet Union. But the king and Loukash were warned that Bulgaria should, just in case, be prepared for an attack from Turkey.

Hitler then briefed the king on his plans for a new offensive on the Russian front. Boris was not impressed. Talking about the possibility of the Allies opening a front in the Balkans, the Fuehrer informed his visitors that the German High Command planned a triple defense line: on the Aegean islands, in Greece, and on the Bulgarian border. But again, he did not give any ultimatum to Bulgaria concerning troops.

It was during this visit that, when asked by Ribbentrop, the king made it clear that he had accepted the deportation of Jews from the occupied territories, over which Bulgaria had no jurisdiction, but never their expulsion from Bulgaria. Among Bulgarian Jews, he might agree to the deportation of certain "Bolshevik elements," he added. As for the others, he intended to put them into camps to build roads. Ribbentrop answered that there was only one right solution to the Jewish problem—the radical one.

There had never been any sympathy between Boris and Joachim von Ribbentrop. The king, who considered the foreign minister a cold, arrogant man, feared that Ribbentrop's hatred for the British was so great that, given the choice of a separate peace, he would prefer to side with the Russians. This was exactly the opposite of what Boris had hoped for since the Munich agreement. Nor did Ribbentrop trust Boris. This was apparent in the last question he asked that day in Berghof: "Could Your Majesty tell us about this man, a certain Poulev, who went recently to Istanbul and met secretly with the former American ambassador Earle? He was traveling with a diplomatic passport, I understand?"

The king remained unperturbed. "Poulev? He is not important. He probably went on a private business trip. And the diplomatic passport? Well, I suppose he must have had it issued long ago and kept it . . ."

Back in Sofia, the king said: "Ribbentrop has a bad influence on the war." Boris was more pessimistic than ever before; he did not like what he had heard in Berghof.

Only two months later, King Boris was invited to another visit to Berchtesgaden on June 3. Again, he left worrying whether the demand for Bulgarian troops for the Russian front would eventuate at this meeting. These trips had become almost routine: the Fuehrer's private pilot Bauer bringing his personal plane to Sofia, the king boarding it at Vrajdebna airport in the company of Handjiev, Colonel Bardarov, Balan and Svilen, his personal valet. Svilen invariably carried the same three pieces of luggage: one suitcase with the king's clothes, the second with the decorations to be worn or given, and the bag with toilet items and an impressive array of pharmaceutical products. Not that Boris used them; he simply liked to have his little pharmacy with him when traveling. Most of the drugs were destined for his father, whom Boris visited on his trips to Germany when he had time. He either brought the drugs to Coburg or had them delivered. The rest he carried as a precaution, especially when he intended to see Ferdinand. "Each time I pay a visit to The Monarque, he manages to upset me," he used to say, only half-jokingly. "I always leave Coburg with ulcers and an upset stomach."

Boris was in a good mood during the flight, spending time in the copilot's seat or chatting with his entourage in the cabin. "How are you enjoying the flight?" he asked his group. "Did Zoupe take a good look at the air hostess's legs?" He liked to tease the formal, dignified Handjiev ("Zoupe") for being an admirer of shapely young ladies.

As the aircraft approached the Salzburg airport, the king took on a more businesslike tone. "Let's see today's welcoming committee," he said. This was the signal to proceed with a well-rehearsed routine. While Svilen was reaching for the medals and decorations, Balan went to the window with a pair of binoculars. Aiming them at the small group surrounding Hitler near the landing strip, he began to announce the names of the officials. An excellent physiognomist, Balan not only identified the delegation but also gave their ranks, titles, and functions, and, most importantly, the order in which they lined up around the Fuehrer. When he could not recognize a face, he asked the German officers who accompanied the king on the plane. This information was very valuable to Boris: learning who was on Hitler's right and who was on his left, who was relegated to the back and who was conspicuously missing, the king deduced the current status of the German hierarchy of power. He drew conclusions about new favorites and declining influences, much as "Kremlinologists" guessed the Politburo's order of precedence from the way its members stood around Stalin in the May parade photograph. On receiving Balan's information, the king, helped by Svilen, quickly rearranged the decorations on his uniform to accord to the composition of Hitler's "welcoming committee."

This little trick always had a great effect. Thus, the ranking Luftwaffe officer would notice with pleasure that the Bulgarian king wore air force insignia, and the veteran party member from Bavaria would be flattered to see a Bavarian decoration displayed prominently on the visitor's chest. On a previous trip, after listening to the names of the waiting officials, King Boris asked Balan, "And what about the 'Pendarliya?' " his nickname for Goering[1]. "I don't see him among the greeters, sire," Balan replied. Indeed, the huge, conspicuous figure of the Reichsmarshal was missing. Boris was puzzled, because Goering, an admirer of the Bulgarian king, was supposed to meet with him during the visit. But without losing a minute, Boris asked Svilen to detach the air force eagle with diamonds that he was wearing. He concluded that the friction that he suspected had existed between Hitler and Goering ever since the invasion of Russia had worsened. Later, during the visit, when the Reichsmarshal arrived at Boris's special request, the impression seemed to be confirmed by the cool reception the Fuehrer's entourage gave Goering. "Your king is definitely the best-informed man about what's going on here," some German officials confided to the members of the royal party. "How does he get the inside information so quickly?" Thinking of Balan's binoculars and Svilen's medals, the Bulgarian visitors only smiled mysteriously.

Hitler's aides were usually very happy to see the Bulgarian king. "You can't imagine the change in the Fuehrer's mood each time King Boris is about to visit him," they used confidentially to tell their Bulgarian colleagues with whom they had become friendly after a few visits. "Hitler is getting more and more tyranical, difficult, explosive . . . He is always in a terrible mood with us, giving us hell constantly. Sometimes it's unbearable to be around him. But as soon as a visit by King Boris is announced, he becomes completely transformed; he calms down; he is in a good mood. 'Now, at last, I'll learn what's really going on in the world!' the Fuehrer tells us. 'You, you don't know anything. And you all lie to me. But King Boris, he knows. He understands the world situation, and he tells me the truth.' So, at least for the few days your king is here, the Fuehrer is pleased and leaves us alone. The whole atmosphere around him becomes more bearable."

The June meeting was not much different from the previous ones, except that this time, because of Boris's insistence that the visit be kept

---

[1]"Pendarliya"—from Pendar, a large gold coin or medallion, slang for someone who wears many medals.

rigorously secret, Hitler installed him not in Berghof, but in the small chalet next door, Bechsteinhaus. Once more Boris felt relieved when no demand for Bulgarian troops for the Eastern front was made. The conversations focused on the situation in the Balkans. Hitler and Ribbentrop, thinking that an Allied invasion from the Adriatic Sea, either of the Peloponnesis or western Greece, was probable, said that the Germans would concentrate troops there. No attack, on the other hand, was expected from the Turkish side. With regard to aid from Bulgaria, the Fuehrer and his foreign minister insisted that Bulgaria extend its occupation duties both in Serbia and in Greece in order to free the German divisions. When the question of Salonika came up, King Boris rejected the idea of Bulgaria occupying the important port city, arguing that this would disturb the Italians as well as the Turks. Salonika should remain under German command, he advised his hosts. Both sides agreed that a German military mission should be sent to Bulgaria to examine the details of the proposed occupations. Boris stressed the need for the promised but still undelivered German armaments, if there were to be additional occupations.

He could learn nothing about the German intentions on the Russian front, but he felt their anxiety over the Balkans, as well as over the attitudes of the Italians and the Hungarians. Hitler had obviously lost confidence in Hungary.

During this short visit, Hitler tried to be even friendlier to Boris than usual, coming for dinner to his chalet, rather than receiving Boris in the villa Berghof, as he had always done in the past.

⁂   ⁂   ⁂

Princess Evdokia, once the closest confidante of her brother, had gradually drifted apart from him, their relations becoming distant and cool. One reason was personal. Evdokia had never resigned herself to the reduced role she had to play in Boris's life since he had brought Queen Giovanna to the palace. Neither did she learn to get along with her sister-in-law. An emotional and touchy woman, she resented living by herself in her villa instead of at the palace—"my father's house"—from which she considered herself exiled. She made remarks such as, "They finally had to invite me to Euxinograd, but I don't know how many days they'll deign to keep me there." Or when asked about the royal children, she would reply that as far as she knew Simeon and Maria-Luisa were all right, but she was "allowed" to see them only occasionally. Increasingly, she showed her hurt feelings, saw herself as the neglected sister, abandoned by old friends, acquaintances, and even the palace personnel.

The second reason for her alienation from her brother was political. Evdokia's disapproval of Boris's "pro-German" policies, which she attributed to the influence of advisors such as "that baleful Gestapo agent" Sevov, had turned to unconcealed hostility. Headstrong and opinionated, she had stormy arguments about politics with her brother, until he stopped asking her advice or even keeping her informed. Not knowing all the reasons behind many of his decisions, Evdokia grew more critical and intolerant of his foreign policy and became totally pessimistic about Bulgaria's future. She developed a hatred for Sevov, Filov, and his "pro-Nazi" ministers, while her once deep sisterly love and admiration for Boris, her life's idol, turned to bitterness and anger.

During a visit to her father in Slovakia, Ferdinand had asked her many questions about Sevov. Some Germans had told him that the architect was the most powerful man in Bulgaria, the liaison between Germany and the Bulgarian government. Back in Bulgaria, Evdokia reported the conversation to King Boris, who became angry, telling her to stay out of things that did not concern her. "Mind your own business!" he snapped.

Evdokia thought, among other things, that her old friend Draganov had been an "accomplice" of King Boris in Bulgaria's involvement with Germany. Resenting this strongly she had stopped corresponding with him. Only when Boris removed Draganov from Berlin to exile him to the Madrid Embassy did she realize that he was not one of the king's favorites anymore. "I am asking you to forgive me for having hated you during these last years," she wrote to Draganov in Madrid by a trusted courier. "Because I did indeed hate and despise you for recommending and promoting this disastrous course, and for being so servile to the ruler, like all the bootlickers around him," she confessed. But now she understood that "Bo" had disappointed him and dropped him, she wrote, as he had disappointed her and all his old companions and true friends.

Isolated, excluded from the intimate, policymaking circle of her brother, this remarkably intelligent, strong woman found herself entrapped in an impossible situation. Publicly, she had no choice but to remain a silent and devoted member of the royal family, loyal to her brother, the king, and the perilous course he was following. Yet, privately, there was nothing she resented more than the policies of the royal government. Disillusioned, lonely, trusting no one and convinced that another national catastrophe was imminent, the spinster princess, at the age of forty-five, could see little in the future worth living for.

\* \* \*

But was Boris really committed to the Axis, and how unswervable was his course of collaborating with Germany? The king was increasingly secretive, but by the summer of 1943 the people around him doubted more and more his intention to stay with the Axis.

The possibility of a change of course had been discreetly mulled over since the beginning of the year. Sofia requested the confidential opinions of the Bulgarian ministers in Switzerland, Spain, France, and Portugal. In March they reported that the consensus in these countries was that Germany could not win the war and probably would not even have a voice in any future peace conference. The four diplomats recommended, however, that Bulgaria should wait, because "the moment for a change of course had not yet arrived," and that the alliance with Germany should be maintained for the moment. But at the same time they recommended, as a matter of utmost necessity, the establishment of direct contacts with the Western Allies, especially the United States, in the hope that neither Washington nor London would agree to "abandon Eastern Europe to the rule of the Bolsheviks."

Before this inquiry, the leader of the Democrats, N. Moushanov, an opposition member of the Sobranié, had urged the government that in view of the German losses in Russia it reorient its foreign policy "according to Bulgaria's national interests." "Moushanov means that if the Germans continue to lose, we should abandon them," Filov noted in his diary.

On July 25, a tremendous event shook the Axis coalition. Mussolini was deposed, and King Victor Emmanuel, Boris's father-in-law, proclaimed the formation of a new Italian government, headed by Marshal Badoglio. "Evidently a preparation for a separate peace," Sevov commented when he telephoned Filov to tell him the news on behalf of King Boris. It was clear that with the collapse of the Fascist regime, Italy's participation in the war was over.

Were the Reich's allies abandoning the endangered ship? Rumania's vice premier Mihai Antonescu had been for some time pressing Bulgaria to discuss, directly and without Germany, the dangers menacing the two countries. On July 27 in Bucharest, Antonescu received the Bulgarian minister, Stoyan Petrov-Tchomakov. "In a very insistent manner Antonescu proposed for the last time that we enter into a direct understanding in order to discuss options and measures we must take together to preserve the interests of our countries," reported the Bulgarian diplomat. This would not change our relationship with the Germans, the Rumanian vice premier assured Petrov-Tchomakov. The matter was so crucial, he went on, that he had made the same proposition to Hungary, despite Rumania's bad relations with the Hungarians.

Later, the Rumanian minister in Sofia submitted to Filov two questions of a delicate nature from his government: Did Bulgaria truly think that the Bolshevik danger could be beaten back by an Anglo-American occupation of the Balkans? And, was Bulgaria not worried that an agreement between Germany and Russia might arise at the expense of the Balkan governments? Rumania was obviously looking for a way out of the German alliance.

Against this background, some unusual moves by King Boris took on special meaning and caused concern in German intelligence circles. To begin with, the king and his advisers privately approached a few well-known pro-Allied opposition leaders whom the palace had persistently ignored since 1941. The consultation of Krustiu Pastoukhov was among the most surprising.

The sixty-nine-year-old Pastoukhov, a life-long Socialist and republican, had opposed both King Ferdinand and King Boris, and, when Bulgaria joined the Tripartite Pact in 1941, he protested strongly. But by the end of the war he declared: "Bulgaria can hold her head proudly before the world because, when every country was sending volunteers to fight against the USSR, it refused to do so. The Bulgarian people refused to permit its leaders to declare war on its liberators, and I, myself, played an active part in this decision against sending troops."

Although opposing King Boris's policies, Pastoukhov was ready to help him pull Bulgaria out of the war. "During the summer of 1943," he declared one year later, "before the capitulation of Italy, I was asked to draw up a list for an anti-German cabinet in order that the country might reverse its allegiances . . . It was done on the initiative of the king and through intermediaries who were in his confidence. If we were unable to carry this out, it was only because the Allies demanded total and unconditional surrender—conditions which were too severe."

Then the former prime minister Georgi Kiosseivanov, exiled since 1940 to the embassy in Bern, suddenly received an order to return and report to Sofia. The call was unexpected, because following his quarrel with the king, Kiosseivanov had not written one single report for over two-and-a-half years, and Boris had never sent him word. But Kiosseivanov recalled that, on sending him to neutral Switzerland, the king had told him cryptically: "Bulgaria may need your services in Switzerland one day . . ." Had that day come? Kiosseivanov did not know, but he took the train, traversed Germany, and arrived in Sofia on August 4. The king received him the next day.

Some secret contacts already had been established with the Allies in Switzerland, the operational base for Allen Dulles, the American OSS representative. The American intelligence officer had been in touch with the former League of Nations' envoy to Bulgaria, René Charron, a good friend of the country and admirer of King Boris. During the war, Charron, a Frenchman, resided in Switzerland and was on close terms with Kiosseivanov.

Early in 1943, Dulles asked Charron to transmit a memorandum to King Boris in which, after asserting that Germany was about to lose the war, the American suggested that the king indicate in some way that Bulgaria intended to withdraw gradually from the Axis. The memorandum did not insist on an immediate break, only advised that Bulgaria signal its willingness to change policies at the first opportune moment. The memorandum further recommended that the existing anti-Jewish measures should, if possible, be annulled. The message concluded that if Bulgaria did not indicate its intention to withdraw from her alliance with Germany, the Allies would be forced to continue military action, even onto Bulgarian soil.

Charron transmitted Dulles's message to Kiosseivanov, who brought it to King Boris. During his short stay in Bulgaria, Kiosseivanov had three audiences with the king, who was very interested in the memorandum and its recommendations. But when Kiosseivanov returned to his post, he had no concrete answer to bring back to Charron and Allen Dulles.

Kiosseivanov also reported another of his indirect contacts with the Allies. In Bern he was on very good personal terms with Marcel Pilet-Golaz, the top Swiss foreign affairs official. Pilet-Golaz, who was sympathetic to Bulgaria, was unofficially asked by Kiosseivanov to sound out the Americans as to whether they would recognize any of the territorial acquisitions Bulgaria had made since the beginning of the war, in case it left the Axis. The answer was disappointing. The United States would not recognize any territorial addition, Pilet-Golaz reported, except perhaps part of southern Dobrudja. This, of course, made any attempts by Bulgaria to change policies even more difficult. After talking to Kiosseivanov, Filov noted in his diary: "He thinks we cannot do anything to go back on our policies which arise from a goal of national unity. By this thesis, he supports the positions which we are able to carry out only with the cooperation of Germany."

Kiosseivanov shared with Filov and his friends in Sofia the news that Germany was in a very serious position and would like to see the war end, even if this meant a separate deal with Russia. But he was extremely cautious in his conversations. Perhaps he knew that by then the ears of the Nazi intelligence in Bulgaria were everywhere, and that to return to Switzerland he would once again travel through Germany. Whatever the reason, he did not voice the opinion that the Reich was certainly going to lose the war, neither did he recommend openly a reversal of Bulgaria's alliances. Convinced that the Western allies had lost interest in the Balkans, Kiosseivanov feared that with a German defeat in Russia, the bolshevization of Eastern Europe would quickly ensue. But while in Sofia he repeated that the Reich with its considerable military possibilities still had a good chance of crushing the Soviets. Unfortunately, he predicted, Bulgaria's future would be decided by Germany and by Russia, not by the Anglo-Saxons.

During the same August week, the former foreign minister, Ivan Popov, calling on the prime minister, was more outspoken about the urgent need of turning to the Western Allies. "He is very pessimistic about relations with Germany, advising us from now on to seek contact with the Americans," Filov wrote. "I told him that it is still too early to think of this . . ."

Simultaneously, however, contact with the Western Allies was being discreetly sought through various channels. Good possibilities were offered in neutral Turkey. After the closing of the American legations in Sofia, Bucharest, Belgrade, Athens, Tirana, and Budapest, the U.S. consul general in Istanbul, Burton Y. Berry, had set up a "Reporting Unit" in his consulate in January 1943 for the purpose of following the developments in the Balkans. The Bulgarian section of the unit was directed by Dr. Floyd Black, the former president of the American College in Sofia and a lifelong friend of Bulgaria. In 1943, Black informed Berry that King Boris was cautiously probing to find a way to extricate Bulgaria from the war. Black, married to a Bulgarian, knew the country extremely well, spoke the language, and kept in close touch with his numerous friends and former students.

During the same period, a more recent American friend of Bulgaria and of the king, George Earle, was also in Turkey, this time as naval attaché. When a "private" Bulgarian citizen, Luben Poulev, arrived in Istanbul with a diplomatic passport, he immediately established contact with Earle.

Another "private" emissary, the industrialist Georgi Kisselov, arrived in Istanbul in May 1943 and called on the American consul. As a result, Berry cabled Washington that the king was determined to avoid active warfare with allied troops in the absence of a direct attack upon Bulgarian soil. Most Bulgarians, Kisselov confirmed, deplored their country's declaration of war on the United States; it had resulted solely from German pressure. Kisselov's message was that if the Allies invaded the country, the ensuing Bulgarian defeat would destabilize the existing order and produce a Communist dictatorship. Stressing that he was acting on his own initiative, he asserted that Bulgaria sought an end to the conflict, although unconditional surrender was unacceptable. Realizing that a separate peace might invite German occupation, Sofia would consider any tolerable solution that would allow retention of the 1941 frontier.

Meanwhile, the former minister to London, Nikola Momtchilov, now a political exile with close contacts with the British government, was urging Sofia to negotiate with the Allies. Through Bulgarian diplomats in neutral countries—Draganov in Madrid, Nikolaev in Stockholm—Momtchilov regularly sent confidential messages to King Boris, adjuring him to break with the Germans.

But in reality, as far as the British were concerned, it was already too late. London was cool to all American suggestions that it open some dialogue with Bulgaria. Its position was summed up in an August 1943 aide-mémoire presented by the British embassy to the Department of State: "His Majesty's government cannot have any dealings with King Boris, whose fate they regard as a matter of indifference, any more than they can have with the present government. The King is a man of no little ability and cunning, but morally weak and incapable of courageous decisions, a true son of his father. Any attempt to give him support in the hope of detaching Bulgaria from the

Axis would probably fail and we should . . . merely compromise ourselves in the eyes of our Balkan allies and the world besides laying up for ourselves incalculable difficulties in our plans for the future of South Eastern Europe."

While looking for a way out, Boris had never shown the Germans his doubts and fears about their deteriorating military position. On the contrary, during his 1942 and 1943 meetings with Hitler, Ribbentrop, and other Reich leaders, including the German espionage chief, Admiral Canaris, whom he received in Sofia in July 1943, he professed—hypocritically, but reassuringly—his belief in the German final victory, as well as his confidence in the Fuehrer's strategy.

Never a man of direct confrontation, Boris was very careful not to arouse any suspicion on the part of the almighty German allies. His tactics paid off well in the case of Beckerle. While reassuring the Reich's envoy about Bulgaria's loyalty and complimenting Hitler's military talents, the king used his meetings with Beckerle to obtain information about the situation and the mood inside Germany, the plans for the next military move, the position of Turkey or of Italy. He shared with him "confidences" about frictions with the Italians in Macedonia or about his own difficulties with Bulgarian right-wingers, knowing well that his complaints would be transmitted immediately to the right place in Berlin.

Gradually, the devout party member Beckerle became convinced of Boris's loyalty to Germany and became an advocate of the king's policies. In his reports, he assured Berlin that the Bulgarians were reliable allies who believed in a German victory. Each time some Nazi informer reported that Sofia was unwilling to help the German war effort, or was sabotaging the deportation of Jews, or was even preparing a betrayal, Beckerle promptly sent denials, often borrowing word for word the official Bulgarian explanation. He became close to Filov and to Sevov and, as a good Nazi, he was happy each time he could send Berlin an optimistic bit of information.

Other Nazi services, however, were less trusting than Beckerle, the messenger of good tidings. The Nazi intelligence was not comfortable with all the talk about Bulgaria's breaking away from the Axis. The alarming part was that most of the speculations and rumors were linked, directly or indirectly, to the palace.

*     *     *

Stanislav Balan, King Boris's junior secretary, was walking down the Boulevard Tsar Osvoboditel, headed for the palace, when he saw the German minister Beckerle coming out of the former Austrian legation. "What a lucky coincidence!" Beckerle said, "I was just about to call you this morning. I have an important message for His Majesty, and I hope that he can receive me today."

Balan promised to call him as soon as he saw the king. Because of his fluent German, Balan served as the usual liaison with the German legation.

King Boris received Beckerle at five o'clock on the same afternoon, Monday, August 9, 1943. After the German minister left, the king called his secretary. "Balan," he said, "get ready, we will travel on Friday! 'Varbàn' is sending his plane to fetch us." "Varbàn" was the king's nickname for Hitler.[2] Balan, used to quick departures, always kept a suitcase ready. He was about to leave his office, when the king appeared at the door. "Sorry, Balan, there's a change. I made a mistake," he said, smiling sheepishly. "I did something foolish that I shouldn't have done, and now you must help me to get out of it." Then he explained, accentuating each word in his nasal timbre: "I do not travel on Friday the 13th!" He was smiling, yet one could hear the determination in his voice. "On Friday the 13th, *je ne fonctionne pas!*" he repeated in French. "Go to Beckerle and tell him anything you want, but cancel the plane for Friday. I'm ready to go on Saturday."

Balan, rushing to the German legation, told Beckerle that some sudden, unforeseen political developments had just occurred, making the king's presence in Sofia absolutely imperative on Friday. "But the plane is already ordered . . ." the diplomat tried to argue. But Balan insisted that state reasons left the king no choice. Beckerle, after hurriedly contacting Germany, was able to report that Saturday suited Hitler too. Boris was pleased. "What did you tell them?" he asked his secretary. "Unforseen political emergency, Your Majesty." The king chuckled. "Well done, Balan! That's what I call good diplomatic work!"

The plane took off on Saturday, August 14, from Vrajdebna. This time the rendezvous with Hitler was not in Berchtesgaden, but at the Fuehrer's headquarters on the Eastern front near Rastenburg in East Prussia. It was a wooded area with numerous lakes in the Königsberg region (now part of Poland).

Soon after cruise altitude was reached, the king left the plane's comfortable lounge to join the pilot Bauer in the cockpit. Always fascinated by engines and mechanics, Boris loved to sit in the copilot's seat, where he would take the controls for awhile. Aviation was quite new to him. Except for a short flight in Switzerland a few years earlier, he had started flying only since the war. He did not have the expertise he had with automobiles, locomotives, and speedboats, but the novelty excited his curiosity as he eagerly explored everything in the cockpit.

The plane was still flying over immense forests, with no clearings visible between the dense trees, when Colonel Bauer announced that they were going to land in a few minutes. The aircraft began its descent and, before the

---

[2]The origin of this nickname is unclear. "Varbàn" is a rather uncommon Bulgarian man's name, derived from the word for "willow tree."

passengers realized where they were, it landed at an incredibly well-camouflaged airfield at the border of a forest almost invisible from the air.

King Boris was greeted by Ribbentrop and Field Marshal Wilhelm Keitel, the armed forces chief of staff, who drove him and his entourage to the Fuehrer's headquarters. It was an amazing underground complex hidden in the midst of the thick Görlitz forest. As a protection against enemy air reconnaissance, the network of roads under the huge pine trees consisted of one-way paths and alleys, just wide enough to permit the passage of one car at a time. The command post, as well as the communications center, offices and conference rooms, living quarters and dining halls, was made up of vast, totally self-sufficient bunkers deep under the ground.

By the end of 1940, the vast forest had been transformed into the "Wolfsschanze" ("Wolf's lair"), Hitler's northern command post. The camouflaged fortifications, underground galleries, living quarters, and landing strip were completed just in time for the attack against the Soviet Union. Reichsmarshal Goering built his own headquarters in the nearby game reserve of Rominten. The Allies never found the spot.

In 1943, after Stalingrad, the Wolfsschanze became Hitler's permanent headquarters. Its central area, occupying about five acres of forest, was divided into three heavily guarded zones. The barracks of the troops that guarded the command post were located in the outer zone, which also contained the landing strip and a small railroad station. The second zone was occupied by the living quarters of the officers of the High Command, including Marshal Keitel, as well as mess halls, movie theaters, storage for the archives, and a telecommunications center.

Hitler and his personal staff occupied the innermost zone, surrounded by two rings of barbed wire separated by a mine field and guarded by sentinels with police dogs posted every thirty yards. The massive bunker with twenty-six-foot-thick walls contained a central conference room with white walls covered with maps, furnished only with a large wooden table and several chairs. To the left of the conference room, there were several small rooms, where Hitler received foreign heads of state, such as King Boris and other distinguished visitors. At the other side of the conference room, Hitler had his private apartment where no one, except for a few of his closest personal aides, could enter. The Fuehrer often lived there for months at a time, conducting the war.

Hitler, flanked by General Kurt Zeitzler, chief of the Army General Staff, received his royal guest at the entrance of his bunker, greeting him warmly as usual. Handjiev, Bardarov, and Balan were shown to their living quarters and had lunch with officers of the Fuehrer's entourage. King Boris began his talks with his German hosts, followed by a working lunch with Hitler, Ribbentrop, and Keitel.

The conversations continued after lunch, with a short intermission during which Boris went to see his three companions in the guest bunker. Later, he had dinner in the main dining room with the Fuehrer, Ribbentrop, Keitel, Zeitzler, and General Alfred Jodl, the chief of operations. After dinner, the king resumed his conversations with Hitler, Keitel, and Ribbentrop until late in the evening. It was already 11:30 by the time he returned to his bedroom to sleep.

＊    ＊    ＊

The windowless concrete cells that served as bedrooms were small and oppressive, and none of the Bulgarians slept well. Overcome by claustrophobia, Balan finally picked up the telephone to ask for the direct line with Sofia and managed to get a connection to his home. He did not say where he was calling from, but the reality of his wife's voice reassured him and he felt better able to cope with his surrealistic surroundings.

Turning off the light, he thought for a moment how embarrassing it would be if anyone was listening to his frivolous conversation. But then he remembered the experience he had had with the German officer in Sofia, Oberst Jordan, when he had expressed some doubts about the safety of the king's direct line. "What about if some switchboard operators are curious and plug into the circuit? Or if somebody at the Sofia Central Post Office branches a listening device directly into this special line?" Balan had asked.

The German officer, visibly shocked at this lack of confidence, simply said, "Come with me! I'll show you." They had gone to the Central Post Office, where Jordan had brought him to the area where the international telephone lines were connected to the switchboards. Then he led him to a locked room in that area, where Balan had seen two cables torn off the wall, connected to each other on the bare floor. A menacing-looking German soldier armed to the teeth was standing sentry over the cables. "This is the special connection between the palace and Germany," the officer explained. "And the guard has orders to shoot to kill anyone who comes near the cables. Anyone. In uniform or not, Bulgarian or German. And we mean it."

Reassured by this memory, Balan went to sleep.

＊    ＊    ＊

In the morning, Handjiev went to the king's bedroom to ask for instructions for the day. Boris, pale and looking tired, was in a depressed mood. He asked his aide how he had slept in the bunker. Hanjiev confessed that he had spent a rather bad night, constantly worried that the electric ventilation system might break down, leaving them all to suffocate underground. "So did I," the king remarked. "I didn't like it. I wouldn't like to sleep in a bunker again."

Leaving the underground quarters, Handjiev asked how the talks were progressing. The king remained silent for a moment, then answered laconically, "Well."

That morning, he had another round of discussions with Hitler, Ribbentrop, and the German High Command in a conference room aboveground. Around noon, he and Hitler withdrew alone into the Fuehrer's personal quarters, where they had lunch by themselves, with no aides or interpreter.

When the two heads of state emerged from the dining room, the aides were amazed to notice the extraordinary transformation in their appearance. The smiles, the friendly expressions, even the politeness had disappeared from their faces. Both Boris and Hitler looked tremendously upset—tense and angry. While the visitors bade farewell and headed for the airstrip, the Fuehrer, looking particularly grim, hardly looked at King Boris when he mumbled an icy "goodbye."

Soon after takeoff, the king again joined Bauer in the cockpit, and the copilot left his seat to join the passengers. A few moments later, Bauer emerged from the cockpit. "The apprentice will replace me for a few moments," he announced to the surprised passengers.

They pretended to be amused but were a little nervous, especially when the aircraft began suddenly to gain altitude. Balan hesitated for a moment, then gathering up his courage, he went into the cockpit. He found the king totally absorbed. "I am curious to find out at what altitude my ear will start ringing," he said, seemingly fascinated by the experiment. Balan knew that the king suffered frequently from otitis in one ear. "You see, when I climb Moussalla[3], the ear doesn't bother me. That's 2.923 meters. But you can't go higher in Bulgaria. Let's see now at what altitude I'll feel it."

"Why don't you try some oxygen?" Balan suggested. "It's invigorating, it eases the breathing, and one feels much better."

The oxygen lines hung from the ceiling of the cabin. As the king nodded his agreement, Balan reached up, took one mouthpiece for himself and, breathing the oxygen mixture, brought another line to the "apprentice-pilot." But instead of accepting that line, Boris reached for Balan's mouthpiece, the tested line he saw was working. "No, give me yours," he said, took it, and started breathing through it. Suspicious? Balan asked himself. Mistrustful? No, simply a natural reflex, acquired after a lifetime with danger. The secretary had observed on many occasions that the king always took a seat facing the window, that he became tense, scrutinizing the road, when driving through a mountain pass, that he could recognize immediately a hostile face in a crowd of thousands. Balan remembered an occasion in Vienna when, arriving at a theater, the king had insisted on exchanging his

---

[3]Moussalla—the Balkan peninsula's highest peak.

reserved seats for two other seats; and once in Berlin he refused at the last minute to take the official limousine, and hailed a taxi instead. So, undisturbed, Balan attached the untested mouthpiece to his own face and joined the rest of the group.

Soon after, when strong winds rose up over the Carpathian mountains, Bauer and the copilot resumed their places in the cockpit. King Boris returned to the cabin, looking happier after his flying experience. When the airplane was about to land at Vrajdebna, he turned to his secretary. "Balan, see who will meet us!" Balan looked for a long moment through his binoculars, then reported, "Nobody is there, Your Majesty." The king was displeased. "So, the men in charge are not at their posts," he commented.

Filov, in Tcham Koria that day, had been alerted by Sevov to meet the king at 4:30 in the afternoon, but he had missed the arrival. Two weeks earlier, after receiving a Horch car as a present from Ribbentrop, he had enthusiastically started taking driving lessons and feeling confident, undertook to drive his new toy to Vrajdebna himself. As he was not as good a driver as he had thought, he arrived at the airport too late. The only people to meet the king were his aide-de-camp General Jetchev and the palace inspector Guentchev, who drove him to Sofia in his car.

Boris was in very low spirits that evening. To the surprise of his aides, he even omitted a small family ritual that he particularly enjoyed each time he returned from a trip abroad. At the airport, he used to inform his companions with a happy smile: "Now I have to go and report to my daughter." As soon as he arrived in the palace, he would rush to the children's apartment or telephone immediately to Vrana, if the family was there, to announce his return to the ten-year-old Maria-Luisa. The princess was always delighted to bring the news to her mother, the queen, who pretended to learn it from her.

On August 15, King Boris did not call Vrana nor did he tell Queen Giovanna that he was back. Instead, he received Prime Minister Filov to tell him that he was not at all happy with the visit to Hitler. On the contrary, he said, he felt so unhappy that, on the flight back, "I wished that we would be shot down by some enemy plane, so that all would be over with me!"

What had happened in Hitler's Wolfsschanze headquarters? None of the Bulgarian aides was present at the conversations, nor did Boris have the habit of briefing his traveling companions about the substance of his confidential talks. He usually only informed the prime minister, his chief of cabinet Grouev and, after the cooling of his relations with Evdokia and Draganov, his new confidant, Sevov.

The little that is officially known about the discussions at Hitler's Rastenburg headquarters on August 15 comes from Filov's diary. On the evening of the king's return to Sofia, the prime minister wrote: "The Germans asked [the king] for two infantry divisions for northern Greece and eventually Albania, so that they would keep the bulk of the German troops in Greece and along the Albanian coast. They think that a Turkish danger does not exist now. The king still called attention to this danger and skillfully brought up other problems. He said that we were prepared to place the 17th Division in readiness in Macedonia, but had not received the necessary arms. They told him that arms would be sent. . . . The king received no information about the position at the fronts . . . In general, they were confident concerning the Russian front; however, they did not indicate in what manner they planned to deal with the situation . . ."

That was all that King Boris shared with the prime minister, a man he knew by now to be irreversibly committed to the alliance with Germany. But the account he gave to his chief of cabinet, Grouev, and which Grouev drafted for Boris's secret archives, was totally different. The king spoke of an unusually stormy meeting during which Hitler insisted that Bulgaria join the war against Russia. The quarrel started when the Fuehrer rejected Boris's old arguments that it was in the interest of everyone, including Germany, that Bulgaria remain neutral *vis-à-vis* the Soviet Union. The king emerged from the meeting extremely upset.[4]

The next day, on August 16, he paid a visit to his oldest adviser, Dobrovitch, his father's former chief of cabinet, who was in bed, dying of cancer of the throat. "I have something to tell you that will make you happy," the king announced as he walked into the old man's bedroom. Dobrovitch was one person in whom Boris had had total confidence since childhood. That day he felt like telling him about his trip to Hitler's headquarters.

Only Mrs. Dobrovitch was present at their conversation, but two weeks after the king's visit, Princess Evdokia went to see Dobrovitch, and he revealed to her, speaking with great difficulty, what her brother had told him. At the Fuehrer's Wolfsschanze, His Majesty had had a terrible fight with the Germans, especially with the military and Ribbentrop, he said. Boris told Dobrovitch that the Germans wanted Bulgaria to declare war on Russia and take an active part in it, but the king had categorically refused.

"Dobrovitch told me that the King said, 'The year 1918 won't happen again! Now my hands are free, I untied them just in time,' " Princess Evdokia revealed much later, in a long handwritten letter to her nephew and niece, Simeon and Maria-Luisa, marked "To be opened after my death."

Dobrovitch went on quoting the king: "But in order to achieve this, I had to put up a terrible fight. Hitler went into a rage when I refused his

---

[4] It was only in the exceptional emotional atmosphere surrounding King Boris's sudden death that the heartbroken Grouev violated his proverbial discretion by discussing briefly, fourteen days later, this event with his son. That day the author was paying his father a visit in his office at the palace.

demands about Russia. Screaming like a madman, he attacked me and Bulgaria in a torrent of accusations and threats. It was horrible! But I didn't give in one inch! He tried to frighten me, but instead, I calmly explained the situation, saying what I had to say, clearly and unequivocally, i.e., that I have decided that we should follow our own road. My hands are now free!"

Once more, he had won, Boris told his old adviser, adding: "I saved you. Even if I have to pay for it!"

\*   \*   \*

# CHAPTER XXIV

# The Mysterious Death

**B**ALAN WAS surprised to find, on the morning after the king's return from Hitler's headquarters, that His Majesty had spent the night at the Sofia palace rather than in Vrana with his family. The secretary was even more puzzled when the king called him early in the morning to tell him to find Colonel Bauer, Hitler's pilot, and ask him to come to the palace at ten o'clock. "Invite him to Vrana for lunch," Boris said. "I want him to see my children." The king sounded composed and rested, in a much better mood than on the previous day. But Balan had the impression from the brief conversation that, curiously enough, the queen was still unaware of her husband's return.

Locating Bauer, who had stayed in Sofia for the day, turned out to be a difficult task. After checking all possible places where the German officer might be, Balan was told that the pilot had gone early in the morning to buy fresh vegetables at Sofia's general market for the Führer's High Command. The secretary rushed to the market, and, indeed, there was Bauer, surrounded by huge baskets, ordering quantities of spinach and melons.

"I cannot go to His Majesty dressed like this. Look at me!" he protested. But the king's instructions were clear, and as it was getting late, the spinach was entrusted to the German driver, while Bauer in his fatigues jumped into the palace car.

The lunch in Vrana was very pleasant, with the king full of charm and the royal children fascinated to meet the pilot. As for the queen, there was no time, before Boris eagerly introduced the guest, for her to ask her husband when he had returned. Graciously welcoming the pilot, she became so absorbed by her role as hostess that she asked very few questions. "A clever husbandly stratagem," Balan thought, amused. But he never understood why King Boris did not want to be seen by the family the previous night.

Later, the royal children were sent to the airport with a present from King Boris to Bauer and permitted to visit the plane before it took off. As they had never been inside an aircraft before, they were immensely impressed by the machine and the gadgets that the pilots showed them.

This was on Monday. That same day Boris received the departing Croatian envoy for a farewell audience. On Tuesday, August 17, he left for Tzarska Bistritza, while the family remained in Vrana. The following day, he went stalking in the mountain forest, his favorite pastime. On Thursday, the nineteenth, he took Prince Kyril, Colonel Bardarov, and Balan on an excursion to Moussalla, the highest peak in the country and one of his favorite mountain sites. They rode on horseback up to the seventh Rila lake, the furthest of the spectacular high mountain ponds, then continued on foot to the barren peak. As the climb was quite strenuous, they rested on Moussalla's top for one hour. Although he had climbed it countless times before, King Boris, with fresh enthusiasm, spent long moments admiring the familiar majestic panorama.

Just before leaving the summit, the king separated for a moment from his companions to perform a special ritual to which they were all accustomed. Facing the peak, he took his hat off and waved it in a friendly salute to Moussalla. As was his habit, he repeated the gesture three times before joining the group to lead them down the mountain path.

During the downhill walk, however, the king's behavior became peculiar. Looking suddenly pale and tired, he continued walking in silence, totally absorbed in his thoughts. He later confessed that for the first time, he had felt a strong fatigue, accompanied by shortness of breath. He even complained to his brother about a "sharp burning feeling in the heart area."

But the malaise did not make him stop and rest. On the contrary, as if following some compulsion to push himself to the limit, he abruptly abandoned the group. Telling the others to continue on the same path, the king took off on a particularly steep shortcut. His companions tried to warn him about the perilous terrain, but this only irritated him. When Kyril asked: "Why do you have to go that way?" Boris barked "Shut up!" and ordered everyone to leave him alone.

Several minutes later, worried about the king's disappearance, Balan took the next steep shortcut over the same ravine to look for him. Balan found himself at the foot of a menacing-looking vertical cliff. Looking up, he was horrified to see King Boris, standing at the very edge of the rock, looking down into the precipice. The tragic memory of King Albert of Belgium immediately came to Balan's mind, as he thought he saw (or imagined he saw?) a very strange expression in King Boris's eyes.

Surprised to see his secretary there, Boris shouted angrily: "What on earth are you doing here? Didn't I tell you not to follow me?"

"But it's a very dangerous spot, Your Majesty," Balan mumbled, "and as my climbing shoes are better than yours, I thought I could be of help, if you needed me."

Grouchy and morose, the king rejoined the party and resumed his silent walk downhill.

At the lake, they mounted the horses to head down to Tzarska. As they were riding across a meadow, Boris suddenly pulled the reins. "Look at the chamois on that crest!" He pointed excitedly in the direction of Sara-Ghyol. At first, his companions could not see anything; then they discerned a dark speck, moving far away on the horizon. The king pulled out his binoculars. "It's a he-goat," he announced, fascinated. "But it's not one of ours. I've never seen this one around. He has definitely come from elsewhere!" He talked as if he personally knew every male mountain goat around Sara-Ghyol, which, in fact, his companions were convinced he did.

For the rest of the trip, Boris could not forget the animal. They reached Tzarska so completely exhausted that, after a quick early dinner, they retired to their rooms and went to bed. At eleven o'clock that night, the telephone rang in Balan's room. It was the king. "Balan, will you come over, I have some work to finish." Then, realizing that he had awakened the secretary, Boris added: "It doesn't matter if you are in your pajamas. Come right away!"

Balan put on his dressing gown and went to the royal apartments. He was surprised to see the king, whom he had thought unusually tired, still dressed and wide awake. Together they went through the voluminous mail that had been brought from Sofia that evening. Balan read several reports aloud until his voice became hoarse. But, as if driven by a demon to exhaust himself, the king insisted on answering more and more letters. It was past 2 A.M. when Boris finally dismissed his secretary.

Everybody was still asleep at five o'clock the next morning, when the king, taking his new rifle, drove from Tzarska Bistritza to Sara-Ghyol in quest of the chamois he had spotted the previous day. After some expert searching, he located the goat and shot him. But when he tried to collect his trophy, he only found a small puddle of blood. The wounded animal had moved. To Boris, crack shot that he was, this was painfully upsetting. He returned to Tsarska in a terrible mood, immediately dispatching Svilen to track the bleeding animal. After a while, the valet returned, carrying the animal, found dead in a bush.

Colonel Bardarov, the first to face the king at the breakfast table, became the natural recipient of the royal displeasure. "The scope on this new gun obviously needs correction," Boris complained. "That's the only explanation. I wouldn't have missed at that distance. You haven't done your job properly, Colonel. Why didn't you have it checked? After all, you were in charge of this gun, weren't you?"

The aide-de-camp was very upset when he told Balan about the dressing-down, insisting that the gun was in perfect order. But the more practical Balan scolded him: "Look, Colonel," he said, "don't you see that the king has been terribly upset ever since we returned from Hitler's Wolfsschanze? What would it cost you to tell him that the gun wasn't shooting straight? Why don't you perform whatever the test is and report at lunch that you have found something wrong with the gun?"

"But that's dishonest! This new gun is a real masterpiece."

"Isn't the king's peace of mind more important at this moment than a small lie? You know hunters. They are funny people in certain ways; they aren't like the rest of us."

Grudgingly, Baradov checked the gun. As they were assembling for lunch, he whispered to Balan, "I tested it. Ten shots, ten bull's-eyes." The king sat at table, still unsmiling.

"Your Majesty, I tested the gun," the aide-de-camp reported. Boris eagerly lifted his eyes from his plate. "We shot ten bullets with the gun in a vise. Nine bullets went into the same hole. But the tenth . . ." Bardarov said, avoiding Balan's eyes. "The tenth bullet showed a marked deviation. Difficult to explain. The humidity, perhaps. We'd better have it sent out for correction."

Boris's face beamed. "I knew it, I knew it!" he exclaimed with an enthusiasm that only hunters would understand. "Didn't I tell you? No wonder I missed the wretched goat's heart."

For the rest of the day, he was a happier man.

On that same day, Friday, he received Slavcho Zagorov, the Bulgarian minister in Berlin, who was in Sofia for consulations. Then he called the queen who was in Vrana with Simeon and Maria-Luisa. "Come on Sunday and bring the children," he suggested cheerfully. "We have splendid weather here today."

Boris remained in Tzarska the following day, August 21, deer-stalking with his brother. During the shoot—for the second time that week—he felt enough discomfort and pressure in the chest to complain to Prince Kyril: "I think I am suffering from angina pectoris." As he had a good knowledge of medicine, he used the term correctly to describe the syndrome characterized by constricting pain below the breastbone, usually precipitated by exertion or excitement. But, as he recovered quickly, the malaise was soon forgotten.

On Sunday he met his wife and children in Samokov, a town 20 kilometers north of Tzarska, delighted as always to spend a day with them. They drove up to Tzarska in his convertible Packard. For the six-year-old prince and his ten-year-old sister, a day with their adored father was the supreme treat. Stopping along the way to point out gorgeous mountain peaks and valleys, showing them rare flowers and trees (using botanical terms, of course), and telling them amusing stories, Boris took the family to Sokoletz, one of the children's favorite playgrounds in the area. Afterwards, they returned to Tzarska, where he received the war minister for a long audience, during which General Mihov reported in detail on the preparations for the big-scale summer maneuvers which were to begin a few days later.

In the afternoon, he took the family for a stroll down to Pessakò, the village square of nearby Tcham-Koria, to the delight of the dwellers of the fashionable mountain resort. Because of recent isolated air raids on Sofia by

British and American planes, several ministers, high officials, and foreign diplomats had been evacuated there. The pleasant chalets and villas, hidden among pine trees, were filled to capacity.

The sight of the smiling royal family, cheerfully returning the greetings of passers-by temporarily dispelled the pessimism which was growing among Tcham-Koria's select population that summer. In spite of the deteriorating situation, Boris's appearance always gave rise to a sort of wishful thinking on the same theme: "The king will, somehow, steer us to a safe shore. The king must have some solution in mind, but only he knows exactly that it is."

While in Tzarska Bistritza with his family, Boris did not mention to his wife the chest pains he had had, nor did he call a doctor. But, perhaps because of worry about his health when kissing the children good-bye the next morning before returning to Sofia, he told Maria-Luisa: "Be a good girl, and while I am away, listen to Uncle Kiki!" Then he promised the queen to try to return to Tzarska that same evening.

He consulted his physicians only on the following day, Monday, August 23, when he returned to the capital. He had asked Sevov to be at the palace at 10:30 in the morning. As soon as he saw his confidant, he started complaining about his health. He believed that he had angina pectoris, Boris said. "Your Majesty, I've heard you complaining about all sorts of illnesses but have never heard you talk about angina pectoris," Sevov remarked. "Did a doctor diagnose it?" "No," Boris replied, adding that the symptoms were obvious—pain in the lower chest and in the left arm, from the shoulder down.

The king then summoned his close friend and ear doctor, Dimitar Balabanov, as well as the palace physician, Dr. Dragomir Alexandrov. They arrived immediately to examine him upstairs, while Sevov waited in the king's study. At 12:30, after a lengthy examination, the king reappeared, asking Sevov to have lunch with him alone. The doctors' visit had obviously reassured him, because during the meal he looked calm and did not mention any ailment. And the architect paid no attention when his host took some drops in a glass of water: Sevov had seen Boris taking medicines before. They had coffee in the adjoining salon, while the king relating his impressions of the recent inspection of an army unit. Then he retired for a short rest, intending to return to the family in Tzarska that same evening.

Later in the afternoon, the king stopped for a moment in Grouev's office on the ground floor. As usual, "Bacho Pavel" reported on the latest developments, showed him a few letters and telegrams, and submitted for the royal signature some decrees as well as a few letters patent for decorations bestowed on foreign dignitaries. The blotter on Grouev's desktop was quickly covered with ink imprints of the ornate, inimitable signature, "Boris III."

At 7:00 the king had a chat on the phone with Princess Evdokia, who had returned from Varna the previous day. After inquiring about her stay at the Black Sea resort, he told her that he had not been feeling too well lately, complaining about pressure in the chest and difficulties in breathing. As she could actually hear him rasping and gasping on the telephone, she urged him to call his doctors. Boris replied that he had already seen them, adding that he had come from Tzarska because he had work to finish in Sofia and, besides, he did not want to have the children around if he was sick. Evdokia inquired whether he had drunk mineral water from the Bankia thermal sources, as he often did for his arthritis. "No," Boris replied, "the trouble is not there. It's with 'the ticker'." He added, after a short silence, "You'll see, I'll die from angina pectoris." She had heard him say this once before during that summer, and when she had objected then that he was too young—only forty-nine years old—to suffer from angina pectoris, he had answered sadly that it was not a matter of age but of harsh times. They discussed the illness of Dobrovitch, who was on his deathbed, and Boris remarked, "That's what's going to happen to me!" Before hanging up, he told his sister that if he felt better the next day, he would pick her up to drive her to Tzarska-Bistritza.

He resumed his work with Grouev, but around 7:30, he said that he was not feeling well at all and left. Shortly thereafter, Grouev heard a commotion outside his office: alarmed lackeys informed him that the king was very ill, vomiting violently. While Svilen was helping him to bed, the palace doctors Daskalov and Alexandrov arrived. Because of the vomiting, their first guess was that the king was having a severe gallbladder attack.

Prince Kyril did not learn about his brother's illness until the next morning, Tuesday the twenty-fourth, when he arrived from Tzarska-Bistritza. As the patient's condition had worsened, Counselor Handjiev rushed to the German air attaché, Colonel Schoenebeck, to urge him to summon the German doctor Rudolf Sajitz, who had treated the king for many years, from Berlin. Schoenebeck immediately relayed the request personally to Goering.

That day, during a heavy air attack, a bomb had hit Sajitz' Berlin clinic. Special teams of rescuers were sent to dig the doctor out of the debris, and he was rushed to the airport in clothes still covered with mortar and dust.

Before Sajitz' special aircraft had landed in Sofia, well after midnight, and as the diagnosis was still gallbladder crisis, Handjiev was again dispatched to Schoenebeck with the request that another well-known physician, the Viennese internist Dr. Hans Eppinger, be called in for consultation. He arrived on a special plane on Wednesday. But in the meantime, the court doctors, together with other reputable specialists, Doctors Tzonchev and Razsolkov, realized that the main problem was with the heart rather than the gallbladder, as there were symptoms of a thrombosis or coagulation of blood in the heart.

But neither on Monday evening, nor all day and all night on Tuesday, was Queen Giovanna informed about her husband's serious condition! (She never understood who had made this decision and resented it all her life.) She was still in Tzarska with the children, assuming that important state business had prevented the king from leaving the capital to join them, as he had promised. The illness was also kept secret during these two days from Filov and the government. Even Sevov was unaware of it. On Tuesday afternoon, when he arrived at the palace unannounced, Sevov met Prince Kyril in the courtyard. After the prince informed him that the king was asleep, Sevov left—without inquiring about his health.

That evening, Kyril drove to Evdokia's house, where he found his sister working in the garden. She had waited the whole day for Boris to call her, as he had promised. "Boris is not well. I don't like it," the prince said. Evdokia's first reaction, knowing that Boris had visited Hitler ten days earlier, was, "Could he have been poisoned? He has been *there*. Do you think *they* fixed him?" (Evdokia used a Bulgarian slang expression for foul play, "moo pogodiha".)

"No, it's the heart. We summoned Sajitz," Kyril answered, adding, "Can you go to the monastery tomorrow to light a candle and say a prayer for Bo?" She promised to do so. Kyril dissuaded her from coming to the palace that evening, as the king had not asked for her. *

Early the next morning, Wednesday, August 25, the prince rang up Sevov who came immediately. Princess Evdokia also arrived. She had already been to the Rila monastery and back, leaving at dawn to say a prayer for her brother. Prince Kyril, unusually pale, met her in the garden. "According to Sajitz, it's an infarct, an embolism," he said.

Dr. Sajitz confirmed this diagnosis to Evdokia, whom he had treated for a gallbladder condition in the past. He told her that the king, having suffered an infarct, was in very serious condition. But, as he was otherwise a healthy man, the doctors hoped to be able to save him. The crisis could be over in three or four days if the patient had complete rest, the doctor added, and went on to insist that the king should not be allowed to work for at least six months thereafter. To the princess's question about the cause of the infarct, Sajitz replied, "Exhaustion—mental exhaustion and emotional stress." As air alerts were becoming more frequent in Sofia that month (British and American planes were passing over Bulgaria on their way to bomb the Rumanian oil fields in Ploesti), Sajitz warned that the shock from an air raid would be fatal to the king. Prince Kyril thereupon instructed the Air Defense not to sound the sirens unless an attack was certain.

Going upstairs to the king's bedroom, Evdokia found Boris surrounded by his doctors, moaning, half-conscious, and waxen. She spent most of the day on the adjacent balcony. At one point, she asked one of the Bulgarian doctors whether her brother had been poisoned. The physician was shocked. "That is absurd!" he snapped. "There has been no poisoning!"

That same Wednesday afternoon, the prime minister was summoned to the palace, where Sevov told him about the king's illness. Filov subsequently informed the war minister, but, otherwise, the secret was kept. Beckerle, the German envoy, had heard the news the previous day, but not before his rival, Colonel Shoenebeck, had already arranged through Goering to have the two German doctors airlifted to Sofia.

The crisis worsened in the early evening, and the palace Orthodox chaplain was brought in. But at eight o'clock, the king's condition improved slightly. Evdokia came in to sit by her brother's bedside. When she took his hand, Boris opened his eyes and said, quite distinctly, "Koka, what are you doing here? What time is it?" As she was answering, he mumbled, "Ah, it's over . . ." and closed his eyes again. After that, he remained silent except for two or three occasions when he asked for a drink of water or to inquire about the time.

Meanwhile, in Tzarska, Queen Giovanna did not suspect anything. Knowing that her husband was particularly busy that week, she was not surprised when he stayed in Sofia and decided not to disturb him by telephoning on Monday night, thinking that he would arrive the following morning. But after waiting in vain on Tuesday, she finally called the palace to find out whether to expect the king for dinner. No, the answer came, he was too busy that evening to answer her call and in fact he did not feel very well. When she called again later, the queen was told not to worry, everything was all right, His Majesty was feeling better. She felt reassured to hear that Prince Kyril had arrived in Sofia and was keeping his brother company.

The next day, Giovanna was told that the king was ill, but that there was no need for her to come: the palace would call her and keep her informed. She was seriously worried by then, and waited all day long for more precise news. By late afternoon, as she wondered whether she should drive down to Sofia, Doctor Daskalov and the palace inspector Guentchev arrived unannounced. Looking very concerned, they told the queen that King Boris was seriously ill. Because they had not wanted to alarm her unnecessarily, they had not called her the past two days, they said, but now that the king's condition had deteriorated, they felt that the queen should know. But they insisted that she should not drive to Sofia that night.

Giovanna, shattered by the news, had a terrible premonition and fell into a state of confusion. Sinking into an armchair, her head in her hands, she experienced nothing but a feeling of desparation, of frightening darkness. She did not even notice that Guentchev and Daskalov had bowed and left the room. Recovering from the first shock, she went down for dinner and had just sat down at table when, at nine o'clock, the telephone rang. It was Guentchev, in Sofia. "Your Majesty, you had better come down," he said. "The king is very ill."

Giovanna leaped from her chair, ordered a car, and went to kiss the two children in their beds. "Faster, faster!" she urged her chauffeur, as the car raced down the dark, winding mountain road to Sofia. She arrived at the palace at 10:30 in the evening.

Surrounded by Prince Kyril, Svilen, and the Bulgarian doctors, King Boris was lying stretched out on his back, eyes closed, his face frighteningly pale. He did not see her as she knelt beside him, nor did he react when she took his hand and kissed it. She went then to her study to wait for Professor Sajitz, who came in a few minutes later. The queen, who knew him well, asked him for his opinion, but he declined to answer before conferring with his colleagues. As the doctors discussed the case, Giovanna waited in the adjacent small salon, until, finally, at 1:00 in the morning, Sajitz emerged. "Your Majesty, the conclusion of our consultation is not final, but we must tell you that the king's condition is grave. We believe that he's suffering from a coronary thrombosis." Then, as if in a nightmare, she heard him say, "If His Majesty survives . . . if! . . . he'll be an invalid." The court physician, Dr. Daskalov, repeated in Latin, "Thrombosis arteriae coronariae sinistrae." According to the diagnosis, the condition had caused double pneumonia, with an edema in the lungs and brain. "Pneumonia bilateralis cum aedema pulmonium et cerebri," Daskalov added.

Later that day, Boris pressed his wife's hand and asked: "What are you doing here?" So as not to appear overly worried, Giovanna answered that she had come to Sofia to do some work for the Red Cross. Then he asked what day it was. When she replied that it was the 26th of August, he said, "On the twenty-eighth, on the twenty-eighth . . ." before falling asleep again.

At some point during the many examinations and consultations, Sevov had heard Dr. Daskalov express some doubts about the cause of the king's illness. Could it be something other than a thrombosis? Some poisoning, for instance? On Thursday noon, the architect asked Professor Eppinger's opinion. The cold, unapproachable Viennese doctor[1] hesitated to give a categorical answer, but admitted that such a possibility could not be excluded. The illness could have been provoked by other causes too, he said.

A new crisis occurred on Thursday afternoon, but again King Boris survived. When his condition stabilized, Sevov once more asked Eppinger about the possibility of poisoning. This time, the Viennese professor's answer was unequivocal: no, he said, he had no doubts, the illness could not

---

[1]Dr. Hans Eppinger, a leading liver specialist, became involved later in medical experiments on inmates in Nazi concentration camps. In 1944, researching ways to make saltwater potable for pilots stranded at sea, he used as guinea pigs forty-four gypsies in Dachau, keeping them on a diet of seawater often mixed with various chemicals for up to a week. Summoned to the Nuremberg war crimes tribunal in 1946, Eppinger committed suicide.

have resulted from poisoning! With Prince Kyril and all the doctors in the room, Sevov asked whether some other specialists should be consulted. But the doctors were positive that none was needed. New drugs were prescribed, and arrangements were made with the German air attaché to speed up their delivery from Germany.

Late on Thursday evening, a first official bulletin announced laconically that the king has been seriously ill for the past three days. The news had a stunning effect—it seemed as if in Sofia and across the country all activity abruptly froze. All talk was silenced, as an anxious population remained glued to the radio. An instinctive fear, undefined yet poignant, gripped the heart of each and every Bulgarian. It was an ominous feeling, begetting new suspicions, too ugly yet to be voiced. In a way, it also contained a selfish concern—while fearing and praying for their beloved king, each was fearing and praying for himself, too. Once again, the personal fate of each Bulgarian seemed to be embodied, for better or for worse, in the man named Boris III.

Three more communiqués were issued, brief texts giving no details. All sorts of rumors inundated the country. Wasn't it strange that the king, a healthy man in his prime, would be stricken just now, when everybody expected momentous changes? people were asking each other.

An improvement in the king's condition was noted on Friday, August 27. The danger of pneumonia seemed to have been overcome, the heart had resumed its more normal functions, and a smiling Doctor Sajitz declared optimistically that the royal patient might recover. King Boris was still asleep most of the time, moaning at times, tossing restlessly in his bed. It was in this state that Prime Minister Filov, accompanied by War Minister General Mihov, had seen him the previous day; they were unable to exchange a single word with him.

Filov came again on Friday and spent most of the day in the palace, talking to Sevov. No visitors were admitted in the bedroom, lest the king be disturbed. The only person who stayed almost constantly in the room was his valet.

During the afternoon, the king opened his eyes for a moment. "Svilen, what time is it?" he asked.

"Twenty past four, Your Majesty."

"Tomorrow, at the same time . . ." Boris mumbled and, without finishing the sentence, fell asleep again.

Because of new complications with the blood supply to the brain, Sajitz and Eppinger suggested sending for a neurologist, Dr. de Crinis, who arrived on Friday afternoon from Vienna.

According to one source, during the last crisis, knowing that her brother liked to talk about metaphysical subjects with Loultchev, Evdokia suggested to Kyril that the mystic be called. But both the prince and Sevov disapproved of the idea. When the king's condition deteriorated again on

Friday evening, the princess insisted. Sevov acceded and brought Loultchev to the palace at 10:00 that night, without the knowledge of the queen. The Dunnovist was allowed into the bedroom, but as Boris did not regain consciousness, Loultchev was soon escorted away.

August 28, the Assumption of Our Lady, is an important religious holiday in Bulgaria. That Saturday morning, the king had a fever but seemed calmer. The queen attended Mass at the palace Catholic chapel with Princess Evdokia.

At around 12:30, Evdokia peeked into the sick man's room. Boris was asleep. After changing the compress on his feverish forehead, she silently left his apartment. Shortly thereafter, she noticed the doctors, looking alarmed, rushing in and out of the patient's room, asking for oxygen bottles and a new supply of injections. Svilen, terribly pale, was frantically looking for the queen, who was found in the palace Orthodox chapel. He also alerted Evdokia to come immediately to the king's bedside.

When Giovanna entered the room, King Boris, in a coma, was being examined by Dr. Sajitz, with the five Bulgarian doctors and the two German specialists. She found Kyril and Evdokia on their knees, and she also knelt near the head of her husband's bed. The state of the patient had worsened alarmingly. At about four o'clock, the final agony began. It was exactly 4:22 P.M. when Boris died.

One by one, stethoscopes in hand, all the doctors approached the bed to listen to the lifeless heart. One after the other, they pronounced the king dead. To witness the death of head of state, Prince Kyril, Filov, and General Mihov, accompanied by Sevov, were admitted to the room, followed a moment later by Gabrovsky. Queen Giovanna, stunned, waited with Evdokia and the first aide-de-camp in the corridor, where Kyril joined them. The official death certificate was drafted, and, at the suggestion of the German doctors, only the six Bulgarian doctors signed it.

The prime minister was the first to present his condolences to the members of the royal family. Kyril, greatly shaken, embraced him emotionally, while the queen, in total shock, was incapable of uttering a word. Evdokia, more composed, found strength to reply, "Now, Mr. Filov, you must hold firmly!"

The prime minister went to the office downstairs, where he, Mihov, and Gabrovsky drafted the texts of two proclamations: one announcing the king's death, the other the accession to the throne of the new king, the crown prince, age six, who would reign under the name of Simeon II, assisted by a council of regents. At eight o'clock in the evening, after approval by the Council of Ministers, Filov read the proclamations over the state radio.

*          *          *

The first suspicions of foul play in King Boris's death arose because it occurred at the time when he was seeking ways of extricating Bulgaria from her alliance with Germany. But by a bizarre twist, the rumors blossomed as a result of the equivocal behavior of the principal suspects, the Nazis themselves. Although the official version—death due to coronary thrombosis complicated by an infarct—sounded logical, Beckerle sent the following disturbing reports, marked "Secret, for the Foreign Minister [Ribbentrop] personally":

Sofia, August 29, 1943:

Today, before their departure, I asked the German doctors de Crines, Eppinger, and Sajitz to come and see me. They told me that they were sorry that during all this time they were unable to get in touch with me. They felt that they were kept, so to speak, prisoners at the palace, in order to prevent any news from leaking out. Even yesterday, after the king's death, they had found it impossible to come here. They understood that King Ferdinand and the Italian royal family had to be notified first. In addition, the entire diagnosis had been left to them. The Bulgarian doctors stayed in the background. Sajitz said that he had spoken to the king while he was still conscious. The king was aware of the gravity of his condition and believed that this time, 'that was it,' and he would not live. The king thought that he had angina pectoris. He attributed it to the strains of an excursion to Mount Moussala, which he had undertaken the previous Wednesday.

Because of suspicions, I asked the gentlemen if the illness and death could have been due to some outside cause (poison). The three doctors answered unanimously and immediately in the affirmative, invoking the similarity of the symptoms. Eppinger spoke of a *typical Balkan death*. But could they say more? Could they reliably attribute the death to such cause? This could not be said with certainty; an autopsy would have been necessary for that. They (the German doctors) have suggested at least a brain autopsy. At the beginning, it was denied altogether, but, later, it was agreed to perform one after the embalmment. At this point, it (the autopsy) would be of no use, so they abstained from the decision to have it performed.[2]

I have the impression that, in spite of the limited scientific hard evidence, the doctors are privately convinced of a violent death. They

---

[2]A partial autopsy (focused on the heart) had been performed, without the German doctors' participation. The queen, who, for emotional reasons, did not give her permission, was informed only after the autopsy had been completed. She never obtained a satisfactory explanation as to *who* ordered it.

told me that, because of professional secrecy, they will make this statement only to me; upon their return to Germany, they will have to restrict their statements to the general diagnosis of the illness. I approved this view and emphasized that keeping the secret is not only a matter of professional ethics, but a citizen's duty to the state. If there is a need, on orders from the highest authorities, they could be questioned again about it. They asked that in such a case, they be questioned not separately but all together. Finally, they declared that they had not accepted any payment nor fee for their services.

I will carefully follow and report all related rumors. In my view, the whole matter should be kept strictly secret, and one should avoid interviewing the doctors again soon. I believe that the Bulgarian future foreign policy will not change, and that the regents who will be appointed will be friendly to Germany and will back our war effort.

Beckerle

The next day, August 30, the German envoy sent the following top secret message:

30 August 1943

For the Reichsminister of Foreign Affairs:

As already reported, I brought to the attention of the prime minister the many rumors blaming the Germans for the death of the king. One states that the stress involved in visiting the Fuehrer's headquarters brought on a heart attack, another purports poisoning following refusal of German demands. Have pointed out necessity to take countermeasures. Filov agreed, saying best way would be to inform the public about king's activities in last days (climbing Moussalla, etc.). Because trip to Germany now known to public it should also be mentioned that the two countries came to a good understanding during this visit. Filov believes it should be stressed that Boris came back looking happy and satisfied. He pointed out how ridiculous the rumors of poisoning, which they at first thought possible, really are. All Bulgarian and all German doctors(!) agree on this. They think the king's illness and death similar to classic examples of those connected to results of severe cold or exertion and fatigue. He had always warned the king about overdoing things. Climbing the Moussalla had been irresponsible. If the press were told all this, the rumors would shortly die down. End of conversation with Filov.

I also believe strong counterpropaganda will halt rumors. I will take measures—have already done so—that should help spread the impression that our enemies are responsible for king's death.

Beckerle

The Nazis were not, of course, the only suspects. After a year of systematic assassinations of anti-Communist leaders by Communist gunmen—General Loukov, Pantev, Yanev—it was only natural to attribute the king's death to the same source. Was Boris a victim of a local Communist conspiracy? Or, following the classical maxim "Cui bono?," was he eliminated by those who would most benefit from his liquidation and the dislocation of the state apparatus that would follow, i.e., the Soviet Union? Who, in the summer of 1943, had a greater interest than the Soviets in depriving the vulnerable Bulgarian ship of its captain and thus turning it into an easy, defenseless prey?

But plausible as such a hypothesis was, no concrete evidence could be advanced to substantiate it, neither then nor in later years.

What Beckerle did not suspect was that Doctors Sajitz and Eppinger, while assuring him that they were held "prisoners" at the palace and could not communicate with him, were in fact in constant contact with another German official in Sofia, the air attaché Colonel von Schoenebeck, Beckerle's rival. Oddly enough, Schoenebeck had sworn to keep all information about the king's illness secret from the German envoy and his legation. Behind Beckerle's back, the two German doctors were sending reports to Hitler and Reichsmarshall Goering through Schoenebeck.

Schoenebeck was in bed with high fever on Tuesday, August 24, when the palace official Handjiev telephoned to say that he had to see him urgently. It was a stifling hot day and the German, feeling sick, tried to postpone the appointment to the next day, but Handjiev insisted that he had to talk to him immediately. Half-an-hour later, Handjiev appeared in the sick man's bedroom. The courtier's usually genial face looked grim as, with no preliminaries, he announced bluntly: "Colonel, you must give me your word of honor that you will not mention a word about my visit to the German minister, or to anybody else!"

Surprised, Schoenebeck hesitated. "Although Beckerle was not my superior, I belonged to the legation, and it was my duty to report anything important to him," he wrote in his diary that day. But Handjiev insisted. "It's a matter of the life of the king. His Majesty asks you, as his friend, not to inform the minister, since the king feels only contempt for him." Although feeling uncomfortable, the colonel shook Handjiev's hand and gave his word of honor.

Wiping the sweat off his forehead with his handkerchief and stuttering with emotion, Handjiev then revealed that the king had been seriously ill for two days and that the diagnosis was angina pectoris. His condition had deteriorated since the previous night, and therefore the king was asking Schoenebeck to contact two German doctors whom the king knew—Sajitz and Eppinger—and fly them to Sofia as soon as possible.

After reporting to Goering personally, Schoenebeck obtained a special plane and the doctors left Berlin and Vienna that same night.

The air attaché spent the next day, August 25, in his steaming bedroom, awaiting news from the palace. Finally, a telephone call announced that the German doctors would visit him in the evening and that he should have his coding machine ready for transmitting confidential messages to Berlin.

Sajitz and Eppinger visited him around seven o'clock, saying that the king's condition was more serious than they had thought. There was no more talk about angina pectoris; instead, they spoke of some more grave, mysterious illness, not yet identified. Schoenebeck's diary reads: "The King requested that the message about his illness be sent to the Fuehrer directly through Reichsmarshall Goering, by-passing Beckerle and Foreign Minister von Ribbentrop. The cipher machine was ready, but in view of the secrecy, I could not trust any operator and had to operate it myself, which was not an easy task for me." The doctors sat with the air-attaché until the early hours of the morning, discussing the king's condition. Although it inspired the worst fears, they still had hope.

The following morning, Thursday, the doctors came again to send messages to Berlin on Schoenebeck's cipher machine. This time they sounded even more pessimistic; King Boris' condition had worsened. Sajitz and Eppinger reported that the king had a very clear idea of his condition and was fully aware of the possible consequences of his illness. But the doctors were still unable to pinpoint the precise causes of the illness.

Finally Schoenebeck managed to convince the royal court to inform the German minister about the situation. As soon as Handjiev had done so, Beckerle telephoned Schoenebeck to reprimand him severely. How was it possible, he asked, that Marshal Goering had been informed by the air attaché without notifying the German legation and the Foreign Ministry? In Berlin, Ribbentrop was furious and rebuked Beckerle, while "Goering laughed," noted Schoenebeck. "The rivalry between Ribbentrop and Goering is already well known. These two gentlemen wouldn't miss any opportunity to do something unpleasant to each other. But this time it all falls on my back . . ." Ribbentrop threatened to recall Beckerle, and Beckerle in turn urged Berlin to have Schoenebeck replaced.

As for the king's condition, Schoenebeck's diary contains a startling entry on August 27: "Medicines were brought (from Germany) by special airplane. King Boris was fully conscious.[3] For the first time the doctor[4] voiced the suspicion that the king could have been poisoned. This suspicion increased with the appearance of odd signs of disintegration in inner organs. Now, things began to take a more dramatic turn. I told the doctors that at the end of May information had reached us from Turkey that the rumor circulated in certain circles there that King Boris would not live to September! I reported this highly disturbing information to the Bulgarian War Ministry. But, in my opinion, they did not take sufficient measures to protect their king. The Balkan lethargy was not shaken even by such alarming information . . ."

On the following day, August 28, Schoenebeck again reported that after a slight improvement in the king's condition during the night, King Boris was fully conscious. But things grew worse by the end of the morning, with the brain also affected, until the afternoon when the king died "in horrendous pain."

As the entire city fell into an unbelievable state of grief at the announcement of the death, the German air attaché wrote: "The two doctors, shaken, met me later on. The town in its anguish still cried and whined. I closed the windows, so we could talk undisturbed. What was the real cause of King Boris's death? I asked the doctors. My question floated in the air, but the answer was not forthcoming. Professor Sajitz lit a cigarette, deeply engrossed in his thoughts. Professor Eppinger scratched his head and said slowly, 'I believe it is a poisoning! This irreproachable King has fallen victim of a most common murder. That's my opinion! What do you think, dear colleague?'

"Prof.Sajitz nodded and said that the spots that had appeared on the body before death indicated absorption of poison. A conclusion, however, could be made with full certainty only after an autopsy, for which the Queen had given her authorization.

"Prof.Eppinger added that, some time ago, he had been called to the sickbed of the Greek prime minister Metaxas, and had seen the same symptoms on his body. Metaxas was certainly the victim of a poisoning. Eppinger spoke of the use of some Indian poison, which becomes effective only after a few months. I remembered the message from Turkey this last May, that King Boris would not live to September. And today was August 28!

"Prof.Sajitz was staring out of the window, vacantly. The other doctor

---

[3] The royal family and other witnesses testify that, on the contrary, the king was unconscious all the time.

---

[4] The diary mentions "the doctor," in the singular, rather than the plural, "the doctors."

sat, holding his head. The ciphering machine stood idle, after the announcement of the king's death had been sent. That message had been brought to me by a messenger from the palace, with the request that it be transmitted to Berlin."

Schoenebeck and the two doctors took a walk in the streets which were filled with people in tears, congregating around the palace. They tried a restaurant, but there was no one to serve—everybody had run to the palace. For a long time, there was no way to move on Tsar Osvoboditel Boulevard to reach the Hotel Bulgaria, where the doctors were staying.

The next morning, Sunday, the German doctors called Schoenebeck and asked him to come to their hotel and see them before their departure. He went, but refused to talk there, suspecting that the hotel rooms were bugged, and brought them instead back to his house. The doctors informed him that the queen had withdrawn her permission for an autopsy, "apparently under pressure from the court clique (among whom there was perhaps someone who knew of the murder plot?). With this, the veil of secrecy fell forever over the death of King Boris III." The same afternoon, the German doctors left Sofia on a special plane.

Beckerle asked Schoenebeck to come to his office at the legation where he informed him that he had demanded his immediate recall. The air attaché couldn't have cared less: he disliked working with the former SA Obergruppenfuehrer and chief of the Frankfurt police, and knew that after King Boris's death, a stay in Sofia would be unbearable. To Beckerle's rebuke that he had not informed him immediately of the king's illness, he only replied that the request to inform Hitler through Goering had been His Majesty's and no one else's. "Could I tell the minister to his face that King Boris resented this 'SA diplomat'?" Schoenebeck wrote in his diary. "The King had once told his cousin, Prince Dietrischsein, in Vienna, that he had no use for police chiefs as envoys to Sofia and felt that the Balkan countries should not be used as 'guinea-pigs' to test decorated SA men as diplomats."

Schoenebeck felt that, immediately after the king's death, the population's normally friendly attitude toward the Germans had been replaced by hostility and mistrust. But this mood, according to him, did not last long: "Five days later, Winston Churchill threatened in a speech, 'What happened to King Boris will also happen to others who side with Germany!' Suddenly, the anti-German was reversed, and the real murderers of the King came under suspicion!"

Schoenebeck did not elaborate, but he ends his diary insisting that "Prof.Eppinger believed until his death that King Boris had been poisoned, and that it was the same poison, extracted from some creeping plant or from a snake, that Eppinger found in the postmortem examination of the Greek premier Metaxas—a poison which causes the appearance of blotches on the skin of the dying man before death. It is a great pity that the palace refused a full autopsy—otherwise one could have had a clearer idea (of the cause of death).

Doctor Eppinger's startling discovery of similar spots on the bodies of King Boris and General Metaxas has never been made public. The raging war and the subsequent suicide of Eppinger contributed to the secrecy surrounding the sudden deaths of the Bulgarian king and the Greek dictator and did not permit a comparison of notes between the two enemy countries. The Greeks, fighting for their survival against Italy, accepted the official explanation—their tough dictator had succumbed to a tonsilectomy, followed by blood poisoning and uremia. Had they been aware of Eppinger's suspicions two years later concerning King Boris, the rumors that circulated briefly in January 1941 concerning Metaxas' death might have taken on new life.

The Greek general, a graduate of the Potsdam Military Academy, had been notorious for his pro-German sympathies. And although he became the leader and the hero of the resistance to the Italian invasion, he firmly declined England's offer to send British troops to Greece. C.M. Woodhouse, the British liaison officer who spent the war years with the Greek resistance, wrote: "Our inadequacies were brutally exposed in the spring of 1941. The Germans were advancing unopposed through Hungary, Rumania, Bulgaria. A British Commonwealth Expeditionary Force was offered to the Greeks. The Prime Minister, Metaxas, declined it for fear that it would only provoke a German attack which it would be too weak to resist. Then he died, and his successor (Alexander Korizis) yielded. The doomed expedition of Australian, New Zealand and British troops arrived in March."[5]

Some people spoke of foul play, but the talk died quickly. But a young aide to the British commander, General Wavell, mentioned in a book he wrote some thirty-five years later: "The next day the Chief asked me to arrange an enormous luncheon at the hotel Grande Bretagne in honor of the Greek prime minister, Metaxas, which I did. I remember that the table was decorated with hundreds of narcissus. I cannot remember anything about the food, but when the unfortunate Metaxas died a few days later, I was accused, by name, on the German radio as having poisoned him . . . It was the only time in my life I have been accused of murder."[6]

On January 29, 1941 (Bulgaria had not yet signed the pact with the Axis), the *New York Times* reported from Sofia that "the news of the sudden death of Premier John Metaxas of Greece has been received with deep regret in Bulgaria, where the greatness of the man is fully appreciated and is the subject of much laudatory comment in the press. . . . Incidentally, the

[5]C.M. Woodhouse, *Something Ventured*, London, Granada Publishing, 1982.
[6]Peter Coats, *Of Generals and Gardens*, London, Weidenfeld and Nicolson, 1976.

interruption of communications between Bulgaria and Greece after General
Metaxas's death, and the general lack of information about his end, gave rise
for a time to rumors that he had not met a natural death. There has been
nothing to confirm such reports."

*       *       *

As for Hitler himself, he also believed that King Boris had been
poisoned. Dr. Goebbels wrote in his diary on September 10, 1943: "The
Fuehrer told me that it must now be regarded as certain that King Boris was
poisoned. The German doctors have reached the conclusion that he was
killed by snake poison. It is not yet known who mixed the poison. The
German doctors wanted to perform an autopsy; the Bulgarian government
agreed, but the royal family refused. I would not regard it as impossible that
the poisoning was engineered by the Italians. After their latest act of
treachery, I am ready to credit the Badoglio regime and the Italians generally
with anything."

Embellishing this version, Hitler in his anti-Italian rage formulated a
grotesque hypothesis. According to the September 11 entry in Goebbel's
diary, which also noted that Prince Kyril, Filov, and Mihov had been named
regents in Sofia and that this regency council was "positively" on the
German side, "The Fuehrer intends to transmit to Prince Kyril the findings
of the German doctors on the poisoning of King Boris, which he believes
was in all likelihood inspired by the Italian court. For it is very suspicious
that Princess Mafalda, the worst wench ('groesste Raabenaas') in the entire
Italian royal house, was on a visit in Sofia four weeks before King Boris's
death. It will be remembered that she is a sister of the Bulgarian queen."[7]

A few pages further in his diary, Goebbels reports that while discussing
the Italian "betrayal" and the fall of Mussolini at lunch, "the Fuehrer again
related how often he had warned the Duce against the monarchy and the
aristocracy, but the Duce was too trustful. He must now pay for it dearly.
The monarchy thanked him in a manner that he certainly had not expected."

"The [Italian] king can no longer be spared in our propaganda. The
Fuehrer once more expressed his conviction that Princess Mafalda was the
trickiest bitch ('geriebenste Aas') in the Italian royal house. He thought her
capable of having expedited the journey of her brother-in-law Boris to the

---

[7]Princess Mafalda, who was married to Prince Philip of Hesse, arrived in Bulgaria
only *after* King Boris's death, to attend the funeral, as all newspaper reports and
photographs can attest. Hitler's allegation that she came to Bulgaria before the king's
illness is absolutely false and has never been taken seriously. After the Fuehrer's first
outbursts of rage and suspicion, the accusation was not repeated by the Nazi
propaganda. Princess Mafalda died tragically in the Nazi prison camp of
Buchenwald, on August 28, 1944.

hereafter. It was also possible that the plutocratic clique administered poison to Mussolini, for Mussolini's illness, too, was somewhat mysterious."

\* \* \*

The two questions about King Boris's death remained open: Was it a natural death? And if not, who was responsible? The Soviets, the Nazis, the Bulgarian Communists, the British?

Or was it a suicide? Not a deliberate act of a man who has decided to end his own life—an extremely unlikely possibility in the case of the profoundly religious Boris. But could some extreme stress and despair lead to a collapse of the will to live, to a form of passive suicide, in which death is welcomed as the only solution to a tragic impasse?

On the evening of his return from Hitler's headquarters on August 15, after most of the lights in the palace had been turned off, Boris, exhausted physically and morally, retired to the solitude of his apartments. As on the night of October 3, 1918, twenty-five years earlier, when the new, frail, and apprehensive twenty-four-year-old king had said good-bye to his family and returned alone from the railroad station to the deserted Sofia palace, he stayed all alone that night, without calling anyone.

Queen Giovanna and the children were in Vrana. Princess Evdokia had left for the Black Sea coast. All court officials and close advisers were in their homes with their families, probably already asleep.

If King Boris ever told anyone how he spent that night or whether he was feeling well or not, there is no record of it. But to Filov, the last person he saw that evening, he confessed: "Today, during our flight back, I wished that enemy fighters had shot our plane down, so it all would be over."

It was a sincere wish. He had just spent one of the worst days in his life, and he had not recovered from the shock. Nor was he ever to recover again. The night before, in the oppressive solitude of Hitler's claustrophobic bunker, he had had ample time for reflection. If he had done any soul-searching, he must have realized that his life's work, his twenty-five-year-old royal mission, was about to collapse. He was losing the game.

He had sworn to keep Bulgaria out of the war, never to send Bulgarian soldiers to fight outside their country. So far, with passive but stubborn resistance, unpalatable compromises, and shrewd maneuverings, he had succeeded. Look at the 1943 map of Europe! he could tell himself. Try to find another country which is enjoying peace while its territory had increased without firing a single shot, another nation which was about to achieve its historical aspirations without going to war! In addition, Bulgaria was more prosperous economically than before. Its army was intact, and as a noncombative ally of the Axis, it had even managed to maintain diplomatic relations with the Soviet Union! Finally, Bulgaria had saved its Jews from deportation. Incredible feats, of which King Boris was proud. But now, everything was about to collapse. Events, bigger than he, bigger than Bulgaria, had driven him to a point where he saw no possible way out.

The long-dreaded day of reckoning had arrived; there was no escape. To say yes to Hitler and send Bulgarian troops against Russia would be to betray his oath, the creed of his entire reign. On the other hand, to refuse Germany's demand was no longer possible—the Wehrmacht's powerful presence in Bulgaria would mean a military occupation and a bloody civil war. Moreover, knowing now for sure that Germany was losing the war, the specter of one more national catastrophe haunted him relentlessly. It seemed to be too late now for a volte-face, a reversal of alliances: the preliminary soundings of the Western Allies indicated no interest in Bulgaria, nor any sympathy for its cause.

Reviewing the internal situation was not any comfort either. Everything that he had really cared for appeared to him now a failure. The coup in May 1934, creating abnormal, undemocratic conditions, had forced him to establish his personal regime, which he had sincerely hoped would be only temporary. But with the beginning of the war, his plans for a gradual return to parliamentary democracy had to be postponed, and the prospects now looked hopeless.

The same coup had curtailed his ability to restrain the death penalty—a point about which he felt deeply. Now Bulgarians who were being sentenced to death for political reasons were executed almost weekly.

Did his compatriots at least back him totally in this impasse? He was not sure anymore. All his old insecurities were reemerging. He had become excessively sensitive to any criticism, and overly suspicious. Under constant pressure, swept by his inner doubts, disillusioned and angry, he tended sometimes to exaggerate the scope of the opposition—the right-wingers, the pro-Western parties, the Communists—and to wonder whether some of it were not directed against him personally.

The last meeting with Hitler had the effect of formalizing the inescapable quandary, causing something to crack inside him, irreparably. His will to live had abandoned him.

King Boris was certainly not a weak man to be broken by a stormy confrontation with the despotic Fuehrer. In spite of his predilection for worry, he possessed a remarkable resilience. But the violent clash with Hitler did not come as an isolate episode in an otherwise normal human life. It came as the climax of a quarter of a century of accumulated tensions, frustrations, and tragic events. For the last three years, the war years, these chronic conditions had erupted into an acute crisis with which Boris had had to cope every single anquished day. The man tossing on his bed in the bunker's cubicle was a man whose body and soul, already severely marked, were particularly vulnerable.

His body had already been affected. That summer, he had told his sister Evdokia of his worries about angina pectoris. But now the desire for life was suddenly extinguished. As if to punish himself, this normally wise and prudent man frantically embarked on a series of unreasonable actions: attempting to fly Hitler's plane as high as his eardrums could bear; climbing Moussalla only four days after the upsetting meeting; insisting on taking the steepest, most dangerous paths; working until 2 A.M. when he was dead tired; getting up at dawn to stalk the mountain goat; hunting again despite the pains in his chest.

Boris, in short, acted like a man who did not care to live anymore. Perhaps Balan was right that day on the edge of the cliff, when he discerned a strange look in the eyes of the king.

Did he feel the first pains in the chest on the evening he returned from his tempestuous meeting with Hitler? If he felt sick that night, that would have been sufficient explanation for his surprising decision to stay by himself at the palace, without calling Vrana to announce his return to his anxious wife. Because he never mentioned to the queen—before or after that day— his suspicions about having angina pectoris. It was Boris's rule never to worry his wife about his ailments and problems.

*       *       *

The gloom and foreboding of another tragic September seeped through the country, just as it had in the fateful autumn of 1918 after the defeat. Twenty-five years to the day had passed between two Septembers, between the time when, diffident and anxious, young Boris was about to be burdened with the crown, and the day of his funeral.

The 1918 disaster had taken place in an atmosphere of near chaos, with the army in splinters and the people too confused and divided to be able to express any common feeling. But in 1943, King Boris's death struck a nation—which though shaken and divided on many issues was nevertheless orderly and intact—with an explosion of desolation. The king's death exposed, abruptly, the hopelessness of Bulgaria's future. Boris's burial became a symbol: It was as though the entire nation attended its own funeral.

How otherwise explain the extraordinary outburst of public grief, a display of unrestrained emotion such as had never been seen before in Bulgaria. During the days before the service at Alexander-Nevsky Cathedral and the burial in the Rila monastery, immense crowds flowed silently toward the church's square, waiting patiently for their turn to enter and pay their last respects to the deceased king. Women made no effort to control their tears; men were not ashamed to cry; rifles shook as guards-of-honor presented arms.

The state funeral took place on September 5. A long procession followed the casket from Alexander-Nevsky, across the city draped in black, to the main railroad station, where the funeral train awaited to take the body to the Rila monastery, the impressive twelfth-century sanctuary hidden in the peace of the mountain forests.

Behind the widowed queen and Prince Kyril, followed by the Princesses Evdokia and Nadejda, walked the cabinet and former ministers, the members of the royal court, generals, officials, the diplomatic corps, and the high clergy. Along the packed Sofia streets, the entire population had come for a last farewell. The ailing King Ferdinand was unable to attend his son's funeral, but Princess Mafalda, the queen's sister, was there, representing the Italian royal family, while Fieldmarshal Keitel and Grand Admiral Doenitz headed the German delegation.

There was not a dry eye in the capital that day. As the crowds were removing their hats and crossing themselves at the passing of the cortege, the silent question became almost audible: "How could you leave us now? What will happen to our country now?"

Later that day, the same anxious question was in the eyes and on the lips of thousands of people—peasants and workers in the fields, women, old folks, youngsters—lined along both sides of the railroad track, as the funeral train crossed the countryside on its way to Rila. "To whom do you leave us now?"

Pious solemnity filled the vast monastery courtyard, no matter the sound of hundreds of footsteps on the old cobblestones. Voices were muffled, as the sun set behind the majestic peaks, towering above the high medieval walls. They were all there—statesmen, notables, generals, advisers—the leading team deprived of a leader.

The bells tolled and, in the silence of the grandiose surroundings, the echo sounded almost surrealistic. Soon, the mountains resounded with the magnificent chant of the Orthodox liturgy, and the smell of incense invaded the pine-scented air. The casket was lowered into the grave, freshly dug in the chapel floor, to the right of the altar. No mausoleum, no statue; just a simple wooden cross bearing the king's name marked the grave. At this precise moment, from a nearby hill, an artillery salvo saluted the departed commander-in-chief, its thunder rolling from peak to peak, to die somewhere far below in the plains.

It was all over. King Boris's life and his mission were over. Night fell on the monastery, and Rila's rocks and forests. The next morning, as from time immemorial, life would go on. Without Boris III. And without his turbulent but engaging, unlucky but proud Kingdom of Bulgaria which he had ruled.

# Epilogue

OUTSIDE OF some circumstantial evidence favoring one or the other of the various hypotheses about King Boris's death, no definitive proof has emerged to this day.

Did he die of coronary thrombosis, as stated in the official communiqué? Was he killed, by poison or by some other means? If so, who committed the crime? Or did King Boris commit suicide, as suggested by some? There really is no conclusive answer. But because of the strange circumstances—Boris III's untimely end at a crucial moment, with the various political implications—the questions and suspicions persist.

Queen Giovanna was never quite satisfied by the official version of the cause of death. But although inclined to believe that the causes were not "natural," she has no hard facts to substantiate her suspicions.

Similar thoughts are not totally dismissed by King Boris's son, King Simeon, and daughter, Princess Maria-Luisa, although they both accept the explanation of a coronary infarct as equally plausible. In fact, King Simeon would prefer to believe it was a natural death.

As for Princess Evdokia, she remained convinced until her death that "the Nazis did it."

Meanwhile, what happened in Bulgaria? For exactly one year after King Boris's death, the country was governed by a three-man regency council (Prince Kyril, Premier Filov, and War Minister General Mihov), which acted in the name of the six-year-old King Simeon II. With the Soviet troops advancing on the Eastern front and the Communist guerrilla activities increasing at home, the three consecutive governments of this dramatic period (headed by Dobri Bojilov, Ivan Bagrianov, and Konstantin Mouraviev) made efforts to extricate the country from its alliance with Germany—secretly under Bojilov, openly uner Bagrianov and Mouraviev—but to no avail. The governments hoped to deal with the Western allies only, in order to forestall a Communist takeover. But the United States and Great Britain refused to meet with the secret Bulgarian delegation sent to Cairo unless their ally, the Soviet Union, also participated in the negotiations.

At the end of August 1944, the advancing Soviet armies crossed Rumania and reached the Bulgarian border. Despite Sofia's continuous diplomatic ties with the Soviet Union, Moscow declared war and the Red army poured over Bulgaria in the beginning of September. Meanwhile, the pro-Western Mouraviev government had severed relations with Germany, and the German troops had begun to pull out. This, however, failed to save the regime. As soon as the Soviet army invaded Bulgaria, the Fatherland Front, a coalition of the Communist party, the left wing of the Agrarian Union, the Zveno group, and a few pro-Russian politicians, executed a *coup-d'état* on September 9 and seized power.

The royal government, simultaneously at war with Germany and (unwillingly) with the Soviet Union, offered no resistance. With the Red army occupying the country and the national authorities in disarray, a few thousand Communist partisans marched into Sofia and other major cities and engaged in a vengeful orgy of arrests and murders. The terror took unprecedented proportions, dwarfing by comparison any blood purges carried out in the other countries formerly allied to Germany. From this coup, made possible only because of the presence of the Red army, the Communist propaganda fabricated the myths of "revolution" and "liberation."

It was not long before the Communists, who had always held de facto power in the Fatherland Front coalition presided over by Kimon Gheorghiev, became the unconcealed and sole rulers of the Stalinist "People's State" of Bulgaria.

On the night of February 1, 1945, the regents—Prince Kyril, Professor Bogdan Filov, and General Nikola Mihov—were executed. Their death sentences had been pronounced earlier that day by a "People's Tribunal." The following persons, mentioned in this book, were shot with them in a remote corner of Sofia' cemetery, on the rim of a bomb crater, which served as their common grave:

Cabinet ministers Ivan Bagrianov and Parvan Draganov, personal friends of the late King Boris; former ministers Peter Gabrovsky, General Theodossy Daskalov, Dobri Bojilov, Nikola Zahariev, and sixteen other former cabinet members; the members of King Boris's chancery Pavel Grouev, Svetoslav Pomenov, General Raphail Jetchev, Dimitar Guentchev, Gheorghi Handjiev, and Petar Kostov, as well as the king's unofficial advisers Yordan Sevov and Lyubomir Loultchev.

The same "People's Tribunal" sentenced to prison, among many others, the opposition (pro-Western) political leaders Nikola Moushanov, Dimitar Guitchev, Konstantin Mouraviev, Athanas Bourov, and Verguil Dimov. Also sent to prison were the royal court's junior secretaries Stanislav Balan and Petar Morfov.

And the remaining characters in this book?

Three new regents were appointed for the child-king, Simeon. One of them was a prominent Communist intellectual, Todor Pavlov, whose life had been spared three times in the past, thanks to the personal interventions of King Boris. A grateful Pavlov treated Boris's widow and children with respect. The monarchy, reduced to fiction, was tolerated by the new regime for another two years. King Simeon was allowed to stay with his mother, Queen Giovanna, and his sister, Princess Maria-Luisa, in their residence in Vrana until the monarchy was abolished at the end of 1946, after a heavily rigged "plebiscite." The royal family was given forty-eight hours to leave the country, and departed first to Egypt, and then to Spain.

Princess Evdokia was arrested in 1945, kept in solitary confinement, and subjected to humiliations and harsh interrogations that lasted for several months. Allowed finally to leave the country with King Simeon, she spent her old age around her Württemberg relatives on the shores of the lake of Constance, where she died in October 1985, a deeply hurt, ailing old lady burdened with nostalgia.

King Ferdinand outlived both his sons. He never fulfilled his dream of seeing Bulgaria again. He died in Coburg in 1948. Princess Nadejda, duchess of Württemberg, died in 1958.

A few among the principal actors in this drama escaped the fate of their colleagues. Former Foreign Minister Ivan Popov committed suicide in Bucharest, where he served as Bulgarian envoy in the fall of 1944. Gheorghi Kiosseivanov, minister in Bern that year, stayed abroad following the Communist takeover, as did most Bulgarian diplomats. He spent his last years in Switzerland and in Spain. Professor Alexander Tzankov escaped to Vienna, where, with the help of the Germans, he tried to form an anti-Communist government-in-exile. He later emigrated to Argentina, where he died. The IMRO leader, Ivan (Vanché) Mihailov, lives in an undisclosed place in Italy and, although in his late eighties, is still active in Macedonian affairs.

The Reich's envoy in Sofia, Beckerle, was intercepted at the Turkish border and sent to Russia, where he underwent long interrogations and imprisonment. Back in his homeland, he was put on trial in the sixties and now lives in Germany, as does the former air attaché, General Schoenebeck.

As for the Communist leaders mentioned in this book, the Soviet officials of Bulgarian origin—Gheorghi Dimitrov, Vassil Kolarov, Vulko Chervenkov, and most of their colleagues—returned to Bulgaria to assume power. As for the internal party, First Secretary Traytcho Kostov was liquidated in 1949, hanged for high treason and accused of being a "British agent." Tzola Dragoytcheva ("Comrade Sonia") remained one of the top members of the Bulgarian Politburo.

The Zveno leaders Kimon Gheorghiev, Damian Veltchev, and Dimo Kazassov, protagonists in the *coups-d'état* of 1923 and 1934, figured once again among the leaders of the September 9, 1944, coup and became ministers in the early Fatherland Front governments. When it became quite clear that this coalition was nothing but a facade, Gheorghiev and Kazassov stayed on as faithful Communist allies while Veltchev fell into disgrace and was exiled as ambassador to Bern. Later, he resigned in protest against the Sovietization of Bulgaria, requested political asylum in Switzerland, and subsequently died there.

The large majority of Bulgarian Jews emigrated to Israel, taking with them the Bulgarian language and customs and a warm feeling for their country of birth and its king, who did not permit their deportation to Nazi extermination camps.

Meanwhile, King Boris's grave became such a popular place of pilgrimage that the authorities ordered his remains exhumed and transferred from Rila to Vrana, where Queen Giovanna, with her two children, had them reburied in the park one gruesome dawn of 1946. After the royal family left Bulgaria, macabre rumors circulated concerning defilement of the grave and removal of the coffin. These rumors were never confirmed, but uncertainty exists about where the king's remains rest today.

*       *       *

# References

## CHAPTER I

Page
| | |
|---|---|
| 1, 2 | Meeting between Ferdinand and Stambolisky Stambolisky, *Dvete mi sreshti s Tsar Ferdinand*. |
| 3 | Letter to Gantchev, King Ferdinand's private archives. |
| 3, 4, 5 | Jekov's report, Ibid. |
| 5 | Prince Boris's telegram, Ibid. |
| 5–9 | Stambolisky, *Dvete mi sreshti . . .* |
| 9–11 | Boris at the front—in *20 godini na prestola, 1918–1938*, commemorative volume published by the army, Sofia, 1938 |
| 10 | Telegram from Boris, King Ferdinand's private archives. |
| 11 | Gen. Bourmov's telegram, Ibid. |
| 12 | Crown Council meeting, Gentizon, *Le Drame Bulgare* |
| 12 | Malinov's letter, King Ferdinand's private archives. |
| 13 | Second Malinov letter, Ibid. |
| 14 | Neklyudov, *Diplomatic Reminiscences*. |

## CHAPTER II

| | |
|---|---|
| 15–18 | Personal interview of the author with Princess Evdokia on the upbringing of the royal children, 1981. |
| 19 | King Ferdinand's private archives, Rumanian queen's visit. |
| 19–20 | Schaufelberger's recollections, in Nikolaev, *La Destinée tragique d'un roi*. |
| 23 | The menu, A. Hepp, *Ferdinand de Bulgarie intime*. |
| 23 | Alexander III to Giers, *Königslöw, Ferdinand von Bulgarien*, 34. |
| 26 | Queen Victoria to Salisbury, *The Letters of Queen Victoria, 1886–1901*, editor Buckle, Vol, I, John Murray, London, 1930. |
| 26 | Bismarck's letter, Königslöw. |
| 27 | Tsar Alexander's remark, Königslöw. |
| 27 | Queen Victoria to Salisbury, *The Letters of Queen Victoria*. |
| 29 | Princess Clémentine to Queen Victoria, Ibid., III series, vol. 2. |
| 30 | Pope Leo to Ferdinand, Sydakoff, *Bulgarien und der Bulgarische Furstenhof*, Berlin, 1896, as quoted in S. Constant, *Foxy Ferdinand*. |
| 30 | Princess Radziwill's letter, as quoted in Constant, *Foxy Ferdinand*. |
| 30 | Anna Stancioff, *Recollections of a Bulgarian Diplomatist's Wife*. |

31        Ibid.
31, 32    Prince Boris's exams, N. Iliev, *Boris III.*
33        Boris's coming-of-age parade—Personal letter from Princess Evdo-
          kia to her niece, Princess Maria-Luisa

CHAPTER III

34–37     Events in Radomir—G. Damianov *Voynishkoto Vazstanie,* 220 ff.,
          J. Bell, *Peasants in Power,* Gentizon, *Le Drame bulgare,* 16, 17.
37        Daskalov's speeches, R. Daskalov, *Voyinishkoto* 190.
38        Daskalov's proclamation, J. Bell, *Peasants in Power.*
39        Daskalov's note to Stambolisky, Kozhukharov, *Radomirskata re-
          publika.*
40        Meeting between Stambolisky and Daskalov, Kh. Khristov, as
          quoted in J. Bell.
40        Daskalov's ultimatum, *Voynishkoto . . .* 209.
41        Blagoev and the rebellion, J. Rothschild, *The Communist party of
          Bulgaria.*
47        Daskalov's analysis of the defeat, *Voynishkoto . . .,* 188

CHAPTER IV

49        Meeting between Ferdinand and Liapchev, N. Iliev, *Boris III, Tsar
          na Bulgarite,* 68;Gentizon, *Le Drame . . .,* 24, 25.
50        Council of Ministers, Gentizon, 25, 26.
50        Meeting between Ferdinand and Malinov, Ibid., 26, 27.
51        Meeting between Ferdinand and Theodorov, Ibid., 28, 29, 30.
52        Rumors of coup d'etat, Ibid., 18, 19, also, *Voynishkoto . . .,* 358, 359
52, 53    Ferdinand's abdication, Gentizon, 31, 32.
53, 54    Ferdinand's departure, Ibid., 32, 33.
56        King Boris's proclamation, King Simeon's archives.

CHAPTER V

58        Boris to Ferdinand, telegrams of Oct. 6, 8 and 11, in King Fer-
          dinand's personal archives.
59        Evdokia's letter, Ibid.
          Dobrovitch's letter, Ibid.
60        Dobrovitch to Ferdinand, Ibid.
61        Boris's message to Ferdinand, Ibid.
61, 62    Nikiforov's letter to Ferdinand, Ibid.
63        As told by Pavel Grouev to the author, his son.
64, 65    Signing of the Neuilly Treaty, N. Muir, *Dimitri Stancioff.*

CHAPTER VI

68        Stambolisky on the Agrarian Union, Gentizon, 154.
69        Dobrovitch letter, July 7, 1922, King Ferdinand's private archives.
73        Boris to Ferdinand, Feb. 21, 1921, Ibid.
74        Boris to Ferdinand, May 25, 1921, Ibid.
75        Stambolisky quotations, Gentizon, 114.
76        Stambolisky to Yugoslav journalists, on Macedonians, "Nov List",
          Sep. 15, 1922, as quoted in Katzarov, *60 Godini . . .,* 313; also,

|         | Report of the Bulgarian consul in Munich to King Ferdinand, Jan. 22, 1923, in King Ferdinand's private archives. |
| 76, 77  | Boris on Stambolisky, interview of the author with Princess Evdokia, 1981. |
| 79      | Boris to Ferdinand, Nov. 11, 1921, King Ferdinand's private archives. |
| 79, 80  | Boris and sisters reunited, Letter from Princess Evdokia to her niece, Princess Maria-Luisa. |
| 83      | Boris to Draganov, March 12, 1923, Draganov diary. |
| 84      | Ibid. |
| 84      | Boris's angry outburst, Ibid. |
| 84, 85  | Draganov on the King's anger, Ibid. |
| 85      | Stambolisky wants martial law in Petrich, Apr. 12, 1923, Ibid. |
| 86, 87  | Boris on Metropolitan Stefan, Apr. 12, 1923, Ibid. |

## CHAPTER VII

| 90       | Draganov diary, June 10, 1923. |
| 90, 91   | D. Kazassov, *V Tumninite na zagovora*. |
| 91–96    | Draganov diary, June 10, 1923. |
| 93–96    | Kazassov, *V tumninite . . .*, and *Burni godini* |
| 96, 97   | Boris's reactions to the coup, Draganov diary. |
| 99       | Stambolisky to the army major, Kozhukharov, 171. |
| 100, 101 | Boris's reaction to Stambolisky's death, Draganov diary, June 15, 1923. |

## CHAPTER VIII

| 103 | Kolarov's statement; Zinoviev criticism, Rothschild, *The Bulgarian Communist party*, 122. |
| 103 | Radek denounces BCP, Rothschild, 122, 123, 127. |
| 104 | Chervenkov's analysis of the defeat, Dimitrov, Kolarov and Chervenkov, *The September uprising*, 90, 91. |
| 105 | Dimitrov's admission, Ibid., 95, 96. |
| 105 | About Roussev, Draganov diary, Oct. 13, 1923. |
| 106 | About Engineer Stoyanov, Ibid. |
| 106 | Opening of the Parliament, Nov. 27, 1923, Ibid. |
| 106 | Scolding Grouev, Ibid. |
| 107 | Dobrovitch letter, Dec. 1923, King Ferdinand's private archieves. |
| 107 | Boris letter of Dec. 3, 1923, to Ferdinand, about 9 June coup, King Ferdinand's private archives. |
| 108 | Boris, on Nadejda's wedding, Ibid. |
| 108 | Boris, on Kyril's return, Draganov diary. |
| 108 | About opening of the Parliament, Dec. 13, 1923, Ibid. |
| 109 | Boris, on vanity—as told by P. Grouev to his son, the author. |

## CHAPTER IX

| 112      | Ivan Mihailov, *Spomeni*. |
| 115–120  | Ibid. |
| 121      | Inauguration of Al. Nevsky, Draganov diary, Sept. 11, 1924. |
| 122      | Boris, on T. Alexandrov's murder, Sept. 20, 1924, Ibid. |
| 123      | Boris's discouragement, Ibid. |

## CHAPTER X

124–126    Meeting with Yankov, Minkov, Dragoytcheva, *Neslomimite.*
126        BCP Vitosha conference, *History of Bulgaria,* Historical Institute, Bulg. Academy of Sciences, 1955, Sofia: 542.
127        BCP's view on the situation in Europe and Bulgaria, *History of Bulgaria,* 527, 528, 529.
128        Meeting with Friedman, Dragoytcheva.
130, 131   Funeral service at Sveta-Nedelia, Stéphane, Archevêque de Sofia, *L'Attentat à notre cathedrale.*
132        Boris, on the day of the cathedral's bombing, Draganov diary, Apr. 16, 1925.
133        Boris, the night after the bombing, Ibid.
135        Pastoukhov's reaction, New York Times, April 21, 1925.
135, 136   Comintern conspiracy, London Times, Apr. 20, 1925.
           Comintern conspiracy, N.Y. Times, Apr. 21, 1925.
138–140    Popov's confession, Personal archives of King Simeon.

## CHAPTER XI

141, 142   Boris's inner conflict, Draganov diary, March 25, 1925.
142        Boris, on the Agrarians, May 1, 1925, Ibid.
142        Boris on abdicating or suicide, Ibid.
143        Boris on the death penalty, June 28, 1924, Ibid.
143        Boris, on opening of the Sobranie, Oct. 28, 1924, Ibid.
144        Boris, on the June 9th coup, Ibid.
144        Strashimirov audience, Oct. 20, 1924, Ibid.
145        Boris's pessimism, Nov. 5, 1924, Ibid.
145        More on the death penalty, Nov. 25, 1924, Ibid.
146        Visit to railroad depot, Ibid.
146        Boris, on Tzankov and Freemasons, Ibid.
146        Boris, more on June 9th coup, Ibid.
148–150    Letter from Marion Stancioff to the author.

## CHAPTER XII

152        Ferdinand signing death sentences, as told to the author by members of King Boris's family.
153        Boris pleased with the change of government, Draganov diary, Jan. 4, 1926.
160        Schaufelberger, in Nikolaev, *La Destinée tragique* . . .
161        Boris's confidences, Ibid.
162        Boris, about staying in Montreux, Ibid.

## CHAPTER XIII

163–167    Personal interviews of the author with Queen Giovanna.
168        Roncalli to Kurtev, Jan. 14, 1949—in P. Hebblethwaite, *Pope John XXIII,* 120.
168        T. Kodding, US Chargé-d' affaires in Sofia, to the Secretary of State, #1589, Jan. 2, 1930, and #1599, Jan. 27, 1930.
169        Report of the US Minister in Belgrade, John Dyneley Prince, to the Secretary of State, #736, Feb. 26, 1930.

| | |
|---|---|
| 170–174 | Details from Draganov diary. |
| 175–178 | Author's personal interviews with Queen Giovanna. |
| 178 | Roncalli to King Boris, P. Hebblethwaite, 138. |

## CHAPTER XIV

| | |
|---|---|
| 181 | Boris to Draganov, Jan. 14, 1933, Draganov archives. |
| 182–184 | Draganov to Boris, Jan. 21, 1933, Ibid. |
| 184 | Roncalli's letter to Boris, Hebblethwaite, 139. |
| 191 | von Neurath's report, RM 252, Berlin, March 1, 1934, in German archives. |
| 193 | Draganov to Boris, Nov. 27, 1933, about Nazi hostility toward the Württemberg family, Draganov archives. |
| 193, 194 | Dr. Meyer's suicide, Draganov diary, Nov. 13, 1933. |
| 194–196 | Meeting between Ferdinand and Draganov, letter from Draganov to King Boris, Dec. 1, 1933, Draganov's archives. |
| 197 | The Military League, Draganov diary, Mar. 2, 1934. |
| 198 | Boris discouraged, Ibid. |

## CHAPTER XV

| | |
|---|---|
| 199 | Kazassov, *Burni godini*, 509; 511. |
| 205, 206 | Macedonian assassinations, reports in dailies *Zora* and *Utro;* Kazassov, *Burni godini*, 388, 389; reports of US Minister in Sofia, Henry W. Shoemaker, to the Secretary of State, dated Jan. 5, Feb. 15 and June 23, 1933. |
| 206 | Gorna-Djoumaia/congress, Report Shoemaker, Feb. 15, 1933. |
| 207 | King Albert's death, P. Grouev to the author; also, interview of the author with S. Balan. |
| 208 | US Minister F. A. Sterling, to the State Department, #21, May 29, 1934. |
| 209, 210 | Kazassov, *Burni godini*, 510, 511, 512. |
| 210, 211, 212 | Personal letter from King Boris to Draganov, describing the coup, and signed "Prometheus"; King's recollections, related to Draganov—in Draganov diary, Feb. 1936; also: Kazassov, *Burni . . .,* 512, 513. |
| 213 | Sterling, to State Department, #21, May 29, 1934. |
| 214 | New York Times, May 25, 1934. |

## CHAPTER XVI

| | |
|---|---|
| 216 | King Boris on "tarpenie", Draganov diary, Dec. 1934. |
| 217 | Interviews of the author with Queen Giovanna. |
| 218 | Ibid. |
| 219 | Ibid. |
| 219 | Young Evdokia's sentimental life, author's interview with Princess Evdokia, 1981. |
| 220, 221 | Interviews, Queen Giovanna. |
| 222 | Kiosseivanov quoted by Prof. A. Tzankov, in *Makedonska Tribuna*, June 18, 1953 |
| 222, 223 | Yugoslav royal couple in Plovdiv, Interview with Queen Giovanna. |
| 223 | Ivan Mihailov, *Spomeni*, vol. II, 499 and 505. |

| 224 | Yugoslav King Alexander's assassination, Mihailov, *Spomeni*, vol. IV, 507. |
| 225 | US Minister Sterling to State Department, #111, Jan. 26, 1935. |
| 228 | Goering, on D. Veltchev's sentence, Draganov diary. |

## CHAPTER XVII

| 230 | Draganov diary. |
| 233 | King Boris reports from Paris, Ibid., Feb. 2 and 5, 1936. |
| 234 | Boris about Bulgarian army, Draganov diary, Feb. 3, 1936. |
| 235 | Sterling, to State Department, June, 1936. |
| 236 | About Guentchev, Letter from King Boris to Draganov, Draganov archives. |
| 237 | Nikolaev, *La destinée tragique* . . . |
| 238, 239 | King Edward VIII's visit, S. Petroff-Tchomakoff, in *Bulgarian Review*, Rio de Janeiro, Dec. 1965. |
| 239 | King Edward, nicknames, as told by the Bulgarian royal family to the author. |
| 241 | About Loukov, letter from King Boris to Draganov—Draganov archives. |
| 242 | King Boris's letter from Paris, Feb. 5, 1936, Draganov diary. |
| 243 | Trade with France, Nikolaev, *La destinée* . . ., 228. |
| 243 | Trade with England, Rendel, *The sword* . . ., 142, 143, 144. |
| 244, 245 | Rendel's impressions of King Boris, Rendel, 148, 151. |
| 246–249 | Various Dunnovist publications in Bulgarian, French and English; also, Loultchev diary and court testimony, as quoted in Paunovsky, *Vazmezdieto*. |
| 251, 252 | About the Munich conference, Rendel, 156; *Documents on British Foreign Policy, 1919–1939*, vol. III, London, 1950–1953; Paunovsky, 145, 146; Sirkov, 65–68; I. Dimitrov, in *Vekove*, Sofia, 1977, #6, 65–67. |

## CHAPTER XVIII

| 257 | Nikolaev, *La destinée tragique* . . ., 227. |
| 258 | Rendel, *The sword* . . ., 155. |
| 261 | Ibid., 164, 183. |
| 262 | Kiosseivanov to Grouev, in Loultchev diary, as quoted in Paunovsky, *Vazmezdieto*. |
| 263 | Conversations of the author with Kiosseivanov. |
| 264 | Rendel, 165, 166. |
| 265 | US Minister Earle, to State Department, Dec. 18, 1940. |
| 266 | Earle, on Dobrudja, June 27, 1940, Ibid. |
| 266, 267 | Letter from King Boris to Draganov, about Dobrudja, July 25, 1940, Draganov archives. |
| 268 | On Dobrudja, Rendel, 145. |
| 269 | Nazis suspect Popov, Reports from German legation in Sofia, Dec. 5, 1940. |
| 269 | Mussolini to Boris, Sirkov, 258; Miller, 35; Toshkova, 24. |
| 269 | Boris's letter to Hitler, Oct. 22, 1940, a copy in Draganov archives. |
| 270 | Boris's visit to Hitler, Interview of the author with the King's secretary S. Balan, 1983. |

| | |
|---|---|
| 270, 271 | Conversation of Boris and Hitler, Toshkova, 28, 29; unpublished memoirs of S. Moshanov, as quoted by Paunovsky, 170–173; US Minister Earle, to Secretary of State, Nov. 21, 1940. |
| 272 | Boris to von Papen, Toshkova, 29, 30. |
| 272 | Sobolev mission, Earle to Secretary of State, Dec. 18, 1940; Also: Miller, 34; Toshkova, 30; Sirkov, 268. |
| 273, 274 | Boris to N. Moushanov, unpublished memoirs of S. Moshanov, according to Paunovsky, *Vazmezdieto*, 174. |

## CHAPTER XIX

| | |
|---|---|
| 276, 277, 278 | Filov diary, Jan. 4, 1941. |
| 279, 280 | Ibid., Jan. 7, 1941; Toshkova, 34; Paunovsky, 212–215. |
| 281, 282 | Draganov to Boris, Jan. 9, 1941, Draganov archives. |
| 282, 283 | Filov diary, Jan. 20, 1941. |
| 284 | Jan. 8, 1941, Ibid. |
| 286, 287 | Donovan's visit, Jan. 20, 1941 Ibid., also: R. Dunlop, *Donovan, America's master spy*, 249–251; and, I. Dimitrov, in Bulg. Historical Review, vol. 4, 1978. |
| 289 | Stalin-Hitler, on Bulgaria, Wm. Shirer, *The Rise and Fall of the Third Reich*, 809, 810. |
| 289, 290 | Operation Marita, Trevor-Roper, *Hitler's War Directives*, 90-92. |
| 291 | Filov diary, March 1, 1941. |
| 292 | Grouev's visit to Lavrishchev, author's interview with S. Balan. |
| 292–294 | Filov diary, March 1, 1941. |
| 294 | The King's reaction to the signing, P. Grouev's court testimony, as quoted by Paunovsky, 257. |
| 294 | Filov diary, March 2, 1941. |
| 295 | Rendel, *The Sword . . .*, 179. |

## CHAPTER XX

| | |
|---|---|
| 297 | Filov diary, March 16 and 28, 1941. |
| 298, 299 | March 30, Apr. 8 and 9, 1941, Ibid. |
| 300 | Hitler's respect for Boris, Balan, to the author; Pavel Grouev, to the author; I. Dimitrov, *"Smurtta na Tsar Boris III"*, 51 |
| 300 | Filov diary, Apr. 18 and 20, 1941. |
| 303 | Ibid., Apr. 23, 24 and 27, 1941. |
| 303 | Balan, to the author. |
| 305 | Ferdinand's letter to E. Karavelova, Apr. 1941—in King Ferdinand's private archives. |
| 306 | Operation Barbarossa, Wm. Shirer, 810; Filov diary; also: Earle, to State Department. |
| 307, 308 | Earle to State Department, Oct. 14, 1941. |
| 309 | Loultchev diary, quoted by Paunovsky, 123, 124. |
| 309 | Naumov cable, Toshkova, 84. |
| 309 | Boris in Alexander-Nevsky, Nikolaev, *La Destinée . . .*, 177. |
| 310, 311 | Ribbentrop to Beckerle, March 26, 1942, RAM 68/R. |
| 312 | Ribbentrop to Beckerle, Apr. 8, 1942, RAM 90/R. |
| 313 | Audience with Ferdinand, Balan, to the author. |
| 314 | Filov, on Popov, Filov diary. |
| 315 | Loultchev diary, as quoted in Paunovsky, *Vazmezdieto*. |

## CHAPTER XXI

316, ff.    F. Chary, *The Bulgarian Jews and the Final Solution*. B. Arditi, *Roliata na Tsar Boris pri izselvaneto na evreite of Bulgaria*.

319, 320    Queen Giovanna, to the author; Balan, to the author.

319    St. Synod's condemnation, Arditi, 41, 42. Disapproval by most Bulgarians, Natan Grinberg, *Documenti* of the Central Consistory of Jews in Bulgaria, Sofia, 1945, as quoted by Arditi, 19; 43, 44. Boris disapproval, Ivan D. Strogov, quoted by Arditi, 12.

320    Sokoloff quote, Arditi, 16.

320    Queen's attitude, Arditi, 17, 35.

320    Boris's telegram to the consistory, Arditi, 22. Boris and rabbi Hananel, Chary, 70. Beckerle's report on Boris's telegram, Arditi, 23.

321    King's interference in favor of Jews, Balan; Arditi, 11.

322    Report Belev from Germany, Chary, 52.

323    German archives: W. Schellenberg to Luther, Nov. 21, 1942.

324    Belev-Dannecker agreement, Arditi, 26; Chary, 208–210.

324    Metropolitan Kyril, Chary, 324.

325    Quote "from the highest place", report from the German legation, Sofia, Apr. 5, 1943.

325    Peshev protest, Filov diary, March 19, 20, 24 and 26; also: Arditi, 38, 39; Chary, 90.

327, 328    Rabbi Tsion, Chary, 149, 150.

328    Protests by Metropolitan Stefan, Mrs. Karavelova, Arditi, 48, 49; Chary, 149, 150; 189.

329    Belev to Hananel, Chary, 151. Boris-Ribbentrop, Ribbentrop telegram to Beckerle, Apr. 4, 1943.

330    Capovilla, quoted in P. Hebblethwaite, *Pope John XXIII*, 188.

330    Roncalli's letter to Boris, June 30, 1943, in *Actes et Documents du Saint Siège, relatifs à la Seconde Guerre mondiale*, 9, Libreria Editrice Vaticana, 1975, 372.

331    Beckerle report on Bulgarian mentality, Chary, 153–155.

## CHAPTER XXII

332    Interview of the author with the King's secretary, Balan, 1983.

335    Communist subversive activities, N. Oren, *Bulgarian Communism*, 175–178; 182, 183; Dragoytcheva, *Neslomimite*.

335    About Tr. Kostov, Balan, to the author.

336    Anecdotes, told to the author by members of the royal family.

340, 341    Assassinations by communist terrorists, Stoinov, *Boinite grupi*, 92–100; Stoinov, *Nespokoen til*, 38–55; Miller, 198; Oren, 202, 203; reports in Sofia's dailies "Zora" and "Utro", in Feb., Apr. and May 1943.

342    Communist guerrillas, interviews of the author with Boris Dimitrov, head of Sofia region's police before Sept. 9, 1944.

342    Defeatism among Bulg. communists, Stoinov, *Boinite Grupi*, 19; Tr. Kostov quoted by Oren, 171 and Stoinov, 19.

## CHAPTER XXIII

344      Filov diary, March 28 and 29, 1943; Hitler on Boris, Trevor-Roper, *Hitler's Table Talk*, 630.
346      Author's interview with Balan.
347      Ibid.
349      Princess Evdokia, private correspondence.
351      Questions about change of policy, SS Obergrupenfuehrer Kalten-brunner's telegram to SS representative in Sofia, Wagner, August 16, 1943. Conversations of the author with G. Kiosseivanov; I. Dimitrov. *Smurtta na Tsar Boris III*, 48.
351      K. Pastukhov's article in *Svoboden Narod*, Sofia, Nov. 4, 1944.
352      Kiosseivanov in Sofia, N. P. Nikolaev archive; Filov diary, Aug. 4, 1943.
353      Letter from Consul B. Berry to the author; Kisselov, Black, Toshkova, 125, 126.
355, 356, 357      Balan, to the author.
358, 359      Ibid.
360      Filov diary, Aug. 15, 1943.
360      Handwritten testimony of Princess Evdokia, addressed to her nephew and niece, King Simeon and Princess Maria-Luisa, to read after her death (in 1985).
361      Ibid.

## CHAPTER XXIV

362      Bauer in Vrana, Balan, to the author.
363      Excursion to Moussalla, Ibid.
364, 365      The goat, the gun, Ibid.
365      Chestpain complaints, I. Dimitrov, *Smurtta . . .*, 54.
366      Boris-Sevov meeting, Ibid., 55; Paunovsky, 413.
367      Telephone conversation Boris-Evdokia, Paunovsky, 414.
367      Letter from Schoenebeck to the author, and his unpublished diary of August 1943.
368      Interrogation of Princess Evdokia after her arrest, as quoted by Paunovsky, 414.
369, 370      Queen Giovanna, to the author.
371      The King and his valet Svilen, Paunovsky, 418.
373      Beckerle report to Ribbentrop, #1292, Aug. 23, 1943.
374      Beckerle report to Ribbentrop, #1304, Aug. 30, 1943.
375      Schoenebeck letter to the author.
376, 377, 378      Schoenebeck diary.
381      Filov diary, Aug. 15, 1943.

# Bibliography

Arditi, Benjamin, "Roliata na Tsar Boris pri izselvaneto na evreite ot Bulgaria", Tel Aviv, 1952

Bell, John D.: "Peasants in Power", Princeton U. Press, 1977

Blet, Pierre, editor: "Actes et documents du Saint Siège relatifs à la seconde guerre mondiale", the Vatican, 1975

Boll, Michael M.: "Cold War in the Balkans", University of Kentucky Press, 1984

Chary, Frederick B.: "The Bulgarian Jews and the Final Solution, 1940–1944", University of Pittsburgh Press, 1972

Chary, Frederick B.: transl. and ed., "The Diary of Bogdan Filov", Southeastern Europe 1 (Spring 1974)

Constant, Stephen: "Foxy Ferdinand", Sidgwick & Jackson, London, 1979

Dimitrov, G., Kolarov, V. and Chervenkov, V.: "The September Uprising", Sofia, 1953

Dimitrov, Gheorghi: "Pisma, 1905-1949", ed. Bulgarian Communist Party, Sofia, 1962

Dimitrov, Iltcho: "Anglia i Bulgaria, 1938–1941", Sofia, 1983

Dimitrov, Iltcho: "Professor Bogdan Filov i negoviat dnevnik", Sofia, 1984

Dimitrov, Iltcho: "Bulgaria na Balkanite i v Evropa", Sofia, 1980

Dimitrov, Iltcho: "Smurtta na Tsar Boris III", Sofia

Dragoytcheva, Tzola: "Neslomimite", memoirs. Partizdat, Sofia, 1980

Dunlop, Richard: "Donovan, America's Master Spy", Rand McNally, Chicago, 1982

Eylan, Claude: "La Vie et la Mort d'Alexandre I, Roi de Yougoslavie", B. Grasset, Paris, 1935

Gentizon, Paul: "Le Drame Bulgare", Payot, Paris, 1924

Giovanna di Bulgaria: "Memorie", Milano, 1964

Girginov, Alexander: "Izpitaniata v voynata 1915–1918", Sofia, circa 1933?

Goebbels, Joseph: "Diaries", Hamish Hamilton, London, 1948

Graham, Stephen: "Alexander of Yugoslavia", Yale University, 1939

Hebblethwaite, Peter: "Pope John XXIII", Doubleday, New York, 1985

Heiber, Helmut: "Der Tod des Zaren Boris", Zeitgeschichte, 1964, #4
Hepp, Alexandre: "Ferdinand de Bulgarie intime", Paris, 1910
Hoppe, Hans-Joachim: "Bulgarien-Hitlers eigenwilliger Verbundeter", Deutsche Verlags-Anstalt, Stuttgart, 1979
Iliev, Nentcho: "Boris III, Tsar na Bulgarite", Sofia, 1936, 1937
Iliev, Nentcho: "Boris III, Tsar Obedinitel", Sofia, 1943
Katzarov, K.: "60 Godini zhiviana istoria", Montreux, 1960
Kazassov, Dimo: "V tumninite na zagovora", Sofia, 1925
Kazassov, Dimo: "Burni Godini", Sofia, 1949
Königslöw, Joachim von: "Ferdinand von Bulgarien", Sudosteuropaeische Arbeiten, vol. 69, Munich, 1970
Kozhukharov, Kunio: "Radomirskata Republika", Sofia, 1948
Kozhukharov, Kunio: "Raiko Daskalov, biographichen ocherk", Sofia, 1956
Kozhukharov, Kunio: "Alexander Stambolisky, biographichen ocherk", BCP Publishing, Sofia, 1968
Markov, Gheorghi: "Bulgaro-Germanskite otnoshenia, 1931-1939", Sofia, 1984
Mihailov, Ivan: "Spomeni", 4 volumes, Italy, 1958, 1965, 1967, and 1973
Miller, Marshall Lee: "Bulgaria during the Second World War", Stanford, 1975
Military Publishing Fund: "Boris III, Tsar na Bulgarite, 3.X.1918-3.X.1938", Sofia, 1938
Moser, Charles: "Dimitrov of Bulgaria", Ottawa, Illinois, 1979
Muir, Nadejda: "Dimitri Stancioff", John Murray, London, 1957
Neklyudoff, A.: "Diplomatic Reminiscences", London, 1920
Nikolaev, N. P.: "La destinée tragique d'un Roi", Uppsala, 1952
Oren, Nissan: "Bulgarian Communism", Columbia University Press, New York, 1971
Palmer, Alan: "The Gardeners of Salonika", Simon and Schuster, New York, 1965
Papen, Franz von: "Memoirs", London, 1952
Paunovski, Ivan: "Vazmezdieto", Sofia, 1971
Popov, Stefan: "Bulgarskata idea", Muenchen, 1981
Rendel, George: "The Sword and the Olive", John Murray, London, 1957
Rothschild, Joseph: "The Communist Party of Bulgaria", Columbia U. Press, New York, 1959
Semerjeev, Peter: "Dimitrov and the Comintern: Myth and Reality", The Hebrew University of Jerusalem, 1976
Shirer, William L.: "The rise and fall of the Third Reich", New York, Simon and Schuster, 1960
Sirkov, Dimitar: "Vunshnata politika na Bulgaria, 1938-1941", Sofia, 1979
Speer, Albert: "Inside the Third Reich", Macmillan Co., New York, 1970

Stamboliiski, Alexander: "Dvete mi sreshti s Tsar Ferdinand", BZNS Publishing, Sofia, 1979

Stancioff, Anna: "Recollections of a Bulgarian diplomatist's wife", London, 1930

Stéphane, Archevêque de Sofia: "L'Attentat à notre Cathedrale", 1926

Stoinov, Boris: "Boinite grupi", BCP, Sofia, 1963

Stoinov, Boris: "Nespokoen til", Sofia, 1964

Stoyanov, Lyudmil: "Alexander Stamboliiski", Sofia, 1979

Tishev, Dimitar (editor): "Voynishkoto Vazstanie 1918", BCP and BZNS publication, Sofia, 1968

Toshkova, Vitka: "Bulgaria i tretiat Reich", Sofia, 1975

Trevor-Roper, H. R.: "Hitler's Table Talk", 1973

Trevor-Roper, H. R.: "Hitler's War Directives", Pan Books, London

Trunski, Slavcho: "Neotdavna", Sofia, 1962

Vinarov, Ivan: "Boitsi na tikhia front", BCP, Sofia, 1969

Vulkov, Gheorghi: "Parola Unterwelt", Sofia, 1984

Unpublished Archives Preserved Abroad:

- King Simeon of Bulgaria: personal archives
- King Ferdinand of Bulgaria: personal archives
- Parvan Draganov: personal archives. (A few years ago, and exceptionally, the author had the opportunity to examine and make copies of parts of Draganov's diary and private correspondence, preserved abroad, after his execution in Sofia. These archives were totally unavailable and were kept at a safe place by the widow of Minister Draganov, who intended to destroy them, because of their highly confidential and intimate character. Mrs. Draganov, as well as her son, have died since.)
- Princess Evdokia: personal notes and letters to members of her family.
- Dr. N. P. Nikolaev: personal archives
- General Carl-August von Schoenebeck: parts of personal diary, kept in August 1943.

Diaries and Testimonies Before the "People's Courts,"
Kept in Sofia and Classified:

- Prime Minister, Professor Bogdan Filov: Diary 1940-1944. Only extracts selected by the Ministry of Justice have been made available for research and publication, and are quoted in:
  Dimitrov, Iltcho: "Professor Bogdan Filov i negoviat dnevnik", Plamak, Sofia, 1984
  Chary, Frederick B., translator and editor, in "Southeastern Europe", 1974, 1975 and 1976, Gary, Indiana
  Paunovsky, Ivan: "Vazmezdieto", Sofia, 1971

Newspaper "Naroden Sud", Sofia, Dec. 1944 to Apr. 1945
"Otechestven Front" daily, Sept. 1944 to Jan. 1945
• Lyubomir Loultchev's diary: selected passages quoted in:
"Naroden Sud", Dec. 1944 to Apr. 1945
"Otechestven Front", Sept. 1944 to Jan. 1945
Paunovsky, Ivan: "Vazmezdieto"

Official Documents:

• German archives (microfilms at the National Archives, Washington, D.C.)
• US State Department files: "Foreign Relations of the United States"—National Archives, Diplomatic Branch, Washington, D.C.

# Index